CRITICAL SURVEY
OF
SHORT FICTION

CRITICAL SURVEY
OF
SHORT FICTION

REVISED EDITION
Hug-Mis

4

Edited by
FRANK N. MAGILL

SALEM PRESS
Pasadena, California   Englewood Cliffs, New Jersey

73906

∞ The paper used in these volumes conforms to the
American National Standard for Permanence of Paper
for Printed Library Materials, Z39.48-1984.

Library of Congress Cataloging-in-Publication Data
Critical survey of short fiction/edited by Frank N.
Magill. — Rev. ed.
    p.   cm.
Includes bibliographical references and index.
    1. Short story. 2. Short stories—Dictionaries.
3. Short stories—Bio-bibliography. 4. Novelists—
Biography—Dictionaries.
I. Magill, Frank Northen, 1907-   .
PN3321.C7   1993
809.3'1'03—dc20   92-41950
ISBN 0-89356-843-0 (set)   CIP
ISBN 0-89356-847-3 (volume 4)

Second Printing

PRINTED IN THE UNITED STATES OF AMERICA

LIST OF AUTHORS IN VOLUME 4

LANGSTON HUGHES

Born: Joplin, Missouri; February 1, 1902
Died: New York, New York; May 22, 1967

Principal short fiction

The Ways of White Folks, 1934; *Simple Speaks His Mind*, 1950; *Laughing to Keep from Crying*, 1952; *Simple Takes a Wife*, 1953; *Simple Stakes a Claim*, 1957; *The Langston Hughes Reader*, 1958; *The Best of Simple*, 1961; *Something in Common and Other Stories*, 1963; *Simple's Uncle Sam*, 1965.

Other literary forms

Although perhaps best known for his poetry, Langston Hughes explored almost every literary genre. His prose fiction includes novels, humorous books, historical, biographical, autobiographical, and cultural works, translations, lyrics, librettos, plays, and scripts. His total output includes more than seventy volumes, as well as numerous articles, poems, and stories that have not yet been collected.

Achievements

Hughes has been acknowledged both before and after his death as the most influential African-American writer in the English-speaking world. As a leader of the Harlem Renaissance, he not only wrote in a variety of genres but also edited and encouraged the literary, dramatic, and musical productions of other people of color. Recognition came during his lifetime as early as 1925, when he won the Poetry Prize given by *Opportunity* magazine and the Spingarn prizes of *Crisis* magazine for both poetry and essay writing. His novel *Not Without Laughter* (1930) won the Harmon Gold Medal in 1931. That year he received his first Rosenwald Fellowship, an award repeated in 1941. The Guggenheim Fellowship in 1935, the National Academy of Arts and Letters Award for Literature in 1946, and the Ainsfield-Wolf Award in 1953 continued to keep him in the forefront of the literary community, particularly in New York, throughout his life. His alma mater, Lincoln University, awarded him an honorary doctorate in 1943, and he received others from Howard University and Case Western Reserve University in 1963 and 1964, respectively.

Biography

James Mercer Langston Hughes came from an educated family whose energies were spent primarily in entrepreneurial efforts to combat poverty and institutionalized racism in order to survive. His life repeats a well-known pattern of early twentieth century African-American families: a resourceful mother who rented out their home to boarders, a father who had to leave home to find work, a grandmother who cared for him during his early years, and a stepfather. He grew up in the Midwest—Kansas, Illinois, and Ohio—and participated in athletics as well as in literary activities in high school.

Graduating from Central High School in Lincoln, Illinois, in 1920, Hughes attended Columbia University before shipping out on liners bound for Africa and Holland. He also traveled extensively in Europe before returning to the United States in 1925. Then, in 1929, he received a B.A. from Lincoln University, Pennsylvania. Hughes at first subsisted with the help of patrons, but gradually began to earn a living on the proceeds from his writings and his poetry readings. Although mainly basing himself in Harlem, New York City, Hughes continued to travel extensively. He won numerous prizes, grants, and fellowships for his literary achievements before his death in 1967.

Analysis

Langston Hughes records in *The Big Sea: An Autobiography* (1940) his feelings upon first seeing Africa: ". . . when I saw the dust-green hills in the sunlight, something took hold of me inside. My Africa, Motherland of the Negro peoples! And me a Negro! The real thing!" The trip to Africa confirmed what he already knew—that the subject matter of his writings would reflect his desire "to write seriously and as well as I knew how about the Negro people." Most of Hughes's short stories concern themselves with black people presented from many different perspectives and in both tragic and comic dimensions. Even when a white is the protagonist of a story, as in "Little Dog," the gentle black man to whom Miss Briggs is attracted is given special focus. Hughes, however, is not racist in his presentation. People, regardless of their racial background, are people first participating in a common humanity before they are individuals distorted by prejudice based on ignorance, by fear, or by social conditions which create a spiritual and psychological malaise, sometimes crippling in its effect.

"Little Dog" tells the story of a white and gaunt middle-aged woman, head bookkeeper of a coal and coke firm for twenty-one years, who, because of her own sense of prudence, responsibility, and concern, sublimates her own desires to care for her mother, and then, after her mother's death, is left alone and lonely. Although she keeps busy, is comfortably situated, and does not think too much of what she may be missing, she occasionally wonders why she knows no one whom she can appreciate as a friend. One day she inexplicably stops the taxicab in which she is riding in front of a pet shop featuring in its window "fuzzy little white dogs," and she purchases for herself a puppy at a very steep price. She arranges with the janitor of her apartment building, "a tow-headed young Swede," to provide food for her dog, which she names Flips, and soon her life revolves around activities centering on Flips.

One day the janitor does not show up to feed the dog; several days pass until Miss Briggs decides she needs to go down to the basement to search out the janitor. With her dog by her side, she knocks at a door behind which she hears sounds of "happy laughter, and kids squalling, and people moving." The door is opened by a small black boy and soon Miss Briggs discovers that the "tall broad-shouldered Negro" standing amidst the children is the new janitor.

The image patterns and juxtapositions in the story now begin to form meaningful patterns. The white woman, living "upstairs" with the "fuzzy white dog," is contrasted with the black man and his "pretty little brown-black" children who live "downstairs." The gentle and kind black man begins to service Miss Briggs's needs, bringing more food than is good for the dog because he believes the woman desires it and because he is being paid for it; Miss Briggs, however, never tells him that meat every few days is sufficient. Soon Miss Briggs finds herself hurrying home, never realizing that it is no longer the dog but rather the nightly visits of the janitor that compel her to hurry. One evening her words inadvertently reveal her subconscious needs. The black janitor has just left after delivering Flips's food and she can hear him humming as he returns to his family. Suddenly Miss Briggs says to Flips: "Oh, Flips . . . I'm so hungry."

Now, although she never consciously knows why, Miss Briggs decides she needs to move; ". . . she could not bear to have this janitor come upstairs with a package of bones for Flips again. . . . Let him stay in the basement, where he belonged." The accumulation of references to bones, meat, and services provides for the reader, if not for Miss Briggs, a moment of epiphany: "He almost keeps me broke buying bones," Miss Briggs says to the tall and broad-shouldered black janitor. "True," the janitor answers her. The sustenance the black man provides for the dog is no sustenance for the gaunt and bony woman, nor is the dog, like children, sufficient to keep memory of the departed alive. Miss Briggs moves and shortly is completely forgotten by the people in the neighborhood in which she had lived.

If Miss Briggs seems a portrait of a woman dead before she is buried, Mrs. Luella Bates Washington Jones of "Thank you Ma'am" is a picture of a middle-aged woman still vital and vigorous, although she, too, lives alone; and although it appears she has no children of her own, she is still potent, giving new life to a young black boy who attempts to mug her. The child is no match for the woman, who is identified with her purse so large "that it had everything in it but a hammer and nails." She drags him home with her, sees that he washes, and shares with him her frugal meal. Her presence is so overpowering that the boy is more fearful of trying to get away than of staying, but she breaks down his resistance when she speaks to him of common problems. "I was young once and I wanted things I could not get." The boy waits expecting the "but" to follow. The woman anticipates: "You thought I was going to say, *but I didn't snatch people's pocketbooks.* Well, I wasn't going to say that. . . . I have done things, too, which I would not tell you, son. . . . Everybody's got something in common." The woman's actions, however, tell the boy more than her words do, and at the end of the story the boy is unable to use words, although his lips try to phrase more than "Thank you Ma'am."

One of Hughes's most frequently praised stories is "Professor." Focused through the point of view of its protagonist Dr. T. Walton Brown (*T* for Tom, Uncle Tom?), the story examines how a black professor of sociology "bows" and "bobs" like a puppet on a string to members of the wealthy white establishment, doing only those things of which they approve, saying what they want to hear, and, although at times he knows the lies diminish him, still allowing his own needs to determine his behavior patterns.

Bitterly ironic in tone, the story begins with the juxtaposition of Brown in dinner dress against the lobby of a run-down segregated hotel and Brown cared for by a white chauffeur who tucks the professor carefully into the luxury of a limousine to carry him through the black ghetto to a private house as large as a hotel. Brown's posture and attire are carefully contrasted with the "two or three ash-colored children" who run across the street in front of the limousine, "their skinny legs and poor clothes plain in the glare of the headlights." So also are the streets and buildings contrasted—"the Negro streets": "pig's knuckle joints, pawnshops, beer parlors—and houses of vice, no doubt—save that these latter, at least, did not hang out their signs" with the "wide lawns and fine homes that lined the beautiful well-lighted boulevard where white people lived."

Brown, of course, has bought entry into the white establishment by prostituting himself, by accepting the degradation of the constant diminishing of his selfhood and his negritude. He listens to his white counterpart say: "Why, at our city college here we've been conducting some fine interracial experiments. I have had some colored ministers and high school teachers visit my classes. We found them most intelligent." Although at times Brown is moved to make slight and subtle protest, in the end he agrees with the biased white people, saying "You are right."

Brown's behavior is dictated by his desire for the money the white people offer him as long as he conforms to their expectation. Money will buy Brown prestige, will enable his college to survive, and will further his career. Money will also "take his family to South America in the summer where for three months they wouldn't feel like Negroes." Thus, he dances to the "tune of Jim Crow education," diminishing both himself and his race. Although carefully constructed, the story offers no subtleties beyond the ironies present; image patterns are at a minimum, complex symbolism nonexistent. Characterization, too, is sparse. The reader learns only enough about the professor to make his behavior immediately credible, but a traditional plot line moves with careful pacing to climax and pointed resolution, and the theme overshadows technique.

Similar in theme and technique to "Professor" is "Fine Accommodations." In this story, a young black porter learns that the Dr. Jenkins, booked into sleeping car accommodations, is not the leader of his race and "fine man" the naïve porter expects, but rather another Uncle Tom who keeps on "being a big man" by "bowing to Southern white customs," by helping to keep poor black people just where they have always been "all the time—poor and black." At the end of the story, the porter makes the point of the story: "The last Negro passenger I had in that drawing room was a pimp from Birmingham. Now I got a professor. I guess both of them have to have ways of paying for such fine accommodations."

From the perspective of complexity, subtlety, and power, "Big Meeting" is a considerably better story. Told in the first person by a young black boy who with a companion is observing a church revival meeting held in the woods, the story recounts the boy's moment of epiphany when he realizes, if only subconsciously, that as a cynical observer rather than a participant in the ritual he is more akin to the white folks gathered to watch than to his own people. Making use of dialect and gospel songs, Hughes builds the story to a powerful sermon where the preacher recounts the betrayal of Christ to the accompaniment of echoing refrains and then moves the sermon to the cadences of poetry:

> They brought four long nails
> And put one in the palm of His left hand.
> The hammer said . . . Bam!
> They put one in the palm of His right hand.
> The hammer said . . . Bam!
> They put one through His left foot . . . Bam!
> And one through His right foot . . . Bam!
> . . . "Don't drive it!" a woman screamed. "Don't drive them nails! For Christ's sake! Oh! Don't drive 'em!"

In the woods observing the action, the narrator and his companion are near enough to a car full of white people to overhear what they are saying as they comment in ways showing their biases, limitations, and prejudices. As the narrator hears these comments, he begins to respond, but not enough to cause him to identify with the participants in the service. Rather, both he and his companion seem more concerned with the behavior of their mothers who are taking part in the church rituals.

At the climax of the story, the narrator hears his mother's voice: "Were you there when they crucified my Lord?/ Were you there when they nailed Him to the tree?" At the same time as the mother cries out the questions, the preacher opens his arms wide against the white canvas tent, and his body reflects a crosslike shadow. As the mother asks the question again, the white people in the car suddenly drive away creating a swirl of dust, and the narrator cries after them, "Don't go. . . . They're about to call for sinners. . . . Don't go!"

The boy's cry to the white people reflects his understanding of the parallel setup between the white people and the betrayers of Christ. Hughes goes further than this, however, and provides in the last sentence of the story an epiphanic moment: "I didn't realize I was crying until I tasted my tears in my mouth." The epiphany projects a revelation dimly understood by the narrator but clearly present—that as bad as the white people's behavior seemed, his own rejection of his people and heritage was worse.

Other major works

NOVELS: *Not Without Laughter*, 1930; *Tambourines to Glory*, 1958.

PLAYS: *Mulatto*, 1935; *Little Ham*, 1936; *Don't You Want to Be Free*, 1938; *Freedom's Plow*, 1943; *Simply Heavenly*, 1957; *Black Nativity*, 1961; *Tambourines to Glory*, 1963; *Five Plays*, 1963; *Jerico-Jim Crow*, 1964; *The Prodigal Son*, 1965.

POETRY: *The Weary Blues*, 1926; *Fine Clothes to the Jew*, 1927; *Dear Lovely Death*, 1931; *The Negro Mother*, 1931; *The Dream Keeper and Other Poems*, 1932; *Scottsboro Limited*, 1932; *A New Song*, 1938; *Shakespeare in Harlem*, 1942; *Jim Crow's Last Stand*, 1943; *Lament for Dark Peoples*, 1944; *Fields of Wonder*, 1947; *One Way Ticket*,

1949; *Montage of a Dream Deferred*, 1951; *Selected Poems of Langston Hughes*, 1959; *Ask Your Mama: Or, Twelve Moods for Jazz*, 1961; *The Panther and the Lash: Or, Poems of Our Times*, 1967.

NONFICTION: *The Big Sea: An Autobiography*, 1940; *The First Book of Negroes*, 1952; *The First Book of Rhythms*, 1954; *Famous American Negroes*, 1954; *Famous Negro Music Makers*, 1955; *The First Book of Jazz*, 1955; *The First Book of the West Indies*, 1955; *A Pictorial History of the Negro in America*, 1956; *I Wonder as I Wander: An Autobiographical Journey*, 1956; *Famous Negro Heroes of America*, 1958; *First Book of Africa*, 1960; *Fight for Freedom: The Story of the NAACP*, 1962; *Black Magic: A Pictorial History of the Negro in American Entertainment*, 1967; *Arna Bontemps-Langston Hughes Letters*, 1980.

TRANSLATIONS: *Masters of the Dew*, 1947; *Cuba Libre*, 1948; *Gypsy Ballads*, 1951; *Selected Poems of Gabriela Mistral*, 1957.

MISCELLANEOUS: *Troubled Island*, c. 1930 (opera libretto); *Popo and Fifina: Children of Haiti*, 1932 (with Arna Bontemps); *Street Scene*, 1947 (lyrics); *The Poetry of the Negro, 1746-1949*, 1949 (with Arna Bontemps); *Simply Heavenly*, c. 1959 (opera libretto); *New Negro Poets: U.S.A.*, 1964; *The Book of Negro Humor*, 1966; *The Best Short Stories by Negro Writers: An Anthology from 1899 to the Present*, 1967.

Bibliography
Dickinson, Donald C. *A Bio-Bibliography of Langston Hughes, 1902-1967*. 2d ed. Hamden, Conn.: Archon Books, 1972. With its preface by Arna Bontemps, a major scholar and critic of the Harlem Renaissance and a contemporary of Hughes, the reader has both older and updated assessments of Hughes's achievement. Part 1 is the biography, which incorporates information throughout Hughes's life; part 2 includes all of his work through 1965, except short newspaper articles, song lyrics, and phonographic records. Even a glance at the bibliography gives an indication of the range of Hughes's imaginative achievement.
Emanuel, James A. *Langston Hughes*. New York: Twayne, 1967. This survey of Hughes's work as a poet and fiction writer emphasizes the reflection of African-American speech patterns, rhythms, and idiomatic expressions in Hughes's work, as well as the folk culture behind these, which he turned into literary devices. The book also points out pan-African themes and the peculiar struggle of a writer with Hughes's background in both the sociological and literary contexts.
Jemie, Onwuchekwa. *Langston Hughes: An Introduction to the Poetry*. New York: Columbia University Press, 1976. This study of the collected poems omits a number of later works but provides an important focus on the poetic techniques and themes of Hughes. Jemie defends Hughes against charges of being merely popular and emotional, pointing out the African oral tradition as well as African-American music as influences on Hughes's poetry and Hughes's role in the development of a black consciousness in American poetry.
Rampersad, Arnold. *The Life of Langston Hughes*. 2 vols. New York: Oxford University Press, 1986-1988. This major critical biography illustrates not only the tri-

umphs but also the struggles of the man and the writer. The importance of Hughes in the Harlem Renaissance and his symbolic significance in the developing artistic and imaginative consciousness of African-American writers come alive in concrete examples in volume 1, *I, Too, Sing America*, and volume 2, *I Dream a World*. These titles, drawn from Hughes's poetry, reveal the themes illustrating the writer's life and the points in his own characterization of his struggle.

Tracy, Steven C. *Langston Hughes and the Blues*. Urbana: University of Illinois Press, 1988. This book uses the folk traditions of African and African-American culture as background but concentrates primarily on the blues tradition within that culture as a way of interpreting Hughes's work. The intellectualizing of this tradition and the deliberate incorporation of the blues dimension in imaginative literature is a major emphasis, along with the oral tradition in African culture. This historical survey of the blues as an art form and its application in criticism seeks to counteract the dismissal of some of Hughes's more popular works by critics such as Donald C. Dickinson (see above).

Mary Rohrberger
(Revised by *Emma Coburn Norris*)

WILLIAM HUMPHREY

Born: Clarksville, Texas; June 18, 1924

Principal short fiction

The Last Husband and Other Stories, 1953; *A Time and a Place*, 1968; *Collected Stories*, 1985.

Other literary forms

Novelist William Humphrey began his literary career in the late 1940's as a short-story writer, contributing to a number of the United States' better magazines—*The New Yorker, Accent, Esquire*, and *The Atlantic*—and publishing a collection of stories before his first novel appeared. His stories have attracted favorable critical comment, but most commentators rate his novels above his stories. Of his novels, the best known are *Home from the Hill* (1958) and *The Ordways* (1965). Many critics think Humphrey's best piece of writing is *Farther Off from Heaven* (1977), a memoir of the first thirteen years of his life. In addition to his fiction, Humphrey is the author of several hunting and fishing stories first published in magazines and later reprinted as small books—*The Spawning Run* (1970), *My Moby Dick* (1978), and *Open Season: Sporting Adventures* (1989).

Achievements

The publisher Alfred A. Knopf called Humphrey's *Home from the Hill* the best novel to come out of Texas. The book earned for Humphrey the Carr P. Collins Award of the Texas Institute of Letters for best book of fiction by a Texas author in 1958. The novel was nominated for—but did not win—the National Book Award. The success of Humphrey's first novel, which was made into a popular motion picture in 1960, led to his winning a grant from the National Institute of Arts and Letters that aided him in the writing of his second novel, *The Ordways*, which was selected by the Literary Guild, went through six printings in its first year, and won for Humphrey a second Texas Institute of Letters prize.

Biography

William Humphrey has been very secretive about his life, saying once that he considered it bragging to fill out forms sent by *Who's Who* and other dictionaries of biography. Therefore, the entries about Humphrey in such publications are limited to the kind of material found on dust jackets. In later years, he became slightly more forthcoming in interviews and has published a memoir that covers the first thirteen years of his life, the years he spent in his native Clarksville, Texas. From notes, hints, and "slips" by the author, it is possible to reconstruct some parts of his life. He is the son of working-class parents (his father was an auto mechanic), and he suffered an affliction as a child that required braces for his legs. He and his mother left Clarksville never to return when his father was killed in a car wreck in 1937. Humphrey and his mother moved to Dallas, Texas. He attended Southern Methodist University and the University of Texas at Austin, apparently never taking a degree. He mentioned in an interview published in 1988 that he left Texas in 1943 during his last semester of college. He decided to leave while sitting in the middle of a German class, so he stood up and walked out, telling the professor that he was headed for Chicago. Where he went is not clear, but for most of the rest of his life he has lived in the state of New York, residing in the city of Hudson beginning in the early 1960's. Humphrey, apparently without benefit of a degree, has lectured at several colleges, but for most of his life he has supported himself, his wife Dorothy, and a daughter by his writing.

Humphrey told interviewer Ashby Bland Crowder that he studied art between the ages of thirteen and eighteen. Then he found, when he tried to join the navy during World War II, that he was color-blind. He gave up art and turned to writing, going to New York with a five-act play about Benjamin Franklin. The play was never produced, and Humphrey turned to the writing of fiction. The short-story writer he most admired was fellow Texan Katherine Anne Porter. She wrote her nephew, after reading two of Humphrey's stories in *Accent*, that the young writer had taken two of her stories, "The Cracked Looking-Glass" and "A Day's Work," and turned them into his own. The Humphrey stories, "In Sickness and in Health" and "Man with a Family," do indeed bear remarkable resemblances to Porter's stories. Later, in a letter cited in Joan Givner's *Katherine Ann Porter: A Life* (1984), Humphrey admitted to Porter that he had stolen his first published story from "A Day's Work" and that he always wrote with her stories open to the paragraphs that he most admired. There is no question that Humphrey's stories owe a great debt to Porter's works, especially in their irony and emphasis on place.

Humphrey, whose interest in hunting and fishing can be traced to his father, has devoted much of his writing in later years to nonfiction stories about outdoor sports, though his interest in the out-of-doors has not produced a large body of work. The same can be said of his fictional output. In more than forty years, he has produced several novels and more than twenty stories.

Humphrey's best work is about Red River County, Texas, but after 1977, the year he published his memoir *Farther Off from Heaven*, about his childhood there, he has written two novels about life in other places. *Hostages to Fortune* (1984) is set in Hudson, New York, and describes the effects of a young person's suicide on his parents; *No Resting Place* (1989) is about the Cherokees' being uprooted from the South and marched to Texas along the "Trail of Tears" in the 1830's.

Analysis

Most of William Humphrey's stories are set in and around his native Red River County, Texas, which is located in the far northeastern corner of the state. The county borders the state of Oklahoma, and many of the stories take place across the Red River in what is called "the Little Dixie" section of Oklahoma. Northeast Texas and southeastern Oklahoma were settled by Southerners who came West before and after the Civil War, Indians driven West when the South was being cleared of Native Americans during the rapid expansion of the 1820's and 1830's, and slaves—later freed—brought in by both whites and Indians.

Humphrey's ancestors came into his part of Texas following the Civil War, and it is this part of the world that Humphrey has always understood best, even though he left Clarksville for good in 1937. His best stories and novels are about the people and places he knew when he was a boy growing up in Clarksville. His first book of stories, *The Last Husband and Other Stories*, shows clearly how much Humphrey is dependent on his homeland for the success of his work. The six best stories in the volume are Texas-based. Five take place in and around Clarksville, and one is about a transplanted Texan isolated in a Northern city and longing for home. The four stories set in the East, where Humphrey was living during his writing apprenticeship, lack the life found in his Clarksville stories. It is not that the themes are deficient or that the style suffers in his Eastern stories. There are excellent scenes and some of the characters are as well developed as those in his regional works. Something is missing, however, and it is very clear that it is a sense of time and place that Humphrey must have in order to tell his stories and develop his points. He understands the people of Red River County and can make them speak a language that is real. When he shifts to New York, his "other" setting, place becomes unreal for him. The sense of kinship with the people who speak his language and share his customs disappears. The stories and novels suffer. Even his later works—produced after a lifetime as a fiction writer—lack the immediacy of his earlier works, his works about Clarksville.

The non-Texas stories, written while he was still in his Katherine Anne Porter phase, are technically correct and usually well written. They are the sorts of things one found in the slick highbrow magazines in the years immediately following World War II. The people are modern and sophisticated, and their lives in the suburbs are as hollow as up-to-date social critics and old-fashioned moralists would like one to believe they are. Furthermore, following the modern mode of fiction, the stories are ironic and ultimately depressing.

The book's title story is about a man named Edward Gavin who has a series of mistresses in a desperate attempt to get his wife, an unsuccessful artist with a successful sister, to pay attention to him and live the kind of life that married people are traditionally supposed to live. Edward, whom the reader knows only through a narrator, loses his battle with his wife of two decades, proving that his infidelities netted him nothing. Of course, his wife's winning gets her nothing either. They are as dead as people in the wasteland always are.

"The Last Husband" is not a bad story until one begins to compare it to Humphrey's best regional work. His early story "The Hardys" makes a nice contrast to "The Last Husband." The Hardys are an old couple closing their home to move in with their children. Mr. Hardy was widowed before he met his present wife, and Mrs. Hardy has spent years being jealous. The reader learns, in this story, told first from one point of view, then the other, that Mr. Hardy has long since forgotten his first wife and that Mrs. Hardy has no need to be jealous. (Interestingly, Edward Gavin summarizes "The Hardys" for the narrator when the two are riding the train home from Grand Central one night.) "The Hardys" is filled with the homey regional details and carefully rendered speech that make for excellent fiction.

"Quail for Mr. Forester" is a typical Humphrey story in that the reader sees the changing ways of the South through the eyes of a young boy—a method Humphrey uses again and again. Mr. Forester's family once made up the local aristocracy, but in recent years the Foresters have come down in the world. The narrator's father, a top-notch hunter, kills some excellent quail and invites Mr. Forester to dine. The dinner conversation is all about the decline of the Old South, which, ironically, is felt much more keenly by the narrator's family of working-class people than by Mr. Forester. At the end of an evening talking about the glory days before the Civil War, the boy, still awed, muses, "I felt that there was no hope for me in these mean times I had been born into." The mean times of the North also trouble the Southern woman in "A Fresh Snow." She married a man from outside her region and is now sitting sadly in her room watching the flakes fall and thinking how far she is from home and how different the customs are. When her young son comes home and speaks in the harsh dialect of the industrial East, "she sat him on her lap and rocked him softly, his head against her breast, while she told him all about the South, where he was born."

The stories in William Humphrey's second volume, *A Time and a Place*, are all set in Depression-era Texas and Oklahoma. Heavily ironic, as most of his stories are, these narratives depict the harshness of life during the years of the Dust Bowl, the oil strikes, and the closing years of the Old South in Texas and Oklahoma, a world eradicated by World War II. There are a number of good stories among the ten in this volume. One of the best and most often discussed is "A Voice from the Woods," which flashes back from the undefined present to the time when the outlaws Bonnie and Clyde and Pretty Boy Floyd were heroes to the poor people of Texas and Oklahoma. The narrator, who grew up in Clarksville, lives in the East. His mother is visiting him and his Eastern wife, and as they sit drinking beer, they hear the cooing of a mourning dove. The sound recalls to the mother the time that a man she once loved and considered marrying robbed the bank in Clarksville and was killed in a gunfight on the street. She and the son, a very small boy at the time, witnessed the death of the robber. She sits thinking how different her life might have been had she married Travis Winfield, who died in the arms of his latest love, a red-headed woman. The mother recalls how she had a good life with a good husband, but she says, "And yet, thinking of that red-headed woman . . . I felt, well, I don't know what else to call it if not jealousy."

There is a certain sentimentality to the story, but Humphrey evokes the time and the place and the attitude of the people as well as anyone writing about Texas in the 1930's ever has. An equally effective story at evoking the era is "Mouth of Brass," about a brief friendship between a small boy and a black tamale vendor. The vendor travels all over town during the week, but on Saturdays he sets up his tamale boxes in the town square, where "the population doubled—in ginning season tripled—as country folks poured in. . . ." One Saturday, Finus—the vendor—sells a dozen tamales to a little boy who is buying them for his redneck family waiting just off the square. When the boy wolfs down five of the tamales on the way back to the family, the father thinks Finus took advantage of the child's age to cheat him, becomes enraged, and confronts the vendor. One thing leads to another, and the man knifes Finus. Naturally, in the Deep South of the 1930's, the white man was provoked and is let off on self-defense. The little boy, who was once allowed to make his rounds with Finus, experiences an epiphany about race relations and will never be the same.

These stories and many others in Humphrey's collections paint vivid pictures of the South as it was when Humphrey was a boy and was learning about the injustices of life. His works are filled with the ironies to be encountered in a merciless universe devoid of justice and quick to plunge human beings into misery. His stories are often bleak and hopeless: men are forced into crime by circumstances and then are punished unmercifully; the underclass are beaten down by the rich; children are jerked suddenly into adulthood by death and destruction. Bad as it is, however, there is a richness to the life found in northeast Texas. There were traditions and stories and customs that were passed down from generation to generation by word of mouth. There were moments of unsurpassable joy to balance—at least partially—the violence and cruelty found there and so well described in the writings of William Humphrey.

Other major works

NOVELS: *Home from the Hill*, 1958; *The Ordways*, 1965; *Proud Flesh*, 1973; *Hostages to Fortune*, 1984; *No Resting Place*, 1989.

NONFICTION: *The Spawning Run*, 1970; *Ah, Wilderness: The Frontier in American Literature*, 1977; *Farther Off from Heaven*, 1977; *My Moby Dick*, 1978; *Open Season: Sporting Adventures*, 1989.

Bibliography

Givner, Joan. "Katherine Anne Porter: The Old Order and the New." In *The Texas Literary Tradition*, edited by Don Graham et al. Austin: University of Texas Press, 1983. Though Humphrey's name does not appear in the title, Givner argues that Humphrey and fellow Texan William Goyen were greatly under the influence of Porter. Here and in the biography that she wrote on Porter, Givner traces Porter's influence on the two younger writers and says that they were eager to imitate Porter and win her favor with letters and flowery dedications. The essay is interesting also in showing the treatment Porter received in the male-dominated Texas literary establishment of the 1930's and 1940's.

Grider, Sylvia, and Elizabeth Tebeaux. "Blessings into Curses: Sardonic Humor and Irony in 'A Job of the Plains.'" *Studies in Short Fiction* 23 (1986): 297-306. The authors of this essay focus on Humphrey's short story "A Job of the Plains," an ironic retelling of the Book of Job as it might have happened in the Dust Bowl of Oklahoma during the Great Depression of the 1930's. Humphrey's story, the authors say, delves into the meaninglessness of life, the cruelty of God's universe, and the pointlessness of human suffering. The theme becomes "the controlling theme for the remaining stories in the collection. In every story, Humphrey weaves a similar naturalism into the Dust Bowl/Depression world view." Grider and Tebeaux compare *A Time and a Place* to Sherwood Anderson's *Winesburg, Ohio* (1919).

Humphrey, William. "William Humphrey: Defining Southern Literature." Interview by Ashby Bland Crowder. *Mississippi Quarterly* 41 (1988): 529-540. Humphrey reveals some hitherto unknown facts about his life and gives a hint about his method of working. The interviewer is at great pains to fix Humphrey in the canon of Southern literature and to question the author closely on his relationship to William Faulkner and others. The persistent attempts to direct the flow of the interview to "southernness" often interrupts Humphrey's commentary on his general attitudes and his view of his place in American literature.

Lee, James Ward. *William Humphrey*. Austin, Tex.: Steck-Vaughn, 1967. One of the volumes in the Southwest Writers series, this pamphlet of sixty pages is the longest work on Humphrey, but it was written when Humphrey had only two novels, a volume of stories, and four uncollected stories in print. The first twenty pages discuss Humphrey's fourteen stories, while the rest of the study analyzes *Home from the Hill* and *The Ordways*. One of the major emphases in the pamphlet is on Humphrey's use of regional materials—the folklore, the naturalistic descriptions, and the customs of northeast Texas.

_____. "William Humphrey." In *American Novelists Since World War II*, 2d ser., edited by James E. Kilber, Jr. Detroit: Gale Research, 1980. In this six-page essay, Lee updates the pamphlet he wrote in 1967, placing more emphasis on the novels, the sporting stories, and the memoir *Farther Off from Heaven*. Lee predicts that *Farther Off from Heaven* may be Humphrey's farewell to Red River County and the Clarksville of his boyhood.

James Ward Lee

ZORA NEALE HURSTON

Born: Eatonville, Florida; January 7, 1903
Died: Fort Pierce, Florida; January 28, 1960

Principal short fiction

Spunk: The Selected Short Stories of Zora Neale Hurston, 1985.

Other literary forms

Though best known for her novels, especially *Their Eyes Were Watching God* (1937), Zora Neale Hurston wrote in most major genres during her forty-year career. In addition to the posthumously published collection of short stories, she wrote a few early poems, several short plays, folklore collections, essays, reportage, and an autobiography.

Achievements

Hurston is best known as a major contributor to the Harlem Renaissance literature of the 1920's. Not only was she a major contributor, but also she did much to characterize the style and temperament of the period; indeed, she is often referred to as the most colorful figure of the Harlem Renaissance. Though the short stories and short plays that she generated during the 1920's are fine works in their own right, they are nevertheless apprentice works when compared to her most productive period, the 1930's. During the 1930's, Hurston produced three novels, all telling examples of her creative genius, as well as two collections of folklore, the fruits of her training in anthropology and her many years of fieldwork. It is Hurston's interest in preserving the culture of the black South that remains among her most valuable contributions. Not only did she collect and preserve folklore outright, but also she used folklore, native drama, and the black idiom and dialect in most of her fiction.

Although Hurston's popularity declined during the 1940's and 1950's, and although she died in relative obscurity in 1960, scholars and critics sparked a Hurston revival during the mid-1970's. Hurston's popularity has never been greater, as her works are considered mainstays in any number of canons, among them African-American literature, folklore, Southern literature, feminist studies, and anthropology.

Biography

Zora Neale Hurston was born in 1903 in the all-black town of Eatonville, Florida, near Orlando. She was the youngest daughter and the seventh of eight children born to John and Lucy Hurston. Her father was a minister and local government official who wrote many of Eatonville's laws upon its incorporation and served several terms as mayor. Her mother was a homemaker who cared not only for her children but also for an extended family that included, at various times, her own mother and her brother Jim. By all accounts, Hurston's childhood was happy, almost idyllic, free from the poverty and racism that characterized much of the black experience in the South. Indeed, this wholesome upbringing informed much of Hurston's later work and earned for her the designation as an early black cultural nationalist.

Whatever idyllic aspects Hurston's childhood possessed were shattered when Hurston was about nine. The death of Hurston's beloved mother, who encouraged the young Zora to "jump at the sun," precipitated a change. This was followed by her father's remarriage to a woman who had no interest in the children and the subsequent dismantling of the relative happiness of the Hurston household. The next several years of Hurston's life found her much displaced, living variously with older siblings and receiving only sporadic schooling.

Although exact dates are difficult to place in Hurston's early chronology because she frequently lied about her age, various sources reveal that Hurston joined a Gilbert and Sullivan traveling show when she was about fourteen as a wardrobe maid to one of the show's stars. Hurston worked for this show for several years, traveling throughout the South, sometimes without pay. It was with this show, however, that Hurston's talents as raconteur were first noticed, as she often entertained the company with stories, anecdotes, and tales from the black South, told with their own humor, mimicry, and dialect.

Hurston left her job with the Gilbert and Sullivan show in Baltimore, and out of an intense desire to complete her education, she enrolled in the high school department of the Morgan Academy (now Morgan State University) in that city, completing the high school program in 1919. From Morgan, Hurston entered Howard University, at that time known as "the Negro Harvard," in Washington, D.C. At Howard, Hurston soon came to the attention of Alain Locke, adviser to the Howard Literary Society and later a principal critic of the New Negro movement. Locke invited Hurston to join the literary society, and she soon began publishing in *Stylus*, the Howard University literary magazine. Her first published short story, "John Redding Goes to Sea," appeared in *Stylus* in 1921.

Hurston's talent soon came to the attention of Charles S. Johnson, founder and editor of the National Urban League's magazine *Opportunity*, which held annual contests for young writers. Johnson encouraged Hurston to submit her works to *Opportunity*, which she did; "Drenched in Light" appeared in December, 1924, and "Spunk" in June, 1925. Both "Spunk" and a short play, "Color Struck," were second-place prizewinners in their respective divisions in *Opportunity*'s 1925 contest, and another short story, "Black Death," won honorable mention.

Hurston traveled to New York to attend the 1925 contest awards banquet and found herself in the midst of the Harlem Renaissance, the great outpouring of artistic expression revolving around Harlem. She became an active member of the Harlem literati and soon became the Harlem Renaissance's most colorful figure. In the fall of 1925, Hurston entered Barnard, the women's college of Columbia University, on a scholarship arranged by Annie Nathan Meyer. There, she studied anthropology under Franz Boas and received her degree in 1928.

Beginning in 1927, Hurston traveled throughout the South, collecting folklore, first under the sponsorship of the Association for the Study of Negro Life and History,

and later through various fellowships, including a Guggenheim, and the private sponsorship of Charlotte Osgood Mason, a wealthy white patron of Harlem Renaissance
writers including Langston Hughes and Alain Locke.

In 1930, Hurston and Hughes collaborated on a black folk play, *Mule Bone*, an
undertaking that severed the personal and professional relationship between Hurston
and Hughes; the break was never mended and kept the play from being published in
its entirety until 1991, long after the deaths of both authors. The dispute, precipitated
by the question of principal authorship, while certainly unfortunate, nevertheless
illustrates the fiercely independent temperament that Hurston maintained throughout
her lifetime.

Though the 1930's got off to a rough start with the controversy with Hughes, the
decade proved to be Hurston's most productive. Hurston published her first novel,
Jonah's Gourd Vine, in 1934, followed in rapid succession by the folklore collection
Mules and Men in 1935; another novel, the now classic *Their Eyes Were Watching
God* in 1937; another folklore collection, *Tell My Horse*, in 1938; and another novel,
Moses, Man of the Mountain, in 1939. In addition, Hurston wrote several short sto-
ries and several essays, notably those on black culture, published in Nancy Cunard's
massive collection, *Negro*, in 1934.

In 1942, Hurston published her autobiography, *Dust Tracks on a Road*. While the
book won the *Saturday Review*'s Ainsfield-Wolf Award for race relations, it proved
to be the last significant work of Hurston's career, although she did publish another
novel, *Seraph on the Suwanee*, in 1948. There are several reasons for the decline in
Hurston's popularity, the most important among them being that her folk-based literature did not fit into protest literature, the dominant literary trend of the 1940's,
coupled with Hurston's growing conservatism. Further, in September, 1948, shortly
before the publication of *Seraph on the Suwanee*, Hurston was falsely charged with
seducing a minor, but before the charges could be dismissed as unfounded, the black
press, in particular the *Baltimore Afro-American*, had spread the story to its readers
and had severely, almost irreparably, damaged Hurston's reputation. Disillusioned
and outraged at her treatment by the court and the black press, Hurston moved back
to the South, where she lived for the remainder of her life.

The 1950's was a tragic decade for Hurston. Her career was stagnant, and although she kept writing, she received rejection after rejection. She did, however, do
some reporting for the *Pittsburgh Courier*, a black paper with a national circulation;
published several essays; and accepted several speaking engagements. She supported
herself with occasional work, including substitute teaching and writing free-lance
articles for various papers.

Toward the end of the 1950's, Hurston's health became increasingly fragile. She
suffered from overweight, hypertension, poor diet, gallbladder trouble, ulcers, and
various stomach ailments. In 1959, she suffered a stroke, and in October of that
year was placed in the Saint Lucie County welfare home, where, alone and penniless, she died on January 28, 1960. She was buried by subscription a week later in
Fort Pierce's segregated cemetery, the Garden of the Heavenly Rest.

Analysis

The bulk of Zora Neale Hurston's short fiction is set in her native Florida, as are most of her novels. Even when the setting is not Florida, however, the stories are informed by the life, habits, beliefs, and idioms of the people whom Hurston knew so well, the inhabitants of Eatonville primarily. One criticism often leveled at Hurston was that she frequently masqueraded folklore as fiction, or, in other cases, imposed folklore on the fictive narrative. Whatever the merits of such criticism may be, Hurston's short stories abound with an energy and zest for life that Hurston considered instructive for her readers.

Hurston's first published short story is entitled "John Redding Goes to Sea." It was published in the May, 1921, issue of the *Stylus*, the literary magazine of Howard University, and was reprinted in the January, 1926, issue of *Opportunity*. While the story is obviously the work of a novice writer, with its highly contrived plot, excessive sentimentality, and shallow characterizations, its strengths are many, strengths upon which Hurston would continue to draw and develop throughout her career.

The plot is a simple one: young John Redding, the titular character, wants to leave his hometown to see and explore parts and things unknown. Several circumstances conspire, however, to keep him from realizing his dream. First, John's mother, the pitifully possessive, obsessive, and superstitious Matty Redding, is determined not to let John pursue his ambitions; in fact, she pleads illness and threatens to disown him if he leaves. Second, John's marriage to Stella Kanty seems to tie him permanently to his surroundings, as his new wife joins forces with his mother to discourage John's desire to travel. Further, his mother's tantrums keep John from even joining the Navy when that opportunity comes his way. Later, when John is killed in a tempest while working with a crew to build a bridge on the St. John's River, his father forbids his body to be retrieved from the river as it floats toward the ocean. At last, John will get his wish to travel and see the world, although in death.

If the plot seems overdone and the sentimentality overwhelming, "John Redding Goes to Sea" does provide the reader with the first of many glimpses of life among black Floridians—their habits, superstitions, strengths, and shortcomings. For example, one of the more telling aspects of the story is that Matty believes that her son was cursed with "travel dust" at his birth; thus, John's desire to travel is Matty's punishment for having married his father away from a rival suitor. Hurston suspends judgment on Matty's beliefs; rather, she shows that these and other beliefs are integral parts of the life of the folk.

Another strength that is easily discernible in Hurston's first short story is her detailed rendering of setting. Hurston has a keen eye for detail, and nowhere is this more evident than in her descriptions of the lushness of Florida. This adeptness is especially present in "John Redding Goes to Sea" and in most of Hurston's other work as well.

By far the most important aspect of "John Redding Goes to Sea" is its theme that people must be free to develop and pursue their own dreams, a recurring theme in the Hurston canon. John Redding is deprived of self-expression and self-determination because the wishes and interpretations of others are imposed upon him. Hurston clearly has no sympathy with those who would deprive another of freedom and independence; indeed, she would adamantly oppose all such restrictive efforts throughout her career as a writer and folklorist.

Another early short story that treats a variation of this theme is "Spunk," published in the June, 1925, issue of *Opportunity*. The central character, Spunk Banks, has the spunk to live his life as he chooses, which includes taking another man's wife and parading openly around town with her. While Hurston passes no moral judgment on Banks, she makes it clear that she appreciates and admires his brassiness and his will to live his life according to his own terms.

When the story opens, Spunk Banks and Lena Kanty are openly flaunting their affair in front of the Eatonville townspeople, including Lena's husband, Joe Kanty. The other town residents make fun of Joe's weakness, his refusal to confront Spunk Banks. Later, when Joe desperately attacks Spunk with a razor, Spunk shoots and kills him. Spunk is tried and acquitted but is killed in a work-related accident, cut to death by a circle saw.

Again, superstition plays an important role here, for Spunk claims that he has been haunted by Joe Kanty's ghost. In fact, Spunk is convinced that Joe's ghost pushed him into the circle saw, and at least one other townsman agrees. As is customary in Hurston's stories, however, she makes no judgment of the rightness or wrongness of such beliefs but points out that these beliefs are very much a part of the cultural milieu of Eatonville.

Another early Eatonville story is "Sweat," published in 1926 in the only issue of the ill-fated literary magazine *Fire!*, founded by Hurston, Hughes, and Wallace Thurman. "Sweat" shows Hurston's power as a fiction writer and as a master of the short-story form. Again, the story line is a simple one. Delia Jones is a hardworking, temperate Christian woman being tormented by her arrogant, mean-spirited, and cruel husband of fifteen years, Sykes Jones, who has become tired of her and desires a new wife. Rather than simply leaving her, though, he wants to drive her away by making her life miserable. At stake is the house for which Delia's "sweat" has paid: Sykes wants it for his new mistress, but Delia refuses to leave the fruit of her labor.

Sykes uses both physical and mental cruelty to antagonize Delia, the most far-reaching of which is Delia's intense fear of snakes. When Delia's fear of the caged rattlesnake that Sykes places outside her back door subsides, Sykes places the rattlesnake in the dirty clothes hamper, hoping that it will bite and kill Delia. In an ironic twist, however, Delia escapes and the rattlesnake bites Sykes as he fumbles for a match in the dark house. Delia listens and watches as Sykes dies a painful, agonizing death.

While "Sweat" makes use of the same superstitious beliefs as Hurston's other stories, a more complex characterization and an elaborate system of symbols are central to the story's development. In Delia, for example, readers are presented with an essentially good Christian woman who is capable of great compassion and long suffering and who discovers the capacity to hate as intensely as she loves; in Sykes, readers are shown unadulterated evil reduced to one at once pitiful and horrible in his suffering. In addition, the Christian symbolism, including the snake and the beast of burden, adds considerable interest and texture to the story. It is this texture that makes "Sweat" Hurston's most rewarding work of short fiction, for it shows her at her best as literary artist and cultural articulator.

Although Hurston turned to the longer narrative as the preferred genre during the 1930's, she continued writing short stories throughout the remainder of her career. One such story is "The Gilded Six-Bits," published in 1933, which also examines relationships between men and women. In this story, the marriage bed of a happy couple, Joe and Missie May Banks, is defiled by a city slicker, Otis D. Slemmons. Missie May has been attracted by Slemmons' gold money, which she desires to get for her husband. The gold pieces, however, turn out to be gold-plated. Hurston's message is nearly cliché—"all that glitters is not gold"—but she goes a step further to establish the idea that true love transcends all things. Joe and Missie May are reconciled at the end of the story.

Hurston's last stories are fables that seem to have only comic value but do, however, advance serious thoughts, such as the ridiculousness of the idea of race purity in "Cock Robin, Beale Street" or the equal ridiculousness of the idea that the North was better for blacks, in "Story in Harlem Slang." While these stories are not artistic achievements, they do provide interesting aspects of the Hurston canon.

In many ways, Hurston's short stories are apprentice works to her novels. In these stories, she introduced most of the themes, character types, settings, techniques, and concerns upon which she later elaborated during her most productive and artistic period, the 1930's. This observation, however, does not suggest that her short stories are inferior works. On the contrary, much of the best of Hurston can be found in these early stories.

Other major works

NOVELS: *Jonah's Gourd Vine*, 1934; *Their Eyes Were Watching God*, 1937; *Moses, Man of the Mountain*, 1939; *Seraph on the Suwanee*, 1948.

PLAYS: *Color Struck*, 1926; *The First One*, 1927; *Mule Bone*, 1991 (with Langston Hughes).

NONFICTION: *Mules and Men*, 1935; *Tell My Horse*, 1938; *Dust Tracks on a Road*, 1942; *The Sanctified Church*, 1981.

MISCELLANEOUS: *I Love Myself When I Am Laughing . . . and Then Again When I Am Looking Mean and Impressive: A Zora Neale Hurston Reader*, 1979.

Bibliography

Glassman, Steve, and Kathryn Lee Siedel, eds. *Zora in Florida*. Orlando: University of Central Florida Press, 1991. This collection of essays by seventeen Hurston scholars explores the overall presence and influence of Florida in and on the works of Hurston. This collection grew out of a Hurston symposium held in Daytona Beach, Florida, in November, 1989, and includes an excellent introduction to the importance of Florida in the study of Hurston.

Hemenway, Robert E. *Zora Neale Hurston: A Literary Biography*. Urbana: University of Illinois Press, 1977. Perhaps the best extant work on Hurston. Hemenway's painstakingly researched study of Hurston's life and literary career was crucial in rescuing Hurston from neglect and establishing her as a major American writer. Although some of the facts of Hurston's chronology have been corrected by later scholarship, Hemenway's study is the most valuable introduction to Hurston's work available. Includes a bibliography of published and unpublished works by Hurston.

Howard, Lillie P. *Zora Neale Hurston*. Boston: Twayne, 1980. A good general introduction to the life and works of Hurston. Contains valuable plot summaries and commentaries on Hurston's works. Supplemented by a chronology and a bibliography.

Lyons, Mary E. *Sorrow's Kitchen: The Life and Folklore of Zora Neale Hurston*. New York: Charles Scribner's Sons, 1990. Perhaps the only straightforward biography of Hurston, written with the younger reader in mind. Especially useful for those who need a primer in Hurston's background in all-black Eatonville.

Newsom, Adele S. *Zora Neale Hurston: A Reference Guide* Boston: G. K. Hall, 1987. A catalog of Hurston criticism spanning the years 1931-1986, arranged chronologically with annotations. This source is an invaluable aid to serious scholars of Hurston. Also contains an introduction to the criticism on Hurston. An especially useful resource for all inquiries.

Warren J. Carson

WASHINGTON IRVING

Born: New York, New York; April 3, 1783
Died: Tarrytown, New York; November 28, 1859

Principal short fiction

The Sketch Book of Geoffrey Crayon, Gent., 1819-1820; *Bracebridge Hall*, 1822; *Tales of a Traveller*, 1824; *The Alhambra*, 1832; *Legends of the Conquest of Spain*, 1835.

Other literary forms

Washington Irving distinguished himself in a variety of genres. His finest and most typical book, *The Sketch Book of Geoffrey Crayon, Gent.*, blends essay, sketch, history, travel, humor, and short story; his first best-seller was a satire, *A History of New York* (1809); he coauthored a successful play, *Charles the Second: Or, The Merry Monarch* (1824); but he devoted the latter and most prolific part of his career to books of travel and especially of history.

Achievements

Irving was America's first internationally recognized author. While he achieved national notoriety with his satiric *A History of New York*, his fame abroad was made with *The Sketch Book of Geoffrey Crayon, Gent.* Irving was a prolific writer throughout his life, from his first collaborations with his brother William and friend James Kirke Paulding, to his many biographies of well-known historical figures, including George Washington. Among his most successful works were his collections of sketches and tales, a distinction then made between realistic and imaginative types of fiction. His sketches often make use of historical sources, while the tales usually derive from traditional folktales. His best-known stories, "Rip Van Winkle" and "The Legend of Sleepy Hollow," although largely copied from German folktales, still maintain an originality through their American settings and Irving's own gently humorous style.

Biography

The eleventh and last child of a successful merchant, Washington Irving studied law and was admitted to the New York bar at age twenty-three. Fond of travel, as a youth he explored his native Hudson Valley and later most of America and Europe. He spent more than twenty years overseas, manning various diplomatic posts and serving as minister to Spain from 1842 to 1845.

Analysis

Washington Irving's masterpiece, *The Sketch Book of Geoffrey Crayon, Gent.*, has a historical importance few American books can match. No previous American book achieved a really significant popular and critical success in England, the only arena of opinion which then mattered; but Irving demonstrated that an American could write not only well but also brilliantly even by British standards. In fact, throughout the century English as well as American schoolboys studied Irving's book as a model of graceful prose.

Irving had achieved some popularity in his own country well before the British triumphs. In 1807-1808, Irving, his brother William, and James Kirke Paulding collaborated on an independently published periodical series, *Salmagundi*. Since the project was a true collaboration, scholars are in doubt as to precisely who deserves credit for precisely what, but two pieces deserve particular notice. "Sketches from Nature" sentimentally sketches two old bachelors, one of whom restores the spirits of the other by leading him through scenes reminiscent of their youth. "The Little Man in Black" is supposedly a traditional story passed through generations of a single family. Irving here introduces another old bachelor, who wanders into the village a stranger to all and sets up housekeeping in a decrepit house rumored to be haunted. First ostracized by the adults, then tormented by the local children, ultimately he dies by starvation, in his last moments forgiving all, a true but misunderstood Christian.

Both pieces display Irving's graceful style, his prevalent sentimentality, and his wholehearted commitment to charming, pleasing, and entertaining his audience. Both feature an old bachelor sterotype which he inherited from the Addisonian tradition and continued to exploit in later works. The pieces differ in their formal focus, however, and aptly illustrate the two poles of Irving's fictional nature. The second shows his fondness for the tale tradition: he cites a source in family folklore; the narrative hangs on striking incident; and he flavors the atmosphere with a suggestion of the supernatural. The first features virtues of the periodical essay: evocation of character divorced from dramatic incident; a style dominated by smoothness (Edgar Allan Poe's term was "repose") and by descriptions strong on concrete detail; and an essentially realistic atmosphere. Irving's unique genius led him to combine the best of both traditions in his finest fiction and thereby to create the modern short story in America.

Irving's early career coincided with the rise of Romanticism, and the movement strongly influenced his greatest book, *The Sketch Book of Geoffrey Crayon, Gent*. Here he capitalized on the element which strongly marks his most successful stories: imagination. Consistently, Irving's most successful characters, and stories, are those which most successfully exploit the imagination.

In "The Spectre Bridegroom," the title character triumphs not through strength, physical skills, or intelligence, but rather through manipulating the imaginations of those who would oppose his aims. The story's first section humorously describes a bellicose old widower, the Baron Von Landshort, who has gathered a vast audience, consisting mostly of poor relatives properly cognizant of his high status, to celebrate his only daughter's marriage to a young count whom none of them has ever seen. In the story's second part, the reader learns that as the count and his friend Herman Von Starkenfaust journey to the castle, they are beset by bandits; the outlaws mortally wound the count who, with his last breath, begs Von Starkenfaust to relay his excuses to the wedding party. The story's third part returns to the castle where the long-delayed wedding party finally welcomes a pale, melancholy young man. The silent stranger hears the garrulous Baron speak on, among other matters, his family's longstanding feud with the Von Starkenfaust family; meanwhile the young man wins the daughter's heart. He shortly leaves, declaring he must be buried at the cathedral. The next night the daughter's two guardian aunts tell ghost stories until they are terrified by spying the Spectre Bridegroom outside the window; the daughter sleeps apart from her aunts for three nights, encouraging their fears the while, and finally absconds. When she returns with her husband, Von Starkenfaust, who had pretended to be the Spectre, they both are reconciled with the Baron and live happily ever after.

By becoming in one sense artists themselves, Herman and his bride both manipulate the imaginations of the Baron, the aunts, and the entire wedding party to make their courtship and elopement possible; here, happily, the dupees lose nothing and share the ultimate happiness of the dupers. There are at least three dimensions to "The Spectre Bridegroom": as it is read, one can imaginatively identify with the duped family and believe the Spectre genuine, or alternately identify with the young couple innocently manipulating their elders. A third dimension enters when the reader recalls the personality of the frame's Swiss taleteller, occasionally interrupting himself with "a roguish leer and a sly joke for the buxom kitchen maid" and himself responsible (it is surely not the modest and proper Geoffrey Crayon or Washington Irving) for the suggestive antlers above the prospective bridegroom's head at the feast.

The narrative perspectives informing Irving's single greatest achievement, "Rip Van Winkle," radiate even greater complexities. At the simplest level the core experience is that of Rip himself, a good-natured idler married to a termagant who drives him from the house with her temper. While hunting in the woods, Rip pauses to assist a curious little man hefting a keg; in a natural amphitheater he discovers dwarfish sailors in archaic dress playing at ninepins. Rip drinks, falls asleep, and awakens the next morning alone on the mountainside. In a subtle, profound, and eerily effective sequence, Irving details Rip's progressive disorientation and complete loss of identity. The disintegration begins mildly enough—Rip notices the decayed gun (a thief's substitute he thinks), his dog's absence, some stiffness in his own body—each clue is emotionally more significant than the last, but each may be easily explained. Rip next notices changes in nature—a dry gully has become a raging stream, a ravine has been closed by a rockslide; these are more dramatic alterations, but still explainable after a long night's sleep.

Upon entering the village, he discovers no one but strangers and all in strange dress; he finds his house has decayed, his wife and children have disappeared; buildings have changed as well as the political situation and even the very manner and behavior of the people. In a terrible climax, when Irving for once declines to mute the genuine horror, Rip profoundly questions his own identity. When he desperately asks if anyone knows poor Rip Van Winkle, fingers point to another ragged idler at the fringe, the very image of Rip himself as he had ascended the mountain. Even Poe or Franz Kafka never painted a loss of identity more absolute, more profound, more credible, more terrible. After a moment of horror, Irving's sentimental good humor immediately reasserts itself. Rip's now-adult daughter appears and recognizes him; the ragged idler turns out to be his son, Rip, Jr. Rip himself hesitates for a moment, but, upon learning that his wife has died "but a short time since," declares his identity and commences reintegrating himself in the community, eventually to become an honored patriarch, renowned for recounting his marvelous experience.

Thus is the nature of the core narrative, which is almost all most people ever read. The reader values the story for its profound mythic reverberations; after all, throughout Western civilization Irving's Rip has become an archetype of time lost. The reader may also appreciate Irving's amoral toying with life-styles; although the Yankee/Benjamin Franklin life-style Rip's wife advocates and which leads to her death (she bursts a blood vessel while haggling) fails to trap Rip, he triumphs by championing the relatively unambitious, self-indulgent life-style Irving identifies with the Dutch. Still, many people feel tempted to reject the piece as a simplistic fairy tale dependent on supernatural machinery for its appeal and effect. This is a mistake.

Those who read the full story as Irving wrote it will discover, in the headnote, that Irving chose to relate the story not from the point of view of an omniscient narrator but from that of Diedrich Knickerbocker, the dunderheaded comic persona to whom years earlier he had ascribed the burlesque *A History of New York*. The presence of such a narrator—and Irving went to some trouble to introduce him—authorizes the reader to reject the supernatural elements and believe, as Irving tells us many of Rip's auditors believed, that in actuality Rip simply tired of his wife, ran away for twenty years, and concocted a cock-and-bull story to justify his absence. Looking closer, the reader discovers copious hints that this is precisely what happened: Rip's reluctance to become Rip again until he is sure his wife is dead; the fact that when his neighbors hear the story they "wink at each other and put their tongues in their cheeks"; the fact that, until he finally established a satisfactory version of the events, he was observed "to vary on some points every time he told it." In the concluding footnote, even dim Diedrich Knickerbocker acknowledges the story's doubtfulness but provides as evidence of its truth the fact that he has heard even stranger supernatural stories of the Catskills, and that to authenticate his story Rip signed a certificate in the presence of a Justice of the Peace. "The story, therefore, is beyond the possibility of doubt." Irving clearly intends to convince his closest readers that Rip, like the couple in "The Spectre Bridegroom," triumphed over circumstances by a creative manipulation of imagination.

In "The Legend of Sleepy Hollow" our source is again Diedrich Knickerbocker, and again, creatively manipulating the imaginations of others proves the key to success. The pleasant little Dutch community of Sleepy Hollow has imported a tall, grotesquely lanky Yankee as schoolmaster, Ichabod Crane. Although he is prey to the schoolboys' endless pranks, he himself ravenously and endlessly preys on the foodstuffs of the boys' parents. Ichabod finally determines to set his cap for the pretty daughter of a wealthy farmer, but Brom Bones, the handsome, Herculean local hero, has likewise determined to court the girl. The climax comes when the principals gather with the entire community at a dance, feast, and "quilting frolic" held at Katrina Van Tassel's home. Brom fills the timorous and credulous Ichabod full of tales of a horrible specter, ghost of a Hessian soldier beheaded by a cannonball, who inhabits the region through which Ichabod must ride that night to return home. As he makes his lonely journey back, Ichabod encounters the dark figure who carries his head under his arm rather than on his neck and who runs him a frightful race to a bridge. At the climax the figure hurls his head and strikes Ichabod, who disappears, never to be seen in the village again. Brom marries Katrina, and years later the locals discover that Ichabod turned lawyer, politician, newspaperman, and finally became a "justice of the Ten Pound Court."

Again it is the character who creatively manipulates the imagination who carries the day; the manipulatee wins only the consolation prize. Again the Dutch spirit triumphs over the Yankee. In this story there is something quite new, however; for the first time in American literature there is, in the characterization of Brom Bones, the figure of the frontiersman so important to American literature and American popular culture: physically imposing, self-confident, rough and ready, untutored but endowed with great natural virtues, gifted with a rude sense of chivalry, at home on the fringes of civilization, and incorporating in his own being the finer virtues of both the wilderness and the settlements. Irving here brilliantly anticipated both the essence of Southwestern humor and of James Fenimore Cooper's seminal Westerns.

Irving wrote a great many other stories, including several romantic tales set in Spain, most of them flawed by superficiality and sentimentality; he also produced a number of Gothic stories, some of which are still read with pleasure today, among them "The Adventure of the German Student" and "The Devil and Tom Walker." Irving, however, reached his highest point in his first published short story, "Rip Van Winkle." He never equaled it in any subsequent story—but then, only a tiny handful of writers ever have.

Other major works

NONFICTION: *A History of New York*, 1809; *Biography of James Lawrence*, 1813; *A History of the Life and Voyages of Christopher Columbus*, 1828; *A Chronicle of the Conquest of Granada*, 1829; *Voyages and Discoveries of the Companions of Columbus*, 1831; *A Tour of the Prairies*, 1835; *Astoria*, 1836; *The Adventures of Captain Bonneville*, 1837; *The Life of Oliver Goldsmith*, 1849; *The Life of George Washington*, 1855-1859 (5 volumes).

Bibliography

Bowden, Mary Weatherspoon. *Washington Irving*. Boston: Twayne, 1981. Bowden's general study of Irving discusses the major works in chronological order of composition. While her focus is literary, Bowden begins each chapter with useful biographical information about Irving at the time. The section dealing with *The Sketch Book of Geoffrey Crayon, Gent.* is particularly successful in describing Irving's attitudes toward England and how these are revealed in the sketches.

McFarland, Philip. *Sojourners*. New York: Atheneum, 1979. While not a conventional biography, this study of Washington Irving's life situates the writer in his various geographic, historic, and literary contexts. McFarland explores in detail the life of Irving, interweaving his biography with those of other important Americans of the time, among them Aaron Burr, the abolitionist John Brown, and John J. Astor.

Myers, Andrew B., ed. *A Century of Commentary on the Works of Washington Irving*. Tarrytown, N.Y.: Sleepy Hollow Restorations, 1976. This collection, divided into four chronologically ordered sections, offers writings on Washington Irving. Part 1 includes essays by contemporaries of Irving, such as William Cullen Bryant and Henry Wadsworth Longfellow; part 2 covers evaluations from the beginning of the nineteenth century. Early twentieth century scholars of American literature, such as Fred Lewis Pattee, Vernon Louis Parrington, and Van Wyck Brooks, are represented in part 3, and part 4 covers the period 1945 to 1975. The collection gives an excellent overview of the development of Irving criticism and provides a point of departure for further investigations.

Rubin-Dorsky, Jeffrey. *Adrift in the Old World: The Psychological Pilgrimage of Washington Irving*. Chicago: University of Chicago Press, 1988. In this study of Irving's short fiction, Rubin-Dorsky sets out to establish Irving's Americanness, thus reversing a critical tradition that marked him as primarily imitative of British prose style. By placing Irving within his historical context, Rubin-Dorsky underscores Irving's central position in early American letters.

Wagenknecht, Edward. *Washington Irving: Moderation Displayed*. New York: Oxford University Press, 1962. Wagenknecht has divided his study of Irving into three parts: The Life, the Man, and the Work. "The Man" is by far the largest section and provides an engaging portrait of Irving's personal life and development as a writer. Wagenknecht's biography offers a more streamlined alternative to Stanley T. William's two-volume work (see below).

Williams, Stanley T. *The Life of Washington Irving*. 2 vols. New York: Oxford University Press, 1935. This very thorough biography of "the first American man of letters" provides a wealth of biographical and literary detail about Washington Irving. Volume 1 is most useful for those interested in Irving's short fiction, as it covers his life and his work up to *The Alhambra*. The chapters are organized according to Irving's places of travel or the titles of his works, an arrangement which highlights the various contexts in which Irving wrote.

Walter Evans
(Revised by *Ann A. Merrill*)

SHIRLEY JACKSON

Born: San Francisco, California; December 14, 1919
Died: North Bennington, Vermont; August 8, 1965

Principal short fiction

The Lottery: Or, The Adventures of James Harris, 1949; *Come Along with Me*, 1968 (Stanley Edgar Hyman, editor).

Other literary forms

Shirley Jackson's dozen published books include novels, humorous fictionalized autobiographies, and children's books. Many of her stories, essays, and public speeches remain uncollected. Several works have been adapted to other media: "The Lottery" for television, *We Have Always Lived in the Castle* (1962) for stage, and *The Bird's Nest* (1954) and *The Haunting of Hill House* (1959) for the cinema.

Achievements

Jackson is probably best known for her short story "The Lottery," which was first published in the June 26, 1948, edition of *The New Yorker*. As with the majority of her works, both short stories and novels, "The Lottery" explores the darker side of the human psyche, often in a manner disturbing to the reader. In addition to using ordinary settings for extraordinary occurrences, Jackson often injects an element of the supernatural. This is seen, for example, in the story "The Visit" and in the novel *The Haunting of Hill House*. In addition, Jackson has published *Life Among the Savages* (1953), a highly humorous account of her home life. In 1961, Jackson received the Edgar Allan Poe Award for her story "Louisa, Please." She was awarded the Syracuse University Arents Pioneer Medal for Outstanding Achievement in 1965.

Biography

Shirley Jackson was born in California on December 14, 1919, and moved with her family to New York when she was sixteen. After an unsuccessful year at the University of Rochester, Jackson enrolled, at age twenty, in the University of Syracuse. This was to be the beginning of an independent life for the author, as she would finally be away from the dominating presence of her mother. At Syracuse, Jackson met Stanley Edgar Hyman, the man she would marry in 1940. Hyman achieved notoriety in his own right as a teacher, writer, and critic. The marriage between Jackson and Hyman was tumultuous in many ways but provided a stabilizing factor for Jackson. Her literary production increased markedly after the marriage and the birth of their four children. Jackson's own phobias, however, keep creeping into this successful, if odd, relationship. She was an agoraphobic and a depressive. Part of the latter affliction was contributed to by her asthma and arthritis, as well as Hyman's extramarital affair in the early 1960's. In addition, Jackson had never really been a social person—she was much too individualistic to fit into any of the polite social molds. In 1963, Jackson began to turn around psychologically. Her husband made a new commitment to the marriage and an enlightened psychiatrist began to help her work with the agoraphobia. Her writing continued to be an outlet for her. Although Jackson recovered emotionally, she never recovered physically. She was obese and a chain smoker. She died on August 8, 1965, at the age of forty-five.

Analysis

Shirley Jackson's stories seem to center on a single concern: almost every story is about a protagonist's discovering or failing to discover or successfully ignoring an alternate way of perceiving a set of circumstances or the world. Jackson seems especially interested in how characters order their worlds and how they perceive themselves in the world. Often, a change in a character's perspective leads to anxiety, terror, neurosis, or even a loss of identity. While it is tempting to say that her main theme is the difference between appearance and reality, such a statement is misleading, for she seems to see reality as Herman Melville's Ishmael comes to see it, as a mirror of the perceiving soul. It is rarely clear that her characters discover or lose their grasp of reality; rather, they form ideas of reality that are more or less moral and more or less functional. For Jackson, reality is so complex and mysterious that one inevitably only orders part of it. A character may then discover parts that contradict a chosen order or that attract one away from the apparent order, but one can never affirm the absolute superiority of one ordering to another. In this respect, Jackson's fictional world resembles those of Stephen Crane and Ernest Hemingway. Perhaps the major differences between her fiction and theirs is that her protagonists are predominantly women; she explores some peculiarly feminine aspects of the problem of ideas of order.

Jackson's middle-class American women seem especially vulnerable to losing the security of a settled world view. Their culture provides them with idealistic dream visions of what their lives should be, and they have a peculiar leisure for contemplation and conversation imposed upon them by their dependent roles. Men in her stories seem so busy providing that they rarely look at and think about the order of things. Her career women are more like these men. In "Elizabeth" and "The Villager," the protagonists succeed, albeit precariously, in preserving ideas of themselves and their worlds despite the contradictory facts that seem increasingly to intrude. In these two stories, one sees a sort of emotional cannibalism in the protagonists as they attempt to preserve belief in an order that reality seems no longer disposed to sustain. Several stories show a woman's loss of an ordering dream. These divide into stories about women who experience the terror of loss of identity and those who may find a liberating and superior order in what would ordinarily be called infantile fantasy.

Among those who lose a dream are the protagonists of "The Little House" and "The Renegade." In "The Little House," a woman's first possession of her own small country house is ruined by the terrifying insinuations of her new neighbors; they leave her alone on her first night after relating to her their fears that the previous owner was murdered and that the murderer will return. In "The Renegade," a mother discovers an unsuspected cruelty in her neighbors and even in her children when her dog is accused of killing chickens. Although Jackson's humorous auto-biographical stories are of a different order, the often anthologized "Charles" tells of a mother's discovery that the nemesis of the kindergarten whose antics her son reports each day is not the mythical Charles, but her own son, Laurie.

Perhaps the most successful escape into fantasy is Mrs. Montague's in "The Island." All her physical needs are provided by a wealthy but absent son and the constant attendance of Miss Oakes. Mrs. Montague lives in her dream of a tropical paradise, virtually untouched by her actual world. This escape is judged by the ironic frame of Miss Oakes's relative poverty and her inevitable envy, suffering, spite, and ugliness; she has no chance of such an escape herself. Some movements into fantasy are terrifying or at least ambiguous. In "The Beautiful Stranger," Margaret resolves a tension in her marriage by perceiving the man who returns from a business trip as a stranger, not her husband. By the end of the story, this fantasy has led to her losing herself, unable to find her home when she returns from a shopping trip. A similar but more ambiguous situation develops in "The Tooth," in which a woman escapes into a vision of an island to evade the pain of an aching tooth. Many of Jackson's protagonists conceive of an island paradise as an ideal order when their control of the immediate is threatened.

Some ideas of order remain impenetrable. In "Louisa, Please," a variation on Hawthorne's "Wakefield," a runaway daughter returns home after a long absence to discover that her family has built a life around her loss and will not be convinced of her return. In "Flower Garden" and "After You, My Dear Alphonse," protagonists find themselves unable to change or to abandon racist ideas because the ideas are too strong or because of community pressure.

A closer look at three especially interesting stories will reveal more about Jackson's themes and give some indication of her technical proficiency. In "The Visit," Margaret comes to visit a school friend, Carla Rhodes, for the summer. The beautiful Rhodes estate includes a dream house with numerous fantastic rooms. The house seems not quite real; nearly every room is covered with tapestries depicting the house in different hours and seasons and there is a mysterious tower of which no one speaks. For Margaret, the house and the family are ideal, especially when Carla's brother, Paul, arrives with his friend, the Captain. This idyll lasts until the evening of Paul's departure, when Margaret discovers that Paul has been a hallucination or a ghost, for the Captain is Carla's brother and no one else has seen Paul. This revelation clarifies several mysteries that have developed, especially that of Margaret's strange visit to the tower. Paul has told Margaret that an old aunt often secludes herself in the tower. When Margaret pays her a visit, she undergoes a not really frightening but certainly haunting experience with old Aunt Margaret. At the end of the story, the reader must conclude Aunt Margaret to be an apparition, that she is probably the Margaret who died for love and whose picture in mosaic appears on the floor of one room. Young Margaret has lost a phantom lover as old Margaret lost her

Paul. Young Margaret realizes this at the same time that she is made aware of time's effect on the house: the age and weakness of the Rhodeses, the bitter darkness of their true son, and the physical decay of the buildings. Furthermore, she begins to doubt her own place and identity as she wonders if her visit to the house will ever end. The home of her dreaming now threatens to become an imprisoning nightmare.

In retrospect, the device by which Jackson encourages the reader to share Margaret's hallucination or haunting may seem contrived. This choice, however, seems effective because the more fully the reader shares Margaret's perceptions and the more subdued (without being absent) are the disturbing elements, the more fully will the reader share the shock of her awakening into nightmare. Also technically effective are the apparent connections with Poe's "The Fall of the House of Usher." Most important among these is the succession of mirror images: multiple pictures of the house, between the house and Mrs. Rhodes, among members of the family, between the two Margarets, and between the decline of the family and of the house. These connections seem deliberately chosen in part to emphasize the contrasts between Margaret and Poe's narrator. Because Margaret's response to the house is so positive, the shock of her discovery is greater by contrast. Furthermore, when she discovers this house to be like what one knows the House of Usher to be, one sees the analogy between her terror at imprisonment and that of Poe's narrator when he sees a universe unnaturally lit by a blood red moon, yet another image of the coffin lit from within. Margaret actually enters one of the dream worlds promised American girls. Under its spell, she overlooks its flaws and forgets about time, but when the Captain breaks the spell, pointing out signs of decay, Paul departs and Margaret becomes acutely aware of time as her nightmare begins.

Time is often the destroyer of feminine ideals in Jackson's stories because they seem to depend on a suspension of time. In "Pillar of Salt," another Margaret loses her secure world. A trip to New York City with her husband forces a new perspective on her which produces her anxiety and, finally, paranoia. It remains unclear, however, whether her paranoia is illness or a healthy reaction to an inimical environment.

The couple's first week in the city is idyllic, and the fast pace is a pleasant change from New Hampshire. At a party at the end of the first week, however, Margaret begins to feel isolated, unnoticed among strangers who behave in strange ways. She learns there is a fire in the building but is unable to convince anyone else to leave. The fire turns out to be two buildings away, but she is the only one to heed the warning and flee the building. She comes to see this nightmarish experience as symbolic of her experience in New York and perhaps of her life as a whole. She begins to notice new details about the city: dirt, decay, speed, stifling crowds. She feels increasingly isolated and insignificant. Of this life she thinks, "She knew she was afraid to say it truly, afraid to face the knowledge that it was a voluntary neck-breaking speed, a deliberate whirling faster and faster to end in destruction." Even her friends' Long Island beach cottage shows the spreading blight; there they find a severed human leg on the sand. Margaret comes to believe that her former order was illusory. Upon returning to the city, she begins to hallucinate, to see the destruction of the city in fast motion. Windows crumble. Her bed shakes. Driven from her apartment, she finds herself unable to return, paralyzed in a fast-moving, anonymous crowd on the wrong side of a mechanical and murderous river of traffic.

Margaret comes to see herself in a modern Sodom, paralyzed not because she has disobeyed God, but because she has seen in prophetic vision the truth about the city: it is no home for man but rather is impersonally intent upon destruction. The allusion of the title and her critique of city life verify her perception; however, those who do not share her vision remain capable of functioning. As in "The Visit," the internal view of Margaret encourages a close identification between reader and character which makes judgment difficult until the reader can step back; but stepping back from "Pillar of Salt" plunges the reader deeper into mystery. In both stories, the protagonist moves from dream to nightmare, but in "Pillar of Salt," the reader is much less certain that the move is to a better or more accurate view of reality.

Shirley Jackson's reputation rests primarily upon her most anthologized story, "The Lottery." Her lecture on this story (printed in *Come Along with Me*) suggests that her creation of a normal setting convinced many readers that the story was largely factual. In fact, the central problem of the story seems to be to reconcile the portrait of typical small-town life in which the characters seem just like the reader with the horrifying ritualistic killing these people carry out. Here apparently incompatible ideas of order are thrust upon the reader for resolution, perhaps in order to complicate the reader's conceptions.

"The Lottery" develops by slowly raising the level of tension in the semipastoral setting until a series of carefully arranged revelations brings about a dramatic and shocking reversal. The villagers gather at mid-morning on a late June day for an annual event, the lottery, around which a great deal of excitement centers. Jackson supplies details which arouse reader curiosity: nearly all towns have a similar lottery; it is as old as the town; it has an elaborate ritual form which has decayed over time; every adult male *must* participate; some believe the orders of nature and of civilization depend on carrying it out correctly. The family of the man who draws the marked lot must draw again to determine the final winner. The tension built out of reader curiosity and the town's moods reverses toward the sinister when the "winner's" wife reveals that she does not want to win. Once this reversal is complete, the story moves rapidly to reveal the true nature of the lottery, to choose a victim for annual sacrifice by stoning. Jackson heightens the horror of this apparently unaccountable act with carefully chosen and placed details.

Several commentators have attempted to explain the story through reconstructing the meaning of the ritual and through carefully examining the symbols. Helen Nebeker sees the story as an allegory of "man trapped in a web spun from his own need to explain and control the incomprehensible universe around him, a need no longer answered by the web of old traditions." These attempts to move beyond the simple thriller seem justified by the details Jackson provides about the lottery. This ritual seems clearly to be a tradition of prehistoric origin, once believed essential for the welfare of the community. Even though its purpose has become obscure and its practice muddled, it continues to unify and sustain the community. Critics tend to underemphasize the apparent health and vitality of the community, perhaps feeling that this ritual essentially undercuts that impression. It is important to notice that one function of the lottery is to change the relationship between community and victim. The victim is chosen at random, killed without malice or significant protest, and lost without apparent grief. This story may be what Richard Eastman has called an open parable, a fable which applies at several levels or in several contexts. "The Lottery" creates an emotional effect of horror at the idea that perhaps in human civilization, the welfare of the many depends often on the suffering of the few: the victim race, the exploited nation, the scapegoat, the poor, the stereotyped sex, the drafted soldier. In these cases, instead of a ritual, other aspects of the social order separate oppressor and victim, yet the genuine order and happiness of the majority seems to depend on the destruction of others. In this respect, "The Lottery" resembles many stories of oppression, such as Franz Kafka's "The Bucket Rider" and some stories by Richard Wright; its purpose may be to jar readers into thinking about ways in which their lives victimize others.

Jackson places the reader of "The Lottery," which lacks a protagonist, in a position similar to that of the protagonists of "The Visit" and "Pillar of Salt." The story moves from a relatively secure agrarian world view to an event which fantastically complicates that view. Here, as in most of her stories, Jackson emphasizes the complexity of reality. Nature and human nature seem unaccountable mixtures of the creative and destructive. Her best people are in search of ways to live in this reality without fear and cruelty.

Other major works

NOVELS: *The Road Through the Wall*, 1948 (also published as *The Other Side of the Street*); *Hangsaman*, 1951; *The Bird's Nest*, 1954 (also published as *Lizzie*); *The Sundial*, 1958; *The Haunting of Hill House*, 1959; *We Have Always Lived in the Castle*, 1962.

PLAY: *The Bad Children*, 1959.

NONFICTION: *Life Among the Savages*, 1953; *The Witchcraft of Salem Village*, 1956; *Raising Demons*, 1957.

CHILDREN'S LITERATURE: *9 Magic Wishes*, 1963; *Famous Sally*, 1966.

Bibliography

Cleveland, Carol. "Shirley Jackson." In *And Then There Were Nine . . . More Women of Mystery*, edited by Jane S. Bakerman. Bowling Green, Ky.: Bowling Green State University Popular Press, 1985. This chapter provides the reader with an overview of Jackson's major works. In addition, Cleveland provides some useful critical insights.

Friedman, Lenemaja. *Shirley Jackson*. Boston: G. K. Hall, 1975. Friedman provides the reader with both a biographical and critical study of Jackson and offers information on both her short stories and novels. The volume includes an extensive secondary bibliography.

Kittredge, Mary. "The Other Side of Magic: A Few Remarks About Shirley Jackson." In *Discovering Modern Horror Fiction*, edited by Darrell Schweitzer. Mercer Island, Wash.: Starmont House, 1985. A useful study of the use of magic and the supernatural in Jackson's works. The author draws interesting comparisons between Jackson's fiction and nonfiction works.

Oppenheimer, Judy. *Private Demons: The Life of Shirley Jackson.* New York: G. P. Putnam's Sons, 1988. This volume is the first extensive biography of Jackson. It is finely detailed and provides the reader an excellent view of this author. Oppenheimer interviewed close to seventy persons for this book, including Jackson's family members, friends, and neighbors. Contains numerous photographs.

Parks, John G. " 'The Possibility of Evil': A Key to Shirley Jackson's Fiction." *Studies in Short Fiction* 15, no. 3 (Summer, 1978): 320-323. This useful article concentrates on Jackson's short stories. Parks draws useful comparisons to authors such as Flannery O'Connor and Nathaniel Hawthorne.

Terry Heller
(Revised by *Victoria E. McLure*)

HENRY JAMES

Born: New York, New York; April 15, 1843
Died: London, England; February 28, 1916

Principal short fiction

A Passionate Pilgrim, 1875; *Daisy Miller*, 1878; *An International Episode*, 1878-1879; *The Madonna of the Future*, 1879; *The Siege of London*, 1883; *Tales of Three Cities*, 1884; *The Author of Beltraffio*, 1885; *The Aspern Papers*, 1888; *The Lesson of the Master*, 1892; *The Private Life, Lord Beaupre, The Visits*, 1893; *The Real Thing*, 1893; *Terminations*, 1895; *Embarrassments*, 1896; *The Two Magics: The Turn of the Screw and Covering End*, 1898; *The Soft Side*, 1900; *The Better Sort*, 1903; *The Novels and Tales of Henry James*, 1907-1909; *The Finer Grain*, 1910; *A Landscape Painter*, 1919; *Travelling Companions*, 1919; *Master Eustace*, 1920; *Stories of Writers and Artists*, 1944; *Henry James: Selected Short Stories*, 1950; *Henry James: Eight Tales from the Major Phase*, 1958; *The Complete Tales of Henry James*, 1962-1965; *Tales of Henry James*, 1984; *The Figure in the Carpet and Other Stories*, 1986; *The Jolly Corner and Other Tales*, 1990.

Other literary forms

Henry James was a prolific writer who, from 1875 until his death, published a book or more every year. Other than short fiction, James wrote novels, dramas, biographies, autobiographies, reviews, travelogues, art and literary criticism, literary theory, and letters. James was a pioneer in the criticism and theory of fiction. Much of his criticism appears in Leon Edel and Mark Wilson's edition of *Henry James: Literary Criticism* (1984). James's creative method and the sources of many of his works are documented in *The Complete Notebooks of Henry James* (1987).

Achievements

James contributed to the development of the modernist novel, invented cryptic tales that border on the postmodern, and laid the groundwork for the contemporary theory of narrative. He completed twenty novels (two uncompleted novels were published posthumously). He also wrote 112 short stories, seven travel books, three autobiographies, numerous plays, two critical biographies, and voluminous works of criticism. James brought the American novel to its fruition and gave it an international flavor. He transformed the novel of physical adventure to one of psychological intrigue. His character studies are probing and intense. His precise use of limited point of view invites the reader to become actively engaged in interpreting events and ferreting out meaning. His works also achieve a masterful blend of summarized action and dramatic scenes. In his short fiction, he created the forerunners of the modern antiheroes and invented metafictional stories about the nature of art and writing. Also, his critical works and many prefaces have given modern critics a vocabulary for discussing character and point of view. James edited a deluxe edition of his complete works, received honorary degrees from Harvard University and the University of Oxford, and was awarded the Order of Merit from King George V. His works have influenced Joseph Conrad, James Joyce, Virginia Woolf, and Graham Greene.

Biography

Henry James's career is usually divided into four periods: his formative years, his apprenticeship, his middle years, and his major phase. James was descended from Irish Protestants. His grandfather, a poor immigrant, lived out the American Dream and died one of the wealthiest men in the United States. James's father, Henry James, Sr., renounced the Calvinistic work ethic and indulged in the mysticism of Emanuel Swedenborg and the socialism of Charles Fourier.

Through most of his youth, James was shuttled back and forth between Europe and the United States, thus gaining an international perspective on art and life. He learned French and received a European education through a variety of tutors and schools. As a young man, he was exposed to the greatest museums and art galleries in the world. His eye for painting aided him in creating a painterly quality in his work. In 1858, his family moved to Newport, Rhode Island, which was to become the scene of some of his early works of fiction. In 1862, he went to Harvard University to study law but attended Robert Lowell's lectures and decided to pursue a literary career. In 1864, he published his first short story and continued to write stories and criticism for the rest of his life. In 1869, he spent a year abroad. With the death of his favorite cousin, Minnie, in 1870, he felt that his youth had come to an end.

James entered his apprentice years between 1865 and 1882. During these years, he published his first collection of short fiction, *A Passionate Pilgrim*, and his first significant novel, *Roderick Hudson* (1876). He achieved popular success with *Daisy Miller* and continued to write *The American* (1876-1877), *Washington Square* (1880), and *The Portrait of a Lady* (1880-1881). These works dealt with the international theme and explored the problems of American innocence exposed to the corrupting influence of European society.

In the 1880's, James began to take up some of the themes of the naturalists. With *The Bostonians* (1885-1886) and *The Princess Casamassima* (1885-1886), James began to treat the issues of social reformers. These novels, along with *The Tragic Muse* (1889-1890), were not successful. Between 1890 and 1895, James attempted to establish his reputation as a dramatist, but he was unable to please theater audiences, and his play *Guy Domville* (1894) was booed.

In 1897, James settled down in Lamb House in Sussex, and by 1900 he had entered his major phase and had written three richly textured novels: *The Wings of the Dove* (1902), *The Ambassadors* (1903), and *The Golden Bowl* (1904). He died in 1916 in London and was buried in the United States.

Analysis

Henry James believed that an author must be granted his *donnée*, or central idea, and then be judged on the execution of his material. James's stories are about members of high society. The characters do not engage in dramatic actions but spend much of their time in cryptic conversations, which slowly reveal the intense psychological strain under which they are laboring. James's narrators are often confused individuals trying to puzzle out and evaluate themselves and the people around them. Romance is frequently at the center of James's tales, but his lovers have difficulty coming to terms with their own feelings, and often love goes unrecognized and unfulfilled. Marriage is often rejected by his characters, and when it does appear, it is often the scene of heartaches and hidden resentments. Death and dying are also a part of James's stories. Even though he focuses on the death of women and children, he avoids both the macabre and the sentimental. His stories can be divided into three categories: international romances, tales about writers and artists, and introspective narratives about wasted lives.

James has not been given the same recognition for his short fiction that Nathaniel Hawthorne and Edgar Allan Poe have received; yet, James devoted much of his literary life to the creation of short fiction and made many attempts to master the form. Several times in his life he expressed the desire to give up writing novels and to devote himself solely to creating short fiction. For half a century, James employed himself in the writing of 112 pieces of short fiction, beginning with "Tragedy of Error" in 1864 and ending with "The Round of Visits" in 1910. He began writing stories ten years before he published his first novel, and over his lifetime, his stories appeared in thirty-five different periodicals on both sides of the Atlantic.

James called his short fiction "tales," and he divided his tales into types. The anecdote, which focuses on one character and one incident, is a brief, compact, and highly distilled story comparable to a sonnet. The longer *nouvelle*, which often ran between twenty thousand and forty-five thousand words, allowed James greater development in his short fiction, not for multiplying incidents but for probing the depths of a character's experience. James expanded his stories because he wanted to explore the richness of human experience that lies hidden behind the surface of everyday life.

James's major tales can be divided into three periods: his early stories focus on the international theme; during his middle years, his stories center on writers and artists; and his final stories focus on older characters who have gone through life but never really lived. James's international stories focus on taking characters with set expectations and placing them in foreign environments. *Daisy Miller* is one of James's early novelettes and deals with a young American girl who finds herself out of place in a European environment.

In *Daisy Miller*, young Frederick Winterbourne, an American living in Europe, becomes fascinated with the garrulous Daisy Miller, who is vacationing on the Continent. The free-spirited Daisy amiably flirts with Winterbourne. Although he is attracted to her, he is aware that she and her negligent mother are the source of gossip among European Americans, who are scandalized by the forward ways of the unchaperoned young American. After seeing Daisy in Vevey, he again meets her in

Rome, where she is frequently seen with Giovanelli, who is thought to be an Italian adventurer. Ostracized by her American compatriots, she continues to be seen with Giovanelli and risks her life by spending a moonlit night with him at the Colosseum, where she contracts malaria and dies. The puzzled Winterbourne attends her funeral and realizes that she is innocent.

In *Daisy Miller*, James explores the dilemma of an innocent American woman who flouts the social codes of European society. More than that, however, he explores the mind of Winterbourne, a Europeanized American who tries to figure out whether Daisy is naïve or reckless. Like other Jamesean heroes, Winterbourne cannot commit himself to a woman with whom he is falling in love. Finding her attractive but shallow, he is compelled to lecture her on mores, and when he sees her at the Colosseum, he "cuts her dead." Unable to break Winterbourne's stiffness, she sends him a message from her deathbed, noting that she was fond of him. Convinced that he has been unjust to her, Winterbourne escapes into his studies and becomes entangled with a foreign woman.

James's heroine, like Herman Melville's Billy Budd, represents American innocence. Both have found themselves in a world order that puts them at risk, and both are sacrificed by those who should have helped them. In addition to introducing the international theme, *Daisy Miller* introduces two Jamesean types: the sacrificed woman and the egotist who rejects her love. Though James later rejected his subtitle *A Study*, the novelette *Daisy Miller* is a study of the complexity of human relationships. The enigmatic but vivacious Daisy is sacrificed at the Colosseum like the early Christians, while the reticent and regretful lover experiences a sense of loss as he retreats from the world of spontaneity and life.

In "The Aspern Papers," James takes the international theme beyond the romance and weaves a darker and more complex tale. In order to obtain the letters of the American poet Jeffrey Aspern, an unnamed American editor takes up residence with Aspern's former mistress Juliana Bordereau and is willing to make love to her middle-aged niece, Miss Tita. He pays exorbitant rent for a room in their Venetian hideaway and spends lavishly to create a garden in their courtyard. Feeling that he is inspired by the mystic presence of Aspern and willing to take any measure to obtain the letters, he breaks into Juliana's drawer and is caught. He retreats, and the dying Juliana hides the papers in her mattress. After Juliana dies, Miss Tita offers to give him the papers if he will marry her. He rejects her proposal only to reconsider it too late, after Miss Tita has burned the papers.

The unnamed narrator goes by an alias. Later, he reveals his name to Miss Tita but not to the reader. He is one version of the unidentifiable American hero who either shuffles names like James Fenimore Cooper's Leatherstocking or assumes various identities like Melville's heroes. He is a man without an identity, a parasite living on the reputation of a famous writer. He is also a typical American monomaniacal quester, fixed on an obsessive quest and willing to sacrifice all in pursuit of it. The narrator sees himself as part of a grandiose scheme; the garden that he plants becomes the symbol of a lost Eden. In Miss Tita, James again sets up woman as a sacrificial victim. Like other Jamesean heroes (and heroes from American literature in general), the narrator rejects marriage. Also, in his quest for knowledge, he is willing to sacrifice the private lives of Juliana and Aspern.

In his next set of stories, which focus on artists and writers, James explores the relationship between life and art, and the conflict between the artist's public and private life. In "The Real Thing," James tells the story of an unnamed artist who hires two highly polished aristocrats forced to earn their living as models. Major Monarch and his wife contrast with the artist's other models, Miss Churm, a feisty cockney, and Oronte, a low-life Italian. The artist discovers that his lower-class models can transform themselves into aristocrats, whereas the real aristocrats present either a static or a distorted picture of reality. He uses the Monarchs to create a set of illustrations upon which his future depends. An old friend tells him to get rid of the aristocrats because they are ruining his work and jeopardizing his career. The artist, however, respects and sympathizes with their plight but eventually has to dismiss them.

In "The Real Thing," James explores not only the relationship between art and life but also the human dilemma of an artist faced with the conflict of saving his career or upholding his responsibility to two people with whom he sympathizes. The story is built on a series of finely balanced contrasts. The Monarchs are pure aristocrats. The artist thinks that they have come to sit for a portrait, but they have come to be hired as models. The Monarchs are aristocrats, yet they cannot model aristocrats, whereas Miss Churm and Oronte are commoners who can easily transform themselves into gentry. Ironically, the Englishwoman models for Italian types, while the Italian model does Englishmen. The servant-class models start out waiting on the Monarchs, but later the Monarchs wait on the servants. Thus, class distinctions are reversed. The artist wants to paint artistic portraits for which the aristocratic Monarchs are suitable, yet he devotes himself to commercial illustrations, using a working woman who can impersonate an empress. The aristocrats display themselves like slaves at an auction, whereas the servants do their job without auditioning. The lower-class models are professionals; the aristocrats are amateurs. The artist friend is supposedly a good judge of models, but he is a second-rate painter. The greatest irony of all is that people who have no sense of self can become transformed into commercial art, while people holding on to their identity, their own clothes, and their own manners become too photographic, too typical, and too much the real thing. Although the artist must rid himself of the two aristocrats, his experience with them has moved him more deeply than his work with the professional models. The story is a gem of balance and contrast that transforms an aesthetic dilemma into an ethical one and explores the relationship of art to life, servant to master, self to role, portraiture to illustration, and commercial art to lived experience. "The Real Thing" is an often-anthologized story and a perfect illustration of James's craft in the anecdote or traditional short story.

The theme of the relationship between art and life is broadened in James's stories about writers. During his middle period, James created a series of stories in which a young would-be writer or critic surveys the life and work of a master writer. In "The Figure in the Carpet," a story about an eccentric writer who has gained significant critical attention, James probes the nature of criticism itself. An unidentified critic trying to gain a name for himself is called upon to review *The Middle*, the latest novel of the famous author Hugh Vereker, because the lead critic, George Corvick, has to meet his fiancée, Gwendolen Erme. The narrator writes a glowing review of Vereker's work, then attends a party in hope of seeing the great author. When a socialite presents Vereker with the narrator's review, he calls it "the usual twaddle." Vereker later apologizes to the critic but says that critics often misunderstand the obvious meaning, which stands out in his novels like a figure in a carpet. The critic probes Vereker for clues, but the author says that the clues run throughout his entire work. After searching for the secret meaning in Vereker's work, the critic gives up the quest as a hoax. His fellow critic Corvick, however, uses the quest for the narrative secret as an excuse to work more closely with his fiancée, Gwendolen. Frustrated in their efforts, Corvick leaves the country. While away, he writes Gwendolen that he has figured out the secret, and he and Gwendolen get married. When Corvick dies, Gwendolen will not reveal the secret to the narrator, who is even willing to marry her to obtain it. Gwendolen does marry a mediocre critic, Drayton Deane. After the deaths of Gwendolen, Vereker, and Vereker's wife, the narrator tries to obtain the secret from Deane, who knows nothing about it.

In "The Figure in the Carpet," James again turns to the monomaniacal unnamed narrator on a quest for secret knowledge hidden in a text. Like the narrator of "The Aspern Papers," the critic is willing to marry a woman to gain greater knowledge about an author's work. James said that the story was about misunderstood authors and the need for more analytical criticism. Yet, the story sets up typical Jamesean paradoxes. Is Vereker being honest or is "the figure" merely a hoax on critics? Does Corvick really know the secret or is he using his knowledge to win Gwendolen? What is the puzzling connection between interpreting a work and exploring the intimate relationships between men and women? Why do the many so-called possessors of the secret die? This story has been cited as a model for the critical act by many modern critics. Its metafictional qualities and its strange mixture of love and death with the act of interpretation give it a distinctly postmodern quality.

The stories written in James's later years take on a mystical tone. The artist is replaced by a sensitive individual who has alienated himself from the world. The characters are few and often focus on only two people. The characters remain obsessive, but now they are in pursuit of that part of themselves that haunts them. The Jamesean love story is played out into old age, with the woman as a patient bystander, a reflector of the man's battle with himself. The image of the hunt found in Cooper, Melville, and Ernest Hemingway is now symbolic of an internal quest for the terrors hidden within the self. The artists, who in earlier stories sought to gain a second chance or find a next time, now become egocentric gentlemen facing the life that they could have had. The venture into the wilderness becomes a metaphor for the descent into the unconscious.

In "The Altar of the Dead," George Stransom constantly memorializes the death of his bride, Mary Antrim, who died of a fever after their wedding day. Like a character from a Poe short story, he maintains an obsessive devotion to his dead love and is chained to the observance of the anniversary of his wife's death. While remembering his wife, he meets his friend Paul Creston and Paul's second wife. In a strange way, James returns to the international theme by making Creston's new wife an American who has married for money. Stransom meditates on Creston's first wife and idealizes her in her death. Later the same day, Stransom learns of the death of his boyhood friend, Acton Hague, a man who betrayed Stransom in some undisclosed manner. Hague becomes the only dead friend that Stransom rejects, as Stransom becomes more and more absorbed with the dead and creates an altar of candles to them. A mysterious woman becomes a fellow mourner at Stransom's shrine. It takes him months to learn her name and years to find out her address. He finally comes to her apartment after the death of her aunt, only to find that her room is a personal shrine to Acton Hague, who rejected the woman. Since Stransom cannot light a candle for Hague, the relationship ends. The loss of the woman casts a shadow over his daily devotions at his altar. Dismayed, he has a vision of his dead wife, Mary, smiling at him from heaven. Just then, the mysterious woman returns to him as he dies in her arms. The last candle on the altar is lit not only for Acton Hague but also for Stransom.

Stransom has left the world of the living and has become obsessed with the dead. He forms a distant relationship with a fellow mourner, but she is only a part of his isolated world. Her feelings are never considered. Instead of forming a meaningful relationship, he continues to withdraw from human love. Stransom, like other heroes in James's later tales, becomes an example of James's reticent lover, a man who has rejected life and embraced death. The death of Stransom in the woman's arms unites the love and death theme predominant in the later tales.

"The Beast in the Jungle" is a powerful story about one man's quest for his illusive identity. John Marcher meets May Bartram when they are both in their thirties. Ten years earlier, Marcher revealed to her that he was singled out for a terrible fate. When Marcher recalls that he told her about his premonition, they form a relationship, and May begins to wait with him. Blindly, he rules out love as the strange fate that awaits him and forms a friendship with May taking her to operas, giving her gifts, and spending hours talking about his fate. As the years pass, he becomes skeptical that the "beast" will ever come. He feels reluctant to take May along with him on a "tiger hunt." Finally, May becomes ill. She knows his fate but will not tell him because she wants to make him a man like any other. He realizes that he might save her, but he is too preoccupied with his own destiny to become involved with her. She eventually tells him that his fate has already passed him by and that he never recognized it. When she dies, he contemplates that her death might be the terrible fate, but he rules out this premise. Marcher, an outsider at May's funeral, eventually goes abroad only to return to the grave of his friend to see another mourner stricken with grief. Suddenly, the beast leaps out at Marcher, as he realizes that he has failed to love and has been unable to feel deeply about anything. He has been an empty man who has watched his life from the outside but has failed to live it.

Marcher, like Stransom, is held prisoner to an obsession that removes him from the world of human relationships. He cannot give himself to another, so he must await his fate. James called the story a negative adventure. Indeed, Marcher's trek into the wilderness is his own confrontation with his unconscious fears. In his mono-maniacal obsession, he sacrifices May, who becomes dedicated to waiting for him to discover his fate, while he prides himself on his disinterestedness. In "The Beast in the Jungle," as in other James stories, the woman becomes useful to the man as a siphon for his own obsessions. Marcher fails to recognize and accept love and wastes his life by projecting all his endeavors onto a nebulous future. He is so wrapped up in his own ego that he fails to believe that the death of a lifelong friend is a terrible fate. In the end, he is brought into the world of the dead. Like Stransom, he has lived outside the present and now has only a lost past on which to look back. Like Winterbourne at the funeral of Daisy Miller, he begins to realize what the woman has meant to him. The cemetery where he stands is compared to a garden, which can be seen as an Eden, where Marcher realizes his own ignorance and comes to a painful awareness of his loss of paradise. The cemetery is also called a wilderness, a wilderness that will take him beyond the settled life and into the terrible recesses of his own heart. Marcher is a version of the American future-oriented pioneer unattached to family and loved ones, an Emersonian hero caught in the void of his own solipsistic world. He also becomes one of the first modern antiheroes, inauthentic men who live outside themselves, men to whom nothing really happens.

Stransom becomes absorbed in the past, in the world of the dead, and he neglects to establish a relationship with the woman who mourns with him. Marcher becomes involved in a vacuous destiny, unable to see the love that surrounds him. In "The Jolly Corner," Spencer Brydon, another alienated man who rejects the present, pursues his obsession with a past that might have been. Having lived abroad, Brydon returns to New York after a thirty-three-year absence only to find that the world has changed around him. James again explores what happens to an individual who finds himself in an alien culture. When Brydon comes to settle some property that he owns in the United States, he begins to wonder about his talents as a businessman and contemplates the kind of man he might have been had he stayed in the United States. He eventually develops a morbid obsession with his alter ego, the other self that he might have been. One night, Brydon enters the empty house called the Jolly Corner in search of his *Doppelgänger*. When he finally comes face to face with it, he faints at the monstrous sight. Upon recovery, he finds himself in the lap of Alice Staverton, who reassures him that she does not find his shadow self so horrible. In the end, he rejoices that he has gained knowledge about himself.

Spencer Brydon's return to the United States plays an ironic twist on James's international theme, as a Europeanized American returns to a United States that he feels alienated from and then conjures up an American self that horrifies him. Like

Marcher, Brydon finds himself on a hunt stalking his secret self, his fate that might have been. Again, James uses the image of the hunt to symbolize an internal journey into the subconscious mind. As the doors of life's options open and close around Brydon in the haunted house of his lost youth, the monster leaps out at him as it did at Marcher. Both men, like Stransom, collapse upon the women they have neglected. Alice Staverton is the woman who waited and shared his destiny, the way that May Bartram did Marcher's. She not only knew his double but also accepted it. The use of the double figure was popular in romantic and gothic literature, but in "The Jolly Corner," James gave a deeper psychological and philosophical undertone to the motif. In his last group of stories, James used the mystery adventure format to probe the inner psyche of his characters and to examine characters obsessed with living life outside the present.

James brought a greater psychological realism to the genre of short fiction, expanded its length in order to encompass an in-depth range of inner experiences, transformed the mystery story into metafictional narratives that have a distinctly postmodern quality, and reshaped the quest motif of American literature into existential probings about authenticating one's identity.

Other major works

NOVELS: *Roderick Hudson*, 1876; *The American*, 1876-1877; *The Europeans*, 1878; *An International Episode*, 1878-1879; *Confidence*, 1879-1880; *Washington Square*, 1880; *The Portrait of a Lady*, 1880-1881; *The Bostonians*, 1885-1886; *The Princess Casamassima*, 1885-1886; *The Reverberator*, 1888; *The Tragic Muse*, 1889-1890; *The Spoils of Poynton*, 1897; *What Maisie Knew*, 1897; *The Awkward Age*, 1897-1899; *In the Cage*, 1898; *The Turn of the Screw*, 1898; *The Sacred Fount*, 1901; *The Wings of the Dove*, 1902; *The Ambassadors*, 1903; *The Golden Bowl*, 1904; *The Outcry*, 1911; *The Ivory Tower*, 1917; *The Sense of the Past*, 1917.

PLAYS: *The American*, 1891; *Guy Domville*, 1894; *Theatricals: Tenants and Disengaged*, 1894; *Theatricals, Second Series: The Album and The Reprobate*, 1895; *The Complete Plays of Henry James*, 1949.

NONFICTION: *Transatlantic Sketches*, 1875; *French Poets and Novelists*, 1878; *Hawthorne*, 1879; *Portraits of Places*, 1883; *A Little Tour in France*, 1884; *Partial Portraits*, 1888; *Essays in London*, 1893; *William Wetmore Story and His Friends*, 1903; *English Hours*, 1905; *The American Scene*, 1907; *Views and Reviews*, 1908; *Italian Hours*, 1909; *A Small Boy and Others*, 1913; *Notes of a Son and Brother*, 1914; *Notes on Novelists*, 1914; *The Middle Years*, 1917; *The Art of the Novel: Critical Prefaces*, 1934; *The Future of the Novel*, 1956; *Henry James: Literary Criticism*, 1984; *The Art of Criticism: Henry James on the Theory and Practice of Fiction*, 1986; *The Complete Notebooks of Henry James*, 1987.

Bibliography

Gage, Richard, P. *Order and Design: Henry James Titled Story Sequences.* New York: Peter Lang, 1988. Gage examines James's published short-story collections, such as *Terminations, Embarrassments,* and *The Soft Side,* in order to show how James collected his stories around a central theme. Focusing on the interrelatedness of James's works, Gage shows how James's stories can be divided into organized units based upon a holistic design.

Hocks, Richard A. *Henry James: A Study of the Short Fiction.* Boston: Twayne, 1990. Hocks's book is a good introduction to James's short fiction. The book divides James's stories into three periods: the early social realism, the middle tales dealing with psychological and moral issues, and the later works of poetic expressionism. Detailed analyses of the major works are provided, along with selections of James's writings on short fiction and a collection of critical articles on selected works.

Kraft, James. *The Early Tales of Henry James.* Carbondale: Southern Illinois University Press, 1969. Kraft briefly covers James's theory of short fiction and gives considerable emphasis to James's little known early stories. He focuses on James's development as a writer of short fiction, beginning with James's first story "A Tragedy of Error" (1864) and ending with "The International Episode" (1879). This book is not for the student interested in James's major works.

Vaid, Krishna Balden. *Technique in the Tales of Henry James.* Cambridge, Mass.: Harvard University Press, 1964. Vaid covers all the major works, gives a comprehensive overview of James's writings on short fiction, and focuses on James's styles of narration and his careful balance of summary and scene. The book contains an excellent chapter on James's later tales.

Wagenknecht, Edward. *The Tale of Henry James.* New York: Frederick Ungar, 1984. The book contains brief analyses of fifty-five of James's major tales as well as thumbnail sketches of other stories. It provides a good reference work for someone looking for short summaries and critical bibliographies (found in the footnotes) but lacks detailed criticism of individual works as well as historical perspective.

Paul Rosefeldt

M. R. JAMES

Born: Goodnestone, Kent, England; August 1, 1862
Died: Eton, England; June 12, 1936

Principal short fiction

Ghost Stories of an Antiquary, 1904; *More Ghost Stories of an Antiquary*, 1911; *A Thin Ghost and Others*, 1919; *The Five Jars*, 1922; *A Warning to the Curious*, 1925; *The Collected Ghost Stories of M. R. James*, 1931 (as *The Penguin Complete Ghost Stories of M. R. James*, 1984); *Book of the Supernatural*, 1979 (U.S. title, *The Book of Ghost Stories*, 1979).

Other literary forms

The scholarly writings of M. R. James were varied and extensive. He cataloged most of the medieval manuscript collections in the Cambridge colleges, the Fitzwilliam Museum, and the Canterbury Cathedral. He was an early researcher in Christian archaeology, contributing dozens of articles and monographs on stained glass, roof bosses, statuary, and wall paintings. James was also one of the foremost biblical scholars of his time and was responsible for producing editions of both the old and new testament apocrypha. He edited a number of ancient books in modern translation or in contemporary editions, researched ancient libraries, as well as works in local history and what might loosely be described as classical studies.

Achievements

James won a number of prestigious awards and scholarships at both Eton College and King's College, Cambridge, including the Newcastle Scholarship at Eton and the Eton Scholarship, the Craven Scholarship, the Carus Undergraduate Prize, a Bell Scholarship, the annual Jeremie Septuagint Prize, and the senior Chancellor's Metal for 1886 at King's. He was elected to a fellowship at King's in 1887, became dean in 1889, and provost in 1905. In addition, he served as both assistant director and later director of the Fitzwilliam Museum, Cambridge, was on the syndicate of the library and the university press, and also became vice-chancellor of the university. James became provost of Eton in 1918 and was awarded the Order of Merit in 1930.

Biography

Montague Rhodes James was reared in a family of academics and clerics. His father was a parish priest who held the living at Livermore in Suffolk where James grew up. He prepared for Eton at Temple Grove where his father had gone before him, entering Eton in 1876 as a King's scholar. His years at Eton were among the happiest of his life, and he demonstrated a scholarly precocity. He was both a popular boy and a successful student and passed on to King's College, Cambridge, on an Eton Scholarship in 1882. He remained at King's for the next thirty-six years as an undergraduate, fellow, vice-provost, and finally provost. During these years he also fulfilled a number of other academic and administrative posts at the university. He was briefly vice-chancellor of the university during the 1914-1918 war. In 1918, partly in response to various changes taking place at Cambridge, James accepted the provostship of Eton, a position he held until his death in 1936.

Analysis

M. R. James, perhaps the most important practitioner of the ghost story between Joseph Sheridan Le Fanu and the modern scene, was, in the very best sense of the word, an "amateur." An antiquarian, bibliographer, theologian, and educator by profession, his fiction writing was an almost accidental avocation; he made up and told (literally as well as figuratively) ghost stories for his own pleasure and that of his friends. His first two tales, "Canon Alberic's Scrapbook" and "Lost Hearts," were composed to be read aloud at an 1897 meeting of the "Chitchat Society," a short-lived literary club. The group disbanded, but James continued the ritual of reading supernatural narratives to friends every Christmas at eleven o'clock in the evening. Publication of the stories was largely due to the encouragement of these friends and never became more than a minor activity in James's long and full, if uneventful, life.

This is not to say, however, that he was less than completely serious about his ghost stories. Although his oeuvre of thirty-two tales is modest in size, especially when compared to his voluminous nonfiction writings, the quality of the stories is uniformly high, and each has a flavor and style that is distinctly M. R. James. Beyond his own fictions, once he had committed himself to the writing of such narratives, James became both a staunch advocate and an important theorist of the genre.

The primary influence on his work was the mid-nineteenth century master of mystery and horror, Le Fanu. James thought himself a writer in the "Le Fanu tradition" and did everything he could to bring public attention to that neglected predecessor. In 1923, he edited a collection of Le Fanu's best short fiction, *Madam Crowl's Ghost and Other Tales of Mystery*, initiating a "Le Fanu revival" which established that writer as the true father of the modern British horror story. James probably overstated his resemblance to his Irish forebear, but there are enough similarities between them to acknowledge a "Le Fanu-M. R. James tradition"—one that emphasizes familiar, contemporary settings instead of exotic, bygone landscapes; narrative distance and indirection rather than blatant sensationalism; and linguistic precision and subtlety over melodramatic verbal excess.

Although, when asked if he had any "theories as to the writing of ghost stories," James responded "none that are worthy of the name or need be repeated," he did, in fact, have a thorough, if succinct and simple, theory of the genre which he articulated—albeit reluctantly—in a few short essays that preface some of his collections. Most of these principles can be seen operating in "Lost Hearts," the most famous of James's early stories.

"Two ingredients most valuable in the concocting of a ghost story are to me," he said, "the atmosphere and the nicely managed crescendo." He begins to create his "atmosphere" and mount his "nicely managed crescendo" in "Lost Hearts" with the picture of a young boy arriving at a very old house; the boy is only sketched in; the house, copied from a real structure, is described in meticulous architectural detail. Like Edgar Allan Poe, a writer in most other respects very different from him, James often endowed his environments and inanimate objects with more reality and vitality than his human characters.

The reader quickly learns that the boy, Stephen Elliott, has come to live with his rich old uncle, Mr. Abney, following the death of his parents. Abney, a bookish scholar, seems benign, if austere and distant. The only odd note in their initial meeting is produced by the old man's insistent repetition of the question: "How old are you?" Abney, however, retreats into the background when Stephen is turned over to Mrs. Bunch, his lively, affectionate, middle-aged housekeeper, who quickly establishes a comfortable setting for the boy—in keeping with James's characteristic strategy.

> Let us, then, be introduced to the actors in a placid way; let us see them going about their ordinary business, undisturbed by forebodings, pleased with their surroundings; and into this calm environment let the ominous thing put out its head, unobtrusively at first, then more insistently, until it holds the stage.

The "ominous thing" makes its unobtrusive entrance into the story when Mrs. Bunch tells Stephen about the mysterious disappearance of two homeless young people, a "gypsy girl" and a "foreign boy," who had also been taken in by Abney. This information is immediately reinforced by a strange and terrible dream Stephen has in which he sees a strange corpselike figure seated in the bathtub, hands over its heart. Two bizarre incidents follow in short order: Stephen awakens one morning to find a series of slits in his nightgown over the heart area, and the butler refuses to go to the wine cellar because he hears voices. James manipulates the ghosts with great skill; the reader cannot be sure whether the rapidly intensifying danger to Stephen comes from these specters or from his uncle, or, perhaps, from both.

The climax of the story is signaled when Abney invites Stephen to an eleven o'clock meeting in his study. Immediately prior to the meeting, Stephen peers out his window and sees two ghosts:

> Whilst the girl stood still, half smiling, with her hands clasped over her heart, the boy, a thin shape, with black hair and ragged clothing, raised his arms in the air with an appearance of menace and of unappeasable hunger and longing. The moon shone upon his almost transparent hands, and Stephen saw that the nails were fearfully long and that the lights shown through them. As he stood with his arms thus raised, he disclosed a terrifying spectacle. On the left side of his chest there opened a black and gaping rent. . . .

Extremely agitated, Stephen rushes to Abney's study, forces the door open, and confronts the horror. The reader, however, is not yet permitted to confront it; instead, he reads an explanation of Abney's actions and motives. Abney was a practicing occultist who attempted to carry out an ancient magic ritual designed to give him almost godlike powers. This required that he consume three hearts taken from "still living human beings" under the age of twenty-one. He had already eaten two (reduced, of course, to ashes and mixed with red wine!), and Stephen's was slated to be the third. Abney's fatal mistake was to ignore the "annoyance . . . experienced from the psychic portion of the subjects, which popular language dignifies with the name of ghosts." Only after reading this explanation is the reader allowed to see the picture of Abney, dead in his chair, his chest slashed open by the dead boy's long fingernails.

The author's reticence in revealing the final assault on Abney is also characteristic of his style. "Lost Hearts" is actually much more direct and visceral than the usual M. R. James story, and it is surprising that Abney's corpse is even described in such detail. The more common technique is to describe the effects of a scene on the observers and leave it to the reader's imagination to fill in the details. When, for example, the unfortunate narrator in "Count Magnus" is found dead, "the jury that viewed the body fainted, seven of 'em did, and none of 'em wouldn't speak to what they see, and the verdict was visitation of God."

For all of its popularity, "Lost Hearts" is atypical of its author in a number of additional ways. The black magic and deliberate malevolence of Mr. Abney are unusual. As a rule, James believed that the machinery of the occult should be left out of a story as much as possible. Although, like Abney, the typical James protagonist is a well-to-do, bookish man of leisure, he is seldom consciously evil. He is more likely to be bored, curious, and a bit naïve, a dangerous combination of qualities. He does not usually summon the dark powers on purpose, but happens on them innocently or in the process of normal scholarly pursuits. Having released the demons inadvertently, he then suffers consequences all out of proportion to his "guilt" (another similarity between the work of James and Le Fanu). Sometimes this hero-victim discovers his error in time to avoid a grisly fate; more often he does not, and the difficulty of dealing with, or even recognizing, the evil forces is compounded by the fact that they are frequently embodied in the most seemingly innocuous and common objects—such things as an old book, a mediocre engraving, a doll house, a swatch of material, a stained glass window, or, as in the case of his best-known story, "Oh, Whistle, and I'll Come to You, My Lad," a small metal whistle.

James's provocative title prepares the reader for a mysterious intruder and is especially effective if he recognizes that it is taken from a Robert Burns song:

> Though father and mother and brother go mad,
> Oh, whistle and I'll come to ye, my lad.

The "lad" of the title is Parkins, a young Professor of Ontography, on a golf-study vacation to the East Coast of Britain. Typically, he is a thorough skeptic who denies the possible existence of ghosts. "Any appearance of concession to the view that such things might exist is equivalent to a renunciation of all that I hold most sacred," he proclaims. Naturally, such an attitude sets him up for what is to follow. A characteristically Jamesian antiquarian, Parkins explores some ancient local ruins where he finds the small bronze whistle hidden in an old altarlike artifact. From the moment

Parkins discovers the whistle, he becomes vulnerable.

En route back to his hotel room he sees a presence lurking behind him, "a rather indistinct personage, who seemed to be making great efforts to catch up with him." It is Parkins' own thoughtless curiosity, however, that puts him in real danger. Despite the ambiguous warning etched in Latin on the instrument ("Quis est iste qui venit?"/"Who is this who is coming?"), he blows the whistle not once, but twice. "Well," he responds aloud to the inscription, "the best way to find out is evidently to whistle for him."

Such minor league hubris is always answered in James; come to Parkins "it" does, but never in a completely recognizable form. The exact nature of the being, its origins, its purposes, and even its capacities, remain unknown. Whatever the creature is, it provokes fear and anxiety in the reader primarily by hint and threat rather than by concrete manifestations of malevolent power.

Skepticism notwithstanding, Parkins' inner emotional security disintegrates as his feelings of being stalked increase. When he first blows the whistle, he sees a mysterious scene of "a lonely figure—how employed he could not tell" and hears a sudden wind crash against the window. Trying to sleep that night, he pictures an agitated man fleeing across a beach, climbing and stumbling over rocks, nervously looking back over his shoulder; then he notices a "figure in pale, fluttering draperies" pursuing in the distance. Parkins also hears the rustling of sheets in a nearby bed and is annoyed by the thinness of the hotel walls. The next morning the maid notices that both beds in the room have been occupied.

Parkins, however, maintains his skeptical façade, even in the face of the Colonel, his more worldly golf partner. It is the Colonel who relates the whistle and strange winds to old fisherman legends. Then both of the men encounter a young boy who swears to have seen a ghostly figure moving about in Parkins' room. The climax occurs when, late that night, Parkins again hears the rustling and realizes that it comes from the bed next to his. A figure rises and approaches Parkins, who backs up against the window, and closes about him, pushing its "face of crumpled linen" into that of the terrified scholar. At this moment, in the best cliff-hanger tradition, the Colonel bursts into the room and the ghost collapses back into a pile of bedding. The following morning, the Colonel casts the whistle into the sea.

Unfortunately, this bald summary may make the story sound rather tame and perhaps corny, especially to a modern reader familiar with more visceral and vicious specters. No simple plot sketch can convey James's ability to manipulate atmosphere, innuendos, images, allusions, language, and tones and these are what sets "Oh, Whistle, and I'll Come to You, My Lad," apart from the mass of fashionable ghostly tales that proliferated during this period.

James's prose style is precise, economical, and understated. As already noted, he seldom describes violence directly, but relies on suggestion and metaphor. Narrative distance is maintained by an adroit control of tone and point of view, and, unlike Le Fanu, James's detached narrators and his framing devices never get cumbersome or distracting. The effect of all of this is to create a running tension between the intense, disturbing reality of the story and the extremely objective voice that describes it. This tension is most obvious in such overt horror stories as "Lost Hearts," "The Ash-tree," and "Wailing Well" but is perhaps even more effective in subtler tales such as "Oh, Whistle, and I'll Come to You, My Lad," "The Mezzotint," and "The Diary of Mr. Poynter," where it amplifies the underlying ambiguity and unresolved fear which bother the reader long after he has finished the story.

James's influence on the supernatural horror story has been pervasive and continuing. His creative years stretched from the end of the Victorian age almost to the pulp era of H. P. Lovecraft and his contemporaries. Thus, he is the primary transitional figure connecting the late nineteenth century with the modern era. It must be admitted, however, that in tone and style James seems more Victorian than modern. One of the best surveys of this genre gives the appropriate label "elegant nightmare" to the ghost story, and of all such nightmares, those of M. R. James are surely the most elegant.

Other major works

NONFICTION: *Psalms of the Pharisees*, 1891 (with H. E. Ryle); *The Testament of Abraham*, 1892; *The Gospel According to Peter*, 1897; *Ancient Libraries of Canterbury and Dover*, 1903; *Wanderings and Homes of MSS*, 1919; *Apocryphal New Testament*, 1924; *Eton and Kings: Recollections, Mostly Trivial, 1875-1925*, 1926.

Bibliography

Briggs, Julia. "No Mere Antiquary: M. R. James." In *Night Visitors: The Rise and Fall of the English Ghost Story.* London: Faber & Faber, 1977. This chapter provides a good overview of James's achievements in the genre, with a discussion of his methods of handling locale, the past, domestic terrors, mythology, and even ghosts themselves within his fiction.

Cox, Michael. *M. R. James: An Informal Portrait.* New York: Oxford University Press, 1983. A good, intimate biography that provides a detailed overview of the life of James. Only one chapter is devoted to the ghost stories, "A Peep into Pandemonium."

Joshi, S. C. "M. R. James: The Limitations of the Ghost Story." In *The Weird Tale: Arthur Machen, Lord Dunsany, Algernon Blackwood, M. R. James, Ambrose Bierce, H. P. Lovecraft.* Austin: University of Texas Press, 1990. This critical chapter by an author who acknowledges his dislike for James's ghost stories nevertheless sheds some light on the drawbacks of his method and general narrative strategies.

Lubbock, S. G. *A Memoir of Montague Rhodes James.* Cambridge, England: Cambridge University Press, 1939. The first and most personal memoir of James's life is both intimate and incomplete, and it makes up in insight for what it lacks in accuracy.

Mason, Michael A. "On Not Letting Them Lie: Moral Significance in the Ghost Stories of M. R. James." *Studies in Short Fiction* 19 (Summer, 1982): 253-260. This essay discusses how James's ghost stories interweave moral values among the accurate evocations of the past, the subtle manipulations of reality, and the unsettling presence of an objective evil, which characterizes his tales of the supernatural.

Pfaff, Richard William. *Montague Rhodes James.* London: Scolar Press, 1980. Pfaff has written the most comprehensive biography of James as well as the most thorough examination of his writings, especially his academic work. Contains a comprehensive bibliography of James's writings.

Sullivan, Jack. "The Antiquarian Ghost Story: Montague Rhodes James." In *Elegant Nightmares: The English Ghost Story from Le Fanu to Blackwood.* Athens: Ohio University Press, 1978. This chapter contains the best analysis of James's ghost stories and their place within the English tradition. Sullivan is especially good in tracing the influence on James. He also traces the influence of James in his chapter "Ghost Stories of Other Antiquaries."

Keith Nelson
(Revised by *Charles L. P. Silet*)

SARAH ORNE JEWETT

Born: South Berwick, Maine; September 3, 1849
Died: South Berwick, Maine; June 24, 1909

Principal short fiction

Deephaven, 1877; *Old Friends and New*, 1879; *Country By-Ways*, 1881; *The Mate of the Daylight, and Friends Ashore*, 1884; *A White Heron*, 1886; *The King of Folly Island, and Other People*, 1888; *Tales of New England*, 1890; *Strangers and Wayfarers*, 1890; *A Native of Winby*, 1893; *The Life of Nancy*, 1895; *The Queen's Twin*, 1899; *Stories and Tales*, 1910; *The Uncollected Short Stories of Sarah Orne Jewett*, 1971.

Other literary forms

Sarah Orne Jewett wrote four novels: *A Country Doctor* (1884), *A Marsh Island* (1885), *The Country of the Pointed Firs* (1896), and *The Tory Lover* (1901). She also published popular books for children, including *Play Days* (1878) and *Betty Leicester* (1890). Her main work of nonfiction was a history, *The Story of the Normans* (1887).

Achievements

Jewett is best known as a local colorist who captured with fidelity the life of coastal Maine in the late nineteenth century in sensitive and moving portraits, mainly of women's lives. Except for *The Country of the Pointed Firs*, widely considered her masterpiece, Jewett's long fiction is thought less successful than her short stories. During her lifetime, she was considered one of the best short-story writers in America. Most of her stories appeared first in popular magazines such as *The Atlantic*, under the editorship of William Dean Howells, and *Harper's*. American literary historian F. O. Matthiessen said in his 1929 study of Jewett that she and Emily Dickinson were the two best women writers America had produced. Willa Cather offered Jewett similar praise and credited her with positively changing the direction of her literary career in a brief but rich acquaintance near the end of Jewett's life.

Biography

Sarah Orne Jewett spent most of her life in South Berwick on the Maine coast, where she was born on September 3, 1849. Daughter of a country doctor, she aspired to medicine herself, but moved toward writing because of early ill health (which led her father to take her on his calls for fresh air), the special literary education encouraged by her family, and her discovery as a teenager of her "little postage stamp of soil" in reading Harriet Beecher Stowe's *The Pearl of Orr's Island* (1862). Her father, especially, encouraged her to develop her keen powers of observation, and her grandfathers stimulated her interest in storytelling. After the death of her father in 1878, she began a lifelong friendship with Annie Fields that brought her into contact with leading writers in America and Europe, such as Henry James and George Eliot. The two friends traveled together in Europe, the Caribbean, and the United States, and after the death of Mr. Fields, they lived together for extended periods.

Jewett began writing and publishing at the age of nineteen. During her career she developed and maintained the purpose of helping her readers to understand and love the ordinary people of her native Maine, and later she told stories about other misunderstood people such as the Irish and Southern whites. In her career, she produced more than twenty volumes of fiction for children and adults, history, prose sketches, and poetry. Her short stories show rapidly increasing subtlety and power. Her early books were well-received, but beginning with *The Mate of the Daylight, and Friends Ashore,* reviewers routinely praised her collections highly. It was not unusual for a reviewer to be a little puzzled by how much he or she liked Jewett's stories. A frequent response was that the stories seemed to lack plot and action and yet at the same time, they were absorbing and charming. Late twentieth century critics, notably feminist critics, have suggested that Jewett was developing a kind of storytelling in opposition to the popular melodramas with their fast-paced romance or adventure plots. Jewett's stories came more and more to focus on intimate relations of friendship, especially between older women, but eventually in one way or another between all kinds of people.

By the time Jewett wrote her masterpiece, the novella *The Country of the Pointed Firs,* she had fully developed a form of narration that pointed toward the James Joyce of *Dubliners* (1914). This novella, and a number of her best stories such as "Miss Tempy's Watchers" and "The Queen's Twin," would set up a problem of tact, of how to overcome barriers to communion between two or more people, and then through a subtle process of preparation would make overcoming these barriers possible. The story would end with an epiphany that involved communion between at least two people. Though she wrote a variety of other kinds of stories in her career, this type of development was probably her major accomplishment, and it achieved its fullest realization in *The Country of the Pointed Firs.*

A tragic carriage accident on her birthday in 1902 left her in such pain that she gave up fiction writing and devoted herself to her friends. In the fall of 1908, she met Willa Cather, to whom she wrote several letters that inspired Cather to write about Nebraska. Cather recognized Jewett's help by dedicating to Jewett her first Nebraska novel, *O Pioneers!* (1913). Jewett died at her South Berwick home on June 24, 1909.

Analysis

When a young reader wrote to Jewett in 1899 to express admiration of her stories for girls, Jewett encouraged her to continue reading: ". . . you will always have the happiness of finding friendships in books, and it grows pleasanter and pleasanter as one grows older. And then the people in books are apt to make us understand 'real' people better, and to know why they do things, and so we learn sympathy and patience and enthusiasm for those we live with, and can try to help them in what they are doing, instead of being half suspicious and finding fault."

Here Jewett states one of the central aims of her fiction, to help people learn the arts of friendship. Chief among these arts is tact, which Jewett defines in *The Country of the Pointed Firs* as a perfect self-forgetfulness that allows one to enter reverently and sympathetically the sacred realms of the inner lives of others. In her stories, learning tact is often a major element, and those who are successful are often rewarded with epiphanies—moments of visionary union with individuals or with nature—or with communion—the feeling of oneness with another person that for Jewett is the ultimate joy of friendship.

"A White Heron," which first appeared in *A White Heron*, is often considered Jewett's best story, perhaps because it goes so well with such American classics as Nathaniel Hawthorne's *The Scarlet Letter* (1850), Herman Melville's *Moby Dick* (1851), and William Faulkner's "The Bear" (1942). With these works, the story shares a central, complex symbol in the white heron and the major American theme of a character's complex relationship with the landscape and society. As a story about a young person choosing between society and nature as the proper spiritual guide for a particular time in her life, however, "A White Heron" is atypical for Jewett. One main feature that marks the story as Jewett's, however, is that the main character, Sylvia, learns a kind of tact during her adventure in the woods, a tact that grows out of an epiphany and that leads to the promise of continuing communion with nature that the story implies will help this somewhat weak and solitary child grow into a strong adult.

Sylvia, a young girl rescued by her grandmother, Mrs. Tilley, from the overstimulation and overcrowding of her city family meets a young ornithologist, who fascinates her and promises her ten dollars if she will tell him where he can find the white heron he has long sought for his collection. Childishly tempted by this magnificent sum and her desire to please the hunter, who knows so much of nature yet kills the birds, she determines to climb at dawn a landmark pine from which she might see the heron leave its nest. She succeeds in this quest, but finds she cannot tell her secret to the hunter. The story ends with the assertion that she could have loved the hunter as "a dog loves" and with a prayer to the woodlands and summer to compensate her loss with "gifts and graces."

Interesting problems in technique and tone occur when Sylvia climbs the pine. The narrative tone shifts in highly noticeable ways. As she begins her walk to the tree before dawn, the narrator expresses personal anxiety that "the great wave of human interest which flooded for the first time this dull little life should sweep away the satisfactions of an existence heart to heart with nature and the dumb life of the forest." This statement seems to accentuate an intimacy between reader and narrator; it states the position the narrative rhetoric has implied from the beginning and, in effect, asks if the reader shares this anxiety. From this point until Sylvia reaches the top of the tree, the narrator gradually merges with Sylvia's internal consciousness. During the climb, Jewett builds on this intimacy with Sylvia. Both narrator and reader are aware of sharing in detail Sylvia's subjective impressions of her climb and of her view, and this merging of the subjectivities of the story (character, narrator, and reader) extends beyond the persons to objects as the narrator unites with the tree and imagines its sympathy for the climber. The merging extends further yet when Sylvia, the reader, and the narrator see with lyric clarity the sea, the sun, and two hawks that, taken together, make all three observers feel as if they could fly out over the world. Being atop the tallest landmark pine, "a great mainmast to the voyaging earth," one is, in a way, soaring in the cosmos as the hawks soar in the air. At this point of clarity and union, the narrative tone shifts again. The narrator speaks directly to Sylvia, commanding her to look at the point where the heron will rise. The vision of the heron rising from a dead hemlock, flying by the pine, and settling on a nearby bough is a kind of colloquy of narrator and character and, if the technique works as it seems to intend, of the reader, too. This shift in "place" involves a shift in time to the present tense that continues through Sylvia's absorption of the secret and her descent from the tree. It seems clear that the intent of these shifts is to transcend time and space, to unite narrator, reader, character, and the visible scene which is "all the world." This is virtually the same technical device which is the central organizing device of Walt Whitman's "Crossing Brooklyn Ferry," and the intent of that device seems similar as well. The reader is to feel a mystical, "transcendental" union with the cosmos that assures one of its life and one's participation in that life.

A purpose of this union is to make justifiable and understandable Sylvia's choice not to give the heron's life away because they have "watched the sea and the morning together." The narrator's final prayer makes sense when it is addressed to transcendental nature on behalf of the girl who has rejected superfluous commodity in favor of Spirit, the final gift of Ralph Waldo Emerson's nature in his essay, "Nature." Though this story is atypical of Jewett insofar as it offers a fairly clearly transcendental view of nature and so presents a moment of communion with the nonhuman, it is characteristic of Jewett in that by subtly drawing reader and narrator into the epiphany, the story creates a moment of human communion.

More typical of Jewett's best work is "The Only Rose," which was first published in *The Atlantic* in January, 1894, and was then collected in *The Life of Nancy*. This story is organized by three related epiphanies, each centering on the rose, and each involving a blooming.

In the first "miracle of the rose," Mrs. Bickford and Miss Pendexter are hypnotized into communion by contemplating the new bloom on Mrs. Bickford's poor bush. In this epiphany, Miss Pendexter enters into spiritual sympathy with Mrs. Bickford, realizing that her silence this time is unusual, resulting not from having nothing to say, but from "an overburdening sense of the inexpressible." They go on to share the most intimate conversation of their relationship. The blooming flower leads to a blooming in their friendship. It also leads, however, to Mrs. Bickford's dilemma: on which of her three dead husbands' graves should she place this single rose? Her need to answer this question points to a deeper need to escape from her comparatively isolated and ineffectual life by shifting from an ethic of obligation to an ethic of love. Her heart has been frozen since her first husband's death, and it is long past time now for it to thaw and bloom again. Miss Pendexter understands something of this and tactfully leaves Mrs. Bickford to work it out for herself.

The second miracle of the rose occurs almost at the end of the story, when John confesses his love for Lizzie to his Aunt Bickford as he drives her to the graveyard. The symbolic rose of young and passionate love moves him to speak, even though he is unsure of the propriety of speaking up to the wealthy aunt from whom he hopes to inherit. His story of young love and hope, however, takes Mrs. Bickford out of herself, and she forgets her troubles in sharing his joy. As a result, he blooms, blushing a "fine scarlet."

The final miracle is that while he is taking the flowers to the graves, she realizes which of her husbands should have the rose. At the same time that John is taking the rose for his Lizzie, Mrs. Bickford is giving it in her heart to Albert, the first husband whom she loved so passionately in her youth. Her realization of this event makes her blush "like a girl" and laugh in self-forgetfulness before the graveyard as she remembers that the first flower Albert gave her was just such a rose.

In the overall movement of the story, Mrs. Bickford is lifted out of herself and prepared for a richer and deeper communion with her friends and relatives. The single rose blossom seems mysteriously to impose an obligation upon her, but probably it really awakens the ancient spring of love within her that was perhaps covered over by grief at losing Albert so young and by the difficult life that followed his loss. When she finally struggles free of the weight of the intervening years, she recovers her hidden capacity for friendship and joy, for forgetting herself and joining in the happiness of others. She has epiphanies, rediscovers tact, and begins again to experience communion.

"Martha's Lady" first appeared in *The Atlantic* in October, 1897, and was then collected in *The Queen's Twin*. This story illustrates Jewett's mature control over her technique and material. She represents a kind of sainthood without falling into the syrupy sentimentality of popular melodrama.

Into a community beginning to show the effects of a Puritan formalism comes Helena Vernon, a young city woman who is unself-consciously affectionate and beautiful and, therefore, a pleasure to please. She delights her maiden cousin, Harriet Pyne, charms the local minister, who gives her a copy of his *Sermons on the Seriousness of Life*, and transforms Martha, Harriet's new and awkward servant girl. In fact, Helena transforms to some extent everyone she meets in the village of Ashford, taking some of the starch out of their stiff and narrow way of life. After Helena leaves to marry, prosper, and suffer in Europe, Martha carries her memory constantly in her heart: "To lose out of sight the friend whom one has loved and lived to please is to lose joy out of life. But if love is true, there comes presently a higher joy of pleasing the ideal, that is to say, the perfect friend." This is the ideal of sainthood that the narrative voice asks the reader to admire. Thanks largely to Martha's living this ideal of always behaving so as to please Helena, she and Harriet live a happy life together for forty years. Helena returns to visit, worn but with the same youthful spirit, and to reward with a kiss what she recognizes as Martha's perfect memory of the services Helena enjoyed as a girl. This recognition acknowledges Martha's faithfulness to her ideal and creates that moment of communion that is the ultimate reward for such faithfulness.

What prevents this story from dissolving into mush? Nearly all the special features of Jewett's technical facility are necessary. She avoids overelaboration. It is not difficult for an alert reader to notice the parallel to the Christ story type; a liberating figure enters a legalistic society to inspire love in a group of followers, which results in an apotheosis after her departure. The disciple remains true to the ideal until the liberator comes again to claim the disciple. Jewett could have forced this analogy on the reader, but she does not. Only a few details subtly suggest the analogy—character names, calling Martha a saint, and her relics—but these need not compel the reader in this direction, which, in fact, adds only a little to the story's power. While avoiding overelaboration, Jewett also avoids internal views. On the whole, the story is made of narrative summary and brief dramatic scenes. Emotion is revealed through action and speech; this technical choice produces less intensity of feeling than, for example, the intimate internal view of Sylvia in "The White Heron." The result is a matter-of-factness of tone that keeps Martha's sainthood of a piece with the ordinary world of Ashford. This choice is supported by nearly every other technical choice of the story—the attention to detail of setting, the gentle but pointed humor directed against religious formalism, and the emergence of Martha from the background of the story. Jewett's intention seems to be on the one hand to prevent the reader from emoting in excess of the worth of the object, but on the other to feel strongly and warmly the true goodness of Martha's faithfulness to love. Another purpose of this narrative approach is to demonstrate tact. In "A White Heron," both Sylvia and the reader enter the quest for the heron with mixed motives, but the nature of the journey—its difficulties, its joys, the absorption it requires—tends to purify motives and to prepare the spirit for epiphany. Sylvia's vision from atop the pine culminates in communion with the wild bird, a vision she has earned and that she may repeat if she realizes its value.

Jewett's light touch, her own tact in dealing with such delicate subjects, is one of her leading characteristics, and it flowers magnificently in the fiction of the last ten years of her writing career. While the stories discussed above illustrate Jewett's most powerful and moving storytelling, they do not illustrate so fully another of the main characteristics of her stories—humor. Humor is often present in her stories and can be found in more abundance than might be expected in "The Only Rose" and "Martha's Lady." She also wrote a number of funny stories that discriminating readers such as Cather would not hesitate to compare with the work of Mark Twain. "The Guests of Mrs. Timms," though more similar to the stories of Jane Austen than Twain, is a popular story of the humorous ironies that result when a socially ambitious widow calls on another widow of higher status without announcing her visit in advance. Among her best humorous stories are "Law Lane," "All My Sad Captains," "A Winter Courtship," and "The Quest of Mr. Teaby," but there are many others that are a delight to read.

Other major works

NOVELS: *A Country Doctor*, 1884; *A Marsh Island*, 1885; *The Country of the Pointed Firs*, 1896; *The Tory Lover*, 1901.

POETRY: *Verses: Printed for Her Friends*, 1916.

NONFICTION: *Letters of Sarah Orne Jewett*, 1911 (Annie Fields, editor); *Sarah Orne Jewett Letters*, 1956 (Richard Cary, editor).

CHILDREN'S LITERATURE: *Play Days: A Book of Stories for Children*, 1878; *The Story of the Normans*, 1887; *Betty Leicester: A Story for Girls*, 1890.

Bibliography

Cary, Richard, ed. *Appreciation of Sarah Orne Jewett: Twenty-nine Interpretive Essays.* Waterville, Maine: Colby College Press, 1973. This book collects a good cross section of the major writing on Jewett from 1885 until 1972. Contains biographical sketches, extended reviews, examinations of her technique, interpretations of some individual works, and evaluations of her career.

──────────. *Sarah Orne Jewett.* New York: Twayne, 1962. This critical study of Jewett includes a chronology, a biographical sketch, and descriptive analyses of most of her published works. Cary divides Jewett's works into thematic groups and shows how Jewett is a product of her New England background. Supplemented by annotated bibliographies of Jewett's books and of secondary sources.

Donovan, Josephine. *Sarah Orne Jewett.* New York: Frederick Ungar, 1980. This critical study includes a chronology and an examination of Jewett's literary career, following the development of her major themes through her works. Donovan is especially interested in Jewett's feminist themes. She provides primary and secondary bibliographies.

Matthiessen, F. O. *Sarah Orne Jewett.* Boston: Houghton Mifflin, 1929. This short biographical study, though it is not the most recent, may be the most readily available in libraries. Matthiessen surveys Jewett's life without going into great detail.

Nagel, Gwen L., ed. *Critical Essays on Sarah Orne Jewett.* Boston: G. K. Hall, 1984. This collection includes sixteen contemporary reviews of Jewett's books, reprints of eight critical essays from 1955 to 1983, and eight original essays. These deal with biography as well as interpretation. The introduction surveys the history of critical writing on Jewett.

Nagel, Gwen L., and James Nagel. *Sarah Orne Jewett: A Reference Guide.* Boston: G. K. Hall, 1978. Introduced with a survey of criticism on Jewett, this reference guide lists and annotates writing about Jewett from 1873 to 1976. It is invaluable as a source for secondary writing and for forming impressions of how Jewett's reputation has developed. For discussions of criticism since 1976, see *American Literary Scholarship: An Annual.*

Weber, Clara Carter, and Carl J. Weber. *A Bibliography of the Published Writings of*

Sarah Orne Jewett. Waterville, Maine: Colby College Press, 1949. This information-filled volume records the original publications and subsequent reprintings of Jewett's known works from 1868 to 1948.

Terry Heller

SAMUEL JOHNSON

Born: Lichfield, Staffordshire, England; September 18, 1709
Died: London, England; December 13, 1784

Principal short fiction

The Rambler, 1750-1752; *The Adventurer,* 1753-1754; *The Idler,* 1758-1760; *Rasselas, Prince of Abyssinia: A Tale by S. Johnson,* 1759 (originally published as *The Prince of Abissinia: A Tale*).

Other literary forms

The range and quality of Samuel Johnson's literary output is almost unparalleled in either English or American literature. He wrote a tragedy, poetry, biography, periodical essays, and travel books. He is most famous for his *A Dictionary of the English Language* (1755), *Rasselas, Prince of Abyssinia,* his critical edition, with notes and a preface, of *The Plays of William Shakespeare* (1765), and his collection of essays *The Lives of the Poets* (1779-1781). Johnson was also known as a brilliant conversationalist, and James Boswell, in his *The Life of Samuel Johnson, LL.D.* (1791), fortunately preserves this fascinating side of Johnson as a critic and verbal artist.

Achievements

As the widely used historical label "Age of Johnson" reveals, Johnson was the most famous man of letters in the second half of the eighteenth century. His neoclassicism, his Christian humanism, and his political conservatism were thoroughly grounded in the rational aesthetic of his predecessors, but he was no slave to the formal standards of his era. He is considered a pioneer in modern scholarship and practical criticism as well as a neoclassical poet. His dictionary, produced almost single-handedly; his introductory essays on English poets, which use the works to illuminate the poet's life and the life to interpret the poet's works; and the combination of philosophy, allegory, and travel adventure in his short novel—all combine to secure his special place in the history of English literature, regardless of literary trends.

Biography

The son of a bookseller in Lichfield, Samuel Johnson failed as a school teacher and settled in London, where for years he barely survived as a hack writer. The first work published in his name was *The Vanity of Human Wishes* in 1749. The same year witnessed the production of his tragedy, *Irene,* by his friend and ex-student David Garrick; but his *The Rambler* essays first brought him general public notice, and his massive *A Dictionary of the English Language* made him the preeminent man of letters of his age. This work was followed by his 104 *The Idler* essays, *Rasselas,* his edition of *The Plays of William Shakespeare, A Journey to the Western Islands of*

Scotland (1775), and *The Lives of the Poets* (1779-1781). Johnson was physically a huge and uncouth man, with tics and personal eccentricities which amused some and frightened others. He was profoundly melancholy, fully aware of his extraordinary intellectual gifts and terrified of the damnation he could expect from God if he did not use his talents well. He was indolent, tending to procrastinate his work until it could be put off no longer and then writing with incredible rapidity. He was a social man in a very social age, the greatest conversationalist of an age of brilliant conversation, but despite his international reputation and his royal pension of three hundred pounds a year, he was constantly beleaguered by debt. His relationship with the Scotsman James Boswell has long intrigued biographers: they have depended greatly on Boswell's record of Johnson amid his circle of friends in an age known for its interest in conversation. His appetite for food, company, knowledge, and ideas was as voracious as his fear of death and judgment for the work he left undone. He died in 1784 at the age of seventy-five.

Analysis

Samuel Johnson is primarily thought of not as a fiction writer, but as a critic, and since his criticism explains so much about the peculiar form which his own fiction was to take, it is wise to discuss his views on criticism. The subject of *The Rambler* 4 is modern fiction. Johnson recognized that fiction underwent a profound change in his lifetime. Gone were the improbabilities of the romantic fiction of the past, expressed in its giants, knights, ladies, hermits, and battles. Contemporary works of fiction, Johnson wrote, "exhibit life in its true state, diversified only by accidents that daily happen in the world, influenced by passions and qualities which are really to be found in conversing with mankind." With this new verisimilitude, fiction acquires a new power, and consequently, a new responsibility. Since these works are chiefly read by the "young, the ignorant, and the idle, to whom they serve as lectures of conduct, and introductions into life," writers must be very careful in choosing their subjects and characters:

> It is . . . not a sufficient vindication of a character, that it is drawn as it appears, for many characters ought never to be drawn; nor of a narrative, that the train of events is agreeable to observation and experience, for that observation which is called knowledge of the world, will be found much more frequently to make men cunning than good.

Fiction, then, has a didactic purpose, whether a writer wishes it or not: readers imitate the behavior of the characters their authors offer as admirable, and authors therefore have a moral responsibility to select their characters and incidents carefully. They must also distinguish the "good and bad qualities in their principal personages," lest, as readers became more involved with these characters, they "lose the abhorrence of their faults, . . . or, perhaps, regard them with some kindness for being united with so much merit."

The type of fictional hero Johnson advocates is virtuous, although not angelic. In the plot, his virtue, "exercised in such trials as the various revolutions of things shall bring upon it, may, by conquering some calamities, and enduring others, teach us what we may hope, and what we can perform." Vice must be shown, but it "should always disgust; nor should the graces of gaiety, or the dignity of courage, be so united with it, as to reconcile it to the mind." The final purpose of fiction is to teach this moral truth: "that virtue is the highest proof of understanding, and the only solid basis of greatness; and that vice is the natural consequence of narrow thoughts, that it begins in mistake, and ends in ignominy."

Johnson was acutely sensitive to the power which people's lives, both fictional and historical, have on the reader. In *The Rambler* 60, he stresses the fundamental "uniformity in the state of man," insisting that "there is scarce any possibility of good or ill, but is common to human kind. . . . We are all prompted by the same motives, all deceived by the same fallacies, all animated by hope, obstructed by danger, entangled by desire, and seduced by pleasure."

An examination of Johnson's fiction reveals that these beliefs about character and the moral function of fiction appear again and again. Many of *The Rambler, The Adventurer,* and *The Idler* essays take the form of short fictional letters, didactic and moral in their intent, which recount more or less artificial tales of hope and misfortune. They are not really what are considered fiction today: plot is stylized, truncated, and undramatic; characterization is minimal; and both are subordinated to the moral lesson. Johnson does not create individual personalities but displays states of minds, generalized experiences, and moral decisions common to all. Carey McIntosh has pointed out that Johnson's fiction characteristically contradicts the pattern of conventional novels: his characters begin in prosperity and success and end as sadder but wiser victims of their own folly or the world's cruelty. These letters commonly take the form of confessions (in which the narrator admits to a fault or mistake), complaints (tales of misfortune told by a victim), or quests (in which the hero goes through a number of opportunities, all of which prove specious). In all three types, the reader is led to a sense of Johnson's usual theme—the vanity of human wishes.

Johnson creates not individuals, but character types, and the character's name, expressed in Latin or English, is frequently the key: Verecundulus (bashful), Hyperdulus (super slave), Misella (miserable), Squire Bluster, Prospero, Suspirius the screech owl. Some papers are sketches of characters in the Theophrastan sense, such as Prospero, the *nouveau riche* (*The Rambler* 200) and Dick Minim, the critic (*The Idler* 60 and 61), typifying a quality, vice, or virtue. Others are moral fables, such as the story of Seged's futile attempt to make one week happy (*The Rambler* 204 and 205). Through each character the reader sees reality generalized and abstracted; he is not expected to believe the reality of the character or the fiction, but rather to recognize, in the formalized patterns and choices depicted, similar patterns and choices of his own life.

Although some of the periodical essay-fictions are obvious, clumsy personifications of moral ideas, *Rasselas* is a powerfully realized book-length fiction, and, while *Rasselas* shares many characteristics with the essay-fiction, these characteristics work together to make it a model of its kind. Johnson wrote this "Eastern tale," as he called it, capitalizing on the popularity of those he had written in *The Rambler* (such as the fable of Seged), to make money to cover the expenses of his eighty-nine-year-old mother, who was dying. He told Sir Joshua Reynolds that he "composed it in the evenings of one week, sent it to the press in portions as it was written, and had never since read it over." His mother died the week of its composition, and the 125 pounds he was paid for the work were used, Boswell was told, to "defray the expense of his mother's funeral, and to pay some little debts she had left."

The sober tale is certainly suited to the occasion. It tells of the inexorable disillusioning of a prince and princess who, unhappy despite their riches and security, search the world to discover what "choice of life" makes people happy. Prince Rasselas of Abyssinia lives in the Happy Valley, a secret earthly paradise walled off from the outside world by mountains and reserved for the successors to the throne and those teachers, artists, and servants whose duties are to make the confinement delightful. The first fourteen chapters are set in this paradise. At the age of twenty-six, growing increasingly dissatisfied, Rasselas contrasts himself to the animals and wonders what is wrong with him. They are content when their physical needs are satisfied; he is not. "Man has surely some latent sense for which this place affords no gratification, or he has some desires distinct from sense which must be satisfied before he can be happy." When an old sage remarks, "if you had seen the miseries of the world, you would know how to value your present state," Rasselas sets his mind on escaping to see for himself. He spends many months dreaming and planning, and although he is unsuccessful, he nevertheless discovers some satisfaction in striving for a goal: one is happier knowing what one wants.

The prince meets Imlac, a poet and man of learning, who tells of his own quest for happiness in the world and eventual retreat to the valley; Imlac, however, is also eager to leave now, and agrees to help Rasselas find a means of escape. They are joined by Rasselas' sister, Nekayah, and with Imlac as their guide through the world, the brother and sister and her maid leave the valley. The next thirty-five chapters recount their futile search for earthly happiness. Indulgence of the senses proves unsatisfactory, but so does stoic control of the passions. The group leaves the city to examine country life: the romance of the pastoral world is quickly dispelled when they discover that shepherds are rude, ignorant, and envious savages; the prosperous country gentleman, although more cultured, lives in constant fear of his life and his possessions; and the wise hermit, about to abandon his own solitude, returns with them to Cairo.

The prince and princess then divide their search; he examines the courts and palaces while she peruses the middle stations of life. They both discover that no station or state of life, not even virtuousness, makes people particularly happy. On a visit to the pyramids, Nekayah's maid, Pekuah, is abducted, and the progress of grief is described. When Pekuah returns at last, she recounts not a romantic Eastern adventure (such as *The Arabian Nights' Entertainments* might depict) but a constant battle with ennui.

When Rasselas then turns to academic studies, Imlac warns him about the dangers of intellectual life by telling the story of an astronomer whose solitary studies led to madness. From this point, however, the book becomes more hopeful since Pekuah's and Nekayah's visits to the astronomer gradually free him from his delusions. Then, when Imlac takes them all to the catacombs, he convinces them of the immortality of the soul: "To me, said the princess, the choice of life [has] become less important; I hope hereafter to think only on the choice of eternity." This clearly is the moral lesson of the book, and in the final chapter, "The Conclusion, in Which Nothing Is Concluded," they decide to return to Abyssinia.

Rasselas possesses some of the qualities of the Oriental tale, a form very popular in the eighteenth century. Most such tales were not Oriental at all, of course, and although Johnson had translated Father Lobo's *A Voyage to Abyssinia* in 1735, he is not attempting to depict a real Eastern society in *Rasselas*. Johnson uses Orientalism, in McIntosh's words, "to simplify and exaggerate experience and thereby clarify its meaning," to create an environment "almost hypothetically pure," and "to raise and ennoble his argument." The language is thus elevated to a level of dignity and generality without any incongruity, and the imaginary setting equally corresponds. At the same time, one has the impression of exploring every mode of existence—high, low, urban, rural, married, single, young, old, social, solitary, ancient, modern—in a formal, ordered, almost scientific way.

Because *Rasselas* is a novel-length piece of fiction, some readers make the mistake of judging it as a novel. It is not, and the reader who expects realistic characterization, vivid settings, suspense, or plot probability will be disappointed. Johnson intended none of these things. *Rasselas* is an apologue, a fictional representation of a moral statement. According to Sheldon Sacks, the statement *Rasselas* dramatizes is that "earthly happiness does not exist, but its absence does not result in unbearable misery in this world for the reasonably virtuous who . . . may turn their eyes with hope toward heaven." As an apologue it is made up of formal, fablelike episodes, which are organized for rhetorical effect rather than for fictional probability; all characters, events, and relationships are subordinated to the theme they exemplify. Consequently, there is almost no characterization. Rasselas, like the remaining characters, has only enough plausibility and individuality to make the episodes convincing fictional examples of the apologue's premise, but no more. Interest in the characterization of Rasselas himself would divert attention from the central idea which must always dominate and shape the fiction. Thus, the reader never knows the color of his hair, his height, or the tone of his voice. He represents a kind of eighteenth century Everyman in whom, despite the elevation of his language and the artificiality of his circumstances, every reader recognizes himself.

In a famous passage, Imlac explains to Rasselas the business of a poet, and in so doing, also explains the purpose of such generality in Johnson's fiction:

> The business of a poet . . . is to examine, not the individual, but the species; to remark general properties and large appearances: he does not number the streaks of the tulip, or describe the

different shades in the verdure of the forest. He is to exhibit . . . such permanent and striking features, as recall the original to every mind. . . .

He must also "consider right and wrong in their abstracted and invariable state; he must disregard present laws and opinions, and rise to general and transcendental truths, which will always be the same. . . . " Johnson believed that such truths shaped existence, and therefore he made them the center of all his fiction. In *Rasselas*, they are given a form which convinces and moves the reader long after such beliefs have gone out of vogue. The central character, then, is not Rasselas or Imlac, but rather the reader himself, who recognizes his own particular experience in the generalized situations of the book and perceives his own life take shape around the truths he finds therein.

Other major works

PLAY: *Irene: A Tragedy*, 1749.

POETRY: *London: A Poem in Imitation of the Third Satire of Juvenal*, 1738; *The Vanity of Human Wishes: The Tenth Satire of Juvenal Imitated*, 1749; *Poems: The Yale Edition of the Works of Samuel Johnson*, 1965 (E. L. McAdam, Jr., and George Milne, editors, volume 6).

NONFICTION: *Marmer Norfolciense*, 1739; *A Compleat Vindication of the Licensers of the Stage*, 1739; *The Life of Admiral Blake*, 1740; *An Account of the Life of Mr. Richard Savage*, 1744; *An Account of the Life of John Philip Barretier*, 1744; *Miscellaneous Observations on the Tragedy of Macbeth*, 1745; *The Plan of a Dictionary of the English Language*, 1747; *A Dictionary of the English Language*, 1755; preface and notes to *The Plays of William Shakespeare*, 1765 (8 volumes); *The False Alarm*, 1770; *Thoughts on the Late Transactions Respecting Falkland's Islands*, 1771; *The Patriot: Addressed to the Electors of Great Britain*, 1774; *Taxation No Tyranny: An Answer to the Resolutions and Address of the American Congress*, 1775; *A Journey to the Western Islands of Scotland*, 1775; *Prefaces, Biographical and Critical, to the Works of the English Poets*, 1779-1781 (10 volumes; also known as *The Lives of the Poets*); *The Critical Opinions of Samuel Johnson*, 1923, 1961 (Joseph Epes Brown, editor).

TRANSLATIONS: *A Voyage to Abyssinia*, 1735; *Commentary on Pope's Principles of Morality*, 1739.

Bibliography

Bate, Walter Jackson. *The Achievement of Samuel Johnson*. New York: Oxford University Press, 1955. An essential place to begin a general study of the accomplishments, the personal life, and the influence of Johnson. Johnson's achievements in both the literary world and the social world are set in their eighteenth century context. Bate provides enough detail to offer a well-rounded picture of a great scholar who was able to speak convincingly of the human world of pain and weakness as well as to write knowingly of poets and poetic achievement in his era.

Bullough, Geoffrey. "Johnson the Essayist." *New Rambler* 5 (June, 1968): 16-33.

This general survey of Johnson's work in periodicals introduces the reader to eighteenth century essay-writing as well as to Johnson's ideas. The article reveals the variety of topics covered in *The Rambler, The Adventurer,* and *The Idler,* and Johnson's emphasis on ideals and standards in matters of religion and morals.

Greene, Donald J. *Samuel Johnson.* New York: Twayne, 1970. An appreciation of Johnson's literary achievement emphasizing its variety and depth and including commentary on the scholar's contributions to the development of modern journalism. The concept of Johnson as a man of letters, with an emphasis on critical theory and practical criticism is addressed. Individual works by Johnson are also treated and bibliographies are included.

Wahba, Magdi, ed. *Bicentenary Essays on Rasselas.* Cairo: Société Orientale de Publicité, 1959. This collection of essays on the short novel includes a number of serious essays by well-known Johnsonian scholars, along with some intriguing and some frivolous commentaries. The book brings together a variety of reactions to what has been called the first philosophical novel.

Wimsatt, William K. *The Prose Style of Samuel Johnson.* New Haven, Conn.: Yale University Press, 1941. This standard work continues to shed light on the sentence structure, the Latinate diction, the rhetorical devices, and other elements that identify Johnson's prose style. The study of rhetoric in the eighteenth century provides the background for this careful analysis, but the treatment is quite contemporary in approach. This volume is essential for a newcomer in understanding how Johnson composed—often in his head—his often lengthy and complex sentences in order to achieve a clarity of meaning.

James W. Garvey
(Revised by *Emma Coburn Norris*)

JAMES JOYCE

Born: Dublin, Ireland; February 2, 1882
Died: Zurich, Switzerland; January 13, 1941

Principal short fiction
Dubliners, 1914.

Other literary forms

James Joyce's name is synonymous with twentieth century fiction, to a revolution in which he devoted himself with remarkable single-mindedness. The results are to be found in three extremely influential works of fiction—*A Portrait of the Artist as a Young Man* (1916), *Ulysses* (1922), and *Finnegans Wake* (1939). Though his work in other genres is of much less significance, Joyce also wrote two books of poetry, *Chamber Music* (1907) and *Pomes Penyeach* (1927), as well as one play, *Exiles* (1918). His youthful critical essays, crucial to an understanding of his artistic origins, were collected posthumously and edited by Richard Ellmann and Ellsworth Mason as *The Critical Writings of James Joyce* (1959). The raw material for *A Portrait of the Artist as a Young Man*, edited by Theodore Spencer, was also published posthumously as *Stephen Hero* (1944).

Achievements

Joyce is acknowledged by many as the twentieth century's greatest prose artist and is also, arguably, that century's most famous author. Despite his small output and the increasing difficulty of his works, Joyce's name stands as a monument to commitment and artistic integrity. Since the end of World War II, there has hardly been a novelist in the West who has not felt Joyce's influence. Continuing interest in his complex mind and work is sustained by a vast array of academic commentators.

The reasons for Joyce's eminence are not hard to find. Each of his works, beginning with the short stories of *Dubliners*, is notable for its startling originality of language and conception. His fiction, moreover, placed his native city, Dublin, indelibly on the map of the world's culture. His life, a continual struggle against ill health, exile, and the almost total neglect of publishers, has come to be perceived as an eloquent expression of self-determination in an age of totalitarian conformity.

Biography

James Augustine Joyce was born on February 2, 1882, the eldest child of John Stanislaus and Mary Jane (May) Murray Joyce. The family was typical of the growing ranks of the Irish Catholic middle class of the day, socially confident, politically optimistic, though less than well established economically. During Joyce's early years, however, the family remained in comfortable circumstances, and at the age of six, Joyce was enrolled in Clongowes Wood College, an elite Jesuit boarding school outside Dublin. After two years at Clongowes, Joyce's education was interrupted because of a decline in family fortunes, the result in large part of John Joyce's improvidence. In 1893, Joyce began to attend Belvedere College, another Jesuit school, in Dublin, where, in addition to undergoing a thorough exposure to the narrow Catholicism of the day, he won a number of academic prizes. In 1898, Joyce entered University College, Dublin, from which he was graduated in 1902.

Throughout the 1890's, the Joyce family continued to experience hard times. Their setbacks had a parallel in the reversal of Ireland's political fortunes during the same period. In 1891, Charles Stewart Parnell, the disgraced leader of the Irish cause, died. This event was the occasion of Joyce's first-known literary work, an accusatory poem directed against the foremost of Parnell's lieutenants, who had turned against him, entitled "Et tu, Healy." The 1890's also saw the rise of a literary and intellectual movement in Ireland. By the time Joyce had begun his undergraduate career, this movement was sufficiently evolved to be criticized, a task that Joyce took upon himself, most notably in a pamphlet entitled "The Day of the Rabblement." While at college, Joyce also distinguished himself by other literary essays, most notably with an article on Henrik Ibsen—an important early influence—which appeared in the prestigious *Fortnightly Review*.

In 1902, Joyce left Ireland for Paris, intending to study medicine in order to secure an income to support his writing. This unsuccessful trip was abruptly curtailed by news of his mother's terminal illness. After her death in 1903, Joyce spent an unproductive year in Dublin, relieved only by writing poems and the initial versions of some of the *Dubliners* stories and by meeting Nora Barnacle, his wife-to-be. With her, he left Ireland in 1904, remaining abroad, with a few brief exceptions, for the rest of his life.

Joyce and his wife began life in Pula, then a backwater in the Austro-Hungarian Empire, later known as the town of Pulj in Yugoslavia. Most of their lives before World War I, however, were spent in Trieste. There, their two children were born, Giorgio in 1905 and Lucia two years later. Joyce earned an uncertain and reluctant living teaching English as a foreign language and worked on the stories of *Dubliners* and *A Portrait of the Artist as a Young Man*. A number of prospective publishers deemed the stories to be too scandalous to issue, and *Dubliners* languished in a limbo of pusillanimity until 1914.

That year was to prove decisive to Joyce's development as a writer. Through the good offices of the Irish poet William Butler Yeats, the American poet Ezra Pound contacted Joyce and arranged for *A Portrait of the Artist as a Young Man* to be serialized. In that year, also, Joyce started his most celebrated work, *Ulysses*, and moved with his family to Zurich, where they lived for the duration of the war. Briefly returning to Trieste in 1919, the family moved to Paris, where *Ulysses* was published in 1922. Beset by ill health and by the mental illness of his daughter, though immune from financial difficulties through the generosity of a patron, Harriet Shaw Weaver, Joyce remained in Paris working on his opaque masterpiece, *Finnegans Wake*, until World War II obliged him to resettle in Zurich. There, Joyce died of complications arising from perforated ulcers on January 13, 1941.

Analysis

In August, 1904, James Joyce wrote to his friend C. P. Curran: "I am writing a series of epicleti. . . . I call the series *Dubliners* to betray the soul of that hemeplegia or paralysis which many consider a city." This note announces, in effect, a transformation of the short story as a form. The note's pretentious jargon reveals the attitude of the young Joyce's artistic demeanor. In addition, it calls attention to some of the main technical and thematic characteristics of a volume that had to wait a further ten years for a publisher to consider it acceptable.

There is still some scholarly debate over the term "epicleti," whose etymology remains obscure. It is clear, however, that Joyce's use of the term shows him to be in pursuit of an aesthetic method. This self-conscious search for a method reveals Joyce as a preeminently twentieth century modernist author. As with his eminent contemporaries and advocates T. S. Eliot and Pound, to write was to articulate a theory of writing. Moreover, the search was successfully concluded, as the closing chapter of *A Portrait of the Artist as a Young Man* records. It culminated in the discovery of the "epiphany," which means "showing forth" and which describes not only Joyce's method but also his objectives in using one.

Joyce used the term "epiphany" to describe some of his own early artistic efforts in prose. These sketches sometimes resemble prose poems, calibrating moments of intense perception and emotional heightening. At other times, they take the form of life studies of banal moments in everyday life. The overall intention is one of unmasking hidden states, whether of the exalted or humdrum variety. In both instances, the pieces are marked by a fastidious language, which clearly anticipates the "style of scrupulous meanness" in which Joyce said *Dubliners* is written.

Artistic theory is not the only novelty of *Dubliners*. Joyce's note to Curran also draws attention to his subject matter. From a strictly historical point of view, Joyce's characterization of his birthplace is to some extent misleading. The stories of *Dubliners* tend to overlook those factors that distinguished the city in Joyce's time. The impact and significance of the establishment in Dublin of Ireland's national theater, the Abbey, for example, which opened in 1904, may be lost on non-Irish readers of Joyce's stories. In general, Joyce is at pains to belittle the various attempts at cultural self-renewal, which were a marked feature of Dublin life in the early years of the twentieth century, as the satire of the story "A Mother" shows—although in "The Dead" this satirical attitude is significantly modified. Joyce also fails to provide a cross section of the city's social composition, there being no stories featuring the upper echelon. The city was not quite the paraplegic of Joyce's diagnostic imagination.

The stories' emphasis is on what Joyce asserts to be typical of his city. This democratic vision of his brings to the reader's notice a range of marginalized citizens. These include children, the alienated, the helpless and hopeless, and particularly women—*Dubliners* has a feminist undercurrent, all the more noteworthy because of its time. These citizens, often known merely by a single name, represent the social, cultural, and moral cost of living in a city that was less a capital than one of the British Empire's provincial administrative centers. The fact that their humdrum and unpromising lives should be subjected to the artistic and intellectual powers that Joyce possessed is significant on a number of counts. From the standpoint of literary history, *Dubliners* combines the two prevailing literary modes of Joyce's day. In a refinement of an approach pioneered by the great French novelist Gustave Flaubert, Joyce subjects material that had hitherto been the artistic property of the naturalists to the aesthetic commitments of the Symbolists. One way of describing the function of the epiphany is to note its author's organization of commonplaces in such a manner that they ultimately yield possibilities of meaning greater than their culturally preconditioned, or factual, appearances admit.

From the point of view of Irish literary history, the stories of *Dubliners* eloquently, though untypically, participate in the overall effort of the Irish Literary Revival to address national realities. The careful delineation of lost lives, which comprises most of *Dubliners*, is a unique contribution to the spirit of the critique, which informs much of the stories' Irish cultural context. It is not surprising to learn that they were considered too controversial to publish with impunity, or that, by virtue of being so, they confirmed their author's belief that they constituted "a chapter in the moral history of my country."

A further notable feature of the book is that, unlike many collections of short stories, particularly those of that period, *Dubliners* is a collection of stories that, however limited in range, is disparate while at the same time functioning as a coherent whole. Its coherence is not merely a matter of Joycean cunning, whereby the collection's opening story is entitled "The Sisters" and centers on a death, while the final story is called "The Dead" and takes place at a party hosted by sisters. The history of the book's composition, to which must be added a recognition of the complications brought about by publishers' lack of commitment, precludes any such facile observation, since "The Dead" was conceived and written after Joyce's initial version of *Dubliners* had been completed and submitted for publication. Two other stories were added to the original dozen, "Two Gallants" and "A Little Cloud." Rather more subtly, the collection achieves coherence by numerous overlapping means. These include the integrity of its style, its thematic consistency, the largely uniform character of its *dramatis personae*, and its use of a major device in the overall scheme of Joyce's aesthetic, repetition and variation.

In addition, Joyce himself had an integrated vision of the work's coherence, one whereby the whole would be seen to be greater than the sum of the parts. This view holds good particularly when applied to the twelve stories of the initial *Dubliners*, where it describes a mode of symmetrical organization as well as a principle of thematic development, so that a case can readily be made for the work as a whole comprising a "moral history." According to Joyce, *Dubliners* may be divided into four consecutive sections. The first of these consists of the three opening stories, "The Sisters," "An Encounter," and "Araby." These are followed by a sequence of stories dealing with adolescence, "The Boarding House," "After the Race," and "Eveline." Three stories of mature life come next, "Clay," "Counterparts," and "A

Painful Case." Finally the volume closes with a trio of stories devoted to public life, "Ivy Day in the Committee Room," "A Mother," and "Grace."

While the symmetry of this quartet of trios is disrupted by the introduction of further stories, two of the new additions, both written in 1906, enlarge rather than negate their respective categories. The range of the stories of adolescence is considerably broadened by the addition of "Two Gallants." Similarly, the motifs of entrapment and disillusion, typical of the stories of mature life, are further adumbrated in the history of Chandler, the protagonist of "A Little Cloud." In "The Dead," written in 1907, Joyce's artistry as a writer of short fiction is seen to best advantage. In addition, this story crystallizes and elevates to a higher plane of intellection and feeling many of the themes of *Dubliners*, the result being what is generally acknowledged to be one of the finest short stories in the English language.

The titles of the stories of *Dubliners* offer a clue to the nature of their contents. Such titles as "An Encounter," "A Painful Case," "Counterparts," "A Mother," and "The Dead"—to take some of the most obvious cases in point—seem deliberately to offer little or nothing to the reader, neither a sense of expectation nor a sense of anything particularly distinctive within the material, for all that Joyce insisted to his publishers that presenting his fellow citizens to the world at large had undoubted novelty value. Yet the very anonymity of many of the titles points with precision to both their character and their method. The stories' protagonists are for the most part colorless, unpromising, defeated, and lacking in interiority. For the most part, they are unaware of these facts about their personalities and conditions, and the stories evolve somewhat remorselessly to a point where these hapless characters are on the threshold of recognizing, or deliberately overlooking, their morally abject lives. The fact, therefore, that the stories' titles frequently evoke generic types or states is a pointer to one of their prominent attributes. The stories that do not conform to this general rule have titles that are extremely localized and opaque in a different sense. Few readers will know automatically that the ivy day referred to in "Ivy Day in the Committee Room" refers to the custom of commemorating the Irish political leader Charles Stewart Parnell, or that "Araby," in addition to its generic connotations, refers to an actual bazaar that was held in Dublin in mid-May, 1894. This obscure fact makes the story's protagonist the same age as Joyce was when the bazaar was held.

The sense of comparative anonymity and insignificance suggested by the titles is replicated in the case of the protagonists, a large number of whom are either anonymous or known by a single name, as though they had not yet succeeded in attaining the measure of identity required to merit being fully named. The very title *Dubliners* is clearly generic, and Joyce, approaching his material from such a standpoint, reveals his interest in the typical, the representative, and the norm. In this sense, Joyce shows his deep sense of the short-story form, with its traditional emphasis on the delineation of representative characters in representative contexts. Such an interest is amplified with great deftness and versatility in the language of the stories, which frequently draws on official, generic codes of utterance. Gabriel's speech on hospitality in "The Dead" is an important example of one such code, particularly when contrasted with the highly wrought meditation that closes the story. The sermon that concludes "Grace" is another, despite being rendered in the narrative mode known as free indirect style for satirical purposes. A third example is the mimicry of the newspaper report of police evidence in "A Painful Case" The collection as a whole is saturated by formal and informal exploitation of the characters' various modes of utterance from which a sense of their cultural orientation and impoverishment may be extrapolated.

As with all Joyce's works, the latently satirical manipulation of cliché is a crucial feature of *Dubliners*. In addition, by virtue of the author's uncanny ear not merely for the demotic but for the quality of consciousness that such utterances reveal, the stories possess a convincing patina of objectivity, as though it is the restless but unobtrusive activity of their language that produces their effects, rather than anything as unrefined as the author's direction and intentions. Thus, the doctrine of the artist's impersonality, which has numerous important implications for modernist aesthetics and which Joyce, possibly following the example of Gustave Flaubert, invokes in *A Portrait of the Artist as a Young Man*, is utilized in *Dubliners* to telling effect.

It is in the matter of the stories' presumed objectivity that *Dubliners* fell foul of the publishing industry of the day. Joyce freely availed himself of the civic furniture of his native city, including by name actual business premises—pubs and hotels, notably—as well as churches and other well-known amenities and distinctive features of the social life of his birthplace. By so doing, he not only went further in his pursuit of documentary verisimilitude than the vast majority of even naturalistic writers of Joyce's generation. He also revealed a conception of language—or of what happens to language once it is written—which, in its mature development in *Ulysses* and *Finnegans Wake*, provided a complex, integrated code of cultural semiotics. Joyce's use of place-names, the names of businesses, and most notoriously the names of English royalty, shows his understanding that a name is a word, not a supposedly photographic facsimile of the entity it denotes. *Dubliners* is replete with names chosen with a sensitivity to their artistic and cultural resonance as well as to their geographical precision. For example, the North Wall, Eveline's terminus in the story that bears her name, is both correct in a documentary sense and thematically appropriate. A subtler instance is Mr. Duffy's residence at Chapelizod, a short distance outside Dublin. Not only does the choice of residence underline Duffy's standoffish nature, but also the name of where he lives is a corruption of Chapel Iseult. This name invokes the legend of the lovers Tristan and Iseult, of whose tragic love Duffy's affair is a banal but nevertheless heartfelt shadow. Use of the legend is an anticipation of the method in *Ulysses*, where the heroic stuff of epic forms an ironic but by no means belittling counterpoint to the trial of twentieth century human beings.

Neither of Joyce's English and Irish publishers was very interested in the long-term consequences or subtle immediacies of Joyce's art. Both feared that his use of actual names would lead them into serious legal difficulties, which would be compounded by what was considered a use of blasphemous language and an impersonation of the thoughts of Edward, Prince of Wales, in "Ivy Day in the Committee Room," Joyce's favorite story in the collection. Joyce, against his better judgment, toned down the impersonation and made a number of other minor adjustments, while basically upholding his right of documentary representation in the service of artistic integrity and objectivity.

The most conclusive evidence for the stories' objectivity, however, is provided by their use of the epiphany. Much critical ink has been consumed in attempting to explicate this device. Undoubtedly it is a key concept not only in the appreciation of the art of Joyce's short stories but also in the comprehension of the form's development under the influence of *Dubliners*. At the same time, the reader who does not possess a firm grasp of the concept may still read *Dubliners* with satisfaction, insight, and sympathy. The epiphany makes its presence felt, typically, at the conclusion of a *Dubliners* story. It is here that the reader is likely to experience a certain amount of distancing from the action, which cannot be accounted for merely by the foreignness of the characters and their locale. These, in themselves, do not inhibit either the forward movement of the narrative or that movement's potential for significance. At the point when that potential might well be expected to be realized, however, it may strike the reader as being deferred or repressed.

This discovery is intended to alert the reader that the narrative technique of a *Dubliners* story only superficially conforms to the introduction-development-denouement model of story organization. Early critics of the work, indeed, complained that for the most part, through their lack of dramatic issue or intriguing theme, the stories were no more than sketches, not seeing that what Joyce was interested in was as much manner as matter, and that only a minimalist approach of the kind he used would grace with art the marginal conditions of his characters and articulate, in a mode that did not violate the impoverished spirit of his paralyzed raw material, its worthiness and the value of bringing it to the reader's attention. Concern for the reader's attention is therefore critical, since so much of what Joyce was writing about had already been effectively written off socially, culturally, politically, and spiritually. The comprehensive nature of this silencing is spelled out in the collection's opening story, "The Sisters."

The strain placed on the reader's attention by the typical conclusion of the stories is Joyce's method of expressing his concern that the material's impact not be diminished by meeting the preconditioned expectations of how its conflicts might be resolved. Rather than have the story reach a conclusion, with its connotations of finality and mastery, Joyce ends the story, breaks off the action before all its implications and ramifications have been extrapolated. He thereby extends to the reader an invitation, which may also be a duty, to draw out the inferences of this act of narrative termination. The development of inferences is the means whereby the story achieves the statement of itself, an achievement that describes the epiphany in action.

In order to participate in the activity of revelation that the term "epiphany" connotes, the reader will note that not only does a *Dubliners* story conventionally, if loosely, observe the Aristotelian unities of time, place, and action. In addition, that unity is achieved by the tissue of correspondences, insinuations, nuances, echoes, and general interplay that exists among the various phases of a given story's action and the language. The introduction of the train at the end of "A Painful Case" is an obvious example of Joyce's cunning and tacit strategies. One of the outcomes of these effects is to offset any purely deterministic sense of plot. The compulsiveness and irreversibility of action, on a sense of which plot tends to be based, is offset, modified, or at the very least has its crudely dramatic character diminished by Joyce's effects. As a result, the reader is placed in a position of assembling what the story's fabric of data signifies. It is the reader, typically, rather than the protagonist, who recognizes the epiphanic moment, the moment at which the tendencies of the action become undeniably clear. At this moment, the reader attains the point of maximum perspective. It is a moment of closure but of reinvestment, of withdrawal and of sympathy, of estrangement and acceptance. Its result is to make the reader morally complicit with the material, since were it not for the epiphany's appeal to the reader the material's significance, or rather its ability to signify, would be moot. The empowered reader becomes the type of citizen whom the representative protagonist of a *Dubliners* story cannot be. The stories represent a mastery over material and circumstances with which the reader is called upon to identify, but which the characters cannot embody.

While it is possible to consider the stories of *Dubliners* from many different artistic, cultural, and moral perspectives, the theme of independence or the lack of it is the one that seems most central to Joyce's concerns. His preoccupation with the paralyzed condition of his native city may be described as an awareness of how little the spirit of independence moved there. The numerous implications of this lack are addressed in story after story. The typical trajectory of the story is the optimistic going out, the counterpart of which is the disillusioned return. In even such a simple story as "An Encounter," the youngster's naïve dream of adventure and access to the adult world is both realized and made unrecognizable and unacceptable by the form it takes. Encounters with worldly others, such as the flirtatious couples at the bazaar at the end of "Araby," or Frank in "Eveline," the sophisticated foreigners in "After the Race," or Ignatius Gallaher in "A Little Cloud," all leave the protagonists reduced and defeated. The world is a more complex and demanding environment than their dreams of fulfillment might have led them to believe. The self withdraws, pained that the world is not a reflection of its needs. As in "Two Gallants," when the world can be manipulated to serve the ego, the process is crude, exploitative, and morally despicable.

Some of the most far-reaching implications of the independence theme may be seen in "Ivy Day in the Committee Room." There, the heirs of a dramatically successful political movement for a constitutional form of Irish independence are depicted as bemused, opportunistic, devoted to rhetoric rather than action, stagnant in thought and deed. Their conspicuous lack of will is matched by their inconsistency of thought. Yet, while satire is a pronounced feature of the story, Joyce also makes clear that the characters cannot be merely scorned. The poem that affects them is certainly not a fine piece of writing, as the story's closing comment would have readers believe. On the contrary, it is a heartfelt performance, genuine in its feeling and authentic in its response. The negative elements of these characters' lives and the bleak outlook for the productive commissioning of their human potential become, in Joyce's view, as compelling a set of realities as the triumph of the will or worldly fulfillment.

This view receives its most comprehensive expression in "The Dead," making the story, for that reason alone, the crowning achievement of *Dubliners*. From the playful malapropism of its opening sentence to its resonant closing periods, this story provides, in scale, thematic variety, psychological interest, and narrative tempo, a complete and enriched survey of Joyce's artistic and moral commitments at the close of the first phase of his writing career. Whereas previously, the collection's stories were representations of a quality, or poverty, of consciousness to which the characters were unable to relate, in "The Dead" Gabriel achieves an awareness of his particular consciousness. The moment of recognition, the epiphany, in which Gabriel realizes what his wife's story of lost love says about his own emotional adequacy, is not an experience whose meaning the reader infers. It is a meaning whose articulation by Gabriel the reader overhears. Unlike many of the other stories, however, "The Dead" does not end on this note of recognition. Gabriel, for all that "The Dead" has shown him having difficulty in being self-possessed and autonomous, acknowledges the force and significance of Gretta's revelation. He relates to those limitations in himself, which the story of Michael Furey underlines. In doing so, he attains a degree of sympathy, honesty, and freely chosen solidarity with the finite, mortal nature of human reality, his mind enlarging as its sense of defeat becomes a central and constraining fact of life. The balance achieved in "The Dead" between subjective need and objective fact, between romance and reality, between self-deception and self-awareness gives the story its poise and potency and makes it a persuasive recapitulation of the other *Dubliners* stories' concerns.

It is by the conclusive means of "The Dead" that Joyce's *Dubliners* identifies itself with the critique of humanism, which was a fundamental component of the revolution in the arts at the beginning of the twentieth century. The invisibility of the author's personality, the tonal and stylistic restraint with which the stories are told, and the aesthetic subtlety of the epiphany add up to rather more than simply a revolution in short fiction. They also, by their nature, draw attention to the force of the negative as a reality in the lives of the characters, a reality that Joyce, by refusing to overlook it, contributed significantly to placing on the agenda of twentieth century consciousness.

Other major works

NOVELS: *A Portrait of the Artist as a Young Man*, 1916; *Ulysses*, 1922; *Finnegans Wake*, 1939; *Stephen Hero*, 1944 (edited by Theodore Spencer).
PLAY: *Exiles*, 1918.

POETRY: *Chamber Music*, 1907; *Pomes Penyeach*, 1927.
NONFICTION: *The Critical Writings of James Joyce*, 1959.

Bibliography

Baker, James R., and Thomas Staley, eds. *James Joyce's "Dubliners": A Critical Handbook*. Belmont, Calif.: Wadsworth, 1969. To some extent supplanted by later critical compilations, this volume is divided in three parts: part 1 is a selection of relevant material from Joyce's letters and essays; part 2 consists of critical overviews; part 3 is a collection of essays on individual *Dubliners* stories, some of them by eminent critics such as Lionel Trilling. Contains an extensive bibliography concentrating on early postwar approaches to Joyce's stories.

Beck, Warren. *Joyce's "Dubliners": Substance, Vision, Art*. Durham, N.C.: Duke University Press, 1969. An extremely comprehensive study of *Dubliners*. After a lengthy introduction, each of Joyce's stories is examined in turn. The author's approach is essentially that of the New Critics. The texts are combed thoroughly for their verbal possibilities, resulting in both exhaustive and dutiful readings.

Beja, Morris, ed. *"Dubliners" and "A Portrait of the Artist as a Young Man": A Casebook*. London: Macmillan, 1973. The student will benefit from encountering commentary on Joyce's first two major works. This volume includes extracts from Joyce's journals and letters and from early criticism. Also includes a section of substantial modern criticism. Contains a bibliography.

Ellmann, Richard. *James Joyce*. 1959. 2d ed. New York: Oxford University Press, 1984. The definitive biography, generally regarded as the last word on its subject's life and widely considered as the greatest literary biography of the twentieth century. Copiously annotated and well illustrated, particularly in the 1984 edition. Contains a considerable amount of informative background on the characters of *Dubliners* and their contexts. Of particular interest is the chapter entitled "The Backgrounds of 'The Dead.'"

Hart, Clive, ed. *James Joyce's "Dubliners": Critical Essays*. New York: Viking, 1969. Arguably, the single most helpful full-length work on *Dubliners*. It consists of essays on each of the stories, each by a different author. The authors are frequently well-known Joyce scholars, such as A. Walton Litz and the editor. Inevitably, the manner of critical approach in the case of a number of the essays is somewhat outdated.

Scholes, Robert, and Richard M. Kain, eds. *The Workshop of Dedalus*. Evanston, Ill.: Northwestern University Press, 1965. Substantially devoted to the artistic genesis of *A Portrait of the Artist as a Young Man*. The presentation of the background for Joyce's aesthetic innovations is extremely helpful to an informed reading of *Dubliners*. Contains an elaborate chronology of Joyce's youth and other background materials. The text of Joyce's epiphanies is most conveniently available in this volume.

George O'Brien

FRANZ KAFKA

Born: Prague, Czechoslovakia; July 3, 1883
Died: Kierling, Klosterneuburg, near Vienna, Austria; June 3, 1924

Principal short fiction

Betrachtung, 1913 (*Meditation*, 1948); *Die Verwandlung*, 1915 (novella; *The Metamorphosis*, 1936); *Ein Landarzt: Kleine Erzählungen*, 1919 (*The Country Doctor: A Collection of Fourteen Short Stories*, 1945); *Ein Hungerkünstler: Vier Geschichten*, 1924 (*A Hunger Artist*, 1948); *Beim Bau der Chinesischen Mauer: Ungedruckte Erzählungen und Prosa aus dem Nachlass*, 1931 (*The Great Wall of China and Other Pieces*, 1933); *Erzählungen*, 1946 (*The Complete Stories*, 1971); *The Penal Colony: Stories and Short Pieces*, 1948; *Selected Short Stories*, 1952.

Other literary forms

Franz Kafka did not attempt to write drama or poetry. His métier was prose. He was a perfectionist who apparently intended only a portion of what he had written for publication. The three novels and several more volumes of short stories were prepared for publication posthumously by the executor of his literary estate, Max Brod.

Kafka also wrote voluminously in other categories of prose that bear the same distinctive style as his creative work. His diaries and letters contain many comments that aid in the understanding of his stories, and his meticulous legal reports are exemplary professional documents.

Achievements

Every year, more secondary literature is published about Kafka than about any other author except William Shakespeare. This attests to the extraordinary power and alluringly enigmatic content of his works. While his inimitable prose style describes everything as if it were self-evident, he invariably introduces elements of the fantastic and surreal and portrays the demise of his characters as inevitable. His works are imbued with a sense of horror as isolated characters struggle futilely against malign forces that they do not understand.

Kafka unintentionally became the voice of the age. Coming after the philosophers Martin Heidegger and Edmund Husserl, and being contemporary with the founder of psychoanalysis, Sigmund Freud, he captured the existential angst of the generation. As a result of the Industrial Revolution, the father no longer worked from the home but dominated the family from a distance. The figure of authority was a stranger.

Biography

Franz Kafka's literary achievements are all the more remarkable when one considers that he lived to be only forty, was increasingly ill with tuberculosis during the last seven years of his life, and up until two years before his death held a full-time position as a lawyer.

While his life-style was in keeping with that of his mother's bachelor brothers, one of whom was a country doctor, Kafka and his father were very different in personality. The efforts of the robust, self-confident, and sometimes abusive businessman to rear a frail, insecure, and sensitive son led to a constant state of friction between the two. Unlike his younger sisters, who married and established families of their own, Kafka lived mainly with his parents, attempting always to relate to the father who could not understand him.

Kafka's parents had a strong marriage but did not have much time for their children, who were cared for by household help. During the day, the parents worked together in their store. In the evening, the two of them played cards. Kafka did well in school, contrary to his fears, and received a good education, especially in Latin, from dedicated teachers.

In 1901, Kafka entered the German University in Prague and obtained his doctorate in law in 1906. He resigned from his first position, stating as his reason that he was upset by the cursing and swearing, even though it had not been directed at him. Through the intercession of a friend, he then obtained a position with the Workers' Accident Insurance Institute and remained with the firm from 1908 to 1922, when his declining health necessitated an early retirement. His work was appreciated, and he received many benefits from the firm.

Kafka was never without friends, and he had a good sense of humor—something that could be emphasized more in the interpretation of his works. He liked to read his stories aloud and sometimes broke down in uncontrollable laughter over the plots that he had invented. Marriage was something that Kafka both desired and feared. He was engaged twice to Felice Bauer, a woman who lived in another city. He had met her briefly through a friend and soon afterward initiated an epistolary relationship. This became a pattern that he repeated with two other women, always being reluctant to be with them in person. Only in the last year of his life did he overcome his inhibitions enough to live for a few months with a woman half his age, Dora Dymant.

Dymant did not realize the value of Kafka's literary works and at his request burned many manuscripts. Kafka also stipulated in his will that his friend and executor, the author Max Brod, was to burn everything not published during Kafka's lifetime. It was an ambivalent request, because Brod had said he would never do so.

Although Jewish, Kafka was relatively unaffected by anti-Semitism. The gravestone for him and his parents is in the Strasnice Cemetery in Prague. His three sisters were later killed in concentration camps.

Analysis

Franz Kafka's stories are not about love or success. They do not leave the reader feeling comfortable. Writing was, for him, a necessity. On August 6, 1914, Kafka wrote in his diary: "My talent for portraying my dreamlike inner life has thrust all other matters into the background; my life has dwindled dreadfully, nor will it cease to dwindle. Nothing else will ever satisfy me." The meaning of the images from his dreamlike inner life was not always clear to him at the time of writing. Sometimes he realized only several years later what he may have subconsciously meant. Toward the end of his life, he decided that psychoanalysis was a waste of time and abandoned that approach in retrospective reading. Critics may not be of the same opinion.

Kafka wrote "Das Urteil" ("The Judgment") in one sitting through the night of September 22-23, 1912. It was an eminently satisfying experience, the only one of his works that he said came out of him like a birth. When he sat down to write, he had intended to depict a war scene. Then, the story took its own direction, and when he finished, early in the morning, he was not sure what it meant. He knew only that it was good.

In the course of "The Judgment," the main character, Georg Bendemann, experiences a complete reversal in his plans. At the outset, he announces his engagement to Frieda Brandenfeld. At the end, he commits suicide. The transition from good news to bad and the descent from normalcy into apparent madness are subtly accomplished. With hindsight, one can see, of course, that warning signs are held up all the way. Yet none of these signs is in itself shocking enough to alienate the reader. Only their cumulative effect is overwhelming. Kafka's stories wield their powerful influence over the reader's mood by always remaining plausible. While never losing the semblance of logical reportage, Kafka creates scenes of horror, which both spring from and give rise to psychological suffering. Anything resembling such scenes is now called "Kafkaesque."

Kafka writes metaphorically, letting characters, actions, and objects represent emotional and psychological states. Thus, the works are understood best not as narrative advancing a plot but in terms of the protagonist's attempts to transcend absurdity, depersonalization, and alienation. There is a strong autobiographical element in all the stories.

Most critics equate Georg Bendemann with Kafka, and Georg's father with Kafka's father. The issue to be dealt with, then, is why the father would violently oppose the son's engagement to a woman from a well-to-do family. To accept that, one has to subscribe to an inverse standard. Kate Flores interprets this aspect of "The Judgment" in an anthropological way, explaining that for precivilized man it was an act of insubordination to supplant the dominant male. Certainly, "The Judgment" does contain elements of a primal struggle. Also consistent with this reading is the father's tenacious hold on Georg's watch chain, as if to halt the inexorable advance of time and the aging process. There is also the fact that Kafka's father did indeed deride one of his engagements, although at a much later date than when "The Judgment" was written.

Kafka's stories support many interpretations. It is important, when reading "The Judgment," that one not concentrate on the apparent polarity of father and son to the exclusion of the curious figure of the friend in Russia, to whom the first third of the story is devoted. In fact, preposterous though it may seem, the most comprehensive reading results from considering all three male figures—the friend in Russia, Georg Bendemann, and his father—to be different aspects of the same person, namely Kafka. It is significant that only one name is provided.

The friend in Russia immediately becomes associated with writing, because Georg has been writing to him for years. This association is reinforced when the father, surprisingly, also claims to have been writing to the friend. After Georg has brought up the matter of an engagement on three separate occasions, the friend in Russia responds by showing some interest, but as with his emotionless reaction to the death of Georg's mother, the friend's interest in human affairs seems perfunctory. He has few social contacts, has let his business slide, and seems to be in a general state of ill health and decline. His life has dwindled dreadfully. This identifies him with Kafka the writer.

Georg Bendemann's business seems to have been operating in inverse proportions to that of his friend in Russia. It is thriving, and he has recently become engaged. The thriving business and the engagement go hand in hand in "The Judgment." Both are traditionally recognized outward signs of success. Kafka, at the time of writing "The Judgment," was already a successful lawyer, well established in his firm and becoming interested in Felice Bauer, who seems to be represented in the story by her close namesake, Frieda Brandenfeld. Frieda makes a remark to Georg that, on the surface, is very puzzling. She tells him that since he has friends such as the one in Russia, he should never have gotten engaged. This is the warning sign that either Frieda or the friend in Russia will have to go. The application to Kafka's life seems clear: either Felice or the writing will have to go.

The most interesting and complex of the three male figures is, of course, the father. While appearing to oppose Georg, the older man can, in this case, actually be relied on to say what Georg wants to hear. Faced with the irreconcilable conflict between loyalty to his longtime friend in Russia and loyalty to his new fiancée, Georg finds himself inexplicably going to his father's room, where he has not been for some time. The sunlight is blocked by a wall, the father is surrounded by ancient newspapers, and the window is shut. It is a trip into the dark and the past, which is sealed off from the outside world. The father represents the subconscious. He is also the progenitor, and he is still, despite some deceptive signs of senility, the figure of authority.

The father's first remark, which points beyond the frame of the surface story, is his question of whether Georg really has a friend in St. Petersburg. What the father really seems to be asking is whether the friend can continue to be called a friend when he has been so neglected. Georg at this point is still inclined to decide in favor of Frieda and an outwardly successful life, so he endeavors to quell the troubling reference to his friend by carrying his father from the dark out into the light and then covering him up, thereby forcibly suppressing the question of the friend.

Contrary to Georg's intent, this results in the father's exploding into action. In an extraordinarily dramatic scene, he hurls off the blankets, leaps to his feet, and, standing upright on the bed and kicking, denounces Georg's plans for marriage and accuses him of playing the false friend all these years. Georg realizes that he should be on his guard against attack but then forgets again and stands defenseless before his father.

The father's second remark that seems rather incredible in terms of the surface story is that the friend in Russia has not been betrayed after all, because he, the father, has also been writing to him all along and representing him. Suppressed talents are only strengthened in the subconscious. The father now unquestionably has the upper hand and pronounces his judgment over Georg: he was an innocent child, but he has been a devilish human being. Presumably, it was during childhood that Georg cultivated the friend now in Russia. As an adult, getting ever more into business and thoughts of marriage, Georg has been devilish by denying his true self, the writer. The father finishes by sentencing Georg to death by drowning. To drown is to be plunged into the creative element.

Georg confirms the validity of his father's verdict by carrying out the sentence. It is important for the reader to remember that as the father crashes on the bed exhausted, the subconscious having asserted itself, and as Georg lets himself fall from the bridge, effectively ending the business career and the engagement, it is the formerly faded and foreign true self, the writer, who remains. Thus, what seems on first reading to be a horror story of insanity and suicide is actually not a disaster at all but an exercise in self-preservation. No sooner had Kafka become romantically involved with Felice than he had worked out subconsciously how detrimental such a relationship would be to his career as a writer. With such personal material, it is no wonder the writer in Kafka felt inspired to finish "The Judgment" in one sitting. Ironically, his conscious mind was at that point still so far behind the insights of the subconscious that he dedicated the story to none other than Felice Bauer.

The subtitle of Heinz Politzer's book on Kafka, *Parable and Paradox*, evokes the elusive nature of Kafka's story lines, which are charged with opposing forces seeking synthesis. Although most of the stories are grim, the reader cannot help but be amused at the outrageous, at times burlesque turns of events. Only the bleak and disquieting desperation of the characters contradicts the humor inherent in their situations. Also, many of the stories end with the main character dead or reduced to a state of utter hopelessness. Many of the longer stories, such as "The Judgment," are so complex that they can be confusing. Kafka's shorter stories, consisting of only a paragraph or a page or two, sometimes leave a more lasting impression, because they each center on one main event.

Politzer begins his study with a lengthy discussion of a 124-word commentary that Kafka wrote late in 1922. In the commentary, which has become known as "Give It Up!," a traveler heading for the train station early one morning becomes disconcerted when he checks his watch against a clock tower and thinks that he must be late. In his haste, he becomes uncertain of the way and has to ask a police officer. The officer repeats the question, then tells the man to give up and turns away from him. The police officer's reply is both hilarious and profoundly unsettling. It is hilarious because it is completely out of line with what a police officer would say. It is unsettling because it lifts the story out of the mundane into a world where not only time but also, apparently, place have lost their relevance and it is impossible to determine one's way. The issue has become existential.

Kafka innately distrusted figures of authority and frequently portrayed them maliciously misleading and abusing those who came under their power. The 1922 commentary is simply a lighter variation on the theme that Kafka stated unforgettably in 1914 in his parable "Vor dem Gesetz" ("Before the Law"). This moving and perfect piece of writing was later incorporated into chapter 19 of Kafka's novel *Der Prozess* (1925; *The Trial*, 1937).

In the two-page parable, a man from the country seeks access to the law. He is told by the doorkeeper that he may not enter at the moment but possibly later. The man is deterred from entering without permission by the doorkeeper's telling him that this is only the first of many doors that are guarded by increasingly powerful doorkeepers. The man spends the rest of his life there waiting for admittance and gives away everything he owns in unsuccessful attempts to bribe the doorkeeper. Finally, in his dying hour, he asks why no one else has come to that door, only to hear the doorkeeper say: "This door was intended only for you. I am now going to shut it."

The parable is not enlightening. By the time the man finds out that he should go through the door after all, it is shut in his face. The story seems, rather, to be a comment on the human condition as Kafka experienced it in early twentieth century Europe. The rise of science and industry had displaced but could not replace religion, with the result that human beings could no longer find their way. The human institutions, the apparent absolutes represented by the law, prove to be fallible, imperfect, and unreliable. Nothing now can fill the human need for direction in life. Reality has become fragmented and disjunctive. "Before the Law" is particularly poignant because the reader cannot help but believe that, before the law, human beings are all people from the country, simple, helpless creatures who have lost their way.

The way out of this impossible situation is brilliantly described with humor and sadness in Kafka's three-page story "Der Kübelreiter" ("The Bucket Rider"), written during a coal shortage in the winter of 1916. The main character has no coal, and it is bitterly cold. He also has no money but goes to the coal dealer anyway, to ask for only a shovelful. To show how desperate he is, he rides there on his empty coal bucket, sailing through the air and calling down from high above the dealer's house. The dealer is deeply moved by the voice of an old customer, but it is his wife who goes to the street to investigate. Once she finds that the bucket rider cannot pay immediately, she claims to see no one and waves him away with her apron. The bucket is too light to offer any resistance. The rider ascends "into the regions of the ice mountains" and is "lost for ever."

This story contains the delightful, dreamlike element of the fantastic that is a source of great beauty in Kafka's works. The moment the main character decides to ride on his bucket, which occurs at the beginning of the second paragraph, he is lifted out of everyday reality, in which he would surely have frozen to death. Kafka shows, once again, that it is useless to plead with others, especially those who have some authority. Rather than send his main character on an empty bucket back to his freezing room, Kafka has the bucket whisk him away into the ice mountains, never to return. Coal and indeed all mundane concerns cease to be a problem as the bucket rider leaves behind the human habitat. Thwarted by everyday pettiness, he has moved instead into a timeless mental space that seems infinitely more interesting. In "The Bucket Rider," Kafka represents that space with the image of distant ice mountains. In his fifty-second aphorism, he writes a literal description of that saving space: "There is only a spiritual world; what we call the physical world is the evil in the spiritual one, and what we call evil is only a necessary moment in our endless development." The bucket rider has transcended the evil phase.

The winter of 1916 was one of Kafka's most prolific periods and one in which he seemed especially visually oriented and inclined toward the fantastic. His seven-page masterpiece "Ein Landarzt" ("A Country Doctor") is one of his most involved works. It contains all Kafka's main themes and the salient features of his style.

As in "The Bucket Rider," the setting of "A Country Doctor" is an icy winter, and the mood is one of confused, melancholy desperation. The situation is hopeless and the doctor sees no way out of it. Unlike "The Bucket Rider," which has only one main event, "A Country Doctor" is a richly textured work. The most rewarding interpretive approach is that employed here in examining "The Judgment." There are three main male characters: the country doctor, the groom, and the sick boy. They seem to represent different aspects of the same person, and the story, once again, seems to be autobiographical.

The country doctor is an older man who has been working for a long time in his profession, and he is disillusioned. The local people, while placing many demands on him, do nothing to help him. Not one of the neighbors would lend him a horse in an emergency. In keeping with the spirit of the age, the people have lost their faith in religion and look instead to science and medicine to perform the miracles, backing up the doctor's efforts with choral chanting as if he were a medicine man. He is the only one sadly aware of the limitations of his profession but plays out the charade in a resigned fashion, eventually lying outright to the boy by minimizing the severity of his fatal wound.

Kafka was a professional as well, a lawyer who in 1916 had already worked nine years after articling. Although he was a dedicated and valued member of his firm, he regarded his work as a necessary evil, as his means of earning a living so that he could write in his spare time. He was not disillusioned with law, but neither did he harbor any cherished illusions about his distinguished profession. He believed that, as it did to the man from the country in "Before the Law," law was wearing him out. Readers will equate the country doctor with Kafka the lawyer.

In order of appearance, the second male character in "A Country Doctor" is the groom. That he belongs to the country doctor or is part of him is evidenced by the servant's girl's remark, "You never know what you're going to find in your own house." Certainly, the groom represents a source not tapped in a long time—so long, in fact, that the country doctor is surprised when the man emerges from the abandoned pigsty. By association with the steaming horses, by the birthlike nature of their emergence, and by his rape of Rose, the groom stands for vitality, sensuality, and sex. He is also associated with savagery and filth.

At the time of writing "A Country Doctor," Kafka had broken off his first engagement to Felice Bauer and had had several short-lived affairs. He was attracted to women but still felt that marriage and his work as a writer were mutually exclusive. His belief that marriage was not for him was based also on his perception of the sexual act as something terrible. Just as the groom represents a repressed aspect of the country doctor, who had all but ignored Rose, so too he represents the sexual fulfillment that Kafka decided again and again to sacrifice in order to continue his writing. Readers will equate the groom with Kafka the lover.

The groom and the two horses emerge from the pigsty together, then go off in different directions. While the groom was pursuing Rose, the unearthly horses transported the country doctor to the sick boy. Perhaps the boy was only to be reached by supernatural means. There is a fairy-tale quality to the ten-mile journey. It took only a moment, and the blinding snow was gone, replaced by clear moonlight. The nature of the journey is significant for the reader's interpretation of the boy. Kafka has placed him in the spiritual world.

Whereas the country doctor is only one of many, as stressed by the indefinite article in the title, the boy is unique. His father, family, and the villagers have no understanding of the boy's condition. Clearly, the boy is having a hard time of it in these surroundings. Even the doctor feels ill "in the narrow confines of the old man's thoughts." Disheartened, the boy at first wants to die. So does the doctor. Once the doctor becomes aware of the unique nature of the boy's great wound, however, which is both attractive and repulsive, rose-colored and worm-eaten, the boy decides that he wants to live. By then, though, it is too late. The blossom in his side is destroying him.

Like the friend in Russia in "The Judgment," the boy in "A Country Doctor" appears sickly but turns out to be of supreme importance. Kafka was not physically strong. In 1916, his tuberculosis had not yet been diagnosed, but he suffered from stomach problems. He lived with his parents, who were concerned that the long hours he spent writing were ruining his health. It is therefore fitting that those characters in his stories who represent Kafka the writer appear to be sickly. Readers will equate the boy with Kafka the writer.

Like the surface level of "The Judgment," the surface level of "A Country Doctor" reads like a tragedy of unequaled proportions. Unable to help the boy, the country doctor finds himself also unable to get home, for the trip away from the boy is as slow as the trip to him was fast. "Exposed to the frost of this most unhappy of ages," the doctor realizes that, as a result of this trip, he has not only sacrificed his servant girl but also lost his flourishing practice to his successor. What this translates into, though, is a triumph. Kafka the writer has subjugated Kafka the lawyer and Kafka the lover. The famous, peremptorily fatalistic last line of the story reveals its double meaning. "A false alarm on the night bell once answered—it cannot be made good, not ever." Once Kafka accepted his gift as a writer, he could never abandon that link with the spiritual world.

Kafka's works show, simultaneously and paradoxically, not only the existential angst inherent in the human condition but also a way out of that hopeless state. If the various characters are considered as elements of a personality seeking integration, the stories end not bleakly but on a transcendent note. Kafka's refuge was in his writing, in the spiritual world, and in laughter.

Other major works

NOVELS: *Der Prozess*, 1925 (*The Trial*, 1937); *Das Schloss*, 1926 (*The Castle*, 1930); *Amerika*, 1927 (*America*, 1938, better known as *Amerika*, 1946).

NONFICTION: *The Diaries of Franz Kafka*, 1948-1949; *Tagebücher, 1910-1923*, 1951; *Briefe an Milena*, 1952 (*Letters to Milena*, 1953); *Briefe, 1902-1924*, 1958; *Briefe an Felice*, 1967 (*Letters to Felice*, 1974); *Briefe an Ottla und die Familie*, 1974 (*Letters to Ottla and the Family*, 1982).

MISCELLANEOUS: *Hochzeitsvorbereitungen auf dem Lande und andere Prosa aus dem Nachlass*, 1953 (*Dearest Father: Stories and Other Writings*, 1954; also known as *Wedding Preparations in the Country, and Other Posthumous Prose Writings*, 1954).

Bibliography

Bloom, Harold, ed. *Franz Kafka*. New York: Chelsea House, 1986. A collection of essays, on Kafka himself and on themes that pervade his oeuvre, by distinguished scholars. Includes essays on the short stories "Up in the Gallery," "A Country Doctor," "Der Bau" ("The Burrow"), and "Die Verwandlung" ("The Metamorphosis"). Contains an excellent index that itemizes specific aspects of the works.

Corngold, Stanley. *Franz Kafka: The Necessity of Form*. Ithaca, N.Y.: Cornell University Press, 1988. Chapter 3 (43 pages) contains what is very likely the definitive analysis of "The Metamorphosis." Also includes excellent analysis of "The Judgment," in chapters 2 and 7, discussions of form and critical method, and comparisons with other authors. Corngold also wrote a critical bibliography of "The Metamorphosis" in *The Commentator's Despair* (1973).

Flores, Angel, ed. *The Problem of "The Judgement": Eleven Approaches to Kafka's Story*. New York: Gordian Press, 1976. An English translation, followed by a valuable collection of essays on the short story that Kafka considered his best. Harmut Binder reveals a surprising number of background sources in literature and legend. Kate Flores writes a convincing analysis based on the nature of human fatherhood. Walter Sokel provides an extensive interpretation. Very worthwhile.

Hayman, Ronald. *K: A Biography of Kafka*. London: Weidenfeld & Nicolson, 1981. More than a biography, this study contains many helpful discussions of the literary works, showing how they arose in response to specific situations and linking them with contemporary passages from Kafka's diary and letters. A moving portrayal particularly of Kafka's last days, when his steps toward liberation coincided tragically with the final stages of tuberculosis.

Pawel, Ernst. *The Nightmare of Reason: A Life of Franz Kafka.* New York: Farrar, Straus & Giroux, 1984. An excellent biography, remarkable in that Pawel's meticulous research has extended beyond Kafka to include the fates of all those lives he touched. Conveys detailed knowledge of the school and university systems of the time and of the stages of social and political unrest in Prague. Beautifully written.

Politzer, Heinz. *Franz Kafka: Parable and Paradox.* Revised and expanded edition. Ithaca, N.Y.: Cornell University Press, 1966. A seminal work in Kafka scholarship. Proceeding from a detailed analysis of one paragraph, Politzer discusses several of the short stories at length ("The Judgment," "The Metamorphosis," and "In the Penal Colony") and touches on all the stories. Entertains many alternative readings and compares the works with one another.

Spann, Meno. *Franz Kafka.* Boston: Twayne, 1976. Meno's familiarity with the 250 books in Kafka's library enables him to identify sources and influences. He corrects many misleading errors in the English translations, provides lucid overviews of diverse critical approaches, and offers his own concise readings of the works. Good discussions of the major short stories.

Jean M. Snook

ANNA KAVAN
Helen (Woods) Edmonds

Born: Cannes, France; 1901
Died: London, England; December 5, 1968

Principal short fiction

Asylum Piece and Other Stories, 1940; *I Am Lazarus*, 1945; *The House of Sleep*, 1947; *A Bright Green Field and Other Stories*, 1958; *Julia and the Bazooka and Other Stories*, 1970; *My Soul in China: A Novella and Stories*, 1975.

Other literary forms

Anna Kavan wrote novels early in her career under the name Helen Ferguson, including *A Charmed Circle* (1929), *The Dark Sisters* (1930), and *Let Me Alone* (1930), which was reprinted under the name Anna Kavan in 1979. As Anna Kavan she wrote several other novels, among them *A Scarcity of Love* (1956), *Eagle's Nest* (1957), and *Ice* (1967), which is highly regarded as a work of science fiction.

Achievements

Largely unrecognized in her lifetime, Kavan has become something of a cult figure since her death. She has been compared to such figures as Franz Kafka, Virginia Woolf, Sylvia Plath, D. H. Lawrence, John Fowles, and Anaïs Nin (who was one of her greatest admirers), and her writing has been classified variously as science fiction, feminist fiction, and surrealist fiction. Her greatest achievement lies in the portrayal of the subjective emotional states of mental illness, drug dependency, and the paranoia that accompany them, as well as the loneliness and the general sense of isolation that many individuals in contemporary society suffer at one time or another. Employing vivid imagery to portray the vague line separating dreams and reality, she is, as Gunther Stuhlmann writes, "one of the most hauntingly remarkable artists of modern English literature."

Biography

A knowledge of Anna Kavan's life is essential to understanding and appreciating her literature, for she is a profoundly autobiographical writer. Echoes of her unhappy childhood, mental illness, and drug addiction appear repeatedly in her stories, and her protagonists are frequently versions of the author herself.

Kavan lived virtually two separate and distinct lives: first as Helen Woods, Helen Woods Edmonds, and Helen Ferguson; and, second, as Anna Kavan. The author was born Helen Woods in Cannes, France, to a wealthy upper-middle-class couple, and details of her early years are sketchy. Little is known about her father, except that he disappeared early in her life. She traveled extensively with her glamorous mother, Helen (Bright) Woods, who eventually remarried a wealthy South African and died young. Kavan's relationship with her mother, who was by all accounts aloof and distant with her young daughter, strongly influenced her life and writing.

In the 1920's, Helen Woods married Donald Ferguson, a successful Scottish businessman, and they settled in Burma, where Helen began writing. Her first book, *A Charmed Circle*, was published in 1929, and by 1937, she had produced twelve novels. The couple had a son, who was eventually killed in World War II, and the marriage ended in divorce, with Helen later marrying painter Stuart Edmonds. Although reportedly happier than her first marriage, this relationship also ended in divorce.

After the dissolution of each marriage, Helen stayed in sanatoriums in Switzerland and England, experiences that she later chronicled in her fiction. By the end of the 1930's, she had also become addicted to heroin, registering as an addict just prior to World War II. This period marked drastic changes in her life, including a name change by deed poll to Anna Kavan (Anna for the protagonist of her novel *Let Me Alone* and Kavan after Kafka's "K") and a complete change in physical appearance from matronly brunette to thin, nearly emaciated, silver blond (a hair color shared with most of her heroines). Her fiction also changed markedly from the more conventional novels of Helen Ferguson, and she enjoyed a measure of critical success when her first book as Anna Kavan, *Asylum Piece and Other Stories*, appeared in 1940.

During the war years, she lived briefly in New York, worked as a researcher in a military psychiatric unit in London, and beginning in 1942 served as an assistant editor on the literary journal *Horizon*, which also published several of her stories. Her critical reputation declined after the war, and by 1956, she was reduced to paying a vanity press to publish *A Scarcity of Love*, while *Eagle's Nest* and *A Bright Green Field and Other Stories* appeared in 1957 and 1958. She spent these years in London, renovating and selling old homes, as well as designing and building a home of her own. Always impeccably groomed, shy, and reclusive, she was given to bizarre behavior, as, for example, when she threw a roast duck across the table during a dinner party.

More than one attempted suicide and bouts with severe depression marked her later years, as well as the humiliation of mandatory attendance at sessions for drug addicts sponsored by National Health, promoting the fear and distrust of authority that play such a prominent role in her stories. She continued writing, including the novel *Who Are You?* (1963) and the well-received *Ice*, which began to revive interest in her career. She died at age sixty-seven, with a loaded syringe, her "bazooka" as she called it, in her hand. Her later stories were published posthumously, collected in *Julia and the Bazooka and Other Stories*, which details her drug addiction, and *My Soul in China: A Novella and Stories.*

Analysis

Anna Kavan's dominant theme, the isolation of the individual in contemporary society, is usually expressed through intensely personal tales of loneliness, mental anguish, and despair set against ominous foreign or institutional backdrops. Her characters, often nameless or merely initialed young women, are psychologically unstable, existing in a vague world where the bounds of dream and reality continually shift. The themes of madness, drug addiction, repressive authority, lost love, and loneliness weave a common thread through each volume of her stories. Although often criticized for speaking to her personal despair rather than to a more universal humanity, Kavan's fiction cannot help striking a deeply responsive and sympathetic chord in the reader.

The stories in *Asylum Piece and Other Stories* explore various states of madness, paranoia, and estrangement from the inside out. In the first story, "The Birthmark," a nameless narrator, away from home for the first time, develops a strong affinity for a girl, known only as H, whom she meets at boarding school. A typical Kavan character, H has "a face unique, neither gay nor melancholy, but endued with a peculiar quality of apartness" which is further accentuated by her peculiarly shaped birthmark, "a circle armed with sharp points and enclosing a tiny shape very soft and tender—perhaps a rose." Despite the attraction they feel for each other, neither can overcome her sense of "apartness" to form a bond with the other. Years later, while touring an ancient fortress in a foreign country, the narrator believes that she sees H, whom she has never forgotten, imprisoned in a subterranean cell, but feels powerless to help her. Typically, the gulf between the two is too great to bridge.

"Going Up in the World" also involves an alienated figure, here a lowly petitioner who begs her Patron and Patroness to "share a little . . . sunshine and warmth." The unnamed narrator can no longer bear her "lonely, cold and miserable" existence and petitions her "patrons" to admit her into the inner sanctum of their luxuriously warm world. Typically, the exact nature of the Patron and Patroness' authority over the narrator remains vague. Possessing the power to banish her to a miserable existence, they speak like scolding parents exhorting their child to "give up [her] rebellious ways." Well-dressed, smug, self-satisfied figures such as these, whether doctors, parents, or unspecified "officials," appear regularly in Kavan's stories, issuing capricious orders that can ruin a life in an instant.

"Asylum Piece," the longest story of the volume, is divided into eight parts, the first of which presents an outsider's view of a mental institution, which looks deceptively like a scene "upon which a light comedy, something airy and gay, is about to be acted." The setting is pastoral, calm, and beautiful and "flooded with dazzling midsummer sunshine." Part 2, however, shifts the perspective to that of a patient, a frightened young woman committed against her will, and the succeeding sections shift to an omniscient view of the inmates' daily lives.

An atmosphere of impotence, imprisonment, and isolation predominates in these sections. In one, a young man, determined to row across the lake to freedom, comes to realize that he is trapped, not just by the physical boundaries of the asylum, but by the boundaries of his own mind. In another, a young woman, perhaps the narrator from part 2, is committed by her husband who "longs to disassociate himself from the whole situation." Lonely and deserted, she is briefly comforted by a sympathetic young cleaning woman. In a later episode, a young woman (again perhaps the same one) spends a holiday from the asylum with her visiting husband, a stern and inflexible man who cannot wait to end the visit and return home. Crushed by her husband's rejection, the young woman is left to the comfort and understanding of a fellow inmate. Unlike many of Kavan's stories, "Asylum Piece" holds out some possibility for human contact, however brief and transitory.

The volume comes full circle with the last story, "There Is No End," which harks back to the motif of imprisonment from "The Birthmark." A nameless woman imprisoned by "unseen and impassable" walls in a place where there is "no love . . . nor hate, nor any point where feeling accumulates" wonders if it is "life then, or death, stretching like an uncolored stream behind and in front of me?" For this narrator and for many of Kavan's characters, prison is only an outer manifestation of an inner sense of isolation, from which no escape is possible.

I Am Lazarus continues the themes of psychological turmoil, paranoia, and isolation introduced in *Asylum Piece and Other Stories* and explores the devastating effects of war on the psyche and the cruelly dehumanizing techniques employed by mental institutions to "rehabilitate" their patients. In the title story, set in an idyllic pastoral sanatorium, "every tree pruned to perfection, . . . brilliant with flowers," a young, aristocratic Englishman has been reduced to an automaton by insulin shock treatments. Although outwardly a model citizen, Mr. Bow is inwardly confused and frightened, feeling in control only while working on his leather belt in craft class. He functions successfully when clear-cut rules exist to guide his behavior but is otherwise debilitated. Although his doctor remarks that "[h]e doesn't know how lucky he is . . . [w]e've pulled him back literally from a living death," the opposite is in fact true. The pathetic young man has been doomed to a living death, not rescued from one.

In "The Palace of Sleep," another victim of destructive "rehabilitative" techniques, drugged to unconsciousness by her doctors, looks "absolutely lifeless, void" and appears to have "forfeited humanity and given . . . over prematurely to death." Her doctor, smug in the knowledge that he has extinguished her pain, fails to perceive a look of "wild supplication, of frantic abysmal appeal" on her lifeless face. Like Mr. Bow, this fair-haired young woman, apparently cured of her madness, no longer a bother to society, is inwardly suffering as intensely as before.

In the novella *The House of Sleep*, referred to by one reviewer as an "autobiography of dreams," Kavan alternates brief bits of "daytime life" with detailed dream sequences, believing that in the "tension between the two polarities night and day, night, the negative pole, must share equal importance with the positive day." This work chronicles a young girl's progressive retreat from the reality of a "remote and starry" mother who seldom had time for her and died young and a distant father who refused to explain her mother's death. Relegated to the "crowded ugliness" of boarding school, the girl regresses ever further into herself, until, living almost entirely in her dream life, she is institutionalized. Although praised for its brilliant dream imagery reminiscent of a Salvador Dalí painting, a critic remarked that "one never feels any desire to read on . . . because Anna Kavan has given too much importance to the negative pole, and thereby destroyed the tension between day and night."

Julia and the Bazooka and Other Stories, perhaps Kavan's best collection of stories, transcends the merely autobiographical to achieve the status of art. Continuing to explore the themes of isolation, loneliness, and mental illness, this volume also deals with drug addiction. Unlike *Asylum Piece and Other Stories* and *I Am Lazarus*, in which she occasionally ventures outside herself to explore other characters, this collection is almost entirely self-referential, most stories told by a first-person narrator, all seemingly about the same character.

In the first story, "The Old Address," the narrator is released from an institution for drug rehabilitation into a threatening and ominous world peopled with "hordes of masks, dummies, zombies" where "everything look[s] sinister." A short-lived feeling of freedom is soon overtaken by the sense of permanent imprisonment within her. Remembering that "I am alone, as I always am" and that "there's to be no end to my incarceration in this abominable, disgusting world," she hails a taxi to drive to the "old address," back to the haven of her drug addiction.

Several stories in this volume use the automobile to symbolize, paradoxically, both the individual's sense of estrangement from her world and her means of dealing with that estrangement. Often used as a symbol of drug addiction, the car represents the syringe or "bazooka" that brings temporary relief from the narrator's suffering. In "The Fog," the narrator, driving in a drug-induced haze, runs down a teenager because she sees him as a "teenage mask," a "dummy made of stuffed clothes and umbrellas," not a real person. As she reasons, "I wasn't really here, so [he] couldn't be either." The narrator longs to be "no more than a hole in space, not here or anywhere at all, for as long as possible, preferably forever."

"The World of Heroes" again deals with cars, this time the world of racing. The narrator finds a sense of security and belonging among the ranks of drivers of high-powered cars. To her a car is "a very safe refuge . . . the only means of escape from all the ferocious and cruel forces lurking in life and in human beings." She finds love with various drivers, moving from one to another, living a "fairy tale" existence. The car, however, which provides this exciting, satisfying life, also takes it away when the narrator is seriously and disfiguringly injured in a race. Her friends disappear, her lovers are gone, and she, like all Kavan's heroines, winds up alone, "back where [she] was as a child, solitary, helpless, unwanted, frightened."

"Julia and the Bazooka," one of Kavan's most critically well-regarded stories, is a moving account of a young woman's drug addiction. As one reviewer commented, "The whole volume has great documentary interest, but 'Julia and the Bazooka' turns the truth of a life into art." Julia's drug addiction is foreshadowed by her childhood love of poppies, although she is told to "throw the poppies away" because they "make a mess dropping their petals all over the house." Even as a little girl, she "feels cut off from people . . . afraid of the world," and by the time of her marriage, she is addicted, carrying her syringe along with her wedding bouquet. Like many of Kavan's heroines, Julia is a good driver, who laughs at danger because "[nothing] can frighten her while she has the syringe." She dies in a bomb blast during the war, lying "in her red-stained dress, her bag, with bazooka inside, safely hooked over one arm," and "[t]here is no more Julia anywhere. Where she was there is only nothing."

My Soul in China: A Novella and Stories, also published posthumously, contains the title novella and several stories in a lighter vein than her previously published work, leaning more toward science fiction and commentary on contemporary society. The novella, much more characteristic of the body of her work, features a typical Kavan heroine, here named Kay, who, like the heroine in "The Old Address," has just been released from an institution. Estranged from her husband, she meets an Australian who offers to take her to California for six months of recuperation before he returns to his wife and family. *My Soul in China* offers one of Kavan's most moving accounts of a tormented soul, a woman who cannot escape her madness no matter how hard she tries to lose herself in others. Kay feels she is "on a narrow bridge without handrails, hair-raisingly suspended above nothingness." At one end lies "security, familiarity . . . a safe vegetable life without risks or emotions . . . while the other end vanishes into dangerous and unknown, stern cloud shapes there coldly assembling." Kay soon discovers, after a brief idyll, that her Australian lover cannot shield her forever from her demons, and as their time together winds down she feels "[a]s indifferent, as vacant as the uninhabited world, the blank empty eye of infinite space stares me down; and the blue unblemished arch of a godless eternity has no consolation to offer me, none at all."

Kay's fear that "[t]he self I inherited from my ancestors, the person I should have been, has been irremediably mutilated and pulled apart, its fragile balance of thoughts and feelings destroyed," echoes the fears of nearly all Kavan's lost, tormented souls. Looking outside themselves, her protagonists find neither love nor faith nor a sense of belonging. Looking inside, they find even less; a soul so destroyed and tortured that they cannot bear to contemplate it. The only hope lies in the oblivion of drugs, madness, or the final oblivion of death.

Other major works

NOVELS: *A Charmed Circle*, 1929; *The Dark Sisters*, 1930; *Let Me Alone*, 1930 (reprinted under Anna Kavan, 1979); *A Stranger Still*, 1935; *Goose Cross*, 1936; *Rich Get Rich*, 1937; *Change the Name*, 1941; *A Scarcity of Love*, 1956; *Eagle's Nest*, 1957; *Who Are You?*, 1963; *Ice*, 1967.

MISCELLANEOUS: *My Madness: The Selected Writings of Anna Kavan*, 1990 (edited by Brian W. Aldiss).

Bibliography

Aldiss, Brian. Introduction to *Ice*. Garden City, N.Y.: Doubleday, 1970. Aldiss, who met and corresponded with Kavan, discusses *Ice* as a work of science fiction and Kavan's reaction to being regarded as a science-fiction writer: "she was surprised. At first, she rejected the idea. Slowly, she came to like it. . . . I fancy she always liked anything that was a novelty." He also offers biographical details and interesting insights into her character.

Byrne, Janet. "Moving Toward Entropy: Anna Kavan's Science Fiction Mentality." *Extrapolation* 23 (Spring, 1982): 5-11. One of the few critical articles available on Kavan, it centers on *Ice* rather than her short fiction, but it nevertheless provides valuable insights into Kavan's fictional style and concerns. Byrne discusses the novel in the context of Kavan's earlier work, in which she "consistently saw the world as peopled by characters who treated each other cruelly or foolishly, or were so lost in their own private hells that they had no relation to each other."

Davies, Rhys. Introduction to *Julia and the Bazooka and Other Stories*. New York: Alfred A. Knopf, 1975. Davies, a good friend of Kavan, reflects on the close relationship between the circumstances of her life (particularly her drug addiction) and her fiction, in particular the story "Julia and the Bazooka." His valuable psychological insights clarify readings of her fiction.

Owen, Peter. "Publishing Anna Kavan." *Anais* 3 (1985): 75-76. Owen, Kavan's publisher, offers interesting personal insights ("Anna Kavan was a lonely person, aloof with strangers, who relaxed only with a few intimate friends. . . . She was an excellent hostess and a good cook") and a valuable insider's look at Kavan's publishing history.

Stuhlmann, Gunther. "Anna Kavan Revisited: The Web of Unreality." *Anais* 3 (1985): 55-62. Stuhlmann's valuable, well-written overview of Kavan's life and career includes many biographical facts unavailable elsewhere and some discussion of her literary influences and fiction. The article also discusses Anaïs Nin's interest in Kavan and her work and includes a photograph of Kavan in her garden.

Wakeman, John, ed. "Anna Kavan." In *World Authors: 1920-1925*. New York: H. W. Wilson, 1980. The entry in this volume provides good background material on Kavan's life and career, placing her fiction in the context of her life, particularly noting the critical reaction to her work as it appeared. The article contains a photograph of Kavan and a bibliography of her principal works, as well as a listing of critical articles and reviews.

Mary Virginia Davis

YASUNARI KAWABATA

Born: Osaka, Japan; June 11, 1899
Died: Zushi, Japan; April 16, 1972

Principal short fiction

Shokonsai ikkei, 1921; *Suishō gensō*, 1934; *Jōjōka*, 1938; *Shiroi mangetsu*, 1948; *Maihime*, 1951; *Bungei tokuhon Kawabata Yasunari*, 1962; *The House of the Sleeping Beauties and Other Stories*, 1969; *Tenohira no shōsetsu*, 1969; *Shui yuch*, 1971; *Honehiroi*, 1975; *Tenjū no ko*, 1975; *Palm-of-the-Hand Stories*, 1988.

Other literary forms

Besides approximately two hundred short stories and fictional vignettes (or short, short stories), Yasunari Kawabata wrote both "serious" novels, which earned for him a Nobel Prize, and "popular" novels, which gained for him financial security. The latter, considered by some critics as vulgarizations, are not included in editions of his complete works. His serious works include juvenile fiction, travel accounts, journalism, letters, reviews, translations, editions, plays, and lectures.

Achievements

Known throughout the world as the only writer from his country to have received the Nobel Prize in Literature, Kawabata was also awarded every major Japanese literary honor, including membership in the Japanese Academy of Arts (1954). In 1972, he was posthumously awarded the First Class Order of the Rising Sun. In his work, Kawabata combines universal themes with literary techniques and conventions typical of Japanese culture. His eminence as a writer of fiction is based on this characteristic of fusing contrary, although not antithetical, elements. He draws upon the East and the West as well as the traditional and the modern, juxtaposes mimetic precision with symbolic evocation, joins the erotic and the spiritual, and fluctuates between dream and reality. In like manner, he cultivated and perfected both long and short genres of fiction and in a sense brought them into conjunction, since many of his long works can be broken down into short, independent elements. His themes embrace both the mundane and the esoteric, his narrative style ranges from the graphic to the lyrical, and his highly original plots and situations touch upon fundamental moral and aesthetic issues of modern life.

Biography

Orphaned at the age of four, Yasunari Kawabata was reared by his grandparents and later by an uncle. Originally attracted by painting, he later decided to follow writing as a career, and at the age of sixteen he published in a little magazine an account of carrying his teacher's coffin. Two years earlier, he had written reminiscences of his grandfather, which he later published under the title "Jūrokusai no

Nikki" ("Diary of a Sixteen-Year-Old"). In 1921, he received his first payment for a
literary work, a review, and published in a student literary magazine an account of a
memorial day commemoration that drew the favorable attention of a prolific novelist, Kikuchi Kan, a dominating force in Japanese literary circles of the time. The
themes of death and loneliness of Kawabata's mature years appeared early in his career and may have been influenced by the loss of his parents and grandparents. During his youth, he came briefly under the influence of a Japanese avant-garde clique
that advocated the adoption of novel Western movements such as Dadaism, Futur-
ism, and Surrealism. These tendencies were wrapped up in the term *Shinkankaku-
ha*, which embraces neo-perceptionism or neo-sensualism, but Kawabata's allegiance
to this extremely many-sided coterie was only temporary and irresolute. His major
work in the experimental mode, "Suishō gensō" ("Crystal Fantasy"), utilizes the
stream-of-consciousness technique.

Kawabata established his reputation as a creative writer with the publication in
1926 of his story "Izu no Odoriko" ("The Izu Dancer") and acquired both critical
and popular acclaim with his novel *Yukiguni* (1947; *Snow Country*, 1956). In 1941, he
visited Manchuria twice, spending a month in the ancient capital of Mukden and
returning to Japan shortly before the breaking out of the Pacific War. Throughout the
conflict, Kawabata's publications consisted in large measure of childhood recollections, and he immersed himself in the study of traditional Japanese culture. In the
aftermath of his country's defeat, Kawabata announced that he would henceforth
write only eulogies, a promise not fulfilled unless his major themes of death, loneliness, and opposition to the Westernization of Japan could be considered elegiac.
These themes dominated the first two of his great postwar novels, *Sembazuru* (1952;
Thousand Cranes, 1958) and *Yama no oto* (1957; *The Sound of the Mountain*, 1970),
and another novel, *Kyoto* (1962; *The Old Capital*, 1987).

The Old Capital, which has as protagonists virginal twins who meet for the first
time in their late teens after being separated as infants, has received relatively little
critical attention in English, perhaps because of the innocence of the characters and
the extensive descriptions of the woodland scenery surrounding Kyoto. Western critics have been more attracted by the novella *The House of the Sleeping Beauties*, concerning an unusual brothel in which old men spend the night with naked girls, who
are voluntarily drugged into unconsciousness. The love of nature in the one and the
eroticism in the other are both typical of Kawabata and are often coalesced in his
other works.

In 1948, Kawabata became president of the PEN Club of Japan, a position he
utilized to continue his perennial occupation of encouraging and promoting the careers of young writers. In 1957, he was the guiding spirit behind the twenty-ninth
congress of PEN, held in Tokyo, and in 1959, he was elected vice president of that
organization, attending three of its congresses in other countries.

In his Nobel Prize acceptance speech, Kawabata remarked that he neither admired
nor was in sympathy with suicide. It was a great shock to his associates and to the
world at large, therefore, when in April, 1972, he took his own life by inhaling gas.

Analysis

The short story or the vignette is the essence of Yasunari Kawabata's literary art. Even his great novels were written piecemeal. Not only were they originally published in serial form, the parts frequently presented as separate stories, but also many segments were rewritten and revised for both style and content. Japanese tradition has applied the term *shosetsu*, loosely "fiction," to both novels and short stories, and as a result, such works as "The Izu Dancer," consisting of only thirty pages, and *The House of the Sleeping Beauties*, forming less than a hundred, have been treated critically as novels.

Kawabata composed his first work "Jūrokusai no Nikki" ("Diary of a Sixteen-Year-Old") at that age and published it eleven years later. The work describes the humiliating last days and suffering of his grandfather and foreshadows the themes of aging and death in his later works. Comparing the diary with his recollections at a later date, Kawabata maintained that he had forgotten the sordid details of sickness and dying portrayed in his narrative and that his mind had since been constantly occupied in cleansing and beautifying his grandfather's image.

With "The Izu Dancer," his first work to obtain international acclaim, the opposite is true. Here, he idealizes a somewhat commonplace autobiographical incident and group of characters. The story, told in the first person, concerns the encounter of a nineteen-year-old youth on a walking tour of the Izu Peninsula with a group of itinerant entertainers, including a young dancer, who appears to be about sixteen. The young man accompanies them on their way, spurred with the hope that he would eventually spend a night with the young dancer. One morning, as he prepares to enter a public bath, he sees her emerging naked from the steam and realizes that she is a mere child, and a feeling akin to a draught of fresh water permeates his consciousness. Learning that she is only thirteen years of age, he, nevertheless, remains with the players and is accepted by them as a pleasant companion until they reach their winter headquarters. There, he takes a boat back to Tokyo, and his eyes fill with tears as the dancer bids him farewell, floating in a "beautiful emptiness."

The situation of a young man joining forces with a group of itinerant entertainers resembles that in Johann Wolfgang von Goethe's *Wilhelm Meisters Lehrjahre* (1795-1796; *Wilhelm Meister's Apprenticeship*, 1824), perhaps the reason that the work was translated into German in 1942, more than twenty years before being rendered into any other Western language. Some years after the original publication, Kawabata revealed that the portrayal of his youthful journey is highly idealistic, concealing major imperfections in the appearance and behavior of the actual troupe. Presumably in real life, moreover, the young age of the dancer would have been no deterrent to his amorous inclinations, since he later portrayed a thirteen-year-old prostitute as the heroine of one of his popular novels concerning Asakusa, the amusement section of Tokyo. The longing for virginal innocence and the realization that this degree of purity is something beyond ordinary attainment is a recurrent theme throughout Kawabata's work, portraying innocence, beauty, and rectitude as ephemeral and tinged with sadness. The sentimental ending of "The Izu Dancer" is considered to symbolize both the purifying effect of literature upon life as well as Kawabata's personal passage from misanthropy to hopefulness.

Kawabata pursues the theme of the psychological effect of art and nature in another autobiographical story, "Warawanu Otoko" ("The Man Who Did Not Smile"), representing his middle years. The author of a film script, impressed by the beauty of the dawn in the countryside, where the script is being filmed, rewrites the last scene with the intention of wrapping "reality in a beautiful, smiling mask." The rewriting is inspired by his notion of having every one of the characters in a mental hospital, locale of the film, wear a laughing mask. On returning to Tokyo, the author visits his own wife in a hospital, where she playfully places one of these masks on her own face. He is horrified by perceiving the ugliness and haggardness of her features in contrast with the beauty of the mask. He meditates on the commonplace that life is ugly but art is beautiful, and he concludes that everyone's smile may be artificial, but he cannot decide whether art in itself is a good thing.

Kawabata gives another unflattering view of life and his own personality in "Kinjū" ("Of Birds and Beasts"). The misanthropic protagonist en route to attend the dance recital of a discarded mistress reflects on a pair of dead birds that he had left at home. Musing that the "love of birds and animals comes to be a quest for superior ones, and so cruelty takes root," he finds a likeness in the expression of his former mistress, at the time of her first sexual yielding, to the placid reaction of a female dog while giving birth to puppies. When he encounters the dancer as she is being made up in her dressing room, he envisions her face as it would be in the coffin. Although the story reveals, as he later admitted, that it was written in a fit of cantankerousness, it embodies the serious theme that human and animal kingdoms share the final destiny of death.

In "Hokuro no Tegami" ("The Mole"), Kawabata looks at life from a woman's perspective, delineating a wife's obsession with a physical flaw. Designed to reveal how the process of loving and being loved differs in men and women, "The Mole" consists of a letter from a wife to her separated husband, describing the disintegration of their marriage in which a bodily blemish acts as a catalyst. Ever since childhood, the wife had played with the mole, shaped like a bean, a female sex symbol in Japan. The habit had at first merely irritated the husband, later driven him to beat her, and eventually induced his indifference. On one occasion, the wife dreamed that the mole came off and she asked him to place it next to a mole on his own nose, wondering whether it would then increase in size. This image of gender reversal suggests what is wrong with the marriage. Her obsession with the mole represents an expression of love that proved counterproductive because the husband failed to recognize its true nature. Although the wife's dilemma arouses the reader's sympathy, Kawabata may have had opposite intentions, since he had originally given the story the title "Bad Wife's Letter."

The feminine perspective is dominant also in "Suigetsu" ("The Moon on the Water"), a story of reciprocated love combining the themes of death, beauty, and sexuality. The story concerns a hand mirror that a dying husband uses while lying in bed to watch the processes of nature outside of his window. The moon as such appears in the narrative in only two sentences, where it is seen in the mirror as itself the reflection of a reflection, thereby introducing the philosophical problem of the nature of reality. The moon in the water is without substance, but in Zen Buddhism, the reflected moon is conversely the real moon and the moon in the sky is the illusion. The moon is also a symbol of virginity, relevant to the wife's continence, enforced by the husband's illness during nearly the entire period of her marriage. After the husband dies, the woman remarries and no longer feels shy when a man praises the beauty of her body. At the same time, she realizes that human anatomy prevents her from seeing her own face, except as a reflection in a mirror. She had loved her first husband because she imagined while he was dying that he had been a child inside her, and she is puzzled because she does not feel an equal degree of devotion toward her second husband. She, nevertheless, becomes pregnant and then revisits the area where she had lived during her first marriage. At the end of the story, she asks, "What if the child should look like you?" leaving the reader with uncertainty concerning the antecedent of the pronoun. The reveries of this paradoxically innocent woman in a second marriage combine and recombine the sexual, the aesthetic, and the metaphysical.

The same elements form Kawabata's somewhat sensational novella *The House of the Sleeping Beauties*, combining lust, voyeurism, and necrophilia with virgin worship and Buddhist metaphysics. The house is an imaginary brothel in which the patrons, old men approaching senility, sleep with naked virgins who are drugged into insensibility. The protagonist is exceptional in that he still has the physical capacity of breaking a house rule against seeking ultimate sexual satisfaction, but he resists the impulse. The circumstances of the story array the beauty of youth and purity against the ugliness of old age and death. Further contrasts are introduced in the protagonist's subsequent visits to the house, in each of which a different girl evokes erotic passages from his early life. The various beauties could be interpreted as composite recollections or dreamlike fantasies from his past. In the three last visits, his sexual meditations are intermixed with thoughts of death, and he asks to be given for his own use the potent drug administered to the girls. The five visits as a whole suggest the human life span, the first featuring a lovely girl, representing "life itself" and giving off the "milky scent of a nursing baby," and the last portraying the actual death and abrupt carrying away of one of the sleeping beauties.

A related story, "Kataude" ("One Arm"), can be interpreted as either more bizarre or more delicate in its eroticism. A young virgin takes off her arm and gives it to a somewhat older man, who takes it home and carries on a conversation with it as he lies in bed, a conversation that makes him recollect the sexual surrender of a previous acquaintance. Along with the erotic descriptions of the arm in contact with parts of the man's body, the narrative introduces New Testament quotations concerning pure and sacrificial love. On one level, the arm is simply a symbol of a woman giving herself sexually to a man, but it may also represent the loneliness of a man who is deprived of a companion with whom to share his thoughts.

Other major works

NOVELS: *Izu no odoriko,* 1926 (*The Izu Dancer,* 1955); *Asakusa kurenaidan,* 1930; *Matsugo no me,* 1930; *Kinjū,* 1933 (*Of Birds and Beasts,* in *The House of the Sleeping Beauties and Other Stories,* 1969); *Hana no warutsu,* 1936; *Hokura no nikki,* 1940 (*The Mole,* 1955); *Utsukushii tabi,* 1947; *Yukiguni,* 1947 (*Snow Country,* 1956); *Otome no minato,* 1948; *Asakusa monogatari,* 1950; *Sembazuru,* 1952 (*Thousand Cranes,* 1958); *Hi mo tsuki mo,* 1953; *Saikonsha,* 1953; *Suigetsu,* 1953 (*The Moon on the Water,* 1958); *Meijin,* 1954 (*The Master of Go,* 1972); *Kawa no aru shitamachi no hanashi,* 1954; *Tokyo no hito,* 1955; *Yama no oto,* 1957 (*The Sound of the Mountain,* 1970); *Mizuumi,* 1961 (*The Lake,* 1974); *Nemureru bijo,* 1961 (*The House of the Sleeping Beauties,* in *The House of the Sleeping Beauties and Other Stories,* 1969); *Kyoto,* 1962 (*The Old Capital,* 1987); *Kataude,* 1965 (*One Arm,* 1967); *Utsukushisa to kanashimi to,* 1965 (*Beauty and Sadness,* 1975); *Shōsetsu nyumon,* 1970; *Aru hito no sei no naka ni,* 1972; *Tampopo,* 1972.

NONFICTION: *Jūrukosai no nikki,* 1925; *Shinshin sakka no shinkeikō kaisetsu,* 1925; *Bungakuteki jijoden,* 1934; *Rakka ryusui,* 1966; *Bi no sonzai to hakken/The Existence and Discovery of Beauty,* 1969 (bilingual); *Utsukushii nihon no watakushi/ Japan, the Beautiful, and Myself,* 1969 (bilingual); *Isso ikka,* 1973; *Nihon no bi no kokoro,* 1973.

TRANSLATIONS: *Ocho monogatari shū,* 1956-1958 (of ancient Japanese stories); *Isoppu,* 1968 (of *Aesop's Fables*).

MISCELLANEOUS: *Kawabata Yasunari zenshū,* 1948-1969.

Bibliography

Keene, Donald. *Dawn to the West: Japanese Literature of the Modern Era.* New York: Holt, Rinehart and Winston, 1984. Fifty-nine pages by this eminent critic and translator of Japanese fiction are devoted to Kawabata. Traces many of Kawabata's themes to his childhood experiences and gives the circumstances of publication and reception of his major works. Keene believes that Kawabata's main preoccupations were Japanese landscapes, Japanese women, and Japanese art. Contains a bibliography and extensive notation.

Petersen, Gwenn Boardman. *The Moon in the Water: Understanding Tanizaki, Kawabata, and Mishima.* Honolulu: University Press of Hawaii, 1979. An excellent critical study, emphasizing nuances of Japanese style and culture. Includes a chronology, a bibliography and explanatory notes.

Swann, Thomas E., and Kinya Tsuruta. *Approaches to the Modern Japanese Short Story.* Tokyo: Waseda University Press, 1982. Analyzes "The Izu Dancer," *The House of the Sleeping Beauties,* and "One Arm."

Ueda, Makoto. *Modern Japanese Writers and the Nature of Literature.* Stanford, Calif.: Stanford University Press, 1976. Devoting forty-five pages to Kawabata, this distinguished Japanese scholar emphasizes the elements of positive thought and action, vitality, beauty, and purity in Kawabata's work. Complemented by a bibliography and an index.

A. Owen Aldridge

1324

GARRISON KEILLOR

Born: Anoka, Minnesota; August 7, 1942

Principal short fiction

G. K. the DJ, 1977; *Happy to Be Here*, 1982; *Lake Wobegon Days*, 1985; *Leaving Home: A Collection of Lake Wobegon Stories*, 1987; *We Are Still Married: Stories and Letters*, 1989.

Other literary forms

Garrison Keillor began his literary career in 1960 as a radio comedian appearing on Minnesota Public Radio. From 1974 to 1987, he hosted a live weekly radio show based in St. Paul, Minnesota, entitled *A Prairie Home Companion*, a variety format that included original monologues that he called "News from Lake Wobegon." Offered as a premium to Minnesota Public Radio contributors, Keillor's *The Selected Verse of Margaret Haskins Durber* (1979) includes fourteen poems about Minnesota that he had read or sung on the air. The short fiction that he subsequently published is largely rooted in the twenty-minute monologues that he composed for his radio shows and that revolve around the places and characters of the mythical Lake Wobegon, Minnesota, in Mist (missed) County.

Some of his monologues have also been released on audiocassette tapes, videocassettes, and compact disc recordings. Keillor's short-fiction pieces began appearing in *The New Yorker* in 1970. Beginning in 1989, Keillor hosted from New York City the weekly radio broadcast *American Radio Company of the Air*, a variety format, which likewise included original monologues, some of which have been anthologized in print or on tape.

Achievements

Keillor, along with Spalding Gray and Eric Bogosian, has achieved fame as one of the most accomplished monologuists in the last half of the twentieth century. His written production initially grew out of both his live and his recorded performances and has succeeded largely because his reputation as a performer preceded the publications. He is a homespun humorist with a droll, low-key, tongue-in-cheek style. His rambling tales emanated from poking fun at the fictional characters of his mythical Lake Wobegon, Minnesota, "the little town that time forgot and that decades cannot improve."

Besides having created and hosted nationally acclaimed radio shows and published best-selling books, Keillor has continued to be a regular contributor to *The New Yorker*. He received a Grammy Award for his recording of *Lake Wobegon Days* and two Awards for Cable Excellence for the Disney Channel productions of *A Prairie Home Companion*. He has also received a George Foster Peabody Broadcasting award and an Edward R. Murrow award. He has appeared with the Chicago, Minnesota, Milwaukee, San Francisco, Pittsburgh, and National symphony orchestras, and in a performance entitled "Lake Wobegon Tonight" at the Apollo Theatre in London.

Biography

Garrison Keillor's roots in small-town Minnesota provided him with the particular brand of midwestern humor that brought him fame and on which he continued to capitalize even after relocating to New York City. Born Gary Edward Keillor, he was the third of six children in the family of John P. Keillor, a railway mail clerk and carpenter, and Grace Denham Keillor. When he was in the eighth grade, he adopted the pen name "Garrison" in place of his given names because, he said, he believed that it sounded "more formidable." He grew up just north of Minneapolis, Minnesota, south of the small town of Anoka in what has since become Brooklyn Park. After his 1960 graduation from Anoka High School, he enrolled in the University of Minnesota, authored a regular column, published stories in the student magazine *The Ivory Tower*, which he later edited, and was student announcer for KUOM, the university radio station. He received a B.A. in English and journalism in 1966, went to New York in an unsuccessful attempt to land a job as a writer, returned to work on a master's degree in English, and then took a job with KSJR-FM in Collegeville, the first station in the Minnesota Public Radio network.

Keillor spent fourteen years on and off, from 1968 to 1982, as a disc jockey in St. Paul, Minnesota. His earliest program, *The Prairie Home Morning Show*, eventually included anecdotes about a mythical Midwestern place that he called Lake Wobegon, situated in the similarly mythical Mist County. One of the hallmarks of the program was inclusion of advertisement from bogus sponsors: Powdermilk Biscuits, Jack's Auto Repair, Bertha's Kitty Boutique, and Ralph's Pretty Good Grocery, among others. Besides broadcasting, Keillor was busy writing. He sold his first story, "Local Family Keeps Son Happy," to *The New Yorker* in 1970, then moved with his wife and small son to a farm near Freeport, Minnesota. He was divorced in 1976.

Modeled after the Grand Ole Opry in Nashville, Tennessee, Keillor's first live segment of *A Prairie Home Companion* aired on July 6, 1974. The monologues, advertisements, and musical entertainment were highlights of the program. Eleven years later, one of the show's monologues concerned a twenty-fifth high school class reunion in which the narrator, Keillor, rekindles an acquaintance with a foreign exchange student that blossoms into a romance. The monologue was biographical in the sense that, at his own class reunion at Anoka High School, Keillor had established a real-life relationship with Ulla Skaerved, Danish exchange student twenty-five years earlier, and they were married on December 29, 1985, in Denmark.

A Prairie Home Companion continued in weekly radio broadcasts for thirteen years, culminating in a farewell performance on June 13, 1987. During these years, Keillor anthologized his monologues on recordings and in books. Perhaps a disenchantment with his celebrity status and an irritation with newspaper reporters in

St. Paul, who printed what Keillor believed to be private information about himself, resulted in Keillor and his new wife relocating to Denmark for a short while, then settling in New York City. There, he continued to write for *The New Yorker* and host a weekly radio broadcast entitled *American Radio Company of the Air.*

Analysis

Garrison Keillor's upbringing in a small town in central Minnesota is the single greatest influence on his work. Many of the experiences and characters that appear in his short fiction are rooted in memories of events that happened to him there or of people whom he knew. In fact, the name for his radio show *A Prairie Home Companion* is taken from a cemetery in Moorhead, Minnesota, called Prairie Home Lutheran Cemetery.

The theme of religion—specifically Christianity—is the most frequently explored concept in Keillor's work. He has, in fact, described *A Prairie Home Companion* as "a gospel show." Growing up, Keillor and his family were members of the Plymouth Brethren, a Protestant sect of Anglican dissenters that closely resembles the "fundamentalists" and the "Sanctified Brethren" in his published works. His upbringing was a conservative one, where drinking, smoking, dancing, attending movies, and watching television were frowned upon; consequently Keillor writes with a conservative, instructional, and highly moral tone. A piece in one of his early books is entitled "Your Wedding and You: A Few Thoughts on Making It More Personally Rewarding, Shared by Reverend Bob Osman." Here, Keillor offers, tongue in cheek, prudent advice and practical suggestions on how to tailor a wedding ceremony to fit the personalities of the bride and groom. A couple he calls Sam and Judy, for example, "chose to emphasize their mutual commitment to air and water quality, exchanging vows while chained to each other and to the plant gate of a major industrial polluter."

Throughout his writing, Keillor writes about ordinary events that evoke a natural piety, *memento mori*, along with an awareness of the transience of all things. His philosophy is consistent with the Christian doctrine that life is basically good. Some of the pieces, for example, offer metaphors for the Christian promise of eternal life. A quotation from "State Fair," a piece that appears in *Leaving Home: A Collection of Lake Wobegon Stories*, perhaps best illustrates this. In it, the narrator remembers riding the Ferris wheel as a child:

> [W]e go up and I think of people I knew who are dead and I smell fall in the air, manure, corn dogs, and we drop down into blazing light and blaring music. Every summer I'm a little bigger, but riding the ferris wheel, I feel the same as ever, I feel eternal. . . . The wheel carries us up high, high, high, and stops, and we sit swaying, creaking, in the dark, on the verge of death. . . . Then the wheel brings me down to the ground. We get off and other people get on. Thank you, dear God, for this good life and forgive us if we do not live it enough.

In other pieces, however, rebellion against his repressive upbringing surfaces in sarcasm, not all of it gentle or good-humored. The most notable example of this is an extended complaint, the "longest footnote in American fiction," entitled "95 Theses

95," which appears in *Lake Wobegon Days.* One of Keillor's important themes here is righteous anger at how the Midwest has shaped him. Keillor uses the character Johnny Tollefson, a fictional, angry son who returns to Lake Wobegon with a new wife from Boston, intent on nailing a set of written complaints about the repressive effects of putative parents and neighbors to the door of the Lutheran church, but "something in his upbringing made him afraid to pound holes in a good piece of wood." So, instead, the treatise becomes "lost" on the overloaded desk of the town's newspaper editor and ultimately appears as a footnote that spans twenty-three pages.

In this complaint, Keillor rails against religious strictures, fear of sexuality, fastidiousness, and his resultant ineptness at sustaining interpersonal relationships. A milder complaint is thesis 7, which states, "You have taught me to fear strangers and their illicit designs, robbing me of easy companionship, making me a very suspicious friend. Even among those I know well, I continue to worry: what do they *really* mean by liking me?" These complaints become increasingly bitter; thesis 14, for example, states:

> You taught me to trust my own incompetence and even now won't let me mash potatoes without your direct supervision. "Don't run the mixer so fast that you get them all over," you say, as if in my home, the walls are covered with big white lumps. I can't mow a lawn or hang tinsel on a Christmas tree or paint a flat surface in your presence without you watching, worried, pointing out the unevenness.

Thesis 21 shows Keillor's anger at having been brought up to feel guilty, "Suffering was its own reward, to be preferred to pleasure. As Lutherans, we viewed pleasure with suspicion. Birth control was never an issue with us. Nor was renunciation of pleasures of the flesh. We never enjoyed them in the first place."

This is an imposing example of Keillor's sarcasm, but it is just as important to bear in mind his knack for comedy, which is, ultimately, more prevalent in his work. With deliberate pacing and mild surprise, many of his stories are gentle, nostalgic, and quiet. Finally, he celebrates, rather than satirizes, the Sanctified Brethren. He believes that, despite ridiculous situations and smallness or meanness in certain people, "life is a comedy" because "God is the author, and God writes an awful lot of comedy." Although he laughs at how foolish humankind can be, it is a good-natured laughter that has his characters' best interests at heart.

When one of Keillor's characters, Clarence Bunsen, discovered that what he thought was a heart attack in the shower one day really was not, he was so grateful that he dropped a check into the collection plate at church the following Sunday, only to realize moments later that he had mistakenly made it out for three hundred dollars instead of thirty, thus cleaning out his bank account.

Lake Wobegon's visitation by twenty-four Lutheran ministers ends in a disaster that is really humorous. Pastor Inqvist had arranged an outing for the clergy on a pontoon boat owned by Wally of the Sidetrack Tap, but the combined weight of all the earnest ministers each holding a can of beer was too much for the *Agnes D.* She took on more water than Wally could bail out, forcibly introducing eight of the clergy to the Baptist heresy of full immersion. Soon, all the ministers were standing chin deep in water, faces uplifted, unable to call out for help "because their voices were too deep and mellow," and "trying to understand this experience and its deeper meaning."

Family gatherings at which his great uncle and aunt told long tales were also influential on Keillor. Keillor often calls himself a "shy person," and, in fact, humorously advocates "shy rights" in some of his tales. His quietly reserved and remote personality is immediately evident in listening to his radio broadcasts. Not surprisingly, one of Keillor's main themes is an idealization of home and family relationships, and another is the evanescence of home. Many of his tales, as well as the title for one of his books, concern his relationship with home.

Happy to Be Here collected witty and urbane pieces that Keillor initially wrote for periodical publication. Though the book includes no Lake Wobegon material, it pokes fun at small-town life in its sly humor and bucolic optimism. Keillor uses an ordinary Minnesota farm as his setting for the ideal "home": "Found paradise. Here it is, and it is just what I knew was here all along. . . . I'm happy to be here." Here also Keillor parodies the styles of writing in magazines such as *Life* and *Rolling Stone*, the swagger of political figures, and the unchecked optimism, grand designs, and little moral dilemmas of his midwestern characters. Two of the pieces, "WLT (The Edgar Era)" and "The Slim Graves Show," draw on his radio experience, and many offer rules to live by or recount lessons that he has learned from life.

Prompted by the popularity of the monologues in *A Prairie Home Companion* broadcasts, Keillor offered in *Lake Wobegon Days* an extended history and geography of the mythical town of Lake Wobegon. Although giving abundant detail of a specific place, Keillor insists on the universality of his myth because he believes that places like it exist everywhere. The book has a pattern of development that is both chronological and seasonal. It chronicles the founding of the town by early settlers and the establishment of its traditions. Emphasizing the cycle of seasons, it also recounts the personal story of a little boy growing up among the Sanctified Brethren, envious of Catholics and Lutherans, who becomes a restless adolescent.

Leaving Home: A Collection of Lake Wobegon Stories is the title of Keillor's second book of Lake Wobegon stories, published after Keillor ended his association with Minnesota Public Radio and moved to Denmark and then, soon afterward, to New York City. If *Lake Wobegon Days* defined the stable and slightly sentimentalized mid-American town, *Leaving Home: A Collection of Lake Wobegon Stories* portrays it in flux and recombination, emphasizing the transience of all things. Every story recounts some kind of leave-taking or homecoming: a waitress quitting her job at the Chatterbox Café, a boy joining the army, Father Emil retiring from Our Lady of Perpetual Responsibility Catholic Church, family members returning to Lake Wobegon for Christmas. During this time, Keillor himself married a second time and left Minnesota, so the book is significant biographically as well as artistically. Keillor laments in the book's introduction that his home territory, Minneapolis and St. Paul, had changed, and not for the better. The Met Stadium, he notes, had been replaced by "a polyester ball field with a roof over it, a ghostly greenish plastic baseball mall, and all those lovely summer nights were lost." The book ends with Keillor himself taking leave of his characters: "This is my last view of [the residents of Lake Wobegon] for a while. If you see them before I do, say hello from me and give them my love."

We Are Still Married: Stories and Letters is a challenging set of essays about life on the edge. The stories are cryptic, cynical, suave, and aggressive. In several, Keillor expresses explicit anger at the media. "My Life in Prison" is a vicious parody about what journalists have done to him. The title story is the piece that closes the book, which describes the near destruction of an ordinary marriage once the media move in to examine it. There is violence in the book as well as sadness and some midcareer anxiety. The rest rooms in New York City's subways are described as a hell unmatched by even the most primitive rural Minnesota gas stations, "full of garbage, filth, killer bees, Nazis, crack heads, [and] flies who carry AIDS." Annie Szemanski is a tobacco-spitting, brass-kneed feminist baseball player in "What Did We Do Wrong?" who insults and abuses her ardent fans. Even the five sketches devoted to Lake Wobegon characters are more complicated and sophisticated than his earlier stories had been, depicting raw emotion and a bit of meanness.

More than one critic of Keillor's work has compared his particular brand of humor and storytelling to that of Mark Twain. Both authors are distinctly American, offering homespun profoundities and cracker-barrel philosophy that are regional in inception and origin. Both tell tall-tales with digressive anecdotes. Both mock pretense, portray comic suffering, and reveal the near-universal indignities of youth. As platform performers, both share the belief that a good tale should be heard as well as read, and both pose as overeager, inept but perceptive witnesses to life experiences. The rich imagination evident in the writings of both authors can be enjoyed by scholars of humor as well as ordinary people who simply want to laugh.

Other major works

NOVEL: *WLT: A Radio Romance*, 1991.
POETRY: *The Selected Verse of Margaret Haskins Durber*, 1979.
RECORDINGS: *A Prairie Home Companion Anniversary Album*, 1980; *News from Lake Wobegon*, 1983; *Ten Years on the Prairie: "A Prairie Home Companion" Tenth Anniversary*, 1984; *Gospel Birds and Other Stories of Lake Wobegon*, 1985; *A Prairie Home Companion: The Final Performance*, 1987; *A Prairie Home Companion: The Second Annual Farewell Performance*, 1988; *A Prairie Home Companion: The Third Annual Farewell Performance*, 1989; *More News from Lake Wobegon*, 1989; *Local Man Moves to the City*, 1991.

Bibliography

Fedo, Michael. *The Man from Lake Wobegon*. New York: St. Martin's Press, 1987. Fedo's biography of Keillor, from early childhood until his departure from Minnesota, is an unauthorized biography. Keillor refused to be interviewed by Fedo and encouraged his staff and the performers on his show to do likewise. Still, Fedo reveals close particulars of Keillor's personal life, his interests and influences, and the phenomenon of his popularity. Particularly useful is Fedo's four-page bibliography, which includes published interviews and articles about Keillor.

Lee, Judith Yaross. *Garrison Keillor: A Voice of America.* Jackson: University Press of Mississippi, 1991. Written with Keillor's consent and input, Lee's scholarly book is primarily a critical study of Keillor's comic imagination. The biographical information is of secondary importance to the focus of the book, which traces the development of Keillor's monologue and the evolution of the themes and techniques used in Keillor's broadcast performances. Lee includes extensive annotation to each chapter, an appendix with the dates of Keillor's published monologues, a comprehensive bibliography of Keillor's works from 1962-1989, and a listing of select secondary criticism.

Scholl, Peter A. "Garrison Keillor." In *Dictionary of Literary Biography, 1987 Yearbook*, edited by J. M. Brook. Detroit: Gale Research, 1988. A very good introduction to Keillor's life and works, giving insights into Keillor's personality, motivation, and career. Recounts the early influences of his literary heroes and of the Grand Ole Opry. Discusses Keillor's childhood, education, and individual published works in some detail and chronicles Keillor's involvement in radio broadcasting.

_____. "Garrison Keillor and the News from Lake Wobegon." *Studies in American Humor* 4 (Winter, 1985-1986): 217-228. Comparing Keillor to Will Rogers and Mark Twain, Scholl stresses the regional, homespun character of Keillor's work. He also draws a distinction between two Keillors, "that of wandering storyteller in exile from Lake Wobegon and that of the urbane wit and writer for *The New Yorker.*" Scholl discusses the unique brand of storytelling that Keillor uses in his monologues, a combination of spontaneity and studied elegance that is evident in the oral narratives as well as on the printed page. He stresses Keillor's focus on the "continuity and resilience of human life" and on the belief that "God is good."

Skow, John. "Let's Hear It for Lake Wobegon!" *Reader's Digest* 128 (February, 1986): 67-71. The inviting and immediate tone of this article makes it very engaging. It details a public performance of a segment of *A Prairie Home Companion* and, in doing so, relates explicitly the tone and mood that infuses all Keillor's work. Some biographical information gives insight into Keillor's career as a performer.

Traub, James. "The Short and Tall Tales of Garrison Keillor." *Esquire* 97 (May, 1982): 108-117. This article, in part an interview, contains an early yet detailed look at Keillor's performance techniques. Formative influences from childhood, college, and adulthood are recounted. Much attention is paid to Keillor's method and technique of written composition as well as the evolution of *A Prairie Home Companion.*

Jill B. Gidmark

BENEDICT KIELY

Born: Dromore, County Tyrone, Northern Ireland; August 15, 1919

Principal short fiction

A Journey to the Seven Streams, 1963; *A Ball of Malt and Madame Butterfly*, 1973; *A Cow in the House*, 1978; *The State of Ireland*, 1980; *A Letter to Peachtree*, 1987.

Other literary forms

Benedict Kiely has published several novels, three of which are set in his native Northern Ireland; others are set mainly in Dublin or in a mixture of Northern Ireland and Ireland topography. *There Was an Ancient House* (1955) is based on his year as a Jesuit novice; *Proxopera* (1977) deals with violence in Northern Ireland in the 1970's. His nonfiction includes *Counties of Contention* (1945), on Northern Ireland; *Poor Scholar* (1947), a life of the nineteenth century Irish novelist William Carleton; and *Modern Irish Fiction* (1950), literary criticism. For many years Kiely has written weekly travel pieces for the *Irish Times*; he has also published numerous book reviews and critical essays.

Achievements

Kiely's approach to short fiction is typically discursive, episodic, and anecdotal, because of the nature of his material as well as his artistic apprehension of it. Kiely's material is drawn less from his own imagination than from the things people say, or write, or sing. His artistic rendering of the material comes from his well-developed sense of oral tradition. This sense is alert not only to the delight of utterance but also to the ways in which utterance stimulates memory and how stories illustrate, like shadow plays, the trials of loss and love that characterize the human journey.

The outcome of these orientations is a body of short fiction that speaks to the rich verbal integument of Irish culture. The adaptation of oral tradition to the context of a society's growing pains is one of Kiely's most significant contributions to modern Irish writing. In addition, his fiction identifies strata of myth in the adventures and careers of its protagonists. This mythic dimension concerns journeying, unearthing, restoring, and rituals of arrival and departure. Kiely's sense of landscape wistfully evinces this dimension. The presence of an archetypal undertow is another means by which Kiely's work reinvigorates certain important strains of Irish literary culture. The flexible and informal conservatism of Kiely's artistic strategies are a distinctive accomplishment in what has been a time of rapid and unnerving change in Irish culture and society. He is a member of the Irish Academy of Letters and received an Honorary Doctorate of Letters from the National University of Ireland in 1984.

Biography

Benedict Kiely grew up in Omagh, County Tyrone, and was graduated from the

Christian Brothers School. He began writing for publication in 1936, entered a Jesuit novitiate in 1937 but resigned with a back injury in 1938, and thereafter was graduated from University College, Dublin, in 1943. In addition to his prolific fiction production, Kiely had a distinguished career as a newspaperman in Dublin, holding among other influential positions that of literary editor of *The Irish Press*, a national daily. Much of the material for his short fiction is drawn from his days as a working journalist. He has also held various teaching positions in the United States. Kiely settled in Dublin, where his reputation as a broadcaster, raconteur, and all-around man of letters exceeds his artistic renown.

Analysis

Benedict Kiely's Northern Ireland background, his attachment to both Ireland and Northern Ireland, his reminiscences about them, his love of poetry, his humor and irony—all can be found in his favorite stories, including "A Cow in the House," "A Ball of Malt and Madame Butterfly," "Down Then by Derry," "A Journey to the Seven Streams," "Bluebell Meadow," and "Maiden's Leap." All of these stories were written between 1960 and 1975; the last three named were first published in *The New Yorker.*

"A Cow in the House" relates a childhood experience of Kiely on his first trip from Omagh to Dublin when the journey was prepared for by an amateurish and embarrassing haircut by a local barber who, for further humiliation, kept a cow in his house. From such adverse beginnings, the child must also clack through Dublin with a loose heel; and his self-consciousness causes him to make another mistake when he sings a bawdy song for a group of nuns. The day's series of disasters turns only when he visits a hall of mirrors, where he becomes conscious of the imperfections of other people; all have "big noses, red faces, legs too long or short, behinds that waggled, clothes that didn't fit. Every one of them had a cow in the house."

Perhaps Kiely's penchant for travelogues derives from his father, who had traveled to South Africa to fight in the Boer War. Kiely reminisces about him in "A Journey to the Seven Streams," in which the father conducts the family among Northern Ireland towns in the vicinity of Omagh and recites history as he points out important features of the landscape. A rickety car, in the days when cars were few, and the family's wry comments on it, provide much of the humor of this story. To the owner the car is "human," but it stops and refuses to start without being pushed uphill; it frightens livestock and attracts congregations. Returning to Omagh, the family decides that decorum demands they alight from the car at the town's entrance and walk the rest of the way home.

At the opposite extreme from youthful remembrance is "A Ball of Malt and Madame Butterfly." To write about his queen of the streets, Kiely chooses the ancient and beautiful symbol of female erotica, the butterfly, and surrounds his Madame Butterfly with attitudes of humor and endearment. This Butterfly owes little but a slightly Japanese appearance to the Puccini opera and her basic occupation, at least, to Guy de Maupassant's story "Ball of Suet." Her favorite "hangout" in Dublin is a pub called the Dark Cow, and "What she is her mother was before her, and proud of it."

The story begins with just a touch of prejudice against prostitutes, unpopular though such sentiment is among Butterfly's loyal followers, the men of the fire brigade. A ladder raised to a smoking upstairs window focuses attention on a partly dressed male who shoves a woman back into the room so that he can escape first. Indignation turns to laughter when Butterfly emerges, and the firemen subsequently make certain that the ungallant man's wife and hometown hear about his deeds.

Images of flight now focus on birds which, like cows, are favored in Irish mythology but, unlike cows, have the further advantage of romantic enhancement by the poet William Butler Yeats and all his entourage of poetry enthusiasts, one of whom is a lonely, shy, forty-year-old Dublin bachelor named Pike Hunter. Painfully self-conscious, he passes through Stephen's Green, where women on park benches seem as "gracefully at rest as the swans on the lake." Then Pike sees the poet himself and observes a touching meeting of Yeats and Maud Gonne in their old age and all their majesty; the sight of Maud Gonne recalls for Pike the poem "When You Are Old" and that "one man loved the pilgrim soul in you, and loved the sorrows of your changing face." His knowledge of a former meeting on Howth Head and the poems "His Phoenix" and "The White Birds" furthers his romantic inclinations, for next he walks into the Dark Cow, frequented by dockers, and into the acquaintance of Butterfly. She will become his personal "phoenix" as in Yeats's poem, the means for him of his transformation and his pilgrimage. The lines "I would that we were, my beloved, white birds on the foam of the sea" will lead later to Butterfly's flight away from Pike. Although Pike knows other poets as well, it is Ireland's greatest that causes his downfall.

Drunk on poetry, views, and visions, Pike buys champagne for Butterfly and meets her fireman friend, Austin, who knew Butterfly's dance hall mother and who always orders "A ball of malt" and adds "and Madame Butterfly" as a joke. Pike becomes acquainted with Jody, the pub owner, and with Butterfly's "stable of girls," all of whom have never before seen the like of Pike Hunter. His lovemaking reminds Butterfly of a Christian Brother: he soon has her "puked" with his continual recitations of poetry, and he loves her with a singularity of devotion that interferes with her normal trade. Nor does she appreciate his efforts to keep the relationship unmercenary by failing to pay her for every performance. Meanwhile, Butterfly invests Jody's five pound note at the races and then buys with her profits a musquash coat of such elegance that she wears it for everything, including a trip to Howth Head to walk around the mountain as the poet had done with Maud Gonne. She could have tolerated the rough walk in high-heeled shoes, topped with a broken heel, the hot sun running sweat under her fur coat, the delays for mending the heel and the resultant shivers when the sun sank; but that the shy Pike should—under the inspiration of poetry—turn into a violent rapist and attempt to flatten her on Howth proves too much indignity for Butterfly, who prefers the privacy of a rumpled bed. The resultant quarrelsome fault-finding ends the relationship.

Thereafter, Pike returns drunk, only once, to the Dark Cow, where efforts to cheer him up fail and evoke from him only a comment, "Boys, Beethoven when he was dying, said: Clap now, good friends, the comedy is done." His aunts, who had presided over his extended virginity, soon find him impossible to live with and place him in Saint Patrick's Hospital where another Irish writer, Dean Swift, "died roaring." Jody dies and his successor ousts all the girls from the Dark Cow. Austin meets Butterfly some time later on O'Connell Street under the Nelson Pillar and tells her the story of the slavey whom Lord Nelson took for wife and made Lady Emma Hamilton. From this Butterfly apparently takes inspiration and eventually marries a dock worker. In this way Kiely blends two of his favorite themes: the literary and historic past of his country and the literary-minded character who quotes poetry, mostly at inopportune moments to unappreciative audiences. In "Maiden's Leap" the protagonist is a writer, Robert St. Blaise Macmahon, whose pride in superiority to his maidenly cousin suffers a rude fall.

Kiely sets "Maiden's Leap" in his home town of Omagh, a garrison town whose people Robert Macmahon despises for their pettiness; but then Robert regards nearly everything as somewhat beneath him: the United States, which he visited and in which he was the only person with sense enough to admire the alligators; Yeats and Joyce, who are "colossal bores"; the town, because his father had "as good as owned it"; his housekeeper and cousin-once-removed, Miss Hynes; and any fleshly contact with other people. He has pride of ancestry and no desire for progeny. At age forty-one with a spinsterish and impoverished housekeeper two years older than himself, he condescends to the civic guard until the man's mission—to inform him of a dead body in the spinster's bed—registers in his consciousness. Yet the dead man, having died "Unhouselled, unappointed, unannealed," as Robert says, evokes from the guard a comment that Robert concedes mentally is worthy of repetition elsewhere: the dead man could not expect the company of a resident chaplain. Robert's thinking in quotations leads him to urge the guard, in the words of Henry James, to "Try to be one of those on whom nothing is lost"; yet the supreme irony of the story is that much is lost on Robert. While awaiting removal of the corpse, Robert learns from the guard good, human stories about the deceased: he once bought and lost—through the open back door of a van—two hundred hens; his brother, a gardener, had died on a lawnmower when it exploded beneath him—lives that would make good writing and that other people live while Robert looks down his nose; yet, again ironically, he despises the Cyrano de Bergerac nose of the corpse. His chief concern about the corpse in his housekeeper's bed is that he, Robert, will be laughed at by the community, "clods he had always regarded with a detached and humorous, yet godlike, eye."

As the guard departs, Robert sits in the room of Miss Hynes and remembers when he tried to kiss her at age sixteen and she slapped him. That she has for many years concealed a lover in his ancestral mansion fails to change his pitying opinion of her. She had come to him an orphan from the cliffs of Glenade, north of Manorhamilton in County Leitrim, where legend described a woman who had leaped from a cliff to save her virtue and smashed to her death on the rocks below; Robert imagined his housekeeper having made a similar leap to his hearthside, where, as a poor relation, she lived a death of all romantic hopes. The image from a book, that of the virile Golden Asse of Lucius Apuleius, that he tried to live with her in a fleeting moment at age sixteen, he had imagined to have been her last prospect for romantic entanglement.

Now he begins reading her diary, however, and finds that, much to his chagrin, instead of admiring him as he deserves to be admired, instead of playing the role of a poor relation grateful to her benefactor, she has always ridiculed and satirized every aspect of his being—his handmade shoes, his writing books no one reads, his arrogance and aloofness which kept him from knowing anything interesting, his fondness for alligators in Florida. Yet the diary reveals her to be a good writer and a good critic, for she sees that "he was twisting life to suit his reading." She scourges him for his thoughtful criticism of the Irish for not marrying young; to her this is more of his ignorance of the conditions of their existence. Finally, he learns, she had rejected his advances when she was eighteen and he sixteen not because of what he was doing but because of the "stupid way he was trying to do it."

Miss Hynes, meanwhile, has made her escape early to report to the civic guard and kept herself at the guard's barracks, but she telephones back long enough to comment on Robert and on her diary. She proves in this conversation that she is in reality more than the housekeeper he has known, and, certainly, she is the witty and insightful writer he has discovered in the diary. She calls him, for his talking in quotations, a two-footed gramophone. Later, when as an employer he tries to demand her return to her duties, the guard informs him she has taken the train to Dublin. Her lover died, he concedes, "looking at the roses," and the two had met as growers of roses. Her second maiden's leap to Dublin is Macmahon's fall into wrenching, dismaying self-knowledge.

In a different perspective, the process by which adults impose their political and religious differences on the otherwise unifying factors of children's friendships is the theme of "Bluebell Meadow," set in Kiely's hometown of Omagh, dominated by the opposing symbols of the British army barracks and the Catholic church spires. From events and ways of the previous centuries, Catholics are called papishes and support the Free State (now the Republic of Ireland) to the south; Protestants are called Black Protestants and remain loyal to the Union (with Britain). Those moderates who would bridge the gap still have a sensitivity to the more intense feelings of others and let discretion dominate social interaction.

Kiely tells this story from the viewpoint of a sensitive teenage girl restricted by a leg brace and her blue convent school costume, but she reads much and has a mind that ranges far beyond this Northern Ireland town. Where she reads in a park, Lofty emerges from the nearby river and gives her one of his fresh-caught trout. His seeking her out she treats as mostly casual friendship; that he is "of the other persuasion" does not immediately occur to her, nor does it especially matter. She remembers a year earlier when Lofty's mother, met on a train to and from Bundoran, seemed "great fun" as she recited jokes and rhymes against both papishes and Protestants, laughed as she smuggled sugar from the Free State, conversed with the girl's uncle and agreed—Protestant and Catholic—on the defects of jerry-built houses.

The girl becomes acquainted with a sense of humor in Lofty and a sensitivity corresponding to her own: his knowing without asking that, in a leg brace, she would not choose to walk with him; his enjoyment of his three sisters who love the company of the British soldiers; his sisters teasing him about a nursemaid whose pram he pushed up a hill and who mistook him for a Catholic. Upon her accusation that he would not associate with her in public view, he did not correct her because she might not like her pram pushed by a Presbyterian.

Such pleasantries between Lofty and the girl are permitted to continue only from April to August, when a black man (not a Negro, but a member of the Black Perceptory of the Orange Order who wears a black sash in the July 12 Protestant parade) sits beside her on her park bench. After some agreeable conversation, he launches into the day's business—to separate her, in the names of God and country and for her own good, from Lofty. The reason, he explains, is that Lofty's uncle is a tiler, "a big man in the Orange Order," one who keeps intruders out and who is responsible to the Worshipful Master, which is himself. Lofty, he says, is a B-Special, a member of the British army pledged "to hold Ulster against the Pope and the Republic of Ireland," one who visits Catholics at night to ascertain their registration. In an irate moment, he adds, "The B-Specials are sworn to uphold Protestant liberty and beat down the Fenians and the I.R.A." It makes no difference to him that she is not a Fenian or a member of the Irish Republican Army, nor that she and Lofty are not thinking of marriage. With further warnings he departs on the terms of a big, friendly man trying to help her. Lofty's friendliness ceases.

At home a sergeant questions her about bullets Lofty had given her and she had placed in an earthenware jug, and she must accompany him to the station. To her uncle, who had seen bullets used in the United States, harboring bullets without a gun seems as harmless as it does to her, but the confiscation of the bullets given in friendship marks the vast division between the two families. Under British rule in the past, no Irish person was allowed to own a knife or gun or weapon of any kind. In spite of tolerance among individuals, the ships of state and church sail divided seas.

The most thoroughly autobiographical of Kiely's stories is "Down Then by Derry," in which the "he" or "dad" of the story is clearly an elderly Kiely, returning to scenes of childhood, recalling a letter from an American correspondent who also had lived in the area, visiting his eighty-five-year-old mother, and having for company a son and daughter. Here is Omagh, with its church spires and army barracks, the town where the rivers Drumragh and Camowen meet and go on "under the name of Strule," and a song about the Strule recurs in the visitor's thoughts. Memories of the past and of people who have traveled elsewhere merge with many nostalgic sights—a sycamore planted a hundred years before; a man who cut down a whitethorn, then saw two ghostly children and died that night with no other forewarning;

his mother's habit of spitting after mention of the devil. Some persons did not leave Omagh, however, and the remembered childhood romances climax in the appearance of an aged face, from which comes a stranger's recognition: "We saw you on the teevee." Her brother now sits in a wheelchair; she dismisses a childhood friend with a brief comment and goes away.

The main story concerns Omagh without military and civil strife. It differs from the reality of the 1970's which Kiely confronted at the close of "Bluebell Meadow": "There are burned-out buildings in the main streets, and barricades and checkpoints at the ends of the town. . . . Still, other towns are worse. Strabane, which was on the border and easy to bomb, is a burned-out wreck—and Newry. . . . And Derry is like Dresden on the day after." The bluebells were appropriate to the life described in "Down Then by Derry," and this former life is the life to remember.

Other major works

NOVELS: *Land Without Stars*, 1946; *In a Harbour Green*, 1949; *Call for a Miracle*, 1951; *Honey Seems Bitter*, 1952; *The Cards of the Gambler*, 1953; *There Was an Ancient House*, 1955; *The Captain with the Whiskers*, 1960; *Dogs Enjoy the Morning*, 1968; *Proxopera*, 1977; *Nothing Happens in Carmincross*, 1985.

NONFICTION: *Counties of Contention*, 1945; *Poor Scholar: A Study of the Works and Days of William Carleton, 1794-1869*, 1947; *Modern Irish Fiction: A Critique*, 1950; *All the Way to Bantry Bay and Other Irish Journeys*, 1978; *Dublin*, 1983; *Ireland from the Air*, 1985; *Yeats's Ireland: An Enchanted Vision*, 1989.

Bibliography

Casey, Daniel J. *Benedict Kiely.* Lewisburg, Pa.: Bucknell University Press, 1974. In this introductory essay, the author tends to cast Kiely as a traditional Irish storyteller. This approach is a reliable guide to one of Kiely's most important characteristics, but it needs to be developed more fully than in this rather generalized work.

Dunleavy, Janet Egleson. "Mary Lavin, Elizabeth Bowen, and a New Generation: The Irish Short Story at Midcentury." In *The Irish Short Story: A Critical History*, edited by James F. Kilroy. Boston: Twayne, 1984. The new generation in question is the one which emerged in the 1950's. Kiely is correctly identified as one of its important members. The case for Kiely's distinctive contribution to the genre is plausibly, if briefly, advanced. A sense of that contribution is clarified by Kiely being seen in the context of the Irish short-story's development.

Eckley, Grace. *Benedict Kiely.* Boston: Twayne, 1972. The most comprehensive account of Kiely's work. In particular, the significance of the relationship between his fiction and nonfiction is discussed. Kiely's novels also receive an attentive reading. Supplemented by a useful chronology and a bibliography.

Foster, John Wilson. *Forces and Themes in Ulster Fiction.* Dublin: Gill and Macmillan, 1974. The most incisive criticism of Kiely's work is to be found here, especially in pages 72 to 81 and 91 to 100. The author relates Kiely's work both to its social and literary backgrounds. In particular, the tendency of Kiely's fiction toward the mythic is the subject of much valuable discussion. The main focus of the discussion is Kiely's short fiction.

Scanlan, Margaret. "The Unbearable Present: Northern Ireland in Four Contemporary Novels." *Études Irlandaises: Revue Française d'Histoire, Civilisation, et Littérature de l'Irlande* 10 (1985): 145-161. Among the works considered is Kiely's novella about civil strife in Northern Ireland, *Proxopera*. Kiely is not generally considered a Northern Irish writer. Not to do so is to distort his achievement in certain key respects. The article isolates the distinct contribution made by *Proxopera* to contemporary writing about Northern Ireland.

Grace Eckley
(Revised by *George O'Brien*)

JAMAICA KINCAID
Elaine Potter Richardson

Born: St. Johns, Antigua, West Indies; May 25, 1949

Principal short fiction
At the Bottom of the River, 1983.

Other literary forms
In addition to her short stories, Jamaica Kincaid has written the novels *Annie John* (1985) and *Lucy* (1990); a book-length essay concerning her native island Antigua entitled *A Small Place* (1988); and a children's book, *Annie, Gwen, Lilly, Pam, and Tulip* (1986), with illustrations by Eric Fischl.

Achievements
Kincaid is noted for her lyrical use of language. Her short stories and novels have a hypnotic, poetic quality that results from her utilization of rhythm and repetition. Her images, drawn from her West Indian childhood, recall Antigua, with its tropical climate, Caribbean food, local customs, and folklore laced with superstitions. Many of her stories move easily from realism to surrealistic fantasy, as would a Caribbean folktale. She is also praised for her exploration of the strong but ambiguous bond between mother and daughter and her portrayal of the transformation of a girl into a woman. Thus her work touches upon the loss of innocence that comes when one moves out of the Eden that is childhood. These are the features that are found not only in her short fiction but also in her novels, the chapters of which *The New Yorker* originally published as short stories, and in *Annie, Gwen, Lilly, Pam, and Tulip*, a children's book that was part of a project designed by the Whitney Museum of American Art, the original publisher, who sought to bring together contemporary authors and artists for a series of limited editions aimed primarily at collectors.

Kincaid's concern with racism, colonialism, classism, and sexism is rooted in her history: "I never give up thinking about the way I came into the world, how my ancestors came from Africa to the West Indies as slaves. I just could never forget it. Or forgive it." She does not hesitate to tackle these issues in her writing. In her nonfictional *A Small Place*, she directs the force of her language toward an examination of her native island of Antigua, presenting the beauty as well as the racism and corruption rooted in its colonial past. In her fiction, these same issues are not slighted; for example, *Annie John* and *Lucy* address various forms of oppression and exploitation.

Her short-story collection *At the Bottom of the River* received the Morton Dauwen Zabel Award from the American Academy and Institute of Arts and Letters in 1983. Her novel *Annie John* was one of three finalists for the international Ritz Paris Hemingway Award in 1985.

Biography

Born in 1949, Jamaica Kincaid, then Elaine Potter Richardson, lived with her homemaker mother and carpenter father on Antigua, a small West Indian island measuring nine by twelve miles. The family was impoverished: their house had no running water or electricity. The young girl's chores included drawing water from a community faucet and registering with the public works so that the "night soil men" would dispose of the family's waste. Even so, her childhood was idyllic. She was surrounded by the extraordinary beauty of the island, was accepted by her community, and was loved and protected by her mother. When Kincaid was nine, however, her mother gave birth to the first of three more children—all boys. At that point, the closeness that Kincaid had enjoyed was at first disturbed and then destroyed. She credits the lies that she began to tell her mother as the catalyst for her fiction writing: "I wasn't really lying. I was protecting my privacy or protecting a feeling I had about something. But lying is the beginning of fiction. It was the beginning of my writing life." Also at this time, she began to comprehend the insidious impact of colonialism. (Antigua was a British colony until 1967, and only in 1981 did it receive full independence.) The Antiguans' docile acceptance of their inferior status enraged her. Thus the serenity she had known as a child was displaced by loneliness and anger.

In 1966, Kincaid, seeking to disassociate herself from her mother, left Antigua not to return for nineteen years and then only after she was a naturalized citizen of the United States and an established writer. Arriving in Scarsdale, New York, the seventeen-year-old Kincaid worked as a live-in baby-sitter. She did not open her mother's letters, and, when, after a few months, she took an au pair position in New York City, she did not send her mother her new address. For the next three years, she cared for the four young girls of Michael Arlen, a writer for *The New Yorker* and a future colleague when she herself would become a staff writer for the magazine. Her childhood and early New York experiences are fictionalized in *At the Bottom of the River*, *Annie John*, and *Lucy*.

During her first few years in New York, she wanted to continue her education at a university but found her Antiguan schooling to be inferior; instead, she first studied for a high school diploma, took a few photography courses at a community college, and then attended Franconia College in New Hampshire on scholarship, leaving after a year because, although only in her twenties, she felt too old. After jobs as a secretary and receptionist, she wrote for a teen magazine. In 1973, she changed her name to Jamaica Kincaid, perhaps suggesting that she had achieved her own identity. Associating with New York writers and artists, she met George Trow (*Lucy* is dedicated to him), who wrote "Talk of the Town" for *The New Yorker*. She collaborated on a few columns, and eventually one of her pieces was accepted by editor William Shawn, who was known for encouraging fledgling writers. In 1978, the magazine published her first short story, "Girl." Soon after, she married Allen Shawn, the editor's son. In 1983, her first collection, *At the Bottom of the River*, was published to generally favorable reviews, as was her subsequent work, which has earned for her a devoted following. She continued to write short stories, usually published in *The New Yorker*, and give lectures and readings. She and Allen Shawn, a composer and professor at Bennington College, along with their two children—Annie, named after her mother, and Harold—settled in Bennington, Vermont.

Analysis

Jamaica Kincaid's short stories, strongly autobiographical, are often set in the West Indies or incorporate images from the islands and include many events from her youth and young adulthood. In general, her stories chronicle the coming-of-age of a young girl. Because the mother-daughter relationship is central to the process, Kincaid often examines the powerful bond between them, a bond that the child must eventually weaken, if not break, in order to create her own identity. Kincaid has been accurately called "the poet of girlhood and place."

The first of the ten stories in *At the Bottom of the River* is the often praised and quoted "Girl." Barely two pages in length, the story outlines the future life of a young girl growing up on a small Caribbean island. The voice heard belongs to the girl's mother as she instructs her daughter in the duties that a woman is expected to fulfill in a culture with limited opportunities for girls. Twice the girl interrupts to offer a feeble protest, but her mother persists.

The girl is told how to wash, iron, and mend clothes; how to cook fritters and pepper pot; how to grow okra; and how to set the table—in short, everything that will enable her to care for a future husband. She is told how to smile, how to love a man, and how to get rid of an unborn baby should it be necessary. Most important, however, her mother warns her about losing her reputation because then the girl (and this is unsaid) loses her value as a potential wife. Almost as a refrain, the mother cautions, "[O]n Sundays try to walk like a lady and not like the slut you are so bent on becoming" or "[T]his is how to behave in the presence of men who don't know you very well, and this way they won't recognize immediately the slut I have warned you against becoming." On the island, a girl's most important asset is her virginity.

The language is a prime example of Kincaid's ability to work a hypnotic spell. The story consists of a series of variations of particular instructions: "[T]his is how to sew on a button; this is how to make a buttonhole for the button you have just sewed on; this is how to hem a dress when you see the hem coming down and so to prevent yourself from looking like the slut I know you are so bent on becoming." The rhythm and repetition create a lyric poetic quality that is present to some degree in all Kincaid's fiction. Her prose demands to be read out loud.

"Girl" suggests the child's future life on the island, but several stories in the collection re-create the atmosphere of her present existence. The story "In the Night" recounts her daily experiences. Thus, details such as crickets or flowers that would be important to her are recorded, often in the form of lists or catalogs: "The hibiscus flowers, the flamboyant flowers, the bachelor's buttons, the irises, the marigolds, the whiteheadbush flowers, lilies, the flowers on the daggerbush," continuing for a full paragraph. Here cataloging, a familiar feature of Kincaid's prose, represents a child's attempt to impose an order on her surroundings. The young narrator does not question her world but only reports what she observes. Thus witchcraft exists side by side with more mundane activities: "Someone is making a basket, someone is making a girl a dress or a boy a shirt . . . someone is sprinkling a colorless powder outside a closed door so that someone else's child will be still-born." This melding of the commonplace with the supernatural occurs frequently in Kincaid's fiction. The narrator's troubles, such as wetting the bed, are those of a child and are easily resolved by her mother. Her plans for the future, marrying a woman who will tell her stories, also are typical of a child. This is an idyllic world before the fall from innocence, a world in which everything is ordered, listed, and cataloged. Nothing is threatening, since the all-powerful mother protects and shields.

In several other stories, including "Wingless" and "Holidays," the girl is again shown to be occupied by the usually pleasant sensations of living: walking barefoot, scratching her scalp, or stretching, but sometimes, as illustrated in "Holidays," experiencing pain: "spraining a finger while trying to catch a cricket ball; straining a finger while trying to catch a softball; stepping on dry brambles while walking on the newly cut hayfields." The trauma, however, is clearly limited to physical sensations. When the child thinks of the future, the images are those of wishful thinking, similar to daydreams. This tranquil state of youth, however, is only temporary, as "Wingless" implies. The narrator, wingless, is still in the "pupa stage."

In "The Letter from Home," the narrator's growing awareness makes it impossible for her to maintain the comforting simplicity of her child's world. Questions about life and death intrude: "Is the Heaven to be above? Is the Hell below?" These inquiries, however, are set aside in favor of the present physical reality—a cat scratching a chair or a car breaking down. Even love and conception are reduced to the simplest terms: "[T]here was a bed, it held sleep; there was movement, it was quick, there was a being." She is not ready to confront the idea of death, so when death beckons, she "turned and rowed away."

Just as the philosophical questions about life and death disrupt the bliss of childhood, so does the journey toward selfhood, which Kincaid symbolically represents as a journey over rough or impassable terrain or water. In "What I Have Been Doing Lately," the obstacle is water: "I walked for I don't know how long before I came to a big body of water. I wanted to get across it but I couldn't swim. I wanted to get across it but it would take me years to build a boat. . . . I didn't know how long to build a bridge." Because the journey is difficult, as any passage to adulthood would be, the narrator is hesitant, afraid of finding the world not beautiful, afraid of missing her parents, so she goes back to bed: she is not ready yet. Soon, however, she will not have that option of retreating and waiting.

The journey toward selfhood necessitates a separation from the mother, as is suggested in the story "My Mother." The protection that was vital during childhood becomes stifling in adolescence: "Placing her arms around me, she drew my head closer and closer to her bosom, until finally I suffocated." Furthermore, the girl's feelings are ambiguous. Realizing that she has hurt her mother, she cries, but then she utilizes those tears to create a pond, "thick and black and poisonous," to form a barrier over which they "watched each other carefully." The all-protecting mother of the earlier stories transforms herself into a mythic monster and thus threatens the emerging selfhood of the daughter. The daughter, however, also grows "invincible" like her mother, and she, too, metamorphoses into a similar beast. Strong as the daughter has become, however, she can never vanquish her mother: "I had grown big, but my mother was bigger, and that would always be so." Only after the daughter completes her own journey toward selfhood is her mother no longer a threat: "as we walked along, our steps became one, and as we talked, our voices became one voice, and we were in complete union in every way. What peace came over me then, for I could not see where she left off and I began, or where I left off and she began."

The concluding and title story is also the longest in the collection, at about twenty pages. "At the Bottom of the River" suggests answers to the questions raised in the other stories. Again, Kincaid employs the symbol of a journey through forbidding terrain to suggest traveling through life. What is the purpose of the journey, for what does one ultimately face but death? One man, overwhelmed, does nothing. Another discovers meaning in his family, his work, and the beauty of a sunrise, but still, he struggles and "feels the futility." How can one live with the paralyzing knowledge that "[d]ead lay everything that had lived and dead also lay everything that would live. All had had or would have its season. And what should it matter that its season lasted five billion years or five minutes?" One possible response is suggested in the life of "a small creature" that lives in the moment, aware only of the sensation of grass underfoot or of the sting of a honeybee.

The narrator, who at first knew only the love of her mother, suffers from its necessary withdrawal. Adrift, she embarks on a symbolic journey in which she submerges herself in a river-fed sea. Discovering a solution at the bottom of the river, she emerges with a commitment to the present. Death, because it is natural, cannot be destroyed, but the joys derived from the commonplace—books, chairs, fruit—can provide meaning, and she "grow[s] solid and complete."

Kincaid's stories are praised for their strong images, poetic language, and challenging themes, and they are criticized for their lack of plot and sometimes obscure symbolism. Any reader, however, who, without reservations, enters Kincaid's fictive world will be well rewarded.

Other major works
NOVELS: *Annie John*, 1985; *Lucy*, 1990.
NONFICTION: *A Small Place*, 1988.
CHILDREN'S LITERATURE: *Annie, Gwen, Lilly, Pam, and Tulip*, 1986 (with illustrations by Eric Fischl).

Bibliography
Als, Hilton. "Don't Worry, Be Happy." Review of *Lucy*. *The Nation* 252 (February 18, 1991): 207-209. Als compares the novel with *A Small Place*, since both are

concerned with oppression. Als emphasizes Kincaid's importance as a Caribbean writer who is not afraid to tackle the issues of racism and colonialism at the risk of alienating readers.

Ellsberg, Peggy. "Rage Laced with Lyricism." Review of *A Small Place. Commonweal* 115 (November 4, 1988): 602-604. In her review of *A Small Place* with references to *At the Bottom of the River* and *Annie John*, Ellsberg justifies the anger that is present in *A Small Place*, anger that is occasioned by exploitation.

Garis, Leslie. "Through West Indian Eyes." *The New York Times Magazine* 140 (October 7, 1990): 42. Based on an interview with Kincaid, this six-page article is the best source of information about Kincaid's life. Contains details about her childhood in Antigua, her relationship with her mother, her early interest in books, her early years in New York, and her marriage to Allen Shawn. Includes illustrations.

Milton, Edith. "Making a Virtue of Diversity." Review of *At the Bottom of the River. The New York Times Book Review*, January 15, 1984, 22. Milton presents the major criticism of Kincaid's fiction—that the stories are obscure, plotless, and too visionary. Milton also discusses the strong Caribbean folktale influence evident in Kincaid's stories.

Onwordi, Iki. "Wising Up." *The Times Literary Supplement*, November 29, 1985, 1374. A brief review of both *At the Bottom of the River* and *Annie John*. Onwordi discusses the similarities, especially in language and themes.

Barbara Wiedemann

STEPHEN KING

Born: Portland, Maine; September 21, 1947

Principal short fiction

Night Shift, 1978; *The Dark Tower: The Gunslinger*, 1982; *Different Seasons*, 1982; *Skeleton Crew*, 1985; *Dark Visions*, 1988 (includes stories by Dan Simmons and George R. R. Martin); *Four Past Midnight*, 1990.

Other literary forms

Stephen King is best known for his horror novels, which he publishes at the rate of approximately one per year. Quite a number of his novels have been turned into films, and he has written several of the screenplays himself. A few of his poems have been included in his short-story collections, and he has written an analysis of horror fiction called *Danse Macabre* (1981).

Achievements

King has become, in a very few years, one of the most popular writers in the United States. Nearly every book he has had published has reached the best-seller lists, whether in hardback or paperback, and has often remained there for months. He is respected in the field of horror fiction, and several of his books have received World Fantasy Award nominations. He has received the World Fantasy Award for his short story "Do the Dead Sing?" (1981), a British Fantasy Award for *Cujo* (1981), and a Hugo Award for his nonfiction work *Danse Macabre*. He has been awarded special recognition for his contributions to horror fiction by both the British Fantasy Awards and the World Fantasy Awards.

King's work follows in the footsteps of such writers of horror stories as H. P. Lovecraft, Edgar Allan Poe, Bram Stoker, and some of the gothic novelists, while he also achieves a horror wrought from ordinary events. He credits Richard Matheson and Robert Bloch, especially, for showing him that the horror story could be brought out "of the foggy moors and the castles and into those 7-Eleven stores and suburbia."

Biography

Stephen Edwin King was born in 1947 in Maine, where he has lived the majority of his life. His parents had adopted his elder brother, David, several years before King was born, since his mother was told that she would be unable to have children. King's father abandoned the family when King was two years old; he has not seen his father since. After his parents' separation, King's mother moved the family to Indiana, then Connecticut, and finally, in 1958, back to Maine to be near her aging parents. King's mother was a strict Methodist with fundamentalist leanings, and the two boys attended church and Bible school several times a week.

Critical Survey of Short Fiction

King began writing young, at age seven or eight, partly to amuse himself during frequent periods of illness. His mother often read to her sons, including some of Classic Comics' adaptations of famous novels; King was impressed by H. G. Wells's *The Time Machine* (1895) and *The War of the Worlds* (1898). He was an avid reader and loved adventure stories and science fiction; thus, even his juvenile work was influenced by fantasy and horror. At the age of twelve, he sent stories to the magazines *Fantastic* and *Fantasy and Science Fiction*; soon afterward, he discovered some stories of Lovecraft and began reading a range of horror fiction, including the works of Lovecraft, Poe, several gothic novelists, and Matheson, whose horror novels, set in modern times, greatly influenced King.

King started high school in 1962, and in 1965, his story "I Was a Teenage Grave Robber" appeared in *Comics Review*, a fan magazine. He wrote all through high school and printed several of his stories on his brother's offset printing press. In 1966, he entered the University of Maine at Orono and made his first professional sale, of "The Glass Floor," to *Startling Mystery Stories*. He also began work on two manuscripts that were eventually published under the pseudonym Richard Bachman in the 1970's. At the university, he received encouragement from several of his professors and was influenced by such naturalist writers as Thomas Hardy and Theodore Dreiser. He wrote a column for the university newspaper and was active in campus politics. In his senior year, while he was working at the college library, he met fellow student Tabitha Spruce, whom he married in 1971. King was graduated from the University of Maine in 1970 with a degree in English and a teaching certificate; unable to find work as a teacher, however, he took a job in an industrial laundry, an experience on which he drew for several of his stories. In 1971, he was hired to teach high school English at Maine's Hampden Academy, where he spent two years.

In 1973, King sold his first novel, *Carrie: A Novel of a Girl with Frightening Power* (1974), to Doubleday. New American Library's purchase of the paperback rights allowed King to quit teaching and write full-time. In 1976, the film version of *Carrie* gave King's popularity a boost, but he was already selling quite well and producing virtually a novel per year. In 1979, King wrote his first screenplay, *Creepshow* (1982), and in 1986, Metro-Goldwyn-Mayer/United Artists released *Maximum Overdrive*, which King had both scripted and directed.

Analysis

"The [horror] genre exists on three basic levels, separate but independent, and each one a little bit cruder than the one before. There's terror on top, the finest emotion any writer can induce; then horror; and, on the very lowest level of all, the gag instinct of revulsion." Stephen King's stories fit onto each of the levels that he describes in a variety of ways. He is not particularly worried about style; he aims for the impact of plot. Not all King's stories can be labeled solely horror; many have elements of science fiction, and some of the best stories contain a sense of psychological tension. Most of the stories, however, even those that cannot neatly be pegged as belonging to a particular genre, attempt to create a sense of uneasiness. King explains the popularity of his stories as follows: "When you've got a lot of free-floating anxieties, the horror story or movie helps to conceptualize them, shrink them down to size, make them concrete so they're manipulable. . . . [T]here's probably some minor catharsis involved."

The kind of horror with which King is most often associated, that of ghosties and ghoulies and things that go bump in the night, is well represented in his short-story collections. Two of the stories, "Jerusalem's Lot" and "One for the Road," are connected by setting and plot elements to King's novel *'Salem's Lot* (1975). In "Jerusalem's Lot," set in 1850 and told in a series of letters and journal entries, Charles Boone, hoping to regain his strength after a serious illness, moves into his ancestral home along with his friend Calvin McCann. They hear noises in the walls and attribute them to rats, but they soon learn that the townspeople of Preacher's Corners believe otherwise. Between the stories they hear from a townswoman and a journal that McCann finds in the house, Boone and McCann discover that Boone's mad great-uncle, Philip Boone, had joined with a malign preacher to unleash the evils found in a satanic bible called *The Mysteries of the Worm*. Boone tries to eradicate the evil by burning the book, and while he starts to set the pages on fire, his friend McCann is killed by an enormous worm. Boone commits suicide, and the story ends with a note written in 1971 by a distant Boone relative, who disbelieves the evidence of the letters of Charles Boone but mentions hearing rats behind the walls of the ancestral home.

"Jerusalem's Lot" has all the trappings of horror in the gothic tradition: a house shunned by the townspeople, inexplicable noises behind the walls, an abandoned town, religion that has been twisted to serve evil, and a monster in the cellar. The tale, written originally for a college class in gothic fiction, is perhaps the only King story that takes place not in modern suburbia but in the past, in a setting somewhat akin to lonely moors and castles.

"One for the Road," though also set in Jerusalem's Lot, is a modern vampire story. Gerard Lumley and his family have gone off the road near Jerusalem's Lot in a bad snowstorm. Lumley leaves his wife and child and goes to get help. When he returns, both his wife and daughter have become vampires. King has commented that "I've always believed that if you think the very worst, then, no matter how bad things get . . . they'll never get as bad as *that*. If you write a novel where the bogeyman gets somebody else's children, maybe they'll never get your own children." Fear for loved ones is a common theme in King's stories. Because Lumley is afraid for his wife and daughter, he risks his own life to get help. While he is gone, the worst happens to his wife and daughter: they have become something alien, something that no longer loves him.

In "The Monkey," King creates a high level of tension from the protagonist's fear for his family, especially for his youngest son. When Hal was young, he discovered a toy monkey with a worn-out mechanism for clanging the cymbals strapped to the monkey's paws. Nevertheless, when someone near Hal is about to die, the monkey clashes the cymbals. Hal attempts several times to get rid of the monkey and finally throws it down his aunt's well. Years later, when Hal and his family are clearing the attic of his aunt's house after her death, Hal's eldest son finds the monkey. Finally, Hal rows out to the middle of the lake and drops the monkey in the water, nearly drowning as his boat breaks up, while his younger son watches. "The Monkey" is an effective story that evokes terror, the highest on King's list of horror-story levels. Like all King's stories, it is highly visual. His settings and characters are familiar and easy to sympathize with, and King uses the monkey well as a symbol of evil that descends despite all one's efforts to keep away from it.

Several of King's stories deal with the destruction wrought by mechanical devices. "The Monkey" is perhaps the most effective, as the monkey is never *seen* to do anything other than strike its cymbals when it should not be able to do so. The connection between the clash of cymbals and death is made in the mind of Hal, and though it seems to be supported by the evidence, the connection could be pure coincidence. In "The Mangler" and "Trucks," however, the machines are clear agents of wholesale destruction. "The Mangler" is set in an industrial laundry: a mangler is a machine that irons and folds material fed into it. This mangler develops a taste for blood and sucks several workers into the machinery inside: "a devil had taken over the inanimate steel and cogs and gears of the mangler and had turned it into something with its own life." After two men unsuccessfully attempt to exorcise the machine, the mangler tears itself loose from its moorings and moves toward the town.

"Trucks" concerns vehicles that turn against their owners, running them down when they try to escape. The trucks encircle a diner, crashing into it after their human hostages refuse to acknowledge a Morse code signal beeped out on a horn to refuel the vehicles. Both "Trucks" and "The Mangler" envisage machines that were built to serve human beings, turning to demand sacrifice and service themselves. King has commented that he finds machines frightening because he does not understand how they work. Both stories, too, while they play on one's fear of death and mutilation, are also rather amusing in a dark sort of way.

Several of King's stories treat death in a far more realistic manner, and in some ways these stories are more disturbing than stories such as "The Mangler." While "The Mangler" graphically describes violent death—fitting into King's third level in the horror genre, the "gag instinct of revulsion"—the plot is clearly unrealistic. It is one of those stories that takes the fear of death and makes it manipulable and even laughable. Industrial accidents do happen but not because machines turn malevolent. A story such as "The Woman in the Room," however, is based on King's own feelings when his mother was dying of cancer. It is highly realistic in both plot and emotion. In it, a son visits his mother in the hospital, where she has just had a "cortotomy," an operation to destroy the pain center in her brain so that she will not be in agony from the cancer in her stomach. The operation has also destroyed 60 percent of her motor control. Seeing her weak, unable to move very much, and with no hopes of any recovery, Johnny considers giving her some Darvon pills that he found in her medicine cabinet at home. On this visit, his mother says, "I wish I was out of this. I'd do anything to be out of this." Finally, he brings the pills to the hospital, shows his mother the box, and shakes six pills into his hand. She looks at them and tacitly agrees to end her life by swallowing all six. Her last request is for Johnny to see if her legs are together: she wants to die with some dignity. She also tells Johnny that he has always been a good son.

"The Woman in the Room" reflects on a very personal, touching level the incredible difficulty of watching a loved one die in pain. King's style is as plain and as colloquial as ever; he does not try to elevate it to suit the subject. The story is told in the present tense, and the very artlessness and transparency of King's style give the story an air of honesty. It is by no means a horror story, yet it evokes what King calls "the finest emotion any writer can induce"—terror: fear that one's own parents will get cancer; fear that one will be faced with the same painful dilemma as Johnny; or ultimately, fear that one oneself will end up lying in agony in a hospital bed.

Another psychologically honest story is "The Body," filmed in 1986 as *Stand by Me*. In it, four twelve-year-old boys walk along a railway track in search of the body of a boy who has been hit by a train. The relationships between the boys, their silly jokes and twelve-year-old bravado, strike the reader as real and true to life. Because they are young, the idea of finding the body excites them; the whole trip is an adventure. It is not until they actually see the boy's body that they finally confront the reality of death: "The kid was dead. The kid wasn't sick, the kid wasn't sleeping. The kid wasn't going to get up in the morning anymore . . . or catch poison ivy or wear out the eraser on the end of his Ticonderoga No 2 during a hard math test. The kid was dead." The quest and the discovery of the body are a rite of passage to which each of the boys reacts slightly differently; soon after they return to town, to their usual lives and to school, they drift apart, growing up in different directions, affected in different ways. King's plain, unornamented style again works to the benefit of the story, making it believable and realistic.

"The Ballad of the Flexible Bullet" is quite different from most of King's other short stories. It is not horror, but neither is it completely realistic. The story concerns a paranoid writer who believes that a "Fornit" inhabits his typewriter to help him write. His editor, humoring him, goes along with the idea and says that he has a Fornit too. Soon, the editor, who has begun to drink heavily, is finding messages on his typewriter from his Fornit when he wakes up from his periodic blackouts. The last message warns him that the writer's Fornit is about to be killed. When the writer hears about this, he buys a gun to protect his Fornit but ends up killing himself after he watches his Fornit die. The flexible bullet of the title is madness; it kills just as surely as a lead bullet but in an unpredictable way. The story walks a neat tightrope between dismissing the Fornits as products of a deranged mind and admitting their existence: the writer's wife wonders if madness is catching when she thinks she hears the dying screams of the Fornit from inside the typewriter.

"The Ballad of the Flexible Bullet" ends in violent death. The writer attempted to kill his wife and the housekeeper and her son besides shooting himself. No matter what type of story King is writing, he usually seems to come back to terror, horror, or the gag reflex. King has commented that "the horror story makes us children. That's the primary function of the horror story—to knock away all this stuff . . . to take us over taboo lines, to places we aren't supposed to be." King does not really need to limit this function of his stories to those of the horror genre; whether his characters are confronting death by mutilation from a mad mangler or death by cancer, King is still taking readers over taboo lines, making them confront by proxy such subjects as madness, fear, and death.

Other major works

NOVELS: *Carrie: A Novel of a Girl with Frightening Power,* 1974; *'Salem's Lot,* 1975; *The Shining,* 1977; *Rage,* 1977 (as Richard Bachman); *The Stand,* 1978; *The Dead Zone,* 1979; *The Long Walk,* 1979 (as Richard Bachman); *Firestarter,* 1980; *Cujo,* 1981; *Roadwork,* 1981 (as Richard Bachman); *The Running Man,* 1982 (as Richard Bachman); *Christine,* 1983; *Pet Sematary,* 1983; *Cycle of the Werewolf,* 1983 (also published as *Silver Bullet,* 1985); *The Talisman,* 1984 (with Peter Straub); *The Eyes of the Dragon,* 1984; *Thinner,* 1984 (as Richard Bachman); *The Bachman Books,* 1985 (omnibus edition, includes *Rage, The Long Walk, Roadwork,* and *The Running Man); It,* 1986; *Misery,* 1987; *The Tommyknockers,* 1987; *The Dark Half,* 1989; *Needful Things,* 1991; *Gerald's Game,* 1992.

SCREENPLAYS: *Creepshow,* 1982; *Cat's Eye,* 1985; *Silver Bullet,* 1985; *Maximum Overdrive,* 1986; *Pet Sematary,* 1989; *Stephen King's Sleepwalkers,* 1992.

NONFICTION: *Danse Macabre,* 1981; *Black Magic and Music: A Novelist's Perspective on Bangor,* 1983; *Bare Bones: Conversations on Terror with Stephen King,* 1988 (edited by Tim Underwood and Chuck Miller).

MISCELLANEOUS: *Nightmares in the Sky,* 1988.

Bibliography

Herron, Don, ed. *Reign of Fear: The Fiction and Film of Stephen King, 1982-1989.* San Francisco: Underwood-Miller, 1988. This collection of essays includes articles by writers as diverse as actress Whoopi Goldberg and science-fiction and fantasy writer L. Sprague De Camp. The quality of the articles varies, though some are helpful, and there are also a few essays on films made from King's tales.

King, Stephen. *Bare Bones: Conversations on Terror with Stephen King.* Edited by Tim Underwood and Chuck Miller. New York: McGraw-Hill, 1988. Though many of the interviews collected in this volume become somewhat repetitive, they provide a good sense, in King's own words, of what he is trying to do in his fiction and why he does it. The interviews were held between 1979 and 1987; the opening transcript of a talk King gave at the Billerica Public Library is most useful.

_____. *Danse Macabre.* New York: Everest House, 1981. King researched and wrote this critical work on horror fiction and film at the instigation of his editor. He focuses on works since the 1940's and discusses novels, B-films, and horror comics to support his thesis that monsters such as Godzilla are a way of making tangible the fear of such things as nuclear war.

Underwood, Tim, and Chuck Miller, eds. *Fear Itself: The Horror Fiction of Stephen King, 1976-1982.* San Francisco: Underwood-Miller, 1982. This is another collection of articles on King's work. The articles vary in quality, with Ben Indick's "King and the Literary Tradition of Horror" providing a good introduction to the history of the horror genre. Douglas Winter's essay, "The Night Journeys of Stephen King," discusses several of the short stories. Includes a bibliography.

Winter, Douglas E. *The Art of Darkness: The Life and Fiction of the Master of the Macabre, Stephen King.* 1984. Rev. ed. New York: New American Library, 1989. Winter's work provides a perceptive critical overview of King's work, with long articles on each novel up to *The Talisman* and a chapter on the short stories in *Night Shift* and *Skeleton Crew.* Winter also includes summaries of King's short stories, a short biography of King, and extensive bibliographies both of King's work and of books and articles written about him.

Karen M. Cleveland Marwick

W. P. KINSELLA

Born: Edmonton, Alberta, Canada; May 25, 1935

Principal short fiction

Dance Me Outside, 1977; *Scars*, 1978; *Shoeless Joe Jackson Comes to Iowa*, 1980; *Born Indian*, 1981; *The Moccasin Telegraph and Other Stories*, 1983; *The Thrill of the Grass*, 1984; *The Alligator Report*, 1985; *The Fencepost Chronicles*, 1986; *Red Wolf, Red Wolf*, 1987; *The Further Adventures of Slugger McBatt*, 1988; *The Miss Hobbema Pageant*, 1989.

Other literary forms

W. P. Kinsella is best known for two novels, *Shoeless Joe* (1982) and *The Iowa Baseball Confederacy* (1986), which combine baseball with fantasy. *Shoeless Joe* is the basis of the popular 1989 film *Field of Dreams*. Because of its use in the film, Kinsella's line "If you build it, he will come" has become a catchphrase. Kinsella has also written poetry and plays.

Achievements

Kinsella has said that his storytelling skills have resulted from growing up in an oral tradition. He and his Yugoslavian grandmother swapped stories, hers set in the hills near Dubrovnik, his in rural Alberta. Through this process, he learned to entertain by making his listener eager to hear what will happen next. Kinsella is a serious writer who sees the writer's first duty as entertainment and thus makes his characters less cynical and angry than he is. He considers himself a realist who does not believe in magic, yet many of his stories are tall tales or fantasies. While his fiction is sometimes sentimental, it is nevertheless effective because of the compassion that he feels for characters confronted by the absurdities of a seemingly meaningless world. Kinsella is also notable for writing a wide variety of stories: realistic, surreal, and fantastic. He has received the Books in Canada First Novel Award, the Canadian Authors Association Prize for Fiction, the Alberta Achievement Award for Excellence in Literature, the Stephen Leacock Medal for Humor, and the Canadian Book Publishers' Author-of-the-Year Award.

Biography

William Patrick Kinsella was born May 25, 1935, in Edmonton, Alberta. His father was a contractor; his mother, a printer. An only child, Kinsella spent his early years in a log cabin near Lac Ste.-Anne, sixty miles northwest of Edmonton. He rarely saw other children and completed grades one through four by correspondence. His parents, grandmother, and aunt read to one another and told stories, and Kinsella began writing fantasies when he was five or six. The family moved to Edmonton when he was ten, and his father, a former semiprofessional baseball player, began taking him to baseball games. In the eighth grade, Kinsella won a prize for "Diamond Doom," a baseball mystery. At eighteen, he published his first story, a science-fiction tale about a totalitarian society, in *The Alberta Civil Service Bulletin.*

Kinsella worked as a government clerk, manager of a retail credit company, account executive for the City of Edmonton, owner of an Italian restaurant, and taxicab driver, the latter two while attending the University of Victoria, where he received a B.A. in 1974. He then attended the Writers' Workshop at the University of Iowa, earning a master of fine arts degree in 1978. He taught at the University of Calgary from 1978 to 1983, but he hated the academic life, quitting to write fulltime. Kinsella was married to Mildred Clay from 1965 to 1978. He married the writer Ann Knight in 1978, and they settled in White Rock, British Columbia, and Iowa City, Iowa, when not traveling to attend major league baseball games. Kinsella has two daughters, Shannon and Erin.

Analysis

W. P. Kinsella calls his short, surrealistic stories "Brautigans" because of the influence of Richard Brautigan on his life and career. According to Kinsella, whose favorite book is Brautigan's *In Watermelon Sugar* (1968), "Brautigan's delicate, visual, whimsical, facetious writing appealed to a whole generation of us who were able to identify with the gentle, loving losers of his stories." Typical of Kinsella's Brautigans is "Syzygy," about Grabarkewitcz, a European immigrant to Vancouver whose cat sleeps in the bathroom sink and disappears down the drain when its owner is shaving: " 'Cats are independent devils,' said Grabarkewitcz. 'They never come when you call them.' "

The Brautigans are Kinsella's most self-consciously literary stories, a fact that he acknowledges in "The Secret" by having Grabarkewitcz confess to the crime of "bookfondling." One of the longest and best of these stories is "The Book Buyers," which satirizes his native country's eccentricities. The narrator wonders why, if most Canadians seem chained to television sets or computers, statistics show that they are buying more books than ever before. Finding himself in Toronto, he decides that this is the perfect place to investigate this phenomenon since "as we all know, there is nothing either west or east of Toronto."

Going to the only bookstore in Toronto that sells books by Canadians, he spots a typical Canadian reader: "He had a bottle opener and ski lift tickets attached to the zipper of his parka." The customer buys $102 worth and says he has to deliver them somewhere. The narrator eventually discovers that the books go to a warehouse, where they are shredded and recycled as packing cases by the government to keep the book business alive. He threatens to make the practice public unless at least one book he has written is included in each pickup. He describes the boxes containing computers and video cassette recorders as representing "the essence of Canadian literature." "The Book Buyers" is typical of Kinsella's satire since instead of becoming angry over Canada's neglect of its writers and his compatriots' general anti-intellectualism, he turns the whole matter into a benign joke.

"Evangeline's Mother," one of the best of his realistic stories, deals with typical Kinsella subjects such as loneliness and class differences. The ambitious Henry Vold goes to work for a savings and loan company after high school, meets Rosalie on a blind date, and impregnates and marries her. Rosalie, who lives for the moment, leaves the dull Henry for a service-station attendant when their daughter, Carin, is a year old. Henry remarries, choosing someone like himself this time—Mona, a financial analyst—and they have a son as practical and unadventurous as they are.

Carin becomes a rebellious, promiscuous teenager and comes to live with Henry when Rosalie can take her behavior no longer. Henry loves Carin uncritically, forgiving her anything. Mona warns him that Carin cannot be trusted and is manipulating him. Despite himself, Henry is attracted to Carin's exotic, vivacious friend Evangeline. He is branch manager of a large savings and loan association and expects to be promoted into senior management, but he allows Evangeline to seduce him. Even meeting her slovenly mother, who once must have been as young and attractive as her daughter, does not deter Henry. He quits his job, withdrawing half his seventy thousand dollars in savings, and the three of them run away together.

Henry makes a mistake in getting involved with Rosalie, since she hardly fits into the carefully planned, conservative world he envisions for himself. His well-ordered world is perhaps too well ordered. He misses the adventure, the risk, and the sex that he associates with a certain type of woman. His world is empty and too lonely without it. Kinsella presents Henry's decision as the fulfilling of a psychological need but does not sentimentalize it. The story ends with a hint of danger: "as he glanced down at Vangy's sepia hand, it seemed to him that the nails . . . curled frighteningly. Images of talons filled Henry's mind." Henry can have order or adventure but not both. Kinsella explores this same theme of longing to recapture the spirit of the past in the equally poignant "Mother Tucker's Yellow Duck" and "K-Mart."

As with his baseball novels, magic and spirituality are at the center of most of Kinsella's baseball stories. These tales are remarkable for the author's ability to find so many ways of looking at how the ritual of baseball can impose order on a chaotic universe and bring a sense of wholeness to shattered lives. In "The Thrill of the Grass," the narrator misses major league baseball during the lengthy players' strike of 1981 and goes to the empty stadium where he is a season-ticket holder. On impulse, he breaks the law for the first time in his forty years as a locksmith by letting himself into the stadium. In love with the game but repelled by the artificial turf, he enlists another fan to replace the turf with sod, square foot by square foot. Each invites a friend to take part, and soon dozens of men armed with sod, sprinklers, rakes, and hoes work until dawn each night to restore the field to its natural beauty, its divinity. With the transformation complete, the narrator feels "like a magician who has gestured hypnotically and produced an elephant from thin air." For Kinsella, the magic of baseball inspires other magical acts.

"The Thrill of the Grass" is one of the best examples of Kinsella's presentation of baseball as a substitute religion. The men's journeys to the stadium are called pilgrimages, and the narrator does not even confide in his beloved wife, since the restoration of the grass is "a ritual for true believers only." Kinsella does not attempt to explain or justify this attitude toward baseball; it must be accepted on faith. The locksmith always watches games from the first-base side and mistrusts anyone, even a daughter, who prefers to sit elsewhere: "The positions fans choose at sporting events are like politics, religion, or philosophy: a view of the world, a way of seeing the universe. They make no sense to anyone, have no basis in anything but stubbornness." Kinsella expresses deep suspicion of organized religion (as well as politics, bureaucracies, academics, and reformers) throughout his fiction, especially in his Native American stories. Baseball is infinitely superior to religion, for it allows the possibility of regaining Eden.

Religion also plays a part in "The Last Pennant Before Armageddon." Al Tiller is considered the stupidest manager in major league baseball. The fifty-five-year-old has never had a winning record as either player or manager in professional baseball. Suddenly, however, he is an apparent genius. The Chicago Cubs, who have not won a National League pennant since 1945, have been in first place all season, and Al should be on top of the world. Managers are essentially lonely people, but Al is lonelier than most, since he has an enormous burden that he is unable to share.

In June, he is listening to a radio sports program in St. Louis, when a caller who says he is an archangel announces that the Chicago Cubs will win the last pennant before Armageddon. Since early August, Al has a nightly dream in which petitioners plead with God to allow the Cubs to win. God replies that the Cubs will win the last pennant before Armageddon. (*The Iowa Baseball Confederacy* also involves the Cubs and apocalyptic events.) Not a religious man, Al is concerned because the Soviet Union has troops in Sri Lanka and the American president has threatened to use force to remove them. Al calls the host of the radio program, but he does not remember anyone claiming to be an archangel.

Al has been faced with a difficult decision before. As a minor leaguer, he fell in love with the perfect woman, but she married someone else. After Al became engaged to a less exciting woman from his hometown, his first love left her husband and asked Al to take her back. He did the honorable thing but always wondered what his life would have been like with his first love, even though she died at thirty. Now, as the Cubs approach the final game of the National League play-offs with the Los Angeles Dodgers, Al has to endure a final dream. In it, a woman petitioner who has always had her back to him turns and is his first love: "Now I have the most important reason of all to manage to win, something beyond honour, beyond duty. For surely, when all is said and done, love is more important." Like Henry Vold in "Evangeline's Mother," Al needs to take a chance for once. Playing it safe has made him a loser. Just as baseball and honor may be more important than religion and politics, love is superior to anything. Kinsella uses baseball and magic or the supernatural to comment on basic human issues.

Kinsella has written dozens of stories about the Cree Indian reserve near Hobbema, Alberta. The characters are generally poor, semiliterate, unemployed, and alcoholic, with little hope for improvement. While these problems lurk in the background of most of the stories—and are the main concern of several—the predominant tone of the tales narrated by Silas Ermineskin is comic. Kinsella comments on racism, social injustice, and political indifference, while creating entertainment through the absurdities and even slapstick surrounding these issues.

The stories originate when twenty-year-old Silas is given a writing assignment in an English class at the technical school that he attends and where he continues with the encouragement of his teacher. Because the teacher corrects only spelling and punctuation, the tales are written in an unlettered, colloquial style. They usually center on the misadventures of Silas; his best friend, the uncouth and uncontrollable Frank Fencepost; Mad Etta, a four-hundred-pound medicine woman; and Bedelia Coyote, the local feminist and political activist. Mad Etta is often a Jeeves to Silas' Bertie Wooster, advising him about how to extract himself and his friends from complicated situations. Silas' stories deal with such subjects as a Native American automobile salesman who cheats other Native Americans, a father who forces his daughter into prostitution, Silas and Frank's trip to Las Vegas, a Native American politician who tries to be white, a Mexican who poses as a Native American doctor, the staging of a buffalo hunt for Prince Philip, and Mad Etta's playing hockey. Silas describes disease, death, and despair and is often bitter: "Sometimes when I have to put up with the Government or the Church I feel so helpless, I get so mad my hands shake." The harsh reality of the Native Americans' situation is counterbalanced by Kinsella's use of mysticism, as when Mad Etta rights a series of wrongs by turning three men into weasels.

Silas' most memorable stories are the comic ones. In one of the best, "The Killing of Colin Moosefeathers," Silas and Frank invent a fellow student at the technical school as a prank, giving him "the silliest name we can come up with." A chain of events leads to Colin's being registered for classes. Silas, Frank, and Bedelia eventually manage to get a credit card for him, making purchases up to the credit limit. Silas quickly learns why they can get away with it all: "people is real greedy and will take a chance if it gonna mean a sale for them." When the bill collectors start arriving, they say Colin is dead. To get liquor for Colin's wake, they allow a white man in a suit to use the credit card: "those kind be the most anxious to make quick money because they all the time have to pay for expensive clothes." Silas and his friends even come up with a grave, cross, and wreath to prove to the police that Colin is dead. The police dig up the grave only to be told that Colin has been cremated.

Throughout Silas' stories, white people ignore, distrust, and hate Native Americans. Colin Moosefeathers gives them the opportunity for revenge and fun at the same time that they exploit a socioeconomic system from which they have been excluded. Their pranks escalate because of the whites' gullibility and greed, their faceless bureaucracy. Anyone can use Colin's credit card, since whites think all Native Americans have funny names and look alike. Whites almost always lose in such confrontations with Kinsella's Native Americans because they underestimate them.

These Native American stories succeed primarily because of Kinsella's virtuosity as a storyteller, and "The Kid in the Stove" celebrates the art of storytelling. Silas entertains his little brothers and sisters with the story that he learned from their mother about how, in 1907, Lazarus Bobtail and four of his five children were murdered by a white man. The fifth child escaped by crawling into a stove: "For such a sad story it almost make a happy ending when you hear at the end that one child got away." Since he is interested in the history of Native Americans in Alberta, Silas wants to find out more about the murder and locates a newspaper account that fails to mention the fifth child. He learns that Mrs. Bobtail, who was away at the time of the killings, gave birth a few weeks later. Her having "one in the oven" has evolved in the Native Americans' oral tradition into a more positive account of what happened. Silas is eager to correct the mistake, until he realizes that the misconstrued version serves a much better purpose than the truth.

The Silas Ermineskin stories often verge on sentimentality because Kinsella, like his hero Brautigan, forces himself to find some virtue arising out of sorrow. "The Kid in the Stove" stands out for reflecting Kinsella's apparent theory of art by acknowledging the healing power of fiction. The audience wants the thrill of the horrifying murders but needs some redemption resulting from their fears. The constant good humor of Silas and his friends in the face of despair is life-affirming.

Other major works

NOVELS: *Shoeless Joe*, 1982; *The Iowa Baseball Confederacy*, 1986.
PLAYS: *The Thrill of the Grass: Three Plays About Baseball*, 1988.
POETRY: *Rainbow Warehouse*, 1989 (with Ann Knight).
NONFICTION: *Two Spirits Soar: The Act of Allen Sapp, the Inspiration of Allan Gonor*, 1990.

Bibliography

Aitken, Brian. "Baseball as Sacred Doorway in the Writing of W. P. Kinsella." *Aethlon* 8 (Fall, 1990): 61-75. Aitken looks at the spiritual aspects of Kinsella's baseball novels and two of his stories, "Frank Pierce, Iowa" and "K-Mart." He concludes that Kinsella shows how North Americans can find as much spiritual fulfillment in sports as in formal religion.

Cameron, Elspeth. "Diamonds Are Forever." *Saturday Night* 101 (August, 1986): 45-47. Cameron shows how most of Kinsella's fiction centers on adolescent males who, unencumbered by women, pursue quests as if they were knights errant.

Horvath, Brooke K., and William J. Palmer. "Three On: An Interview with David Carkeet, Mark Harris, and W. P. Kinsella." *Modern Fiction Studies* 33 (Spring, 1987): 183-194. Kinsella explains how he came to write about baseball and his attitude toward literary criticism.

Kinsella, W. P. "W. P. Kinsella, the Super-Natural." Interview by Sheldon Sunness. *Sport* 77 (July, 1986): 74. Kinsella discusses his fondness for baseball, calling it the chess of sports, and his disdain for Canada's native game of hockey. He wishes he could be a major league baseball player in another life.

Murray, Don. *The Fiction of W. P. Kinsella: Tall Tales in Various Voices.* Fredericton, New Brunswick, Canada: York Press, 1987. This brief but excellent study provides an overview of Kinsella's fiction, placing emphasis on the short stories. Murray includes three interviews with Kinsella, a bibliography, and an index.

_____. "A Note on W. P. Kinsella's Humor." *The International Fiction Review* 14, no. 2 (1987): 98-100. Humor is the basic ingredient in Kinsella's fiction, according to Murray. He argues that anarchy is justified and funny in Kinsella's works.

Michael Adams

RUDYARD KIPLING

Born: Bombay, India; December 30, 1865
Died: Hampstead, London, England; January 18, 1936

Principal short fiction

In Black and White, 1888; *Plain Tales from the Hills*, 1888; *Soldiers Three*, 1888; *The Story of the Gadsbys*, 1888; *The Phantom 'Rickshaw and Other Tales*, 1888; *Under the Deodars*, 1888; *Wee Willie Winkie*, 1888; *Life's Handicap*, 1891; *Many Inventions*, 1893; *The Jungle Book*, 1894; *The Second Jungle Book*, 1895; *Soldier Tales*, 1896; *The Day's Work*, 1898; *Stalky & Co.*, 1899; *Just So Stories*, 1902; *Traffics and Discoveries*, 1904; *Puck of Pook's Hill*, 1906; *Actions and Reactions*, 1909; *Rewards and Fairies*, 1910; *A Diversity of Creatures*, 1917; *Land and Sea Tales for Scouts and Guides*, 1923; *Debits and Credits*, 1926; *Thy Servant a Dog*, 1930; *Limits and Renewals*, 1932.

Other literary forms

Rudyard Kipling's literary career began in journalism, but his prose sketches and verse brought him early fame. He wrote several novels, most lastingly *Kim* (1901), and he also wrote works of history, including a study of his son's military regiment from World War I. In his lifetime as well as posthumously, however, his fame depended upon his poetry and short stories, both of which he wrote for adult audiences and for children. Kipling's autobiography, *Something of Myself: For My Friends Known and Unknown* (1937), was published after his death.

Achievements

By his early twenties, Kipling had become one of the best-known writers in the English language. His first poems and stories were written and published in India, but his popularity quickly spread throughout the English-speaking world and beyond. Although he published several novels, the short-story form proved to be his most successful métier. Drawing upon his experiences in India, many of his early stories featured the adventures of ordinary soldiers, junior officers, and civil officials, and his use of dialect was a recognized feature of his literary technique. Awarded the Nobel Prize in Literature in 1907, he also received honorary degrees from many universities.

Kipling wrote extensively about the benefits of the United Kingdom's paramount position in the world, and over time his public persona was perceived to be that of a political reactionary. Although some of his finest short stories were written in the last two decades of his life, by that time, to many of his contemporaries, he had become yesterday's man, irrevocably associated with political imperialism, a dying creed even before his death in 1936. After his death, however, his stories received much critical study and acclaim, and Kipling is considered to be one of the major practitioners of the short-story art ever to write in English.

Biography

Joseph Rudyard Kipling was born in Bombay, India, in 1865. His father, John Lockwood Kipling, was an artist and teacher. His mother, Alice Macdonald Kipling, was from a family of exceptional sisters. One married the Pre-Raphaelite painter, Sir Edward Coley Burne-Jones, and another was the mother of Stanley Baldwin, the British prime minister in the years between the two world wars.

As was customary at the time, Rudyard and his younger sister remained in England when their parents returned to India, and Kipling dramatized his misery at being left behind in his later writings. He attended a second-rank private school that prepared middle-class boys for careers in the military; small, not athletic, and forced to wear glasses, Kipling was not an outstanding or popular student, but his literary interests proved a defense and a consolation. The university was not an option for him, primarily for financial reasons, and he returned to India, where his parents had found a position for him on an English-language newspaper.

Kipling was fascinated by India. Often unable to sleep, he spent his nights wandering the streets. He had written some poetry as a schoolboy and continued to do so, while also composing newspaper sketches featuring his Anglo-Indian environment. By the end of the 1880's, he had already published several volumes of short stories and poems. No British writer since Charles Dickens had become so well known, and Kipling was only in his mid-twenties. His works were often satiric, and some readers believed that he cast aspersions upon the British army and imperial authorities in India, but the opposite was closer to Kipling's own feelings. He doubted that the English at home understood the sacrifices that the average soldier, the young officer, and the district commissioners were making to preserve Great Britain's prosperity and security.

Kipling left India in 1889 and established himself in London, where he became acquainted with the major literary figures of the day, including Thomas Hardy and Henry James. In 1890, he published his first novel, *The Light That Failed*. With the American Wolcott Balestier, Kipling, in spite of his previous unwillingness to attach himself to any literary partnership, wrote a second novel, *The Naulahka: A Story of East and West* (1892). Kipling's relationship with Balestier was very close, and after the latter's death, he married Balestier's sister, Caroline (Carrie), in 1892. Kipling subsequently settled in Vermont, near his wife's family. Although residing there for four years before returning to England, Kipling never admired the United States and had difficulty with Carrie's family.

His fame reached its pinnacle in the years before the South African Boer War broke out in 1899. His portrayal of the Empire struck a chord in the British psyche during the 1890's; a changing political climate, however, began to make Kipling's public posture as an imperialist less acceptable. Still, he continued to write, both for children and for adults. In 1902, he purchased Bateman's, a country house in Sussex, which remained his home for the rest of his life.

Long a frustrated man of action and a Francophile from his schoolboy years, he vehemently opposed Germany during World War I. His only son was killed in action in 1915. Kipling's health had begun to decline, his marriage was less than fulfilling, and although he received much formal praise, his later stories were not widely read. He died in 1936 and was buried in Westminster Abbey, more a recognition for his earlier than his later career. Only after his death was it possible to separate the public man—imperialist and antiliberal—from the literary artist whose best stories have continued to survive.

Analysis

Many of Rudyard Kipling's earliest short stories are set in the India of his early childhood years in Bombay and his newspaper days in Lahore. The intervening years at school in England had perhaps increased his sensitivity to the exotic Indian locale and British imperial presence. Kipling was a voracious reader of English, French, and American writers, trained by his newspaper experience in the virtues of conciseness and detail. His art arrived almost fully revealed in his earliest works. Kipling focused, however, not on the glories and conquests of empire but on the lives—work and activities, passions and emotions—of ordinary people responding to what were often extraordinary or inexplicable events. Love, especially doomed love, terror and the macabre, revenge and its consequences—these were the elements upon which his stories turned, even later when the settings were often English. His fame or notoriety was almost instantaneous, in part because of the locations and subject matter of the stories, because of his use of dialect in re-creating the voices of his nonestablishment characters, and because Kipling's early writings appeared at a time when England and Western civilization as a whole were caught up in imperial dreams and rivalries.

A number of his stories pivot around the relations between men and women. Kipling has been called a misogynist, and often his characters, particularly those in the military, blame women for their own and others' misfortunes. Most of his stories employ a male voice, and many critics agree that Kipling's women are not often fully realized, particularly in his early years. The isolation of British soldiers and officials in India could itself explain these portrayals. There were boundaries in that esoteric environment—sexual, social, racial—that were violated only at a cost, but in Kipling's stories they are crossed because his characters choose to do so or cannot help themselves.

In "Beyond the Pale," Christopher Trejago seduces and is seduced by a young fifteen-year-old Hindu widow, Bisea, before misunderstanding and jealousy cause the lovers to terminate the relationship. Later, Trejago returns to their place of rendezvous only to discover that Bisea's hands have been cut off at the wrists; at the instant of his discovery, he is attacked by a sharp object that injures his groin. One of Kipling's shortest stories, it exhibits several of his continuing concerns. Love, passion, even understanding are often doomed, whether between man and woman or between British and Indians, while horror and unexpected shock can occur at any time and have lasting effects; revenge is a human quality. Stylistically, the story is rich in the descriptive detail of the dead-end alley where Bisea and Trejago first met but is enigmatic in explaining how the affair became known, leading to Bisea's maiming. The story does not end with the assault on Trejago. As often with Kipling, there is a coda. Trejago is forced to carry on, with a slight limp and the remembrance of horror leading to sleepless nights.

Dangerous boundaries and illicit relationships also feature in his "Love-o'-Women," the story of Larry Tighe, a gentleman who had enlisted as a common soldier, a gentleman-ranker who stepped down out of his proper world. Kipling often used the technique of a story-within-a-story, told by a narrator who may or may not be telling the total truth but whose own personality and perception are as important as the plot itself, accomplished most notably in "Mrs. Bathurst." Here, in "Love-o'-Women," the tale opens with Sergeant Raines shooting one of his own men, Corporal Mackie, who had seduced Mrs. Raines. After Raines's trial, several soldiers ruminate on the dead Mackie's fate. One of them, Terrence Mulvaney, comments that Mackie is the lucky one: he died quickly. He then tells the story of Tighe, who claimed the nickname of Love-o'-Women and made a career in the military of seducing daughters and wives, governesses and maids. When Tighe attempts to commit suicide by exposing his body to enemy fire during a battle, Mulvaney saves him and learns that Tighe deeply regrets what he has done, including his treatment and loss of his only real love, a woman named Egypt who turned to prostitution. Dying of syphilis, Tighe collapses in Egypt's arms; she then shoots herself. Kipling did not necessarily believe in justice in the world and although reared a Christian, he was not orthodox in his religious beliefs but believed that there was a morality for which one must answer. In "Love-o'-Women," sin required confession, contrition, and penance.

Ghosts or phantoms also often played a role in Kipling's stories. In "The Phantom 'Rickshaw," Jack Pansay, an English official in India, begins a shipboard flirtation with a married woman, Mrs. Keith-Wessington, while returning from England. The affair continues in India, but Pansay grows tired of her, becoming engaged to someone else. Mrs. Wessington refuses to accept the termination of the romance and subsequently dies after losing control of her rickshaw while attempting to renew the affair. Soon, as a ghostly presence, she and her rickshaw begin to appear to Pansay, and feeling that his rejection had killed her, he himself sinks into decline. Although his doctor believes that his illness is merely the result of overwork, Pansay believes otherwise: his death is the payment required for his treatment of Mrs. Wessington.

From the beginning of his literary career, Kipling was considered to be a master in the use of dialect. Mulvaney's telling of Tighe's tale was rendered in an Irish dialect. In Kipling's Indian stories, Mulvaney's Irish was joined by characters speaking London Cockney, Yorkshire in northern England, and others. In many of his later stories, Kipling incorporated various English dialects, such as the Sussex dialect spoken by Grace Ashcroft and Liz Fettley in "The Wish House." He generally used dialect when portraying the speech of persons from the undereducated classes or foreigners—persons different from his middle-class readers—and his treatment is often successful, even though some critics have claimed that his dialect re-creations were not entirely accurate. It has also been argued that at times, the use of dialect gets in the way of the reading and understanding of the story itself, although this is more true of his early stories than his later ones.

On occasion, Kipling attempted to create the speaking style of the middle or upper classes. Here the use of words and phrases can be disconcerting to the reader, particularly after the diction and slang of an era has become dated. In "The Brushwood Boy," George Cottar, the perfect public-school graduate and heroic young officer, resorts to "By Jove" on a regular basis. Possibly accurate then, it is artificial and stereotyped to a later generation. The same might be said about Kipling's attempts to re-create the voices of children: sometimes they are successful, sometimes not. If dialogue and dialect can deepen and extend the meaning and quality of a story, they can also date a story and detract from it.

In the 1890's, after his marriage to Carrie and the birth of his three children, Kipling, although continuing to write short stories and novels for an adult audience, also turned his hand to works for children. Kipling had an empathetic feeling for children; some critics suggest that he never entirely outgrew his own childhood, with its traumas and rewards. *The Jungle Book* was published in 1894 and *The Second Jungle Book* the following year. The series of stories of the baby Mowgli reared by wolves in the jungle is perhaps the most enduring of Kipling's many short-story collections. Several generations of children read about Father and Mother Wolf, the tiger Shere Khan, the sleepy bear Baloo, the panther Bagheera, and Kaa, the python. In later decades, other children came to know them through the Walt Disney cartoon feature, but there is a quality in the Kipling stories that did not translate fully to the screen. Like authors of other animal stories, Kipling anthropomorphized his creatures, and they exhibit recognizable human characteristics, but his jungle contains a quality of danger, of menace, which was not replicated in the Disney production.

Kipling's City of the Cold Lair in "The King's Ankus," inhabited only by the evil White Cobra, places the reader in a dark, dangerous, and claustrophobic building, a house of fear and death. A continuing motif in the stories involves references to the Law of the Jungle—Charles Darwin's survival of the fittest—an ideology very prominent in the imperialist years of the late nineteenth century. The villainous Shere Khan, Mowgli's rival who is always eager to put Mowgli to death, belonged to that jungle world, while the Monkey-People as portrayed in "Kaa's Hunting" and human beings, driven from their village in "Letting in the Jungle," did not. Both species did not properly follow the law; both were cowardly, vindictive, thoughtless, greedy, and irrational.

The *Just So Stories* were published in 1902. These were composed for an audience younger and more innocent than the readers of *The Jungle Book* stories. The teller of the tales, or fables, addresses his hearer as "O my Best Beloved," who was Kipling's eldest child, Josephine, who died at the age of six, in 1899. The *Just So Stories* appeal on two levels. First, they purport to answer some of the eternal questions of childhood such as "How the Camel Got His Hump" and "How the Leopard Got His

Spots." In so doing, Kipling's genius for specific details captivates the reader. From "How the Whale Got His Throat" comes the following:

> If you swim to latitude Fifty North, longitude Forty West (that is magic), you will find sitting *on* a raft, *in* the middle of the sea, with nothing on but a pair of blue canvas breeches, a pair of suspenders (you *must* not forget the suspenders, Best Beloved), and a jack-knife, one shipwrecked Mariner.

Second, the settings of the tales enchant with their exotic locale, such as the Howling Desert of the camel, the High Veldt of the leopard, and "the banks of the turbid Amazon" in those High and Far-Off Times.

The fourth collection of Kipling's children's stories was *Puck of Pook's Hill*, published in 1906. Now ensconced in the English countryside at Bateman's, Kipling turned to the history of England. Puck, "the oldest Old Thing in England," appears to two young children, Dan and Una, and through the use of magic conjures up for them various past eras from pre-Roman times onward. The nationalistic bias of the tales is not heavy-handed, and generally the narrative and the conversations of the characters are appropriate for children, while Puck's world, if not Puck himself, is more familiar and less exotic than Kipling's earlier children's books. Among re-created practical Romans, patriotic Saxons, and archetypal peasants, the most evocative tale is "Dymchurch Flit," recited by the narrator in a Sussex dialect. In the aftermath of Henry VIII's Protestant Reformation, England's fairies ("pharisees") wished to flee from the land, and a peasant woman gives her two disabled sons through a "pure love-loan" to ferry them to the Continent. At the end of each conjuring of the past, however, Puck causes the children to forget him and his creations; he and his magic belong in the stories, not in so-called real life. Although Puck uses magic, the stories themselves are more realistic, being grounded in history, than either the fables of *The Jungle Book*, *The Second Jungle Book*, or *Just So Stories*.

One of Kipling's most successful short stories was "Mrs. Bathurst," published in 1904 and set in South Africa. On one level, the story is told through an unidentified first-person narrator. He and his friend Inspector Hooper, a railway investigator who had just returned from surveying railway equipment in the interior, are passing time drinking beer on a hot day. Hooper has something in his pocket for which he occasionally reaches but never quite removes. They are shortly joined by Pycroft, a sailor, and Sergeant Pritchard, whom the narrator knows but Hooper does not. Pycroft and Pritchard begin to reminisce about sailors whom they have known: Boy Niven who led them astray in the forests of British Columbia supposedly searching for his uncle's farm, Spit-Kit Jones who married "the cocoanut-woman," and Moon, who had "showed signs o'bein' a Mormonastic beggar" and who deserted after sixteen years of service. The talk then turns to "V" who had disappeared just recently while up-country, only eighteen months before his pension. "V" was also known as Click because of his false teeth, which did not quite fit. Hooper is interested in what Pycroft and Pritchard have to say about "V" and asks them if "V" has any tattoos. Pritchard takes umbrage, believing that Inspector Hooper is seeking information in order to arrest his friend "V." Apologies are made, and then Hooper asks to hear more about "Vickery," though until that moment only "V" had been used in the discussion.

The narrator asks why Vickery ran away, and Pycroft, through a smile, lets it be known that there was a woman involved. Mrs. Bathurst, a widow, owned a hotel in New Zealand frequented by sailors and others. Asked to describe her, Pycroft answered that " 'Tisn't beauty, so to speak, nor good talk necessarily. It's just It." Pycroft has now become the primary narrator, and Vickery and Mrs. Bathurst are filtered through his memories and perceptions. According to Pycroft, Mrs. Bathurst had "It," and Vickery was captivated although he did not let that be known to Pycroft at the time. Last December, as Pycroft tells the story, while on liberty in Cape Town, he ran into Vickery who, visibly disturbed, demanded that Pycroft accompany him to a biograph or cinematograph. This early motion picture—a recent novelty—featured scenes from England. Sitting in the front row, Vickery and Pycroft watched various London views appear on the "magic-lantern sheet." The scene shifted to London's Paddington Station, and among the passengers who came down the platform in the direction of the camera was Mrs. Bathurst who "looked out straight at us with that blindish look. . . . She walked on and on till she melted out of the picture—like a shadow jumpin' over a candle."

At Vickery's urging, Pycroft accompanies him for five consecutive evenings to the cinematograph. On one occasion, Vickery agitatedly claims that Mrs. Bathurst is looking for him. Then, under obscure circumstances, Vickery is assigned up-country, and before he leaves he tells Pycroft that the motion picture of Mrs. Bathurst would appear again in a town where he would be able to see her once more. Vickery also abruptly informs Pycroft that he is not a murderer, for his wife had died during childbirth after Vickery had shipped out. Confused, Pycroft asked for the rest of the story but was not enlightened: " 'The rest,' 'e says, 'is silence,' " borrowing from *Hamlet* (c. 1600-1601). Pycroft heard no more from Vickery.

At this point Hooper again reaches into his pocket and makes a reference to false teeth being acceptable evidence in a court of law. He then tells of his recent experience in the interior. Told to watch for a couple of tramps, Hooper recites how he could see them from a long way off, one standing and one sitting. They were dead.

There'd been a bit of a thunderstorm in the teak, you see, and they were both stone dead and black as charcoal. That's what they really were, you see—charcoal. They fell to bits when we tried to shift 'em. The man who was standin' up had the false teeth. I saw 'em shinin' against the black. . . . Both burned to charcoal.

Again, Hooper reaches to his pocket, and again he does not bring forth anything. Although no other evidence appears, Pritchard for one seems to assume that the other body, unidentified by Hooper, is Mrs. Bathurst. Pycroft concludes that he for one is glad that Vickery is dead, wishing only to drink the last of the beer.

Throughout the story, Mrs. Bathurst is perceived through a series of images, as seen and related by Pycroft and Pritchard, who had known her in New Zealand, as told by Vickery to Pycroft, as she appears flickering on the motion-picture screen, and as the unidentified narrator recites these varying images to the reader. If one theme in "Mrs. Bathurst" is the difficulty of perceiving the reality behind the images, another is the compulsive and destructive power of love. This was not a new aspect in Kipling's work, but perhaps never before had the woman, and even the man, Vickery, been quite so filtered from the reader through the various narrators and now including her image on the screen. Vickery's death apparently resulted because of his experience with Mrs. Bathurst. What was that experience? Was he escaping from her or seeking her out? Was he guilty of something? Apparently he was not guilty of murdering his wife. Had love or its consequences driven him mad? One critic has pointed out the element of "synchronicity," or the significant coincidence as an element in "Mrs. Bathurst." Many twentieth century writers, from James Joyce to Anthony Powell, have employed this device. In "Mrs. Bathurst," the most notable example was the coincidence of Vickery and then Pycroft discovering Mrs. Bathurst on the motion-picture screen. The story is of seemingly disjointed events, like individual scenes in a motion picture. Combined they may have a coherence, but what that coherence is, or means, remains obscure, merely flickering images. Readers have puzzled over "Mrs. Bathurst" ever since the story first appeared.

Several of Kipling's later stories continue to develop his earlier themes. In 1904, Kipling wrote "They." A ghost story, or perhaps a fantasy, its setting is a beautiful, isolated country house in England inhabited by a young blind woman who, through her sheer need, has been able to bring back the spirits of dead children and thus to transcend the grave, the ultimate barrier. Like Mrs. Bathurst and other of Kipling's female characters, the blind woman has a power that profoundly affects the world around her. In "The Wish House," Grace Ashcroft goes to an abandoned house, inhabited by wraiths, where it was possible to take on the pain of some loved one; for her, it was her former lover. Like the blind woman in "They," however, she is driven by a love that is ultimately a selfish one: she is willing to accept his pain as hers not only because she loved him but also because she hopes that he will never marry and find happiness with anyone else.

"Mary Postgate," a powerful story of repression and revenge, portrays a middle-aged spinster and companion who passively accepts the abuse of the young boy of the house, Wyndham Fowler. He treated her shabbily for years, throwing things at her, calling her names such as "Posty" and "Packhead," and belittling her abilities. Then, while in training as a pilot in World War I, Wynn is accidentally killed. Postgate has long repressed and denied any feelings and does so again when his death is announced; her only regret is that he died before he had the chance to "kill somebody." While she is in town getting paraffin to burn Wynn's effects, a building collapses, killing a young girl; although the local doctor tells her that the crash occurred from natural causes, she refuses to accept it, convinced that the Germans have bombed the house. Returning home to light the fire, she comes across an injured pilot in the garden and, assuming that he is German, refuses to summon a doctor, electing instead to watch him die. In choosing the pilot's death, Postgate not only is having her revenge for the death of Wynn and the girl killed supposedly at the hands of the hated German enemy but also is gaining her personal revenge for the hollowness of her own life. The pilot in the garden might well be German, but for Mary it made no difference: it could have been anyone. As he dies and as the fire consumes Wynn's effects, Mary experiences a rush of ecstasy comparable to a sexual release. "Mary Postgate" is a deeply felt exploration of a damaged human psyche.

"Dayspring Mishandled" is one of Kipling's last and finest stories. It too is a story of revenge, but revenge ultimately not taken. It tells of two writers, Manallace and Castorley, cynically writing for pulp publication: "If you save people thinking you can do anything with 'em." After they quarrel, Castorley decides to write real literature and becomes a pseudoexpert on Geoffrey Chaucer; Manallace, who does have literary abilities, chooses not to pursue his talent and continues the easy path. Over an unspecified insult by Castorley to a woman for whom Manallace has been caring—typically in Kipling, much is left unsaid—Manallace vows revenge, creating a fake Chaucerian manuscript that Castorley publicly proclaims as legitimate, thus earning a knighthood. Manallace plans to reveal the fake, perhaps to the press, perhaps to Castorley himself to drive him insane, but he delays his plan as Castorley's health begins to fail and as he is put under the care of a doctor Gleeag, who Manallace later suspects is poisoning Castorley. Lady Castorley urges Manallace to help Castorley assemble his collected works for publication and implies that she knows about the forgery; Manallace believes that she is having an affair with Gleeag, the doctor, and that she wants knowledge of the fake Chaucer manuscript to come out in hopes that the shock will kill her husband. On his deathbed, Castorley confesses his fears to Manallace: the manuscript was "*too* good," and his wife has reminded him that "a man could do anything with anyone if he saved him the trouble of thinking," which is exactly what Manallace has done with Castorley by allowing him to validate the fake without really thinking. Castorley dies of what Gleeag, Lady Castorley's paramour, said was "Malignant kidney-disease—generalized at the end."

Like most of Kipling's best stories, "Dayspring Mishandled" explores the recurring themes of passion and revenge, the failure of human nature, the confusion in relationships, frustrated ambition, and the inability to see clearly, even in the understanding of oneself. It is rich in allusions and references that remain unexplained and are left for the reader to explore. Kipling's most popular stories were the product of his early life, but some of his greatest stories—too often ignored for a time—were written toward the end.

Other major works

NOVELS: *The Light That Failed*, 1890; *The Naulahka: A Story of East and West*, 1892 (with Wolcott Balestier); *Captains Courageous*, 1897; *Kim*, 1901.

POETRY: *Departmental Ditties*, 1886; *Barrack-Room Ballads and Other Verses*, 1892; *The Seven Seas*, 1896; *Recessional and Other Poems*, 1899; *The Five Nations*, 1903; *The Years Between*, 1919; *Rudyard Kipling's Verse*, 1940 (definitive edition).

NONFICTION: *American Notes*, 1891; *Beast and Man in India*, 1891; *Letters of Marque*, 1891; *The Smith Administration*, 1891; *From Sea to Sea*, 1899; *The New Army in Training*, 1914; *France at War*, 1915; *The Fringes of the Fleet*, 1915; *Sea Warfare*, 1916; *Letters of Travel, 1892-1913*, 1920; *The Irish Guards in the Great War*, 1923; *A Book of Words*, 1928; *Something of Myself: For My Friends Known and Unknown*, 1937; *Uncollected Prose*, 1938 (2 volumes); *Rudyard Kipling to Rider Haggard: The Record of a Friendship*, 1965 (Morton N. Cohen, editor).

MISCELLANEOUS: *The Sussex Edition of the Complete Works in Prose and Verse of Rudyard Kipling*, 1937-1939 (35 volumes).

Bibliography

Birkenhead, Lord. *Rudyard Kipling.* London: Weidenfeld & Nicolson, 1978. This work was initially completed in 1948 but was not published until much later because of the opposition of Elsie Bambridge, Kipling's daughter. It contains some information from documents later destroyed.

Carrington, C. E. *The Life of Rudyard Kipling.* Garden City, N.Y.: Doubleday, 1956. The first major published study of Kipling's life, the author succeeded with Elsie Bambridge where Lord Birkenhead did not. Also contains some material later destroyed. Sympathetic but not entirely uncritical of Kipling's politics.

Rutherford, Andrew, ed. *Kipling's Mind and Art.* Stanford, Calif.: Stanford University Press, 1964. Subtitled *Selected Critical Esays*, it includes commentaries by Edmund Wilson, George Orwell, and Lionel Trilling, among others.

Seymour-Smith, Martin. *Rudyard Kipling.* New York: St. Martin's Press, 1989. The author of this provocative and controversial work probes deeply into Kipling's personality and sexuality and argues that they are the key to the understanding of Kipling's writings.

Tompkins, J. M. S. *The Art of Rudyard Kipling.* Lincoln: University of Nebraska Press, 1965. First published in 1959, this major critical study of Kipling's literary work should be consulted in any discussion of Kipling's art.

Wilson, Angus. *The Strange Ride of Rudyard Kipling: His Life and Works.* London: Martin Secker & Warburg, 1977. Wilson, literary critic and novelist, sees Kipling's ability to remain in part a child as the key to his imagination. Wilson's own background in fiction gives insight into Kipling's own works.

Eugene S. Larson

HEINRICH VON KLEIST

Born: Frankfurt an der Oder, Prussia; October 18, 1777
Died: Wannsee bei Potsdam, Prussia; November 21, 1811

Principal short fiction:
Erzählung, 1810-1811 (2 volumes; *The Marquise of O, and Other Stories*, 1960).

Other literary forms
Heinrich von Kleist considered himself primarily a dramatist, and each of his several plays is recognized today as a masterpiece of its type. *Der zerbrochene Krug* (1808; *The Broken Jug*, 1930), Kleist's comedy of unmasking, is one of the liveliest exhibitions of comic misunderstanding and double entendre in European drama. In *Penthesilea* (1808; English translation, 1959), Kleist restructures a Greek myth as a psychological tragedy. Under the spell of a Dionysian frenzy, Penthesilea murders Achilles when she misinterprets his gesture of reconciliation and love. When she realizes what she has done, she wills herself to die. *Das Käthchen von Heilbronn* (1810; *Cathy of Heilbronn*, 1927) and *Penthesilea* are paired by Kleist as opposite expressions of identical inner impulses. *Cathy of Heilbronn* is a fairy tale in which the heroine's forbearance and inner surety guided by dream win her a life of true happiness. Kleist also wrote a family tragedy, *Die Familie Schroffenstein* (1803; *The Schroffenstein Family*, 1916), a patriotic play, *Die Hermannsschlact* (1821), and *Amphitryon* (1807; English translation, 1962), an adaptation of Molière's comedy of the same name. Kleist's fragmentary tragedy, *Robert Guiskard* (1808; English translation, 1962), prompted Wieland's celebrated comment that the play, if finished, would unite the spirits of Aeschylus, Sophocles, and Shakespeare. Kleist's last play, the internationally known *Prinz Friedrich von Homburg* (1821; *The Prince of Homburg*, 1875), follows the career of a young prince whose dream of future glory is playfully encouraged by the Elector and his guests, who come upon the prince walking in his sleep. The prince wins a military victory but is sentenced to death for violating orders. When he sees his grave being dug, he recoils in horror and begs for his life. Later he accepts his guilt and passionately yearns for death. When he is pardoned and celebrated as a hero after all, reality seems more illusory than the dream which opens the play.

Kleist was also a journalist, and he wrote a group of war poems and several aesthetic and political essays. These along with several of his stories first appeared in newspapers.

Achievements
Although he received little recognition during his lifetime, Kleist is today considered a masterful writer of fiction and one of the greatest German dramatists. Critics rank his work second only to that of his great contemporaries, Johann Wolfgang von Goethe and Friedrich von Schiller. His short fiction (novellas), as well as his dra-

mas, all confront the central problem of the elusive quality of truth, and even his highly individual writing style and syntax seem to reflect that problem by using an objective tone and a complex pattern of a clause within a clause, breaking the logical sequence of the reader's thoughts. The world is presented as problematic or "torn," bereft of its logical or sensible wholeness, and his characters are confronted with an irrational universe, barring the possibility of justice and happiness. Kleist's tragic view of the contradictions in the world present an essentially modern viewpoint, a forerunner of the feelings of isolation and alienation in an unpredictable world so often presented by twentieth century writers.

Biography

Following the military tradition of his family, Heinrich von Kleist joined the Prussian army at the age of fifteen, but he resigned his commission in 1799, declaring that he had wasted seven valuable years. He returned to Frankfurt an der Oder, the city of his birth, where he entered the university. Kleist plunged himself into a rigorous study of mathematics and philosophy, believing that through virtuous discipline and knowledge, one could achieve moral perfection and happiness. He became engaged to a general's daughter, Wilhelmine von Zenge, and began teaching her his eudaemonistic precepts by letter. In 1801, Kleist announced the total collapse of his convictions, which he claimed resulted from reading Kant's philosophy. This so-called "Kant crisis" set Kleist forth on the erratic and intense search for meaning which was to characterize the remaining eleven years of his life.

Kleist traveled to France, hoping to accomplish "something good, absolutely." When his decision to become a Swiss farmer came to naught, he began to write. In 1803, he outlined several plays and finished a draft of *The Schroffenstein Family*. Favorable reviews of the play encouraged him, and he probably outlined several stories as well. Kleist's exhilaration soon gave way to despondency; he broke his engagement, journeyed through Switzerland and Italy, and returned to Paris, where he burned the fragment of *Robert Guiskard*. He then left Paris to join Napoleon's forces in hopes of dying during the invasion of England, but he was located by a friend and sent back to Germany.

In 1804, Kleist was given work by the Finance Minister of Berlin. He held that post and others like it for two years, and despite continual bouts of illness, he completed several stories and plays. While traveling to Dresden in 1807, Kleist and several friends were arrested as French spies. Kleist continued writing in prison and upon his release was celebrated by the literary society of Dresden. He met Adam Müller there, and the two founded the literary journal, *Phöbus*, which, after a promising start, failed. Disillusioned with the instability of the literary world, Kleist moved to Austria and then to Prague where he tried to found a patriotic journal called *Germania*. His political activism and publishing plans came to nothing when Austria fell to Napoleon.

In 1810, Kleist appeared back in Berlin. His first volume of *Erzählungen* was published that year, and he founded the *Berliner Abendblätter*, Germany's first daily newspaper. The *Abendblätter* became an immediate popular success, but the government soon censored much of its news. The last issue appeared just six months after the first.

Kleist appealed to the king for a civil service post or a stipend but got no response. A second volume of five of Kleist's *Novellen* appeared later that year, but his dramas and stories did not earn him a living. As a final resort, Kleist turned again to the military. He joined the Prussian army just as an alliance was signed with France. Once again French victories signaled Kleist's defeats. With his last resource exhausted, Kleist appealed to his family but found that they were no longer willing to help. Weary and embittered by the years of struggle and rejection, Kleist feared that his love of art was beginning to wane. In 1811, he met a terminally ill young woman, and the two made a suicide pact. On November 21, 1811, on the shores of Wannsee near Berlin, Heinrich von Kleist shot Henrietta Vogel and then himself.

Analysis

"Das Erdbeben in Chili" ("The Earthquake in Chile") was the first of Kleist's *Novellen* to appear in print, and in many ways it is emblematic of all of his tales. The refugees from the earthquake, which hit Santiago in 1647, experience in literal fashion what Kleist regards as the general condition of human existence—people are set adrift from the regular order of their days, and the visible framework of the world falls into unexpected collapse. Life's cataclysms, be they geological or psychological, are not inevitable, but they are unpredictable. Kleist's stories are fraught with accidents and unexpected reversals which confound human response.

When Jeronimo hears the bells signaling his lover's execution, he vows to die with her. He is preparing to hang himself when the earthquake hits, destroying the prison and setting him free. Each lover thinks the other is dead, but they find each other, and Josepha has their baby with her. In the company of other refugees, they experience a night of Edenic calm, convinced they have been saved by divine miracle. Those who have fled with them do not mention their illicit love, which had sentenced Josepha to death and Jeronimo to prison. Drawn together in extremity, the human family is as one. By morning the tremors stop, and Josepha is eager to go to the cathedral to give thanks. As she and Jeronimo enter, they hear the priest describing the earthquake as a punishment for moral laxity, and he mentions the young lovers by name. They try to leave but are recognized. The outraged crowd turns murderous and beats them to death in front of the cathedral.

Kleist's later protagonists do not fall victim to the sort of direct, unanswerable force which destroys Jeronimo and Josepha. Later characters are more active and articulate; their fates are more complex. No matter how involved their stories, however, all Kleist's heroes share a native ingenuousness with the two young lovers in "The Earthquake in Chile." These characters attempt to keep a strange world at bay by allegiance to an inner certainty which is precarious and enigmatic but deeply felt. Such convictions may produce suffering and confusion or, on occasion, redemption. Kleist's characters ask questions, faint, describe the world or themselves as mad, but they cling to their own sense of truth as best they can. This haphazard bravery has its wellspring in human feeing, which in Kleist's world endows it with a sort of purity and honor.

In "Über das Marionettentheater" ("The Marionette Theater"), Kleist describes the difference between a marionette and a human dancer. Because the puppet is built around a center of gravity, its limbs move effortlessly and in harmony; it is possessed of every grace. Perfectly controlled from above, it is so light its feet barely touch the earth. Human dancers, although free from strings and able to move as they desire, are weighted to the earth. Their motions are typically awkward and artificial attempts to mime the weightless grace of the marionette. Characters such as Littegarde and Friedrich in "Der Zweikampf" ("The Duel") and several of Kleist's heroines intimate that some dancers can locate the center of gravity and dance with intuitive grace.

The Marquise of O is one such character. She is a young widow rearing her children quietly in the shelter of her father's house. To her great disbelief, she learns that she is pregnant. Her parents are shocked and then mortified when she denies any knowledge of how such a condition could have arisen. An examining doctor makes jokes at her expense; she is scorned by her brother and driven from the house by her father. Retaining her dignity and poise, the marquise settles herself and her children in new quarters and advertises in the newspaper for the unknown man to come forth.

A few months before, Count F—, commander of forces which had the marquise's father's castle under siege, had rescued the young widow from a band of his own men. She called the count her angel and fainted, but the commander himself then took advantage of her. Count F— returns months later and asks to marry the marquise. He is in love with her and ashamed of his deed, but he does not admit to the rape. By then, the marquise has discovered her pregnancy and rejects him, declaring herself unworthy.

In great embarrassment, Count F— answers the newspaper ad. The family is happily relieved. Ashamed of their past conduct, they are anxious to put the embarrassing incident aside. They welcome the count into the family and make wedding plans. It is the marquise who hesitates. Her trust had been betrayed, and she is too honorable to capitulate immediately to the count's advances; she is also too honest to deny love for the sake of revenge. She marries Count F— and the two produce a houseful of children and live happily ever after. The marquise, who answers to no force except her own honorable convictions, is one of the strongest heroines in all of short fiction. Toni, the heroine of "Die Verlobung in St. Domingo" ("The Engagement in Santo Domingo") is a similar character, but her faith and confident actions cost her her life.

Tension between inner convictions and the confusions of the external world is at the center of most of Kleist's stories. Only in "Der Findling" ("The Foundling") does Kleist allow unexpected tragedy to assume the proportions of perverse malevolence. "The Foundling" is an oddity in Kleist's corpus, and it lacks the authenticity of his other tales which present life as paradox. Kleist's finest and most complex study of ambiguity is *Michael Kohlhaas* (1810), which purports to be the story of one man's search for justice.

While taking a group of horses to market, Kohlhaas is illegally detained at the Brandenburg-Saxony border and charged a tax. He is forced to leave two horses as substitute payment and also a man to tend them. When he has proof that the tax is illegal, he presses charges. Upon his return, he finds that his horses have been abused and his man is missing. He is still patient, confident that the law will redress his grievances. Kohlhaas presses his case further, but it is ignored by the magistrates. When his wife is accidentally killed while trying to bring his case to an authority's attention, Kohlhaas vows to take things into his own hands. His fervor for justice turns to self-righteousness and violence when he attacks a nunnery and begins burning towns. His band of marauders is feared throughout the land, and Kohlhaas, swept up by his own sense of power, names himself an emissary of the Archangel Michael and has himself carried by porters. Justice and revenge become inseparable.

Martin Luther issues a proclamation declaring Kohlhaas' actions evil and appeals to him to stop. Since he respects no man more than Luther, Kohlhaas goes to him and humbly follows his directives. A series of unfortunate events follow which eventually cost Michael Kohlhaas his life. The incompetence and inattention of government authorities turn out to be the horse dealer's greatest enemies. Kohlhaas is an earnest individual who is unable to elicit honorable redress from a disorganized bureaucratic system. In his quest for individual justice, he resembles many a twentieth century protagonist. This theme appears to be the central one of *Michael Kohlhaas* until the last several pages of the story, at which point the plot is riven in two.

As the story reaches its conclusion, the reader is told that Michael Kohlhaas carries a locket around his neck in which is contained a piece of paper which reveals the fate of the House of Saxony. Kohlhaas was given the paper by a Gypsy Woman at a carnival shortly after his wife died, although this event is not reported in the narrative. When the Elector of Saxony learns that Kohlhaas is the man with the prophecy, he offers to spare the doomed man's life if he will give him the paper. The Gypsy Woman visits Kohlhaas in prison and warns him that the Elector will take the amulet from him after death if he does not relinquish it. She also tells him that the bit of paper can save his life. Kohlhaas, however, does not give up the paper. He reads it, peers straight into the Elector's eyes, places it in his mouth and swallows it. Then he walks to the scaffold to meet his death.

This unexpected turn of events has a disorienting effect on the entire story. What seemed to be a complex tale of an unfortunate individual in a bureaucratic society is redirected into another realm of human experience. The Gypsy Woman makes a reader reexamine all the earlier events of the story. Is it the government which is disordered and disorienting to an individual like Michael Kohlhaas or is it the nature of life itself? Human foolishness and sloth cause government's inconsistencies, but what causes universal inconsistencies? The Gypsy Woman is a supernatural force associated with irrationality and accident. Her presence is evidence that magic and mystery are at large in the cosmos whether man recognizes them or not.

Kleist's themes are remarkably echoed by his prose style. His language is objective in tone and apparently sequentially presented, but what is connected in the orderly schemata of the German sentence is often neither logical nor sequential.

"Das Bettelweib von Locarno" ("The Beggarwoman of Locarno"), Kleist's briefest story, illustrates the power the author could create almost solely from the force of language. The plot *per se* is but the sketchiest of anecdotes. An Italian count orders an old woman to sleep behind the stove. As she crosses the room, she slips and hurts her back but does manage to get behind the stove. The next morning she is dead. Some time later a prospective purchaser of the castle is hosted in the room where the beggarwoman died. During the night, he hears a ghost and leaves the next morning. The count and countess spend a night in the room themselves. They hear scratchings as if someone is crossing the room. The countess rushes away and the count, "weary of life," burns down the castle. The reader is never told whether there is a ghost or whether the count believes there is. The old woman's ghost prompts all the action and yet her presence is questionable. She might be called a palpable sense of nothingness. If her spirit is present, the reader has no sense of what it is, what its motives are, or what it means. Such moments of complete and eloquent silence are a hallmark of Kleist's narrative style.

In Kleist's stories, supernatural power is visible in every human turning, but its meaning seems to pose the same questions for the narrator as it does for his readers and his characters. At best, the artist can describe a multiplicity of perceptions which might be regarded as true. Kleist calls one of his stories a legend and draws further attention to its ambiguous meaning when he names it "Die heilige Cäcilie: Oder, Die Gewalt der Musik" ("St. Cecilia: Or, The Power of Music.")

During a period when iconoclasm is rife, four brothers take it upon themselves to rid the world of one particularly obvious popish relic, the convent of St. Cecilia. They gather a band of like-minded protesters and, on the Feast of Corpus Christi, enter the church intending to reduce it to rubble. The nuns, although outwardly composed, are quite undone. The men are milling around awaiting a signal from their leaders when a pale nun enters and approaches the orchestra. The other sisters are surprised to see the orchestra conductor, whom they believe to be deathly ill. As the first notes of the glorious festival music sound, the four brothers fall on their knees before the altar and remain motionless throughout the concert. Their baffled followers wait in vain for a signal. Hours later the four have to be removed to a lunatic asylum. There they keep their prayerful attitude which is broken only when they bellow the *gloria in excelsis* each night at midnight.

Six years later their mother arrives in Aachen. She hears the festival described by one of the protesters as a youthful misadventure. The Mother Superior describes the feast as a miracle, since St. Cecilia herself apparently conducted the music. No one, however, accounts for her insane sons whose ghostly singing still splits the night. Such is the pitch of Kleist's miracles and mysteries. They have as many meanings as observers, and one meaning as good as cancels out the others. Paradox remains at the center: Count F— is a devil and an angel, Michael Kohlhaas is an honorable and terrible man, and the miracle of St. Cecilia is both glorious and horrible. Contradiction is life's basic truth.

Other major works

NOVELS: *Michael Kohlhaas*, 1810 (novella; English translation, 1844); *Die Marquise von O . . .*, 1810 (*The Marquise of O . . .*, 1960).

PLAYS: *Die Familie Schroffenstein*, 1803 (*The Schroffenstein Family*, 1916); *Amphitryon*, 1807 (English translation, 1962); *Penthesilea*, 1808 (English translation, 1959); *Der zerbrochene Krug*, 1808 (*The Broken Jug*, 1930); *Robert Guiskard*, 1808 (English translation, 1962); *Das Käthchen von Heilbronn: Oder, Die Feuerprobe*, 1810 (*Cathy of Heilbronn: Or, The Trial by Fire*, 1927); *Prinz Friedrich von Homburg*, 1821 (*The Prince of Homburg*, 1875); *Die Hermannsschlacht*, 1821.

Bibliography

Dyer, Denys. *The Stories of Kleist: A Critical Study.* New York: Holmes & Meier, 1977. An excellent study of Kleist's masterpieces of short fiction, intended for students and general readers with little knowledge of German literature. After a chapter on Kleist's life and works, Dyer treats the stories individually so that each chapter is a self-contained interpretation. Chapter 8 summarizes the main points about Kleist's themes and style. Contains an index and a bibliography, including some sources on individual stories (many in German).

Gearey, John. *Heinrich von Kleist: A Study in Tragedy and Anxiety.* Philadelphia: University of Pennsylvania Press, 1968. A helpful and readable study of Kleist's life and works. In studying the works, Gearey focuses on the problem of conflict, which he believes is caused by Kleist's own puzzlement over the problem of human experience. Includes plot summaries and analyses of Kleist's early dramas, some of his novellas, and his later major works. Supplemented by a chronology of Kleist's life and a bibliography.

Grandin, John M. *Kafka's Prussian Advocate: A Study of the Influence of Heinrich von Kleist on Franz Kafka.* Columbia, S.C.: Camden House, 1987. This study tracks parallels of style and theme in the works of the two writers. It is Grandin's belief that much of Kafka can be better understood through "Kleistian eyes" and that some Kleist stories can be read "from the more modern Kafka perspective." The comments on *Michael Kohlhaas* are particularly helpful. Complemented by an index and a bibliography.

Maass, Joachim. *Kleist: A Biography.* Translated by Ralph Manheim. New York: Farrar, Straus & Giroux, 1983. A comprehensive biography of Kleist including detailed information about his family background, life, and attitudes. His works are also discussed in context. Includes photographs, a select bibliography, and an index of works and names.

Mehigan, Timothy J. *Text as Contract: The Nature and Function of Narrative Discourse in the "Erzählungen" of Heinrich von Kleist.* Frankfurt am Main: Peter

Lang, 1988. A discussion of Kleist's short fiction from the point of view of language and communication. Mehigan believes that the narratives have a "strong sense of structure," even when describing disorder, and he uses a narrative paradigm to show the relationship between pattern and disorder in the individual works. Contains an extensive bibliography.

Silz, Walter. *Heinrich von Kleist: Studies in His Works and Literary Character.* Philadelphia: University of Pennsylvania Press, 1961. A collection of essays on various works and aspects of Kleist's literary expression. Includes separate chapters on "Das Erdbeben in Chili," *Amphitryon,* "Über das Marionettentheater," *Michael Kohlhaas,* and *Prinz Friedrich von Homburg,* and an excellent chapter on the recurrence of certain concepts and expressions in Kleist's work. Supplemented by notes to each chapter, bibliographical references, and an index of names.

Ugrinsky, Alexej, et al., eds. *Heinrich von Kleist Studies.* New York: AMS Press, 1980. A collection of studies prepared for the Heinrich von Kleist bicentennial (1777-1977) and published in both English and German. After an introduction on Kleist's life by Ilse Graham, the discussions are divided into various headings: drama; novellas; marionettes; comparative studies; education, linguistics, and science; and new perspectives. Includes an index and a reprint of the catalog of materials available on Kleist.

Helen Menke
(Revised by *Susan L. Piepke*)

JOHN KNOWLES

Born: Fairmont, West Virginia; September 16, 1926

Principal short fiction
Phineas, 1968.

Other literary forms
In addition to his short fiction, John Knowles has published a volume of nonfiction, *Double Vision* (1964), and several novels, including *A Separate Peace* (1960), *Indian Summer* (1966), *Spreading Fires* (1974), *A Stolen Past* (1983), and *The Private Life of Axie Reed* (1986). He has also written articles for *Saturday Evening Post*, *Story*, *New World Writing*, *Reader's Digest*, and *Holiday*.

Achievements
John Knowles established his literary reputation in the 1960's when *A Separate Peace* won the William Faulkner Foundation Award for a first novel, the Rosenthal Award of the National Institute of Arts and Letters, and an Independent Schools Education Board award. *A Separate Peace* explores the process of growing up, and it became a favorite with younger people in the 1960's, along with William Golding's *Lord of the Flies* (1954) and J. D. Salinger's *The Catcher in the Rye* (1951). In the novel, Knowles reveals the typical precise craftsmanship and handling of characteristic themes that run throughout all of his later work.

Knowles writes about environments he himself has experienced, and his descriptive technique is one of his most appealing qualities. Frequently he uses place description to indicate the environmental shaping of his protagonists' personalities. He ties this to the themes in his work. Knowles is interested in the self-knowledge derived from his protagonists' continual attempts to integrate the two elements of the American character, savagery and cautious Protestantism, into a reasonable whole. His later novels continue to explore the strategies his protagonists invent to reconcile this dualism. Despite their neatness of plot and description, none has received the critical attention given to *A Separate Peace*.

Biography
John Knowles, the third of four children of James Myron and Mary Beatrice Shaw Knowles, was born in Fairmont, West Virginia. At fifteen he left home to attend Phillips Exeter Academy in New Hampshire. After graduating in 1945, he enlisted in the U.S. Army Air Forces' Aviation Cadet Program, qualifying as a pilot. After his discharge, he attended Yale University where he served as editor of the *Yale Daily News*. He graduated in 1949 and went to work as a reporter for the Hartford *Courant*. In 1952, he became a free-lance writer, living for the next several years in southern Europe.

When he returned in 1955, he settled in New York City, but a year later moved to Philadelphia where he worked as an associate editor of *Holiday* magazine and wrote his first novel, *A Separate Peace*. When it was clear that the book was successful, Knowles resigned his position to travel abroad. During his two-year trip, he gathered material for a travel book. A second novel was published when he was abroad. Now an established writer, he returned from Europe to live in New York City. Throughout the 1960's, he traveled, served at several universities as writer-in-residence, and completed another novel and a book of short fiction. After his father died in 1970, Knowles moved to Long Island where he has continued to write novels.

Analysis

John Knowles's *Phineas* consists of six stories, "A Turn with the Sun," "Summer Street," "The Peeping Tom," "Martin the Fisherman," "Phineas," and "The Reading of the Will," which are not linked thematically but which possess a universality which leaves the reader with an insight into the condition of man. Structurally, all the stories are orthodox and follow the traditional plot structure, but their final effect is aimed at more than one level, a symbolic timelessness coming from the context of each story. The plot is only half of each story; the other half is the matrix of the earth from which the author, the story, and the phenomenon of life emerge.

The first story in the volume, "A Turn with the Sun," is set in New Hampshire, and although the immediate locale is Devon, a sophisticated prep school, nature plays a larger role in the story. The plot is simple and concerns the attempts of Lawrence Stewart to break the barrier of the "foggy social bottomland where unacceptable first year boys dwell." Lawrence, the protagonist, has entered Devon in the fall in the fourth form and instantly finds out that he possesses nothing distinct to make him accepted by his "sophisticated" peers. He is from an unknown and small West Virginia town; he does not have outstanding athletic ability; his clothes are wrong; his vocabulary is common; and he engages in conversation about the wrong things. He is assigned to live in a small house with "six other nebulous flotsam," and as early as his fourth day at school, Lawrence shows signs of becoming a person to be considered. Lawrence is standing on the bridge and does not have anything in mind when he dives from it. He is like everyone else when he initially plunges from the bridge, an unknown newcomer, but his dive is so remarkable that when he breaks the surface of the water he has become to his peers a boy to be regarded. His achievement is capped by an invitation to dinner from Ging Powers, a senior from his own town who, previous to his dive, has religiously avoided him.

The dinner that evening is Lawrence's waterloo. In his own mind he is sure that this is the beginning of a new career at Devon. As he walks into the dining room, he sees his host and his friends huddled at a corner table. Ging then introduces him to Vinnie Ump, the vice-chairman of the senior council, and Charles Morrell, the sportsman laureate of Devon, an outstanding football, baseball, and hockey player. During the course of the conversation, Lawrence realizes that Ging is a social climber and immediately feels superior to him. He also understands by looking at Morrell that the important aspect of the athlete is not his ability but his unique personality, the "unconscious authority" which his diverse skills give him. Then his own visions of being the next Captain Marvel get the better of him and he lies, "I have some cousins, two cousins, you know—they're in clubs at Harvard. . . ." Suddenly aware that the others are interested, Lawrence goes on with his diatribe on the clubs of Harvard, capping it eventually with a restatement of his dive from the bridge. When Morrell asserts that "I saw you do it," Lawrence is overwhelmed because the most important athlete in school saw him in his moment of triumph. He envisions the distinct possibility of becoming Morrell's protégé and jumps at the chance by talking continuously about his house and family and anything he can think of to make himself sound important. His downfall occurs when he asks which of the men at chapel the first day of school was the dean; when the other boys describe him, Lawrence responds in his loudest voice, "Like my beagle, that's the way he looks, like the beagle I've got at home, my beagle looks just like that right after he's had a bath." The consternation of the three seniors calls Lawrence's attention to the elderly couple making their way toward the door; his questions ("Was that the dean? . . . Did he hear me?") go unanswered, and Lawrence responds symbolically by slipping under the table. Only then does Lawrence realize the ridiculousness of his position, "under a table in the Anthony Wayne Dining Room of the Devon Inn, making a fool of himself." Immediately Ging, Morrell, and Vinnie make excuses and leave; numbed, Lawrence can only smother his sobs and keep his anguish to himself.

After this evening, all Lawrence's attempts to be "regarded" backfire, until suddenly with the change of seasons he is redeemed to an extent. He plays intramural football and is on the junior varsity swimming team; his housemates start accepting him and calling him "Varsity." Yet there are still sensitive incidents, and he has confrontations with several of his housemates regarding his undistinguished background.

When he returns to Devon after the spring break, the bleakness of winter has given way to the peripheral beauty of spring. Then unexpectedly he begins to slip in his studies. For two successive French classes he is unprepared, but the undercutting from his peers does not seem to bother him. Soon after this he achieves a "minor triumph" when he scores his first goal for his intramural team; but the event is actually of little magnitude and does nothing about furthering his quest to be "regarded." The day of this "minor triumph" turns out to be the final day of his life. After a shower Lawrence goes to the trophy room and fantasizes that 1954 will be the year that he will win the Fullerton Cup, the trophy awarded to the outstanding athlete of each year. Then he suddenly realizes the "finiteness of the cup" and that with the passage of time the cup and the inscriptions on it will all fade from human memory. The room suddenly feels like a crypt, and he steps outside to the freshness and aroma of spring. That night Lawrence drowns in the river. Bruce and Bead, who have gone swimming with him, try to save him, but fail. At a conference two days later Bruce remembers distinctly that Lawrence "had looked different, standing up there on the bridge." The dean asks if Lawrence had looked happy. "Something like that. He wasn't scared, I know that," Bruce answers, unable to fathom the enigma. Structurally "A Turn with the Sun" is a modern short story following in the mode of such writers as Katherine Mansfield, James Joyce, and Sherwood Anderson and sharply distinct from the contemporary mode of stories with a surreal surface structure. The story begins *in medias res*; there is no formal introduction or exposition. The positioning of words in the first sentence, however, together with the punctuation and the soft vowel sounds grouped together, suggests the softness of dusk and is in direct contrast to Lawrence's experience. Moreover, the serene setting sets the area of thematic concern. The atmosphere created in the first sentence is then maintained throughout the story. Everything that Lawrence does or experiences is set against a backdrop of changing seasons, of a beautiful nature indifferent to the upheavals around it. The important images and recurring motifs—the steamy heat, the bridge and the stream, the quest for athletic glory—come together at the end of the story to symbolize Lawrence's intense efforts to be "regarded." Thus "Devon" achieves microcosmic proportions not through the story line, but by repetitive patterns. Parallel scenes (the two dives), motifs, and events juxtaposed with each other create metaphors and achieve symbolic levels; thus Lawrence's accidental death assumes universal meaning.

The narrative technique of flashback which Knowles deploys in "A Turn with the Sun" is also used in the title story of the volume. The flashback in "Phineas" is framed by a prologue and an epilogue in the present tense designed to link the narrative to the present moment. The setting is "Devon," the same as that used in the earlier story, and the cast of characters includes the narrator and his roommate, Phineas or "Finny." Thematically the focus in this story is more on the process of initiation of the young narrator than on the quest to be regarded. When the narrator arrives in Devon during the summer session, he is thrown off by the outgoing attitude of his roommate, Phineas. At the very moment of arrival, Finny lectures him on all subjects, "beginning with God and moving undeviatingly through to sex." The narrator chooses not to reveal his own confidences, however, because he takes an immediate dislike to Phineas.

Phineas is an excellent athlete. He excels in soccer, hockey, and lacrosse and has the queer notion that an athlete is "naturally good at everything at once." When the narrator asks him why he chose these teams, he replies nonchalantly that they give him the freedom to develop and display his individual talent—"to create without any imposed plan." This lack of discipline makes Finny a weak student, and the narrator begins to suspect that Finny is interfering with his studies because "He hated the fact that I could beat him at this. . . . He might be the best natural athlete in school, the most popular boy, but I was winning where it counted." The narrator suddenly feels that he is equal to Finny and that Finny has human frailties after all.

One evening in summer, five students including Finny and the narrator go to the river with the intention of jumping into it from a tree which leans out slightly over the river's edge. Finny jumps into the river impetuously, expecting the others to follow. Everybody refuses except the narrator, who "hated" the idea but jumps anyway because he does not want to "lose" to Phineas. Soon after this event, Phineas draws up a charter for the *Super Suicide Society of the Summer Session*, inscribing his name and the narrator's as charter members and enrolling Chet, Bobby, and Leper as trainees. The society meets almost every evening and all members are required to attend and jump.

On a Thursday evening, the day before a French examination, Phineas goes over to the narrator's room and asks him to attend a meeting of their select society because Leper has finally agreed to jump. The narrator is visibly irritated and says sarcastically, "Okay, we go. We watch little lily-liver Leper not jump from a tree, and I ruin my grade." Finny is taken aback at this and says simply, "I didn't know you needed to study. . . . I thought it just came to you." The narrator realizes for the first time that Phineas has assumed that the narrator's intellectual capacity comes as easily as his own natural ability at sports. Truth dawns on the narrator and he realizes that Phineas has never been jealous of him or considered him as a rival—he has simply considered himself a far "superior" person. This realization causes the narrator, as they both climb the tree by the river, to shake the limb, and Phineas falls into the river with a "sickening natural thud." One of his legs is shattered in the fall and he is maimed for life.

Later, when the narrator goes to see Phineas at the infirmary, his guilt almost makes him reveal the truth. When he asks Phineas if he remembers how he fell, Phineas answers "I just fell, that's all." The narrator finally has a total conception of Phineas' character and realizes that he has not been jealous of Phineas' popularity, background, or skill at sport—he has envied Finny's total and complete honesty.

"Phineas" also has a universal quality stemming from its classic initiation theme. The narrator is initiated into the ways of men within three months of his first meeting with Phineas. Phineas himself is not only the touchstone but also a symbol of an ideal state of being. His lack of human frailties sets him apart from the snobbish class struggle and the Machiavellian quest for athletic fame which Knowles satirizes in "Phineas" and in "A Turn with the Sun." This quest is responsible for the undertone of pessimism in both stories, for it makes victims not only of the involved, but also of the innocent. Thus Lawrence is drowned and Phineas is maimed for life, a victim of his roommate's moment of jealousy in a self-seeking, hostile world.

This negative view of human striving contrasts sharply to the serenity of nature in Knowles's stories. Unlike Thomas Hardy, who depicted nature as a viable force responding directly to human predicaments, Knowles's nature is beautiful, peaceful, and distant. "Phineas" opens with a nostalgic description of an old Massachusetts town with its "ancient impregnable elm" and proceeds to Devon where the pace of summer is sketched in a beautiful metaphor: "Summer moved on in its measureless peace." The story ends with the approach of dusk, which seems to have a special meaning for Knowles; "A Turn with the Sun" opens with a soothing detailed description of the sun going down, and "Martin the Fisherman" ends with the "warm crimson glow" of the sun setting over the ocean. This peaceful beauty is in stark contrast to the social and moral conflict in the stories and symbolizes the other half of life—the latent allure beneath the external conflagration of life.

Epiphany is an element common to all of Knowles's stories. The sudden realization, the dawning of the truth, is quite marked in "Phineas" but is more subtle in "Martin the Fisherman," in which the patron of the fishing boat finally sees the problem of his crew from their perspective after he gets an accidental dunking in the sea. In the later story, Christopher realizes that his father did not leave him anything because he, Christopher, did not need any help. This effect is complemented by Knowles's use of metaphor and a simple uncomplicated style, which is often the vehicle for stories of universal significance.

Other major works

NOVELS: *A Separate Peace*, 1960; *Morning in Antibes*, 1962; *Indian Summer*, 1966; *The Paragon*, 1972; *Spreading Fires*, 1974; *Vein of Riches*, 1978; *Peace Breaks Out*, 1981; *A Stolen Past*, 1983; *The Private Life of Axie Reed*, 1986.

NONFICTION: *Double Vision*, 1964.

Bibliography

Degnan, James. "Sex Ex Machina and Other Problems." *The Kenyon Review* 31 (Spring, 1969): 272-277. By analyzing "Phineas," the source of material for *A Separate Peace*, Degnan shows how Knowles succeeds when he adheres to treating the torments of the sensitive intelligent male adolescent. In other novels, however, he fails because he leaves this theme.

Gardner, John. "More Smog from the Dark Satanic Mills." *The Southern Review* 5 (Winter, 1969): 224-244. Gardner places Knowles's *Indian Summer* among other 1960's novels that he considers trivial because, instead of examining things closely, they make easy distinctions between good and evil. The result is mechanical neatness, but simpleminded morality. This evaluation is a sample of Knowles's criticism dealing with novels other than *A Separate Peace*.

Halio, Jay. "John Knowles' Short Novels." *Studies in Short Fiction* 1 (Winter, 1964): 107-112. In discussing Knowles's first two novels, Halio compares him with Saul Bellow and Angus Wilson in terms of craftsmanship and handling themes that concern looking inward and then coming to terms with society.

McDonald, John. "The Novels of John Knowles." *Arizona Quarterly* 23 (Winter, 1967): 335-342. McDonald places Knowles in the American tradition of Henry James and F. Scott Fitzgerald and examines subjects, themes, and techniques that show his affinity with this group of writers.

Weber, Ronald. "Narrative Method in *A Separate Peace*." *Studies in Short Fiction* 3 (Fall, 1965): 63-72. To show how Knowles's narrative method relates to his themes, Weber explores comparisons with J. D. Salinger's *The Catcher in the Rye* (1951). He shows how, because he is such a precise craftsman, Knowles provides the clearer statement about life.

Zia Hasan
(Revised by *Louise M. Stone*)

MILAN KUNDERA

Born: Brno, Czechoslovakia; April 1, 1929

Principal short fiction

Směšne lásky: Tri melancholicke anekdoty, 1963; *Druyh sešit směšných lásek,* 1965; *Třetí sešit směšných lásek,* 1968; *Směšne lásky,* 1969 (partial translation as *Laughable Loves,* 1974).

Other literary forms

Milan Kundera began his literary career as a poet, playwright, and critic before turning to short fiction. In the late 1960's, he began devoting himself almost exclusively to long fiction, publishing several highly acclaimed novels and a miscellany, *L'Art du roman* (1986; *The Art of the Novel,* 1988), as well as a dramatic "variation" on a favorite eighteenth century novel, entitled *Jacques et son maître* (1970; *Jacques and His Master,* 1985). With director Jaromil Jires, he wrote the screenplay for *Žert* (1969), adapted from his first novel.

Achievements

Published at the very beginning of the reform movement that would culminate in the short-lived Prague Spring of 1968, the novel *Žert* (1967; *The Joke,* 1969, revised 1982) was, in the words of R. C. Porter, "one of those rare literary events which occur when a people suddenly finds its history, accumulated anger and frustration given voice in one masterful stroke." Kundera, along with playwright-president Václav Havel, is one of contemporary Czechoslovakia's two most important writers and, after Franz Kafka, the country's most interesting, influential, and international novelist—"the other K," as Mexican novelist Carlos Fuentes called him. Such flattering comparisons are fully merited, for not only is Kundera, in his own largely apolitical and anti-ideological way, as devoted as Havel to resisting totalitarianism in its various guises; as Kafka did before him, he has changed the very shape and scope of the twentieth century novel, giving it a new form and a new importance. For a writer so intellectually complex and aesthetically uncompromising, he has achieved a surprisingly large but wholly deserved following increased by, perhaps, but certainly not owing to, the popularity of Philip Kaufman's 1987 film version of Kundera's fifth novel, *L'Insoutenable Légèreté de l'être* (1986; *The Unbearable Lightness of Being,* 1984). Included among his many literary honors are the Prix Médicis for *La Vie est ailleurs* (1973; *Life Is Elsewhere,* 1974) and the Jerusalem Prize for Literature on the Freedom of Man in Society, in 1985.

Biography

Milan Kundera's life has followed as curious and circuitous a course as the plots of his polyphonic novels. Influenced by his father, Ludvík, a noted pianist and musicologist, Kundera attended Charles University and the Academy of Music and Dramatic Arts in Prague, where he studied piano, composing, film directing, and screenwriting. He joined the Communist Party in 1948, was expelled in 1950, and was reinstated in 1956. He published three volumes of poetry during the 1950's, joined the academy's film faculty in 1958, and began writing plays and stories in the early 1960's.

The year 1967 proved to be an especially momentous one in Kundera's life. That year saw his marriage to Vera Hrabankova; the publication and immediate success of his first novel, *The Joke*; and his provocative speech at the fourth Writers Union meeting. Warning against the threat that political repression posed to Czech literature, he spearheaded efforts to speed reform and extend freedom. The reformers carried the day. Antonín Novotný fell from power; Alexander Dubček rose, and with him the Prague Spring of 1968, which ended when the Soviet army, "legitimized" by the token participation of its Warsaw Pact allies, invaded Czechoslovakia on August 20. Kundera was soon branded a counter-revolutionary; he was dismissed from his faculty position, was expelled from the party for a second time, and found his plays banned and his books removed from libraries and bookstores.

Silenced in his own country, Kundera soon began to be heard abroad. In 1975, two years after his second novel, *Life Is Elsewhere*, won France's prestigious Prix Médicis, Kundera was allowed to leave Czechoslovakia to accept a faculty appointment at the Université de Rennes. The Communist government proved less generous in responding to the publication of his fourth novel, *Le Livre du rire et de l'oubli* (1979; *The Book of Laughter and Forgetting*, 1980), revoking his citizenship. In 1980, he accepted a position at a university in Paris and became a naturalized French citizen one year later. Although comfortable in France—largely, he said, because of his early interest in, and affection for, Denis Diderot, François Rabelais, and the French Surrealists—Kundera has been as critical of Western forms of censorship as of Communist ones. Asked in 1987—two years before the Havel-led Velvet Revolution, which ended Communist rule in Czechoslovakia—whether he believed he would ever be allowed to return to his native land, Kundera said he would not want to: "One emigration suffices for a lifetime."

Analysis

That the West expects writers from Eastern (or what Milan Kundera prefers to call Central) Europe to be political was something Kundera learned the hard way when an English publisher, in the wake of the Soviet invasion, restructured and to some extent even rewrote *The Joke* to make it into what Kundera subsequently claimed it was not: a political protest against Communism rather than a work of fiction (or, as Kundera countered at the time, a love story only). In terms of ideological preference, Kundera describes himself as "an agnostic" no more interested in a literature of politics than in a literature of the author's personality. He is, in other words, no more and no less opposed to Communist ideology than he is to capitalist (or Communist) "Imagology," as he terms the assault upon individual freedom in his sixth novel, *Nesmrtelnost* (1990; *Immortality*, 1991). His fiction is neither political nor didactic (moralistic), autobiographical nor journalistic. Rather, it is deeply meditative—more an exploration than an explanation.

Kundera traces his literary lineage back to Cervantes, Rabelais, Diderot, Laurence Sterne, and more recently to the great twentieth century Central European writers Hermann Broch, Jaroslav Hašek, Kafka, Robert Musil, and Witold Gombrowicz. What attracts him to the first four is their sense of play, and to the latter five their "search for new forms," a search that is at once "impassioned" yet "devoid of any avant-garde ideology (faith in progress, revolution, and so on)." "The great Central European novelists ask themselves what man's possibilities are in a world that has become a trap," or, as Kundera explained to fellow novelist Philip Roth, a pair of traps: fanaticism on the one side, absolute skepticism on the other, with human beings attempting to negotiate the narrow path between the two. Kundera conceives of his negotiation not in terms of mimetic plots but instead as existential inquiries that raise questions rather than offer answers, preferring the demystifying "wisdom of uncertainty" to the "noisy foolishness" of received ideas. Thus, instead of the plot and characters of conventional fiction, Kundera offers a theme and variation approach and characters who are not mimetic representations but instead "experimental egos" and the author's "own unrealized possibilities." Yet for all the open-ended complexity of Kundera's fiction, his writing proves remarkably clear and concise, almost classically chaste in style despite its often erotic subject matter. It is also a prose that strives to be what Kundera believes Sterne's *Tristram Shandy* (1759-1767) and Diderot's *Jacques le fataliste et son maître* (1796; *Jacques the Fatalist and His Master*, 1797) are: "absolutely irreducible" and "totally unrewritable," qualities as necessary in the media-maddened West as they were in a police state.

Kundera's stories have received little critical attention, overshadowed by his better-known and more ambitious novels. He began writing the stories as a way of relaxing while working on his first play. He soon realized, however, that fiction would serve him far better than drama or poetry as the means for dealing with the "fascinating and enigmatic" reality in which he then found himself and his compatriots. Just as important, only when he began to write the first of his stories was Kundera able to find "my voice, my style, and myself." Kundera, who completed the last of the stories only three days before the Soviet invasion, said that *Laughable Loves* is the book that he is "fondest of because it reflects the happiest time of my life." *Laughable Loves* is important for another reason, for in these early stories one finds the wellsprings of Kundera's later novels (which some convention-bound reviewers have complained are not novels at all but instead story collections). The form of the novel as Broch and Kafka practiced it and as the Soviet critic Mikhail Bakhtin came to define it provided Kundera with the scope and flexibility that his imagination came to require, but a scope and flexibility already manifest in miniature as they were in *Laughable Loves*. In them, the reader finds ample evidence of Kundera's early interest in, and mastery of, the theme and variation approach, which would provide him with a potent means for countering what Terry Eagleton has called "the totalitarian drive of literary fiction."

Laughable Loves is more than the title of three slender volumes published during the 1960's and of the collection of eight of the ten original stories published in 1970 (seven in the French and English editions, 1970 and 1974 respectively). *Laughable Loves* refers as well to the theme on which each of the stories plays its variations—a theme that Kundera also treats in each of his six novels. Love figures prominently and ambiguously throughout Kundera's fiction: partly as a release from everyday reality, partly as a way of achieving at least a momentary personal freedom, partly as a revelation of character, and partly as an epistemological delusion (in *Immortality* Kundera writes that love gives one "the illusion of knowing the other"). Love then, is not so much a state of being as it is the intersection of various social, sexual, political, and epistemological forces, a struggle against power that all too often— and perhaps all too predictably—turns into the exercise of power over another. In *The Book of Laughter and Forgetting*, for example, "Love is a constant interrogation," and in *La Valse aux adieux* (1976; *The Farewell Party*, 1977), an unfaithful yet in his own way loving husband is "always suspecting his wife of suspecting him." The relation between love and totalitarianism proves both close and comic, "laughable," a word that here means more than simply "amusing." Kundera conceives of laughter as the antidote to the seriousness that he believes characterizes the modern, journalistic age. As he explains in his introduction to *Jacques and His Master*, taking the world seriously means "believing what the world would have us believe." Not surprisingly, given the complexity of his meditative style of fiction making, Kundera defines laughter in a twofold way: as an expression of the sheer joy of being and as a more or less existential negation of the world's seriousness. Kundera as hedonist and kitsch destroyer approves of both and also understands that, taken to the extreme, each poses its own danger: the fanaticism of the totalitarian idyll often associated with a youthful lyrical (poetic) idealism and the absolute skepticism of the unbeliever.

Both extremes manifest themselves in the opening story of *Laughable Loves*. "Nobody Will Laugh" bears a striking resemblance to Kundera's slightly later first novel. The story's main character (and narrator) receives a pleading and obsequious letter from a stranger, Mr. Zaturetsky, asking him to read and recommend his enclosed essay for publication in the *Visual Arts Journal*, which, unbeknown to Zaturetsky, rejected the narrator's "controversial" study which that very day appeared in a less orthodox but also less prestigious publication. Seeing that Zaturetsky's essay is unoriginal to the point of being unintentionally plagiaristic, but on the other hand unwilling to do the hatchet work of the very editor who had rejected his essay, Klima, the narrator, decides to amuse himself by writing a long and cynically sympathetic letter in which he manages to make no final evaluation whatsoever. Klima has, however, underestimated his petitioner's desperation and persistence. Zaturetsky begins to appear at the university and even shows up at Klima's attic apartment, where he finds not Klima but the beautiful Klara, who has been sleeping with Klima while he fulfills his promise of finding her a better job. Klima's efforts to elude Zaturetsky prove as desperate and humorous as Zaturetsky's attempts to locate him: Klima changes his teaching schedule, pretends to be in Germany, dresses up a student in his hat and coat, has the department secretary lie for him, and finally, when at last confronted by his nemesis, charges Zaturetsky with having made sexual advances toward Klara.

Following the zany yet terrifying logic of Kundera's fiction and Eugène Ionesco's plays, the consequences of Klima's little joke grow more and more serious, even as Klima continues to believe that everyone will laugh once his story is told. Klima, however, is wrong: "Nobody will laugh." The local committee finds him lacking in seriousness; he will lose his faculty position and with it his future and of course Klara, who has already found someone better suited—and more powerfully placed— to get her what she wants. Klima does find some comfort in the knowledge that his story "was not of the tragic, but rather of the comic variety." Humor such as this comes perilously close to horror, particularly the horror of absurdity without end, an absurdity that permeates every corner of existence, including Mrs. Zaturetsky's dedication to her husband and his essay, which, of course, she has never even read. "It wasn't a question of willful plagiarism," Klima realizes, "but rather an unconscious submission to those authorities who inspired in Mr. Zaturetsky a feeling of sincere and inordinate respect" of the very same kind that the woefully inadequate and inept Mr. Zaturetsky inspires in his utterly sexless and wholly humorless and therefore laughable wife.

Submission of a different kind plays a key role in "The Hitchhiking Game." Here, instead of Klima's friendly first-person narration, Kundera adopts an emotionally distant prose reminiscent of the existential gaze described by Jean-Paul Sartre. A "young man," twenty-eight, and a "girl," twenty-two, lovers, are driving toward the resort where they will spend the next two weeks on vacation. He values her modesty; she wishes she were more open about her body. Making clear that she does not enjoy his little game of running out of fuel and making her hitchhike to the nearest station, she makes him stop for gasoline. Instead of precluding their usual game, however, this stop enables him to play a variation on it. He pretends that she is a hitchhiker to whom he is giving a ride. Although there are still only two bodies in the car, there are now at least four "possible selves": the young man, the girl, the young man whom the young man is pretending to be, and the girl pretending to be the hitchhiker who was picked up by the young man. The dizzying proliferation of fictive selves signals considerably more than narrative gamesmanship; there arises the complex question of whether, and to what degree, these pretended, or possible, selves conceal or reveal the nameless and perhaps identity-less young man's and the girl's actual selves (and the related question of whether a phrase such as "actual self" can now be said to mean anything at all). No longer on the road to their planned destination (the resort where they had reserved a room), they discover that "fiction was suddenly making an assault upon real life" and, worse, that "there's no escape from a game," least of all a game involving the politics of sexual power and identity. Just as "the game merged with life," multiple images merge, stacked one upon the other in the eye of the lover turned beholder. Freed to play the part of whore, the girl ironically achieves a greater sexual freedom and pleasure than she had known before, but she immediately feels she has paid too high a price: her self. Hearing her repeat her plaintive and "pitiful tautology"—"I am me, I am me"—the young man understands "the sad emptiness of the girl's assertion." This emptiness recalls Klima's recognition of his comical fate at the end of "Nobody Will Laugh," but the last lines of "The Hitchhiking Game" are bleaker still: "There were still thirteen days' vacation before them."

Similarly bleak prospects, coupled with a dizzying array of possible selves, characterize "Let the Old Dead Make Room for the Young Dead." The title suggests an ironizing of the familiar *carpe diem* theme. Two lovers meet after ten years. He is now thirty-five, divorced, living alone in a provincial town, working at a job that affords him no satisfaction. She is now nearly fifty, a widow who has just discovered that she has forgotten to renew the lease on her husband's grave. Thus she takes the cemetery administrator's words to her, which form the story's title, first as a reproach and then as her rationale for having sex with her former lover. No act in Kundera's fiction is ever quite so simply motivated, however, and hers involves as much revenge as love—revenge against the son who has forced her to play the widow's role—and it involves, too, as much self-assertion as self-accusation. The lovemaking proves no less ambiguously motivated for the man who wishes to possess at last the woman who has eluded him (along with so much else in his inconsequential life) for so long, even though he knows that their encounter will end in disgust. Yet he finds this prospect oddly exciting:

... he, whether he realized it or only vaguely suspected it, could not strip all these pleasures that had been denied him of their significance and color (for it was precisely their colorfulness that made his life so sadly dull), he could reveal that they were worthless, that they were only appearances doomed to destruction, that they were only metamorphosed dust; he could take revenge upon them, demean them, destroy them.

Kundera's two Dr. Havel stories treat much the same theme but in a far more playful way. "Symposium" draws its title from Plato and its five-act structure from drama. Its five characters—the chief physician, Havel, the aging Nurse Alzbeta, the attractive thirty-year-old woman doctor, and the young intern Flaishman—offer a host of sexual possibilities (permutations based as much on misreadings, misstatements, and expectations as on sexual preferences). The story focuses on Nurse Alzbeta's efforts to attract Havel's attention, efforts that nearly result in her death (variously read—and misread—as a suicide attempt). Her striptease becomes an apt metaphor for the story itself insofar as the story reveals more and more of the characters' deceits and self-deceptions while nevertheless managing, like any good striptease, to conceal the very mystery it entices the viewer/reader into believing will be exposed (revealed as well as made vulnerable). In "Dr. Havel Twenty Years Later," Havel is made to play Alzbeta's part, with, however, considerably more success, thanks to his established position, his reputation as a Don Juan, and especially his marriage to a beautiful and well-known actress. As in "Symposium," there is a youth (here it is a young editor, and in "Symposium" it is the intern) willing to take one of Havel's little jokes seriously because the joke appeals to his naïve sense of self-importance and his need to have his identity validated by someone older and more authoritative.

Edward, in "Edward and God," proves less naïve and more manipulative though perhaps no less self-deluded. A joke played at the expense of the ultra-Stalinist Miss Chekachkova costs Edward's brother his job but indirectly helps secure for Edward a teaching position at the school that she now runs. Far more self-aware than either Flaishman or the editor, Edward divides his life into two spheres: the serious and obligatory on the one hand and the unserious and nonobligatory on the other (teaching he places in the latter). Edward, however, is not nearly as free as he thinks. His pursuit of Alice, a churchgoer, jeopardizes his position at the state school; in parallel fashion, his radical skepticism, cynical in nature, jeopardizes his relationship with Alice (whose religious fervor is more political than spiritual in origin, a fact of which she remains serenely unaware). During his private reeducation session, Edward turns the tables on the spinsterish Miss Chekachkova, ordering this ardent Communist to strip, kneel, and recite the Lord's Prayer. Finding her humiliation sexually exciting, he carries her off to bed. He also—and again under false pretenses—overcomes Alice's very different scruples (she mistakenly believes Miss Chekachkova and the other Communists are persecuting him for his religious beliefs). Although he finds any God that would forbid extramarital sex "rather comical," Edward becomes angry when Alice consents to his sexual advances, believing that she has betrayed her God too easily. In "Edward and God," as in all Kundera's stories and novels, reversals and incongruities such as these abound, nowhere more ambiguously than in this story's closing paragraphs. Edward, still a nonbeliever, sits in a church, "tormented with sorrow, because God does not exist. But just at this moment his sorrow is so great that suddenly from its depth emerges the genuine *living* face of God." In describing Edward as having "a sorrow in his heart and a smile on his lips," the narrator is drawing on the poetry of the Czech writer Karel Hynek Mácha and the romantic lyricism that Kundera has often criticized for making a value of feeling and the excesses it engenders. "For my part," Kundera has explained, "I'm always tempted to reverse the terms, 'a faint sadness on one's lips and a deep laugh in one's heart.' " From such a depth of heart—"and art"—Kundera's "laughable loves" emerge as early variations on a persistent theme.

Other major works

NOVELS: *Žert*, 1967 (*The Joke*, 1969, revised 1982); *La Vie est ailleurs*, 1973 (*Life Is Elsewhere*, 1974; in Czech as *Život de jinde*, 1979); *La Valse aux adieux*, 1976 (*The Farewell Party*, 1977; in Czech as *Valčik no rozloučenou*, 1979); *Le Livre du rire et de l'oubli*, 1979 (*The Book of Laughter and Forgetting*, 1980; in Czech as *Kniha smíchu a zapomnění*, 1981); *L'Insoutenable Légèreté de l'être*, 1984 (*The Unbearable*

Lightness of Being, 1984; in Czech as *Nesnesitelná lehkost bytí*, 1985); *Nesmrtelnost*, 1990 (*Immortality*, 1991).

PLAYS: *Majitelé klíčů*, 1961; *Ptákovina, čili Dvojí uši—dvojí svatba*, 1968; *Žert*, 1969 (screenplay); *Jacques et son maître: Hommage à Denis Diderot*, 1970 (*Jacques and His Master*, 1985).

POETRY: *Člověk zahrada širá*, 1953; *Poslední máj*, 1955, revised 1963; *Monology*, 1957, revised 1964.

NONFICTION: *Umění románu: Cesta Vladislava Vančury za velkou epikou*, 1960; *L'Art du roman*, 1986 (*The Art of the Novel*, 1988).

Bibliography

Brand, Glen. *Milan Kundera: An Annotated Bibliography*. New York: Garland, 1988. The starting point for any serious student of Kundera's work. Includes an excellent introduction, an exhaustive primary bibliography, and a well-annotated bibliography of reviews and criticism.

Pochoda, Elizabeth. Introduction to *The Farewell Party*. New York: Viking Penguin, 1977. Pochoda situates Kundera's fiction and the private lives of his characters within a larger political context. Their lives are marked by helplessness and a sense of missed opportunities. Instead of freeing them from political oppression, love seems to refigure the system of political oppression on a more intimate scale.

Porter, R. C. *Milan Kundera: A Voice from Central Europe*. Århus, Denmark: Arkona Press, 1981. In separate chapters, Porter discusses *Laughable Loves*, Kundera's three plays, *The Joke, Life Is Elsewhere*, and *The Book of Laughter and Forgetting*. The introduction is especially useful for establishing the political context of Kundera's writings.

The Review of Contemporary Fiction 9 (Summer, 1982). This special issue devoted to Kundera and Zulfikar Ghose includes Lois Oppenheim's interview with Kundera, Glen Brand's "Selective Bibliography of Kundera Criticism," and Maria Nemcova Banerjee's "The Impossible Don Juan" on the Don Juan theme in *Laughable Loves*. An expanded version of Banerjee's essay appears in her *Terminal Paradox: The Novels of Milan Kundera* (New York: Grove Weidenfeld, 1990).

Roth, Philip. "Milan Kundera." In *Reading Myself and Others*. New York. Farrar, Straus & Giroux, 1975. First published as "Milan Kundera, The Joker" in *Esquire*, in April, 1974, and as "Introducing Milan Kundera" in *Laughable Loves*, 1974. Roth provides a capsule biography, a brief history of contemporary Czechoslovakia, and then discusses the relation between "erotic play and power" (the Don Juan theme) and offers brief but interesting comments on specific stories, "The Hitchhiking Game" and "Edward and God" in particular.

Salmagundi, no. 73 (Winter, 1987). This special issue devoted to Kundera is framed by two indispensable interviews and includes seven important essays on his work, chiefly the novels. "Estrangement and Irony," by Terry Eagleton, and "On Milan Kundera," by Clavin Bedient, are especially noteworthy.

Sturdivant, Mark. "Milan Kundera's Use of Sexuality." *Critique: Studies in Modern*

Fiction 26 (Spring, 1985): 131-140. Sturdivant offers a detailed reading of the sexual theme first raised by Elizabeth Pochoda and Philip Roth, examining *The Joke*, *The Book of Laughter and Forgetting*, "Symposium," "The Hitchhiking Game," and "Edward and God."

Robert A. Morace

TOMMASO LANDOLFI

Born: Pico, near Frosinone, Italy; August 9, 1908
Died: Rome, Italy; July 7, 1979

Principal short fiction
Dialogo dei massimi sistemi, 1937; *Il Mar delle Blatte*, 1939; *La spada*, 1942; *Le due zitelle*, 1945 (*The Two Old Maids*, 1961); *Cancroregina*, 1950 (*Cancerqueen*, 1971); *Ombre*, 1954; *Se non la realtà*, 1960; *Racconti*, 1961; *In società*, 1962; *Gogol's Wife and Other Stories*, 1963; *Tre racconti*, 1964; *Racconti impossibili*, 1966; *Cancerqueen, and Other Stories*, 1971; *Le labrene*, 1974; *A caso*, 1975; *Landolfi: Le più belle pagine*, 1982 (partially translated in *Words in Commotion and Other Stories*, 1986).

Other literary forms
While Tommaso Landolfi wrote mainly short stories and short works called *novelle*, he also published some long fiction. Examples include *La pietra lunare* (1937; the moonstone) and *Un amore del nostro tempo* (1965; a love story of our time). He wrote for the theater: *Landolfo VI di Benevento* (1958; Landolph VI) and *Faust '67* (1969). He published two highly regarded volumes of poetry; *Viola di morte* (1972; the violet shade of death) and *Il tradimento* (1977; betrayal). In Italy, he also enjoyed a reputation as an observant literary critic and a witty and ironic essayist. A selection of critical essays are gathered in *Gogol a Roma* (1971; Gogol in Rome), while *Del Meno* (1978; this and that) is a collection of columns which Landolfi published over the years on the "terza pagina" (the literary page) of the *Corriere della Sera*. To this steady and voluminous activity must be added the writer's numerous translations from French, German, and Russian literature.

Achievements
Landolfi is a unique and eccentric writer who fits into no obvious category of Italian literature, past or present. Italian fiction in the twentieth century follows the tradition laid down by the nineteenth century masters, Alessandro Manzoni and Giovanni Verga, both of whom dealt directly with the historical forces at work on human society and who emphasized realistic description of the social backdrop. Landolfi appears to have had no interest in dealing overtly with those historical crises of his time which had such a formative influence on his own generation (Fascism and World War II). Instead, Landolfi's cosmopolitanism is reflected in his continuous output as a translator—mainly from Russian, but also from French and German literature, which always paralleled his literary production. In the 1930's, Landolfi was associated with the hermetic movement in Italian poetry and prose, as a part of that generation of writers who, in response to the pressures of the Fascist regime, turned in upon themselves to rediscover a poetic voice or simply to maintain private integrity, while they also looked to foreign traditions in search of stylistic and thematic

mentors. In those years, Landolfi, who had taken a degree in Russian literature at the University of Florence, continued to reside in that city and published his early fiction in reviews such as *Letteratura* and *Campo di Marte*. The hermetics made their anti-Fascist comments obliquely, never attacking the regime directly, but rather withdrawing from its vulgarity, militancy, and stridency.

The hermetics had attracted Landolfi most, not for their political attitude but rather for their exploration of the metaphysical, especially as expressed in the humble and the mundane. Increasingly obsessed with the spiritual and existential, Landolfi became more and more isolated during the postwar period, when the intellectual climate became intensely political, with mounting claims made on writers for commitment and partisan allegiance. He consciously neglected issues he deemed outside his own art, and an important consequence of his withdrawal from fashion was the delayed recognition of his work. His columns in the *Corriere della Sera*, however, earned him a wider audience, and he won repeated recognition in Italy for his achievements over a broad area of the literary landscape. To list only a few of his awards: the Premio Viarregio for fiction (1958); the Bagutta (1964) and Elba (1966) awards; the Premio D'Annunzio (1968, 1974); the Pirandello Theater Award (1968, for *Faust '67*); the Premio di poesia Fiuggi (1972); and the Strega Prize for fiction (1975, for *A caso*).

Biography

The biographical facts pertaining to Tommaso Landolfi can be briefly stated. His life was without major incidents, and he chose to live in obscurity, away from the glare of publicity. Landolfi is known for consciously establishing barriers between himself and any would-be biographer. This jealously guarded privacy amounted to something of an obsession.

He was born in Pico (in the province of Frosinone) in 1908. His mother died in his second year, and as a young adolescent he was sent away to boarding school. He later attended the University of Florence, from which he was graduated, having specialized in Russian literature. He spent most of the 1930's in Florence, participating in the literary activities of the time, publishing his early fiction. It is known that, on the eve of World War II, he was arrested and spent some time in prison for activities deemed inappropriate by the regime. Landolfi's political demeanor, however, took the form of a rather generic anti-Fascism rather than that of an overt militancy. During the war, he lived with his father in his ancestral home in Pico, which at different times during the war was occupied both by German forces and by Moroccan troops of the Free French Army. Landolfi married later in life, fathered two children, and devoted himself to literature. He divided the years after the war between Pico and Rome, where he died in 1979.

Analysis

It is appropriate to begin with a psychological portrait of the man before proceeding to an analysis of the writer's principal themes and works. For one who made such a cult of privacy, Tommaso Landolfi proved remarkably confessional, revealing much of a complicated inner life, the details of which are far richer than the external events of his career. In this respect, the critic's task was made much easier with the publication in the 1950's and the 1960's of such autobiographical works as *La Bière du pecheur* (1953; the sinner's bier/coffin), *Rien va* (1963; no more), and *Des mois* (1968; months). These works are not strictly diaries; they are more like private jottings in which the writer reminisces but also attempts to define personal responses to crises in his own life and to clarify his position vis-à-vis all human experience. These volumes have their nineteenth century antecedents in Giacomo Leopardi's *Zibaldone* (1898-1900; notebooks) and Charles Baudelaire's *Mon cœur mis à nu* (1887; *My Heart Laid Bare*, 1950).

The following psychological patterns are quite visible in Landolfi's personality and in the fiction that they have nourished. The loss of his mother before his second birthday left scars on the psyche of the child and adolescent that were to stay with him the rest of his life, bestowing on him a profound sense of privation and an equally strong sense of guilt. To the child's trauma one can trace the origins of an ambivalence toward women, who, on the one hand, stirred in the writer erotic and even violent impulses, and, on the other, as repositories of a sacred motherhood suggested an ineffable purity accessible only through dream and memory. In the absence of the mother stood the father—in reality an affectionate if gruff man with a taste for solitude, and a forthright anti-Fascist. The fictional father figure loomed menacingly over vulnerable offspring, often in a gloomy manor in an abandoned corner of the provinces. The son may never have fully pardoned the father for sending his hypersensitive child to a private boarding school at the age of twelve: for the second time in his young life, Landolfi felt rejected, cast off and set afloat in a hostile universe. Thereafter the fiction bristled with the theme of Oedipal conflict and incestuous temptation. In the novella *La morte del re di Francia* (the death of the King of France, published in *Gogol's Wife and Other Stories*), the father, So-and-So, broods over his daughter Rosalba's ripening adolescence and supervises her daily bath, while he is also the object of her erotic dream. In the fable *Racconto d'autunno* (1947; *An Autumn Story*, 1989), an old man keeps his daughter imprisoned in an isolated villa, where she serves as a high priestess to an almost necrophiliac cult of his dead wife. The Landolfian antihero is solitary and impotent in a much larger than sexual sense: his essential form of communication is the monologue, which he commits to the page of his diary. He is convinced of his own uselessness in an existence that he finds insufficient.

The Two Old Maids, published just after the war, offers few concessions to the fashion of contemporary realism. Both the setting and the style of this novella place it within the tradition of nineteenth century fiction, which Landolfi acknowledges, and from which he detaches himself in the second sentence. The reader can be thankful, he writes, that he (the author) would not dream of describing this house and district in every detail. His satire of a literature to which he remains devoted and of a way of life that he knows rather too intimately remains unerring. The district is "disheartening"; dust lies on the buildings and trees. In the apartment which the reader is invited to enter, the old maids Lilla and Nena sacrifice their lives to their seemingly indestructible mother, who dominates them to her dying day.

The hero of this tale is the monkey, the family pet, more or less domesticated and living, as all objects of love do (says Landolfi), in a large cage. The sisters have inherited him from their brother, a sea captain, who brought him back from one of his voyages; and they lavish on him an affection that is their memorial to the departed mariner. The monkey is the only male in the house, summing up in his diminutive frame the roles of father, brother, even husband, and certainly that of the children the barren sisters never bore. Like a child or lover, he likes to sleep in Lilla's lap and sometimes clutch her breasts when she lies down for a nap. The animal introduces a contrapuntal principle of virility and spontaneity into a shared existence predicated on a pious suppression of instinct.

The crisis comes when the monkey, Tombo, is accused by the Mother Superior of the convent next door of stealing the consecrated host and drinking the communion wine from the chapel. Nena vehemently denies these charges, but on closer inspection she learns that the ingenious Tombo can indeed unlock his cage, make his way over the wall into the convent garden, and pay a visit to the chapel. Following him, Nena hides herself in that sacred place together with a young nun and observes with her own eyes the sacrilegious trespass of the monkey. What she sees horrifies her far more than the accusations of stealing heard from the Mother Superior. Every gesture that the little creature makes—the way he wraps himself in the holy corporal as if it were a stole, the pouring of the wine into the chalice, the salutation to a nonexistent congregation—can spell only one thing: "Tombo was saying Mass!" For such desecration he is immediately condemned. Nena declares, "He must die."

If the tale is read simply as social satire, then the monkey's comic imitations of the gestures of the priest do not go beyond a parody of the mass and the devalued rituals of the Church. Tombo, however, is not the damnable heretic for which he is mistaken. In effect, his visits to the chapel are his way of following in his mistresses' footsteps, of identifying with their faith, of adoring their God as best he might. Tombo's gibbering and untidy imitation, had Nena the charity or piety to stop and reflect, is rather a reminder, or memory, of masses conducted under primitive conditions in the distant colonies under missionary supervision. Improvised and scruffy, garbled but sincere, it is the sort of thing Lilla and Nena's sea captain brother—and his pet monkey—might have witnessed many times in his travels. It is within this simple probability that much of the tale's irony, and tragedy, lie.

The demise of the monkey is finally consummated. Landolfi communicates the terror of an animal that knows no guilt, but knows it is about to die, betrayed for having dared to love. Nena victoriously snuffs out a flickering life, and in her victory achieves a terrible irony. By his crucifixion she elevates the blasphemer Tombo to actual martyrdom. The last event in the sisters' life is over, and until their death all can return to normal, or, as Landolfi puts it, a gray dust can settle over everything once more.

Cancerqueen is linked thematically to Landolfi's previous fiction in that it explores the human search for freedom along with the foundering of that quest. It marks at the same time an anticipated development in his career and a point of crisis. It is in part an exercise in science fiction which suggests that the writer's imagination was finally working its way free of earthbound experience and needed to test itself against the dimensions of space. The tale is divided into two parts. The first recounts the author's meeting with a mad scientist who invites him on a voyage to the moon aboard his spaceship, christened *Cancerqueen*. This fantasy is told in chronological order in punctilious detail, as if it belonged to the tradition of narrative realism. Part 2 is composed of a diary in which the protagonist, marooned alone in the spaceship, jots down his thoughts on his isolation, on life in general, on his fears and obsessions. Artistically this part marks a rupture with the first forty pages of the tale; it also provides an interesting indication of the diaristic direction of Landolfi's prose less than three years before the publication of *La Bière du pecheur*. This diary also indicates the growing inversion of Landolfi's point of view and his preference to write in the first person singular and to adopt the form of the monologue.

The protagonist is a failed writer forced to return to his native village and house as a result of gambling debts and disappointments in love. He receives a visit from an escapee from the local insane asylum, who tries to interest him in a bizarre story of his invention of a wonderful machine designed to fly them to the moon. Can there be any method in this madman? Is he the victim of the prejudice of rival professionals jealous of his superior genius? Is he the expression of human fears of science and fascination with the forces beyond human control—the fears that humanity's moral development has not kept pace with technological advance? Might this maniac not represent the gambler's instinct in Landolfi come to whisper in his ear that it is better to risk all for a flight through the cosmos than to accept stagnation and death in a moldering mansion without hope or a future?

The author is tempted, and the two men rush out of the house to embark on their "singular excursion" into the mountains in search of the treasured creation of Filano (the mysterious visitor and architect of *Cancerqueen*). The remarkable description of this journey by moonlight up steep slopes, across vertiginous peaks, and over dizzying chasms is another example of Landolfi's fascination with the wild nature of his native hills around Pico. They are built into the texture of many of his tales, and he invests them with a strange, gothic beauty, attractive and terrifying. The journey ends with a descent into a cave at the pit of which is the miraculous *Cancerqueen*, a creation of almost mythic dimension and faith more than of scientific calculation. She—and she must be granted her sex—is presented not as a triumph of physics but rather is anthropomorphized as an extension of the human imagination now poised to conquer space.

The human imagination, however, is impeded by human paranoia. Filano goes mad and, concluding that the voyage will be jeopardized by the extra weight of his companion, determines to jettison him. In the ensuing struggle it is Filano who is plunged into the void, with the protagonist facing space alone. Not quite alone, however, for the laws of physics decree that the ejected Filano cling eternally to the sides of his beloved craft, and he is transformed into an irremovable mute companion on a voyage without end.

Characters in Landolfi's stories who resort to violence are obliged to live with the consequences of their acts. The child murderer in "La muta" ("The Mute") must await the arrival of his executioners. Kafka, imagined in "Il babbo di Kafka" (Kafka's father) as killing his father, who has assumed the form of a spider, can never be certain whether the spider he killed really did contain his father's soul. In like manner, the protagonist of *Cancerqueen* must live forever with the image of Filano grimacing at him from space beyond the window. In seeking to liberate himself, the protagonist has turned himself into a prisoner. Would it not have been better to stay amid the ugly confusion of human society than to seek the rarefied purity of space? The final irony is that the writer has begun to write again, but there is no audience. No one will recover the manuscript. His works are like Filano's corpse, empty husks cast into space.

Passing from the eventual madness of the writer lost in space to that of another, unable to free himself from an obsession, the reader encounters similar concerns in Landolfi's best-known short story, "La moglie di Gogol" ("Gogol's Wife"). This story first appeared in the 1954 collection of short stories and autobiographical pieces entitled *Ombre* (shadows). The title and protagonist are a reminder of Landolfi's lifelong interest in the author of the 1842 novel *Dead Souls* (a study of Gogol is included in Landolfi's critical essays, in *Gogol a Roma*), to whom he was drawn for a narrative style that depended less on meticulous observation than on audacious leaps of the imagination. Undoubtedly, Landolfi was also interested in Gogol as an example of an unbalanced mind that descended into religious mania and a fatal melancholy that led to his early death. Like his Gogol, many of Landolfi's heroes fall victim to hallucinations and obsessions, and the author deals convincingly with acute states of psychological isolation, undoubtedly similar to his own.

The tale reads like a surrealistic joke conceived as an entertainment which ultimately reveals much more about its author than was originally intended. Gogol's wife is an inflatable rubber doll which can be blown up to the size and dimensions chosen by her spouse. She possesses a rudimentary spine and rib cage for rigidity. She is nude at all times, and the narrator, in the guise of an intimate of the great Nikolai, draws attention to the remarkable anatomical exactitude of her exposed genitalia. Yet what appears to be a perfect human replica is only an epidermis, with no inner organs, no mind, no character of her own.

What is the reader to make of this simulacrum of a wife? Since this Gogol is an invention of Landolfi, one is to assume that some of the observable fetishes and the transference of affection from people to objects belong to him. A doll is preferred to a proper wife out of the fear of a real woman's independence and judgment. The doll, naked and placid, with her changes of wigs, able to assume a variety of shapes according to the caprice of the inflator, is quite literally a sex object, ready at all times to satisfy the whims of the husband. The fact that she cannot answer back makes her always passive, subservient and obedient. (The narrator, however, recalls one occasion when she does appear to talk, childishly expressing a desire to go to the lavatory, which throws Gogol into a fit of rage, causing him to deflate her for the evening.) The doll also brings out sadistic impulses in the male; indeed, she seems designed to be humiliated. To inflate her, a pump is inserted in her anus, and she is deflated by forcing one's hand down her throat to release a nozzle.

Subservient as she is, her master is convinced of a stubborn insubordination in her nature, a kind of passive resistance to his whims, perhaps even an unspoken mockery, which he interprets as a challenge to his authority. The wife-doll, Caracas, represents a taunting sexual presence to Gogol which his growing religious mania persuades him to eradicate from his life. She must suffer the same fate as the manuscript of the second part of *Dead Souls*, and in the final conflagration one sees a murderous assault on female sensuality, the world of the flesh and even art (in that Caracas is part muse and the inspirer of the literature of love). In addition, Gogol throws into the flames what appears to be a baby doll of the same material as Caracas, identified as her son. Once more, a father exerts a fearful, fatal authority over his offspring.

Landolfi's symbolism is rich and suggestive, never formulaic or precise. Caracas is a projection of a host of male fears of the female, of the ambiguous relations between the sexes. She offers both physical partnership and challenge to her companion, but the reader can never say with certainty that she equals one value or meaning rather than another. Furthermore, each reading of the tale will yield different levels of interpretation. The story goes well beyond a psychological portrait of Gogol. The fears of the eternal feminine, the impotence of the protagonist, the failure to establish a relationship with another, the sadism of the father—all are familiar themes in Landolfi's fiction. The reader is directed to "La beccaccia" (the woodcock), also in *Ombre*, which focuses on a hunter's cruelty toward an innocent creature following his disappointment in love.

The thematic links between these stories offer a guide to a complete reading of Landolfi's work. In different ways, they deal with aspects of freedom in psychological and aesthetic terms. Tombo introduces into the house of the old maids disturbing motifs of vitality and an alternative form of religious expression. His death is the price he must pay for their lives to remain unruffled. The association of space flight with artistic freedom is quite clear in *Cancerqueen*, but the dream runs into conflict with human limitations, leaving the artist-protagonist suspended in the void. Gogol may immolate his wife to free himself of a degrading dependence, but his creative will is not restored by that brutal expedient. The fate or crisis of the artist is a serious matter for Landolfi.

In *Cancerqueen*, he reveals the ultimate isolation of the writer, who passes with tragic inevitability from dialogue to monologue to silence. Two fellow writers whom he includes in his tales, Franz Kafka and Nikolai Gogol, are presented as being insane, suggesting that this condition accompanies that of the artist. Either one risks mental balance by choosing art as a way of life, or one must be part mad in order to write (or paint or compose). Either way, life in art amounts more to tyranny than to freedom. The caverns and labyrinthine mansions where many of Landolfi's dramas occur suggest that he is interested only in the hidden experience. What lies below the surface of life alone is worth writing about, revealing secret truths of which we are unaware, including destructive impulses that society has a right to control. Landolfi is by no means an aesthete who has chosen literature as a means of refining a style for the pleasure of a handful of insiders. He is a disturbing writer who reveals the cracks in the human façade.

Other major works

NOVELS: *La pietra lunare*, 1937; *Racconto d'autunno*, 1947 (*An Autumn Story*, 1989); *Ottavio di Saint-Vincent*, 1958; *Un amore del nostro tempo*, 1965.

PLAYS: *Landolfo VI di Benevento*, 1958; *Scene della vita di Cagliostro*, 1963; *Faust '67*, 1969.

POETRY: *Viola di morte*, 1972; *Il tradimento*, 1977.

NONFICTION: *Un paniere di chiocciole*, 1968; *Gogol a Roma*, 1971; *Del meno*, 1978.

MISCELLANEOUS: *La bière du pecheur*, 1953; *Rien va*, 1963; *Des mois*, 1968.

Bibliography

Brew, Claude. "The 'Caterpillar Nature' of Imaginative Experience: A Reading of Tommaso Landolfi's 'Wedding Night.' " *Modern Language Notes* 89 (1974): 110-115. Although focusing on one story, Brew's attentive analysis of narrative technique, cryptic imagery, and surreal action—especially as these apply to imagined rather than literal experience—illuminates many other stories by Landolfi.

Calvino, Italo. "Introduction: Precision and Chance." *Words in Commotion and Other Stories.* New York: Viking, 1986. Master fantasist and personal acquaintance of Landolfi, Calvino utilizes Landolfi's real-life obsession with gambling to identify and analyze his "rules" for the "game" (literature) between writer and reader. As described by Calvino, necessity, chance, uncertainty, and suffering are as significantly interwoven for Landolfi the man as they were for Landolfi the artist.

Capek-Habekovic, Romana. *Tommaso Landolfi's Grotesque Images.* New York: Peter Lang, 1986. Landolfi's stories are analyzed through their grotesque imagery, which the author claims he uses to combat the toll of scientific logic and modern technology on humanity: too much perfection produces dehumanization. Excerpts in Italian; notes; thorough bibliography.

Rosenthal, Raymond. "A Note on Landolfi." In *Cancerqueen, and Other Stories.* New York: Dial Press, 1971. A short but lucid essay. Rosenthal emphasizes the creative effort both reader and author must exercise in confronting Landolfi's works. Paradox, ambiguity, and doubt are highlighted as primary aspects of the stories, both because of the experience of reading and because of Landolfi's own obsession with conflict and the reality of the spirit.

Weales, Gerald. "Fiction Chronicle." *The Hudson Review* 24, no. 4 (1971-1972): 716-

730. Weales' very short review of *Cancerqueen* reveals an unanticipated disappointment: "What I find at work in Landolfi is a professional story-teller, one who uses the traditional materials—loss, death, cruelty—sometimes to explore man in his greatest pain, at others simply to play games with the reader."

Harry Lawton
(Revised by *Terri Frongia*)

RING LARDNER

Born: Niles, Michigan; March 6, 1885
Died: East Hampton, New York; September 25, 1933

Principal short fiction

Bib Ballads, 1915; *Gullible's Travels,* 1917; *Treat 'Em Rough,* 1918; *The Real Dope,* 1919; *Own Your Own Home,* 1919; *How to Write Short Stories,* 1924; *The Love Nest and Other Stories,* 1926; *Round Up: The Stories of Ring Lardner,* 1929; *Lose with a Smile,* 1933.

Other literary forms

Ring Lardner is known today chiefly as a short-story writer, but in his own time was better known as a sportswriter, columnist, and humorist. He also wrote two novel-length works, *You Know Me Al* (1915) and *The Big Town* (1921), and he tried his hand at writing musical comedies, *June Moon* (1930; in collaboration with George S. Kaufman) being his only successful one. Most of Lardner's nonfictional prose remains uncollected, although a few works have appeared in book form, including an early piece about the return of the Chicago White Sox from a worldwide tour, a book of verse about successful business and professional men (*Regular Fellows I Have Met,* 1919), three humorous essays, "The Young Immigrunts," "Symptoms of Being Thirty-five," and "Say It with Oil," and a burlesque autobiography, *The Story of a Wonder Man* (1927).

Achievements

Lardner added significantly to a tradition dating back at least as far as Mark Twain's *The Adventures of Huckleberry Finn* (1884). Using first-person monologue (usually humorous, always steeped in colloquialisms, occasionally in the form of correspondence), Lardner allowed his characters to reveal themselves, warts and all. As such, the superficiality and insincerity of his narrators is starkly contrasted with the often harsh truths they unintentionally reveal. This allowed Lardner to illustrate some of the less edifying aspects of American society and human nature in general. He also captured the spoken language (and slang) of ordinary people, rendering it as an art form unto itself. Thus, in addition to their entertainment value, Lardner's stories provide a telling picture of American manners and morals during the first third or so of the twentieth century. Finally, Lardner was a pioneer in the fruitful marriage between the game of baseball and American letters, laying the foundation for later works by prominent authors such as Mark Harris (*Bang the Drum Slowly,* 1956), W. P. Kinsella (*Shoeless Joe,* 1982, filmed as *Field of Dreams,* 1989), Bernard Malamud (*The Natural,* 1952), and Philip Roth (*The Great American Novel,* 1973).

Biography

Ring Lardner was born into a wealthy, genteel family and educated at home by his mother and a tutor before he attended the public high school. After a brief stay at the Armour Institute in Chicago, where his father sent him to study mechanical engineering, he held a series of jobs with newspapers, chiefly as a sportswriter, which led him into writing fiction about ball players and athletes. He married Ellis Abbott in 1911 and subsequently had four sons. He died in 1933 of a heart attack.

Analysis

The question that inevitably arises in any discussion of Ring Lardner's stories is: what is Lardner's attitude toward his characters and by extension toward the culture out of which they come? Is Lardner, in other words, a misanthrope who hated not only his own characters but also himself, or is he, rather, a disappointed idealist who found in the world of his immediate experience constant instances of cruelty, vulgarity, and insensitivity? Those who point to Lardner's sheltered upbringing and the apparently happy family life both of his early years and of his later married life favor the latter view, while those who wish to find in his fiction some affirmation of the goodness of man prefer the former. Obviously, no final answer to the question is possible.

If one reads an early story such as "Champion," one sees a heavy-handed author stacking the cards against his brutal hero, Midge Kelly. Midge beats up his crippled brother to steal his half dollar and when their mother objects beats her up too. Thereafter Midge's life is a succession of victories and brutalities: he becomes a prizefighter who wins fight after fight and, at the same time, does in those who have befriended him. Although his crippled brother is sick and unable to get out of bed and longs to have a letter from his famous brother, Midge refuses to write. When his wife and son are ill and destitute, he tears up a letter from his wife begging for help. He fires the manager who has helped make him a champion fighter and heaps money on a woman who is obviously using him, although he later casts her off, too, and takes himself the wife of his new manager. Through the obvious cardstacking one sees Lardner's intention. He hates brutality and he hates the way brutality is not only ignored but also rewarded in our society. Midge Kelly is not a believable character; he is a symbol on which Lardner heaps all of the abuse he can muster. If it were not for the brutality, "Champion" would be a maudlin tear-jerker.

The truth seems to be that underneath the pose of the realist, observer, and reporter of American crudities, Ring Lardner was a sensitive, even a sentimental man. The monologue form exactly suited his need to keep the sentimentality out of sight while letting his crude, vulgar, insensitive types condemn themselves out of their own mouths, but it was also a way of allowing the victims of the bullies to engage the reader's sympathies without having to make them stereotyped victims: cripples who are beaten, mothers knocked down by their sons, abandoned wives and babies. Lardner's best stories present the reader with a story in which the real author has all but disappeared while his narrator tells his ironically revealing, self-condemning tale.

The best of Lardner's stories, "Haircut," is told by a barber who is giving a haircut to an unnamed stranger in a small Midwestern town. The hero of the barber's tale is Jim Kendall, a practical joker, whom the barber describes as "all right at heart," but whom the reader quickly sees as a man who enjoys inflicting pain on other human beings under the guise of being funny. To pay his wife back for getting his paycheck (he gives her no money to run the household), Kendall tells her to meet him with their children outside the tent of a visiting circus. Instead of joining her there with the tickets as he promised, he hides out in a saloon to savor the joke he is playing on his family. Meanwhile, a new doctor in the town, "Doc" Stair, appears on the scene, and feeling sorry for the mother with the crying children, buys the tickets for them. When Kendell hears how Doc Stair spoiled his fun, he gets furious and vows revenge. He tricks a young woman, Julie Gregg, who is "sweet on" Doc Stair, into coming into the doctor's office late at night. No one is there but Kendell and his friends hiding in the dark. When Julie calls out the doctor's first name, "Oh, Ralph," Kendell and his crowd leap out and mimic her. When she retreats, they chase her home. Another frequent victim of Kendall's jokes, a "cuckoo" named Paul who is fond of Julie and the doctor and who hears the doctor say that a man like Kendell ought not to be allowed to live, invites himself to go duck hunting with Kendell. Kendell gives Paul his gun to hold, the gun goes off, and Kendell is killed. Doc Stair, the coroner, rules the shooting accidental. Although in this story the chief villain is given his comeuppance, a subtler cruelty is revealed by the barber who says of Kendell that in letting a man like Paul hold his gun, he probably got what he deserved.

Another of Lardner's best stories, "Golden Honeymoon," is a gentler satire; indeed, critics have disagreed about whether this is the portrait of a happy marriage or a vicious attack on marriage in general. Doubtless the truth lies somewhere in between, for the old man who tells the story of his and his wife's trip to Florida on their golden honeymoon is a boring windbag, impressed with himself and his son who is "high up in rotary" and with the commonplace, vulgar, details of their trips to cafeterias, church socials, card games, and movies, and their encounter with his wife's old beau. The main action of the story concerns the conflict that arises between the couple over the reappearance fifty years later of the suitor, who is married to a woman the narrator describes as a rotten cardplayer. Although he is not as brutal or despicable as other Lardner narrators, he has many of the same faults: insensitivity, vanity, pettiness, and even a little cruelty. When he wins a game of checkers, he gloats; when he loses at horseshoes, he pouts. When his wife hurts her back on the croquet court, he laughs at her, and when he is beaten at horseshoes, he quarrels with his wife and she quits speaking to him. The story ends "happily"—that is, the two make up and get "kind of spoony"—but the essential portrait remains that of a boring, vain, pompous old man.

"Some Like Them Cold" is a story told through the exchange of letters between a young woman named Mabelle Gillespie who allows herself to be picked up by a young man in the La Salle Street Station in Chicago. Chas. F. Lewis (as he signs his letters) is on his way to New York to break into the songwriting business. He is a typical Lardner monologuist—vain, crude, and cruel—and Mabelle is the familiar

Lardner victim—sensitive, trusting, and foolish. Her letters to Lewis play up her virtues as a "home body"; his become increasingly short, emphasizing how well he is getting on in the Big Town and offering accounts of women who chase him. After he announces his marriage to a woman whom he had earlier described as cold and indifferent to home life, he advises Mabelle not to speak to "strange men who you don't know nothing about as they may get you wrong and think you are trying to make them." "Some Like Them Cold" was later converted by Lardner into the successful musical comedy *June Moon*.

A story technically subtler is "Ex Parte," told in the first person by a man attempting to justify his part in the breakup of his marriage. As he tells it, he and his wife were happy on their honeymoon but as soon as they moved into the house he had bought as a surprise for her (he had promised they would choose a house together), their marriage began to go bad. The trouble is that the house and furniture (picked out by a decorator) are too shiny and new-looking to suit his wife; she hates the house and admires the converted barn and early American furniture of her school friend. Even the nicks and burns on her friend's dining room table seem beautiful to her. So the narrator, after consuming a large quantity of "early American Rye," goes home and mutilates their table with a blow torch. His wife leaves him and he is now trying to get his friends to take his side in the quarrel.

What is unusual about this story is that instead of the typical opposition of bully and victim, there is rather a battle between two people equally insensitive and shallow: the husband who likes bright, shiny new things and the wife who likes antiques. For both, marriage is simply a matter of having the right things.

To call Ring Lardner either a misanthrope or a humorist, or even a realist who observed American manners, is to miss the point. Lardner was a moralist, like his friend F. Scott Fitzgerald, and although at times he could be merely funny or sentimental or tiresome, his best stories are homilies, camouflaged by humor, on meanness, cruelty, and vanity. Lardner had a remarkable ear for a certain kind of native American speech, and he used that talent for giving his stories the ring of truth and passing on to succeeding generations a small but enduring collection of excellent short stories.

Other major works

NOVELS: *You Know Me Al*, 1915; *The Big Town*, 1921.

PLAYS: *Elmer the Great*, 1928; *June Moon*, 1930 (with George S. Kaufman).

NONFICTION: *My Four Weeks in France*, 1918; *Regular Fellows I Have Met*, 1919; "The Young Immigrunts," 1920; "Symptoms of Being Thirty-five," 1921; "Say It with Oil," 1923; *What of It?*, 1925; *The Story of a Wonder Man*, 1927.

Bibliography

Bruccoli, Matthew J., and Richard Layman. *Ring Lardner: A Descriptive Bibliography*. Pittsburgh: University of Pittsburgh Press, 1976. This highly accessible and useful summary of Lardner's work provides a good starting point for getting a sense of Lardner's overall achievements, range, and productivity.

Elder, Donald. *Ring Lardner.* Garden City, N.Y.: Doubleday, 1956. This early biography is helpful because it includes much firsthand testimony from those who knew Lardner throughout his career, including the very early days when his affection for baseball and overall philosophy of life were formed.

Friedrich, Otto. *Ring Lardner.* Minneapolis: University of Minnesota Press, 1965. An admirably concise work that discusses Lardner's command of different dialects. Puts the darker side of Lardner's psyche into the context of myths and misconceptions popular at the time he wrote. An expert on the historical period both in the United States and Europe, Friedrich provides a lucid and insightful introduction to Lardner's main themes and techniques.

Geismar, Maxwell. *Ring Lardner and the Portrait of Folly.* New York: Thomas Y. Crowell, 1972. Probably the most ambitious work of literary criticism devoted entirely to Lardner. Geismar draws a full blown critique of American materialism out of Lardner's work, arguing that Lardner's sarcasm and satire masked a deeply felt idealism.

Lardner, Ring, Jr. *The Lardners: My Family Remembered.* New York: Harper & Row, 1976. Lardner's third son, a successful screenwriter, provides a charming portrait of the Lardner family. As portrayed here, Ring Lardner, Sr., was humble and completely unpretentious about his work. He was also a good family man and had an interesting circle of friends, including F. Scott Fitzgerald.

Yardley, Jonathan. *Ring.* New York: Random House, 1977. This well-written, thorough biography is especially good at drawing the very strong connection between Lardner as journalist and Lardner as short-story writer. According to Yardley, the journalistic desire of unadorned facts that Lardner had to present leads logically to an unflinching examination of human nature and American society through the medium of fiction.

W. J. Stuckey
(Revised by *Ira Smolensky*)

MARGARET LAURENCE

Born: Neepawa, Manitoba, Canada; July 16, 1926
Died: Lakefield, Ontario, Canada; January 5, 1987

Principal short fiction
The Tomorrow-Tamer, 1963; *A Bird in the House*, 1970.

Other literary forms
Margaret Laurence's best-known books are the series of four novels and the short-story collection that have been called the Manawaka works, named after the fictional town in central Canada from which all the major characters originate. The series consists of *The Stone Angel* (1964), *A Jest of God* (1966), which was made into the motion picture *Rachel, Rachel* in 1968, *The Fire-Dwellers* (1969), *A Bird in the House*, and *The Diviners* (1974). Although this is not a series in the sense of sequels, the characters are related through their birthplace and memories, as well as some by birth, as in William Faulkner's imaginary Yoknapatawpha County.

Laurence also translated Somali folktales and poetry, published as *A Tree for Poverty: Somali Poetry and Prose* in 1954, the first collection of Somali literature ever published in English. The novel *This Side Jordan* (1960) tells the story of Ghana's emergence as a nation. *New Wind in a Dry Land* (1964) is an account of Laurence's first two years in Somaliland, describing both her experiences and the life of Somali nomads; it was also published under the title *The Prophet's Camel Bell*. In the field of literary criticism, Laurence wrote *Long Drums and Cannons* (1968), a study of Nigerian novelists and dramatists writing in English. She also wrote four novels for children.

Achievements
Laurence is not only a great Canadian writer but also a universal voice for understanding, independence, and brave experimentation with life. Her African work helps to point up the evils of colonization, whether of a country, a people, or an individual. Her Manawaka series more specifically looks at the oppression of women by societal expectations that are irrational and sexist and that result also in the lessening of individual men.

In 1967, Laurence became an Honorary Fellow of United College, University of Winnipeg; she was the first woman and the youngest person to be honored in this way. The novel *This Side Jordan* won for her Canada's Beta Sigma Phi Award, a prize for the best first novel by a Canadian, in 1960. In 1971, Laurence was made a Companion of the Order of Canada; in the following years, she was awarded seven honorary degrees. Her novel *The Diviners* won the Governor General's Medal for Fiction in 1974 and the Molson Prize. She received the Woman of the Year Award from B'nai B'rith Toronto Women's Branch in 1976 and won the Periodical Distributors' Award for the mass paperback edition of *A Jest of God* in October of 1977.

Biography
Jean Margaret Wemyss was born on July 16, 1926, in Neepawa, Manitoba, Canada. She began writing at the age of eight, and at age thirteen she sent a story to a *Winnipeg Free Press* competition; in that story, she first used the name Manawaka for a town similar to her native Neepawa. She contributed stories to her school magazines and later to the university magazine when she attended United College in Winnipeg. She completed a B.A. in honors English from that institution in 1947 and went to work as a reporter on the *Winnipeg Citizen*. She married Jack Laurence, an engineer, and moved with him to England in 1949. In 1950, her husband was offered a job in Somaliland to build dams in the desert, and so the Laurences moved to Africa, a place that would have a strong effect on Margaret Laurence's writing career. It was there that she began to write seriously.

In 1952, the couple moved to Ghana, where Jocelyn was born. Laurence had been translating Somali folktales and poetry, which were published as *A Tree for Poverty: Somali Poetry and Prose* by the Somali government in 1954. That same year, the Laurences' son David was born. In 1957, the family returned to Vancouver, Canada.

In 1960, her novel *This Side Jordan* was published simultaneously in Canada, England, and the United States. Two years later, she separated from Jack Laurence and moved with her children to Buckinghamshire, England. There, she published her first collection of short stories, *The Tomorrow-Tamer*, begun while she was in Africa and based on her experience of that continent. It was while she was in Great Britain that she began to write her Canadian or Manawaka books, the group of five great works centered on the prairies. The first book in this series, *The Stone Angel*, established her as a leading Canadian novelist.

Beginning in 1970, Laurence wrote for *The Vancouver Sun*, and in 1971, for *Maclean's* magazine. In 1973, she moved back permanently to Canada, where she was writer-in-residence at the University of Western Ontario. In 1974, she was writer-in-residence at Trent University and published *The Diviners*, her last adult novel and the final in the Manawaka cycle. In 1976, she published *Heart of a Stranger*, a collection of essays.

For the last twelve years of her life, Laurence wrote no more novels but focused on children's stories and an autobiography, which was incomplete at the time of her death, on January 5, 1987, in Lakefield, Ontario.

Analysis
Margaret Laurence's short stories are collected in two volumes, which display the two major places of her concern: *The Tomorrow-Tamer* is set in Africa and explores the effect of imperialism and colonialism on the people there, while *A Bird in the House* is a part of the Manawaka cycle, telling the story of a young Canadian girl and her family in a series of interconnected stories. Both collections, however, display Laurence's ongoing concerns with the dignity of the individual; the effects of societal events on families; the politics of dominance; the themes of death, freedom, and independence; and racial, social, and gender inequities. The collections also

display her skillful control of narrative voice, her ability to render the dialects of English-speaking people from a broad range of places and ages, her imaginative use of metaphor, and her delight in wordplay.

The Tomorrow-Tamer was written out of Laurence's experience of living in Ghana just before it gained its independence from the British, and the major themes are the pains of imperialism and the problems of independence. These are explored in stories that alternate between the tragic or ironic and the comic. While she worked on these stories, she read *Psychologie de la colonization* (1950; *Prospero and Caliban: The Psychology of Colonization*, 1956) by Dominique O. Mannoni, a French ethnographer, and later acknowledged his work as the only theoretical influence on her fiction.

Some of the stories in this collection would seem to have their roots in the oral tradition of the Somali works that Laurence had recently translated for her book *A Tree for Poverty*. For example, the title story, "The Tomorrow-Tamer," focuses on a young man, Kofi, who has grown up in a traditional village setting, made a traditional marriage, and expects to live as his ancestors did. The government, however, has brought in a crew to build a bridge over the Owura River, seen as a god by Kofi's people, and he is chosen by the village to be the first to work on it. In the process, he transposes his loyalties from his ancestral gods to those of the bridgemen, among whom he wishes to be counted. He knows, however, how to give of himself only as he has been taught, so that when the ironically named Emmanual, a bridgeman who travels from place to place living only for the earning of money and the spending of it, asks him what he will do next, he decides that he will be the priest of the bridge. Indeed he becomes so, as, in a moment of transcendence, he gazes at the sun while painting the peak of the bridge and as a result falls into the water. The village people see his drowning as a sacrifice from the bridge to the river. What gives the story a talelike, oral feel is that the death of Kofi becomes a legend in the village, and even his bereaved father is proud, for "a man consumed by the gods lives forever." This thought leaves the reader with a feeling of completion, despite the tragic nature of the story.

Another story in a similar vein is "The Voices of Adamo," which is also a tale of the inability of disparate cultures to communicate, despite good intentions. In it, Adamo is an almost epic heroic character who loses his whole village in an epidemic yet manages to survive incredible odds in the jungle, only to end up in a British regimental band as a drummer. He is taken on by Captain Fossey, the bandmaster, and he transposes his tribal loyalties to the captain. As independence nears, however, the captain, totally unable to read Adamo in any way but in terms of his own British culture, tries to find Adamo a better place in the world, while Adamo, who has very little grasp of English, thinks that Fossey is trying to dismiss him. All he can sense is that he is being sent off, another loss, like the loss of his village, his family, his place in the scheme of things, and so in despair, he kills Fossey. This is the only peace that he can obtain, the knowledge that he will be allowed to stay in his new home until he dies, which unfortunately will be very soon under the end of British rule.

In contrast to the tragic sense of the imperialistic contribution to the African continent is the story "The Perfume Sea," which tells the tale of two people without a home, Archipelago and Doree, who run a beauty salon for European women. With the coming of independence, their livelihood is destroyed: not only are they penniless, but also they have no resources to fall back on, like strangers in a strange land. Both misfits—one small and round (the Italian man, Archipelago), the other tall and gawky (the woman from no one knows where, Doree)—they face a bleak future until, in a moment of epiphany, they realize that there is a whole new market out there, that of African women who desire to look like city women. Their new shop begins to prosper only after Mercy, the daughter of their African landlord, tries their services and is immensely satisfied; thus they are saved, as Archipelago says, by an act of Mercy, one of the delightful puns in which Laurence occasionally indulges herself.

All the stories in this collection deal with outsiders, either native Africans who have been dispossessed by Europeans, Europeans who have settled in Africa but are forced by the independence movement to recognize that they do not belong, or colonizers who believe that they are in the right but have never been a part of the real life of the country. Archipelago and Doree are unusual outsiders, touching in their delicate affection for each other, unacceptable to the European community because they are service class and have possibly shady backgrounds but viewed by the Africans as a part of the European community. It is only when they are completely down on their luck that the African community accepts them. A number of the other stories in the collection display more typical colonial types, although never in the form of stereotype.

In "The Drummer of All the World," Matthew, the son of a missionary, grows up playing with an African child, nursed by an African woman. His Africa is exotic, warm, and exciting, but when he returns after schooling in England, he learns that his Africa has disappeared. Although he regrets this, he realizes that he never saw the disease (and dis-ease) below the surface of his experience. Matthew is a typical European in love with an unreal image of an African world, but at the same time he is more in touch with the reality of that world than his father, an iconoclast in a nearly literal sense, since he destroys the fetishes of the people. Matthew thinks, "Moses broke the idols of his own people."

In contrast, *A Bird in the House* is peopled by characters who grew up in the fictional small town of Manawaka, Manitoba, Canada. Unlike the African stories, in which Laurence employs either the first-person or the third-person voice, these Canadian stories are all told in the first person by a single narrator, Vanessa, whose voice is a true accomplishment; although she ranges in age from a very young child to a young adult, the voice simultaneously presents the experience appropriate to her age with insights of the adult mind. Also, as Vanessa is preparing herself to be a writer, she sees things from a writer's vantage point, even though she is also involved. She is also constantly gathering material, which means that she listens closely to, even eavesdrops on, adult conversations, thus allowing her to know more of what is happening in her world than many first-person narrators would, particularly a child. Laurence has admitted that *A Bird in the House* is the most autobiographical of her works.

Vanessa's world is a restricted one, hemmed in by the power of adults, particularly her maternal grandfather, who is a patriarch of the most oppressive sort, and by the breakdown of society, which results in wars (both World Wars I and II touch Vanessa's life) and depression. She escapes this world by writing stories of the most lurid, romantic, and impossible sort; at least, she does this as a youngster, but exposure to the reality of the world around her gradually forms a more mature approach to life.

The title story, "A Bird in the House," like many of the stories in the collection, centers on the theme of death. Vanessa's father dies of pneumonia, and the young girl loses her faith, thus feeling more isolated from her community. Another story, "The Mask of the Bear," depicts the loss of her grandmother and her anger and anguish over her grandfather's implacable patriarchal coldness and selfishness. Both of these stories have epilogues in which a more mature Vanessa recognizes the disappointments and humanity of these men in her life, and how they too were trapped by their societies.

Margaret Laurence is a major world author whose compassionate understanding of what forms the individual character and the character of nations, combined with her ability to render this knowledge in clear, distinctive prose so that all who read her will feel the same (at least while reading), has added to the wealth of the global reading community.

Other major works

NOVELS: *This Side Jordan*, 1960; *The Stone Angel*, 1964; *A Jest of God*, 1966; *The Fire-Dwellers*, 1969; *The Diviners*, 1974.

NONFICTION: *The Prophet's Camel Bell*, 1963 (published in the United States as *New Wind in a Dry Land*, 1964); *Long Drums and Cannons: Nigerian Dramatists and Novelists, 1952-1966*, 1968; *Heart of a Stranger*, 1976.

CHILDREN'S LITERATURE: *Jason's Quest*, 1970; *Six Darn Cows*, 1979; *The Olden Days Coat*, 1979; *The Christmas Birthday Story*, 1980.

ANTHOLOGY: *A Tree for Poverty: Somali Poetry and Prose*, 1954.

Bibliography

Buss, Helen M. *Mother and Daughter Relationships in the Manawaka Works of Margaret Laurence*. Victoria, British Columbia: University of Victoria, 1985. A Jungian reading of the four Manawaka novels and *A Bird in the House*, this book raises some interesting issues about the mother-daughter relationships that Laurence depicts, although at times the archetypal readings can be somewhat dense. Includes a select bibliography of criticism on Laurence and some later feminist criticism that informs the critic's work.

Hind-Smith, Joan. *Three Voices: The Lives of Margaret Laurence, Gabrielle Roy,*

Frederick Philip Grove. Toronto: Clarke, Irwin, 1975. Designed for students and the general reader, this volume is very helpful as an introduction to Laurence's work. It includes biographical information, at the same time providing narrative summaries of the major works.

Morley, Patricia. *Margaret Laurence*. Boston: Twayne, 1981. An extremely helpful and complete study of Laurence's work, which the author approaches by first arguing that Laurence, despite the fact that her work tends to focus on two very disparate places, Africa and Canada, has shown a consistent development of ideas and themes. She then looks at the African works, followed by the Manawaka cycle. Includes a complete chronology up to 1980, biographical information, an index, and an annotated select bibliography. A useful reference tool.

New, William, ed. *Margaret Laurence: The Writer and Her Critics*. Toronto: McGraw-Hill, 1977. This volume is an anthology of criticism on Laurence and interviews with her. Contains an informative introduction by the editor and, most important, three central essays by Laurence herself, which are invaluable aids to the understanding of her fiction.

Nicholson, Colin, ed. *Critical Approaches to the Fiction of Margaret Laurence*. Vancouver: University of British Columbia Press, 1990. An excellent collection of critical essays on Laurence, most written specifically for this book. They cover such topics as Laurence's place in the Canadian tradition in fiction, her work on Africa, close readings of specific works, comparison with Tillie Olsen and Jack Hodgins, and the use of autobiography in her writing. Includes a helpful preface and an index.

Thomas, Clara. *The Manawaka World of Margaret Laurence*. Toronto: McClelland and Stewart, 1976. A close reading of the works in the Manawaka cycle combined with an argument that although Laurence's characters talk Canadian, Laurence cannot be restricted to the category of Canadian or prairie writer, as her concerns, experiences, and philosophy are far from limited to one nation, or even one continent. Supplemented by a complete bibliographic checklist.

Woodcock, George. *Introducing Margaret Laurence's "The Stone Angel": A Reader's Guide*. Toronto: ECW Press, 1989. A close reading of the novel *The Stone Angel*, the first of the Manawaka series. Examines the novel's plots, characters, themes, origins, comparisons, and critical reception, as well as Laurence's work as a whole. Includes a useful chronology of Laurence's life, a brief biography, and an index.

Mary S. LeDonne

MARY LAVIN

Born: East Walpole, Massachusetts; June 11, 1912

Principal short fiction

Tales from Bective Bridge, 1942; *The Long Ago and Other Stories*, 1944; *The Becker Wives and Other Stories*, 1946; *At Sallygap and Other Stories*, 1947; *A Single Lady and Other Stories*, 1951; *The Patriot Son and Other Stories*, 1956; *Selected Stories*, 1959; *The Great Wave and Other Stories*, 1961; *The Stories of Mary Lavin*, 1964-1985 (3 volumes); *In the Middle of the Fields and Other Stories*, 1967; *Happiness and Other Stories*, 1969; *Collected Stories*, 1971; *A Memory and Other Stories*, 1972; *The Shrine and Other Stories*, 1977; *A Family Likeness and Other Stories*, 1985.

Other literary forms

Mary Lavin's novel *Gabriel Galloway* was serialized in *The Atlantic Monthly* in 1944 and was later published as a book under another title, *The House in Clewe Street* (1945). *The House in Clewe Street* and the novel *Mary O'Grady* (1950, 1986) are a loosely connected series of episodes in family life, structured to dramatize the lives of family members over several generations. Without an overall unity, the novels lack direction and force; there are, however, numerous examples within the novels of the social mores and restrictive attitudes more artfully handled in the short stories. Lavin's fine children's stories, *A Likely Story* (1957) and *The Second-Best Children in the World* (1972), capture the imaginative life of children.

Achievements

As a major Irish writer, Lavin is a realist in the tradition of Frank O'Connor and Seán O'Faoláin. The resemblance to those important Irish writers, however, stops there. Her characters are usually solidly middle class, and they tend to be shopkeepers and clerks, a population that is, perhaps, less "submerged" than that of O'Connor's fiction. For Lavin, social class is a determining factor in a character's behavior and fate. She stresses the limitations imposed by a character's social role. In addition, she does not use humor as a major fictional device. Instead of humor, there is often an ironic twist to the plot. Lavin's plots also tend to avoid the simple solution provided by techniques such as reversal and recognition. Instead, she closely examines the problems that her characters encounter. If there is a resolution, it is by no means a simple one.

Lavin is the recipient of numerous awards and honors, including the James Tait Black Memorial Prize in 1944, the Katherine Mansfield-Menton Prize in 1962, the Ella Lynam Cabot Fellowship in 1971, the Gregory Medal in 1974, and the American Irish Foundation Award in 1979. Lavin was president of the Irish Academy of Letters from 1971 to 1973, and she received the American Irish Foundation award in 1979.

Biography

Born in East Walpole, Massachusetts, on June 11, 1912, and the only child of Irish-born Nora Mahon and Tom Lavin, Mary Lavin emigrated to Ireland in her ninth year. Educated at Loreto Convent in Dublin and University College, Dublin, she wrote her M.A. thesis on Jane Austen; she then taught French at Loreto Convent for two years while preparing her unfinished Ph.D. thesis on Virginia Woolf. In 1942, she married William Walsh, and they had three daughters: Valentine, Elizabeth, and Caroline. After the death of her husband in 1954, Lavin had little time to write fiction since she had to bring up her children and run the farm at Bective. A Guggenheim Fellowship in 1959, however, and another in 1962, gave her the time and confidence to create fiction once more. She published a number of stories that were then collected in *The Great Wave and Other Stories*. Thereafter, the years became serene and productive. Lavin received a number of awards and prizes, including a third Guggenheim Fellowship, in 1972, and a D.Litt. from the National University of Ireland in 1968. In 1969, she married an old friend from her university days, Michael MacDonald Scott, a laicized Jesuit. Her *Collected Stories* was a fitting testimony to the depth and range of her fiction.

Analysis

Neither national nor international events find their way into Mary Lavin's fiction, which is crammed with incidents from the lives of Dublin shopkeepers, countrypeople, island fishermen and their families, nuns, priests, her parents, children, and husbands. Lavin's characters, much more important than the plots, which are rather mundane, are usually autobiographical. They represent their author and acquaintances at various stages in her lifetime: childhood, student life, marriage, motherhood, and widowhood.

Whereas James Joyce was haunted by a father-son conflict, Lavin was plagued by a mother-daughter conflict, resulting in an Electra complex. It partially accounts for the frequent revelations of unhappy marriages between mismatched couples although the differences were a source of attraction before the birth of children or the assumption of responsibilities. More often than not, the wife characters are domineering, practical, slaves to social mores, and unhappy. Some other women characters—nuns, spinsters, sisters, and widows—are vain, flighty, insecure, and emotionally labile. Husband characters, on the other hand, no matter how beaten they are by their wives and circumstances, have poetic vision while the priests, bachelors, brothers, and widowers appear robust, in command of life and their emotions.

"Miss Holland," Lavin's first short story published in *Dublin Magazine* (1938) and reprinted in *Tales from Bective Bridge*, is the story of a typical spinster. Agnes Holland, lonely and ill-prepared to face life, traveled for years with her father, who made all the decisions. At his death, Agnes must adjust to the world without anyone to help her. The story, set in England, begins with Agnes searching for a place to live; she finally decides to live at the guest house of Mrs. Lewis because of a playful cat.

Living there are two men and three women with whom Agnes has nothing in common. She is not a conversationalist and cannot join in the spirited exchanges held during dining hours. Since the other boarders are younger, age is a further obstacle. Agnes feels trapped in her surroundings; there is nothing from the past which she can recollect that will bridge the gap between her and the boorish boarders. Agnes thinks she must try to enter this strange world and wants to discover something to share with the group, needing to be part of her environment.

The black cat affords the opportunity. Agnes sees him jumping in the sun after running through the flower bed where he plucked one red carnation; the image is like that of a Spanish dancer, and she can hardly wait to tell the group. At dinner she and a male guest begin to speak simultaneously, so Agnes waits to let him tell his story. To her horror, she learns that he has shot the black tomcat. Amused, the other guests begin to laugh. Agnes is silent, withdrawing from the boisterous group; no longer can she associate with such people. Having no place else to go because she must live on the small amount of money left to her by her father, she determines to live on past memories of more genteel days. All the ugly characteristics of the uncultured men and women rush to her mind, separating her from them. Loneliness will become a fixed part of life, borne with dignity. Agnes' emotional drama is the conflict of the story. Forever opposed to vulgarity, Agnes realizes she can no longer use her imagination to disguise poor taste and must protest "because my people before me went that way."

Annie Ryan in "At Sallygap" and Ella in "A Happy Death" are typical examples of the wife characters who pressure their husbands. Childless, Annie is a real terror. Artistic Manny Ryan, a fiddler who years earlier was heading to Paris with a band, jumped ship for Annie. He thought she was loving, fragile, and in need of him. Their marriage, however, symbolizes the paralysis and stagnation of Irish urban life. After years of labor, they have nothing more tangible than a tiny Dublin shop where they work and live. Manny knows that "All the Dublin people were good for was talking." Annie was no exception. Her tongue lashes out at Manny usually because he is not aggressive enough in commercial dealings. Annie dominates him while wishing he would be the dominant spouse. Manny's gentility, unfortunately, serves as a red flag for Annie's temper.

By ordering him to go to Sallygap to set up a trade in fresh eggs, Annie gives him a brief escape from his hateful marriage. A lover of nature, Manny draws strength from the rural scenes. On missing the last bus, he walks home, free "at last from the sordidness of the life he led." While Manny feels elated, however, Annie, accustomed to her husband's regularity, goes through a variety of emotions awaiting his return. First, she plans to taunt him. Then thinking he is out drinking to get the courage to fight back, she relishes that prospect and prepares herself for a grand battle. Next, fear overcomes her: perhaps Manny is dead. No, he would be brought home alive with a "latent mutinous instinct" activated, which she hopes will enliven their relationship. On hearing his footstep, however, Annie realizes nothing has changed. Manny is sober and servile, "imprisoned forever in her hatred."

In "A Happy Death," Ella, with three daughters to rear, has to control her emotions in dealing with her dying husband Robert. To supplement their income, Ella rents rooms in their home, using some of the money to buy clothes for Robert so he can get a better job at the library. Outraged when he is demoted from clerk to porter because of his coughing, she demands that he quit, but he refuses and works as a porter. Ella cannot comprehend Robert's need to work and bring her his wages, so she convinces herself that he works to spite her and lower the family's social class. The emotional charges between Ella and Robert build up until his death and explode in Ella afterward.

Through a series of flashbacks, a device Lavin uses in most of her stories, the reader learns of Ella's happy courtship with Robert, her admiration of his white skin and his interest in poetry, and their elopement against her parents' wishes. Their happiness is fleeting. After they are married, she burns his poetry books, sees his white skin as a sign of weakness, and understands why her shopkeeping parents opposed her marriage to unemployed Robert. When Robert is hospitalized, with a flush of excitement, Ella insists on keeping up appearances. He must have the best ambulance, a private ward, a new nightshirt, and oranges which he cannot eat.

The daughters are embarrassed by their mother's vain fussing over Robert; it is so unnatural, being sent out for grapes, apples, and newspapers when they know he can neither eat nor read. Ella, however, wants everyone to know Robert is a person of importance with people who care for him. More fruit, biscuits, and sweets are brought to him, making it difficult for the nurses to find space for the thermometer.

Eventually, Ella realizes that the unconscious Robert is dying and prays for his happy death; meanwhile, her prayers and behavior at the bedside are a continued source of distress to her daughters. Thrusting a crucifix in Robert's face, Ella tries to get him to say an act of contrition; he does not. Then he regains his senses long enough to call out for Ella with the lovely golden hair. Misunderstanding her request for him to repeat "I am heartily sorry," Robert thinks she is sorry for having offended him and says, "There's nothing to be sorry about. You always made me happy, just by being near me." Robert's delirious mind recollects their youth and plans for "just the two of them," ignoring the daughters, and a look of "rapturous happiness" returns to his face before he dies. Bewildered, Ella refuses comfort from the priest, nurse, and her daughters. Screaming and sobbing, she is led from the ward, disbelieving God's refusal to answer her prayers for Robert's happy death. Ironically, she does not know that her prayers have been answered.

The young boy in "Say Could That Lad Be I," an early story in the first collection, *Tales from Bective Bridge,* and Tom in "Tom" from the collection *The Shrine and Other Stories,* are portraits of Lavin's father. The farm boy, mischievous and carefree, has a dog, White Prince, the greatest fighter in the countryside. On a visit to his grandmother, the boy takes along White Prince. It is a great mistake to lock him in the cottage when he goes on an errand for his grandmother, since the dog flies through a closed window and follows his master to the village. After a disturbance in a shop, White Prince flies through its window, causing even greater destruction. Pretending that it is not his dog, the boy walks back to his grandmother. On the road, White Prince, dragging a leg of mutton in his mouth, joins his master. There is not much the lad can do but wash the mutton, present it to his grandmother, and head home before the townspeople pounce upon him.

In "Tom," Lavin opens the story by saying, "My father's hair was black as the Devil's, and he flew into black, black rages." Everything about him was black except for "the gold spikes of love with which he pierced me to the heart when I was a child." The author leaves little doubt about the affection she held for her father. In this story she recounts with pride his exploits at school, his walks under a sky filled with birds, his travels to Dublin, Liverpool, Scotland, and America, plus his return to Ireland.

Her portrait of her mother is quite different. Lavin states with disinterest that her mother had numerous memories filling her head, but they could all be reduced to her mother at the piano with her singing sisters and their beaux about her. Her courtship with Tom was more ardent on his part than hers. Yet she, at thirty years, realized she had snared a desirable fifty-year-old bachelor even though she disliked him at first because of his coarseness, ignorance, and arrogance. Lavin surmises her mother would have preferred her Protestant suitor, Mr. Barrett, a land agent on a large estate. Because of the age difference, Nora lived twenty-four years after Tom's death; Lavin agrees it was an unfair relationship. Her father had her "mother's beauty when he could proudly display it but she did not have his support when she needed it most."

Mary, on the other hand, had Tom's support when she needed it. While at the university, he took her to Roscommon, revisiting his boyhood haunts and sharing his memories. Ignoring the material changes, he points out the unchanging mounds, stone walls, and streams running over mossy stones. Although he recognizes old friends, very aged and worn, they do not recognize him. A childhood friend, Rose Magarry, on seeing him says he is Tom's son, "Sure, you're the dead spit of him!" Silently, they leave without correcting the woman.

Tom does not follow the same rules which Nora does, and Mary accepts his lifestyle without complaint. If he was ever a burden to her, it does not appear in her fiction. Incidentally, the old mother in "Senility" from the same collection is an exquisite portrait of a widowed woman who lives with her daughter. The emotional tension between them is acute, and neither mother nor daughter will release it. The son-in-law acts as a referee in a continuing war of nerves.

When not writing about her family, Lavin presents other people's problems. Always busy with her own difficulties as the correspondence with Lord and Lady Dunsany reveals, she records some fresh insights about psychotic behavior in a tightly structured society. In writing about insanity, she is more comprehensive in *Mary O'Grady*, her second novel, with a description of Patrick's withdrawal from his family and its effect upon the members, but the short stories also document the exploits of schizophrenic people, giving the impression that such people are an integral part of Irish society.

Eterna, the nun in "Eterna," is an excellent example of a woman who cannot face life. A young doctor called to treat the novice Eterna finds her arrogant despite an outward appearance of humility. He discovers that her infected arm was caused by turpentine soaking through the bandage over a cut which she received by falling off a ladder. Eterna, he learns, is an artist. As the eldest of ten from a poor family, she was educated by the nuns because of her talent and joined the order to continue her work; she could not remain with her impoverished family, and the doctor learns that in time she could not remain with the order.

Years after his calls at the convent in a provincial town, he sees Eterna again at the National Gallery in Dublin. She has a crazed look, wears outlandish clothes, and fixes her daft gaze upon him. It brings back his memories of her former life and his brief, questioning visits with her. He flees from the gallery and rushes to his car to await his wife. She, who also knew Eterna, is nonchalant about his encounter with the artist, saying, "If she'd gone a bit cracked, what about it . . . she was probably headed that way from the start." She then tells her husband that people have to clip their wings in order to keep their feet on the ground.

The many widows in Lavin's fiction have their feet on the ground, representing their author after the death of her first husband. Mary and Maudie from "In a Café," Brede from "Bridal Sheets," the unnamed widow from "In the Middle of the Fields," and Vera Traska from "The Cuckoo-spit," "Happiness," "Trastevere," and "Villa Violella" trace Lavin's battle against loneliness and her eventual adjustment to another self and remarriage. Vera in "Happiness" is a central widow character. Her story is told in the first person by her eldest daughter, an unusual technique for Lavin, who generally uses the omniscient third-person point of view. Kate, the eldest daughter in "The Will," the novice in "My Vocation," the neighbor-narrator in "The Small Bequest," the niece-narrator in "A Wet Day," the daughter in "The Mouse," and the husband in "My Molly" are other exceptions to the omniscient viewpoint.

The daughter in "Happiness" describes Vera's thoughts about happiness and how it must not be confused with pleasure or perceived as the opposite of sorrow. The narrator then introduces her younger sisters, Bea and Linda (the latter was only a year old at their father's death), Father Hugh (Michael Scott), a family friend filling the place of the lost father, and Grandmother, who "God Almighty couldn't make happy." This, of course, is a portrait of Lavin's family. Episodes from Lavin's life with husband Robert (William Walsh) and grandfather Tom reveal happy moments. The black period immediately after Robert's death is an unhappy period when the narrator and Bea guard against their mother's suicide. Their trips to Europe are in vain because Vera cannot forget her husband, but since the children learn geography and history, they are not completely wasted. In rearing her daughter after returning home, Vera rejects advice from relatives, friends, and strangers who want her to accept life as a vale of tears.

By accepting life's chaos, symbolized by her disordered study, Vera painfully pursues life. Father Hugh is there to help, but at times she has him "as distracted as herself." Writing, working for her family, and gardening consume much energy, and it is not surprising that Vera eventually collapses while working in her garden. Father Hugh carries her into the house, where she dies four hours later, recalling the day Robert died. It is necessary for Vera to die and natural that she would remember Robert's last day. A finality to that relationship opens new doors for Mary Lavin through which she and Father Michael Scott can pass. "Happiness," more autobiographic than fictive, is the story of an insecure, emotionally fragile woman dealt some cruel blows.

Other major works

NOVELS: *The House in Clewe Street*, 1945; *Mary O'Grady*, 1950, 1986.

CHILDREN'S LITERATURE: *A Likely Story*, 1957; *The Second-Best Children in the World*, 1972.

Bibliography

Bowen, Zack. *Mary Lavin*. Lewisburg, Pa.: Bucknell University Press, 1975. A very concise introduction in the Irish Writers series to Lavin's life and work. Bowen touches on the social background of the fiction and a few themes. Nearly half the book is a discussion of Lavin's novels *The House in Clewe Street* and *Mary O'Grady*.

Caswell, Robert W. "Political Reality and Mary Lavin's *Tales from Bective Bridge*." *Eire-Ireland* 3 (Spring, 1968): 48-60. Caswell argues that Lavin's stories lack the "political reality" found in the works of Frank O'Connor and Seán O'Faoláin. He also states that she does not show nationalism as a driving force of her characters. Yet Caswell still feels that Lavin captures a distinctly Irish identity.

Kelly, A. A. *Mary Lavin: A Study*. New York: Barnes & Noble Books, 1980. The best critical book available on Lavin. Kelly discusses Lavin's use of the social hierarchy in her fiction. There are also excellent chapters on the themes of the family and religion found in Lavin's work.

Murray, Thomas J. "Mary Lavin's World: Lovers and Strangers." *Eire-Ireland* 7 (Summer, 1973): 122-131. Murray finds much "sterility" in the characters and situations in Lavin's fiction. The role of women in many of the stories, Murray argues, is to destroy the life-affirming fantasies of men.

Peterson, Richard F. *Mary Lavin*. Boston: Twayne, 1980. This book offers a brief biography of Lavin and then examines specific examples of the stories and novels. A useful introduction to the writer.

Eileen A. Sullivan
(Revised by *James Sullivan*)

D. H. LAWRENCE

Born: Eastwood, England; September 11, 1885
Died: Vence, France; March 2, 1930

Principal short fiction

The Prussian Officer and Other Stories, 1914; *England, My England,* 1922; *The Ladybird, the Fox, the Captain's Doll,* 1923; *St. Mawr: Together with the Princess,* 1925; *Rawdon's Roof,* 1928; *The Woman Who Rode Away and Other Stories,* 1928; *The Escaped Cock,* 1929 (best known as *The Man Who Died*); *Love Among the Haystacks and Other Stories,* 1930; *The Lovely Lady and Other Stories,* 1933; *A Modern Lover,* 1934; *The Complete Short Stories of D. H. Lawrence,* 1961.

Other literary forms

D. H. Lawrence is one of the most prolific writers in English literary history. His major works include ten volumes of poetry, a collection of critical essays, four books of travel writings, several translations, and plays, in addition to the four novels (among others) for which he is popularly known. His most famous novel, *Lady Chatterley's Lover* (1928), brought him notoriety and further assured that he would be remembered as a novelist rather than a poet and short-story writer. After his novels, his most widely read and anthologized works are short stories and poems. In many of his works, Lawrence uses identical situations, plots, images, and themes.

Achievements

The subject and style of Lawrence's works, of whatever kind, are so distinct and consistent that his name has given birth to an adjective, "Lawrentian," to describe a way of looking at the world and a method for presenting it. The bold originality and powerful style of his early novels attracted the attention of upper-class British writers and intellectuals such as the philosopher Bertrand Russell and even the prime minister Herbert Asquith. Lawrence's values, however, were not the same as theirs, and he spent most of his life as a nomad, searching for amenable landscapes and cultures. All of his works record that search and reveal its remarkable unity of purpose.

After Lawrence's death, his critical reputation eventually declined, though his works continued to sell. Then, in 1955, the influential modern English critic F. R. Leavis published a study of the novels and declared Lawrence to be the most important writer of his generation and as good as Charles Dickens. He praised *Sons and Lovers* (1913) as the first honest treatment of the British working class. Also in 1955 the American critic Harry T. Moore published the first authoritative biography, *The Intelligent Heart,* introducing Lawrence to a public as fascinated by his life as by his work. His reputation is worldwide; in 1982, there were nearly three hundred titles pertaining to Lawrence translated into thirty languages.

Biography

David Herbert Lawrence's life went through four distinct stages. The first may be indicated as the Nottingham or Eastwood years, the formative years before March, 1912. Lawrence's father, Arthur, was a miner, and his mother, a teacher. Married beneath her status, Lydia Beardsall Lawrence detested the commonness of her husband and vowed that her sons would never work the pits. She therefore doggedly saw Lawrence through a teacher-training program at Nottingham University College. The class struggle at home mirrored the larger class struggle, of which Lawrence was acutely aware.

Within the grim industrial village life there remained a lyrical beauty in intimate relations. In Eastwood, Lawrence was romantically involved with two women who represented the contradictory nature of love. Jessie Chambers (Muriel in *Sons and Lovers*), his mother's choice, was too spiritual and possessive for Lawrence. He was physically attracted to another, Louie Burrows, but the oedipal bonds were too strong to break. When Lydia Lawrence died in December, 1910, Lawrence drifted aimlessly, and over the next few months severed all romantic attachments. Then, in March, 1912, he met Frieda Weekley, the wife of his modern languages professor. They were married in May.

The next period lasted until the end of World War I and his subsequent departure from England. Lawrence published poems that treat his marriage to Frieda as at once physical and spiritual. He was at work on a long novel, *The Sisters*, which he split into two and published the first part, *The Rainbow*, in 1915. The work was suppressed by British censors because of its frank portrayal of sexual relations, and Lawrence was unable to find an American publisher. In 1917, he and Frieda applied for passports, which they were denied, ostensibly because Frieda's family was German and some of her relatives (notably, the infamous Red Baron) served prominently in the German army. For the next two years, the Lawrences lived in dire poverty, in cottages and on funds lent by friends.

Years of wandering characterize the third period. After relatively short residencies in various Italian towns, Lawrence visited Ceylon (now Sri Lanka) and Australia, and then from September, 1922, until September, 1925, lived in Taos, New Mexico, and Chapala and Oaxaca in Mexico, interspersed with a short return to England in late 1924. He traveled to the United States at the invitation of Mabel Dodge Luhan, who had read *Sea and Sardinia* (1921) and was convinced that only Lawrence could describe the "soul" of the Southwest landscape and Indians. His American works lyrically reveal the landscape but show little empathy for the people and their history.

In November, 1925, the Lawrences moved to Spotorno, Italy. In June, 1926, Lawrence declared that he no longer wanted to write fiction and began a series of watercolors and large oil paintings. From a villa near Florence in 1927, Lawrence wrote his last novel and *succès de scandale*, *Lady Chatterley's Lover*, and collected his lyrical accounts of travels in Mexico and the American Southwest. His last works, just before he moved to Bandol and then Vence in the French Provence, included his studies of the Etruscan tombs at Tarquinia; a short novel, *The Escaped Cock*, which is an idiosyncratic account of Christ's death and resurrection; *Apocalypse* (1931), a study of the Book of Revelation; and *Last Poems* (1932), which deals with the experience of dying. All of them reflect Lawrence's preparation for his own death, from tuberculosis, in March, 1930.

Analysis

D. H. Lawrence's early stories are set, except for "The Prussian Officer," in the English Midlands; their plot and characters are a thinly veiled autobiography and are built on incidents that Lawrence would develop at length in other forms, notably the novels and plays that he was writing concurrently. Some readers prefer the stories over Lawrence's longer forms, which they regard as too insistent and repetitious; his stories, like his poems, are more structured, their images more intense. Like the longer works, however, the stories reveal Lawrence's central belief in a "fatal change" in the early twentieth century: "the collapse from the psychology of the free human individual into the psychology of the social being." Lawrence tried always to see unity in the behavior of human beings and the historical changes through which ages lived. In the longer works and in many essays, he developed a didactic style appropriate to his sweeping interpretation of human history and types of personality. In the stories, he lyrically and more intimately explores how the quality of individuals' lives is affected by their human relationships.

A majority of the stories more frequently treat the failure of human relationships. "Odour of Chrysanthemums" is one of five accounts of such a discovery of lost human possibilities; other versions appear in three novels and a play, *The Widowing of Mrs. Holroyd* (1914), from this period. A proud miner's wife, Elizabeth Bates, waits with her two children for her husband, who is late coming from the pits. At first, she angrily surmises that he has gone to a pub; as time passes, the anger changes to fear. The husband has been killed in a mining accident, and his fellow colliers bring his body home. The climax of the story is one of Lawrence's best scenes, as the miner's mother and wife wash the corpse. In early versions of the story, from 1911, Lawrence treated the mother's and wife's whimperings and reveries equally; in the collected version in 1914, however, he added the powerful dramatic epiphany of Mrs. Bates's feeling of shame for having denied her husband's body. "She had denied him what he was . . . refused him as himself." The discovery is also liberating: "She was grateful to death, which restored the truth. And she knew she was not dead." The symbol of flowers is a derivative, almost gratuitous device. Their fragrance equates to memory, as the wife recalls the events of her married life: birth, defeat and reconciliation, and death.

Before Lawrence's own fulfillment with Frieda Weekley, it is problematic whether he could have known, or treated so honestly, the complex nature of human sexuality or the separateness of lovers. Without the revisions, the story is successful only as an account of lost love and patent realizations, much like others in *The Prussian Officer and Other Stories.* "The Shadow in the Rose Garden" and "The Shades of Spring" are stories about return and realization, but they lack dramatic climaxes. In "The

Shadow in the Rose Garden," an unnamed woman returns on her honeymoon to the town where she first fell in love. There, she discovers that her first lover, whom she believed a Boer War casualty, is alive but confined to an insane asylum. In an unresolved ending, her husband learns that she is still attached to the soldier and concludes that it "would be violation to each of them to be brought into contact with the other." In "The Shades of Spring," Hilda Millership—rejected by a cultured suitor, John Syson—gives herself to her gamekeeper, Arthur Pilbury, on Syson's wedding night. Later, still foppishly attached to Hilda, Syson returns to her farm, learns about Hilda's affair, and is taunted by the gamekeeper for not having seduced her.

Both stories lack the dramatic structure of "Odour of Chrysanthemums." They exemplify a style that Lawrence told his literary agent in 1914 he wanted to outgrow: a method of "accumulating objects in the light of a powerful emotion, and making a scene of them." Nevertheless, these early stories use situations, characters, and symbols that one finds in all Lawrence's work. At the end of "The Shades of Spring," for example, a bee stings Pilbury, and Hilda sucks the wound and smears his mouth with bloody kisses. This gesture is one of the first symbolic statements of a Lawrentian paradigm: blood symbolizes natural, unconscious life, in contrast to the mechanically intellectual and socially correct existence of Syson.

These two ways of living are also represented in a contrast between *feeling* and *seeing*, between intuitive knowledge and acquired, social knowledge. "The Blind Man" is Lawrence's most powerful treatment of both the necessity and the consequence of intimate physical contact. Isabel Pervin is married to Maurice, who was blinded and scarred in World War I and is completely dependent on her. The focus of the story is not their love but Maurice's sudden passion for his wife's cousin and former admirer, Bertie Reid. Maurice asks Isabel to invite Bertie for a visit, hoping that he can become his closest friend. Isabel's ambivalent feelings about Bertie, fond yet contemptuous, derive from her knowledge of his life-style. "He had his friends among the fair sex—not lovers, friends." She knew that he was "unable to enter into close contact of any sort." This failure at relationships, Lawrence bitingly asserts, made him a "brilliant and successful barrister, also a litterateur of high repute, a rich man, and a great social success"—in short, the epitome of the aristocratic Englishman. The story, however, is more serious than it is satirical. At the electrifying climax, Maurice first runs his hand over Bertie's face and body, and then, to Bertie's horror, puts Bertie's hand over his scars and into his eye sockets. Maurice tells Isabel of the experience, which he regards as a ritual of undying friendship, but she sees Bertie's revulsion and his urge to flee such intimacy.

In his own life, Lawrence was attracted to the ritual of *Blüdbrudershaft*, in which two male friends mix their blood from self-imposed cuts, and he used that ritual, along with a nude wrestling scene, in *Women in Love* (1920). The equivalent contact in "The Blind Man," heightened by Maurice's disfigurement, shows the failure of male relationships as a corollary of failed sexual love. Lawrence had been reading Carl Jung's "Psychology of the Unconscious" and "found much truth" in the oedipal "mother-incest idea." At times, Frieda could become for Lawrence the devouring mother: a man "casts himself as it were into her womb, and . . . the Magna Mater receives him with gratification. . . . It is awfully hard, once the sex relation has gone this way, to recover. If we don't recover we die." Lawrence professed to "believe tremendously in friendship between man and man, a pledging of men to each other inviolably."

While male friendship remained for all Lawrence's life an ideal, he was never able to produce an account of successful male relations, whether the bonds were sexual or not. "The Blind Man" symbolically rejects male friendship as a way out of an unavoidable sexual regression, despite what Lawrence professed to believe. In an earlier story, "The Prussian Officer," Lawrence had not yet acquired the skill of using symbolic gestures. He thus treats more directly the destructive nature of suppressed desires—in this case, for an overtly sexual male relationship. Originally entitled "Honour and Arms," the story's title was changed by an editor, much to Lawrence's chagrin. While the revised title focuses on the dominant character and necessarily minimizes another, it removes the pun and limits Lawrence's intent to show how repressed or unconscious desires can erupt in sadistic violence in any relationship. The Prussian captain, attracted to his young orderly, Anton Schoner, vents his forbidden attraction, first in sadistic assaults and then by refusing to let the orderly see his sweetheart. The orderly's "normal" heterosexuality eventually yields to unconscious responses toward the captain, which drive Schoner to murder him. Lawrence treats the murder like a rape: "It pleased him . . . to feel the hard twitchings of the prostrate body jerking his own whole frame. . . ." The theme common to both "The Prussian Officer" and "The Blind Man" lies in the similarity between otherwise dissimilar characters. Anyone who has avoided his feelings, or acknowledged but repressed them, on being forced to recognize them, destroys himself—or, more usually, as in Bertie's case, flees to avoid entrapment in any permanent sexual relationship.

In contemporaneous stories of heterosexual love, physical contact has the opposite effect. A woman is, like Sleeping Beauty, awakened by physical touch to know and accept, usually gradually, her unconscious desires. In "The Horse Dealer's Daughter," a doctor rescues a drowning girl, takes her to his home, and strips off her wet clothes. When she awakens, she embraces him and stirs him into love for her. (Lawrence develops the same plot in a longer version in *The Virgin and the Gipsy*, 1930.)

"You Touched Me" also explores the theme of touch, complicated by an additional motive of inherited wealth. The lower-class male, ironically named Hadrian, has been adopted from a charity house. After wartime service, he returns to his adoptive father, Ted Rockley, a dying invalid cared for by his two natural spinster daughters, Emmie and Matilda. One night, Matilda goes into Hadrian's room, genuinely mistaking it as her father's, and caresses his face before discovering who he is. The touch stirs Hadrian's desire and determines him to conquer the proud Matilda. Ted Rockley approves Hadrian's offer to marry and threatens to leave his estate to Hadrian if Matilda refuses. Matilda's reason for agreeing to marriage is not the point, though it adds a realistic, common touch. The point is that her touching Hadrian validates his desire and gives him rights.

"You Touched Me" shares its plot with a longer work of this period, *The Fox*. In both narratives, a young man returns to England from Canada and falls in love with an older woman. In *The Fox*, the plot complication is not inheritance but a romantic and economic liaison of the loved one, Nellie March, with another woman, Jill Banford. As he does with other homosexual characters, Lawrence simply kills Jill: the young man, Henry Grenfel, cuts down a tree so that it falls where Jill is standing. Henry's repeated warnings to Jill to move and her refusal to do so leave vague whether the act was suicide or murder.

Homoeroticism in stories such as *The Fox* and the subject of sexual awakenings in all of his works elicited the popular view of Lawrence's works as being pornographic. It was a charge against which Lawrence vigorously defended himself. His narratives were erotic, designed to awaken readers to their sexuality when they identified with his characters, but they were not pornographic, designed for genital arousal. Pornography offered a life-denying and self-consuming masturbatory release; the erotic stimulated the need for fulfillment with another. According to Lawrence, the British public was not accustomed to the open treatment of sexual relations as healthy. Instead, earlier writers had denied normal sexuality and reduced virile male characters to enervated victims of accidents or war. Nineteenth century readers could accept such vital characters as Rochester in Charlotte Brontë's *Jane Eyre* (1847) only when they were physically ruined or subjugated to a feminine domesticity. The impotent characters, Lawrence believed, that recur so often are both cause and effect of the decline of modern British civilization. In 1917, hoping to flee to the United States, Lawrence wrote to Bertrand Russell, "I cannot do any more work for this country . . . there is no future for England: only a decline and fall. That is the dreadful and unbearable part of it: to have been born into a decadent era, a decline of life, a collapsing civilisation."

Even a dying civilization has its beauty, Lawrence decided, but it was a demonic and apocalyptic one. In the most important essay for understanding his credo, "The Crown," Lawrence characterized modern society as the end of a civilization. It was self-indulgent, self-destructive, sensuous, power-seeking, monotheistic, and light-denying. A new and balanced society would eventually follow. Meanwhile, for generations caught at the end of such epochs, the only way out of a narcissistic egoism was to indulge demonically in sex or bloodlust. Destruction, like creation, required vitality. Lawrence hoped that demonic vitality, spent at last, would lead to a new civilization. Even if it made things worse, it was preferable to apathy.

Lawrence always saw correspondences between individuals, the kinds of societies that they fostered, and the religious myths that they created. The most cogent interpretation that Lawrence gives of the Christian myth is an oedipal one recorded in an unpublished foreword to *Sons and Lovers*:

> The Father was flesh—and the Son, who in himself was finite and had form, became Word. For form is the uttered Word, and the Son is the Flesh as it utters the word, but the unutterable Flesh is the Father.

And God the Father, the Inscrutable, the Unknowable, we know in the Flesh, in woman. She is the door for our ingoing and our out-coming. In her we go back to the Father.

Much of this echoes Jung's "Psychological Approach to the Trinity." For both Lawrence and Jung, father and son constitute polarities in the male psyche. At the personal level, Lawrence has been separated from his father by the mother's interventions. The only way back to the father was to reject the mother and replace her with another female object of desire. The wife replaces mother and restores the son to the father.

Like civilization, Christianity had hardened into meaningless dogma. Lawrence's travels were undertaken not only to avoid a dying British culture but also to discover the nature of other, pre-Christian religions. In the Native American culture, Lawrence found, for a while, what he was seeking: the "oldest religion," when "everything was alive, not supernaturally but naturally alive." The Native Americans' "whole life effort" was to "come into immediate *felt* contact and, so derive energy, power, and a dark sort of joy." Their efforts to become one with the cosmos, without intermediation, was the "root meaning" of religion. Such rapturous description suggests an equivalence to Lawrence's "blood-consciousness" as an attempt to revive a vital religion. The stories and short novels set in the American Southwest and Mexico blend religious vitality and demonic indulgence. Many readers, unaware of Lawrence's metaphysical framework, disparage the stories for what they see as his approval of brute, male force against women. At the naturalistic level, the stories are gratuitously violent, but in the context of Lawrence's credo, they become fabulistic, not realistic. Character and action should be interpreted as symbolic. The presentation of a scene does not necessarily indicate the author's approval.

The juxtaposition of characters in three stories of the Southwest—"The Princess," "The Woman Who Rode Away," and the short novel *St. Mawr*—recalls the structure of earlier stories. Egotistical, haughty, coddled but unfulfilled American and European women come under the sway of dark-skinned heroes who embody Lawrence's ideal. Lawrence's male Native Americans are distinguished from even the most intuitive British men, like Maurice in "The Blind Man" or Henry in *The Fox*: they have rejected a white culture, including religion, that threatens to demean and confine them. Having escaped the coming Christian apocalypse, they are neither self-indulgent nor spiritual but living embodiments of a phallic mystery, the "only mystery" that the female characters have not unravelled. Their attempts to "know" that mystery leads to their alienation or destruction.

In "The Princess," Dollie Urquhart travels, after her aristocratic father's death, to a dude ranch in New Mexico. There, she is drawn ineluctably to Domingo Romero, a guide at the ranch and the last of a line of great Native American landholders. Romero is himself unfulfilled and waits for one of two Lawrentian fates: to die or to be "aroused in passion and hope." One day, Dollie arranges a trip, with a female companion and Romero as guide, over the Rockies to a spot where animals can be observed in their "wild unconsciousness." Even though the companion's horse is injured, Dollie and Romero continue the trip. The cold mountains both terrify and seduce Dollie, as Lawrence makes the mountains represent what she is seeking, in perhaps his most successful use of settings as symbols. The guide and his charge spend the night in a miner's shack. Frightened by dreams of snow, a symbol of spiritual death, Dollie goes to Romero for "warmth, protection" and to be "taken away from herself," and Romero obliges. The next day, when Dollie tells him that she does not like "that sort of thing," Romero is broken and angry. Like Hadrian in "You Touched Me," he argues that Dollie's coming to him has given him the right to marry her. When she refuses, he strips her and violates her repeatedly, but she refuses to relent. Romero had successfully reached some "unrealised part" of her that she had never wanted to feel. Soon, rangers rescue Dollie and kill Romero. Unable to find her old self, "a virgin intact," she goes "slightly crazy."

In "The Woman Who Rode Away," the knowledge sought by the unnamed woman is much more profound. She wants to visit a remote tribe of Chilchui Indians and "to know their gods." She does not know that for years the Chilchui have waited for a female sacrificial victim to appease their gods. The woman uses the ploys that society has taught her to engage the Indians, but they remain indifferent. They "were not human to her, and they did not see her as a beautiful white woman . . . no woman at all." Instead, she sees in the dark eyes of her guard a "fine spark" of derision. In a masterful confusion of object and metaphor, Lawrence has the Indian ask if the woman will "bring her heart to the Chilchui." Her affirmative response convinces the Indians that she was sent in fulfillment of the prophecy. An aged Chilchui appears, drugs her, cuts away her clothes, and touches her body with his fingertips, which he has moistened at his mouth. At the dawn of the winter solstice, four Indians lay her on a stone and hold her legs and arms. At her head, with knife poised and one eye on the sky, the old priest figure waits for the moment to strike.

In _St. Mawr_, Lawrence uses not a Native American or even a human figure but a red stallion to symbolize ideal maleness. Lou Witt's husband, typically for Lawrence, has lost his sense of what it means to be a man. The other two male characters, the grooms Phoenix and Lewis, a Navajo and a Welshman respectively, retain some of their fierce male separateness. None of them, however, measures up to the horse, who "stands where one can't get at him" and "burns with life." When _St. Mawr_ throws Rico, an event full of symbolic suggestion, Lou plans to sell the horse. Then she discovers that the new female owner plans to geld him. To avoid that fate Lou moves with the horse to New Mexico. St. Mawr thrives in the new, stark, mountain landscape, but Lou feels thwarted and diminished. As in "The Woman Who Rode Away," Lawrence ritualizes Lou's quest and transforms her into another mythic sacrificial figure. "She understood now the meaning of the Vestal Virgins. . . . They were symbolic of herself, of woman weary of the embrace of incompetent men." So she turns to "the unseen gods, the unseen spirits, the hidden fire" and devotes herself "to that, and that alone."

In Lawrence's last major story, Lou's character and function as the waiting Vestal Virgin are transformed into the mythological figure of Isis, although with a peculiarly Lawrentian twist. *The Man Who Died* is Lawrence's ultimate revision of Christianity's emphasis on the Crucifixion. The work is divided in two parts. The first, published with the title that Lawrence wanted for all editions, "The Escaped Cock," follows the traditional story of Christ's rising and healing. He perceives intellectually the life around him but laments, "The body of my desire has died and I am not in touch anywhere." In 1927, when Lawrence wrote "The Escaped Cock," he may have seen the ending as incomplete, but he did not return to create a second part for two years.

In part 2, Lawrence recasts Christ as the dismembered Osiris whose parts are reassembled by Isis. Reborn in part 1, Christ can function only as a pagan male seasonal deity, dying in winter, while the eternal feminine, symbolized in Isis, waits for his rebirth in spring to reanimate her. Lawrence thus effectively unites two themes that obsess all of his works: the renewal of the sexes and the concomitant discovery of a revitalized religion. At one level, Christ and Isis are merely man and woman, but as both deity and man, this new Christ integrates the physical and the spiritual. Lawrence is not advocating a return to paganism, as a facile reading might conclude, but a return of Christianity to its archetypal origins. The new Christ says, "On this rock I built my life," the rock of the living woman. It is not the rock of Saint Peter, of masculine control, but of phallic marriage.

Other major works

NOVELS: *The White Peacock*, 1911; *The Trespasser*, 1912; *Sons and Lovers*, 1913; *The Rainbow*, 1915; *Women in Love*, 1920; *The Lost Girl*, 1920; *Aaron's Rod*, 1922; *Kangaroo*, 1923; *The Boy in the Bush*, 1924 (with M. L. Skinner); *The Plumed Serpent*, 1926; *Lady Chatterley's Lover*, 1928; *The Virgin and the Gipsy*, 1930; *Mr. Noon*, 1984 (wr. 1920-1922).

PLAYS: *The Widowing of Mrs. Holroyd*, 1914; *Touch and Go*, 1920; *David*, 1926; *A Collier's Friday Night*, 1934; *The Complete Plays of D. H. Lawrence*, 1965.

POETRY: *Love Poems and Others*, 1913; *Amores*, 1916; *Look! We Have Come Through*, 1917; *New Poems*, 1918; *Bay*, 1919; *Tortoises*, 1921; *Birds, Beasts, and Flowers*, 1923; *Collected Poems*, 1928; *Pansies*, 1929; *Nettles*, 1930; *The Triumph of the Machine*, 1931; *Last Poems*, 1932; *Fire and Other Poems*, 1940; *Phoenix Edition of Complete Poems*, 1957; *The Complete Poems of D. H. Lawrence*, 1964 (Vivian de Sola Pinto and Warren Roberts, editors).

NONFICTION: *Twilight in Italy*, 1916; *Movements in European History*, 1921; *Psychoanalysis and the Unconscious*, 1921; *Sea and Sardinia*, 1921; *Fantasia of the Unconscious*, 1922; *Studies in Classic American Literature*, 1923; *Reflections on the Death of a Porcupine and Other Essays*, 1925; *Mornings in Mexico*, 1927; *Pornography and Obscenity*, 1929; *A Propos of Lady Chatterley's Lover*, 1930; *Assorted Articles*, 1930; *Apocalypse*, 1931; *Etruscan Places*, 1932; *The Letters of D. H. Lawrence*, 1932 (Aldous Huxley, editor); *Phoenix: The Posthumous Papers of D. H. Lawrence*, 1936 (Edward McDonald, editor); *The Collected Letters of D. H. Lawrence*, 1962 (Harry T.

Moore, editor, 2 volumes); *Phoenix II*, 1968 (Harry T. Moore and Warren Roberts, editors).

TRANSLATIONS: *Maestro-Don Gesualdo*, 1923; *Little Novels of Sicily*, 1925; *Cavalleria Rusticana*, 1928.

Bibliography

Balbert, Peter. *D. H. Lawrence and the Phallic Imagination*. New York: St. Martin's Press, 1989. This book is a well-reasoned response to feminist critics, who, especially since the 1970's, have accused Lawrence of misogyny. For "The Woman Who Rode Away," Balbert gives a revisionist study that shows the causes for misreadings in other works.

Black, Michael. *D. H. Lawrence: The Early Fiction*. New York: Cambridge University Press, 1986. In this sensitive study, Black discovers new layers of meaning in five of the eight stories that he examines. He rejects earlier psychoanalytic readings as too reductionist. As soon as critics characterized Lawrence's works as oedipal, they went no further.

Flora, Joseph M. *The English Short Story, 1880-1945: A Critical History*. Boston: Twayne, 1985. Lawrence's stories are placed in a historical literary context with their contemporaries. Though Flora offers no interpretations, he does effectively show Lawrence's influences, how Lawrence absorbed and rejected early forms, and how his works both belong to and surpass their time.

Harris, Janice Hubbard. *The Short Fiction of D. H. Lawrence*. New Brunswick, N.J.: Rutgers University Press, 1984. Harris' book is the first to treat chronologically all Lawrence's short fiction. Weak discussions of some works (for example "England, My England") are more than compensated for by enlightening readings of others (such as *The Man Who Died*).

Moore, Harry T. *The Priest of Love: A Life of D. H. Lawrence*. Rev. ed. New York: Farrar, Straus & Giroux, 1974. In preparing this first objective biography, Moore lived for several years at Lawrence sites and interviewed Lawrence's family and friends. Moore's work remains the standard source for accuracy and completeness.

Schneider, Daniel J. *The Consciousness of D. H. Lawrence: An Intellectual Biography*. Lawrence: University Press of Kansas, 1986. Tracing all the major works chronologically, Schneider treats Lawrence's religious nature at all stages of his life. Nineteen stories, both early and late, are briefly analyzed to show how Lawrence shaped, over the years, his credo about kinds of consciousness and knowledge.

Widmer, Kingsley. *The Art of Perversity: The Shorter Fiction of D. H. Lawrence*. Seattle: University of Washington Press, 1962. Widmer focuses on the satirical and demonic forces at work in the stories. While his conclusions have been weakened by later studies of Lawrence's use of myth and psychology, the book remains a useful survey of many stories.

Alvin Sullivan

HENRY LAWSON

Born: Grenfell, Australia; June 17, 1867
Died: Sydney, Australia; September 2, 1922

Principal short fiction
Short Stories in Prose and Verse, 1894; *While the Billy Boils*, 1896; *On the Track*, 1900; *Over the Sliprails*, 1900; *Joe Wilson and His Mates*, 1901; *The Rising of the Court*, 1910; *Mateship: A Discursive Yarn*, 1911; *Triangles of Life and Other Stories*, 1913; *Henry Lawson: The Bush Undertaker and Other Stories*, 1971; *Henry Lawson: Selected Stories*, 1971; *Henry Lawson: Short Stories and Sketches, 1888-1922*, 1972.

Other literary forms
While Henry Lawson is now known primarily for his short stories and prose sketches, he also wrote a substantial amount of verse. Collections of his poetry include *In the Days When the World Was Wide and Other Verses* (1896), *Verses, Popular and Humorous* (1900), and *When I Was King and Other Verses* (1905). *Henry Lawson's Collected Verse* is published in three volumes (edited by Colin Roderick, 1967-1969).

Achievements
Lawson, while at the height of his career in the 1890's, was a truly popular writer: he wrote for and about the common people of Australia, and he was read by those people. Fortune, however, did not follow fame for him, and though his work was published, read, and admired, he lived most of his life in penury and often misery. Even so, he was the first Australian writer ever to receive a state funeral, and his portrait was put on the ten-dollar note in 1965. His reputation, then, has always been high in Australia, though with different people for different reasons at different times; he has yet, however, to receive the recognition he no doubt deserves among readers of fiction in the rest of the world. By any acceptable standard, Lawson, at his best, is a masterful short-story writer.

Biography
Born on the goldfields of New South Wales at Grenfell in 1867, Henry Lawson was the eldest of the five children of Peter Larsen, a former Norwegian sailor, and Louisa Albury, his Australian wife. Henry's name was registered as Lawson and that became the family name. His childhood was not a happy one: from the age of nine he had difficulties with deafness; the family was poor and moved frequently; the parents disliked each other and fought bitterly. Peter and Louisa finally separated by mutual consent in 1883, Louisa taking the younger children to Sydney; Henry remained briefly with his father before joining his mother to help support the family—he was fifteen at the time. Lawson seems to have been fond of his ne'er-do-well father, while he found Louisa overbearing and lacking in human warmth. A number

of stories, presumably autobiographical, touch upon this period of his life, especially "A Child in the Dark, and a Foreign Father."

Lawson worked in Sydney as a coach painter and, for a while, went to night school. His mother was ambitious for him and encouraged his intellectual endeavors, for by this time she was herself a considerable figure in feminist and republican circles in Australia. Idealistic in nature, Lawson soon became imbued with lifelong radical and Socialist convictions. As a young writer, Lawson's first break came in 1887, when he published a ballad, "The Song of the Republic," in the prominent magazine *The Bulletin*, which also published his first story, "His Father's Mate," in 1880, a few days before his father died. In 1890, Lawson traveled to Western Australia and worked as a journalist, and in 1891, he moved to Brisbane to write for the radical newspaper *Boomerang*. Before the end of the year, however, he was back in Sydney.

At this point in his career, Lawson began to develop his mastery of the short story; indeed, he was then known more for his poetry than his prose. In 1892, he wrote his first important story sequence, the Arvie Aspinall series, and a number of his most important stories, including "The Drover's Wife" and "The Bush Undertaker." During that same year, he took what became a crucial trip to Bourke, in the Outback, and farther, to "back of beyond." There, on the frontier, the virtues of "mateship" and solidarity, and the terrible realities of Bush life, were impressed upon him and became important thematic features of his subsequent work. Returning to Sydney, Lawson worked at a number of jobs and published his first book, *Short Stories in Prose and Verse*, in 1894. His reputation now growing, he brought out *While the Billy Boils* in 1896, perhaps his best collection of stories, and a volume of verse. That year, he fell in love with, and married, Bertha Bredt. In the midst of the Depression of the 1890's, they went to New Zealand and ran a Maori school until 1896, when again Lawson returned to Sydney. Lawson, by this time, had developed serious alcoholism, which was exacerbated by his frequenting the bohemian Dawn and Dusk Club. Nevertheless, he was able to bring out two more collections of prose in 1900, *On the Track* and *Over the Sliprails*, as well as another book of verse.

Having become dissatisfied with pursuing a writing career in Australia, Lawson took his wife and children to Great Britain, where he hoped to gain recognition. He met with some limited success there, and wrote a number of important stories, particularly the Joe Wilson series. Yet he was not happy; there was still poverty, illness, and drunkenness with which to contend, and increasingly, he and his wife were becoming estranged. In fact, it appears that Lawson had fallen in love with another woman, Hannah Thornburn, before leaving for Great Britain, and his return in 1902 may well have been motivated by his desire to be with Thornburn. Upon arrival in Sydney, Lawson learned that Thornburn had died several days before. Lawson separated from his wife and the children, and his life thereafter steadily disintegrated. Not only were there the twin personal tragedies of death and estrangement, there was an artistic crisis as well: his creative faculties were clearly in decline. Added to this was the painful recognition that the Socialist political values he had so long espoused were permanently in eclipse. Whatever relationship each difficulty bore to the other, taken together they were a severe blow, and the remaining twenty years of Lawson's life saw him periodically in prison for indebtedness and drunkenness (out of which comes the famous ballad "One-Hundred-and-Three"), in convalescent or mental hospitals, and simply on the streets. Lawson's friends were generous to him, particularly his landlady, and often helped him; even his political friends assisted with some government support. Lawson continued to write and publish, and his following continued to grow. Yet his best work was now mostly retrospective and autobiographical. In 1921, Lawson had a partially disabling cerebral hemorrhage, though he still wrote, and in 1922, he died at home. He was accorded a state funeral by the government of New South Wales, and a statue was erected in commemoration.

Analysis

Henry Lawson is a popular writer, both with the reading public at large and with professional critics, and for not dissimilar reasons: his limpid and engaging prose style seems a marvel of easy craftsmanship, and his sardonic wit, lively humor, and compassion render his stories attractive. He had a gift for realism that seemed to capture the authentic experience of people, his characters are believable and memorable, and his presentation of the harshness of life in the Bush, with its melancholy overtones of pessimism, has entered into the mythic structures of the Australian consciousness. Lawson mastered the difficult craft of artlessness, allowing the reader to enter into the world of his stories as one might enter a familiar room.

From his earliest collections come many of Lawson's best stories, such as "The Bush Undertaker," "The Drover's Wife," "Rats," and "The Union Buries Its Dead," a frequently anthologized story. In the latter story, Lawson describes the funeral procession in the Outback for a young man who, though a stranger in town, is nevertheless given a funeral because he was a fellow union laborer. This mateship or union solidarity is an ideal that underwrites much of Lawson's thinking, but it is rarely embodied in the world he presents. Most of the gathered crowd are too drunk to follow once the procession begins; the horseman who leaves to join his friend at the bar is an emblem of how good intentions get undermined in the Bush. The tone of the story wavers between an ironic and minimal affirmation of mateship and an almost nihilistic portrayal of the grimness of life on the margins. The comic touches are like gallows humor, and the respects paid to the corpse are the conditioned responses of human indifference. The confusion over the man's identity and name becomes significant: he is a stranger; then he is called James Tyson, according to his union papers; that proves to be a pseudonym; later his real name is learned, but is unfortunately forgotten by everyone. Identity becomes unimportant in the face of the absoluteness of death; it does not matter what his name is. The speaker, both involved participant and distant narrator, refuses the comforts of stock responses and conventions and leaves the reader with a bittersweet regard for the isolation of men striving to survive. The light he casts over the scene is harsh because it is real. As he says, "I have left out the 'sad Australian sunset' because the sun was not going down at the time. The burial took place exactly at mid-day."

In "The Drover's Wife," Lawson delineates the drab and yet dangerous conditions of life for a woman alone in the Bush with her young children while her husband is away for long periods of time. The story is often taken as a tribute to the strength and stoicism of the pioneer woman, but Lawson is less concerned with her character (in certain respects she is a stereotype) than he is with the pattern of life in the Bush. As the drover's wife stands guard against a snake all night, the reader learns about her in a series of flashbacks or reminiscences that reveal the pitiable elements of her lonely life as well as the physical courage and resourcefulness on which she draws. Whether it is fighting a bushfire, trying to stem a flood, or protecting herself from animals and men (the difference is not always clear), the woman does what she must, what she can, because she has slowly adjusted to her existence. There is, however, a cost involved: though she loves her children, she seems harsh to them. As Lawson puts it, "Her surroundings are not favourable to the development of the 'womanly' or sentimental side of nature." Lawson indicates that her fight with the snake is a symbol of her condition when he writes that the dog, helping her, "shakes the snake as though he felt the original curse in common with mankind." The monotonous Bush, with its "everlasting, maddening sameness of . . . stunted trees," is a false and fallen Eden, and she struggles not with the desire for a forbidden consciousness but with the consequences of male sexuality, with her confinement in isolation and "her worn-out breast."

Lawson never wrote a novel, but his stories often fall into sequences, which, though written in a haphazard order, suggest the outlines of a fragmented novel. Such stories tend to revolve around fictional characters that some critics regard as aspects of Lawson's personality and others see as composite figures from his past. There is Steelman, the clever trickster; his dim-witted sidekick, Smith (whom Lawson spoke of as "my conception of the weaker side of my own nature"); Jack Mitchell, who figures in almost forty pieces, often as an engaging and laconic narrator; Dave Regan, an amusing practical joker who is sometimes his own victim; and Joe Wilson, perhaps Lawson's most complex and developed character. The Joe Wilson series is the closest Lawson came to the expansive connectedness of long fiction; it was written at the height of his career (actually completed during his stay in London), just before his precipitous decline. There are four stories closely interconnected: "Joe Wilson's Courtship," "Brighten's Sister-in-law," "'Water Them Geraniums,'" and "A Double Buggy at Lahey's Creek." The central story in the sequence, "'Water Them Geraniums,'" is often regarded as Lawson's finest achievement as a short-story writer.

Like "The Drover's Wife," "'Water Them Geraniums'" is primarily a story of women in the Bush. Yet it is a deeper, more psychological analysis of what the Bush does to a person than the earlier story. Ostensibly, it is about the narrator, Joe Wilson, and his wife, Mary, and their move to a new home in the Outback. The central portrait, however, is of Mrs. Spicer, a woman in her forties who lives nearby with her children. Like the drover's wife, Mrs. Spicer is often left alone while her husband is away working, but unlike that capable woman, Mrs. Spicer is "haggard," pathetic and even slightly mad, the vitality of her spirit having been eroded by the appalling life she leads. As such, she represents for Mary, Joe's wife, a frightful example of what could become of her; indeed, she and Joe are already experiencing a breakdown in communication with each other, which seems exacerbated by the alienating, dehumanizing force of the Bush itself. More than once, Mary cries out to Joe that this life is killing her; "Oh, Joe! you must take me away from the Bush." The process is one of disintegration, and Mrs. Spicer has succumbed to it. Though she clings to the remnants of respectability, she has been brutalized by the coarseness of her desperate existence. Her death at the end is as pitiful as it is inevitable. Lawson gives his readers a compassionate but dismal rendering of these people, whose lives are not quite redeemed by infrequent touches of tenderness. The fear of madness that constantly surfaces in the story is the fear of losing one's tenuous connection to humanity, of falling into an inward isolation that mirrors the outer circumstances of loneliness. This powerful and affecting story is one of Lawson's most detailed studies of character, and it is impossible not to sense behind it some of his own melancholic desperation with failure.

Lawson's stories are not always grim; his ironic sensibility often carries him into humor, at which he can be extremely successful. Some of his finest stories are his most amusing, in particular "The Loaded Dog," "The Ironbark Chip," and "Bill, the Ventriloquial Rooster." Even when he is comic, however, there is a sense that contact between people is at best precarious and often unsatisfying. For Lawson, the need for camaraderie, for a warmth of relations, is crucial, but it is constantly undercut by the overwhelming difficulties of life. At times, his stories seem to fall into self-pity and sentimentality, but at his best, he maintains a fine balance between an unflinching realism and a compassionate idealism. His easy, colloquial style, with its sardonic self-consciousness, has subsequently become a characteristic and abiding voice in Australian literature and culture.

Other major works

POETRY: *In the Days When the World Was Wide and Other Verses,* 1896; *Verses, Popular and Humorous,* 1900; *When I Was King and Other Verses,* 1905; *The Skyline Riders and Other Verses,* 1910; *For Australia and Other Poems,* 1913; *My Army! O My Army! and Other Songs,* 1915; *Selected Poems of Henry Lawson,* 1918; *Poetical Works of Henry Lawson,* 1925 (3 volumes); *Henry Lawson's Collected Verse,* 1967-1969 (3 volumes).

NONFICTION: *The Romance of the Swag,* 1942; *Henry Lawson: Letters, 1890-1922,* 1970; *Henry Lawson: Autobiographical and Other Writings,* 1972.

MISCELLANEOUS: *Children of the Bush,* 1902.

Bibliography

Matthews, Brian. "Eve Exonerated: Henry Lawson's Unfinished Love Stories." In

Who Is She?, edited by Shirley Walker. New York: St. Martin's Press, 1983. Matthews examines the role of women in Lawson's fiction and finds them to be idealized creatures whose contact with the masculine world of reality inevitably scars them. There is little communication between men and women, who are seen essentially as victims.

Phillips, A. A. *Henry Lawson.* New York: Twayne, 1970. After identifying Australian cultural nationalism ("mateship," "common man," "socialism"), Phillips provides a biographical chapter as well as chapters on Lawson's folk art, his "personal views" (including guilt and melancholy), and his craft. Contains several fairly lengthy readings of short stories, as well as a chronology and an annotated bibliography.

Prout, Denton. *Henry Lawson: The Grey Dreamer.* Adelaide, Australia: Rigby Limited, 1963. The only full-length biography of Lawson, Prout's book is essential reading. It contains information, not criticism, about Lawson's fiction and approximately twenty illustrations, mostly photographs. The well-researched volume also contains numerous lengthy quotations from Lawson's work and from his contemporaries and places Lawson within the context of his time.

Roderick, Colin. *Henry Lawson: Poet and Short Story Writer.* Sydney, Australia: Angus and Robertson, 1966. A sympathetic evaluation of Lawson's poetry and short stories. Roderick's monograph-length study examines the "modernity" of the stories, the literary influences on Lawson's work, and the role Lawson played in establishing the "Australian" short story. Roderick is especially helpful in placing Lawson within an Australian context and in discussing his use of Australian idioms and speech rhythms.

Wilding, Michael. "Henry Lawson's Radical Vision." In *The Rise of Socialist Fiction, 1880-1914*, edited by H. Gustav Klaus. New York: St. Martin's Press, 1987. Wilding examines Lawson's short stories in terms of their socialist philosophy. He discusses the Arvie Aspinall and Joe Wilson stories, and he devotes several pages to "The Drover's Wife," which he reads as an Australian Edenic story with Oedipal overtones.

Paul Kane
(Revised by *Thomas L. Erskine*)

DAVID LEAVITT

Born: Pittsburgh, Pennsylvania; June 23, 1961

Principal short fiction
Family Dancing, 1984; *A Place I've Never Been*, 1990.

Other literary forms
In addition to his short-story collections, David Leavitt writes novels: *The Lost Language of Cranes* was published in 1986 and *Equal Affections* was published three years later, in 1989.

Achievements
While still a student at Yale University, Leavitt won the Willets Prize for fiction in 1982 for his story "Territory," and a subsequent story, "Counting Months," won the 1984 O. Henry Award. His first published collection of short fiction, *Family Dancing*, was nominated for best fiction from the National Book Critics Circle in 1984, and in 1985 it was a finalist for the PEN/Faulkner Award for Fiction. Leavitt received a John Simon Guggenheim Foundation Fellowship in 1989; he was also foreign writer-in-residence at the Institute of Catalan Letters in Barcelona, Spain.

Biography
David Leavitt was born June 23, 1961, in Pittsburgh, Pennsylvania. His father, Harold Jack, was a professor, and his mother, Gloria Leavitt, a housewife who fought a battle with cancer for many years. This struggle is reflected in many of Leavitt's stories and particularly in one novel, *Equal Affections*, which deals with cancer and its impact on family life.

The young Leavitt grew up in Palo Alto, California, and some elements of his adolescence are to be found in a 1985 *Esquire* magazine article, "The New Lost Generation," where Leavitt discusses and compares the late 1960's and early 1970's generation of youth to his own of the late 1970's and early 1980's. Leavitt attended Yale University, where he published, at age twenty-one and while still a student, his first short story in *The New Yorker*. He received his B.A. from Yale University in 1983 and worked for a time as a reader and editorial assistant at Viking Penguin in New York, where he was, he has said in interviews, a reader of the "slush" manuscripts.

Leavitt's first collection of short fiction was published by Alfred A. Knopf and received considerable literary acclaim in 1984. That volume, *Family Dancing*, did, however, generate some negative criticism for its limited choice of themes. Nevertheless, Leavitt was soon considered to be among the more promising group of young American writers first appearing in the 1980's. In addition to two stories in *The New Yorker*, he published short fiction in *Harper's*. His first novel, *The Lost*

Language of Cranes, appeared in 1986 and generated controversy over its straightforward depiction of a homosexual youth's life-style compared to the closeted sexuality of the boy's father, who also had homosexual yearnings in secret. His second novel, *Equal Affections*, appeared in 1989 and centers on a family in which a dominant mother figure fights a long battle with cancer. One child in the family is homosexual and living with his lover in the East, while a daughter is a lesbian folksinger caught up in the world of concerts, travel, and performing. A second collection of short fiction, which picks up many themes from the first collection and also some of its characters in later stages of their lives (much as the Southern writer Ellen Gilchrist has done with her fictional characters in several short-story collections), was published in 1990 under the title *A Place I've Never Been*. Leavitt has continued to write full-time and has settled in East Hampton, New York.

Analysis

David Leavitt is one of a number of openly homosexual young writers whose work began to appear in the 1970's and 1980's, but who, in spite of their declared homosexuality, have achieved a far wider audience than that normally restricted to "gay" writers. While Leavitt (and other writers) may deal in their fiction with the topic of homosexuality and the difficulties posed by heterosexual society for those who are "gay" or are so perceived, that theme is not the entire focus of his fiction, and his handling of the homosexual experience is not of some isolated, hidden world (as homosexual writing tended to be in the decades of the 1940's and 1950's). Instead, the homosexual experience in Leavitt's work is directly related to the family experience in which parents, brothers, sisters, and relatives are an integral everyday part. Thus, there is little homosexual eroticism present and no homosexual exoticism; homosexuals are present, everyday, and all around, rather as earlier homosexual activists liked to say: "We are everywhere." To that generalization, Leavitt's characters add the generalization, "and we are just like you, for the most part." To this homosexual theme which is found in Leavitt's fiction can be added two other areas that are sometimes linked (but sometimes unrelated) to homosexuality. One is the recurring fragility of human life and the threat to it by terminal illness such as cancer, acquired immune deficiency syndrome (AIDS), or even a sudden fatal allergy. Another discernible theme is the fragility of the American family and the pressures upon it in contemporary life, particularly the fragmenting effect of divorce.

Several stories in Leavitt's collections deal with the complications resulting from the confrontations of heterosexual and homosexual lives. This difficult relationship is seen particularly in a group of stories involving the characters of Celia, Nathan, and Andrew from their initial encounters as college students to their later lives, as their sexual relationships change, new ones are developed, and the later loves affect their friendships.

In "Dedicated," the final story in the *Family Dancing* collection, the trio of Nathan (dark and Jewish, from a wealthy family), Andrew (blond and the definitive

WASP), and Celia (attracted to and friends with both Nathan and Andrew) is introduced at the residence of Nathan's parents while they are spending a leisurely weekend away from their Manhattan jobs. In a story seen primarily from Celia's point of view, the contentious sexual relationship between Nathan and Andrew is explored in the present-time setting of the story and also in flashbacks to college, to scenes in New York, and to scenes recalled from a European trip, when Nathan and Andrew became lovers in Florence. The story centers on Celia's somewhat frustrated attempts to comprehend her attraction to homosexual men, which she sees not as an accident but as what she terms "a career."

Celia is, of course, a confidant to both Andrew—who professes not to love Nathan—and Nathan—who likes talking endlessly and analytically with her. While Nathan and Andrew constantly attempt to define for her their conflicting affair, Celia tries to determine why she is attracted only to men who, ultimately, can be attracted only to one another. Additionally, there are discussions among the trio in which current issues such as whether one should be a gay activist or whether to discuss one's homosexuality with one's parents are argued. The complexities of Nathan and Andrew's lives are further explored in scenes in which both Nathan and Andrew tell Celia of their first night of love together, and she becomes aware of the discrepancy of their points of view while experiencing her own ongoing sense of isolation from the men and their lives. She finally realizes that her happiness with each results in part from their unhappiness with each other. She also is aware of how much of her awareness comes from her repeated partings with the two young men.

In Leavitt's second collection, *A Place I've Never Been*, he again deals with the trio in several stories. In the book's title story, Nathan returns from a lengthy trip to Europe to find his apartment a shambles and immediately calls upon Celia, who continues to be for him a dependable prop in his life. Nathan's former lover, Martin, has tested positive for HIV, and Nathan has vowed to give up sex entirely. In Nathan's absence, Celia has discovered her own sense of being and has come to understand her own beauty and appeal. She also knows that as long as she is the only solace in Nathan's life, she cannot have a life of her own, and Nathan now is paralyzed by his fear of getting—or worse, giving—AIDS to someone he loves.

In "When You Grow to Adultery," Andrew resurfaces, having long been separated from Nathan and Celia, the friends of his college years. Andrew momentarily is suspended between his relationship with his established lover, Allen, and his new attraction to an architect named Jack Seldon. Andrew thus is torn between his love for Allen (who needs Andrew) and his need for Jack, a need that is underscored by the story's final scene, where, as he and Allen make love at the house of Allen's parents, Andrew traces Jack's name on Allen's back.

In the story "I See London, I See France," Celia goes to Europe with Seth, a man she has met through a telephone dating service, and she discovers on their first date that they share a love of Italy. At the heart of Celia's life is an essential unhappiness about what her life is and has been and the impossibility of ever making it anything truly different. That realization comes to her vividly as she and Seth visit a "beautiful" couple—Alex and Sylvie Foster and their two daughters, Adriana and Francesca, at the Foster's Italian farmhouse, Il Mestolo. Yet, after an idyllic afternoon at the Italian house, Celia Hoberman, who grew up with her mother, Rose, and her grandmother, Lena, in an apartment in Queens, also comes to know that she, too, can change her life and live in Italy, but she will never break the umbilical cord that life uses to attach everyone to his or her undeniable past.

Other problems associated with homosexuals appear in stories such as "Ayor," "Houses," and "My Marriage to Vengeance" in *A Place I've Never Been*, and in the story "Territory" in *Family Dancing*. In "Territory," a young man, Neil, whose mother supports liberal causes, brings his male lover, Wayne, home to visit. The confrontation with his lover brings about a subtle epiphany of suppressed feelings of guilt and responsibility between mother and son. The same kind of shared responsibility of one friend for another's life is seen too in "Ayor," where an unnamed narrator (Nathan, possibly?) tells of his sexual longing for a college friend, Craig Rosen, who later becomes the narrator's guide to the seedy underside of New York's homosexual life. After a trip to France—where he has an affair with a young Frenchman named Laurent, the narrator again meets Craig, who tells him that he has been raped by a man in Spain, a revelation that conjures up for the narrator a complex of feelings questioning the extent to which human beings all are, indeed, somewhat responsible for the lives they impinge upon.

In yet another story, "My Marriage to Vengeance," Ellen Britchkey is invited to the wedding of her former lesbian lover, Diane Helaine Winters. In this story, Leavitt fully explores both the ironies and the humor inherent in this situation: Ellen's being a lesbian is just how things are, while with Diana, it is merely the exploration of one of several options in life, which leads the narrator (Ellen) to comment, "Rich people are like that, I have noticed. They think a love affair is like a shared real estate venture they can just buy out of when they get tired of it." In actuality, Ellen comes to see, after witnessing Diane cry in desperation about her own wedding, that Diane simply has made a life of compromise for herself, but Ellen also knows that for many like Diane, dishonest compromise in life is easier than difficult honesty.

A similar theme is explored in "Houses," where Paul, a real estate broker married to Susan, suddenly and impetuously enters into a sexual relationship with a local dog groomer, Ted, who cares for the couple's dog, Charlotte. Paul and Ted meet on their first "date" at a local restaurant frequented by homosexuals, the Dunes, and begin a three-month affair. Eventually, however, Paul decides to return to his wife, only to find that she views their marriage as something false and questions whether he ever truly loved her and if he really was not thinking of men as he made love to her. Paul's business occupation with houses is also a personal one, since he professes to "love" houses. After his second departure from his wife, he lives hit-or-miss in a succession of empty houses, a poignant symbol of his sexual life. As he states his condition at one point, it is possible in one's heart to love two different people in differing ways, but it is not possible to do so in life.

As Leavitt examines subtly the many ways in which homosexuality alters perceptions of family relationships and values, so too does he look regularly at how divorce can suddenly create a major shift in family values and alliances. In "The Lost Cottage," a story in *Family Dancing*, Leavitt presents the Dempson family, where the parents, Lydia and Alex, six months earlier have announced to their children that they are divorcing. Yet, in spite of the changed nature of the parents' relationship to one another, the family—at the mother Lydia's insistence—still assembles, as they always have for twenty-six years, at their summer cottage on Cape Cod. The Dempsons' three children are Mark, a homosexual who lives in Manhattan doing odd jobs; his sister Ellen, an unmarried lawyer; and Douglas, who, with his girlfriend of the past five years, conducts oceanographic research in Hawaii. All assemble at the family cottage, "Under the Weather," where Lydia, their mother, attempts to continue the same family gathering they long have observed each summer. Yet, this summer's reunion soon disintegrates as Lydia is unable to bear her husband's new relationship, an anxiety that is heightened to crisis proportions for the family when Alex's new girlfriend, Marian Hollister, shows up in the New England village to be near him as he spends time with his family and former wife. Amid the growing tensions set off by Marian's presence, Lydia reveals the blunt fact of her own—and her family's—problem: she still loves her husband, Alex, and always has, and even if he has left her, he cannot escape the simple fact of that love. The situation among the family, however, is one that cannot be resolved by any family member; the complexities set in motion by the parents' divorce are such that they are as insurmountable as Mark's trying to comprehend his brother's heterosexual indulgence of his girlfriend's demands. It is a confusion also mirrored in Mark's sister, who cannot understand Mark's ability to go to bed with someone he has just met. The shifts that occur in human relationships—like homosexual and heterosexual desire—may simply be, ultimately, inexplicable and irreconcilable despite the good intentions of all involved. The tragedy is, as Ellen tells her family at one point, not that they do not care but that they *do*.

Sexual complications and divorce's ramifications are two principal themes in Leavitt's short fiction. The impact of terminal illness forms a third major topic. In the stories "Counting Months" and "Radiation" (in *Family Dancing*), the manifestations of family problems surrounding the last days of cancer patients and their medical treatment are explored. In "Gravity" (in Leavitt's second collection), a mother's reaction to her son's fatal AIDS is seen. This frequent invocation of fatal illness (especially that of cancer) is one to which the author frequently returns, and it is again treated in his novel *Equal Affections*, where the mother, Louise Cooper, has been involved in a twenty-year struggle with cancer.

Another story, "Spouse Night," also presents a group of characters whose lives have been suddenly altered by the loss of a mate. The title refers to a postdeath support meeting, where persons attempt to come to grips with their individual loss. Arthur has lost his wife, Claire, to a sudden but quickly fatal skin disease, while his new companion, Mrs. Eve Theodorous, recently has lost her husband, Spiro. The survivors have begun a tentative sexual affair and even have acquired a new "child," a puppy that Mrs. Theodorous envies for its ability to forget its family connections and for being spared the sense of loss that humans must accept. Arthur's hesitancy in committing himself to his new relationship with Mrs. Theodorous is emphasized in his passionate scene of grief, when he attempts to scatter his wife's ashes from a boat in the harbor. This scene suggests in vivid detail (which Leavitt is so good at selecting) the anguish encountered in transitional moments in life from one form of commitment to another.

Leavitt's systematic return to certain themes—homosexuality, sexual infidelity, the family, terminal illness—in his short fiction certainly is a vivid portrayal of contemporary American social mores, rendered all the more acute by the author's ability to select situations and details that become metaphors for his stories' issues. Leavitt, in a discussion of other contemporary fiction writers whom he admires, has suggested that a number of contemporary fiction writers are concerned with the shattering of the familial, or parental, edifice. Many today write of a world "where very little can be taken for granted or counted on, where potentially dangerous change looms around every corner, and where marriages and families, rather than providing havens, are themselves the fulcrum of the most sweeping upheavals." His comment about the works of a number of other contemporary fiction writers could, quite easily, be applied to his own work.

Other major works

NOVELS: *The Lost Language of Cranes*, 1986; *Equal Affections*, 1989.

Bibliography

Iannone, Carol. "Post Counter-Culture Tristesse." *Commentary* 84 (February, 1987): 57-61. Iannone's article discusses representative themes of Leavitt's work, including his short stories and his first novel, *The Lost Language of Cranes*.

Leavitt, David. "Interview with David Leavitt." Interview by Jean Ross. In *Contemporary Authors*, vol. 122, edited by Hal May and Susan M. Trosky. Detroit: Gale Research, 1988. Leavitt, in a telephone interview transcript, discusses his writing habits, his training in creative writing at Yale University, the *Family Dancing* collection, and his novel *The Lost Language of Cranes*. Also reflects on his short editorial assistant's work at a New York publishing house.

_____. "Interview with David Leavitt." Interview by Sam Staggs. *Publishers Weekly* 237 (August 24, 1990): 47-49. Leavitt reveals some autobiographical aspects of his youth and talks in some detail about what he terms risk-taking in fiction writing. There is also a discussion of ACT Up and comment about how AIDS has altered the perspective of younger homosexuals' writing.

_____. "The New Lost Generation." *Esquire* 103 (May, 1985): 85-88. In an autobiographical remembrance of adolescence in California, Leavitt compares the activist, socially conscious late 1960's generation with that of his own "Yuppie" era.

_____. "New Voices and Old Values." *The New York Times Book Review*,

May 12, 1985, 1, 26-27. In a lengthy review of several books by contemporary authors, including Marian Thurm, Peter Cameron, Meg Wolitzer, Elizabeth Tallent, and Amy Hempel, Leavitt cites similarity of themes in their handling of crises in the traditional family and reveals as well elements of his own work and concerns.

_____. "The Way I Live Now." *The New York Times Magazine*, July 9, 1989, 28-29, 32, 80-82. Leavitt, in a personal revelation about his homosexuality, discusses the way in which AIDS has affected his life. He also discusses his involvement with ACT UP, the radical AIDS activist organization, and his views of that organization's necessity and positive influence.

White, Edmund. "Out of the Closet, Onto the Bookshelf." *The New York Times Magazine*, June 16, 1991, 22-24. White writes about the 1980's generation of openly homosexual writers and how the AIDS epidemic has both decimated their ranks and at the same time created a maturity of creative writing as writers react to the disease and its threat.

Jere Real

JOSEPH SHERIDAN LE FANU

Born: Dublin, Ireland; August 28, 1814
Died: Dublin, Ireland; February 7, 1873

Principal short fiction

Ghost Stories and Tales of Mystery, 1851; *Chronicles of Golden Friars*, 1871; *In a Glass Darkly*, 1872; *The Purcell Papers*, 1880; *The Watcher and Other Weird Stories*, 1894; *A Chronicle of Golden Friars*, 1896; *Madam Crowl's Ghost and Other Tales of Mystery*, 1923 (M. R. James, editor); *Green Tea and Other Ghost Stories*, 1945; *Best Ghost Stories of J. S. LeFanu*, 1964; *Ghost Stories and Mysteries*, 1975.

Other literary forms

Joseph Sheridan Le Fanu is most famous for such horror and mystery novels as *Uncle Silas* (1864) and *Wylder's Hand* (1864), but he also wrote historical novels (*The Cock and Anchor*, 1845; *The House by the Churchyard*, 1863) which depict the social, political, and religious conflicts that were surfacing in the Ireland of his day. Although not a prolific or generally important poet, his verse does contain two popular and memorable "Irish Ballads," "Shamus O'Brien" and "Phaudhrig Crochoore." Since, in the course of his literary career, he owned and edited a number of Irish periodicals, Le Fanu wrote numerous articles and essays which have not, as yet, been republished. Late in the nineteenth century his novel *Uncle Silas* was successfully adapted to the stage, and in 1971 his most famous short story, "Carmilla," was filmed as *The Vampire Lovers*.

Achievements

Like many Anglo-Irish writers, Le Fanu's achievements are of two kinds. On the one hand, because he possessed the advantages of education, culture, and leisure, he was equipped to participate in, and contribute to, contemporary developments in fiction. In this regard, his role in the evolution of the English Gothic novel has been widely noted. The modulation from merely sensationalist effects to psychological verisimilitude in Le Fanu's works is an example of a more general development in nineteenth century fiction.

In an Irish context, however, this modulation has a particular resonance. Its emphasis on withdrawal and duress, with failed fortunes and alienated circumstances, may be regarded as an unnervingly accurate representation of the declining importance of the Anglo-Irish as a culture-creating, and value-bearing, class. Le Fanu's artistic interests also led him toward the adaptation of Irish folklore material, a development which also presages, like much of his career, important shifts of emphasis in the cultural history of modern Ireland.

Biography

Descended from an upper-class Irish Protestant family on his father's side and a vitally artistic one on his mother's (his forebears included the playwright Richard Brinsley Sheridan and the actor Thomas Sheridan), Joseph Sheridan Le Fanu was well equipped by inheritance and upbringing for a successful writing career. Although he studied law at Trinity College, Dublin, and was admitted to the Irish bar, he never practiced law, going immediately into literature and journalism after graduation. When his first historical novels were dismissed by the critics in the 1840's, he turned almost exclusively to journalism and editing for fifteen years. Le Fanu's journalistic commitments culminated in 1861 in his purchasing the leading Irish intellectual organ of the day, the *Dublin University Magazine*. He continued to own and edit this journal, in which most of his work had been and continued to have its initial publication, until 1869, some four years before his death. It was in this period of public engagement and cultural commitment that Le Fanu's major fiction was produced. In 1844, he married Susan Bennett, daughter of a prominent Dublin attorney; they had four children. This idyllic marriage ended prematurely, however, with her death in 1858. Le Fanu thereupon became a recluse, and it was during these last solitary years that he produced the bulk of his most memorable fiction.

Analysis

Joseph Sheridan Le Fanu's method for writing horror fiction was unusual. After drinking copious amounts of tea for stimulation, he would retire around midnight to his dismal bedroom, where he would nap for approximately two hours, having, if possible, a few provocative nightmares. Upon awakening about two o'clock in the morning, he would begin to write and continue until daylight. He would then sleep again until noon. Unlikely and bizarre as this routine sounds, it was the ritual that Le Fanu followed during the last fifteen years of his life. This was the period in which he produced his best work, a body of fiction that entitles him to rank with Edgar Allan Poe as an innovator in the development of the modern horror and mystery genres.

Le Fanu began these curious compositional procedures following the premature death of his wife. The grief and shock of her passing were instrumental in turning him gradually from a socially active, convivial editor-journalist-writer to a recluse. This progressively increasing self-absorption, isolation, and preoccupation with the dark side of human experience found objective expression in the supernatural stories of his last years, as well as in such outstanding novels as *Uncle Silas* and *Wylder's Hand*. This is not to say, however, that his concentration on the morbid and supernatural represented an abrupt shift in Le Fanu's work. Although his earliest stories and novels focused more on Irish history and society, the macabre was an important ingredient in virtually everything he wrote, especially his shorter fiction. During his fifteen-year "dry spell" (1848-1863), the only book of fiction he published was *Ghost Stories and Tales of Mystery* in 1851.

"Schalken the Painter" is vintage early Le Fanu, although in a brief summary it probably sounds as overblown and chaotic as the worst examples of Le Fanu's Gothic predecessors. Schalken, a promising Flemish artist, is in love with Rose Velderkaust, the ward of his painting master, Gerard Douw. Because he is poor, Schalken's proposal of marriage to Rose is rejected by Douw in favor of a suit pressed by a rich, mysterious old man, "Minheer Wilken Vanderhausen of Rotterdam." When the principals finally get a good look at Vanderhausen, however, they are horrified: he looks to be a walking corpse. His face has a "bluish leaden hue," his eyes "an undue proportion of muddy white . . . a certain indefinable character of insanity," his lips "nearly black," and "the entire character of the face was sensual, malignant, and even satanic." Nevertheless, the marriage is contracted and takes place.

Some months later, after the couple has vanished and Vanderhausen has been exposed as a fraud, Rose suddenly comes to Schalken and Douw, dressed in a strange white garment, and babbling hysterically that "the dead and the living never can be one"; she eats ravenously and begs for protection. They attempt to guard her but fail, and she vanishes from behind a locked door, never to reappear in the flesh. Years later while in Rotterdam for his father's funeral, Schalken sees her in a dream. Dressed in her white costume, she leads him to a small apartment containing a curtained four-poster bed. She spreads the curtain apart, and Vanderhausen sits up. Schalken faints and is found unconscious the next day in the burial vaults, stretched out beside a coffin.

This narrative clearly leaves more questions than it answers; the reader who expects everything to be neatly tidied up and explained in the end will be disappointed. The *experience* it offers, however, is both unified and potent. Three factors enable Le Fanu to order the chaos in the story quite effectively: the precision with which he controls the structure and point of view; the careful balance in his language between graphic realism and suggestive abstraction; and strong suggestions of an underlying worldview in which such horrible events really do not seem out of place. The title notwithstanding, the main action of the story does not focus on Schalken, but on the bizarre fate of the innocent Rose Velderkaust. The painter simply provides the eyes through which these strange events are viewed in bits and pieces. Since most of the action happens offstage, the reader is forced to share the rejected lover's anxiety and puzzlement. Like Schalken, the reader must guess at the awful details of her marriage, and, in the end, the reader is left with the same unanswered questions. As is typical of the best modern practitioners in this genre, Le Fanu stimulates fear and horror as much by what he omits as by what he includes, leaving it to the reader's imagination to make concrete horror out of his many dark hints.

When Le Fanu is specific, however, he is very precise, visual, and visceral. Vanderhausen is no wispy, floating ghost of the sort that haunted old Gothic mansions. He is a physically solid—if rotting—corpse, who acts directly and purposefully. The reader cannot avoid identification with the distraught bride as she contemplates intimacy with such a creature. Later, when she makes her sudden appearance dressed in white, her agitation and hysteria are described with powerful visual images and telling details; and lastly, the dream sequence, although brief, ends with the sharp picture of Vanderhausen sitting up in his bed-coffin and grinning at Schalken, a striking final image of perverse sexuality and death.

"Schalken the Painter" bridges the gap between the old Gothic and the modern horror story. The plotting probably belongs to the realm of the old—innocent girl sold to the highest bidder, walking corpses, kidnaping, violence behind locked doors, and necrophilia—but the manner of the telling—the carefully controlled structure, point of view, language, and imagery—is definitely new. In the later stories, the transition is complete; both form and content are modern. The best examples of the mature Le Fanu style can be found in his last and finest collection of short stories, *In a Glass Darkly*. All of the horror stories in this anthology—"The Familiar," "Mr. Justice Harbottle," "Carmilla," "Green Tea"—are fully realized, with the last two generally acknowledged as his masterpieces.

The *In a Glass Darkly* stories all ostensibly come from the papers of the late "Dr. Martin Hesselius, the German Physician," as edited by his secretary. Le Fanu had used this kind of framing device in his first collection in a relatively superficial way. In this anthology, however, the technique is handled in a more sophisticated manner. In addition to gathering the stories, Hesselius personally "analyzes" each "case" and in one story, "Green Tea," plays a major role. If Hesselius, himself, is unconvincing as a personality and "psychic detective," the character type he represents was to become prominent in modern literature; he is, in fact, the first practicing (meddling?) psychiatrist in English fiction.

Hesselius is a mixed blessing. The concept of the psychic detective is a provocative one, and Hesselius' comments give the anthology some overall unity. On the other hand he is such a long-winded bore, with arrogant claims of infallibility that contrast sharply with his inept handling of the situations at hand, that he becomes an irritation. More annoying yet is the ambiguity regarding his ultimate function in these stories. Is he Le Fanu's spokesman or is he simply a pedantic fool? Or, which is more likely, might he be both? Is it possible that beneath the pompous rhetoric of his philosophical diatribes are the clues to Le Fanu's own worldview? Hesselius, however, has almost no role in the best-known of Le Fanu's short stories, "Carmilla." The secretary, in a short prologue, simply records that the doctor had much to say about the narrative and goes no further. "Carmilla" is probably the only pre-Dracula vampire story that can still be read for pleasure as well as historical interest. The vampire in this tale is no distant, forbidding male shrouded in a black cape and hovering in the shadows of a decaying castle, but is, rather, Carmilla, a pretty, bright—if "langorous"—young girl who, after ingratiating herself with the family, wins the trust and affections of the story's heroine.

The reader is prepared for her entrance by two ominous events; in the first, at about age six, Laura, the narrator, has a dream in which she is accosted in bed by a beautiful young girl and experiences two needle-like pains in her breast; in the second, an expected visit from a potential girlfriend is canceled by the girl's mysterious death, caused, her guardian reports, by "the fiend who betrayed our infatuated hospitality." Then Carmilla appears suddenly when her carriage has an accident in front of the heroine's family chateau. Claiming she cannot wait for her daughter's recovery, Carmilla's "mother" manipulates Laura's father into accepting the young girl as a house guest.

Shortly after Carmilla is ensconced in the household, a mysterious illness begins to ravage the countryside, which kills only young peasant girls; an "oumpire" is suspected. The reader learns of these depredations, however, only in an indirect, fragmentary fashion. Life in the household is largely unaffected. Thus, the horror in "Carmilla" is much more psychological and less visceral than it was in "Schalken." As Le Fanu carefully reveals clues about Carmilla's demonic nature and sinister purposes, he also intensifies the emotional tie between the two girls. Carmilla woos Laura with the ardor of a lover. Le Fanu is most contemporary in the way he makes explicit (although restrained) use of the sexual connotations of the vampire myth. The lesbian implications in "Carmilla" have been strongly emphasized by some critics and, while there is some distortion and faddism evident in this approach, these elements are too overt to ignore. There is more here, however, than sexuality; the eroticism is linked to thoughts of death: Eros meets Thanatos. This association is central to the long, powerful appeal of the vampire myth and few writers since have treated it so directly and provocatively.

Paradoxically, however, this female-female relationship also creates Le Fanu's most serious artistic problem. Having created a villainess who, if not actually sympathetic, is at least very real and deeply involved with her victim, how can he mete out the just but gory punishment that Carmilla deserves without destroying the mood and direction of the story? His solution is to shift the focus completely away from Laura to a new set of characters. It is they who trap and destroy Carmilla in her coffin. Although this tactic does resolve Le Fanu's plotting problem, it also damages the momentum of the story; the ending of "Carmilla" is logically sound, but emotionally unsatisfying.

If "Carmilla," however, is a flawed masterpiece of the macabre, Le Fanu's shorter and more subtle "Green Tea" has no such defects; it is the supreme example of the modern horror story. The simplicity of this tale contrasts with the Gothic complexity of "Schalken the Painter" or even "Carmilla." Dr. Hesselius meets a pleasant middle-aged cleric, the Reverend Mr. Jennings, at a dinner party. Upon learning the doctor's identity, the clergyman seeks him out and requests treatment. Hesselius thus learns of his strange and frightening condition. Jennings has been plagued for nearly three years by a small black spectral monkey, which has harassed, abused, mocked, and threatened him with increasing fury. Although the clergyman has managed to maintain a calm demeanor, he is desperate, almost suicidal, when he finally contacts Hesselius. The German doctor, however, can offer only a little ineffective advice. Shortly thereafter, Hesselius goes into isolation, causing him to receive the cleric's last frantic communication a day too late; they find Jennings with his throat cut, a suicide.

Again, it is Le Fanu's skill in telling the story that separates "Green Tea" from the work of his contemporaries. Because the narration is indirect, the reader is drawn slowly and carefully into the story, thus allowing the horror to manifest itself gradually and muting the potentially comic effect of a monkey as specter. This subtlety in presentation is one of the important qualitative differences between even the best early Le Fanu stories, such as "Schalken the Painter," and his mature works. Jennings does not actually reveal his problem to Hesselius until the story is almost half over; and, as the reader learns the facts in this case, he also comes to understand the personalities of the two principal characters. The arrogance and insensitivity of Hesselius contrasts sharply with the intelligence, sensitivity, and muted desperation of Jennings. In only a few pages the reader comes to like the doomed cleric; and although his final act comes as no surprise, it is a shock.

During Hesselius' first casual conversations with Jennings, he is surprised to hear of the cleric's interest in "Metaphysical Medicine," Swedenborgian philosophy, and pre-Christian religions. From others the doctor learns some additional facts about Jennings' life and background: that his father had conversed with a ghost; that he was addicted to strong green tea; that, despite his apparently vital appearance, his health always failed him whenever he attempted to assume his pastoral duties; and that he had the odd habit of staring into space as though actually seeing something. These bits of information, coupled with the sense of dread and desperation that increasingly shows beneath Jennings' controlled behavior, prepare the reader for the revelation of the troubled cleric's secret.

Jennings' red-eyed monkey is certainly one of the most memorable fiends in literature, a far cry from the disembodied, innocuous ghosts typical of Le Fanu's predecessors. Le Fanu chronicles the course of the relationship between cleric and creature with a meticulousness of detail and imagery that makes it vividly real. This relationship is described in three distinct stages: the initial meeting on an omnibus and Jennings' reactions to it; the protracted conflict between the clergyman and his specter; and the creature's intensified assault on his victim, which finally pushes Jennings to suicide. The monkey is a solid physical presence to Jennings, although he touches nothing when he attempts to run his umbrella through the thing. The focal point of the beast is its "smokey red eyes," which are never off of Jennings. Although black as pitch, the creature remains visible in the dark "in a halo that resembles a glow of red embers"; even with his eyes closed, Jennings sees the malevolent beast. Its absences, sometimes up to three months in duration, add to Jennings' torment, since he knows that the monkey will return with intensified malice when least expected. It also talks to him constantly, becoming most vociferous whenever the clergyman attempts to worship or carry out his pastoral duties; in the midst of sermons, it squats on the minister's text, forcing him to flee the lectern. As the clergyman becomes increasingly debilitated, the monkey becomes correspondingly more active, as though it were draining off his energies for its own use, until Jennings has no way out but suicide.

Of course Dr. Hesselius never sees the specter himself, nor does Jennings do more than paraphrase the monkey's words. Thus, Le Fanu follows the dictum later articulated by his successor M. R. James to "leave a loophole for a natural explanation, but . . . let the loophole be so narrow as not to be quite practicable." Is it all a figment of Jennings' imagination or is the fiend truly a being from another order of reality? Or could it somehow be both?

Critics have used this "loophole" to develop a variety of interpretations of "Green Tea." To one critic, Jennings, a bachelor, is a classic schizophrenic having a breakdown and the monkey represents repressed sexuality surfacing. To an analyst of the Christian persuasion, the monkey is a demonic punishment for hidden sins or perhaps an embodiment of original sin. More mundane critics have simply cited the effects of green tea on the nervous system and have left it at that. All such views, which unduly narrow the story to a case history of one sort or another, miss the point of James's "loophole" theory. An inadequate or incomplete "rational" explanation in a supernatural fiction actually reinforces the sense of horror by heightening the ambiguity that underlies it. Certainly Jennings is made vulnerable to the unseen by virtue of his heredity, his addiction to green tea, his metaphysical bent, and his taste for primitive religion, but none of these things explains his fate, and nothing he does that the reader knows of—his religious views, his social behavior, or his sex life—indicates that he deserves it.

Perhaps the key lies in the Swedenborgian references as interpreted (and distorted) by Hesselius. Although the doctor is too much of a bore to be taken with complete seriousness, his ideas do seem to point toward Le Fanu's own vision, a vision that is both conceptually powerful and artistically convenient for the writer of horror fiction who would go beyond the conventional heaven/hell, black magic/white magic, good/evil dichotomies. In this view, there exists all about us a world of the unseen of which only a few, by design or accident, get a glimpse, and those who do are in great peril. Evil is neither accidental nor gratuitous nor external, but is everywhere, all the time, within as well as without. It is this sense of the pervasiveness of evil that separates Le Fanu's best work from that of his predecessors and contemporaries; the demonic exists just at the edge of our existence, just out of sight, and can force itself into vision at any time through almost any opening, even one created by so trivial a substance as green tea.

Other major works

NOVELS: *The Cock and Anchor*, 1845; *The Fortunes of Colonel Torlogh O'Brien*, 1847; *The House by the Churchyard*, 1863; *Wylder's Hand*, 1864; *Uncle Silas*, 1864; *Guy Deverell*, 1865; *All in the Dark*, 1866; *The Tenants of Malory: A Novel*, 1867 (3 volumes); *A Lost Name*, 1868; *The Wyvern Mystery*, 1869; *Checkmate*, 1871; *The Rose and the Key*, 1871; *Morley Court*, 1873; *Willing to Die*, 1873 (3 volumes).

POETRY: *The Poems of Joseph Sheridan Le Fanu*, 1896.

Bibliography

Begnal, Michael H. *Joseph Sheridan Le Fanu*. Lewisburg, Pa.: Bucknell University Press, 1971. Although this volume is only an essay-length discussion of Le Fanu's works, it is valuable in providing general commentary about Le Fanu's intellectual and artistic interests, especially his sensitive understanding of women.

Browne, Nelson. *Sheridan Le Fanu*. London: Arthur Barker, 1951. This short critical exposition places emphasis on Le Fanu's "essentially Gothick quality." The author believes Le Fanu to be at his best in his short fiction, advancing familiar objections to his novels' prolixity. Old-fashioned in tone and attitude, but a pioneering study.

McCormack, W. J. *Sheridan Le Fanu and Victorian Ireland.* Oxford, England: Clarendon Press, 1980. The standard work on Le Fanu. The author's approach is twofold. First, this study is a detailed biography of Le Fanu. Second, it locates, with much intellectual sophistication, Le Fanu's life in his times, giving to what might remain mere biographical data the stamp of historical significance. A second, enlarged edition of this important work was issued in 1991.

Melada, Ivan. *Sheridan Le Fanu.* Boston: Twayne, 1987. Melada's approach is chronological, proceeding from Le Fanu's early short fiction to the major novels with which his career ends. The critical emphasis sees Le Fanu as a writer of popular fiction, the quality of which entitles him to serious academic consideration. Contains a chronology and a bibliography.

Sullivan, Kevin. *"The House by the Churchyard:* James Joyce and Sheridan Le Fanu." In *Modern Irish Literature: Essays in Honour of William York Tindall,* edited by Raymond J. Porter and James D. Brophy. New Rochelle, N.Y.: Iona College Press, 1972. Le Fanu's novel *The House by the Churchyard* has some of its significant scenes set in the village of Chapelizod, a few miles west of Dublin and at the western end of the Phoenix Park. James Joyce's *Finnegans Wake* (1939) contains numerous important allusions to both these Dublin settings. This essay traces the presence of the earlier work in the later. The undertaking is both an academic rehabilitation of Le Fanu's novel and an illustrative instance of Joyce's method in *Finnegans Wake.*

Keith Neilson
(Revised by *George O'Brien*)

URSULA K. LE GUIN

Born: Berkeley, California; October 21, 1929

Principal short fiction

The Word for World Is Forest, 1972; *The Wind's Twelve Quarters*, 1975; *Orsinian Tales*, 1976; *The Water Is Wide*, 1976; *Gwilan's Harp*, 1981; *The Compass Rose*, 1982; *The Visionary: The Life Story of Flicker of the Serpentine, with Wonders Hidden*, 1984; *Buffalo Gals and Other Animal Presences*, 1987.

Other literary forms

Ursula K. Le Guin is best known for her novels, especially the Earthsea books, which include *A Wizard of Earthsea* (1968), *The Tombs of Atuan* (1971), *The Farthest Shore* (1972), and *Tehanu: The Last Book of Earthsea* (1990). Other well-known novels include *The Left Hand of Darkness* (1969), *The Lathe of Heaven* (1971), *The Dispossessed: An Ambiguous Utopia* (1974), and *Always Coming Home* (1985). She has also published poetry, including *Wild Angels* (1975) and *Hard Words and Other Poems* (1981). *The Language of the Night: Essays on Fantasy and Science Fiction* (1979) and *Dancing at the Edge of the World: Thoughts on Words, Women, and Places* (1988) are important collections of her critical writing.

Achievements

Le Guin is recognized as a leading American writer of science fiction and fantasy. Her short stories, especially "The Ones Who Walk Away from Omelas," winner of a 1974 Hugo Award, often appear in college literature anthologies, suggesting that her work, like that of Kurt Vonnegut, Jr., stands above much that has been produced in these popular genres. Le Guin has received many awards and honors for her work. *The Left Hand of Darkness* and *The Dispossessed* received both the Nebula and Hugo awards. Volumes of the Earthsea books earned awards for adolescent literature, including the Boston *Globe* Horn Book Award for *A Wizard of Earthsea*, a Newbery Honor Book Citation for *The Tombs of Atuan*, and the National Book Award for Children's Literature for *The Farthest Shore*. Her other awards include a Hugo for *The Word for World Is Forest*, a Nebula in 1974 for "The Day Before the Revolution," and Jupiters for *The Dispossessed* and "The Diary of the Rose."

Le Guin has been a guest writer at several universities, including the University of Washington, Portland State University, Indiana University, and the University of Reading in England. She has edited several anthologies. In 1980, an adaptation of *The Lathe of Heaven* was broadcast on public television.

Not all of Le Guin's work has been as well received as her fantasy and science fiction. As literary scholars and critics give more attention to fantasy and science fiction, Le Guin attracts a large share of their interest because she creates possible worlds that cast an informative light on perennial human problems.

Biography

Ursula Kroeber was born on October 21, 1929, in Berkeley, California, the daughter of anthropologist Alfred L. Kroeber and author Theodora Kroeber. She received her B.A. from Radcliffe College in 1951 and her M.A. from Columbia University in 1952. While on a Fulbright Fellowship in Paris in 1953, she married Charles A. Le Guin. They had three children: daughters Elisabeth and Caroline and a son, Theodore. She taught French at Mercer University and the University of Idaho before settling in Portland, Oregon, in 1959. In 1962, she began publishing fantasy and science fiction. In addition to writing, she has been active in the Democratic Party and in writing workshops.

Analysis

When Ursula K. Le Guin writes about her craft and her works, she often refers to Jungian psychology and Taoist philosophy as major components of her worldview. In her 1975 essay "The Child and the Shadow," Le Guin uses Jungian psychology to support her contention that fantasy is "the language of the night," an important means by which the collective unconscious speaks to the growing individual. In Le Guin's understanding of Jungian thought, consciousness, the part of the self that can be expressed in everyday language, emerges from the unconscious as a child matures. The individual's unconscious is shared in its essentials with all other humans and so is called the collective unconscious.

To become an adult, an individual must find ways of realizing the greatest potential of the unconscious. For Le Guin, these are summed up in the recognition by the individual that on unconscious levels, he or she is identical with all other humans. This recognition releases the irrational forces of social binding, such as compassion, love, creativity, and the sense of belonging to the human community.

A major problem in achieving this recognition is learning to deal with "the shadow." Choosing to be one person involves choosing not to be other persons that one could be. Both the positive and the negative choices must be maintained to sustain an identity; the negative choices become one's shadow. The process of achieving adulthood is blocked by the shadow, an unconscious antiself with which one must deal in order to take possession of the rest of the unconscious.

For Le Guin, a child becomes an adult when he or she is able to cease projecting evil impulses onto others and to recognize that these impulses are part of the self. This process, she believes, is symbolically represented in the many fairy tales and fantasies in which an animal helps the protagonist to discover and attain his true identity. Such stories speak to the unconscious, telling the child by means of myth and symbol how to achieve wholeness of self.

Taoism, a Chinese philosophy expressed about two thousand years ago in the *Tao-te Ching*, seems closely related to Jungian psychology in Le Guin's mind. This philosophy is expressed in the Circle of Life, or yin and yang symbol. The circle is divided into dark and light halves. Within the light half is a dark spot; within the dark half, a light spot. The dark half represents nonbeing—not nothingness, but rather the potential for all forms of being. That potential for being in nonbeing may be represented by the white spot. Out of this nonbeing comes being, represented by the white half of the circle. Because all that is exists in time and must end, it contains its end within itself, this end represented by the dark spot that refers to nonbeing. The Circle of Life is a diagram of the dynamic relationship between being and nonbeing in the universe.

This metaphysic leads to an ethic of passive activity. All acts in the world of being imply their opposites, the assertion of being activating the potential for nonbeing of the end one seeks. Acts of coercion aimed at controlling human behavior are especially prone to produce equal and opposite reactions. Therefore, the wise person tries not to influence people's actions by direct persuasion or by force but rather by being a model of the desired activity.

Several of these aspects of Le Guin's worldview appear in "Darkness Box," one of her earliest publications. "Darkness Box" is a fairy tale/allegory that takes place in a world of cycles. In this world, time does not pass. There is no source of light, though it is always mid-morning. Certain events repeat themselves exactly and perpetually. A young prince rides with his army to the seashore to repel an invasion by his rebel brother. The brother always comes from the sea; he is always defeated and killed. At the same time that he leaves, the prince returns to the palace of his father, who exiled the brother. The prince always rides out again with his army to meet the restored and returning invaders. Into this cycle intrudes what appears to be a unique set of events that are sequential rather than cyclical. The son of a witch finds a box on the shore and gives it to the prince. The king recognizes it as a box he cast into the sea and warns the prince not to open it. The prince's longing for music that ends, for wholeness, leads him to knock the box open and restrains him from closing it. Darkness spills out, the darkness of shadows and their opposite, the sun. He begins to experience conflict, death, and the passing of time. Having achieved a shadow, he has entered into time and being.

Read as a Jungian myth of maturation, the tale represents the collective unconscious as a place of unrealized potentials for identity. The prince is a potential ego, his exiled brother a potential shadow, their endless battle a portent of the struggle consciousness must undergo to create a mature personality. Opening the box that lets out darkness becomes a symbolic representation of the birth of the ego, the entrance into time, and self-creation with real consequences for the self, such as the creation of a shadow and the acceptance of mortality.

Read as a Taoist allegory, the tale represents nonbeing, the dark half of the Circle of Life, as a place of unrealized potential for being. Nonbeing is timeless and changeless yet full of possibilities. In this reading, opening the box realizes some of the potentials for being. A real world begins, a world of cause and effect in time, a world bounded by nonbeing as reflected in the introduction of true death. Though not all of Le Guin's stories so directly communicate the Jungian and Taoist aspects of her worldview, many become richer and deeper when viewed in this context.

Le Guin defines fantasy as the manipulation of myths and symbols to communicate with the unconscious. Some of her fantasies she calls psychomyths: "more or less surrealistic tales, which share with fantasy the quality of taking place outside any history, outside of time, in that region of the living mind which . . . seems to be without spatial or temporal limits at all."

"The Ones Who Walk Away from Omelas" is probably her best-known psychomyth. This story combines fiction and essay in an unusual way. The narrator describes the beautiful and happy city of Omelas beginning its summer festival. Gradually, she reveals that this is an imagined city. The narrator cautions the reader against doubting that a utopian city filled with joy might also be a place of dynamic and meaningful life. The reader is encouraged to follow his own fancy in imagining a truly happy city. She suggests attitudes toward technology, sexual pleasure, and drug use that would foster happiness, then returns to a description of the festival.

Guessing that the reader will be skeptical even after helping to imagine this wonderful city, she then reveals two more facts. First, the happiness of Omelas depends upon one small child being locked forever in a dark room, deprived of all comfort and affection. Any effort to provide care and justice for that child would destroy the happiness of Omelas. Second, there are people who cannot bear to accept their happiness under this condition. These are the ones who walk away.

Structured as a mutually imagined myth, this story seems designed to provoke examination of the tendencies of human imagination. Why must people find a dark side of beauty in order to believe in it? Why is happiness unimaginable without suffering? How do people manage to find ways of accepting life under these terms? Why are some people unable to accept that living inevitably entails gaining from the suffering of others? While this story is somewhat different in form from her more typical fantasies, it seems to share with them the central aim of fantasy Le Guin described in "The Child and the Shadow": to reduce the reader's inclination "to give up in despair or to deny what he sees, when he must face the evil that is done in the world, and the injustices and grief and suffering that we must all bear, and the final shadow at the end of all."

Le Guin's science fiction differs from her fantasy and psychomyths in that the distinguishing feature of the story's world is technology rather than magic. Her best science-fiction stories accept the unique technology as a given and center on fully realized characters coming to terms with the problems or implications of that technology. "The Eye Altering" recounts the struggle of colonists trying to adjust to a new planet that does not quite mesh with their metabolism, especially the difficulties they encounter when they discover that they are bearing children who, in fact, are better suited to this new planet than to Earth. In "The Diary of the Rose," the psychoscope, a therapeutic tool, allows a form of mind reading. An apprentice analyst confronts the problem of how to treat a patient who seems perfectly sane but who is accused of political deviation. Several of Le Guin's best science-fiction stories became the seeds of later novels or developed in relation to her novels. "Winter's King" led to *The Left Hand of Darkness*. Written after *The Dispossessed*, "The Day Before the Revolution" is about the death of Odo, the woman who founded

Odonianism, the anarchist philosophy of Anarres society in *The Dispossessed*. In "The New Atlantis," Le Guin combines psychomyth and science fiction. While a future America sinks into the sea under the weight of political tyranny and ecological sin, a mythical new world awakens and rises from the sea. In each of these stories, the fates of fully realized characters are more central than the science-fiction settings and technology.

Though Le Guin's stories nearly always contain multiple layers of meaning that repay rereading, they are usually also engaging and entertaining on first reading. She interests the reader in her characters or she sets up her problems in images and symbols that stimulate the imagination and lead to speculation. Many of her stories are also witty. Sometimes the wit is broad, as in "The Author of the Acacia Seeds," which tells of efforts to translate the writings of ants. Sometimes, her wit is more subtle, as in "Sur," an account of the "real" first expedition to the South Pole, made by a group of women who kept their feat a secret to avoid embarrassing Roald Amundsen.

This brief account cannot deal with many of Le Guin's themes. She has shown significant interest in feminism and other political and social themes. Her family background in anthropology has contributed to her interest in imagining cultures and contact between alien cultures. Over the span of her career, she has tended to move from more traditional forms of fantasy and science fiction toward imagining alternative cultures and their interactions. Throughout her career, she has continued to draw themes from Jungian psychology and Taoism.

Other major works

NOVELS: *Rocannon's World*, 1966; *Planet of Exile*, 1966; *City of Illusions*, 1967; *A Wizard of Earthsea*, 1968; *The Left Hand of Darkness*, 1969; *The Tombs of Atuan*, 1971; *The Lathe of Heaven*, 1971; *The Farthest Shore*, 1972; *The Dispossessed: An Ambiguous Utopia*, 1974; *Very Far Away from Anywhere Else*, 1976; *Leese Webster*, 1979; *Malafrena*, 1979; *The Beginning Place*, 1980; *The Eye of the Heron*, 1982; *Always Coming Home*, 1985; *Catwings*, 1988; *Catwings Return*, 1989; *Tehanu: The Last Book of Earthsea*, 1990.

POETRY: *Wild Angels*, 1975; *Hard Words and Other Poems*, 1981; *In the Red Zone*, 1983; *Wild Oats and Fireweed: New Poems*, 1988.

NONFICTION: *From Elfland to Poughkeepsie*, 1973; *The Language of the Night: Essays on Fantasy and Science Fiction*, 1979 (Susan Wood, editor); *Dancing at the Edge of the World: Thoughts on Words, Women, and Places*, 1988; *Napa: The Roots and Springs of the Valley*, 1989.

CHILDREN'S LITERATURE: *The Adventure of Cobbler's Rune*, 1982; *Solomon Leviathan's 931st Trip Around the World*, 1988; *A Visit from Drokatz*, 1988; *Fire and Stone*, 1989.

Bibliography

Bittner, James W. *Approaches to the Fiction of Ursula K. Le Guin*. Ann Arbor: UMI

Research Press, 1984. This author discusses both Le Guin's short stories and novels, making connections among her works to show how certain themes are apparent in all of them.

Bucknall, Barbara J. *Ursula K. Le Guin.* New York: Frederick Ungar, 1981. The main emphasis in this book is a discussion of Le Guin's novels, mainly in chronological order. It does include one chapter devoted to her short fiction.

Cogell, Elizabeth Cummins. *Ursula K. Le Guin: A Primary and Secondary Bibliography.* Boston: G. K. Hall, 1983. A detailed bibliography of Le Guin's writings, including her fiction (short stories and novels), nonfiction, and miscellaneous media (including poetry), as well as critical studies of her work. The introduction provides an overview of Le Guin's biography and writing career.

Cummins, Elizabeth. *Understanding Ursula K. Le Guin.* Columbia: University of South Carolina Press, 1990. An analysis of Le Guin's work emphasizing the different worlds she has created (Earthsea, the Hannish World, Orsinia, and the West Coast) and how they provide the structure for all of her fiction.

De Bolt, Joe, ed. *Ursula K. Le Guin: Voyager to Inner Lands and to Outer Space.* Port Washington, N.Y.: Kennikat Press, 1979. This volume is a collection of critical essays that discusses Le Guin's work from a variety of perspectives, including anthropology, sociology, science, and Taoist philosophy.

Olander, Joseph D., and Martin Harry Greenberg, eds. *Ursula K. Le Guin.* New York: Taplinger, 1979. The authors of this collection of critical essays use various approaches, including mythological archetypes, psychological interpretations, and political influences to interpret Le Guin's work.

Terry Heller
(Revised by *Eunice Pedersen Johnston*)

STANISŁAW LEM

Born: Lvov, Poland; September 11, 1921

Principal short fiction

Sezam i inne opowiadania, 1954; *Dzienniki gwiazdowe*, 1957, 1971 (*The Star Diaries*, 1976, and *Memoirs of a Space Traveler: Further Reminiscences of Ijon Tichy*, 1982); *Inwazja z Aldebarana*, 1959; *Księga robotów*, 1961; *Bajki robotów*, 1964; *Cyberiada*, 1965 (*The Cyberiad*, 1974); *Polowanie*, 1965; *Ratujemy kosmos i inne opowiadania*, 1966; *Opowieści o pilocie Pirxie*, 1968 (*Tales of Pirx the Pilot*, 1979); *Doskonała próżnia*, 1971 (*A Perfect Vacuum*, 1979); *Wielkość urojona*, 1973 (*Imaginary Magnitude*, 1984); *Maska*, 1976; *Suplement*, 1976; *Mortal Engines*, 1977; *Golem XIV*, 1981; *More Tales of Pirx the Pilot*, 1982; *Prowokacja*, 1984 (partial translation, *One Human Minute*, 1986).

Other literary forms

Stanisław Lem may well be the best-known Continental European science-fiction writer. He has written teleplays (produced in his native country), but his short stories and particularly his many novels have brought him an even wider circulation. In whatever form, he has concentrated on speculative fictions in which he frequently describes the future of society, combining philosophical argument with imaginative technological fantasies. He has also published book-length studies and collections of essays on technology, general literature, and science fiction. A valuable selection of those essays is available in English translation in *Microworlds: Writings on Science Fiction and Fantasy* (1984), which also includes the autobiographical essay "Reflections on My Life."

Achievements

Lem has been called by a number of critics, Darko Suvin in particular, the best European writer of mature science fiction. A member of the post-World War II Polish "Columbus" generation (a name derived from the novel by Roman Bratney), Lem has been praised for his intellectual abilities, his imaginative writing, and his grasp of modern science. His books, widely popular in Poland, Eastern Europe, and the Soviet Union as well as in the West, have been translated into more than thirty languages. They have sold well despite the handicap of often being translations of translations: *Niezwyciżony i inne opowiadania* (1964; *The Invincible*, 1973), for example, is available for readers of English in a version not from the original Polish but from German; *Solaris* (1961; English translation, 1970), his best-known work in the United States, comes to American readers through the intermediary language of French. Yet these linguistic difficulties have not prevented Lem's talent from being recognized both in his own country and abroad: he won the Polish State Literary

Award for 1973, and for a brief and controversial period he was the recipient of an Honorary Membership in the Science Fiction Writers of America.

Biography

Stanisław Lem was born in Poland in 1921, a particularly bad time for countries located between great powers. His study of medicine was interrupted by the German occupation of Poland in World War II, and he did not receive his M.D. until 1946. Lem married Barbara Lesniak in 1953, and their son, Tomek, was born in 1968. In 1982, he left Poland, living for a year in Berlin before establishing a residence in Vienna. He retained his Polish citizenship and returned home after Poland successfully separated from the Warsaw Pact. As the publication dates of his fiction show, he turned to speculative writing early, but his output increased greatly beginning in 1956, when Poland, among other Eastern European countries, offered a brief challenge to Soviet hegemony. During the next twenty years, Lem has commented, he gained a reputation in his own country primarily as a writer of adventure stories for juveniles and was therefore not seriously considered as a writer. Translations of his works, however, were reaching adult audiences both in the Soviet Union and in the West. As sales of the translations mounted and his reputation grew abroad, critical attention followed at home, and today he is recognized as a major European writer within the genre of prose science fiction. His work has appeared in other media as well, even reaching visual media in a number of cases: he has himself written scripts for television adaptations; his novel *Astronauci* (1951; the astronauts) was filmed in a joint East German-Polish venture; and his most popular novel, *Solaris*, was made into a motion picture in 1972, at the beginning of the decade that saw his readership increase in Great Britain and the United States.

One result of his increased exposure in the United States was the invitation, in 1973, to become an honorary member of the Science Fiction Writers of America (SFWA), a voluntary association of published writers in the field. Lem accepted, becoming (after J. R. R. Tolkien) only the second writer to be awarded honorary membership in the SFWA. Lem's acid comments on the quality and marketing of American science fiction appeared in print soon after, leading a number of SFWA members to protest his membership and to call for his ouster. The motives for Lem's eventual dismissal depend on who is telling the story, but the full sequence of events, presented from several sides, may be found in the July, 1977, issue of the journal *Science Fiction Studies*. The outcome was that Lem's honorary membership was withdrawn, and he was invited to apply for regular membership, an invitation which he refused.

Lem has strong opinions; he is especially scornful of writers who think of science fiction as mere entertainment. He has great respect for the genre as a valid means of speculating on serious questions, and he resents those who he thinks trivialize it. Many American writers share those opinions, and many protested Lem's treatment in the controversy. In the long run, however, readers will decide for themselves the importance of such biographical incidents to an understanding of the writer's life, and it is most likely that it is Lem's fiction on which his reputation will ultimately depend.

Analysis

Readers fond of the short story will find much both conventional and unconventional in the works of Stanisław Lem. He has published several collections of short stories of the familiar kind; he has also contributed to a form perhaps peculiar to the twentieth century, one that contains all the same elements as a short story or novel—characters, setting, theme, and plot—but which adds an additional fiction that removes the author one step further from his creation. In this form, Lem pretends that the author of the work is someone else; instead of telling the story, Lem summarizes and reviews it.

A Perfect Vacuum and *One Human Minute* consist of just such reviews of nonexistent books, and *Imaginary Magnitude* plays slight variations on the theme, being composed of an introduction to the work, three introductions to nonexistent works, an advertisement for a nonexistent encyclopedia, and a final set of six pieces bearing the general title "Golem XIV." Golem XIV is a reasoning, self-programming supercomputer that has composed several "lectures"; the pieces in this section consist of an introduction and a foreword to those lectures, instructions for consulting the computer, and an afterword. For perfect consistency, Lem should have left the lectures themselves unwritten, but (perhaps unable to resist) he supplies two of them.

Although these forms are unusual, Lem did not create them: he cites the Argentine writer Jorge Luis Borges as his predecessor at the labor of reviewing nonexistent books and suggests that the practice predates even Borges. Lem, however, consistently attempts to add further levels of complication. For example, the introduction to *A Perfect Vacuum* is a brief essay by the same title. "A Perfect Vacuum" (the introduction) functions like the usual preface or foreword, but it is itself also a review and—like the rest of the essays in the book—in part a critique of a work that does not exist. The essay that the reader sees presupposes that the collection *A Perfect Vacuum* begins with an introduction by Stanisław Lem, a fictitious introduction titled "Auto-Momus." What the reader sees, therefore, is at the same time an introduction to the real book in hand and a critique of the nonexistent introduction to that book. Reading "A Perfect Vacuum" is an excellent way to begin one's experience of these unusual forms because it discusses at some length why a writer would choose to write them. A writer, says "S. Lem," may simply be producing parodies or satires, may be producing drafts or outlines, or may be expressing "unsatisifed longings." Yet a final reason is suggested as well:

> Books that the author does not write, that he will certainly never undertake, come what may, and that can be attributed to fictitious authors—are not such books, by virtue of their nonexistence, remarkably like science? Could one place oneself at any safer distance from heterodox thoughts?

It should be added, however, that in keeping with the convolutions of the form, this opinion is immediately contradicted in the next sentence.

It is tempting to believe that the reviews of fictitious books imply Lem's dissatisfaction with conventional forms; this belief is buttressed by what the author has called "Lem's Law": "No one reads; if someone does read, he doesn't understand; if he understands, he immediately forgets." Lem's Law notwithstanding, it is far safer to resist attributing a motive to so subtle and comic a writer, especially since Lem has also written (and become famous for) the kind of fiction that he here claims no one reads.

In those more conventional short fictions, Stanisław Lem has shown a fondness for stories of two general kinds: those with human space voyagers as the central characters, and those set in a world of robots. There is no hard-and-fast separation; almost all the stories show some kind of man-machine interaction or confrontation. Both types demonstrate that one of Lem's especially noteworthy abilities is his talent for the comic in a field—science fiction—that is not on the whole rich in humor. A second simple preliminary division of Lem's short fiction, in fact, can be made by separating the comic adventures of Ijon Tichy from the serious tales of Pirx the Pilot; both heroes are space travelers of the future, but they inhabit stories quite different in tone and language, although the stories are often similar in the themes they examine.

Lem worked on the stories with Ijon Tichy as a hero for well over a decade, and the publishing history of the work is complicated enough to warrant a word of explanation. There are two Polish versions of the work originally titled *Dzienniki gwiazdowe:* the first was published in 1957, was translated in 1976, and carries the English title *The Star Diaries.* The second Polish edition, that of 1971, contains a number of stories not included in the 1957 collection. These later stories were translated into English and published in 1982 under the title *Memoirs of a Space Traveler.* The two collections in English, *The Star Diaries* and *Memoirs of a Space Traveler,* together with the short novel *Bezsenność* (1971; partial translation in *The Futurological Congress,* 1974), make up the complete adventures of Ijon Tichy available in English.

Tichy, the comic side of Lem's vision, is described by the anonymous narrator not only as the discoverer of 83,003 new stars but also as someone to rank with Baron Münchhausen and Lemuel Gulliver. The literary allusions warn the reader that Tichy's truthfulness is not guaranteed, but since his creator employed him as a character for fifteen years, Tichy must provide a useful vehicle for his author's statements. In fact, many readers may find Tichy the best introduction to Lem: the comedy of the stories is easy to appreciate regardless of the nationality of the reader. The stories are comic not only in their exaggerated space-opera action and in the wildness of their plots but also in their often pointed satire: in these works, Lem parodies an astonishing range of targets. Critics have noted that the author makes fun of his own early attempts at science fiction, and he burlesques many of the more shopworn themes and plots of the genre—for example, time travel. In "Ze wspomnień Ijona Ticheyo IV" ("Further Reminiscences of Ijon Tichy: IV"), in *Memoirs of a Space Traveler,* Tichy is approached by the inventor of a working time machine for capital to continue his research. Greatly impressed, the explorer agrees to approach potential investors, but both to save time and to provide a demonstration of the machine, the inventor offers to go thirty years into the future, find out who the investors were historically, and return with the information on exactly which backers to approach. Unfortunately, the inventor forgets that thirty years in the future he will be thirty years older. He steps into his machine, turns it on, and as he fades from sight before Tichy's eyes in the present, dies of old age. Tichy concludes by observing that everyone travels in time, and if we age when we travel together at the same rate, why not expect that if the speed of travel is accelerated, the speed of aging will also increase? Readers of science fiction will recognize some subtle thrusts at the genre in Tichy's complaint that science fiction, like the inventor, forgets this problem.

Lem satirizes not only science fiction; in fact, critics' most frequent applause is reserved for Lem's linguistic inventiveness as a tool for his satire: his coinage of new words, his skill with names, and especially his fluent parodies of different styles of writing (scientific reports, political speeches) provide commentary on the whole spectrum of the ways in which people communicate (or fail to communicate). In questions of the style of the author, the reader is entirely dependent on the skill of the translator, but even without considering style, the humor of the stories is abundant and genuine.

Two larger targets of the satire of the Tichy stories are human imperfection and human philosophy. The way in which systems of thought have explained or failed to explain human flaws is one of Lem's constant themes. Lem does not hesitate to explore large questions: the purpose of an imperfect creature in a puzzling universe, why evil exists, the possibility of perfection of the human or another species, the utopias for which the human race strives—all these are among the themes that Lem examines in both the comic and the serious stories.

Tichy's serious counterpart is Pirx, a spaceman whose career the reader follows (in *Tales of Pirx the Pilot*) from cadet to commander. Pirx in many ways seems absolutely ordinary as a human being, if not as a literary character. Although in excellent physical condition, he is no superman like Edgar Rice Burroughs' John Carter, but rather a rounded character who changes as he matures. Through the tales, Pirx is subjected to a series of challenges of increasing difficulty, ones that bring all of his abilities into play. He has courage, skill, and training, but he often confronts as adversaries machines with powers far superior to his. Tichy, by contrast, is frequently only a bystander or an observer of such a machine. In the first tale of Pirx, "Test" ("The Test"), for example, the malevolent machine is the cadet's own ship. Through a series of mechanical failures, it seems to threaten to end his maiden flight by splattering him across the surface of the Moon. Yet Pirx always survives, through intuition when systematic thought is fruitless, through indecision when action fails, or simply through being more adaptable than his adversaries or his competitors.

Pirx is called a dreamer in that first story, but his dreams are sometimes nightmares. In "Patrol" ("The Patrol") two space pilots disappear while routinely surveying an uninhabited region of space. Their disappearance is a mystery until Pirx himself almost falls prey to a mental aberration caused by yet another ship malfunction. The breakdown produces the illusion of a light outside the ship, a will-o'-the-wisp that the two earlier pilots followed to their destruction. Only by using pain to bring himself back to reality is Pirx able to regain control and survive. Here the emphasis is on the fragility of the human endeavor in space: the vulnerable humans inside the ships are totally dependent on the machines that enclose and guard them. They are at the mercy of the machines that make it possible for them to exist. If the machines fail, the humans die. "Albatros" ("The Albatross") drives home this message; in it, the line between safety and disaster is even thinner, because Pirx witnesses a suspenseful but unsuccessful rescue attempt from a luxury passenger liner complete with swimming pools and motion-picture theaters.

Such brief descriptions may make the stories sound pessimistic, but students of Lem have traced in these tales the seemingly contradictory theme that humanity's weakness, its very vulnerability, defines its strength. One might point out that in "The Test," Pirx succeeds when a cadet whom he considers far better qualified fails. The other cadet, Boerst, is handsome and brilliant. Boerst always has the right answers in class and always knows the accepted procedures. Yet the final examination for the cadets aims to test their capacity for innovation and imagination: no procedure covers what to do when a cover falls off a control panel at the same time that a fly has stowed away. No procedure covers what to do when the fly crawls into the open panel and shorts out an electric circuit. In a crisis for which the standard operating procedures are not enough, even perfect knowledge of those procedures is useless. Boerst fails in just such a crisis.

Pirx, by contrast, makes mistakes and—even more important—knows that he makes mistakes. He will not, therefore, stick with a procedure if it does not yield immediate results; rather, since he has failed before, he will assume he is failing again and try something else. With enough tries, he is bound to hit on something that works. The method may seem irrational, but it simply takes into account that humans cannot plan for every eventuality and must therefore leave open an avenue for new solutions. The situation of the electrocuted fly might not occur in a thousand years, but someone in charge of the examination has realized that some unforeseen circumstance is bound to occur, and probably sooner rather than later. One must therefore keep one's mind open. This openness, as Pirx himself comments, results from the fact that we are "the sum of our faults and defects." Pirx's own success in the test can be explained in these terms. Since he lacks superior or outstanding ability in any one dimension, he cannot afford to become one-dimensional; he cannot become a specialist like the humans who fail before him or like the machines that failed them. He must remain open to possibilities from every direction. In short, he must be adaptable. In the final analysis, Pirx is not simply a sympathetic yet bungling hero, as one commentator has called him, nor is his success merely good luck; he is simply human in the best sense—adaptable.

In a third set of stories, Lem asks the question, "What does *simply human* mean?" As Bullpen, one of the instructors at cadet school, likes to remind his pupils, "A computer is only human." Even in the tales of Pirx or of Ijon Tichy, machines sometimes take on human attributes and characteristics. In "Further Reminiscences of Ijon Tichy: V," competing washing-machine manufacturers escalate their competition by building models that seem more and more human: they converse, they instruct, they even make love. By the end of the story, their original purpose has been so submerged that they have room to wash only a handkerchief or two, but they look like Jayne Mansfield. The stories in *The Cyberiad* and *Mortal Engines* carry this development into the far future, when computers and other machines have become only too human. In that distant setting, humans are no longer the central figures in the drama of civilization. Robots occupy the center stage, but the play seems familiar. Although the robots disparage and scorn humans, the robots' fairy tales have the forms and plots of human ones. Endow robots with consciousness and freedom of action, the stories seem to argue, and the meaning of "human" is called into question. The robot societies even show the same weaknesses as earlier human ones. They have their own villains and heroes, who show the same vices and virtues that humans do. There is not much difference between the men and the machines.

Lem reaches the same conclusion as the American science-fiction writer Isaac Asimov, who began his robot stories only a short time earlier: it is behavior, not biology, of which one is proudest in one's best moments and most ashamed in one's worst. Whether the creature is made of flesh or metal is not ultimately the most important factor. Lem may be saying, "Human is as human does," and in his stories, that is ultimately an optimistic definition.

Other major works

NOVELS: *Człowiek z Marsa*, 1946; *Astronauci*, 1951; *Obłok Magellana*, 1955; *Czas nieutracony*, 1957 (3 volumes, includes *Szpital przemienienia*, *Wśród umarłych*, and *Powrót*; partial translation, *Hospital of the Transformation*, 1988); *Eden*, 1959 (English translation, 1989); *Śledztwo*, 1959 (*The Investigation*, 1974); *Pamiętnik znaleziony w wannie*, 1961 (*Memoirs Found in a Bathtub*, 1973); *Powrót z gwiazd*, 1961 (*Return from the Stars*, 1980); *Solaris*, 1961 (English translation, 1970); *Niezwyciężony i inne opowiadania*, 1964 (*The Invincible, 1973*); *Głos pana*, 1968 (*His Master's Voice*, 1983); *Bezsenność*, 1971 (partial translation in *The Futurological Congress*, 1974); *Katar*, 1976 (*The Chain of Chance*, 1978); *Wizja lokalna*, 1982; *Fiasco*, 1987 (English translation, 1987).

PLAY: *Jacht Paradise*, 1951 (with Roman Hussarski).

POETRY: *Wiersze młodzieńcze*, 1966.

NONFICTION: *Dialogi*, 1957, 1984; *Wejście na orbitę*, 1962; *Summa technologiae*, 1964; *Wysoki Zamek*, 1966; *Filozofia przypadku*, 1968; *Fantastyka i futurologia*, 1970; *Rozprawy i szkice*, 1975.

MISCELLANEOUS: *Noc księżycowa*, 1963; *Powtórka*, 1979.

Bibliography

Davis, J. Madison. *Stanisław Lem*. Mercer Island, Wash.: Starmont House, 1990.

Though Davis does not discuss all Lem's works in detail, he does provide thorough discussions of his major novels and many of his short stories, showing the development of Lem's thought as reflected in his fiction. Includes a chronology, a biographical sketch, and extensive annotated primary and secondary bibliographies.

Macdonald, Gina. "Lem, Stanisław." In *Twentieth-Century Science-Fiction Writers*, edited by Curtis C. Smith. 2d ed. Chicago: St. James Press, 1986. Macdonald offers a brief biographical sketch and overview discussion of Lem's work.

Mullen, R. D., and Darko Suvin, eds. *Science Fiction Studies: Selected Articles on Science Fiction, 1973-1975.* Boston: Gregg Press, 1976. This volume contains essays on Lem by one of his best translators, Michael V. Kandel, and by Jerzy Jarzebski. Kandel's short "review" is a witty introduction to some of Lem's themes. Jarzebski's "Stanislaw Lem, Rationalist and Visionary," is an overview of Lem's career that provides a good introduction to his major themes and techniques, as well as to phases of his development during his career.

Slusser, George E., George R. Guffey, and Mark Rose, eds. *Bridges to Science Fiction.* Carbondale: Southern Illinois University Press, 1980. This volume contains essays on Lem by Gregory Benford and Stephen Potts. Benford deals mainly with *Solaris*, discussing Lem's use of the unknowable alien being. Potts discusses Lem's major theme of the limits of human knowledge and human ability to understand the unknown, comparing him to other authors, such as Franz Kafka.

Solataroff, Theodore. "A History of Science Fiction and More." *The New York Times Book Review*, August 29, 1976, 1, 14-18. This appreciative review of a few of Lem's books, including *The Cyberiad*, is a helpful introduction to Lem's themes and works.

Ziegfeld, Richard E. *Stanisław Lem.* New York: Frederick Ungar, 1985. This introduction to Lem surveys his translated works and his themes. It includes a biographical sketch, two substantial chapters on the short fiction, an annotated primary bibliography, and a select secondary bibliography.

Walter E. Meyers
(Revised by *Terry Heller*)

NIKOLAI LESKOV

Born: Gorokhovo, Oryol, Russia; February 16, 1831
Died: St. Petersburg, Russia; March 9, 1895

Principal short fiction

Povesti, ocherki i rasskazy, 1867; *Rasskazy*, 1869; *Sbornik melkikh belletristiche-skikh proizvedenii*, 1873; *Tri pravednika i odin Sheramur*, 1880; *Russkie bogonostsy: Religiozno-bytovye kartiny*, 1880; *Russkaia rozn'*, 1881; *Sviatochnye rasskazy*, 1886; *Rasskazy kstati*, 1887; *Povesti i rasskazy*, 1887; *The Sentry and Other Stories*, 1922; *The Musk-ox and Other Tales*, 1944; *The Enchanted Pilgrim and Other Stories*, 1946; *The Amazon and Other Stories*, 1949; *Selected Tales*, 1961; *Satirical Stories*, 1968; *The Sealed Angel and Other Stories*, 1984.

Other literary forms

Although Nikolai Leskov's most memorable work was in the shorter forms of fiction, he also attempted to meet the characteristic nineteenth century demand for "major works" with two full-length novels, *Nekuda* (1864; no way out) and *Na nozhakh* (1870-1871; at daggers drawn). Recognizing that novels were not his forte, he also tried to develop a different long form, the "chronicle," the major result of this effort being *Soboriane* (1872; *The Cathedral Folk*, 1924). Leskov also wrote one play, *Rastochitel'* (1867; the spendthrift), and a large body of journalistic nonfiction.

Achievements

Despite the continued output over more than thirty years of much high-quality fiction and despite his popularity among Russian readers, Leskov's immense narrative talent went largely unrecognized by the critics of his time. He was to some extent eclipsed by his great contemporaries: Ivan Turgenev, Fyodor Dostoevski, and Leo Tolstoy. He was also adversely affected by the view that only big novels really "counted." Finally, he was caught in political cross fire and early in his career was virtually read out of literature by certain radical critics for his supposed retrograde views. Nevertheless, the first twelve-volume edition of his collected works (1889-1896) was a symbolic acknowledgment of his status as a classic, and that status has been more and more widely recognized in the decades since his death. New Russian editions of his works are frequent, and there is now a substantial body of scholarship dealing with him. His reputation has also spread abroad, and many volumes of translations and of books about him have been published in English, French, German, Italian, Dutch, Swedish, and other languages. He is regarded as a major narrative artist and a thoughtful critic and moralist, a keen and often caustic observer of Russian society, and an especially penetrating and well-informed commentator on Russian religious life.

Biography

Nikolai Semyonovich Leskov was born on February 16, 1831, in Gorokhovo, a village in Oryol Province. His class background was varied and unusual. His father, a priest's son, had become a government official, receiving technical membership in the hereditary gentry when he attained the required rank. His mother was the daughter of an impoverished gentleman married to a merchant's daughter. Leskov grew up partly in the country, where his father had bought a tiny estate, and partly in the town of Oryol, where he attended the *gymnasium*. He did not complete the course, however, dropping out to take a lowly civil service job, first in Oryol and later in Kiev, where an uncle was a university professor. Though in later years by wide and incessant reading he educated himself enough for several university degrees, the lack of a formal one remained a sore point for Leskov. In Kiev, he worked in an army recruiting bureau, a position that obliged him to witness and take part in some of the gross injustices and cruelties of Nicholas I's regime. In 1857, Leskov took leave from the service and entered private business, working as a factotum for an uncle by marriage, a Russified Scotsman who managed the estates of some wealthy grandees. This work necessitated much travel within Russia, and Leskov drew heavily on these experiences in his later writings, which exhibit a connoisseur's knowledge of colorful nooks and crannies of Russian provincial life. The success of a few early experiments with writing convinced Leskov to move to St. Petersburg with the intention of becoming a professional journalist.

Leskov obtained a position as editorial writer for a leading newspaper, but in 1862 he fell afoul of the radicals. At issue was an article in which he suggested that a recent series of fires in the capital might actually have been set by revolutionary arsonists, as had been rumored; he urged the police to make public its list of suspects so that popular anger would be deflected from the general body of university students. The threats and attacks on him infuriated Leskov, and he retaliated with an antiradical *roman à clef*, *Nekuda*, which incensed the radicals against him even more. He struck again with a second novel, *Na nozhakh*, and there are also antiradical sallies in *The Cathedral Folk*. In fact, however, despite all the anger and name-calling, Leskov's views on society and politics were consistently progressive. He called himself a "gradualist." He hailed the reforms of Alexander II, especially the abolition of serfdom, and he favored equality of all citizens before the law, freedom of speech and of the press, and an independent judiciary. Yet he was often discouraged, as were many others, by the enormity of the country's problems and the inadequacy of the resources, human and material, it could bring to bear on them. The age-old demons of hunger and cold still haunted the lives of all too many Russians, making other problems seem trivial luxuries.

As early as 1862, Leskov began to publish short stories, and he soon became convinced that fiction was his true calling. Some of his most famous stories date from this early period; he went through no phase of literary maturation. In the 1870's, after the termination of his long war with the radicals, Leskov produced another series of classic stories. Many were published in the organ of the right-wing ideologue Mikhail Katkov, and for some time Leskov was considered an established member of the Katkov camp. In 1874, Leskov broke with Katkov, ostensibly because of high-handed editing of one of his stories; in fact, their political differences would eventually have led to rupture anyway.

Because of *The Cathedral Folk* and other works with clerical heroes, Leskov had been typed as Russian literature's chief expert on the clergy and its most ardent proponent of Orthodoxy, but actually, by 1875 his own religious development had led him to break with that church. Meditation, rereading of the Gospels, and contacts with Protestants during an extended trip to Western Europe in 1875 brought about this major reorientation. "I no longer burn incense to many of my old gods," Leskov wrote to a friend. His alienation from Orthodoxy only deepened during the remainder of his life. Eventually he went so far as to assert categorically that Orthodoxy was "*not* Christianity." By that time, his ideas had "coincided," as he put it, with those of Tolstoy. Though he acknowledged the brighter light cast by Tolstoy's "enormous torch," Leskov had valid reason to claim that in many respects he became a Tolstoyan even before Tolstoy did. Leskov had suffered from heart disease for several years; he died suddenly on March 9, 1895.

Analysis

Nikolai Leskov, early in his career, developed a characteristic form for his short stories: the "memoir"—half fiction, half fact—with a narrating "I" who regales the reader with tales of the colorful personalities and unusual events that he has experienced in his adventurous life. The border between "fiction" and "fact" is left intentionally blurred—an adroit illusionistic stratagem in an age that claimed the label "realism." In "Ovtsebyk" ("The Musk-ox"), for example, the narrator is presumably to be equated, at least by unsophisticated readers, with the actual author. Indeed, the story contains, in a lengthy digression, a lyrical account of what are believed to be the actual pilgrimages to monasteries on which the real Leskov as a boy accompanied his grandmother. The main focus of the story, however, is on the mature narrator's encounters with a character who illustrates Leskov's conviction of the futility of the radical intellectuals' efforts to stir the peasantry to revolt.

"Iazvitel'nyi" ("The Stinger") evokes a theme Leskov touched on many times later, the difficulties encountered by the foreigner in Russia. An Englishman working as an estate manager in Russia comes to grief and brings disaster on his peasant charges through his inability to understand their mentality. The story avoids the impression of chauvinism, however, by the narrator's clear recognition that the downfall of the humane Englishman is caused not by any Russian superiority of soul but by the peasants' stubborn barbarism and backwardness.

"Voitel'nitsa" ("The Amazon") remains one of the classic examples of what the Russians call *skaz*, in which a frame narrator, more or less identifiable with the author, hears and records an inner, oral narrative, which is related in picturesque, "marked" language by a folk character. In this case, the inner narrator is one of Leskov's most colorful literary offspring, a Petersburg procuress. Catering to the secret sexual needs of the capital, she has entrée into all levels of society, and her language is a mixture of correspondingly disparate layers, the substratum of local dialect being overlaid with upper-class words, often of Western origin, but not always perfectly understood or accurately reproduced. Her motley language is in perfect harmony with her personality: vulgar, down-to-earth, cynical, yet endlessly vital.

"Ledi Makbet Mtsenskogo uezda" ("Lady Macbeth of the Mtsensk District"), though somewhat atypical in technique, remains one of Leskov's most famous stories; it was the basis for the libretto of Dmitry Shostakovich's opera. Like Turgenev's earlier "Gamlet Shchigrovskogo uezda" ("Hamlet of the Shchigrovsky District"), the title oxymoronically situates a regal Shakespearean archetype in a maximally unromantic, provincial Russian setting; the story itself demonstrates that such human universals know no boundaries of place, time, or class. Presented in a more conventional omniscient-author format than the pseudo-memoirs, "Lady Macbeth of the Mtsensk District" is a lurid tale of adultery and murder in a provincial merchant milieu.

In 1866, Leskov began the most ambitious literary enterprise of his career: to encapsulate in a single artistic work, class by class, the provincial Russia he knew so well. The life of a single town would serve as its microcosm. The huge project was never completed, but the section dealing with the clergy eventually emerged in 1872 as a full-length book, the celebrated novel *The Cathedral Folk*. This volume opened up for Russian literature a hitherto unexplored social territory, the provincial clergy, presented in a highly attractive form, with a winning mixture of sentiment and humor. Leskov insisted that *The Cathedral Folk* was not a novel (*roman*), a genre he considered hackneyed in form and limited in content to man-woman "romance," but rather a "chronicle," a genre already made classic in Russian literature by Sergei Aksakov. The chronicle had the advantage for Leskov of legitimizing almost unlimited structural looseness, since its only explicit guiding principle is the sequence of events in time.

Leskov sustained a high level of narrative art through his works of the early 1870's. "Zapechatlennyi angel" ("The Sealed Angel") is one of his most virtuoso performances in the art of *skaz*. Its narrator is a former Old Believer whose speech combines two highly marked linguistic stocks: the religious jargon of the "ancient piety" and the technical language of icon-painting. In this picturesque language, he relates a stirring, skillfully paced tale of his comrades' struggle to recapture a confiscated icon. "Ocharovannyi strannik" ("The Enchanted Pilgrim") is the life story of a monk purportedly encountered by the "author" on a steamer plying Lake Ladoga. This character, Ivan Severyanovich Flyagin, a former serf whose life has been a kaleidoscopic series of extraordinary adventures, is made to epitomize some of the essential qualities of the Russian national character as Leskov perceived it. These generalizations, however, are incarnated in a vivid sequential narrative that grips the reader from beginning to end.

In "Na kraiu sveta" ("At the Edge of the World"), Leskov explored in fictional form an issue concerning which he had strong personal opinions: the missionary activities of the Orthodox Church among primitive tribes in Siberia. It was a risky subject, but Leskov cleverly camouflaged his subversive message by having his tale told by a sympathetic and unimpeachably Orthodox bishop. Intense experiences in Siberia convince the bishop that there is more natural Christianity among the heathen tribesmen than among all the lazy clerics and rapacious, hard-drinking officials then engaged in bringing "civilization" to Siberia. The bishop's tale includes one of the most powerful blizzard stories in Russian literature.

Religious subjects did not occupy Leskov exclusively. "Zheleznaia volia" ("Iron Will") again takes up the theme of the difficulties of the foreigner working in Russia. This time, a German engineer who carries Teutonic discipline and self-control to the point of absurdity is vanquished by the "doughy" formlessness of Russian life. Again, Leskov avoids any impression of chauvinism by showing that it is Russian weaknesses—insouciance, irresponsibility, and hedonism—that bring the German to his doom.

Even when not dealing directly with religious themes, Leskov took very seriously his responsibility to teach morality through literary art. He produced a whole cycle of portraits of *pravedniki* or "righteous ones," people who demonstrate that moral beauty and even sainthood are still possible in the tainted modern world. For all their differences of form and style, these stories are intended to function much like medieval hagiography: While entertaining the reader, they inculcate ideas of virtue. Among the most successful are "Odnodum" ("Singlethought"), "Nesmertel'nyi Golovan" ("Deathless Golovan"), and "Chelovek na chasakh" ("The Sentry"). Leskov took pugnacious pride in his ability to depict virtuous characters. "Show me another writer who has such an abundance of positive Russian types," he demanded. In some of these latter-day moralities, to be sure, artistic performance far overshadows morality. The left-handed hero of the famous "Levsha (Skaz o tul'skom kosom lefshe i o stal'noy blokhe)" ("Lefty: Being the Tale of the Cross-eyed Lefty of Tula and the Steel Flea") is indeed a "righteous one"—not only a craftsman of extraordinary skill but also an (unappreciated) patriot. Yet the principal impact of this classic *skaz* comes from its manner, not its message—its marvelous display of verbal acrobatics. "The Sentry," on the other hand, is cast in a more somber key. There, an omniscient author, moving through a series of terse chapters, builds up extraordinary tension by focusing on the hour-by-hour movement of the clock.

The memoir form employed in many of his stories had many advantages for Leskov. It at least ostensibly transposed a "story" from the realm of fiction to that of history or fact, thus not only enhancing the illusion of reality but also avoiding the charge of deception and even lying that troubled such creators of imaginary realities as Tolstoy. Furthermore, reminiscences of the past provide both philosophical perspective and didactic impetus. The memories Leskov resurrects are drawn mainly from the period of his youth, the reign of Nicholas I. It was not only enlightening to show Russians how far their country had evolved since those dark days, largely through the reforms of Czar Alexander II, but also disturbing to reveal how dangerously reminiscent of the tyrannies of Nicholas' time were the reactionary tendencies prevalent under Alexander III. Finally, the ultimate paradox of the memoir form lies in the nature of art: concrete images, even explicitly dated memories of a vanished past, may be a vehicle for universal, timeless truths about man's nature and fate.

From Leskov's memoir tales of the era of Nicholas I, one could construct a comprehensive sociology of Russia as it was then. Its most egregious evil was serfdom, and in "Tupeinyi khudozhnik" ("The Toupee Artist") Leskov created one of the most searing evocations in Russian literature of the horrors of that institution, especially its corrupting effect on both master and slave. For all his abhorrence of serfdom, however, Leskov never succumbed to the populist tendency to idealize the "people." From the beginning of his career to the end, he demonstrated again and again the "darkness" of the peasant world. Characteristically, the terrible famine of 1891-1892 inspired Leskov to recollect, in "Iudol" ("Vale of Tears"), the equally terrible famine of 1840. The comparison revealed that society had measurably advanced in that interval: relief measures were now open, energetic, and public. Yet the peasants were as benighted as ever, superstitious, and prone to senseless violence. By no means all of Leskov's memoir pieces, however, are so somber. One of the most humorous is "Grabezh" ("A Robbery"), another superb example of *skaz*, which evokes the atmosphere of the prereform provincial merchant class as a setting for comedy.

After his "conversion" to Tolstoyanism, Leskov placed even greater stress on the didactic function of literature. He plumbed a medieval Russian translation of the ancient Greek text *Synaxarion* for materials for an entire cycle of moralistic stories, slyly doctoring their plots to fit Tolstoyan specifications. The most substantial of these stories is "Gora" ("The Mountain"). In another *Synaxarion*-based fable, "Povest' o Fedore-khristianine i o druge ego Abrame zhidovine" (the story of Theodore the Christian and his friend Abraham the Hebrew), Leskov preached a much-needed sermon of tolerance and fraternity between Christians and Jews, thus demonstratively reversing the anti-Semitic tendency of some earlier stories.

Perhaps the most memorable and artistically most successful works of Leskov's late years were his satires of contemporary Russian society, which he viewed with deep pessimism, seeing little but corruption and folly among the elite and savagery in the masses. "Polunoshchniki" ("Night Owls") ridicules as a fraud (though without naming him) the highly touted Orthodox thaumaturge, Father Ioann of Kronstadt; the contrasting figure is a saintly Tolstoyan girl. In "Zimnii den'" ("A Winter's Day"), Leskov depicts another pure-hearted Tolstoyan girl alone in a degenerate milieu of police informers, extortionists, and sexual delinquents. Perhaps the greatest of these satires, Leskov's swan song, is "Zaiachii remiz" ("The March Hare"). Here, beneath a humorous camouflage—the narrator is a lovable Ukrainian lunatic who relates muddled memories of his adventurous youth—Leskov ridicules the "police paranoia" so pervasive in Russia (and elsewhere) at that time and later, the mentality that sees a subversive plotter lurking behind every bush. The camouflage, however, proved insufficient; no magazine editor could be found brave enough even to submit the story to the censors.

In his depiction of nineteenth century Russian life, Leskov's sociological range is broader than that of any other writer before Anton Chekhov. For those who can read him in Russian, his verbal pyrotechnics are simply dazzling, and his *skaz* technique has inspired many twentieth century imitators, notably Aleksei Remizov, Yevgeny Zamyatin, and Mikhail Zoshchenko. For non-Russians, such as Walter Benjamin, Leskov remains the storyteller *par excellence*, a practitioner of pure, uncontaminated narrative art. This description would doubtless have surprised and perhaps annoyed Leskov, who set greater store by his efforts as a moralist, but it seems to be the verdict of history.

Other major works

NOVELS: *Nekuda*, 1864; *Oboidennye*, 1865; *Ostrovitiane*, 1866; *Na nozhakh*, 1870-1871; *Soboriane*, 1872 (*The Cathedral Folk*, 1924).

PLAY: *Rastochitel'*, 1867.

NONFICTION: *Velikosvetskii raskol*, 1876-1877; *Evrei v Rossii: Neskol'ko zamechanii po evreis komu*, 1884.

MISCELLANEOUS: *Sobranie sochinenii*, 1889-1896; *Polnoe sobranie sochinenii*, 1902-1903 (thirty-six volumes); *Sobranie sochinenii*, 1956-1958 (eleven volumes).

Bibliography

Benjamin, Walter. "The Storyteller: Reflection on the Works of Nikolay Leskov." In *Illuminations*. New York: Harcourt, Brace & World, 1968. In this general study of the short story as an oral and written genre, Benjamin discusses Leskov and the technique of *skaz* by linking it to the oral transmittance of stories either by foreign travelers or by natives familiar with their own oral tradition.

Eekman, Thomas A. "The Genesis of Leskov's *Soborjane*." *California Slavic Studies* 2 (1963): 121-140. Eekman traces the genesis of *Soboriane*, the first great novel about the life of the Russian clergy, and examines its relationship to some of Leskov's stories that may have been planned for future volumes of the novel.

Lantz, K. A. *Nikolay Leskov*. Boston: Twayne, 1979. A brief biography and a general study of Leskov's works. A useful book for quick reference.

Lottridge, Stephen S. "Nikolaj Leskov and the Russian *Prolog* as a Literary Source." *Russian Literature* 3 (1972): 16-39. A detailed discussion of Leskov's *Prolog* tales of 1886-1891, which he patterned after Russian religious legends from various sources, and how they influenced him in writing these tales and in his overall development. Lottridge also touches upon culture and literature in the second half of nineteenth century Russia.

──────────. "Solzhenitsyn and Leskov." *Russian Literature TriQuarterly* 6, (1973): 478-489. Although Lottridge deals here primarily with Solzhenitsyn, by commenting on Leskov's short stories he provides valuable insights into Leskov, whom he considers Russia's greatest pure storyteller.

McLean, Hugh. *Nikolai Leskov: The Man and His Art*. Cambridge, Mass.: Harvard University Press, 1977. The standard work in English on Leskov, satisfactory in every respect. McLean presents Leskov in both scholarly and interesting fashion, making Leskov less foreign to the English-speaking reader. The first book on Leskov to be recommended to those interested in him.

Hugh McLean
(Revised by *Vasa D. Mihailovich*)

DORIS LESSING

Born: Kermanshah, Persia; October 22, 1919

Principal short fiction

This Was the Old Chief's Country, 1951; *Five: Short Novels,* 1953; *No Witchcraft for Sale: Stories and Short Novels,* 1956; *The Habit of Loving,* 1957; *A Man and Two Women,* 1963; *African Stories,* 1964; *Winter in July,* 1966; *The Black Madonna,* 1966; *Nine African Stories,* 1968; *The Temptation of Jack Orkney and Other Stories,* 1972 (also known as *The Story of a Non-Marrying Man and Other Stories*); *This Was the Old Chief's Country: Volume 1 of Doris Lessing's Collected African Stories,* 1973; *Sunrise on the Veld,* 1975; *A Mild Attack of Locusts,* 1977; *To Room Nineteen/Her Collected Stories,* 1978; *The Temptation of Jack Orkney/Her Collected Stories,* 1978; *Stories,* 1978.

Other literary forms

Doris Lessing's more than forty books include poetry, memoirs, reportage, plays, essays, and reviews. She is best known, however, for her novels, particularly *The Golden Notebook* (1962), and the five-volume *Children of Violence* series, which includes *Martha Quest* (1952), *A Proper Marriage* (1954), *A Ripple from the Storm* (1958), *Landlocked* (1965), and *The Four-Gated City* (1969). She has explored the genre she terms "space fiction" in the volumes *Shikasta* (1979); *The Marriages Between Zones Three, Four, and Five* (1980); *The Sirian Experiments* (1980); *The Making of the Representative for Planet 8* (1982); and *Documents Relating to the Sentimental Agents in the Volyen Empire* (1983), as well as "inner space fiction" in novels such as *Briefing for a Descent into Hell* (1971) and *The Memoirs of a Survivor* (1974). In the mid-1980's, she returned to more realistic fiction, publishing, among others, two novels under the pseudonym Jane Somers.

Achievements

Lessing has engaged in a lifelong process of self-education, becoming involved with all the important intellectual and political movements of the twentieth century: Freudian and Jungian psychology, Marxism, feminism, existentialism, mysticism, sociobiology, and speculative scientific theory. All these interests appear in her fiction, which consequently serves as a record of the changing climate of the times. She has also displayed in her writing an increasing anxiety about humanity's ability to survive. Lessing has been a nominee for the Nobel Prize in Literature, but her continuing eclectic exploration of the human condition has not won her that prize.

Biography

Born to British parents in Persia where her father, Alfred Cook Tayler, worked in a bank, Doris May Lessing moved to Southern Rhodesia in 1925, when she was five.

There she lived on a remote farm, south of Zambezi. "Our neighbors were four, five, seven miles off. In front of the house . . . no neighbors, nothing; no farms, just wild bush with two rivers but no fences to the mountains seven miles away." In her teens, she moved to a "very small town that had about ten thousand white persons in it. The black population, of course, did not count, though it was fairly large." This was the Africa of apartheid; Lessing would later chronicle its horrors.

While still in her teens, Lessing married and had two children. She later married again and, in 1949, left her second husband to go to England, bringing her son with her. The emptiness of the African veld and the life of small African towns are the themes of much of her earlier work, including the early volumes of the *Children of Violence* series. The scene then shifts in her fiction, as it did in her life, to England, and particularly London.

Lessing was a member of Communist groups both in Africa and in England. In Africa, she describes the group as "having no contact with any kind of reality. . . . I found this when I came to England and had a short association with the British Communist party."

Lessing's disillusionment with the difference between the official Communist Party and the "beautiful purity" of the ideas which lie behind Communism becomes an extremely important theme in her fiction. For many of her characters, disillusionment with the possibility of a political solution to the inequities and horror of modern life, leads them, first, to madness, suicide, or acquiescence; and later, beginning with *The Four-Gated City*, it leads them to visionary solutions. Once her characters give up politics as a solution, they come more and more to accept the mystic resolutions of the Eastern traditions, especially those of Sufism, an ancient form of Islamic human-centered mysticism. In *Prisons We Choose to Live Inside* (1987), a series of lectures she gave for the Canadian Broadcasting Corporation, she reaffirms her view that the survival of the human race depends on its recognizing its connection to all nature rather than stressing a sense of separation. She returned to a more realistic form of fiction, in the Jane Somers novels and *The Good Terrorist* (1985), exploring the phenomena of aging and of mindless ideology, but her 1988 novel, *The Fifth Child*, created some confusion in critics not familiar with her body of work.

Analysis

In Doris Lessing's short fiction, the reader meets characters remarkable for their intelligence, their unceasing analysis of their emotions, and their essential blindness to their true motivations. The people who move through her stories, while very vividly placid in the details of their lives, are in essence types. As Lessing says in her preface to *The Golden Notebook*, they are "so general and representative of the time that they are anonymous, you could put names to them like those in the old Morality Plays." Those whom the reader meets most frequently in the short fiction are Mr. I-am-free-because-I-belong-nowhere, Miss I-must-have-love-and-happiness, Mrs. I-have-to-be-good-at-everything-I-do, Mr. Where-is-a-real-woman, and Ms. Where-is-a-real-man; and there is one final type Lessing names, Mrs. If-we-deal-very-well-with-this-small-problem-then-perhaps-we-can-forget-we-daren't-look-at-the-big-ones. This last type is the character so often met at the beginning of Lessing's stories, the character who has become uneasily aware of a discrepancy between intention and action, between the word and the deed, but who would prefer not to take the analysis too far. Lessing is inexorable, however, and in story after story characters are driven to new, usually unpleasant, knowledge about themselves and their motivations. Usually, the stories end with the situation unresolved. The reader sees the awakening but not the translation of new knowledge into action. For Lessing, the jump from dealing very well with small problems to looking at the big ones is the jump from History to Vision and lies beyond the scope of short fiction.

The great obstacle facing Lessing's characters in their movement toward self-knowledge, toward vision, is emotion—particularly romantic love. Lessing sees romantic love as essentially egocentric; people love what they wish to see in the beloved, not what is really there. They love so that they will feel loved in return. They love, in the terms of the title story of one of her collections, from "The Habit of Loving." This, Lessing insists, is nothing but masochistic self-indulgence. Love robs people of their ability to reason clearly, diverts their energy into useless and potentially harmful channels, causes them to agonize over choices which make, in the end, very little real difference.

Worse, in terms of her visionary philosophy, romantic love, by keeping people focused on the particular, prohibits their making the necessary connections between the individual and the collective consciousness. In story after story, readers watch people live out the same patterns, search for love at all costs, focus on the small problems, the matter at hand: does he love me? Readers watch them try to believe that this is fundamentally what matters, that there is meaning in the small patterns of their lives. Lessing would deny that this is so. There is meaning, she seems to say, but it lies beyond these insignificant details. One must break through them, destroy them, in order to find it.

Some of her characters, although by no means all, do so. Anna Wulf, the writer-heroine of *The Golden Notebook*, succeeds in first dismantling the old patterns and then in synthesizing new ones, as does the anonymous narrator of "How I Finally Lost My Heart."

An uncharacteristic story in its resemblance to fable, "How I Finally Lost My Heart" is fascinating in its diagrammatic exposition of Lessing's views on romantic love. The story opens as the unnamed "I," a woman, is awaiting the arrival of her escort for the evening, a man designated only as C. The narrator explains that C is the third "serious" love of her life, the first two being, of course, A and B. Earlier in the day, the speaker has had lunch with A and tea with B and is pleased that she has been able to enjoy their company with equanimity; she is, finally, "out of love" with them. Recognizing her sensation at this discovery as one of relief, the speaker begins to question her exhilaration at the thought of spending the evening with C, "because there was no doubt that both A and B had caused me unbelievable pain. Why, therefore, was I looking forward to C? I should rather be running away as fast as I could."

Her questioning leads her to a new recognition of what lies behind the human desire to be "in love." It is not, she concludes, that "one needs a person who, like a saucer of water, allows one to float off on him/her, like a transfer." It is not, then, that one needs to "lose one's heart" by blending with another. Rather, "one carries with one a sort of burning spear stuck in one's side, that one waits for someone else to pull out; it is something painful, like a sore or a wound, that one cannot wait to share with someone else." One needs to "lose one's heart" literally, to get rid of it by giving it to someone else. The catch, of course, is that we are expected to take their heart in return. Lessing envisages a grotesque sort of barter, two people demanding of each other, "take my wound."

Moving to the telephone to call C and suggest that they agree to keep their hearts to themselves, the speaker is forced to hang up the phone:

> For I felt the fingers of my left hand push outwards around something rather large, light and slippery—hard to describe this sensation, really. My hand is not large, and my heart was in a state of inflation after having had lunch with A, tea with B, and then looking forward to C. . . . Anyway, my fingers were stretching out rather desperately to encompass an unknown, largish, lightish object, and I said: Excuse me a minute to C, looked down, and there was my heart, in my hand.

There her heart stays, attached to her hand, for four days, growing to the flesh of her palm. She cannot remove it by any "act of will or intention of desire," but when, distracted by events outside her window, she temporarily forgets herself, she feels it begin to loosen. One can "lose one's heart" only by forgetting about it; but it is still attached, and who is one to give it to?

She has previously covered the heart with aluminum foil, in part because it is messy and in part because, unaccustomed to the air, "it smarts." Now wrapping a scarf around her hand, heart and all, she walks about London, finally taking a train on the underground. In the train, she sits across from a woman maddened by love, who ceaselessly, jerkily, accuses her lover or husband of giving his mistress a gold cigarette case. The woman is on the verge of total breakdown, of lapsing into total immobility and, watching her, the narrator forgets herself. She feels the heart loosen from her hand, plucks it off and gives it to the mad woman:

> For a moment she did not react, then with a groan or a mutter of relieved and entirely theatrical grief, she leaned forward, picked up the glittering heart, and clutched it in her arms.

The woman has "taken heart"; she now has the energy of the heart and the "theatrical" grief it brings with it. She can once again play love as a game, insisting that her husband or lover "take her wound." The narrator, finally, is free. "No heart. No heart at all. What bliss. What freedom."

"How I Finally Lost My Heart," although uncharacteristic in its style, can serve as a paradigm for most of Lessing's stories on the relations between men and women. It is valuable because it points out so clearly her vision that the important choice is not among A and B and C, but it is rather the choice of freedom or bondage. If people choose freedom and break out of the patterns of romantic love, they are then able to see clearly and can move on to new ways of loving. This will necessitate new forms of the family, which Lessing sees, in its traditional structure, as the institutionalized destruction of its individual members. If, however, they remain convinced that the important choice is that of who to love, not how to love, they remain in delusion.

This same lesson is exemplified in the more traditional story "A Man and Two Women," one of Lessing's many explorations of the strains and restrictions of marriage. The plot is simple. Two couples, good friends, arrange to spend some time together in a country cottage. The couple who own the cottage, Dorothy and Jack, have recently had a baby. Of the visiting couple, Stella and Paul, only Stella is able to come. The story is impressing in its precise delineation of the relationships among the members of the quartet and in its explorations of Dorothy's languor and withdrawal after childbirth. The real excitement, however, lies in Stella's slow examination of her own marriage, in the light of the situation she finds between Jack and Dorothy. Both marriages are perceived by the couples to be extraordinary in their strength and exuberance, yet both are strained. The connection between Jack and Dorothy is threatened by the strength of Dorothy's attachment to her new son. Also, Stella realizes that her connection with Paul has been more strained by their occasional infidelities than she has realized.

In the final scene, Jack begins to make love to Stella, something Dorothy has goaded him into, declaring that she does not care what he does; he has become insignificant to her. At first, Stella responds:

> She thought: What is going to happen now will blow Dorothy and Jack and that baby sky-high; it's the end of my marriage. I'm going to blow everything to bits. There was almost uncontrollable pleasure in it.

Remembering the baby, however, she pulls back and waits for Jack to drive her to the station, making the final comment "It really was a lovely night"; a mundane comment for a return to the usual.

Using the paradigm of "How I Finally Lost My Heart," readers see that the story ends with Stella's struggle over choosing A or B, Jack or Paul, and with her desire to abandon herself to love. "There was almost uncontrollable pleasure in it." She agonizes only over whom she will ask to "take my wound." Although she perceives that both her marriage and Jack's marriage are failures, she leaves with her heart in her hand, carrying it back to Paul. She sees more clearly than she did at the opening of the story, but she is not yet able to act on her perceptions. She has not yet lost her heart.

"A Man and Two Women" ends, then, in ambiguity but not in pessimism. Stella may not yet be able to act on her perceptions, but she is admirable in her willingness to reexamine her life. Readers should consider emulating her. They are left not with a blueprint for action but with feelings and emotions that must be examined. It is typical of Lessing's short fiction that they, like Stella, are awakened to reality and then are left to take their own directions.

Other major works

NOVELS: *The Grass Is Singing*, 1950; *Martha Quest*, 1952; *A Proper Marriage*, 1954; *Retreat to Innocence*, 1956; *A Ripple from the Storm*, 1958; *The Golden Notebook*, 1962; *Landlocked*, 1965; *The Four-Gated City*, 1969; *Briefing for a Descent into Hell*, 1971; *The Summer Before the Dark*, 1973; *The Memoirs of a Survivor*, 1974; *Shikasta*, 1979; *The Marriages Between Zones Three, Four, and Five*, 1980; *The Sirian Experiments*, 1981; *The Making of the Representative for Planet 8*, 1982; *Documents Relating to the Sentimental Agents in the Volyen Empire*, 1983; *The Diary of a Good Neighbour*, 1983 (as Jane Somers); *If the Old Could . . .* , 1984 (as Jane Somers); *The Diaries of Jane Somers*, 1984 (includes *The Diary of a Good Neighbour* and *If the Old Could . . .*); *The Good Terrorist*, 1985; *The Fifth Child*, 1988.

PLAYS: *Each His Own Wilderness*, 1958; *Play with a Tiger*, 1962.

POETRY: *Fourteen Poems*, 1959.

NONFICTION: *Going Home*, 1957; *In Pursuit of the English: A Documentary*, 1960; *Particularly Cats*, 1967; *A Small Personal Voice*, 1974; *Prisons We Choose to Live Inside*, 1987; *The Wind Blows Away Our Words*, 1987.

Bibliography

Brewster, Dorothy. *Doris Lessing*. New York: Twayne, 1965. The first book-length study of the fiction. Provides a good general overview of Lessing's work up to the fourth novel in *The Children of Violence* series, *Landlocked*. Includes a brief biography and a discussion of the early novels, including *The Golden Notebook*. Contains a chapter on the short fiction, which analyzes stories published up to 1964, and a concluding chapter on attitudes and influences. Select bibliography, index, and chronology.

Lessing, Doris. *A Small Personal Voice*. New York: Alfred A. Knopf, 1974. This collection of interviews and essays by Lessing gives the reader an insight into the novelist's constantly expanding consciousness and agenda.

Pickering, Jean. *Understanding Doris Lessing*. Columbia: University of South Carolina Press, 1990. A brief, clear overview of Lessing's work. Begins with a chapter providing a biographical and analytical look at Lessing's career, then continues with a short but sharp analysis of her fiction through *The Fifth Child*. Includes an index and an annotated bibliography of books and articles about Lessing.

Schleuter, Paul. *The Novels of Doris Lessing*. Carbondale: Southern Illinois University Press, 1969. One of the earliest and most intelligent works on Lessing, which discusses the novels through *Briefing for a Descent Into Hell*.

Taylor, Jenny, ed. *Notebooks/ Memoirs/ Archives: Reading and Rereading Doris Lessing*. London: Routledge & Kegan Paul, 1982. A collection of essays by British women, mostly from a political standpoint defined in the introduction, which looks at Lessing and Sufism, mysticism, comparison with Simone de Beauvoir, and so on. Supplemented by a select bibliography of Lessing criticism and a complete index.

Thorpe, Michael. *Doris Lessing*. Essex, England: Longman, 1973. A good general introduction, very thorough, including a select bibliography, with an emphasis on the short fiction. Although only thirty-five pages in length, this volume includes a biography and discussion of Lessing's life and attitudes, and a sociopolitical analysis.

Whittaker, Ruth. *Doris Lessing*. New York: St. Martin's Press, 1988. A short but excellent overview of the fiction through *The Good Terrorist*. Ideal for a first reader of Lessing or to clarify points for those familiar with her work. Includes background and influences, the colonial legacy, in-depth analysis, an index, and a select bibliography that lists all Lessing's work and the major books, articles, and interviews published to 1988. Also includes reference to the *Doris Lessing Newsletter*, published by the Brooklyn College Press.

Mary Baron
(Revised by *Mary S. LeDonne*)

WYNDHAM LEWIS

Born: Amherst, Canada; November 18, 1882
Died: London, England; March 7, 1957

Principal short fiction

The Wild Body, 1927; *Rotting Hill*, 1951; *Unlucky for Pringle*, 1973.

Other literary forms

In addition to his short fiction, Wyndham Lewis published more than forty books in his lifetime, including a number of novels. He wrote some poetry and plays, two autobiographies, a considerable amount of art criticism and literary criticism, a volume of letters, and a mass of materials published posthumously. His "Human Age" trilogy was successfully performed as British Broadcasting Corporation (BBC) radio drama, and his novels partake of a number of genres: Nietzschean novel, fantasy, political thriller, travelogue, murder mystery, detective thriller, and country house weekend novel. Lewis' canon is diverse and his productivity stunning. Lewis was interested in the political, cultural, and philosophical repercussions of art and literature; he enjoyed polemic. His subjects included Adolf Hitler (whom he initially praised and later condemned), James Joyce, D. H. Lawrence, all Bergsonian advocates of stream of consciousness (of which he disapproved on artistic grounds), the Bloomsbury Group, and Gertrude Stein. His best-known critical work is *Time and Western Man* (1927).

Achievements

A man of multiple talents—poet, novelist, essayist, satirist, critic, editor, philosopher, political thinker, journalist, revolutionary, and painter—Wyndham Lewis was one of the major controversial intellectual figures of his age. He originated the British neoclassic, vorticist movement in the arts, together with Ezra Pound founded the journal *Blast* to further vorticism, and was a longtime contributor to such periodicals as *The Egoist*, *Athenaeum*, *The Little Review*, and *The Listener*. Although Lewis never won a large readership, the literary greats of his age admired his work. T. S. Eliot called him "the most fascinating personality of our time" as well as "the greatest prose master of style" of their generation; William Butler Yeats praised his philosophical work, and Pound believed that Lewis should have won the Nobel Prize for his novel *Self Condemned* (1954). If Lewis had been less irascible, dogmatic, and self-destructive, if he had not tainted his public image with anti-Semitic and Fascist political tracts, he might be better received today. Yet, in spite of everything, as Marvin Lachman notes in his *Dictionary of Literary Biography* article on Lewis, he was "an independent, courageous artist and brilliant social observer," a gadfly for contemporaries and well deserving of modern consideration.

Biography

Percy Wyndham Lewis was born on November 18, 1882, on his father's yacht moored near Amherst, Nova Scotia, Canada. Lewis was the son of an American army officer who had fought in the Civil War, Charles Lewis, and a British woman, Anne Prickett. He kept the Canadian nationality all of his life. When he was eleven, Lewis' parents separated, and he lived for some years in genteel poverty with his mother in the London suburbs. At Rugby, Lewis ranked at the bottom of his class, but at the Slade School of Art he began to write poetry and make friends with poets such as Thomas Sturge Moore and Lawrence Binyon. In the early 1900's, Lewis resided mainly in Paris (in Montparnasse, the artist's quarter) but also visited Spain, Holland, and Germany and spent summers in Normandy and Brittany. During this time, he studied painting and lived a profligate life of garrets and mistresses (by several of whom he had illegitimate children); as a consequence, he suffered several bouts of illness and venereal disease. His first novel, *Tarr* (1918, 1928), was set amid the Parisian student and café life.

When he returned to England in 1909, he began publishing his first stories and became associated with various art movements. Together with Pound he publicized the vorticist revolution. He met Henri Gaudier-Brzeska, Richard Aldington, Rebecca West, and Ford Madox Ford, among others, but, arrogantly brash, argumentative, and egotistical, he made more enemies than friends. In 1913, when he led an active opposition against Roger Fry, he lost his former friends among the Bloomsbury Group and began a critical exchange that led eventually to his satiric novel *The Apes of God* (1930). In 1914, he and Pound founded *Blast*, "Review of the Great English Vortex," a publication edited and largely written by Lewis but with later contributions by T. S. Eliot. It advocated abstract art, hard geometrical lines, African and Polynesian motifs, classical detachment but an underlying explosiveness that would capture urban life and its machinery. In 1916, he joined the military to battle "German barbarism," trained as a gunner and bombardier, received a commission in the Royal Artillery, and was sent to France. He describes his war experiences in *Blasting and Bombardiering* (1937). Demoralized by the war, he returned to London to pursue his interests in architecture and art, producing drawings and editing the art review *The Tyro*.

For Lewis, the 1920's were a productive period of literature and criticism. Calling himself "The Enemy," he blasted those whose ideas or style offended him. In 1929, Lewis married Gladys Anne Hoskyns. He visited Germany in 1930 and traveled in North Africa in 1930. After a period of illness and controversy in the early 1930's, particularly about his pro-Fascist, anticommunist stance, several of Lewis' books were withdrawn from publication. Ernest Hemingway, stung by Lewis' criticism of his novels in "The Dumb Ox" (1937), retaliated much later with a vicious portrait of Lewis in *A Moveable Feast* (1964). In 1938, his portrait of Eliot was refused by the Royal Academy, and, when Sir Winston Churchill defended the academy's action, Lewis attacked him for his "passionate advocacy of platitude." Condemned in England for his association with the British Union of Fascists, for his right-wing tracts, and his book praising Hitler as a true democrat and a "Man of Peace," Lewis went to the United States (Buffalo, New York City, and Long Island) in 1939 and moved to

Canada in 1940 (Toronto and Windsor), where he lectured for a year at Assumption College in Windsor, Ontario. When faced with the true nature of Hitler's fascism, Lewis recanted his previous stance but was permanently tainted by it. His novel *Self Condemned* is a subjective analysis of his own self-destructive patterns.

In 1945, Lewis returned to London to Notting Hill Gate and became art critic for *The Listener* until his eyesight failed in 1951. At that time, he was granted a small government pension, and a friend, Agnes Bedford, came to help his wife care for him and to help him continue to write. In 1952, the University of Leeds awarded him a doctorate of literature. In 1953, Lewis went totally blind. The Tate Gallery put on a Retrospective Exhibition in 1956: "Wyndham Lewis and Vorticism." Lewis died March 7, 1957, after a lifetime of controversy and criticism, his final words being "Mind your own business."

Analysis

A staunch elitist whose barbed wit won for him many enemies, Wyndham Lewis began his literary career writing the first literary form with which he had become familiar: the short story. Later, he claimed that the short story was "the crystallization of what I had to keep out of my consciousness while painting." Despite this seemingly negative attitude toward a form in which he continued to write throughout most of his lifetime, Lewis' stories reflect the diversity, values, and creative concerns of his other artistic endeavors. In fact, literary critic E. W. F. Tomlin says of *The Wild Body* that it contains "almost the whole of Lewis." Lewis himself is occasionally a character in his stories, and even when he is not there personally, many of the figures reflect his experiences as a student, a lover, a soldier, and an artist, as if the fictive and the nonfictive merge. His lifelong belief was that art should be about something, that politics, theology, philosophy—all human beings' intellectual concerns—are implicit in any serious work of art. Most of his short stories are satires that focus on the divided person: the split between mind and body, between good intentions and negative results, between the creative spirit and commercial needs, between surface appearances and hidden realities. The imagery reinforces these ideas: in them, clean and hard is good; soft and mushy is bad.

Lewis' prose style is unforgettable; characterized by structural clarity, vivid visual descriptions, striking metaphors, a range of diction, and a sense of discord, all with a biting edge. Stories such as "Some Innkeepers and Bestre" and "The Cornac and His Wife" are small gems, beautifully conceived. In keeping with his artistic theories of the vortex, continually in motion round a fixed and motionless center, his short fiction shifts perspective and attention but maintains a still, unchanging artistic center. His is the eye of a painter, who, in a few words, can capture the essence of "a slut of a room, dribbling at the sink, full of unsavoury pails, garishly dirty" ("Unlucky for Pringle") or of an athletic Frenchwoman on a cold day ("Some Innkeepers and Bestre"):

The crocket-like floral postiches on the ridges of her head-gear looked crisped down in a threatening way: her nodular pink veil was an apoplectic gristle round her stormy brow; steam came out of her lips upon the harsh white atmosphere. Her eyes were dark, and the Contiguous color of her cheeks of a redness quasi-venetian, with something like the feminine colouring of battle.

The Frenchman in the hotel window of "A Soldier of Humour" and Carl in *The Wild Body* are sketched in black and white with "dazzling skin and black patches of hair alternating"; many of the early stories describe the small things (such as a fishing boat, an athletic interest, an arrested conversation) that become the focus of human obsessions.

Lewis' first collection of short stories, *The Wild Body*, began as a travelogue, a sociological documentary characterized by realistic detail and a fragmentary vision, but developed into a far more complex dramatization of modern human beings. "Inferior Religions" and "The Meaning of the Wild Body" comment on the stories' meaning and construction and emphasize Lewis' vision of human absurdity, echoing Henri Bergson's idea of man as "a thing behaving like a person" and therefore comic. A Lewis character is often driven by obsessions beyond his control and mechanically repeats patterns that create both comedy and pathos. In *The Wild Body* the inhabitants of the Pension Beau Séjour, Francis the wandering musician, Bestre, and Cornac and his wife (poverty-stricken traveling entertainers savagely at odds with their village audiences) are just such creatures, while the Soldier of Humour, Ker-Orr, Lewis' projected persona, is self-described as a "barbarian clown . . . large, white and savage" and as a "forked, strange-scented, blond-skinned gut-bag, with its two bright rolling marbles with which it sees, bull's-eyes full of mockery and madness." The innkeeper in "A Breton Innkeeper" is a study of a domineering personality, a bullying, bellowing menace, a murderous "buffoon" characterized by empty and mechanical behavior patterns. Patient Eldred in "The Room Without a Telephone" is at times a "clown" whose mind was "blotted out by his frantic vanity" and his "spiteful animal" self. Lewis' detached narrator provides a surreal edge to even his most realistic tales.

Lewis' metaphors provide clues to his themes. He describes many of his characters as animals, a bestiary of modern people: horses, camels, walruses, sea lions, ferrets, dogs, placid cows, silly goats, sharp sheep, or even "some strenuous amoeba." John Leslie in "Junior" declares "We are a beastly race"; the head of Misrow in "The War Baby" reminds one of a "snake's sling-like extremity," and diners at a popular restaurant are "a lot of glum-looking cattle" who need stirring up. One character has "clam" eyes. *The Wild Body*, in particular, focuses on humans as primitive, like "big, obsessed, sun-drunk insects." Lewis as anthropologist scrutinizes strange new species of human beings and categorizes them according to their animal parallels, from the French or Spanish settings of *The Wild Body* stories or the English settings of his later tales. The French landlord in "Unlucky for Pringle" has an "animal-like selfishness and self-absorption," while Pringle's portmanteau lets loose its squashed contents "like a flock of birds and pack of dogs." "Cantleman's Spring-Mate" describes humans as "the most ugly and offensive of the brutes because of the confusion caused by their consciousness" and Cantleman as "an animal disguised as an officer and gentleman"; it advocates a return to raw animal nature. Eldred in "The Room Without a Telephone" is "like a sea beast—but blowing blood."

Lewis was particularly disturbed by the modern movement toward standardization and mechanization. His stories repeatedly attack human beings for "herd" behavior and "herd" philosophies. Similar to his herd images is his description of man as "a pea disguising itself from a million other peas . . . soft, subtle, clever, insolent." His other images focus on machines: the sun appears "bitterly and mechanically." Many of his characters seem little more than robots or automatic machines, endlessly repeating the same dull tasks, the same inescapable patterns, the same windup dialogue. For Lewis, stupidity, primitive behavior, and mechanical patterns are interrelated and sum up the absurdity of all mankind. Bestre, Brocatnaz, and various other inhabitants of the Breton Coast (*The Wild Body*) are elemental figures, seemingly rugged individualists who give rein to their "wild bodies" but in fact are cogs, "bobbins," "puppets," and mere "shadows of energy" caught up in "the complexity of the rhythmic scheme," "a pattern as circumscribed and complete as a theorem of Euclid" ("The Soldier of Humour"). The Frenchman in "Bestre" fixes Ker-Orr "with the blankness of two metal discs"—his eyes; at a trapeze performance the clown is "a cheerful automaton" and his barker, inspired by him, springs back and forth "as though engaged in a boxing match" as the audience howls with delight. Mr. Patrick, a shopkeeper in *Rotting Hill* is like "a wound-up toy," while the socialist parson, Rymer, is at times "an infuriated animal"; "X" in "Tyronic Dialogues" defines himself as an "animal" and his friends as "automata"; Arghol yawns in "mechanical spasms," "Father" François is described as "automata," the face of a woman reclined in bed is "a flat disc . . . sideways on the pillow," and a young boy's face might physically change as he imagines himself "a steamroller" or a "sightless Juggernaut" (all in *The Wild Body*). The pugilists in "The Man Who Was Unlucky with Women" spring left and right like mechanical toys or batter away like "a compact, seemingly heavily-loaded machine."

Related to his emphasis on the animalistic and the mechanistic is Lewis' interest in sudden, unpredictable violence, the meaningless events that will have a country parson scuffling with an angry opponent in the local pub and ignominiously kicked in the genitals ("The Bishop's Fool") or the cuckold husband of "The Man Who Was Unlucky with Women" frustratedly picking vicious fights with strangers at every opportunity and being unexpectedly killed by an enraged wolfhound that takes his warlike exhibitionism as a direct challenge. All the early stories in *The Wild Body* include violence, brutality and callousness. Brobdingnag dispels the bruises left on his wife by an unknown rival by adding his own, while Brotcotnaz believes that he can kill an invalid woman with impunity. The patterns are behavioristic: cause-effect patterns of stimulus-response. "The French Poodle" connects the motives that would cause an animal lover to kill his own pet with the horrible death that the pet owner is doomed to face in the trenches.

In contrast to the mechanistic and animalistic are a few characters who have learned to control mind and body, ones Lewis sometimes calls puppet-masters. For example, Ker-Orr in "A Soldier of Humour" operates with detachment as he uses his body as "a stalking horse." Cantleman is another such figure, for he imitates the murderous callousness of nature to assert his own superiority amid a world of trench warfare and inescapable horror.

Lewis' sense of place is directly related to his sense of humanity. The distant foreign settings of *The Wild Body*—the hotels and boardinghouses, cafés and bars— emphasize the narrator's alienation, while the insufferable restrictions of domestic hells in other tales contrast with the lonely but open spaces of homeless vagabonds. Frequently Lewis depicts rooms and flats as microcosms reflecting the world of their owners, their personality and essence. "Unlucky for Pringle," for example, traces the rootless Pringle's search, from Morocco to Canada to Chelsea, for the perfect accommodations, ones harmonious with his sense of self and with his need to extract sensations from his environment while imposing his own personality on it. With a gusto for common things, he might pass "like a ghost . . . through a hundred unruffled households," whose peaceful landladies he enjoys; yet Pringle awakens such hostility in observant landlords that his lodging houses "vomit him forth" unassimilated. "The Rot" in *Rotting Hill* in turn describes the narrator and his wife's encounters with both the dry rot of his own apartments and the dry rot of the new socialism as a stream of lazy, unmotivated repairmen make them feel like bruised grapes "in a basketful of glass marbles"; they dream of workers accusingly declaring that the couple themselves are the dry rot that infects the heart of their home and country. "The Room Without a Telephone" attacks socialized medicine as a diseased system that turns the individual into a guinea pig, promotes monumental waste, and endangers human life, accusations summed up in the treatment of patient Paul Eldred, whose confinement in a room without a telephone spells near doom.

Rotting Hill sketches the bedraggled people and patterns of post-World War II London, a place that Lewis describes as rotting, both physically from the wartime bombing and the dry rot produced by neglect and metaphorically from the political and social decay. Basically a political treatise, it captures a period of shortages, rationing, and depressing poverty. In "Time the Tiger," Lewis describes a London morning as "a constipated mass, yellowed by the fog, suspended over a city awaiting the Deluge" and city streets "like Pompeii with Vesuvius in catastrophic eruption, a dull glare, saffronish in colour, providing an unearthly uniformity." As is frequent in Lewis' books, many of the stories depend on a conflict or disagreement between two characters representing totally opposite points of view, morality, politics, or social conditions, with Lewis' literary persona sometimes appearing as the representative of one side of an argument. In "Bishop's Fool," for example, Lewis describes a chance meeting with a village rector, whose admirable but foolish views sum up what Lewis saw going wrong all over England: a Christian-influenced movement toward socialism, the dominance of the Labour Party, and the potential for England to perpetuate the abuses of a godless communism—socialism without Christian restraint. In "Time the Tiger," two old friends, a Tory and a socialist, exchange views and insults in a friendly fashion until an opinionated woman turns the disagreement into a permanent separation and the predatory "tiger," time, consumes the last of the world that they once knew. In "My Disciple," the Lewis persona is accosted by an advocate of spontaneous, undisciplined child art, in "My Fellow Traveler to Oxford" by a leftist undergraduate with firm opinions, and throughout the *Rotting Hill* stories by plumbers, carpenters, and other assorted repairmen halfheartedly trying to shore up the decay that threatens to engulf him, while Britannia herself (in "The Rot Camp") begs alms and sings "Land of Hope and Glory" in "a cracked wheeze."

Some of Lewis' stories focus on the artist, his life and vision. A bitter central theme is the hostile treatment of artists and the fate of the artist in modern society— beset by poverty, fearful of failure, tempted to compromise his talent for short-term financial gain. "Doppelganger" argues through its portrait of Thaddeus Trunk, an aging and purposefully eccentric artist, that "a man's publicity is a caricature of himself." Beset by adoring students, Trunk has chosen to play "the Dispenser of Culture" and in doing so has submerged his creative and spiritual self for the applause of "a horde of anonymous beings." His *Doppelgänger*, in the guise of a distant cousin, calls attention to Trunk's concern with his reputation and his betrayal of his art simply by being what Trunk should be but is not, a quiet, private artist, true to his artistic vision, a gadfly showing up the limitations of Trunk's admirers. As such, the *Doppelgänger* wins the heart of Trunk's wife, who sees in the double the real "Thaddeus," and the two leave the publicity-seeking Trunk "a shadow, a shell" of whom "the vulgar" would have the last word about "what his actions signified." "The Cornac and His Wife" portrays a melancholy showman who is a victim of his own audiences; as he manipulates them, they demand and elicit the kind of humor that they prefer, so that instead of puppet-master he becomes in part puppet, contorted to conform to the desires of his audience.

Related to his concern with artists is Lewis' Nietzschean belief that women are traps set for the creative man. In "The Code of a Herdsman," he voices his contention that "women, and the processes for which they exist, are the arch conjuring trick." He calls women "chocolate-cream traps" or "lush red sex-fruit" and find situations such as those in "The War Baby" and "Junior" all too typical. The women in such stories are overweight, indolent, soft, and determined. "Junior" describes mankind as "walking factories for procreation" and women as walking "time-bombs" whose "delight-producing machinery" will inevitably produce a child to trap a man in marriage and domesticity. The hero of "Junior" flees his mewling son, his wife, and a home transformed by marriage into a woman's club; forced by bad publicity to return home, he renounces them all, only to be taunted that the child was not his anyway and that he does not have "the guts to have a child." The young man in "The War Baby," desperate to find just the right kind of woman to seduce before going off to war, is reminded of another more subtle battle, the battle of the sexes: "all women seemed to feel that they should have their luxurious battles too; only they were playing at dying, and their war was fruitful." In this case, a woman chosen to affirm life before frontline confrontations pursues the young man with letters and after her death leaves him obliged to support their child, a dull, homely daughter, "a blast of God's irony." "Children of the Great" focuses on a similar irony, the child of a famous historian, totally lacking his father's arrestingly handsome looks, his sharp intelligence, and his interest in the world of the mind yet courted and pursued by women who adored his father, until captured by a rich, clever girl who sees him as the holder of valuable genes and a potential breeder of remarkable children, throwbacks to their grandfather, and uses him as such. Cantleman, the main character in "Cantleman's Spring-Mate," treats women with the same animalistic power that makes him a successful soldier. Assuming that "all women were contaminated with Nature's hostile power" and might be dealt with as secret agents or enemies, he craftily plans to outwit Nature by paving the way for the sexual "devouring of his mate" with the courtship niceties that women demand but then committing the sexual act with "the same impartial malignity" that he displayed "when he beat a German's brains out." The brutality of some of Lewis' male characters is directly linked to their sexual drive and their fear of the power it might give women over them.

Lewis effectively depicts neurotic compulsives. For example, he details the lunatic behavior of Captain Polderdick, in "The King of the Trenches," who races about pretending to be a "flying pig" (a nickname for a World War I British bomb) and who sends fusillades into the enemy camp, precipitates retaliatory attacks, and then heads for the safety of the back lines. The busybody Lionel Letheridge (nicknamed "Pish-Tush") rushes about spraying DDT to drive out a supposedly ghostly inhabitant of a neighbor's apartment, while the beach bum (a comic Cuchulainn) who finds a yachting cap (in "The Yachting Cap") is convinced that it has overpowered his consciousness and led him to challenge the sea to battle and that he can escape the sea's clutches only by giving the cap back to the sea. Some of Lewis' stories follow traditional genre lines, made slightly offbeat, such as the ghost story in "Pish-Tush" or the bank robbery and con game in "The Two Captains."

Lewis believed that "true satire must be vicious," and his stories reflect this viciousness in their attack on mechanistic behavior, scheming women, brutish men, dull heads, compromising artists, wrongheaded liberals, and general social and political corruption and decay. Lewis' fiction seems modern, and indeed his avant-garde stance anticipated the self-conscious, surrealistic fiction of later generations.

Other major works

NOVELS: *Tarr*, 1918, 1928; *The Childermass*, 1928; *The Apes of God*, 1930; *Snooty Baronet*, 1932; *The Revenge for Love*, 1937; *The Vulgar Streak*, 1941; *Self Condemned*, 1954; *The Human Age: Monstre Gai and Malign Fiesta*, 1955; *The Red Priest*, 1956; *The Roaring Queen*, 1973; *Mrs. Dukes' Million*, 1977.

PLAYS: *Enemy of the Stars*, 1914, 1932; *The Ideal Giant*, 1917.

POETRY: *One-Way Song*, 1933.

NONFICTION: *The Caliph's Design: Architects! Where Is Your Vortex?*, 1919; *Harold Gilman*, 1919; *The Art of Being Ruled*, 1926; *The Lion and the Fox: The Role of the*

Hero in Shakespeare's Plays, 1927; *The Enemy: A Review of Art and Literature*, 1927, 1929; *Time and Western Man*, 1927; *Paleface: The Philosophy of the Melting Pot*, 1929; *Satire and Fiction*, 1930; *Hitler*, 1931; *The Diabolical Principle and the Dithyrambic Spectator*, 1931; *The Doom of Youth*, 1932; *Filibusters in Barbary*, 1932; *The Old Gang and the New Gang*, 1933; *Men Without Art*, 1934; *Left Wings over Europe*, 1936; *Blasting and Bombardiering*, 1937; *Count Your Dead, They Are Alive*, 1937; *The Jews, Are They Human?*, 1939; *Wyndham Lewis: The Artist from "Blast" to Burlington House*, 1939; *The Hitler Cult*, 1939; *America, I Presume*, 1940; *Anglosaxony: A League That Works*, 1941; *America and Cosmic Man*, 1948; *Rude Assignment: A Narrative of My Career Up-to-Date*, 1950; *The Writer and the Absolute*, 1952; *The Demon of Progress in the Arts*, 1954; *Letters of Wyndham Lewis*, 1963 (W. K. Rose, editor); *Wyndham Lewis on Art*, 1969; *Wyndham Lewis: An Anthology of His Prose*, 1969 (E. W. F. Tomlin, editor); *Hitler, the Germans, and the Jews*, 1973 (5 volumes); *Enemy Salvoes: Selected Literary Criticism*, 1976; *Creatures of Habit, Creatures of Change*, 1989.

MISCELLANEOUS: *Collected Poems and Plays*, 1979.

Bibliography

Grigson, Geoffrey. *A Master of Our Time: A Study of Wyndham Lewis.* London: Methuen, 1951. Grigson, a strong admirer of Lewis, argues that "all Lewis's work is one work" and that, whether he was right or wrong about life and politics, one can profit from his intellectual passion and his "crystalline" understanding of art. Grigson also praises Lewis' prose as "Nashe-like," a prose that "demands reading" and that "cannot be absorbed effortlessly like air."

Jameson, Fredric. *Fables of Aggression.* Berkeley: University of California Press, 1979. Jameson, ironically, applies Marxist criticism and psychoanalysis to a staunch anticommunist to argue that Lewis' explosive language practice was a symbolic political act. He explores in Lewis' canon his aggressiveness, sexism, flirtation with Fascism, and polemics against the countercultural trends of his age. He finds Lewis contemplating a sham world filled with unreal puppets, "a paper world of falsefaces and hollow effigies, walking caricatures, split-men, scarecrows and automata," and ultimately denouncing himself for the innocence that led him to misread the political trends of his age.

Kenner, Hugh. *Wyndham Lewis.* Norfolk, Conn.: New Directions, 1954. This critical estimate of the importance of Lewis' writings is reliable and convincing, though its style might be daunting for students. Lewis himself called it a "splendid study." It places each work in the progression of Lewis' career to argue that "Lewis reveals the time's nature" and that "this tough-minded failure . . . was right . . . about Western Man" though wrong about himself as an antithesis. He calls Lewis' harangues "electrifying" and traces themes and concerns throughout his fiction as a whole: his interest in the unreal and in gradations of unreality, in the disharmony of reason and power and the mechanistic nature of human behavior.

Meyers, Jeffrey, ed. *Wyndham Lewis: A Revaluation.* London: Athlone Press, 1980.

Describing Lewis as "the most neglected and underrated major author of this century," Meyers hopes to "stimulate critical appreciation of the depth and diversity of Lewis' fifty years of creative life" by providing essays on his prose style and imagery, his philosophical influences, and representative works in a variety of genres (autobiography, short story, mystery, play, Nietzschean novel, fantasy, satire, political tract, travelogue, and literary criticism). Along with Saul Bellow, he praises Lewis as "a brilliant, thoughtful and original observer" of contemporary society.

Pritchard, William. *Wyndham Lewis.* New York: Twayne, 1968. Pritchard examines Lewis' canon by exploring his various roles: as satiric humorist, sage and mocker, dystopic social critic, literary critic, vulgarian, and self-appraiser. He calls *Rotting Hill* Lewis' "greyist and least artistic" fictive work.

Wagner, Geoffrey. *Wyndham Lewis: A Portrait of the Artist as Enemy.* London: Routledge & Kegan Paul, 1957. Wagner discusses Lewis' interest in group rhythms and herd instinct, his elitism, and his attack on "time." He labels his antagonism toward women partly French and partly antiromanticism. Wagner is puzzled "that a man so sensitive to words could use them so wildly and irresponsibly" in his political writings, finds his satire lacking in universality and his later works indicative of artistic decline, but he praises *The Apes of God* as Lewis' best book: its ideas honest, its every page functional. This study contains a large bibliography but its mine of information about Lewis itself overwhelms the critique.

Gina Macdonald

CLARICE LISPECTOR

Born: Chechelnik, U.S.S.R.; December 10, 1925
Died: Rio de Janeiro, Brazil; December 9, 1977

Principal short fiction

Alguns Contos, 1952; *Laços de Família*, 1960 (*Family Ties*, 1972); *A Legião Estrangeira*, 1964 (*The Foreign Legion*, 1986); *Felicidade Clandestina: Contos*, 1971; *A Imitação da Rosa*, 1973; *Onde Estivestes de Noite*, 1974; *A Via Crucis do Corpo*, 1974; *A Bela e a Fera*, 1979.

Other literary forms

Clarice Lispector achieved almost equal success in the short story and the novel. Her novels include *Perto do Coração Selvagem* (1944; close to the savage heart), *O Lustre* (1946; the chandelier), *A Cidade Sitiada* (1949; the besieged city), *A Maçã no Escuro* (1961; *The Apple in the Dark*, 1967), *Água Viva* (1973; *The Stream of Life*, 1989), and *A Hora da Estrela* (1977; *The Hour of the Star*, 1986). Lispector also wrote a limited number of works for children, the most famous of these being *O Mistério do Coelho Pensante* (1967; the mystery of the thinking rabbit) and *A Mulher Que Matou os Peixes* (1968; the woman who killed the fish). She also wrote nonfiction prose pieces.

Achievements

It is no exaggeration to suggest that Lispector was one of the most original and singular voices to be found in twentieth century Western literature. In a career that spanned more than thirty years, Lispector produced a series of novels and short stories that not only helped lead a generation of Brazilian writers away from the limitations of literary regionalism but also gave Western literature a unique body of narrative work characterized by a highly personal lyrical style, an intense focus on the subconscious, and an almost desperate concern for the individual's need to achieve self-awareness. Though her works earned for her numerous literary awards during her lifetime (including an award she received in 1976 from the Tenth National Literary Competition for her contributions to Brazilian literature), Lispector is only beginning to receive the attention she deserves from critics and readers alike as her spellbinding narratives attract a growing international audience.

Biography

Clarice Lispector was born in the tiny Ukrainian village of Chechelnik on December 10, 1925, while her family was emigrating from the Soviet Union to Brazil. The family settled in the city of Recife in northeastern Brazil before moving to Rio de Janeiro, when Lispector was twelve years old. A precocious child, Lispector began composing stories as early as age six, even attempting to have them published in a local newspaper. A voracious reader in general and a devotee of writers such as

Hermann Hesse and Katherine Mansfield in particular, it was a well-read Clarice Lispector who enter the National Faculty of Law in 1940, from which she was graduated in 1944. While in law school, she first took a job on the editorial staff of the Agência Nacional (a news agency) and then as a reporter for the newspaper *A noite*. It was while working for the newspaper that Lispector began writing her first novel, *Perto do Coração Selvagem*. It was during this period that she met Lúcio Cardoso, an innovative novelist who would serve as her mentor.

Lispector married Mauri Gurgel Valente in 1943 and after being graduated from law school accompanied him to his diplomatic post in Naples, Italy. She followed her husband to Berne, Switzerland, and to Washington, D.C., before separating from him in 1959 and returning with the couple's two children, Pedro and Paulo, to Rio de Janeiro, where she lived and wrote until she died of inoperable cancer only one day before her fifty-second birthday, in 1977.

Analysis

Although Clarice Lispector achieved fame as a novelist as well as a writer of short stories, most critics agree that it is the shorter genre to which the author's storytelling talents, writing style, and thematic concerns are more suited. The bulk of Lispector's stories (particularly those published before 1970, for which the author is most famous) are intense and sharply focused narratives in which a single character (almost always female) is suddenly and dramatically forced to deal with a question concerning an integral part of her existence, and, by extension, on a thematic level, human existence itself. Save for a single act that prompts the character to look inward, there is little action in Lispector's stories, as the author seeks not to develop a plot but instead to capture a moment in her character's life. The central event of each story is not nearly so significant as the character's reaction to it, as he or she is shocked out of complacency and forced into a situation that will lead to self-examination and, in most cases, self-discovery.

Because Lispector's stories focus on the rarefied world of her characters' subconscious, many of the short narratives possess a dreamlike quality. Adding to this quality is the lyrical prose in which the stories are written, a prose in which not only every word but the syntax as well seems to have been very carefully selected, frequently making the reading of the pieces more like reading poetry than prose.

In spite of the emphasis on the inner world of her characters and the subjective and highly metaphorical language, Lispector's stories still maintain contact with the world that exists beyond the confines of her characters' minds. While the characters' reaction to a given situation is intensely personal, the theme dealt with in that reaction is always a universal one, such as frustration, isolation, guilt, insecurity, uncertainty, or the coming of age; in other words, fundamental questions of human existence. Also, the events that trigger these questions in the characters' minds are everyday events of modern society. In this way, Lispector manages to examine both private and universal human concerns while still keeping her stories grounded firmly in reality.

Lispector's first collection of short stories, *Alguns Contos* (some stories), appeared in 1952 and was immediately praised by critics. In fact, this one collection not only placed the author among the elite of Brazil's writers of short fiction of the time, but also it showcased her as a leader among the new generation of writers in this genre.

Alguns Contos contains six stories: "Mistério em São Cristóvão" ("Mystery in São Cristóvão"), "Os Laços de Família" ("Family Ties"), "Começos de Uma Fortuna" ("The Beginnings of a Fortune"), "Amor" ("Love"), "A Galinha" ("The Chicken"), and "O Jantar" ("The Dinner"). All six narratives are lyrical pieces that focus on the act of epiphany—that is, a single moment of crisis or introspection from which the character emerges transformed. The story most representative not only of this collection but also of all Lispector's short fiction is "Love." Its central character, Ana, is a basically satisfied, middle-class wife whose world is stable, controlled, predictable. Taking the tram home from shopping one afternoon, however, she spots a blind man chewing gum. For some reason, Ana's world is totally and inexplicably shaken by the sight of him. Disoriented, she gets off the tram well past her stop and finds herself in the relatively primitive and hostile setting of a botanical garden. Feeling out of place and even threatened, she makes her way home and attempts to resume her normal patterns, but while she is happy to be back in the security of her predictable domestic life-style, she has been profoundly affected by her brief and confusing excursion into a world foreign to her own, and she wonders if she can ever be as happy in her world as she was before.

This story is a Lispector classic, both because it presents a single character whose normal existence is shaken by a seemingly insignificant event, an event that destroys the stable life-style of the character and takes him or her to a new level of awareness concerning life, and because, in large part a result of its language, the story takes on a dreamlike quality that reflects the disoriented state of the protagonist. This story, however, is not unique; it is simply the best of a collection of six similar tales.

As good as *Alguns Contos* is, Lispector's next collection, *Family Ties*, surpasses it. In fact, this collection, the high point of Lispector's work in short fiction, is truly one of the masterpieces of Brazilian literature, regardless of period or genre.

Family Ties is composed of thirteen enigmatic stories, six of which had already appeared in *Alguns Contos*, and once again the stories focus on the act of epiphany. For example, in "Preciosidade" ("Preciousness"), a girl going through puberty experiences both fear and confusion after an ambiguous encounter with some boys. This story is particularly interesting in that the event that triggers the protagonist's reaction is never fully described to the reader. The reader sees the character's reaction to the event, however, and it is that reaction, full of anxiety and uncertainty, that constitutes the story, demonstrating that Lispector is not so concerned with the central event of her stories as she is with her characters' reaction to the event. By not providing details concerning the event in this particular story, she assumes that her reader's concerns are the same as her own. Another interesting story included in this collection is "O Crime do Professor de Matemática" ("The Crime of the Mathematics Professor"), which recounts the story of a man who buries a stray dog he has found dead in a desperate attempt to relieve himself of the guilt he feels for having once abandoned his own dog. Finally, there is "Feliz Aniversário" ("Happy Birthday"), the story of an old woman surrounded by her family on her eighty-ninth birthday. Rather than celebrate, she observes with disdain the offspring she has produced and, much to the shock of those in attendance, spits on the floor to show her lack of respect. All the stories in this collection present individual characters in turmoil and how each deals with this turmoil from the inside out.

Lispector's preoccupation with personal growth through epiphany continues in her third collection of stories, *The Foreign Legion*. Here again, Lispector's protagonists grow as a result of some sort of circumstance in which they find themselves. There is a difference in this collection, however, as the author appears more overtly interested in an existentialist angle concerning her characters' reactions to the situations they confront. For example, in one story, "Viagem a Petrópolis" ("Journey to Petrópolis"), an old woman, told to leave the house in which she has been living, realizes that she is no longer of any use to the world and that she is not only alone but unwanted as well. Her "growth," her manner of dealing with the truth surrounding her existence, is quite fatalistic, existentialist in nature: she dies. In stories in previous collections, the character might well have emerged with some sort of new insight that would have made life more interesting if not better. Here, however, the character merely dies, reflective perhaps of Lispector's growing interest in existentialist thought.

Lispector's fourth collection of stories, *Felicidade Clandestina* (clandestine happiness), follows much the same track as her previous collections. The style is still lyrical, the focus is internal, and the thematic concerns are self-awareness and self-discovery. Yet there are some differences between this collection and the earlier ones. In this work, for example, Lispector is more sharply ironic, at times bordering on an almost cruel humor. Also new, or at least intensified, is the author's criticism concerning the condition of both women and the elderly in modern society, concerns that are present in earlier works but never brought before the reader in such an obvious manner.

After publishing *A Imitação da Rosa* (the imitation of the rose), a collection of some of her best previously published stories, Lispector published *Onde Estivestes de Noite* (where were you last night?). While a number of the pieces included in this collection are indeed stories, fictions in the truest sense, several pieces are personal commentaries or reflections by the author, while still others seem to be a mixture of both fiction and commentary. In the pieces that are in fact stories, it is easy to see that Lispector has abandoned neither her thematic concerns nor her interior perspective. This is best seen in the story entitled "A procura de uma dignidade" (the search for dignity), which focuses on a nearly sixty-year-old woman who becomes lost in the maze of halls and tunnels that run beneath the mammoth soccer stadium of Maracanã. While wandering the halls in search of an escape route, she comes to the realization that she is not only physically lost but psychologically lost as well, that it is indeed possible that her life up to this point, a life lived in large part through her husband, may have been a wasted, empty existence. By the end of the story, she is seeking an escape route from both her physical and her psychological confinements.

A *Via Crucis do Corpo* (the via crucis of the body) is somewhat of a departure from the stories previously published by Lispector—so much so, in fact, that it has confounded critics, most of whom admire it for its quality but nevertheless are left uncertain as to how to interpret it since it does not fit neatly into the Lispector mold. The two main differences between this collection and the others before it is that the stories in this collection contain not only eroticism but also open sexuality, as well as an ample dose of sardonic humor, neither of which is found, at least not to such a degree, in her earlier stories. There is, for example, the story "Miss Ruth Algrave," in which the protagonist is visited by an alien being from Saturn named IXTLAN. He makes love to her and in so doing raises Miss Algrave to a new level of existence. She quits her job and becomes a prostitute while awaiting her extraterrestrial lover's return. Then there is the story "O corpo" (the body), about a bigamist who is murdered by his two wives. Rather than going to the trouble of arresting the two women, the police tell them to leave the country, which they do. This collection is nothing if not entertaining.

Published after her death, *A Bela e a Fera* (the beauty and the beast) is a collection of Lispector stories put together by her friend Olga Borelli. Some of the stories included in this collection were written when the author was a teenager and had never been published. Given the time they were written, these stories and the collection in which they appear are potentially revealing for those interested in the evolution of Lispector the short-story writer. Unlike other collections, however, such as *Alguns Contos, Family Ties,* and *The Foreign Legion, A Bela e a Fera* is not considered a major collection of the author's stories but rather a literary curiosity piece.

Between 1952 and 1977, Clarice Lispector produced a consistent body of short narratives characterized by a sharpness of focus, a lyrical presentation, and a deep and sincere interest in the psychological growth of the individual human being. These three qualities, which pervade all the author's short stories, are the same ones which form her individual literary voice and which will guarantee that the popularity of her short fiction not only endures but also increases as more readers gain access to it.

Other major works

NOVELS: *Perto do Coração Selvagem,* 1944; *O Lustre,* 1946; *A Cidade Sitiada,* 1949; *A Maçã no Escuro,* 1961 (*The Apple in the Dark,* 1967); *A Paixão Segundo G. H.,* 1964 (*The Passion According to G. H.,* 1988); *Uma Aprendizagem: Ou, O Libro dos Prazeres,* 1969 (*An Apprenticeship: Or, The Book of Delights,* 1986); *Água Viva,* 1973 (*The Stream of Life,* 1989); *A Hora da Estrela,* 1977 (*The Hour of the Star,* 1986); *Um Sopro de Vida: Pulsa Cões,* 1978.

NONFICTION: *Para Não Esquecer,* 1978.

CHILDREN'S LITERATURE: *O Mistério do Coelho Pensante,* 1967; *A Mulher Que Matou os Peixes,* 1968.

MISCELLANEOUS: *Selecto de Clarice Lispector,* 1975.

Bibliography

Cook, Bruce. "Women in the Web." Review of *Family Ties. Review 73*, Spring, 1973, 65-66. Cook discusses the lack of Brazilian local color in Lispector's stories and then focuses on the writer's ability to penetrate the internal realities of her characters. He also briefly compares Lispector to Virginia Woolf. Limited reference to selected stories, most notably "The Imitation of the Rose." Descriptive more than analytical.

Fitz, Earl E. *Clarice Lispector.* New York: Twayne, 1985. An excellent, book-length study of Lispector's writings. Chapters include "Biography and Background," "The Place of Clarice Lispector in the History of Brazilian Literature," "Some Intrinsic Considerations: Style, Structure, and Point of View," "Novels and Stories," and "The Nonfiction Work." Both descriptive and analytical. This insightful and extremely readable book is written by the foremost authority on Lispector's works. A must read for serious readers of the Brazilian writer's fiction or for anyone seeking a deeper understanding of both Lispector and her works.

_____. "Freedom and Self-Realization: Feminist Characterization in the Fiction of Clarice Lispector." *Modern Language Studies* 10 (Fall, 1980): 51-61. Fitz explains and defends Lispector's method of characterization and discusses the Brazilian writer's "unique interpretation of feminism," a feminism that encourages her characters "to break the bond of stagnant quiescence that imprisons [them]." This feminism, Fitz contends, "actually pushes [the characters] forward, occasionally with deleterious results, toward freedom and self-realization." Essential reading for the reader who seeks a better understanding of Lispector's characterization methods, her particular brand of feminism, and her characters themselves.

Lindstrom, Naomi. "Clarice Lispector: Articulating Woman's Experience." *Chasqui* 8 (November, 1978): 43-52. Lindstrom examines the narrative voice employed in the short story "Love" (from *Family Ties*) and said voice's relationship to the emerging (and then fading) self-awareness of the protagonist, Ana. Lindstrom shows how the narrator first dominates the story, then allows Ana to speak more, before retaking the narrative in the end as the protagonist "finds no supportive response." An interesting slant on an important story in Lispector's body of work.

Moisés, Massaud. "Clarice Lispector: Fiction and Cosmic Vision," translated by Sara M. McCabe. *Studies in Short Fiction* 8 (Winter, 1971): 268-281. A study of how the thematics of Lispector's short fiction reflect and support the author's "cosmic vision." Moisés discusses, for example, "the privileged moment," in which "the 'I' and the universe meet as if for the first time, framed in a halo of original 'purity,' causing the mutual discovery to become suspended in time, a vision of the most intimate part of reality, without deformation of thought or prejudice." An excellent article on the themes in Lispector's short fiction.

Nunes, Maria Luisa. "Narrative Modes in Clarice Lispector's *Laços de Família:* The Rendering of Consciousness." *Luso-Brazilian Review* 14 (Winter, 1977): 174-184. Citing several stories in *Family Ties*, Nunes examines how Lispector renders the consciousness of her protagonists, stating that the Brazilian writer employs "*style indirect libre* or narrated monologue, interior monologue, internal analysis including sensory impressions, direct discourse in the form of 'asides,' and the mixture of many of the above techniques." Nunes explains each technique and demonstrates how each is used by Lispector to reveal the inner workings of her characters. Insightful and very readable.

Peixoto, Marta. "*Family Ties*: Female Development in Clarice Lispector." In *The Voyage In: Fictions of Female Development*, edited by Elizabeth Abel, Marianne Hirsch, and Elizabeth Langland. Hanover, N.H.: University Press of New England, 1983. Peixoto focuses on the protagonists of the stories in *Family Ties*, stories that the critic believes "can be read as versions of a single developmental tale that provides patterns of female possibilities, vulnerability, and power in Lispector's world." Peixoto examines the epiphanies experienced by the female protagonists of several stories, epiphanies that allow the characters, although only momentarily, to break out of their "metaphoric prisons formed by their eager compliance with conforming social roles." An excellent piece.

Keith H. Brower

JACK LONDON

Born: San Francisco, California; January 12, 1876
Died: Glen Ellen, California; November 22, 1916

Principal short fiction

The Son of the Wolf, 1900; *The God of His Fathers and Other Stories,* 1901; *Children of the Frost,* 1902; *The Faith of Men and Other Stories,* 1904; *Tales of the Fish Patrol,* 1905; *Moon-Face and Other Stories,* 1906; *Love of Life and Other Stories,* 1906; *Lost Face,* 1910; *When God Laughs and Other Stories,* 1911; *South Sea Tales,* 1911; *The House of Pride and Other Tales of Hawaii,* 1912; *A Son of the Sun,* 1912; *Smoke Bellew Tales,* 1912; *The Night-Born,* 1913; *The Strength of the Strong,* 1914; *The Turtles of Tasman,* 1916; *The Human Drift,* 1917; *The Red One,* 1918; *On the Makaloa Mat,* 1919; *Dutch Courage and Other Stories,* 1922.

Other literary forms

Jack London's more than fifty published books include plays, children's fiction, novels, sociological studies, essays, and short stories. Although generally known as a writer of short fiction, London is remembered today also for two novels, *The Call of the Wild* (1903) and *The Sea-Wolf* (1904), both of which have been made into motion pictures several times. London is also credited with pioneering work in the development of tramp fiction (*The Road,* 1907) and science fiction (*The Star Rover,* 1915).

Achievements

London's numerous stories and his many novels capture with a bold and sometimes brutal reality the confrontation between humans and nature, which by some writers may easily have been portrayed romantically. Instead, London was at the forefront of the move toward naturalistic fiction and realism. He was influenced by social Darwinism, and his stories often reflect the idea that human beings, to survive, must adapt to nature yet are themselves creatures of nature, subject to forces they do not really understand. London was also interested in Marxism, and his work often employs a working-class hero.

London's realistic stories were very popular in the United States when they were first published and continue to be so. He has also achieved wide popularity abroad, with his work being translated into more than fifty languages. His stories in the naturalistic mode continue to influence writers.

Biography

Largely self-educated, Jack London was the product of California ranches and the working-class neighborhoods of Oakland. London's rise to fame came as a result of the Klondike Gold Rush. Unsuccessful in his attempt to break into the magazine market, he joined the flood of men rushing to make instant riches in the Yukon. Although he found little gold, he returned after the winter of 1897 with a wealth of memories and notes of the Northland, the gold rush, and the hardships of the trail. London married Elizabeth May Maddern in 1900, and the couple settled in Oakland, soon adding two daughters to the family. The marriage, however, was not successful, and London divorced his wife in 1905 and married Charmian Kittredge the same year. With Charmian, he sailed across the Pacific aboard a small yacht, intending to continue around the world on a seven-year voyage. The trip ended in Australia, however, when ill-health forced London to abandon the voyage after only two years. London's last years were spent in the construction of a scientifically run ranch complex in Glen Ellen, Sonoma County, California. It was there that he died at age forty, on November 22, 1916. His death still has not been satisfactorily explained.

Analysis

London's fame as a writer came about largely through his ability to interpret realistically humans' struggle in a hostile environment. Early in his career, London realized that he had no talent for invention and that in his writing he would have to be an interpreter of the things which are rather than a creator of the things which might be. Accordingly he turned to the Canadian Northland, the locale where he had gained experience, for his settings and characters. Later on he would move his setting to the primitive South Seas, after his travels had also made him familiar with that region. By turning to harsh, frontier environment for his setting and themes, London soon came to be a strong voice heard over the genteel tradition of nineteenth century parlor-fiction writers. His stories became like the men and women about whom he wrote—bold, violent, sometimes primitive. London was able to give his stories greater depth by using his extraordinary powers of narrative and language, and by infusing them with a remarkable sense of irony.

"To Build a Fire" has often been called London's masterpiece. It is a story which contrasts the intelligence of human beings with the intuition of the animal and suggests that humans alone cannot successfully face the harsh realities of nature. The story begins at dawn as a man and his dog walk along a trail which eventually could lead them, thirty-two miles away, to a companion's cabin and safety. The air is colder than the man has ever experienced before, and although the man does not know about the cold, the dog does. While the animal instinctively realizes that it is time to curl up in the snow and wait for warmer weather, the man lacks the imagination which would give him a grasp of the laws of nature. Such perception would have enabled him to see the absurdity of attempting to combat the unknown, especially since an old-timer had warned him about the dangers of the cold to inexperienced men. With his warm mittens, thick clothes, and heavy coat, the man feels prepared for the cold and protected while the dog longs for the warmth of a fire. As the man walks along the trail, he looks carefully for hidden traps of nature, springs under the snow beneath which pools of water lie, since to step into one of these pools would mean calamity. Once he forces the dog to act as a trail breaker for him, and, when the dog breaks through and ice immediately forms on its extremities, the man helps the dog remove the ice.

At midday the man stops, builds a fire, and eats his lunch. The dog, without knowing why, feels relieved; he is safe. The man, however, does not stay beside the fire; he continues on the trail and forces the dog onward too. Finally, inevitably, the man wets his feet. Although he builds a fire to dry out, snow puts out the fire, and before he can build another fire, the cold envelops him, and he freezes to death. The dog senses the man's death and continues on the trail toward the cabin, wherein lies food and the warmth of a fire.

The irony of the story, of course, is that the man, even with the benefit of all the tools with which civilization has provided him, fails in his attempt to conquer nature and instead falls victim to it, while the dog, equipped only with the instinct which nature has provided, survives. The story, representing London's most mature expression of pessimism, stresses the inability of human beings to shape their environment and conquer the unknown. Unlike the dog, they cannot draw from instinct since civilization has deprived them of it. They are therefore unfit and totally unequipped to face the unknown and conquer the cosmic power.

"Law of Life" exhibits another recurring theme in London's work, the inability of humans to assert positive values. It tells the story of the last moments of life for an old Indian. As the tale begins, the old man, son of the chief of the tribe, sits by a small fire with a bundle of wood nearby. The tribesmen are busy breaking camp in preparation for departure since they must go to new hunting grounds in order to survive. The old man, too old to benefit the tribe further, represents only a burden to the rest of his society and must therefore stay behind. As the man sits beside the fire, he remembers the days of his youth and an incident when he tracked an old moose. The animal had become separated from the rest of the herd and was being trailed by wolves. Twice the young Indian had come across the scene of a struggle between the moose and the wolves, and twice the moose had survived. Finally, the Indian witnessed the kill, the old moose dying so that the wolves might live. The moose-wolf analogy to the old Indian's situation, of course, is obvious, and as the story closes, the old Indian feels the muzzle of a wolf upon his cheek. At first he picks up a burning ember in preparation for battle, but then resigns himself to the inevitability of fate and extinguishes it.

London uses several vehicles to express his pessimism. Like the protagonist in "To Build a Fire," the old Indian is a man of limited vision. Encircled by an ever-constricting set of circumstances, he waits by a dying fire for his own death. Finally, as the moose-wolf analogy has foretold, the inevitability of nature dominates. As the story ends, the fire goes out, the wolves are no longer kept at bay, and the reader is left repulsed by the knowledge of the Indian's horrible death. London employs a number of symbols in this story as well. The fire gives light which symbolizes life, as does the white snow which falls gently at the beginning of the story. As the fire ebbs, the man remembers the grey wolves, and at the end of the moose-wolf analogy, London writes of the dark point in the midst of the stamped snow, foretelling the end of the fire, and thus of life.

Although London's earlier stories embody a pessimism which reflects humans' helplessness in challenging the unknown, his later ones mark a dramatic changeover. Following an intensive study of Carl Jung and Sigmund Freud, London began writing stories in the last years of his life which reflected his discovery of some unique human quality that enabled humans to challenge successfully the cosmos and withstand the crushing forces of nature. One of London's last stories, also with a Northland setting, reflects this change of philosophy and contrasts markedly with the earlier "To Build a Fire" and "Law of Life." "Like Argus of Ancient Times" begins as a largely autobiographical account of London's trek to Dawson City with a man known as "Old Man" or "John" Tarwater. Unlike the unnamed protagonist of "To Build a Fire," Tarwater is totally unequipped to face the rigors and challenges of the north. He is old and weak; furthermore, he arrives on the trail without money, camping gear, food, and proper clothing. Somehow he manages to join a group of miners, serve as their cook, and earn his passage to Dawson. Although the winter snows force the group to make camp until spring, Tarwater (who is also called "Old Hero" and "Father Christmas") is driven by gold fever. He strikes out on his own, gets lost in a snowstorm, and falls to the ground, drifting off into a dreamlike world between consciousness and unconsciousness. Unlike London's earlier characters, Tarwater survives this confrontation with nature, awakens from his dream, turns toward the "rebirthing east," and discovers a treasure of gold in the ground. Couched in Jungian terms, the story is directly analogous to the Jungian concepts of the wandering hero who, undertaking a dangerous night journey in search of treasure difficult to attain, faces death, reaches the highest pinnacle of life, and emerges in the East, reborn. "Like Argus of Ancient Times" marks London's return to the many stories he wrote in which the hero feels the call of adventure, encounters difficulties and confronts nature, battles with death, and finally achieves dignity.

Often called the successor to Edgar Allan Poe, an imitator of Rudyard Kipling, or a leader of writers emerging from the nineteenth century, London wrote stories which mark the conflict between the primitive and the modern, between optimism and pessimism. He created fiction which combined actuality and ideals, realism and romance, and rational versus subjective responses to life. More than a new Poe, imitator of Kipling, or new genre writer, however, London is a legitimate folk hero whose greatness stems from his primordial vision and ability to center upon the fundamental human struggles for salvation and fears of damnation.

Other major works

NOVELS: *A Daughter of the Snows*, 1902; *The Call of the Wild*, 1903; *The Sea-Wolf*, 1904; *The Game*, 1905; *White Fang*, 1906; *Before Adam*, 1906; *The Iron Heel*, 1907; *Martin Eden*, 1909; *Burning Daylight*, 1910; *Adventure*, 1911; *The Abysmal Brute*, 1913; *The Valley of the Moon*, 1913; *The Mutiny of the Elsinore*, 1914; *The Scarlet Plague*, 1915; *The Star Rover*, 1915; *The Little Lady of the Big House*, 1916; *Jerry of the Islands*, 1917; *Michael, Brother of Jerry*, 1917; *Hearts of Three*, 1920; *The Assassination Bureau, Ltd.*, 1963 (completed by Robert L. Fish).

PLAYS: *Scorn of Women*, 1906; *Theft*, 1910; *The Acorn-Planter*, 1916.

NONFICTION: *The Kempton-Wace Letters*, 1903 (with Anna Strunsky); *The People of the Abyss*, 1903; *The War of the Classes*, 1905; *The Road*, 1907; *Revolution and Other Essays*, 1910; *The Cruise of the Snark*, 1911; *John Barleycorn*, 1913; *Letters from Jack London*, 1965 (King Hendricks and Irving Shepard, editors).
CHILDREN'S LITERATURE: *The Cruise of the Dazzler*, 1902.

Bibliography
Hedrick, Joan D. *Solitary Comrade: Jack London and His Work*. Chapel Hill: University of North Carolina Press, 1982. Hedrick interweaves a discussion of London's stories and novels with details of his life in an attempt to see behind London's self-created myth. She does some close reading of the stories and includes a useful bibliography and an index.
Labor, Earle. *Jack London*. New York: Twayne, 1974. Labor combines a biographical look at London with extensive discussions of London's short stories and novels. He puts London's work into a biographical, historical, and political context and clearly presents London's major thematic concerns. Includes an annotated bibliography and an index.
London, Jack. *The Letters of Jack London*. Edited by Earle Labor, Robert C. Leitz III, and I. Milo Shepard. 3 vols. Stanford, Calif.: Stanford University Press, 1988. Includes the most significant letters of the thousands London wrote during his lifetime. The editors have thoroughly annotated each letter, explaining references and identifying people. The letters include love letters, letters to editors and publishers, and to fellow writers on London's ideas and methods, as well as to friends and family.
McClintock, James I. *White Logic: Jack London's Short Stories*. Grand Rapids, Mich.: Wolf House Books, 1975. McClintock's work is the only one to focus solely on London's short stories. He provides a detailed analysis of the stories in a clear and useful way.
Sinclair, Andrew. *Jack: A Biography of Jack London*. London: Weidenfeld & Nicolson, 1978. A well-researched, extensively documented biography that focuses on London's life rather than his work. Includes a bibliography and many photographs.
Stone, Irving. *Sailor on Horseback: The Story of Jack London*. Boston: Houghton Mifflin, 1938. Stone's popular biography seems somewhat dated, but it was the biography that helped to perpetuate the myth that London created for himself of the self-educated, self-reliant adventurer. There is no bibliography or index.

David Mike Hamilton
(Revised by *Karen M. Cleveland Marwick*)

AUGUSTUS BALDWIN LONGSTREET

Born: Augusta, Georgia; September 22, 1790
Died: Oxford, Mississippi; July 9, 1870

Principal short fiction

Georgia Scenes, Characters, Incidents, Etc. in the First Half Century of the Republic, 1835.

Other literary forms

Although Augustus Baldwin Longstreet's unquestioned masterpiece is *Georgia Scenes*, he also published a variety of books, pamphlets, letters, and other materials, most of which deal with politics, religion, or the South, and often with the intersection of the three. Perhaps the most significant is *Letters on the Epistle of Paul to Philemon: Or, The Connection of Apostolic Christianity with Slavery* (1845), a closely reasoned defense of slavery on biblical grounds. *A Voice from the South, Comprising Letters from Georgia to Massachusetts* (1847) vehemently sets forth antebellum Southern political positions. Late in life he published a long-contemplated didactic novel on the folly of indulging youth, *Master William Mitten: Or, A Youth of Brilliant Talents Who Was Ruined by Bad Luck* (1864).

Achievements

Longstreet is best known for his collection of humorous tales, *Georgia Scenes*. His use of the tall-tale form, vernacular speech, and the setting of the Georgia frontier (then considered part of the "southwest") marks him as foremost among the Southwest humorists. In a form known for its combination of oral folklore with more traditional forms such as the sketch, Longstreet's contributions are marked for their polished, literary quality. Like the border region that comprises his settings, Longstreet's stories reveal a literary territory that combines genteel prose with raucous renderings of local scenes and characters. He often uses an Addisonian-type gentleman narrator who describes the less civilized, more outrageous behavior of the "locals." Later writers such as Mark Twain and William Faulkner make similar use of the contrast between exaggerated storytelling and vivid, even cynical, realism. Longstreet's renderings of unique Georgia characters, who speak in uncensored and often hilarious voices, place him firmly within the tradition of Southern literature.

Biography

Augustus Baldwin Longstreet was born in Augusta, Georgia, on September 22, 1790. He was graduated from Yale and from the Litchfield Law School, then widely considered the finest in America, and returned to Augusta in 1814. He became a successful lawyer and subsequently a judge. He left the bench, became a farmer, and, a little later, a newspaper editor. It was during this period that he published, first periodically and then in book form, his *Georgia Scenes* (1835). In 1838, Longstreet became a professing Christian and a most active Methodist minister; the next year he was appointed the first president of Emory College, a Methodist institution, and in following years he served as president of Centenary College in Louisiana, the University of Mississippi, and the University of South Carolina. Longstreet died July 9, 1870, and was buried in Oxford, Mississippi.

Analysis

Augustus Baldwin Longstreet's *Georgia Scenes* covers such a remarkably wide variety of behavior that he largely succeeds in his ambition to be a social historian. He vividly pictures men involved in such noble occupations as "The Horse-Swap," "The Fight," "The Militia Company Drill," and "The Foxhunt." He portrays women as charming their beaux with an impromptu concert in "The Song," engaging in polite battles of status and manipulation in "The Ball," or simply gossiping into the wee hours in "A Sage Conversation." Longstreet structures some "scenes," less typical but often more interesting, around elaborate practical jokes: "The Character of a Native Georgian" follows Ned Brace through an involved series of capers that bewilder dozens of people; in "The Debating Society," two young men confound their peers by putting up for discussion a completely incomprehensible question; and in "The Wax-Works," a group of touring rowdies try to swindle enough for their tavern bill by masquerading as wax figures at an exhibition.

Longstreet combines many of these elements in the book's brief opening sketch, "Georgia Theatrics." The narrator begins in uncharacteristically precise fashion: "If my memory fail me not, the 10th of June, 1809, found me, at about eleven o'clock in the forenoon, ascending a long and gentle slope in what was called 'The Dark Corner' of Lincoln [County]." In a kind of thematic prelude to the volume as a whole, he explains that the corner was "Dark" from a "moral darkness" which, he avers, by "wonderful transitions," has been dispelled in the past quarter century. The narrator takes care, however, to distinguish the area's former "*moral* condition" from its "*natural* condition." The latter, in terms of physical contours, trees, streams, birds, flowers, he characterizes as idyllic. Early in the sketch, as the narrator mounts a slope, the aura of Edenic grace shatters with a concatenation of "loud, profane, and boisterous voices," the source hidden in the undergrowth. Violent oaths give way to sounds of muffled blows and terrific thrashings; the narrator watches the largely obscured back of one man rise briefly, then plunge heavily, "and at the same instant I heard a cry in the accent of keenest torture, 'Enough! My eye's out!' " The victor rises bragging until he sees the narrator, then looks "excessively embarrassed." The narrator orders the swaggering bully to help him aid the horribly maimed victim, but the young victor defiantly replies that there has been no one else involved: "I was jist seein' how I could 'a' *fout.*" He then bounds over to a plough that he had left in a fence corner several yards off. The narrator surveys the battlefield; in the soft dirt, he sees two thumb prints, about as far apart as a man's eyes; ". . . would you believe it, gentle reader? his report was true. All that I had heard and seen was nothing more nor less than a Lincoln rehearsal, in which the youth who had just left me had played all the parts of all the characters in a court-house fight."

The brief sketch effectively introduces several of the book's dominant motifs: violence, crude humor, cultural conflict, close attention to physical detail, and a style that abruptly alternates between the narrator's polite affectation and the powerful dialect of the lower classes.

Many of these elements reach a sort of climax in "The Gander-pulling," a sketch which none of the others can top for sheer crudity and high spirits. Longstreet sets the scene in 1798, just beyond the outskirts of Augusta proper and not far from three very close satellite "towns." He opens reprinting an "advurtysement" for the gander-pulling, a notice every bit as enthusiastically unconventional in its phrasing as in its spelling. After elaborately describing the general area and petty rivalries of the neighboring towns, he details the immediate scene of action. The locals have outlined a circular path about forty yards in diameter around which the entrants will ride their horses. At one point on each side of the path, about ten feet apart, stands a post; between the posts a rope is slung loosely enough that a gander attached can vibrate in an arc of four or five feet. The gander-pull impresario, Ned Prator, first passes a hat into which each contestant tosses twenty-five cents, the sum to be the victor's prize. He next proceeds to bind the gander's feet and then to coat the bird's neck liberally with goose grease—inspiring in the narrator an ironic paean to the gander's former mate. Finally Prator attaches the gander to the rope directly over the path, stations men at the posts to whip any horse inclined to dawdle, arranges in a rough line the contestants mounted on their increasingly spooky horses, and sets them off. The riders make three raucous but uneventful rounds until one man, riding a horse aptly named Miss Sally Spitfire, finally makes a solid grab, jerks the gander's neck close to his startled horse's head, while at the same instant each of the two lashers lays on with all his might. The crazed horse gives one look at the gander, feels both lashes, and bolts through the crowd carrying along a circus worth of bawling dogs, alarmed and belled cattle, and three tobacco-rollers, hauling over all in her path until she arrives at not just one airborne gander but a whole flock immediately at her feet. She stops suddenly enough to convert her rider into an unguided projectile. Gridiron, a second and rather more coolly rational horse, ignores his rider's whoops, kicks, and lashings, while he pauses to examine and consider Miss Sally Spitfire's experience, and then heaves a deep sigh.

> It was plain that his mind was now made up; but, to satisfy the world that he would do nothing rashly, he took another view, and then wheeled and went for Harrisburg as if he had set in for a year's running. Nobody whooped at Gridiron, for all saw that his running was purely the result of philosophic deduction.

One of two of the remaining contestants seems most certain to win on each succeeding round, especially after one breaks the neck, but finally a third jerks away the head to win the prize. He brags and struts outrageously, but, as he and his audience are all aware since he triumphed through luck rather than skill, his vaunting puts the whole crowd in a high good humor—except for one little man who lost his bet of six quarts of huckleberries: "*He* could not be reconciled until he fretted himself into a pretty little *piny*-woods fight, in which he got whipped, and then he went home perfectly satisfied."

Much of the piece's charm derives from the relaxed focus which easily shifts from the advertisement to the area's history to the field of competition to the organizer to the gander to the competitors to the horses to the victor and on to the end, no one element taking precedence over another. Longstreet focuses where and how he pleases to gain maximum local effect from each element of his sketch—which is precisely the sum of its parts. What the sketch does not have is a controlling fictional perspective that can compel the piece to do more than merely sum up its parts, more than exploit a fascinating, bizarre, and self-sufficient surface. Longstreet vividly represents the gander-pulling but merely represents it rather than significantly developing a meaningful experience arising out of that activity; consequently, he produces here one of his typical sketches rather than a story.

In the final section of *Georgia Scenes*, "The Shooting-match," Longstreet does produce a genuine short story, although—compared to earlier pieces in the book— in some ways a rather bland one. About a year ago, the narrator tells the reader, traveling on business in Northeastern Georgia, he encountered a small man carrying a massive old rifle and bound for a shooting-match. The native, Billy Curlew, learns that this well-dressed stranger (the narrator) is the same person who, years ago as a child barely large enough to hold a shotgun, had earned a lasting reputation in a shooting match—and incidentally a fine silk handkerchief for Billy's father who had bet on the boy. The narrator admits that the shot years before had been pure luck, but Billy talks him into coming along to see the fun.

When they arrive, Billy, unreservedly a partisan of the man who won his father's bet so long ago, startles the narrator by arranging for him to have a shot in the match, but none of the locals fear much from the strange dude. The narrator then vividly details the rules, target, prizes, contestants, and finally the shifting fortunes of all in the match. Hoping to delay his humiliation as long as possible, the narrator insists on shooting last. The dreaded time arrives, his arms cannot hold the ponderous rifle without trembling, and he paradoxically begins bragging (quite unconvincingly) to relieve somehow his own acute embarrassment. Finally, on impulse he halfheartedly fires and amazes absolutely everyone—except Billy—by making the second best shot of the day, missing first prize (won by Billy) by only fractions of an inch. Except for a handful of agnostics, the narrator converts the whole crowd, who promise to vote for him no matter what office he is seeking. When he objects that he is seeking no office, they insist he let them know when he does, for they would all back him to the death. "If you ever come out for anything," Billy vows, "jist let the boys of Upper Hogthief know it, and they'll go for you to the hilt, against creation, tit or no tit, that's the *tatur.*"

The story capitalizes on some nice ironies: generous backwoods Billy seems fated to share in the narrator's humiliation but has judged better than anyone else. The narrator's nervous bragging during his ludicrous preliminaries ironically helps him to carry the day once he fires his shot. The narrator deserves a rich load of back-woods contempt for his lack of manliness but winds up with a whole region ready to back him to a man. Here Longstreet uses a fine rhetorical sensitivity to prepare, develop, and capitalize on his climactic surprise. Unlike a typical Georgia "scene," this story has no extraneous characters, no long descriptions or discussions of purely local interest, and no digressions to include bizarre comic incidents. Longstreet fo-cuses not, as usual, on broadly representing typical scenes, characters, or actions, but more narrowly on re-creating the narrator's experience, an experience which encompasses his sympathy for the sympathetic Billy Curlew. Here Longstreet has created a genuine short story by concentrating, uncharacteristically, on form at the expense of content. Later frontier humorists and local-color writers learned tech-niques which allowed them the best of both dimensions, but they could hardly have written as well as or as intelligently without the pioneering example of *Georgia Scenes.*

Other major works

NOVEL: *Master William Mitten: Or, A Youth of Brilliant Talents Who Was Ruined by Bad Luck*, 1864.
NONFICTION: *Letters on the Epistle of Paul to Philemon: Or, The Connection of Apostolic Christianity with Slavery*, 1845; *A Voice from the South, Comprising Let-ters from Georgia to Massachusetts*, 1847; *Letters from President Longstreet to the Know-Nothing Preachers of the Methodist Church South*, 1855.

Bibliography

Blair, Walter. *Native American Humor, 1800-1900.* New York: American Book, 1931. This classic in American humor studies provides a general discussion of nine-teenth century humorists, an extensive bibliography (which is outdated but useful in its listing of "Individual Writers of Native American Humor"), and more than one hundred selections from a wide range of authors. The chapter on "Humor of the Old Southwest" discusses Longstreet among his contemporaries.
Brown, Carolyn S. *The Tall Tale in American Folklore and Literature.* Knoxville: University of Tennessee Press, 1987. Brown traces the origins of the popular tale in both folklore and literature. Chapter 3, "Flush Times: Varieties of Written Tales," has an extended analysis of Longstreet's *Georgia Scenes.* Brown does not over-simplify in her discussion of Longstreet's sketches but rather explores the com-plexity of his work within the tall-tale tradition.
Fitzgerald, Oscar Penn. *Judge Longstreet: A Life Sketch.* Nashville: Methodist Epis-copal Church, 1891. Bishop Fitzgerald's biography covers Longstreet's life and work in eloquent terms—and at times does little to dispel some of the reigning legends surrounding Longstreet. Exaggerations aside, this biography distinguishes itself by the inclusion of many letters to and from Longstreet, allowing a more personal glimpse into the life of a complex and talented man.
King, Kimball. *Augustus Baldwin Longstreet.* Boston: Twayne, 1984. King's study

provides an excellent general discussion of Longstreet's life and work. Much of the book discusses *Georgia Scenes*, Longstreet's major work of short fiction, and gives a wealth of background material on both the writing and subject matter of *Georgia Scenes*. The annotated list of secondary sources is a very useful component of this book.

Wade, John Donald. *Augustus Baldwin Longstreet: A Study of the Development of Culture in the South*. New York: Macmillan, 1924. This engaging biography of Longstreet, the result of Wade's extensive research, tells about the life of a literary man whose interests and activities ranged far beyond that of writing humorous sketches. Wade refers not only to the *Georgia Scenes* but also to Longstreet's career as a lawyer and judge, his religious and political interests, and his terms as president of several leading universities in the South.

Walter Evans
(Revised by *Ann A. Merrill*)

H. P. LOVECRAFT

Born: Providence, Rhode Island; August 20, 1890
Died: Providence, Rhode Island; March 15, 1937

Principal short fiction
The Dunwich Horror and Others, 1963; *Dagon, and Other Macabre Tales*, 1965; *The Horror in the Museum, and Other Revisions*, 1970.

Other literary forms
Except for his personal correspondence, H. P. Lovecraft's total output was quite modest, even considering his relatively short life. Like that of his illustrious predecessor, Edgar Allan Poe, almost all of Lovecraft's narratives are in the shorter forms, with at most three works qualifying as novelettes. Other than fiction, his writings consist of some poetry, a few essays on literature and science, and a voluminous amount of personal correspondence, much of which has been published. In addition to his own work, Lovecraft revised, rewrote, and "ghosted" a large number of works for other authors, including one short story for Harry Houdini. Although a number of his stories have served as the basis for films, the products have seldom resembled the originals. Indicative of this is the ironical fact that probably the most successful adaptation of Lovecraftian material was released under the title "Edgar Allan Poe's *Haunted Palace.*"

Achievements
Lovecraft brought an intimate knowledge of the short story to his horror-story creations. Beginning as a ghost writer and pulp-fiction hack, Lovecraft produced a body of tales that is still viewed as important by those who write fantasies on the dark side: Robert Bloch and Stephen King, to name only two who cite Lovecraft as an important influence on their own work. Of equal importance is Lovecraft's study of horror literature, *Supernatural Horror in Literature* (1945), in which he outlines the structure of the tale of terror. This work is still cited as an important study in the narrative structure of the horror story.

Biography
Except for a few trips with friends in the last years of his life and residence in New York City during part of his brief marriage to Sonia Greene, Howard Phillips Lovecraft spent almost all of his life in Providence, Rhode Island, living with aunts in genteel poverty on the diminishing family capital. Most of the money he made as a writer came from collaborative efforts and ghost-writing. As a pulp-fiction author he wrote too little to make much money and was too reticent to sell much of what he did produce. By far, the bulk of his writing was done for unpaying amateur publications and in personal correspondence. Lovecraft died at age forty-six of intestinal cancer.

Analysis

The critical acceptance of H. P. Lovecraft as an important American writer, and as the finest exponent of dark fantasy since Poe, has not come quickly or easily. Much of this neglect was due to a blanket rejection of the "pulp writer," reinforced by the fact that Lovecraft published nothing in book form during his own lifetime. The primary outlet for his stories was *Weird Tales*, a pulp magazine whose circulation barely reached twenty thousand a month although its influence on horror fiction has been enormous. Moreover, Lovecraft's entire oeuvre was modest in size and, for reasons both personal and commercial, a considerable portion of it never saw print during his lifetime.

There are, perhaps, even more obvious reasons for this general critical dismissal: in many ways Lovecraft was a poor writer. The prose is often vague, ornate, and studded with overblown adjectives such as "eldrich," "uncanny," "hellish," and "weird." At a time when even the pulps featured the hard, lean prose of a Dashiell Hammett or James M. Cain, Lovecraft's purple verbosity sounded like a relic from the mid-nineteenth century. His characterization tends to be flat and undifferentiated. His plots sometimes collapse in the middle or disintegrate altogether, and his strain for sensational effect occasionally becomes painful. Lovecraft's characteristically italicized last-line climaxes—"*and the Monster was Real!!!*"—sometimes evoke more laughter than dread.

How then can the reader take this author seriously, let alone grant him status as an important writer? The answer lies in the two unique contributions Lovecraft made to the supernatural horror genre in particular and to modern literature in general: his original approach to dark fantasy revitalized the genre and has influenced every important new writer in the field, and the vision that animates his fictions transcended the limits of the popular genre to offer a provocative and significant view of modern man's predicament.

Because it has been so frequently anthologized, Lovecraft's best-known work is probably the somewhat uncharacteristic short story "The Outsider." An unnamed narrator laments his unhappy, bizarre youth. Having grown up bereft of human contact in a dismal, decaying castle, filled with damp "crumbling corriders" that smell like "piled-up corpses of dead generations," he resolves to escape by ascending a partly ruined black tower whose top "reaches above the trees into the unknown outer sky." After a difficult, perilous climb the narrator reaches a trapdoor, which he pushes open. To his amazement, he finds that he is not, as expected, on some "lofty eminence," but is, instead, "*on the solid ground.*" Wandering about, he then comes upon a castle where a party is in full progress. As he enters, the guests run screaming. He assumes that there is a horrible presence lurking near him and becomes frightened. Sighting the beast, he overcomes his fears and approaches it, finally touching the thing's "*rotting outstretched paw.*" Terrified, he flees back to the trapdoor but finds it blocked. Thus, he is forced to linger on the fringes of the world of the living, alienated from all contact with its inhabitants. In the last sentence of the story, the speaker reveals what he touched that so frightened him: "*a cold and unyield-*

ing surface of polished glass."

The effect of this story on the reader is chilling—even if the story, when analyzed, is a bit absurd. Lovecraft succeeds in gaining the reader's sympathetic identification with the narrator so the revelation of its monstrous being is a shock; and the experience itself is almost archetypal. One ingenious critic has offered five separate and different interpretations of the tale: autobiographical, psychological (Jungian), metaphysical, philosophical, and political. Although none of these readings is completely satisfying, they all have some merit and illustrate the important point: "The Outsider" evokes emotional responses that are not fully explained by critical exegesis.

At the same time, the story turns essentially on a clever deception: the reader is tricked into identifying with a creature who turns out to be a corpse or zombie or ghoul or something of that sort, a fact that is not revealed until the punch line. So the sensitive reader is likely to be moved and irritated by a story that seems both profound and trivial. This mixed reaction is characteristic of many of Lovecraft's stories, and any attempt to assess his importance must somehow take it into consideration.

Despite its popularity, "The Outsider" does not suggest the full range of the author's powers. At best it is a story with more resonance than substance, a very clever exercise in imitating Poe. To truly appreciate Lovecraft one must examine his central vision—the somewhat misnamed "Cthulhu Mythos." (The term was coined by August Derleth, but Cthulhu is not really the major figure in the hierarchy. Contemporary Lovecraftians prefer to call it the "Lovecraft Mythos.")

The Mythos did not spring full blown from Lovecraft's head but emerged in bits and pieces. In "Nyarlathotep," a fragment, Lovecraft presented the first important figure in his pantheon. "The Nameless City" introduced the "mad Arab, Abdul Alhazrad," author of the *Necronomicon*, a fictive text of magical spells and arcane knowledge which became the Bible of the Mythos. The book itself was brought into "The Hound" and "The Festival," the latter story being the first set in the "Arkham, Massachusetts" region, site of most Mythos tales. It was not until 1926, however, that Lovecraft really consolidated his ideas and presented them in a single story, "The Call of Cthulhu."

The artistic assumption behind the Mythos is that by the 1920's the usual menaces of horror fiction—such as Satan, demons, werewolves, and vampires—had become overworked and obsolete. A new set of menaces, he felt, one more in keeping with contemporary views of humans and their place in the universe, was needed to breathe life into the genre.

The metaphysical assumption behind the Mythos is stated in the famous first paragraph of "The Call of Cthulhu":

> The most merciful thing in the world, I think, is the inability of the human mind to correlate all its contents. We live on a placid island of ignorance in the midst of black seas of infinity, and it was not meant that we should voyage far. The sciences, each straining in its own direction, have hitherto harmed us little; but some day the piecing together of dissociated knowledge will open up

such terrifying vistas of reality, and of our frightful position therein, that we shall either go mad from the revelation or flee from the deadly light into the peace and safety of a new dark age.

In the Cthulhu Mythos, that "terrifying reality" consists of an order of beings, vast, powerful, and immortal, who hover at the edges of humans' consciousness, poised to enter their world and sweep them away like so much useless debris. These creatures—the "Great Old Ones" or "Ancient Ones," with exotic forbidding names and titles such as "Cthulhu," "the messenger Nyarlathotep," "the blind, idiot god Azathoth," "the key to the gate Yog-Sothoth"—had dominated the earth long before human beings but lost the power eons ago for reasons that vary from story to story (in early tales, they tended to be supernatural creatures from another dimension; in later ones, they were usually powerful extraterrestrials).

The Old Ones remain on the periphery of man's reach in outer space or lie dormant in vast submerged cities, and they strive to reenter the human domain or to awaken from their enforced sleep. Since this reentry is barred to them without human assistance, the Old Ones have established contact with various degenerate groups, families, or individuals, who attempt to utilize the occult knowledge found in forbidden books such as the *Necronomicon* to summon their "masters."

Thus, the typical Mythos story pits the degenerate servants of the Old Ones against the harried but valiant human defenders (most often professors from Miskatonic University). In a few stories the Old Ones can be banished by various magical defenses, but, for the most part, once they are reanimated, they are invulnerable; only accident, luck, or whim saves humanity. Perhaps the most frightening thing about the Old Ones, however, is that, despite their horrendous appearances and destructive capacities, they are not truly evil or consciously malevolent. They simply regard humankind with total indifference and would destroy it for mere convenience without concern or rancor, as a human would step on a pesky insect.

The narrator of "The Call of Cthulhu" states that "he has had a glimpse" of that awful reality, which "like all dread glimpses of truth, flashed out from an accidental piecing together of separated things—in this case an old newspaper item and the notes of a dead professor." Lovecraft wisely maintains this fragmentary approach in narrating his tale. Instead of a simple chronology, the reader has isolated events and revelations which slowly form into a pattern. This indirect, quasi-journalistic approach also enables Lovecraft to mix real historical events, places, characters, and references with the fictional ones, and to insert newspaper clippings and interviews into the text along with straight narrative; the effect is to give the story a strong feeling of authenticity that not only underscores the horrors described but also implies that horrors even more profound lurk just beyond the limits of perception.

"The Call of Cthulhu" is presented in three self-contained sections, which are brought together in the narrator's final conclusions. In the first section, "The Horror in Clay," he describes a set of notes left to him by his granduncle, George Gammell Angell, a Brown University Professor Emeritus of Semitic Languages, who has recently died mysteriously after being jostled by a "nautical looking negro."

Angell's package contains a number of interesting items: a strange bas-relief covered with odd hieroglyphics, including a symbol suggesting "an octopus, a dragon, and a human caricature"; a document headed "Cthulhu Cult"; a number of notes on queer dreams, as well as references to secret cults; and occult, mythological, and anthropological texts. As the narrator examines these fragments, a frightening picture gradually coalesces, from dreams and hints, to accounts of the sinister machinations of the Cthulhu cults and the lore surrounding the creature, to a final confrontation with the thing itself. This semidocumentary approach works brilliantly. The dreams of a young sculptor, as relayed to Angell and reinforced by a series of weird events around the world, give the reader a feeling of pervasive cosmic evil on the brink of erupting.

That evil is made more concrete in the second part, "The Tale of Inspector Legrasse," which chronicles the apprehension of a mysterious, bestial swamp cult in the midst of human sacrificial rituals. From the cultists and an old mestizo named Castro, the officers hear the story of the Great Old Ones, the first articulation of the Mythos in Lovecraft's stories.

In the third part, "The Madness from the Sea," the reader meets the dreaded Cthulhu itself in the grotesque experiences of Gustaf Johansen, a Norwegian sailor. Although Johansen has apparently been killed by the cultists, the narrator obtains his journal which describes the encounter. After meeting and subduing a boatload of bizarre, savage sailors, Johansen and his comrades discover a mysterious island and inadvertently release Cthulhu from his slumber. All but Johansen and one other are killed; chased by Cthulhu they flee and survive by ramming the monster head-on. The actual meeting with the beast is the least satisfying moment in the story. It is unlikely that any other writer, and certainly one not given to Lovecraft's extravagant use of language, could depict a creature as awful as the one suggested in the story prior to the actual meeting. Even the reader's disappointment in the monster, however, does not seriously undermine the power of Lovecraft's conception; the meeting with the creature is brief and sketchy, leaving the momentum of the story largely undamaged. Neither Lovecraft nor his successors ever made the mistake of bringing Cthulhu back to the surface again.

With "The Call of Cthulhu" Lovecraft established his Mythos, but the story is uncharacteristically expansive and fragmentary. It lacks one element that was typical of most of his best fiction, a solidly realized setting. The hierarchy of supernatural beings was only one side of Lovecraft's coin; the other was the very real, believable New England world into which they usually intruded, "Arkham, Massachusetts," and environs. As the elements of his cosmic design grew and became more subtle and intricate, so, too, the world of Arkham became more concrete and familiar. Like William Faulkner's Yoknapatawpha County, the real area it was modeled after (Salem and vicinity) can easily be identified, but the fictional region takes on a separate identity of its own. The importance of this milieu is nowhere better illustrated than in "The Dunwich Horror," as underscored by the fact that Lovecraft devotes the first five pages to convincing the reader that the township of Dunwich, located in Northern Arkham County, is a particularly desolate, forboding, and degenerate area. Only after thoroughly establishing this realistic environment and eerie atmosphere does he introduce the diabolical and perverse Whateley family, the subjects of the narrative.

Once an important, aristocratic family, the Whateley clan has split into two factions, one that clings to normality and some sense of respectability, the other that has thoroughly degenerated into bestiality, viciousness, and black magic. The story proper begins with the birth of Wilbur Whateley to Lavinia, "a somewhat deformed albino woman of about 35"; the father is unknown. Lavinia's aged, half-mad, "wizard" father publicly rejoices and tells the villagers that "*some day yew folks' ll hear a child o' Lavinny's a-callin' its father's name on the top o' Sentinel Hill!*" The child grows rapidly and strangely. At a year and a half he is as big as a four-year-old; at ten he is fully grown; at thirteen he assumes the role of an adult—and a height of more than seven feet. Other odd events occur around the Whateley household: extra rooms are built for no apparent reason; whippoorwills crowd about the house and sing constantly; cattle mysteriously disappear—as does Lavinia; and finally the old man dies, mumbling incoherently about "Yog-Sothoth" and "the old ones as wants to come back."

Shortly thereafter Wilbur attempts to secure the Miskatonic University Library copy of the *Necronomicon*. He fails but excites the curiosity of the librarian, Henry Armitage. Some time later Wilbur is killed by a guard dog while attempting to steal the forbidden text during the night. When young Whateley's clothing is ripped off, he is revealed to be a monster whose torso is covered with black fur, tentacles, unformed eyes, feelers, and the legs of a lizard; instead of blood a greenish-yellow ichor flows out. As people watch, the dead creature dissolves into a putrid mess.

With Wilbur dead, something in the house breaks loose and begins to terrorize the countryside. Armitage recruits two colleagues, and they study the dangerous, arcane books in hopes of finding a defense against the invisible creature, who leaves only huge footprints at the scenes of its carnage. At last they encounter the thing, make it momentarily visible with a powder spray, and deliver the magical chants. As it dissolves, it cries for help to "FATHER. YOG-SOTHOTH!," thus fulfilling old Whateley's prediction, but not in the manner he had desired. As usual, Lovecraft gives us the final explanation of things in the last line: "You needn't ask how Wilbur called it out of the air. He didn't call it out. *It was his twin brother, but it looked more like the father than he did.*"

"The Dunwich Horror" is probably the most direct and visceral of Lovecraft's major horror stories. If it lacks some of the subtlety and complexity of other masterworks such as "The Colour Out of Space," *At the Mountains of Madness* (1964), and "The Shadow Out of Time," it is a potent, memorable narrative that perhaps conveys the essence of the Mythos more clearly than any other single story.

Lovecraft continued to flesh out his Mythos for the rest of his life, producing a number of impressive stories, notably "Pickman's Model," "The Whisperer in Darkness," "The Shadow over Innsmouth," *At the Mountains of Madness*, "The Dreams in the Witch-House," and "The Shadow Out of Time." At the same time it should be remembered that at least half of Lovecraft's fictional output had little or nothing to do with the Cthulhu group. Even if there had been no Mythos, Lovecraft's place as America's foremost master of the macabre after Poe would have been assured by non-Cthulhuian works such as "The Outsider," "The Rats in the Walls," "Cool Air" (after Poe's "The Facts in the Case of M. Valdemar"), the eerie science fictional "The Colour Out of Space," the Salem witchcraft novelette *The Case of Charles Dexter Ward* (1943), and his most enigmatic nightmare/heroic fantasy, *The Dream-Quest of Unknown Kadath* (1943).

The thing that sets the Mythos narratives apart from Lovecraft's other fiction, however, is their collective power and the fact that the Mythos has continued to grow and prosper many years after its originator's death. Fortunately, however, the power of the original concept, at least in Lovecraft's own stories, comes through safely; and, in the end, it is that cosmic vision which gives primary stature to Lovecraft among modern horror writers. Lovecraft was a materialist in belief and attitude who viewed all supernatural ideas, whether conventionally religious or occult, as make-believe. The previously quoted opening paragraph from "The Call of Cthulhu" is a succinct summary of its author's own thinking. Thus, his Old Ones, with their indifferent cruelty and overwhelming powers, were, to Lovecraft, metaphors for a cruelly indifferent universe that provides a fragile, temporary refuge for the most ephemeral and insignificant of creatures—man.

In essence, Lovecraft's cosmic view resembles that of many modern writers, including artists as different as Thomas Hardy and Robinson Jeffers. Like them, Lovecraft's art was an attempt to find a set of metaphors and images with which to express that worldview. The power of the Cthulhu Mythos lies in the fact that, despite the clumsiness, turgidity, and triteness of much of the writing, it presents a powerful metaphorical construct of the modern world and the extremely precarious place of human beings in it.

Other major works

NOVELS: *The Case of Charles Dexter Ward*, 1943; *The Dream-Quest of Unknown Kadath*, 1943; *At the Mountains of Madness and Other Novels*, 1964.

POEMS: *Collected Poems*, 1963; *A Winter Wish*, 1977.

NONFICTION: *Supernatural Horror in Literature*, 1945; *Selected Letters*, 1965-1976 (edited by August Derleth and Donald Wandrei); *Lovecraft at Last*, 1975 (with Willis Conover).

MISCELLANEOUS: *The Outsider and Others*, 1939; *Beyond the Wall of Sleep*, 1943; *Marginalia*, 1944; *The Something About Cats*, 1949; *The Shuttered Room, and Other Pieces*, 1959; *The Dark Brotherhood, and Other Pieces*, 1966; *To Quebec and the Stars*, 1976.

Bibliography

Burleson, Donald R. *H. P. Lovecraft: A Critical Study.* West Port, Conn.: Greenwood Press, 1983. A very helpful consideration of Lovecraft's fiction, nonfiction, and poetry. Provides a good overview of his work as well as placing him among other writers in the genre.

Carter, Lin. *Lovecraft: A Look Behind the "Cthulhu Mythos."* New York: Ballantine, 1972. An extended examination of Lovecraft's mythic horror pantheon. Useful for following the development of his fictive world of demons and altered "realities."

DeCamp, L. Sprague. *Lovecraft: A Biography.* Garden City, N.Y.: Doubleday, 1975. A controversial biography that provides insights into Lovecraft's personal life but little critical material on his writings.

Joshi, S. T. *H. P. Lovecraft and Lovecraft Criticism: An Annotated Bibliography.* Kent, Ohio: Kent State University Press, 1981. A thorough presentation of Lovecraft scholarship. Including both primary and secondary works.

_____, ed. *H. P. Lovecraft: Four Decades of Criticism.* Athens: Ohio University Press, 1980. Contains essays by Barton Levi St. Armand, J. Vernon Shea, and Dirk W. Mosig, as well as a survey of Lovecraft criticism by Joshi.

Joshi, S. T., and L. D. Blackmore. *Lovecraft and Lovecraft Criticism: An Annotated Bibliography: Supplement.* West Warwick, R.I.: Necronomicon Press, 1985. Supplement to the 1981 Joshi bibliography, covering materials published between 1981 and 1985.

Lévy, Maurice. *Lovecraft: A Study in the Fantastic,* translated by S. T. Joshi. Detroit: Wayne State University Press, 1988. A useful consideration of Lovecraft's fiction as examples of the fantastic in literature. Helpful to those interested in genre study and critical theory.

Keith Neilson
(Revised by *Melissa E. Barth*)

LU HSÜN
Chou Shu-jên

Born: Shao-hsing, China; September 25, 1881
Died: Shanghai, China; October 19, 1936

Principal short fiction

Ah Q cheng-chuan, 1921 (serial), 1923 (in *Na-han*; *The True Story of Ah Q*, 1927); *Na-han*, 1923 (*Call to Arms*, 1981); *P'ang-huang*, 1926 (*Wandering*, 1981); *Ku shih hsin-pien*, 1935 (*Old Tales Retold*, 1961); *Ah Q and Others: Selected Stories of Lusin*, 1941; *Selected Stories of Lu Hsün*, 1960, 1963; *The Complete Stories of Lu Xun*, 1981.

Other Literary forms

Lu Hsün wrote prolifically throughout his life, producing essays, verses, reminiscences, and translations of other writers as well as the short fiction for which he is known in the West. The bulk of Lu Hsün's writing consists of polemical essays, written between 1907 and 1936, directed against aspects of Chinese culture and politics of which he disapproved. These writings have been collected from time to time and make up more than twenty volumes. Varying in style, these essays were published in newspapers and magazines and are journalistic in design compared to the sensitive, imaginative, and carefully constructed short stories.

Much of Lu Hsün's writing as a whole consists of the translations of foreign authors, a practice he continued during his entire career. His translations were rendered from Japanese or German, the only foreign languages he knew. As early as 1903, he translated the science fiction of Jules Verne. In 1909, he and his brother, Chou Tso-jên, collaborated in publishing *Yü-wai hsiao-shuo chi* (collection of foreign stories). In two volumes, it included works by Anton Chekhov, Leonid Andreyev, Vsevolod Mikhaylovich Garshin, Henryk Sienkiewicz, Guy de Maupassant, Oscar Wilde, and Edgar Allan Poe. In the 1930's, Lu Hsün translated works by many other Russian authors. He and his brother also issued an anthology of Japanese authors titled *Hsien-tai Jih-pên hsiao-shuo chi* (1934; a collection of modern Japanese short stories), which included works by Mushakoji Saneatsu, Kunikida Doppo, Mori Ōgai, and Natsume Sōseki.

Lu Hsün also produced autobiographical sketches in *Chao hua hsi shih* (1928; *Dawn Blossoms Plucked at Dusk*, 1976) and prose poems and reminiscences in *Yeh ts'ao* (1927; *Wild Grass*, 1974). He composed verses in *wên-yên* (classical Chinese) as well as in the vernacular, *pai-hua*. According to the late scholar and critic, Tsi-an Hsia, Lu Hsün's classical verses are superior to those in the vernacular and are at least equal to his best *pai-hua* prose. Lu Hsün also kept copious diaries, which have been published in facsimile in twenty-four volumes.

Lu Hsün maintained a lifelong interest in graphic art. In 1929, he published a volume of British wood engravings and another which featured the work of Japanese, Russian, French, and American artists. In 1934, he published selected works of young Chinese artists in *Mu-k'o chi-ch'êng* (the woodcut record). He also published, in collaboration with Chêng Chên-to, two collections of traditional-style stationery by the seventeenth century artist Wu Chêng-yên. He developed a strong interest in the wood engravings of Socialist artists in Western Europe and the Soviet Union, and he published books on the form.

Achievements

Lu Hsün is generally regarded as one of the most important of modern Chinese writers. His short story "K'uang-jên jih-chi" ("The Diary of a Madman"), modeled on Nikolai Gogol's story of the same title, was the first Chinese story written in the style of Western fiction and Lu Hsün's first story written in the modern vernacular. His reputation as a short-fiction writer rests primarily on two volumes of stories written between 1918 and 1925, *Call to Arms* and *Wandering*. After these, Lu Hsün wrote little fiction. His best-known story is the novella, *The True Story of Ah Q* (first collected in *Call to Arms*).

Lu Hsün developed a narrative style of pointing without commentary, allowing silence to generate meaning within the form of the short story, a method reminiscent of Poe, who may have influenced Lu Hsün's sense of structure. Like many Chinese writers of short fiction, Lu Hsün was influenced by Western masters of the form, especially those whom he translated. It was Lu Hsün, however, who pioneered the movement in short fiction that helped launch a new literary era in China, and his assimilation of Western ideas became the new reality in Chinese fiction.

Lu Hsün's tales often tend toward satire, and his sense of irony is masterful and pervasive. Reminiscent of the traditional Chinese painter, Lu Hsün renders a whole person from a few deft strokes and evokes atmosphere without elaborate detail. Considered a pioneer of modern Chinese realism, he has been translated more than any other modern Chinese writer. Because he believed that the literature of a nation reflected its character or spirit, he also believed that in order for his country to emerge from centuries of torpor there must be a reawakening in its literature. The prevailing view of Lu Hsün has been that he was a writer who considered literature to be propaganda for social ends; Mao Tse-tung called him "not only a great writer but a great thinker and a great revolutionist." It is true that Lu Hsün was fervently committed to his nation's future and the development of Chinese society, but his fiction is redeemed from didacticism by his humanism and the high quality of his art.

The Communists attacked Lu Hsün at first as a bourgeois writer but later accepted him as a proletarian. After they established the Chinese People's Republic in Peking, they considered him to be the Maxim Gorky of China. Mao Tse-tung referred to him as a "national hero." In 1939, the Communists established the Lu Hsün Academy of Arts in Yenan. Following the fall of Shanghai to the Japanese in 1937, the magazine *Lu Hsün Fêng* (*Lu Hsün's Style*) was started by a group of Communist writers. After Communist troops shattered the Chinese Nationalist defenses of Shanghai in 1949 and occupied the city, the Lu Hsün Museum was established in

Peking. Lu Hsün's tomb is located in northeast Shanghai.

Many books and articles have been written about Lu Hsün. For his pioneering efforts in restructuring the Chinese short story and in developing vernacular speech into a new form of written prose, Lu Hsün deserves to be considered the leader of the Chinese Literary Renaissance of 1917-1937. As a writer of short stories, however, he has formidable contenders in such colleagues as Ch'ang T'ien-i, Shên Ts'ung-wên, and Mao Tun.

Biography

Lu Hsün (the pen name of Chou Shu-jên) was born on September 25, 1881, into an upper-middle-class family in the village of Shao-hsing, Chekiang Province, China. He was the eldest of the four sons of Chou Fêng-i (or Chou Po-i), an old-style Chinese scholar, and Lu Jui, the daughter of a minor government official. Of Lu Hsün's three younger brothers, Chou Tso-jên became a writer, Chou Chien-jên became a scientist, and the youngest died of pneumonia at the age of five.

The Chou family was prosperous until 1893, when Lu Hsün's grandfather, Chou Fu-ch'ing, a *chin-shih* (entered scholar), was convicted of attempting to bribe a provincial examination official and sentenced to be beheaded. His execution, however, was postponed until he was fortunate enough to be released from prison under a general amnesty. This scandal and the prolonged illness and death of Lu Hsün's father in 1896 brought the family to the brink of poverty.

Lu Hsün's formal education began at the age of five under the tutelage of his granduncle Chao-lan, who taught him to love books. Grandfather Fu-ch'ing, always unorthodox, required him to read history but encouraged him to read popular novels as well. At the age of eleven, Lu Hsün was enrolled in a private school supported by the Chou clan, where he was obliged to study the Confucian classics known as the Four Books.

Although as late as 1898 Lu Hsün was still practicing the writing of the *pa-ku-wên*, or the eight-legged essay, and the poetry required for the civil service examinations, he decided to pursue an unorthodox path to social advancement. He enrolled in the Kiangnan Naval Academy at Nanking. Dissatisfied with the poor quality of education offered there, however, at the end of the year he returned to Shao-hsing.

Deciding now to attempt the orthodox route, he presented himself at the K'uanchi District examination for the *hsiu-ts'ai* (flowering talent) degree. Although he passed this examination, he never sat for the prefectural examination. Instead, he returned to Nanking and transferred from the Naval Academy to the School of Mines and Railroads attached to the Kiangnan Army Academy. He was graduated in 1901.

Lu Hsün obtained a government scholarship to study medicine in Japan. Arriving in Tokyo in 1902, he entered the Kōbun Institute to study the Japanese language. After being graduated from Kōbun in 1904, he enrolled in the medical school at Sendai, Honshū. In 1906, however, he received a severe shock. In viewing a news-slide of the Russo-Japanese War, he witnessed a bound Chinese man awaiting execution as a spy for the Russians while a crowd of Chinese stared indifferently at him.

As a result, Lu Hsün was convinced that the soul and not the body of China needed curing. Withdrawing from medical school, he returned to Shao-hsing. There, he submitted to an arranged marriage to a woman he never afterward regarded as his wife. Then, in company with his brother, Chou Tso-jên, he returned to Japan, this time resolved to devote himself to literature.

The brothers spent their time reading, writing, and translating foreign literature. Although able to read German and Japanese, Lu Hsün used these languages mainly to gain access to the cultures of the "oppressed peoples" of Russia, Eastern Europe, and the Balkans. He also composed essays in classical Chinese on a variety of cultural topics. Near the end of his stay in Japan, the brothers published their *Yü-wai hsiao-shuo chi* (collection of foreign stories), rendered in classical Chinese. Succeeding in obtaining a teaching position at the Chekiang Normal School at Hangchow, he returned to China in 1909.

Lu Hsün quit teaching at Hangchow in 1910 to return to Shao-hsing to serve as the school principal. On October 10, 1911, the Republican Revolution, led by Sun Yat-sen, burst forth, throwing the country into turmoil. With the overthrow of the monarchy in 1911, Lu Hsün composed his first short story—in classical Chinese—which was entitled "Huai-chiu" ("Remembrances of the Past") when published in 1913.

When Sun Yat-sen resigned the presidency of China in favor of Yüan Shih-k'ai. Lu Hsün was called to Peking to serve in the ministry of education. Soon disgusted with reform party politics, he buried himself in the study of ancient Chinese texts and inscriptions and developed a strong interest in the history of Chinese literature. This latter interest resulted in his famous volume *Chung-kuo hsiao-shuo shih lüeh* (1923-1930; *A Brief History of Chinese Fiction*, 1959).

Awakened to creative activity by the Literary Revolution of 1917, the following year Lu Hsün wrote his first short story in *pai-hua*, or colloquial Chinese, "The Diary of a Madman," employing Western technique. From this time until 1926, he would write twenty-five such stories that would appear in two collections—fourteen stories in *Call to Arms* and eleven in *Wandering*. His novella *The True Story of Ah Q* brought him national recognition. After 1926, however, Lu Hsün wrote only brief satirical tales, collected in *Old Tales Retold*, devoting himself mostly to writing polemical essays.

Following the massacre of demonstrating students in Peking on March 18, 1926, by the Tuan Ch'i-jui government, Lu Hsün was looked upon as a dangerous radical and was forced into hiding. Leaving Peking, he joined the faculty of Amoy University. In 1927, he moved to Sun Yat-sen University in Canton, where he taught and served as academic dean. Resigning in the spring, Lu Hsün and Hsü Kuang-p'ing, a former student who had become his common-law wife, left Canton for Shanghai.

In 1930, Lu Hsün, having studied Marxism-Leninism, lent his name to the founding of the League of Left Wing Writers. He joined the International Union of Revolutionary Writers. In 1933, he became associated with the Far Eastern Conference against Imperialist War. A close friend of Ch'u Ch'iu-pai, former general secretary of the Communist Party, Lu Hsün provided him with a safe haven from arrest and acted as a courier for the Communists. He himself lived in constant fear of arrest and possible execution.

Although by 1930 Lu Hsün had apparently concluded that the Chinese Communist Party rather than the Kuomintang was the only viable force to reform China, he neither accepted Marxist-Leninist dogma fully nor became a member of the Communist Party. Although from 1927 until his death from tuberculosis on October 19, 1936, Lu Hsün produced no original creative work, he has continued to be viewed by many Chinese as China's leading writer of short fiction in the twentieth century.

Analysis

Nearly all Lu Hsün's short stories were written between 1918 and 1925. The time they deal with is from the eve of the Republican Revolution of 1911 until the May Fourth movement of 1919. The characters they present are mostly women whom Lu Hsün considers victims of traditional Chinese society—he calls them "unfortunates"—whether a failed *litteratus*, a *maudit révolté* (cursed rebel), an unlucky ricksha puller, or a young village woman plagued by widowhood. Although Lu Hsün seems more comfortable as a writer when he deals with the downtrodden, he also sometimes concerns himself with certain members of the ruling class, the scholar-gentry either in or out of office, who are opportunists, compromisers, or oppressors of the common people. Although the stories usually focus on a single protagonist and expose either his or her misery or hypocrisy and cruelty, sometimes they also condemn the entire Chinese populace. This view is developed in "The Diary of a Madman," in which the protagonist goes beyond tradition and sees the people as cannibals—the weak devouring the strong. Lu Hsün was a moralist who viewed contemporaneous China as a sick and degenerate society badly in need of treatment. Ironically, the young man's concern for the health of China gains for him the diagnosis of "mad."

Lu Hsün is usually termed a "realist" as a writer of short fiction. Communist critics call him a "critical realist," a "militant realist," and even a Socialist Realist. Although Lu Hsün sought to make his stories conform to reality as he had experienced it and wanted his readers to credit them as based on the truth, he was not realistic in the sense of the fiction of the great European exponents of nineteenth century realism and naturalism, such as Ivan Turgenev, Gustave Flaubert, and Émile Zola, in whom he never showed any interest. His realism was very personal and highly subjective. He was not interested in the material but in the spiritual. In his short stories, he probes into the human spirit as that has been affected by environment and tradition. If one considers the men he took for his intellectual mentors, T. H. Huxley, Max Stirner, Søren Kierkegaard, Henrik Ibsen, Friedrich Nietzsche, Georg Brandes, Lord Byron, Gogol, and Andreyev, one sees a curious thing: the majority are associated with the Romantic spirit of individualism, and only two of them, Huxley and Brandes, with the anti-Romantic spirit of positivism. Lu Hsün had an ironic view of reality that was highly subjective and tempered by strong Romantic elements. It was this view that attracted him to writers such as Gogol and Andreyev, both of whom attempted the fusion of Romanticism and realism and then the fusion of realism and symbolism, and Lu Hsün adopted similar practices. Therefore, as a writer, Lu Hsün might be more usefully termed a subjective realist or an expressionist rather than a social realist. He was surely not a Socialist Realist. One wonders how he would have taken Mao's Yenan Forum Talks of 1942. A satirist must exaggerate, draw sharp contrasts between good and evil. Although he exposed the faults of Chinese society, Lu Hsün never offered any remedy except that it should honor the individual and free the spirit.

Lu Hsün's short stories, for the most part, grew out of his personal experience. He enhanced this subjectivity by the power of his imagination and taut artistic skill. His stories are characterized by their brevity but above all by their compactness of structure and their pithy, sharp style, in which each word is needed and apposite. His prose is strongly imagistic, especially in its visual appeal. Lu Hsün seldom employs the figures of metaphor or simile; when he does use such a figure, however, it is usually highly effective. He makes use of historical and literary allusion, and one or more such allusions are to be found in the vast majority of his stories. He sometimes resorts to symbolism. Dialogue is usually kept to a minimum. Irony is a pervasive element in nearly all Lu Hsün's stories, with satire a frequent weapon used in defense of individual freedom. He shows unusual skill in fusing an action with its scene. Although description is suppressed, atmosphere emerges strongly. Perhaps Lu Hsün's major weakness as a writer of fiction is his fondness for nostalgia, his lapses into sentimentality, and his inability always to deal fairly with persons other than the downtrodden.

Of Lu Hsün's stories collected in *Call to Arms*, "The Diary of a Madman," although it made its author prominent, is not one of his best. The first story to be written in the Western manner, it is more clever in conception than effective as a well-constructed tale. As C. T. Hsia, a judicious critic, has pointed out, the story's weakness lies in the author's failure to provide a realistic setting for the madman's fantasies.

The story "K'ung I-chi," about a failed scholar who has become a wine bibber at a village tavern, where he is the butt of jokes, is a much stronger story than "The Diary of a Madman." K'ung I-chi has studied the classics, but he has failed to pass even the lowest official examination. With no means of earning a living, he would have been reduced to beggary except for his skill in calligraphy, which enabled him to support himself by copying. He loved wine too much, however, and he was lazy. When he needed money, he took to stealing books from the libraries of the gentry. For such actions he was frequently strung up and beaten. After being absent from the tavern for a long time, he reappears, dirty and disheveled, his legs broken. Partaking of warm wine, he is the butt of the jokes and taunts of the tavern yokels. He departs from the tavern, but he is never seen again. It is presumed that he has died. As a commentary on the Chinese social order, the story presents a man who is a part of the detritus left by the examination system. At the same time, he must take responsibility for his own weaknesses of character. In addition, the story shows how cruel and unfeeling people can be to those who are less fortunate than they.

"Yao" ("Medicine") is another powerful story. It shows especially careful construction and makes effective use of symbolism. The story concerns two boys who are unknown to each other but whose lives follow equally disastrous courses to become linked after their deaths. Hua Hsiao-chuan is the tubercular son of a tea-shop owner, Hua Lao-chuan, and his wife. The boy is dying. Anxious to save his life, the parents are persuaded to pay a packet of money for a *man-t'ou* (steamed bread-roll) soaked with the blood of an executed man, which is alleged by tradition to be a sure cure for tuberculosis. The beheaded man is young Hsia Yu, the son of the widow Hsia. A revolutionary seeking the overthrow of the Manchu or Ch'ing Dynasty, he was betrayed to the authorities by his conservative Third Uncle, who collected a reward for his treason. Thus, the blood of a martyr and hero, a representative of the new order, is used in the service of a superstitious and useless medical cure. If the parents are ignorant and superstitious, they also truly love their son and try by all the means they know to save him, but he dies, regardless. Nobody has sought to save Hsia Yu from execution; indeed, all the customers at the tea shop highly approve of his arrest and beheading. His widowed mother, who loved him dearly, was powerless to help her son.

Influenced by his admiration for the Russian writer Andreyev, Lu Hsün sought to emphasize the story's purport through the use of symbolism. Since the two boys in the story are linked in the action purely by accident, Lu Hsün reinforces the connection through their surnames, "Hua" and "Hsia," which as "Hua-hsia" literally means "glorious and extensive"; this compound is also an ancient name for China. It is a story of the opposition between the old China—the China of darkness, superstition, and lethargy under foreign rulers—and the new China—the China trying to emerge into the light, the China of the awakened, of the revolutionary. The symbolism is especially dense at the conclusion of the story, when the two mothers meet at the graves of their sons, who are buried opposite each other. Natural flowers are growing on the grave of the Hua boy, but on Hsia Yu's grave has been placed a wreath of red and white flowers. When Hsia Yu's mother perceives the wreath, she cannot understand its presence. She believes that her son has wrought a miracle as a sign of the wrong done to him, that he desires that his death be avenged. Perplexed, she looks around her but sees only a crow perched on a leafless bough. She tells her son that heaven will surely see that a day of reckoning will come. Uncertain of his presence, though, she requests him to make the crow fly onto his grave as a sign to her that he is really there. The crow remains still perched on its bough, as if made of iron. Mrs. Hsia and Mrs. Hua have, in their mutual grief, formed a bond of sympathy. Mrs. Hua now suggests that the two of them might as well leave for home. As they depart, they hear a loud caw behind them. Startled, they turn their heads to look behind them. They see the crow stretch its wings and fly off toward the horizon.

The True Story of Ah Q is Lu Hsün's longest and most important story. It originally appeared serially on a weekly basis in the Peking *Ch'en Pao* (weekly post) in

its Sunday supplement; these circumstances may have been responsible for its rambling, episodic plot and other literary defects. The story made a powerful impact,
however, on its Chinese audience. It saw in the protagonist, Ah Q, what Lu Hsün
wanted it to see: the embodiment of all the weaknesses of the Chinese national
character, which just prior to the fall of the Ch'ing Dynasty had constituted a national disease. Ah Q is a homeless peasant who lives in the temple of the tutelary
god of Wei village. Since no one knows his true surname, the narrator calls him
simply "Ah Q" because the foreign letter "Q" resembles a man's head with a queue,
or pigtail, hanging down. Thus, "Q" is a pictograph of every Chinese man during
the rule of the Manchus, since the conquerors required Chinese men to shave their
heads and wear queues. Ah Q is a Chinese Everyman.

Ah Q is a dunce whose foolish actions result in repeated humiliating defeats. He
just as repeatedly glosses over these defeats by convincing himself that, if he has
been physically overcome, he has nevertheless won a "spiritual victory." Ah Q is a
perfect antihero, but he is an unusual one in that he is, as William A. Lyell, Jr., has
pointed out, "victimizer as well as victim." He is bullied and mistreated by those
stronger than he, but he, in turn, bullies and mistreats those who are weaker. Like
the other inhabitants of Wei village, he follows the Chinese social principle: *P'a
ch'iang ch'i jo* (fear the strong, bully the weak). He is opposed to revolutionaries
until he learns that the village power elite is terrified of them. He tries to join them,
but they arrest him for thievery. He is condemned to death, not by the sword but by
the rifles of a firing squad. He tries to be brave, but, his soul ripped, he is about to
utter, "Help." Yet, as Lu Hsün writes, "Ah Q never said that. Blackness had already
covered his eyes. He heard the shots ring out and felt his body scatter like a heap of
dust."

Ah Q may personify the Chinese social sickness of his time. According to the
perceptive scholar, Lee Ou-fan Lee, Ah Q's life revolves around subsistence in a
world that he does not understand. He is only a face in the crowd without spirit,
interior self, or self-consciousness. His negative qualities combine to depict a slave
mentality. He may suggest how the people of Wei village responded to the Republican Revolution of 1911. He suggests as well why the revolution eventually failed.

On the whole, the stories collected in Lu Hsün's second volume *Wandering* are
superior to those of his first. He himself favored them and pointed out the reasons
for their superiority: his having outgrown his foreign influences; his more mature
technique; his more incisive delineation of reality; and his having cooled his personal anger and sorrow. Of the eleven stories included in *Wandering*, three of them
are particularly noteworthy: "Chu-fu" ("The New Year's Sacrifice"), "Tsai chiu-lou
shang" ("Upstairs in a Wineshop"), and "Li-hun" ("Divorce").

"The New Year's Sacrifice" is the story of the tragic lot and cruel treatment
accorded a peasant woman, Hsiang Lin-sao, who, widowed at twenty-six, is forced
to remarry against her will, is then widowed a second time, has her infant son carried off by a wolf, and is hired as a servant by a scholar-gentry family named Lu.
The head of the Lu family, Han-lin, the neo-Confucian scholar Fourth Uncle Lu,

thinks that Hsiang Lin-sao, as a twice-married widow, is impure and unfit to touch any food or implement connected with the family ancestral sacrifices. Despite her religious efforts to atone for her "sin," she is rejected by the Lus and turned into a beggar. She dies in poverty just as the Lus are about to invoke a New Year's blessing. The news of her death annoys Fourth Uncle Lu. In anger, he berates her for dying at such an unpropitious time. He remarks to his wife, "You can tell from that alone what a rotten type she is." Thus, this renowned neo-Confucian scholar and rationalist reveals himself to be an inhumane, unfeeling, superstitious, rigid traditionalist whose narrow and inflexible morality is the executioner of a good, simple-hearted peasant woman. The twice-widowed woman is the victim of tradition and superstition. Being a widow, she must bear the stigma of carrying the ghosts of her two husbands; in fact, it may even be believed that she caused their deaths. When she asks the noncommittal narrator if he believes a person's soul goes on after death, she seems to be clutching for meaning in a realm of existence beyond the world she has known, where she can be reunited with her child who was eaten by wolves.

"Upstairs in a Wineshop" is the story of the chance reunion one winter evening of two former friends and colleagues upstairs in a village wineshop, back home after a ten-year interval. The story is obviously autobiographical and the unnamed narrator a mask for Lu Hsün himself. The narrator arrives at the wineshop alone. He goes upstairs, orders wine and some dishes, and sits drinking and eating while looking out over the snow-covered courtyard outside. The atmosphere here is beautifully evoked by Lu Hsün—inside warm wine and food, outside snow. The snow introduced at the beginning, the symbolism of the crimson camellias blossoming in the snow (suggesting the homeliness of the south as opposed to the strangeness of the north), and the snow and wind at the end that wash away the bittersweet taste of the remembrances of the past give to this story a special pictorial quality in respect to its text—reminiscent of those scholar-painters who did *Wên-jên-hua* (literary men's painting), harmonizing text with picture. When the narrator's old friend and colleague Lü Wei-fu appears by chance, each is surprised at meeting the other, and they greet each other warmly. Both recollect their younger days when they were avid reformers who had rejected the Old Learning in favor of the New. Now they are both middle-aged. To his dismay and disappointment, the narrator learns that his friend is changed, has lost his nerve and rejoined the Confucian establishment. He lives with his mother in a northern province where he tutors the children of a prosperous family in the Confucian classics. He also deceives his mother by making up white lies in order to shield her from a painful reality. Lü Wei-fu has given up "pulling the beards of the gods."

Perhaps the most remarkable feature of "Upstairs in a Wineshop" is Lu Hsün's seeming ambivalence of his anti-Confucian position. As C. T. Hsia has observed, although Lu Hsün undoubtedly intended to present Lü Wei-fu as a weak-kneed, broken man, "the kindness and piety of Lü Wei-fu, however pathetic, also demonstrate the positive strength of the traditional mode of life, toward which the author must have been nostalgically attracted in spite of his contrary intellectual conviction." Hsia concludes that the story, then, with an irony contrary to its author's intention, "is a lyrical confession of his own uncertainty and hesitation."

"Divorce" provides a vivid portrait of a tough, uncouth, rebellious country girl as well as a picture of how the power structure of traditional Chinese society works in a rural setting to cow such a female rebel. As the story opens, a family feud has been going on for three years between the Chuangs and the Shihs. The girl, Ai-ku, born a Chuang, married young Mr. Shih. After a time, however, she and her husband did not get along and his parents disliked her. Soon, her husband took up with a young widow and informed his wife that he no longer wanted her. Since that time, she has been living with her father, Chuang Mu-san, and her six brothers. For the past three years, the two feuding families have entered into negotiations several times without any settlement being reached. Preferring to be an unloved wife with honor rather than a dishonored divorcée, Ai-ku has insisted each time that her husband take her back despite an offer of money by the Shihs to effect a separation, and until now her father has supported her position. Father and daughter are now traveling by boat to the village of P'ang, where another meeting between the Shihs and the Chuangs has been arranged by Old Gentleman Wei in a final effort to produce a settlement of the family feud. When they arrive, Wei announces that Seventh Master, a prestigious urban relative of the Weis, visiting him for the New Year's celebration, has agreed to preside over Ai-ku's case and will attempt to persuade the Chuangs to accept the terms of divorce proposed, with which he, Wei, already agrees. To make the settlement more agreeable, Seventh Master has persuaded the Shihs to add ten dollars to the sum of money already offered to the Chuangs. Although Ai-ku is confident that her father will again reject the divorce proposal, she becomes alarmed when he remains silent. In desperation, she speaks out in her own defense.

Seventh Master reminds her, however, that a young person ought to be more compliant in adjusting to reality, for "compliance produces riches." Furthermore, he informs her, since her in-laws have already dismissed her from their presence, she will have to suffer a divorce, regardless of whether there is a money settlement. At this point, Young Shih takes the opportunity to remind Seventh Master that if Ai-ku acts in this manner here, she must have acted much worse in his father's home. He complains that at home she always referred to his father and to himself as "beasts." Indeed, she even called him a *szŭ-shêng-tzŭ* (bastard). Ai-ku breaks in to deny this charge and counters that he called her a *p'in-ch'üan* (bitch).

At Ai-ku's response, Seventh Master cries out a command: "Come in!" Silence immediately follows. Ai-ku is thunderstruck. A servant enters and hurries up to the dignitary, who whispers some order to him which nobody can understand. The man replies: "Yes, venerable sir," and departs. Fearfully, Ai-ku blurts out to Seventh Master that she always meant to accept his decision. Wei is delighted. The families exchange wedding certificates and money. The servant enters and gives something to Seventh Master, who puts his hand to his nose and then sneezes; the whispered order was for snuff. Chuang Mu-san and Ai-ku leave after refusing to take a cup of New Year's wine.

Lu Hsün was a highly sensitive man with a strong sense of justice. He was not content to endure evil with passive indifference. A sedentary literary man (a *wên-jên*), he admired action more than anything else but had no heart for it himself. An acute observer of human nature, but one with a limited range, he had a special knack for sketching what he saw with deft, swift strokes of his pen and with a minimum of words. He was a very gifted writer of short fiction but a mediocre thinker. His thinking fell short of complete clarity. A "wanderer" in the wasteland of hopes and broken dreams, he was at first inspired by Charles Darwin and Friedrich Nietzsche but misunderstood both. His later excursions into Karl Marx and Vladimir Ilich Lenin curtailed his imagination, aroused in him resentment and prejudice, and ran counter to his natural instinct for freedom, independence, and appreciation of individual worth. It was unfortunate that as a creative writer he thought that changing the face of China was more important than painting its portrait. As an individual, he could do little about the former but could have done much about the latter. He never realized this truth until the last year of his life.

If in his short fiction Lu Hsün had depicted humanity as he found it in all its richness, splendor, and nobility together with its poverty, stupidity, and moral degeneracy—in a spirit that extended charity to all and with a sense of the brotherhood of man that included tolerance and a readiness on his part to pardon, leaving moral lessons for others to proclaim and class distinctions for others to condemn—he might have been a great writer rather than simply a gifted one whose full potential as a creative artist was never realized.

Other major works

POETRY: *Yeh ts'ao*, 1927 (*Wild Grass*, 1974).

NONFICTION: *Chung-kuo hsiao-shuo shih lüeh*, 1923-1930 (*A Brief History of Chinese Fiction*, 1959); *Jê fêng*, 1925; *Hua-kai chi*, 1926; *Fên*, 1927; *Hua-kai chi hsü-pien*, 1927; *Êr-i chi*, 1928; *Chao hua hsi shih*, 1928 (*Dawn Blossoms Plucked at Dusk*, 1976); *San hsien chi*, 1932; *Êrh hsin chi*, 1932; *Wei tzŭ yu shu*, 1933; *Chi-wai chi*, 1934; *Nan ch'iang pei tiao chi*, 1934; *Chun fêng yüeh t'an*, 1934; *Hua pien wên-hsüeh*, 1936; *Ch'ieh-chieh-t'ing tsa wên*, 1937; *Ch'ieh-chieh-t'ing tsa wên êrh chi*, 1937; *Ch'ieh-chieh-t'ing tsa wên mo-pien*, 1937; *Lu Hsün jih-chi*, 1951.

TRANSLATIONS: *Yü-wai hsiao-shuo chi*, 1909 (with Chou Tso-jên; of works by Anton Chekhov, Leonid Andreyev, Vsevolod Mikhaylovich Garshin, Henryk Sienkiewicz, Guy de Maupassant, Oscar Wilde, and Edgar Allan Poe); *Hsien-tai Jih-pên hsiao-shuo chi*, 1934 (of short stories by Mushakoji Saneatsu, Kunikida Doppo, Mori Ōgai, and Natsume Sōseki).

ANTHOLOGY: *Mu-k'o chi-ch'êng*, 1934 (2 volumes).

MISCELLANEOUS: *Selected Works of Lu Hsün*, 1946-1960 (4 volumes); *Silent China: Selected Writings of Lu Xun*, 1973.

Bibliography

Chen, Pearl Hsia. *The Social Thought of Lu Hsün, 1881-1936*. New York: Vantage

Press, 1976. Chronicles the development of Lu Hsün's thought against his cultural background, including his encounter with Western ideas, his belief in women's rights, his involvement with liberal socialism, and his reevaluation of traditional Chinese culture. The preface, by Franklin S. C. Chen, is an essay on traditional China's economic structure as it related to social thought.

Hanan, Patrick. "The Techniques of Lu Hsün's Fiction." *Harvard Journal of Asiatic Studies* 34 (1974) 53-96. Using a broad definition of "technique," Hanan discusses possible influences of writers such as Nikolai Gogol, Vsevolod Mikhaylovich Garshin, and Leonid Andreyev, as well as Lu Hsün's use of symbols and different types of irony.

Lee, Lee Ou-fan, ed. *Lu Xun and His Legacy.* Berkeley: University of California Press, 1985. This collection of essays by various scholars discusses Lu Hsün's perception of traditional and modern literature, his development of form, and his intellectual and political views.

――――――. *Voices from the Iron House.* Bloomington: Indiana University Press, 1987. The stated purpose here is to "demythify" Lu Hsün with the aim of evaluating his literary accomplishments on their own ground. Good discussions include biographical information but emphasize analysis.

Lyell, William A., Jr. *Lu Hsün's Vision of Reality.* Berkeley: University of California Press, 1976. The first third of this book provides a biography, and the remainder is devoted to good basic discussions of Lu Hsün's fiction.

Seminov, V. I. *Lu Hsün and His Predecessors.* White Plains, N.Y.: M. E. Sharpe, 1980. Describes Lu Hsün's role as innovator in Chinese fiction from a moderate Soviet perspective.

Shiqing, Wang. *Lu Xun: A Biography.* Beijing: Foreign Languages Press, 1984. Traces Lu Hsün's life, particularly his political and intellectual development. Includes several photographs.

Richard P. Benton
(Revised by *Mary Rohrberger*)

JOHN LYLY

Born: Canterbury(?), Kent, England; c. 1554
Died: London, England; November, 1606

Principal short fiction
Euphues, the Anatomy of Wit, 1578; *Euphues and His England*, 1580.

Other literary forms
In addition to *Euphues, the Anatomy of Wit* and *Euphues and His England*, John Lyly wrote several plays, including *Campaspe* (1584), *Sapho and Phao* (1584), *Endymion* (1591), *Gallathea* (1592), *Mother Bombie* (1594), and *Love's Metamorphosis* (1601).

Achievements
Lyly's two works of prose fiction were among the most popular literary works of their period. *Euphues, the Anatomy of Wit* first appeared in 1578, and fourteen editions were printed by 1613. *Euphues and His England* also went through fourteen editions by 1609. Between 1617 and 1638, four editions containing both works were printed.

Lyly's witty prose style was probably responsible for the enthusiastic reception accorded to him by his contemporaries. The term "euphuism" was coined to describe his characteristic techniques: appeals to proverbial lore, analogies based on natural history, and rhetorical antithesis. His sentences contain syntactically parallel clauses that are antithetical in meaning, while alliteration and assonance are used to highlight the antithesis (for example, "The earth bringeth forth as well endive to delight the people as hemlock to endanger the patient. . . . If my lewd life, gentlemen, have given you offence, let my good counsel make amends; if by my folly any be allured to lust, let them by my repentance be drawn to continency.") In his prose romances, Lyly debates issues such as which is more important, nature or nurture, learning or experience. Like his courtly dramas, these prose romances comment on court politics, showing that Lyly was a humanist who had indeed become a courtier.

Biography
John Lyly was the grandson of the grammarian, schoolmaster, and friend of Desiderius Erasmus, William Lyly. Although he did not approach his grandfather in profound zeal for learning, he was an educated man (Oxford, B.A. 1573, M.A. 1575) who could write confidently and elegantly and could move deftly the traditional counters of classical mythology. The sometimes seemingly arid rhetorical training of the university provided him with the structures of argumentation found throughout the essentially didactic *Euphues, the Anatomy of Wit*. He married in 1583 and at about the same time became attached to the household of the Earl of Oxford. He wrote and produced plays performed by children in private theaters and at court and

in 1588 seems to have been "promised" by the Queen the post of Master of the Revels, a promise never fulfilled. Frustrated in his hope, Lyly wrote nothing for the last twelve years of his life. He did serve as a member of Parliament several times but died without the rewards his years of court attendance had led him to expect.

Analysis

Euphues, the Anatomy of Wit, a first effort and astounding "best seller" in its day, is often discussed as an *Ur*-novel, but its narrative aspect is minimal and its didactic purpose puts it closer in essence to the courtesy books of the time. The most striking feature is the style in which it is written, a prose marked by balance, alliteration, and images drawn from the tradition of unnatural natural history (such as toads with diamonds in their foreheads) which stems from Pliny and is best known to modern readers in Falstaff's parody of the style in the tavern play of *Henry IV, Part I* (1597-1598). It has been demonstrated by G. K. Hunter that the plot of *Euphues* is organized rather much in the way John Lyly created his plays, that is, with the five-act structure of Terence which he (along with contemporaries, including William Shakespeare) learned at school. Euphues reaches Naples and meets Philautus, with whom he becomes fast friends (act 1); the two friends visit the love of Philautus, the fair Lucilla (act 2); Euphues chooses love over friendship, deceives Philautus, and temporarily wins the heart of Lucilla (act 3); the two friends now quarrel (act 4); Lucilla finds a third lover and the two friends quit her and restore their friendship (act 5).

Thematically, the story deals not merely with the idea that masculine friendship is superior to romantic love but also with the still more overarching issue of experience as a greater teacher than theory. The importance of experience is revealed as Euphues (a youth of natural ability, as his name suggests) leaves Athens (rather clearly the Oxford of Lyly's own life) and arrives in Naples (clearly London with all its temptations). On the rough path to hard-won wisdom, Euphues fails to heed wise counsel (from Eubulus) or honor his friendship (with Philautus) or perceive the limitations of passionate love (in the form and nature of Lucilla). Indeed, Euphues is the favored son gone wrong but ultimately recovered; he is one of the Prodigal sons, like Falstaff's companion Hal, who appear so frequently in English Renaissance literature. That experience is the greatest teacher, that it is the reverse of "the common lie—that experience is the Mistress of Fools" is made clear in the letters which conclude the volume, and while these letters are not, as in the epistolary novel, integrated into the narrative, they are evidence of the wisdom earned by Euphues through the difficulties described in that narrative.

Euphues' reward is a return to Athens and something of a chair in moral and social omniscience, but the groves of academe do not hold him, for he reappears in 1580 in *Euphues and His England*, a work less serious in tone and narrative throughout which shifts focus from the bachelor Euphues to the ultimately wived Philautus. Although Euphues himself is no longer the Prodigal Son, he tells of or meets several such born-again folk in Callimachus, the uncle of Callimachus, and Fidus the beekeeper, each one of whom illustrates the force and value of experiential knowledge.

Letters of moral instruction are part of the narrative in this sequel. Lyly has produced carefully developed and extensive excursuses on traditional topics such as the difficulties of foreign travel, the frustrations of expectations, the mixed nature of wine, the intelligence of women, and so forth, sometimes to the point of almost exhausting the reader if not the topic. The copiousness of Lyly's examples is in keeping with the desires and pedagogical doctrine of the Elizabethan period, but it naturally retards and at times replaces the narrative itself.

Although there are signs that Lyly hurried in the composition of *Euphues and His England* the better to capitalize on the extraordinary success of *Euphues, the Anatomy of Wit*, he did double the length of the story without, however, fully shaping the work to its expected conclusion. At times he seems uncertain of the nature of his audience, addressing in different sections of the work first "Gentlemen" and then "Gentlewomen." Women do seem to have been a large part of his intended readership.

There are structural weaknesses resulting from design and inexperience in both *Euphues, the Anatomy of Wit* and *Euphues and His England*, but in his prose comedies Lyly not only taught Shakespeare how to write romantic dialogue with scenic balancing but also demonstrated his command of comedic structure in large. The standard division of Lyly's plays by material—historical, allegorical, pastoral, and realistic—has proved less fruitful than the investigation of Lyly's structural techniques which give his works such unity. This mastery of the principles of unification was reached in his very first play, *Campaspe*, some five years after the rousing success of *Euphues, the Anatomy of Wit*. Lyly seems to have structured his play upon the central issue of a debate which originated in ancient history and is preserved in both Pliny's *Natural History* (A.D. 77) and Baldassare Castiglione's *Il Cortegiano* (1528; *The Courtier*, 1561) as to whether one should more "commend in Alexander's victories, courage or courtesy."

The play in five acts demonstrates Alexander's conquest of his own passion (for Campaspe) and his keen sense of justice and *noblesse oblige* in his dealing with the painter, Apelles, who is himself smitten with love for the same girl, who reciprocates the painter's affection. In the midst of the carefully wrought prose there is the celebrated lyric which is sung by Apelles, "Cupid and my Campaspe played at cards for kisses." The plot is particularly satisfying in that the poor painter wins out over the powerful ruler (and the girl is quite content with the painter over the king, unlike the version in Castiglione), although the ruler wins a larger moral triumph. By returning to his ostensibly more demanding role in politics, having shown a control over his passions, he makes a clear parallel, however masculine, to Queen Elizabeth, the chief audience for this court play. The charm of all these noble gestures was increased by their having been made by boys dressed in the roles of maidens and conquerors. Further, the natural energy of young boys doubtless made the characters of the pages to the philosophers more naturalistically appealing. In their witticisms these pages provide a parodic melody to the lofty hymn sung by their philosophic masters and noble rulers. Shakespeare learned from Lyly how to make a humorous subplot echo ironically the issues of the main story, and, seeing that Lyly did not scruple to engage in the anachronism of having the philosophers of different ages brought simultaneously upon the stage, he himself cared little to have clocks strike in *Julius Caesar* (1599-1600) and a Trojan hero cite Aristotle in *Troilus and Cressida* (1601-1602).

Endymion is concerned with the unbridgeable distance between the love of a man and the goddess Cynthia in a plot which reveals the dangers of court intrigue which can be defeated only by Cynthia's intervention. Cynthia is rather clearly the unique Queen Elizabeth herself (who elsewhere in Elizabethan literature is called "Cynthia" by Sir Walter Raleigh and Ben Jonson), and the lesser characters dominated by the passion of love and baser affections are her courtiers, some of whom are the victims of the more calculating others. In spite of the Prologue to the play, critics have frequently attempted to read the work allegorically, but no satisfactory interpretation has appeared short of that which views the play as a compliment to the queen and an indictment of the kind of court intrigue from which Lyly himself doubtless suffered. Of particular structural interest is the reversal of the relationship of Endymion and Cynthia in his source (in which the moon goddess is in love with the man), the use of the symbolic dumb show, the multiplication of parallel situations, and the use of comic figure (Sir Thopas), who in the intensity of his infatuations parodies the commitments of the other lovers in the play including Endymion himself. Sir Thopas is not so clever a figure as certain of the pages in earlier Lyly comedies, but he better parodies the theme of the main plot. In allegorical interpretation of the play Sir Thopas is sometimes thought to be modeled upon Gabriel Harvey, the pedantic friend of Edmund Spenser. If this is so, then Shakespeare may have gotten the idea of modeling his own Malvolio in *Twelfth Night* (1599-1600), a play with another Sir Thopas, upon the same unlucky Harvey (the victim also of Thomas Nash) from Lyly, several of whose other devices and techniques became part of Shakespearean comedy.

Modern critics find in Lyly's reliance upon balance and antithesis in his sentences and in his fictive universe a self-limiting view of life as filled with simple oppositions, such as good and bad, friendship and love, success and failure. They believe that this was most likely the result of his university training in scholastic disjunctives of an old logic developed in rhetorical debate coupled with a keen appreciation of the ins and outs of court politics. Perhaps, but not all forms of art need be "realistic," and there is little doubt that as a teacher Lyly taught by examples selected from the world at large without claiming that they were exhaustive, but rather implicitly arguing by his syntax and thematic structures that reason is choice and most choices do not admit of the luxury of the "both-and" alternative.

Still other readers, noting the intelligence that plays upon the surface of the dramas and the "novels" and genuinely admiring the stylistic genius if not every passage in that style, seek to rehabilitate Lyly by making him an ironist of a substantial kind, a writer profoundly parodic who by his women-hating protagonist in *Euphues, the Anatomy of Wit* seeks to undercut the world of courtly grace expounded in the courtesy books of the English and Continental Renaissance. Such a view would make Lyly a satirist rather like Nash.

What is perhaps most modern in Lyly is his awareness and frequent presentation of the fact that things are seldom what they seem. A first reading of Lyly's works may suggest that lovers are fickle, that change of heart is everywhere, but further reflection suggests that the alternations of affection in episodes of romantic love are chiefly versions of the alternation in support and trust found throughout life. Deceit is a central theme in Lyly, and whether he learned of its pervasiveness in the slippery court of Elizabeth or discovered it elsewhere, his heightened and baroque images of it show a modern awareness in an outlandishly nonmodern style. The day was longer in Lyly's time and the long, slow-moving, drawn-out story was expected. The reader does not have the leisure of Lyly's original audience today.

Other major works

PLAYS: *Campaspe*, 1584; *Sapho and Phao*, 1584; *Endymion*, 1591; *Gallathea*, 1592; *Midas*, 1592; *Mother Bombie*, 1594; *The Woman in the Moone*, 1597; *Love's Metamorphosis*, 1601.

NONFICTION: *A Whip for an Ape*, 1589; *Pappe with a Hatchet*, 1589.

MISCELLANEOUS: *The Complete Works of John Lyly*, 1902 (3 volumes; R. Warwick Bond, editor).

Bibliography

Berry, Philippa. *Of Chastity and Power: Elizabethan Literature and the Unmarried Queen*. New York: Routledge, 1989. This study traces developments in the cult of Queen Elizabeth and comments on how Lyly's works reflect his political views. Treats changes in Lyly's views of the ideal relationship between the poet courtier and the monarch.

Henderson, Judith Rice. "Euphues and His Erasmus." *English Literary Renaissance* 12 (Spring, 1982): 135-161. An analysis of euphuism, particularly the often-overlooked treatises and letters appended to *Euphues, the Anatomy of Wit*, as a variety of the sort of rhetoric encouraged by the humanist school curriculum. Footnotes provide a useful summary of the source scholarship on Lyly's prose.

Hunter, G. K. *John Lyly: The Humanist as Courtier.* London: Routledge & Kegan Paul, 1962. The first major study of Lyly's life and works. Discusses the changing relationship of humanist scholars to the Elizabethan court and argues that by Lyly's time the scholar's role had deteriorated from political adviser to "mere entertainer." Includes a chapter on Lyly's influence on William Shakespeare.

Lyly, John. *The Complete Works of John Lyly.* Edited by R. Warwick Bond. 3 vols. Oxford, England: Clarendon Press, 1902. This volume remains the standard edition of Lyly's complete works.

May, Steven W. *The Elizabethan Courtier Poets: The Poems and Their Contexts.* Columbia: University of Missouri Press, 1991. Contains a valuable corrective analysis of the connections between the court and poets such as John Lyly. Discusses

Lyly's patronage connections with the Earl of Oxford but observes that Lyly had little independent status as a courtier.

Stephanson, Raymond. "John Lyly's Prose Fiction: Irony, Humor, and Anti-Humanism." *English Literature Renaissance* 11 (Winter, 1981): 3-21. A revisionary study arguing that Lyly's prose fiction is heavily ironic. Stephanson cites evidence that Lyly exposes the logical inconsistency of analogies made between the natural world and human affairs.

J. J. M. Tobin
(Revised by *Jean R. Brink*)

MARY McCARTHY

Born: Seattle, Washington; June 21, 1912
Died: New York City, New York; October 25, 1989

Principal short fiction

The Company She Keeps, 1942; *Cast a Cold Eye*, 1950; *The Hounds of Summer and Other Stories*, 1981.

Other literary forms

Mary McCarthy began writing as a drama critic for the *Partisan Review*. She wrote six novels. *The Group* (1963), the most widely read of these, was subsequently made into a film in Hollywood. She also wrote two autobiographies as well as numerous articles and books on art and politics. Most ground-breaking among her nonfiction is the autobiography *Memories of a Catholic Girlhood* (1957), an idiosyncratic combination of fiction and nonfiction. McCarthy comments on the proportions of fact and fantasy in each selection in italicized bridges between each essay/ story. In her second autobiography, *How I Grew* (1987), she presents her life as an artist. Reviewers responded quite well to the second autobiography but typically noted the superiority of the first. McCarthy's literary criticism for *The New Republic* and *The Nation* earn her an important place in American literature.

Achievements

McCarthy's exceptional skill as a writer won her immediate recognition. An essay she wrote for the College Entrance Examination Board (CEEB) was published anonymously in a CEEB journal of the early 1930's as an example of a high scoring essay. Recognition for her excellence includes the 1949 *Horizon* literary prize for *The Oasis* (1949), an O. Henry short-story prize in 1957 for "Yellowstone Park," and in 1984 both the National Medal of Literature and the Edward MacDowell Medal for outstanding contributions to literature. McCarthy, a Guggenheim fellow in both 1949 and 1959, was a member of the American Institute of Arts and Letters from 1960 until her death. Recognized for her astute observation of literary works, she was a judge for a number of fiction awards, including the Prix Formentor, the Booker Prize, and the National Book Award.

McCarthy's own writing style is classic: her sentences, architectural structures of balance and cadence; her rebellious point of view, a rainbow prism of satiric wit. The typical McCarthy story is realistic and satirical, revealing the self-deception of the supposedly intelligent and well educated. Her fiction is peopled with veiled portraits of those whom she knew well. Critical opinion tends to cast each of McCarthy's husbands, except James Raymond West, as the model for one or more of her male "antagonists": Harold Johnsrud for Harald Peterson in *The Group* and the husband in "Cruel and Barbarous Treatment"; Edmund Wilson for Miles Murphy in *A Charmed Life* (1955) and a legion of short-story husbands; and Bowden Broadwater for John Sinnot in *A Charmed Life* and a young American in "The Cicerone." Generally, McCarthy's characters are viewed ironically from a vantage point of cool detachment. Known as much for her criticism as for her own fiction, McCarthy earns an important place in literature.

Biography

Mary Therese McCarthy's biography is unusually significant for understanding her fiction, since various clusters of biographical details seem to generate all of her stories and characters. McCarthy's childhood began in Seattle with a doting, extravagant mother and a romantic, imaginative father. Her early life was an eden of picnics, parties, and stories, which ended abruptly in 1918, when the flu killed both her parents within the same week. McCarthy was then remanded to the harsh and punitive custody of an Aunt Margaret and Uncle Meyers, but she survived in this new environment, which included beatings and deprivation, by excelling in school. These early triumphs led her to Vassar College, the crucible of her imaginative life and scene of her most popular work, *The Group*. All of these details can be variously found in the lives of her fictional heroines, principally Meg Sargent's, the recurring figure in *The Company She Keeps* (indeed, Sargent was her great grandmother's maiden name).

On her graduation from Vassar College, McCarthy married an actor, Harold Johnsrud, and at the same time she became drama critic for the *Partisan Review*; the marriage lasted three years, her career ten. By 1938, she had branched out into fiction and had a new marriage with Edmund Wilson. After six cataclysmic years and one son, Reuel, McCarthy divorced Wilson and married Bowden Broadwater, from whom she was divorced in early 1961. Later in the year, McCarthy married James Raymond West, a State Department official, in Paris. She and West spent half of each year in their Paris home and half in Maine. During the last few years of her life, McCarthy had several operations for hydrocephalus but continued to work on her memoirs, plan a study of Gothic architecture, teach literature at Bard College, study German, and write literary criticism and commentary. She died in New York City on October 25, 1989, of cancer.

Analysis

Mary McCarthy's stories are, on the whole, about errors endemic to intellectuals, which lead them to indignity, despair, and sterility. McCarthy's typical intellectuals are political radicals or artists who fail to comprehend that their analytical acumen or talent does not raise them sufficiently from the common dilemma to empower them either to save the rest or to live more beautifully than do others. Meg Sargent, who, like Hemingway's Nick Adams, reappears continually in a series of short stories, is McCarthy's Every-intellectual, her voyage the purgatory of those with pretensions to education. "Cruel and Barbarous Treatment" is a good example of McCarthy's literary universe, and Meg's.

In this story, Meg is going through a divorce, orchestrating the breakup of her marriage with the self-image of a diva in her greatest role. Meg considers herself to be a member of the intelligentsia, but McCarthy etches her as a grandiose fraud whose view of her situation is riddled with tired clichés. McCarthy comments on Meg economically by simply capitalizing strategically to turn Meg's thoughts into a series of buzz words. Meg is anxious to hear "What People Would Say" and "How Her Husband Would Take It." Finally, even the heroine realizes what she is doing. She will go ahead with her divorce, but she understands that The Young Man whom she thought she had waiting in the wings has been her factotum, not her passion. She will not be fool enough to fly into his arms. Unfortunately, her insight does not last, and on the train to Reno, she is fabricating a new opera for her fellow passengers, deciding what to answer to queries concerning her destination. She will not be vulgar enough to blurt out, "Reno," nor will she equivocate and reply "San Francisco." At first, she will say, " 'West,' with an air of vagueness and hesitation. Then, when pressed, she might go as far as to say 'Nevada.' But no farther."

The most pointed and, some might say, best treatment of McCarthy's theme, however, is "The Man in the Brooks Brothers Shirt," her most widely anthologized story. In this story, Meg is traveling West to tell her aunt in Portland that she is to be married again. As a result of her trip, she realizes that she will never marry her new intended. The source of Meg's revelation is her encounter with Mr. Breen, a middle-level corporate executive in the steel business whose wife, Leonie, and three children live comfortably in the Gate Hills section of Cleveland. Meg begins the trip flashing an advance copy of a very unimportant novel with which she intends to impress her suitor with her cultural superiority.

A political radical, Meg patronizes Breen's position in the corporate structure. Along with her self-dramatized contempt for the man, however, McCarthy explores attitudes of which Meg is not aware. Meg is a poseur and she envelops others in mythological poses. Despite her initial characterization of Breen as a "middle-aged baby, like a young pig, something in a seed catalogue . . . plainly Out of the Question," when Breen reveals that beneath his Brooks Brothers shirt beats a heart that wants to vote for Norman Thomas, Meg immediately romanticizes him as the last of the old breed of real American men. Stringing along behind her fantasy, she allows herself to get drunk in Breen's private compartment; the predictable revelry and sex follow in short order.

The next morning Meg is filled with shame, but Breen is wildly in love with her and wants to divorce Leonie and throw himself into an unconventional life with his Bohemian Girl. For Meg, sudden realization follows her drunken, sensual orgy; she begins to feel that she is not so much a free spirit, as she has always prided herself, but a sort of misfit. All the men in her life have suited her because they, like her, were in some way "handicapped" for American life. Although Breen seems to break the pattern, he does not. He is fifty, she thinks, over the hill. Would he, she wonders, have been in such hot pursuit if he were ten years younger?

What is clear, at least to the reader, is that each character is ambivalent about the characteristic of the other that holds the most attraction. Meg is contemptuous of

Breen's conventionality, and Breen is critical of Meg's individualism. He tells her to shape up, because if she does not, "In a few years you'll become one of those Bohemian horrors with oily hair and long earrings." The liberation that each affords the other does not mitigate these streaks of aversion. Meg and Breen do not run off together, but Meg also knows that she cannot marry her intended, and Breen manages to tryst with Meg several times before disappearing from her life. Meg has gained, through Breen, some humility about her elite self-image, but only temporarily; ultimately, she writes Breen off. Her last contact with him is a telegram she receives from him after the death of her father: "SINCEREST CONDOLENCES. YOU HAVE LOST THE BEST FRIEND YOU WILL EVER HAVE." Meg disposes of the missive, disgusted and embarrassed by Breen's middle-class sentimentality.

The portraits of Meg's individualism and Breen's conventionalism are ironic, but, although both characters are supremely flawed, the story nevertheless treats Breen's limitations more charitably than Meg's. If Breen is corny, at least he fulfills the obligations of social convention to be nurturing, even if he is a bit obtuse. The nature of the intellect is to enlighten society, and Meg is too cliché-ridden to fulfill her obligations; all we see are her limitations. In the end, her Bohemianism is merely another form of convention. She shreds Breen's telegram at the end of the story because, "It would have been dreadful if anyone had seen it." No bourgeoise could have better phrased the sentiment. McCarthy is a mistress of such deft, deflating touches. In the final ten words of the story she irretrievably nails Meg to the wall, just as she did at the end of "Cruel and Barbarous Treatment." She frequently uses a parting shot to devastate her protagonists.

McCarthy also grants her characters an occasional victory. When she does, the victory is hard-won and painfully small, but it can be lyrically affecting, as in "Ghostly Father, I Confess." In this story, Meg is now the wife of Frederick (perhaps based on Edmund Wilson) and is in analysis with Dr. James. Through numerous digressions, we learn much about other people in Meg's life, but the story takes place almost entirely during a session with her analyst. The beginning of the session is awash with stereotype; Meg stereotypes Dr. James, and he counters with the routine Freudian castration theory and dream interpretation. They move past this initial standoff, however, and begin to examine the effect of Meg's childhood on her terrible marriages. The details are all recognizable from McCarthy's own biography.

Meg explains how her marriage to Frederick shows that she is in a downward spiral initiated by the cruelty of her childhood guardians. James comes forward with a surprising inversion of Meg's rather obvious, although painfully arrived at, analysis, suggesting that "This marriage took more daring on your part than anything you have done since you left your father's house." He goes on to say that with the marriage to Frederick, Meg has stopped denying the trauma of her childhood because she is now strong enough to face it and work it through. James quiets Meg's doubts by referring to her brains and beauty, which he tells her will overcome her problems. The session comes to a sudden close as James snaps shut his notebook, though clicking the interview off. He is transformed, now uninvolved. Meg is upset by the abruptness, but somewhat intoxicated by her discovery that James has given her five extra minutes and by his parting remark about her brains and beauty.

Once in the street, Meg is suddenly struck by the meaning of the dream for which James had given her an unsatisfying, conventional interpretation during the session. In her dream, she had seen herself loved by a Byronic figure who slowly metamorphosed into a Nazi war prisoner. She understands that the changing figure is her own mind revealing its true identity, not truly Byronic, after all, but a victim of rigidity and cruelty. As in the other stories, Meg has an insight into her fraudulent self-images, but this time the self-awareness seems to take hold. The story closes with the image of Meg in front of a window full of hot water bottles begging God to let her hold onto her uncomfortable revelation. McCarthy cryptically ends her narrative with the statement, "It was certainly a very small favor she was asking, but . . . she could not be too demanding, for, unfortunately, she did not believe in God."

McCarthy's sly portrait explores the enormity of trying to think at all. The mind tends to fall in love with its own creations and perpetrate frauds on itself. There is the fraud of the analyst who can turn his involvement on and off; the vanity of Meg's greed for five more minutes; the possible disingenuousness of James's remark about brains and beauty; the war between flesh and spirit, one of which desires the vulgar comfort of the hot water bottle, the other the irritant of enlightenment; and James's inordinate pleasure about his various interpretations, although we do not know if they are true or false. Finally, there is the magnitude of the universe for which we desire the comfort of a caretaker, whom McCarthy would deny as a vulgarity equal to the hot water bottle. The mind is surely nine-tenths dissembler, but Meg, by intuiting profoundly her own shabby role-playing has made an inroad on that great disabler of the intellect, its own narcissism. Such an inroad is the outer limit of McCarthy's concept of human achievement.

Other major works

NOVELS: *The Oasis*, 1949; *The Groves of Academe*, 1952; *A Charmed Life*, 1955; *The Group*, 1963; *Birds of America*, 1971; *Cannibals and Missionaries*, 1979.

NONFICTION: *Sights and Spectacles: 1937-1956*, 1956; *Venice Observed*, 1956; *Memories of a Catholic Girlhood*, 1957; *The Stones of Florence*, 1959; *On the Contrary: Articles of Belief*, 1961; *Mary McCarthy's Theatre Chronicles, 1937-1962*, 1963; *Vietnam*, 1967; *Hanoi*, 1968; *The Writing on the Wall and Other Literary Essays*, 1970; *Medina*, 1972; *The Seventeenth Degree*, 1974; *The Mask of State*, 1974; *Ideas and the Novel*, 1980; *Occasional Prose*, 1985; *How I Grew*, 1987.

Bibliography

Gelderman, Carol W. *Mary McCarthy: A Life.* New York: St. Martin's Press, 1988. Gelderman offers an objective biography of McCarthy. Although much of the narrative is familiar, the book is well written and amply documented. The photographs provide important perspective on McCarthy's childhood and a satisfying glimpse into her adult life. This biography makes good reading for a general audience as well as for a student of McCarthy.

Goldman, Sherli Evens. *Mary McCarthy: A Bibliography.* New York: Harcourt, Brace & World, 1968. Goldman explains that Mary McCarthy was "more collaborator than subject" in this work. The book is divided into five categories: books, contributions to books, contributions to periodicals, translations into foreign languages, and appendix of miscellanea. The appendix lists interviews, McCarthy's own translations of French works, and Braille and recorded editions of books by McCarthy.

Kufrin, Joan. *Uncommon Women.* Piscataway, N.J.: New Century, 1981. In a book that examines women who have succeeded within several different fields, McCarthy is "The Novelist" for the chapter so named. The portrayal of the writer is friendly and informal, largely the transcription of an interview in McCarthy's home in Maine. McCarthy comments on her writing process of extensive revision. The two photographs capture a sense of fun and humor in McCarthy. A light and readable piece.

McKenzie, Barbara. *Mary McCarthy.* New York: Twayne, 1966. McKenzie offers a one-page chronology of McCarthy's life as well as an opening chapter titled "The Fact in Biography." The fourth chapter, titled "The Key That Works the Person," concerns the short stories in *The Company She Keeps* and *Cast a Cold Eye.* The final chapter assesses McCarthy's overall contribution to literature. McKenzie's book, with notes, a bibliography, and an index, would benefit the serious student of McCarthy's work.

Stock, Irvin. *Mary McCarthy.* Minneapolis: University of Minnesota Press, 1968. Stock's forty-seven-page essay includes overall critical comment on McCarthy's work, noting the moral concerns evident in her fiction. Stock also provides a brief biography. He summarizes and then provides analysis of *The Company She Keeps, Cast a Cold Eye, The Oasis, The Groves of Academe,* and *The Group.* Stock's character studies are particularly good.

Martha Nochimson
(Revised by *Janet T. Palmer*)

CARSON McCULLERS

Born: Columbus, Georgia; February 19, 1917
Died: Nyack, New York; September 29, 1967

Principal short fiction

The Ballad of the Sad Café: The Novels and Stories of Carson McCullers, 1951; *The Ballad of the Sad Café and Collected Short Stories*, 1952; *The Shorter Novels and Stories of Carson McCullers*, 1972.

Other literary forms

Carson McCullers' remarkable first novel, *The Heart Is a Lonely Hunter* (1940), establishes the themes that were to concern her in all her other writing: the spiritual isolation of individuals and their attempt to transcend loneliness through love. Thereafter, she wrote short stories, some poetry (mostly for children), three other novels, and two plays. The most popular of the novels, *The Member of the Wedding* (1946), she adapted for the stage; the play was a great success on Broadway and was also made into an award-winning film. *The Heart Is a Lonely Hunter* and her somber Freudian novel, *Reflections in a Golden Eye* (1941), were also adapted for film. McCullers also wrote a number of significant essays, which are collected in *The Mortgaged Heart* (1971). The essays that are most important to understanding the method and content of her fiction, especially her use of the grotesque, are "The Russian Realists and Southern Literature" and "The Flowering Dream: Notes on Writing."

Achievements

McCullers was the winner of a number of literary awards during her lifetime, including membership in the National Institute of Arts and Letters, two Guggenheim fellowships, and an Arts and Letters Grant. She also won the New York Drama Critics Circle Award, a Gold Medal, and the Donaldson Award (all for the play version of *The Member of the Wedding*). Her fiction and nonfiction prose were published in a number of reputable magazines, including *The New Yorker, Harper's Bazaar, Esquire*, and *Mademoiselle*. For her story "A Tree. A Rock. A Cloud," she was nominated for an O. Henry Award.

As a writer of short fiction, McCullers' success with objective narration, the theme of loneliness, and her lyric compression are praiseworthy. While McCullers is perhaps not as great a writer of short stories as her peers Flannery O'Connor, Eudora Welty, and Katherine Anne Porter, she is nevertheless successful at affecting her readers' emotions. The brevity and compression of stories such as "The Jockey" and "The Sojourner" are remarkable based on any standards. Although her fiction may not, in the long run, be influential on the craft of many other writers, and although her techniques are not as innovative as those of many other postmodern fiction writers, she has influenced, among others, Truman Capote, Flannery O'Connor, and Anne Tyler, particularly with the expert use of the grotesque and the freakish, and the portrayal of human alienation. Her knowledge of human psychology also makes her a great spokesperson for the complexity of human experience.

Biography

Carson McCullers, born Lula Carson Smith, was reared in a small Southern town, a milieu which she used in much of her fiction. Exhibiting early talent in both writing and music, she intended to become a concert pianist but lost her tuition money for the Juilliard School of Music when she went to New York in 1935. This loss led her to get part-time jobs while studying writing at Columbia University. She earned early acclaim for her first novel, *The Heart Is a Lonely Hunter*, written when she was only twenty-two. Her friends included many prominent writers, including Tennessee Williams, W. H. Auden, Louis MacNiece, and Richard Wright. Her health was always delicate; she suffered early paralyzing strokes, breast cancer, and pneumonia. She stayed remarkably active in literature and drama, however, even when confined to bed and wheelchair. She died of a stroke at the age of fifty.

Analysis

Carson McCullers' short stories (ruling out for the moment "The Ballad of the Sad Café," a short novella) often explore the intense emotional content of seemingly undramatic situations. Plot is minimal, although there is often at least one unusual or grotesque element. "Wunderkind," for example, deals with the confused feelings of a gifted fifteen-year-old girl at a piano lesson. Her social development has been sacrificed to her musical talent; now her mastery of the keyboard is faltering and she is profoundly humiliated. The reader realizes that part of her difficulty is the awakening of sexual feelings for her teacher, Mister Bilderbach. Neither the teacher, who thinks of her as a child prodigy, nor the young girl herself understands her tension and clumsiness.

"The Jockey" has an even more ordinary situation—a brief encounter in a restaurant between a jockey and three other men identified as a trainer, a bookie, and a rich man whose horse the jockey has ridden. The dwarflike jockey, called Bitsy Barlow, is one of those grotesque figures who seem like an embarrassing mistake in nature. The point of the story is the ironic contrast between the three "normal" men's callous pretense of sympathy for a rider's crippling accident on the track and the jockey's bitter grief for that rider, who is his closest friend. Although the jockey, because of his physical deformity, seems a caricature of humanity, the intensity of his sorrow makes the other men's callousness seem the more monstrous.

"Madame Zilensky and the King of Finland" is, on the most obvious level, at least, a revelation of the emotional price of artistic excellence. Like "Wunderkind" and "The Jockey," the story concerns the subjective significance of seemingly minor events. Mr. Brook, head of a college music department, hires Madame Zilensky, a famous composer and teacher, for his faculty. He is tolerant of her several eccentricities, her tales of adventures in exotic places, and even her somewhat shocking assertion that her three sons are the offspring of three different lovers. When she claims to have seen the King of Finland, however, Mr. Brook realizes that she is a pathological liar, since Finland has no king. Mr. Brook is sensitive enough to intuit the motive for her prevarications: the terrible constriction of her actual experience. "Through her lies, she lived vicariously. The lies doubled the little of her existence that was left over from work and augmented the little rag end of her personal life."

Point of view is vital in this story. The pathetic emotional dependence of Madame Zilensky upon fantasy is the explicit and obvious content, but the story's real focus is on the growing perception of Mr. Brook, who has himself led a somewhat dull, repetitive life in academia. It is his character which receives the more subtle delineation. He represents those countless ordinary people whose individuality has been subdued, but not utterly extinguished, by professional duties. When Mr. Brook, in his official capacity, feels he must reprimand Madame Zilensky for propagating lies about herself, he comes face to face with stark tragedy. The terrible emotional deprivation he is about to expose echoes in his own solitary soul. Compassion for her loneliness and his own makes him realize that truth is not the highest virtue.

This terrified retreat from reality into the most banal of polite conversation ironically combines tragedy and sardonic humor. To use the name of love in this context is surprising, at once accurate and absurd. A final symbolic image captures the grotesque irrationality embedded in the most familiar landscape. As Mr. Brook looks out of his office window later, he sees, perhaps for the hundredth time, a faculty member's old airedale terrier waddling down the street. This time, however, something is strange: the dog is walking backwards. He watches "with a kind of cold surprise" until the dog is out of sight, then returns to the pile of student papers on his desk.

This story is thematically typical of McCullers' fiction. Love, which has little or nothing to do with sexuality, is the only way to bridge the terrible isolation which separates individuals. Too many other factors in the situation, however—habit, social custom, human perversity, the demands of artistic creativity, or simply devotion to duty—conspire against the goal of giving love and comfort to one another. Each person is trapped, incommunicado, in the little cage he has chosen.

The irrational persistence of love and its inadequacy to solve the everyday problems of existence are also apparent in "A Domestic Dilemma." Here, too, the story is told from the point of view of a patient, kindly man whose attitude toward his alcoholic wife is a curious blend of compassion, love, and angry exasperation. He fears for the welfare of his two children. He comes home to the suburbs from his New York office to find his children unattended, playing with Christmas tree lights, a supper of cinnamon toast on the kitchen table, untouched except for one bite. The little boy complains, "It hurt. The toast was hot." His wife, Emily, had mistaken cayenne pepper for cinnamon.

The bewildered children do not understand the painful scene between mother and father, in which Emily vacillates drunkenly between belligerent defense of her behavior and tearful shame. Martin finally persuades her to go to bed and let him feed the children, bathe them, and put them to bed. He successfully reestablishes an atmosphere of tender solicitude, hoping the children will not remember their mother's puzzling behavior. How long will it be, he wonders, before they understand and despise her? There are moments when Martin hates his wife, imagining "a future of degradation and slow ruin" for himself and his children. When he finally lies down beside Emily and watches her sleeping, however, his anger gradually dissipates. "His hand sought the adjacent flesh and sorrow paralleled desire in the immense complexity of love."

One interpretation offered for "A Domestic Dilemma" points to the stresses of an urban life-style upon a woman reared in an emotionally supportive small Southern town. In suburbia, Emily is isolated from everyone she ever knew, while Martin commutes long distances into the inner city. Thus, it is social isolation which is destroying her. This interpretation has considerable validity, although the cause of her alcoholism is not really central to the story; isolation and loneliness occur in all kinds of social situations in McCullers' fiction, and small southern towns are as deadly as urban suburbs in that regard. Isolation is a metaphysical affliction more than a cultural one. Emily's social isolation is analogous to Bitsy Barlow's physical deformity or even Madame Zilensky's enslaving musical genius—one of the many accidents of nature or situation over which people have little control. As Mr. Brook's empathy for Madame Zilensky cannot alleviate her isolation, Martin's love for his wife will not necessarily save her from her unhappiness. In McCullers' fiction it is usually the act of love, not the comfort of being loved, that has power to transform the lover.

One of the most anthologized of McCullers' stories is "A Tree. A Rock. A Cloud," which was chosen for the O. Henry Memorial Prize Stories of 1952, even though it may be inferior, in some ways, to "A Domestic Dilemma," "Wunderkind," and "Madame Zilensky and the King of Finland." It deals more philosophically and perhaps more ironically with the art of loving. The lover, in this case, is an old, boozy wanderer who waylays a newspaperboy in a café. He is compulsively dedicated to explaining how he learned to love "all things both great and small." The quotation comes not from the story, but from *The Rime of the Ancient Mariner* (1798), which is quite possibly its inspiration. The irony of Samuel Taylor Coleridge's Ancient Mariner waylaying an impatient wedding guest with his story of salvation through love is translated here into a somewhat different context.

Three persons, rather than two, are involved. Although the tale is addressed to the naïve newspaperboy, it is overheard by Leo, the proprietor of the café, who is early characterized as bitter and stingy. When the wanderer accosts the boy and says distinctly, "I love you," the initial laughter of the men in the café and their immediate return to their own beer or breakfasts suggest both a widespread cynicism and an utter indifference concerning the welfare of the boy. Although Leo is also cynical and often vulgar, he listens to the conversation carefully. When the old man orders a beer for the boy, Leo brings coffee instead, reminding the other man, "He is a minor."

Although Leo soon understands that the old man's intention is not to proposition the boy, he continues to interject insulting remarks into the wanderer's sad tale of love for a wife who deserted him for another man. The old man struggles to explain the unifying effect of love upon the fragmented psyche. Before his marriage, he says, "when I had enjoyed anything there was a peculiar sensation as though it was laying around loose in me. Nothing seemed to finish itself up or fit in with other things." His wife, however, transformed his experience of himself—"this woman was something like an assembly line for my soul. I run these little pieces of myself through her and I come out complete." Yet, after years of frantic search for the lost wife, the man realizes with horror that he cannot even remember distinctly what she looked like. It was then that he began his "science" of love.

At this point, Leo explodes in exasperation:

> Leo's mouth jerked with a pale, quick grin. "Well none of we boys are getting any younger," he said. Then with sudden anger he balled up a dishcloth he was holding and threw it down hard on the floor. "You draggle-tailed old Romeo!"

The wanderer solemnly explains that one must practice the art of loving by starting with small or inanimate things—a tree, a rock, a cloud—and graduate from one thing to another. He learned to love a goldfish next. Now he has so perfected the science of loving that he can love anything and everyone. By this time, Leo is screaming at him to shut up.

As an explanation of Platonic love, this, to be sure, may be feeble. The reactions of Leo and the boy do, however, provide depth to the story. The newsboy is puzzled and confused—presumably because he has yet to pass through adolescence, when the importance and complexity of love will become clearer to him. After the old man leaves, the boy appeals to Leo for answers. Was the man drunk? Was he a dope fiend? Was he crazy? To the first two questions Leo says, shortly, "No." To the last he is grimly silent. Probably Leo responds so emotionally to the old man's tale because it makes him too keenly aware of his own barren lovelessness. His role is somewhat analogous to that of Mr. Brook in this respect. He recognizes, perhaps, that the old man, unlike himself, has found a way to transcend his wretchedness. Can it be "crazy" to be at peace with oneself, in spite of outwardly miserable circumstances? If so, it is a craziness a sane man might covet. The boy, thinking of nothing else to say, comments that the man "sure has done a lot of traveling." As the story ends, McCullers emphasizes therefore that the story is about adolescent versus adult perceptions of love.

McCullers' short fiction, like her most popular novel, *The Member of the Wedding*, has many autobiographical elements. Her own absorption in music and early aspirations to be a concert pianist are reflected in "Wunderkind" and "Madame Zilensky and the King of Finland." The particular mode of Madame Zilensky's escape from a narrowly focused existence is even more pertinent to McCullers' short, intense life. She escaped the limitations of her frail body through fantasy, transforming it, of course, into fiction and drama.

Even the situation in "A Domestic Dilemma" echoes her own life curiously altered. She lived both the Emily role, that is, the maimed personality who desperately needs love and companionship, and the Martin role, the hopeless lover of the psychologically crippled person. McCullers' husband, whom she divorced and later remarried, was an alcoholic whose drinking was aggravated by the fact that, although he fancied himself a writer, she was so much more successful than he. She has disguised the personal element in the situation by changing the presumed cause of the alcoholism (although she, too, knew the effect of migrating from a small Southern town to New York) and by projecting her role more upon the husband than the wife.

Both Martin and Mr. Brook exhibit qualities ordinarily ascribed to women— intuition, gentleness, patience, and unselfish love. McCullers' blurring of gender roles (Miss Amelia in "The Ballad of the Sad Café" is strikingly masculine) was probably not motivated by a feminist revolt against stereotyped sex roles; she was not a polemicist, but a lyrical writer, projecting her own personality, feelings, dreams, and fears. If her men act like women or vice versa, it is because she was herself decidedly androgynous. She loved both men and women and somehow contained them both. Some of her most ardent attractions were for women who repudiated her attentions (or at least did not remain in her vicinity), which may account for the wistful need for love in some of her fictional characters.

In spite of her personal sorrows and her emotional isolation and loneliness, McCullers was beloved by many friends and generous in her own affections. Even the odd triangular love affairs which appear in *The Member of the Wedding* and *Reflections in a Golden Eye* have some autobiographical parallels. Both Carson and her husband, according to McCullers' biographer, Virginia Spencer Carr, were intimately involved with Jack Diamond, a concert musician. It is not an accident that McCullers was one of the first American writers to deal openly (in *Reflections in a Golden Eye*) with repressed homosexuality. In the case of her husband, at least, his homosexual orientation was not always repressed; whether she was an active bisexual is more ambiguous.

Her personal life and her fiction both seem marked by a curious combination of sophisticated intuition into human motives and an odd childlike quality which sometimes verges on immaturity. Most writers, for example, would not write of Mr. Brook that he could not speak until "this agitation in his insides quieted down"; nor would many writers try to express the blurred Platonic idealism of "A Tree. A Rock. A Cloud." Although the situational irony of that story saves it from being naïvely expressed philosophy, one has a lingering impression that the writer is mocking a sentiment that she really wants to advocate.

"The Ballad of the Sad Café," sometimes grouped with novellas, sometimes with short stories, is the most successful of McCullers' ventures into the grotesque. The melancholy mood suggested by the title is appropriate; like many a folk ballad, it tells a mournful tale touched with sardonic humor. The story celebrates the love of a cross-eyed, mannish woman for a conceited, hunchbacked dwarf. It also involves a curious love triangle, for the climax is a grotesque battle between the protagonist,

Miss Amelia, and her former husband for the affection of the dwarf.

True love, paradoxically, is both a cruel joke and the means of redemption, not only for the lover, Miss Amelia, but also for the whole in-grown, backwoods community, which otherwise dies of emotional starvation. The inhabitants of this stifling Southern village, like a somber chorus in a Greek tragedy, observe and reflect the fortunes of Miss Amelia, their leading citizen. Cousin Lymon, the hunchback, appears out of nowhere at the door of Miss Amelia, who runs the town store and the best distillery for miles around. To everyone's amazement, instead of throwing him out, as she has done to others who claimed kinship, Miss Amelia takes in the wretched wanderer and even falls in love with him. Cousin Lymon becomes a pompous little king of the castle, although not, apparently, her bed partner. Love transforms the mean, hard, sexless Miss Amelia into a reasonable facsimile of a warm-hearted woman. She opens a café in her store because Cousin Lymon likes company, and her place becomes the social center of the community. Miss Amelia blossoms; the community blooms with goodwill, until the arrival of another person who is to destroy this interlude of happiness and peace.

Miss Amelia had once married the town bad boy, who had unaccountably fallen in love with her. Her motivation had apparently been solely commercial, the hope of acquiring a strong helper in her business; when the bridegroom expected sexual favors, Miss Amelia had indignantly refused. After ten stormy days, she threw him out entirely, earning his undying hatred for causing him such frustration and humiliation; he turned to a life of crime and landed in the penitentiary. Now he is out of jail and returns with malevolent thoughts of revenge. Poor Miss Amelia, now vulnerable in a new and surprising way, accepts his unwelcome presence in her café because Cousin Lymon is fascinated with him, and Miss Amelia and her former spouse become rivals for the affection of the dwarf.

This rivalry culminates in a ludicrous variation of the western showdown, solemnly witnessed by the whole community, when Miss Amelia and her former husband have a battle of fisticuffs in the café. Moreover, Miss Amelia, who has been quietly working out with a punching bag in preparation for the event, is winning. At the last moment, however, the traitorous Cousin Lymon leaps onto her back and the two men together beat her senseless. Afterward, they vandalize her store and her still in the woods and flee. Miss Amelia thereafter closes her business and becomes a permanent recluse in a town now desolate and deserted.

Although many readers prefer her mood piece, *The Member of the Wedding*, McCullers has hardly surpassed in originality and skill her achievement in this sardonically humorous fable. Although it may be vaguely reminiscent of Mark Twain or perhaps Bret Harte, there is really no other story like it; yet it gives the impression of archetypal myth. Much rustic humor suffers from an artificial quality, as though the author has put on a mask quite alien to his true nature. This strange tale seems to issue from the subconscious, having the authenticity of dream life; yet it is controlled by a fully conscious intelligence, capable of irony and humor. Thematically, it attests to both the power of love and its fragility. Love ennobles the lover, but not the beloved. Indeed, the beloved, who often has done nothing at all to deserve such affection, may perversely despise and destroy the lover. Since love chooses its object with all the obliviousness to reality of Titania pursuing the assheaded Bottom, it can seldom last; and with the defeat of love, human existence becomes a desolation.

Other major works

NOVELS: *The Heart Is a Lonely Hunter*, 1940; *Reflections in a Golden Eye*, 1941; *The Member of the Wedding*, 1946; *Clock Without Hands*, 1961.

PLAYS: *The Member of the Wedding*, 1950; *The Square Root of Wonderful*, 1957.

CHILDREN'S LITERATURE: *Sweet as a Pickle and Clean as a Pig*, 1964.

MISCELLANEOUS: *The Mortgaged Heart*, 1971 (short fiction, poetry, and essays; Margarita G. Smith, editor).

Bibliography

Carr, Virginia Spencer. *The Lonely Hunter: A Biography of Carson McCullers.* Garden City, N.J.: Anchor Press, 1975. This definitive biography offers an interesting read and provides significant biographical elements that are related to McCullers' works. The complexity, pain, and loneliness of McCullers' characters are matched by their creator's. Includes an extensive chronology of McCullers' life, a primary bibliography, and many endnotes.

Cook, Richard M. *Carson McCullers.* New York: Frederick Ungar, 1975. A good general introduction to McCullers' novels, short stories, and plays. Cook's analyses of the short stories and *The Ballad of the Sad Café* are especially good, though the book includes chapters on each of the novels, McCullers' life, and her achievements as well. Cook, while admiring McCullers, recognizes her limitations but nevertheless praises her success with portraying human suffering and isolation and enabling readers to relate to the most grotesque of characters. The book's endnotes and primary and secondary bibliographies may be useful in finding other sources.

Graver, Lawrence. *Carson McCullers.* Minneapolis: University of Minnesota Press, 1969. An early, though still useful extended essay in the University of Minnesota pamphlet series. Offers a chronological overview of McCullers' life and career. Particularly good are the brief analyses of the novels and *The Ballad of the Sad Café*, but some of Graver's comments, especially some psychoanalytical observations, are outdated. Graver's admiration of McCullers is questionable since at times he does not admit her fiction's power at the psychological and mythical level and instead praises male authors' superiority, reducing McCullers to a mere lyricist. Complemented by a brief bibliography of primary and secondary sources.

McDowell, Margaret B. *Carson McCullers.* Boston: Twayne, 1980. A good general introduction to McCullers' fictions, with a chapter on each of the novels, the short stories, and *The Ballad of the Sad Café*. Also included are a chronology, endnotes, and a select bibliography. Stressing McCullers' versatility, McDowell emphasizes the lyricism, the musicality, and the rich symbolism of McCullers' fiction as well as McCullers' sympathy for lonely individuals.

Westling, Louise. *Sacred Groves and Ravaged Gardens: The Fiction of Eudora Welty, Carson McCullers, and Flannery O'Connor.* Athens: University of Georgia Press, 1985. In this study, important comparisons are made between these three major Southern writers of short fiction and novels. While Westling is not the first to use a feminist approach with McCullers, the book offers useful insight concerning the portrayal of the female characters and the issue of androgyny in McCullers' fiction. Her analysis of *The Ballad of the Sad Café* is particularly good. Supplemented by useful endnotes and a bibliography of secondary material.

Katherine Snipes
(Revised by *D. Dean Shackelford*)

JOAQUIM MARIA MACHADO DE ASSIS

Born: Rio de Janeiro, Brazil; June 21, 1839
Died: Rio de Janeiro, Brazil; September 29, 1908

Principal short fiction

Contos Fluminenses, 1870; *Histórias da Meia-Noite*, 1873; *Papéis Avulsos*, 1882; *Histórias Sem Data*, 1884; *Várias Histórias*, 1896; *The Psychiatrist and Other Stories*, 1963; *The Devil's Church and Other Stories*, 1977.

Other literary forms

Joaquim Maria Machado de Assis' first published works were poems and literary criticism, including two frequently cited studies on Brazilian literature. He wrote comedies for the theater, was master of a journalistic genre known as the *crônica* (literally, "chronicle"), and carried on an extensive correspondence, since published. He is best known for his novels, especially the last five, for which *Dom Casmurro* (1900) and *Memórias Póstumas de Bras Cubas* (1881) are probably the best known outside Brazil.

Achievements

At the time of his death, in 1908, Machado de Assis was revered as Brazil's most important and influential man of letters, a distinction many critics feel he deserves even today. An innovator in such areas as the use of irony and of self-conscious but unreliable narrator/protagonists, Machado de Assis was instrumental in leading Brazilian literature toward an appreciation of both technical sophistication and authenticity of expression. Although he did outstanding work in all the literary genres, including poetry, drama, translation, and critical theory, it was in narrative—the novel and short-story forms especially—that he achieved his greatest successes. His extraordinary work *Memórias Póstumas de Bras Cubas* (1881; *Epitaph of a Small Winner*, 1951) can, for example, be regarded as the first modern novel of either North or South America, while the text widely held to be his supreme achievement, *Dom Casmurro* (1900; English translation, 1953), ranks as one of the outstanding novels of its time. Perhaps even more brilliant as a writer of short fiction, however, Machado de Assis is credited with having originated the modern short-story form in Brazil, where tales such as "The Psychiatrist," "Midnight Mass," "A Singular Event," "The Companion," and "Dona Paula" are still judged to be masterpieces of his laconic, metaphoric art.

Biography

A lifelong resident of Rio de Janeiro, Joaquim Maria Machado de Assis was the son of a Portuguese mother and a mulatto father. Despite humble origin, epilepsy, and a speech defect, this self-taught intellectual not only attained the highest civil service position open to him but also founded the Brazilian Academy of Letters and served as its president until his death in 1908. While still living, Machado de Assis saw himself acknowledged as Brazil's greatest writer.

Analysis

To some modern readers it may appear lamentable that Machado de Assis' works bear neither overt references to his racial heritage nor arguably even oblique ones. In this regard the Brazilian mulatto will be seen to be fully integrated with the concerns and priorities of the European-leaning dominant bourgeois society in late nineteenth century Brazil. Nevertheless, Machado de Assis wrote on the fringes of "polite" society in a way that did not specifically derive from race, although a sense of social inferiority may well have contributed to his development of a cynical and biting stance toward the higher spiritual aspirations of the socially dominant Brazilian of his day. Specifically, this stance can be seen in his critical analyses of the ambiguities of the human soul (his "Jamesian" quality) and in his dissection of the pious self-sufficiency of the ignorant bourgeoisie (his "Flaubertian" and "Tolstoian" qualities). Like many of the great realists, Machado de Assis lends himself to a Lukacsian or Marxist analysis. His works bespeak, beneath the surface of the comings and goings of polite, ordered society, the tremendous conflicts, passions, and irreconcilable tensions of a society that fragments human experience and strives to metaphorize, in terms of a myth of spiritual transcendence, humans' carnal and materialistic nature. The patterned texture of an ordered society remains permanently at odds with fundamental aspects of the human soul which it chooses to ignore or metaphorize.

In this regard, Machado de Assis' story "Singular Occurrência" ("A Singular Event") may be considered a metatext not only of the Brazilian's concern with ambiguities of the human experience that polite society cannot account for in terms of its own ideological construction of the world, but also of his typically nineteenth century rhetorical strategies for the framing of ambiguous narrative. The story concerns the "singular event" in the amorous relations between a young married lawyer and a woman of unspecified occupation ("she was not a dressmaker, nor a landlady, nor a governess; eliminate the professions and you will get the idea") who becomes not only his devoted lover but his "pupil" as well. The relationship described between the two goes beyond simply the sexual bond between a gentleman and his extramarital companion (a Latin American sociocultural cliché). The lawyer undertakes to form the woman, teaching her to read and to appreciate the "finer" things in life in the form of the high cultural artifacts of the period. Then one night the woman undertakes a sordid adventure with another man in such a way that it appears she is flaunting her perfidy. The idolizing lawyer is possessed with despair; yet she remains silent as to the reasons for her infidelity or at least for the "dramatization" of an apparent flagrant infidelity. The lovers are reconciled, she bears him a child who soon dies, he subsequently dies while out of town, and she spends the rest of her days conducting herself as a proper widow: when the story opens she is seen going to church clad in somber black.

The semantic contrasts put forth by the narrator's story of the beautiful "widow" and the singular event that colors it are the overt markers of the ambiguities of human nature involved: the intensely correct and well-bred man versus the woman of questionable occupation; her natural goodness versus his cultural refinement; her acquisition of ennobling culture versus subjugation to an all-consuming passion willing to accept even her putative fall from grace; the predictable patterns of behavior that characterize their socially acceptable liaison versus the traumatic and inexplicable flaunting of propriety that the woman seems to have gone to such lengths to accomplish; her refusal to give an accounting of her actions versus his need to reimpose the security of a proper relationship; and her past—particularly the singular event—versus her insistence on assuming the role of a dutiful widow.

There are many ways in which the foregoing semantic contrasts may be interpreted as they are given narrative form in the story. First, the woman's dramatic rebellion may be seen as a gesture of class differences: the socially inferior courtesan must affirm her status by reminding her lover of her sordid origin. Second, the singular event may be seen as a dramatic farce in a game of sexual politics: the woman ensures her dominance of her lover by threatening to deceive him with other men. Third, the relationship may be seen in feminist terms: the unstable and degrading situation of a woman who, despite the social acceptance of the man's extramarital affairs, is a social outcast, treated as an adoring child by the man-father who educates her to his own sociocultural norms. Fourth, in larger social terms, the story concerns exploitation with sex in the guise of ennobling love the instrument of dominance on both sides. Which of these interpretations is the "true meaning" of Machado de Assis' story is less important than our understanding of the text's narrative strategies for ranging semantic contrasts and for underscoring the fundamental ambiguities of the human relations these ambiguities signal. "A Singular Event" is a metatext of Machado de Assis' fiction not so much because it typifies a prominent thematic preoccupation in the Brazilian's works but because it is paradigmatic of the narration of an event that is strikingly ambiguous and lacking in any reductionary meaning that will make either it or the narrative that tells about it a transparent explanation of human experience.

The narrative framing of "A Singular Event" is the direct correlative, in terms of literary *écriture*, of the paradox of ambiguity: how to explain what has no coherent explanation. The reader reads a formal literary text (with all the external trappings of literature, from title to the inclusion in a self-identified literary work, to the complete graphic array of grammatological texts) which is ostensibly the verbatim transcription of a natural narrative. By natural narrative we understand a tale or a story told in a formal, semiformal oral register that does not purport to be written literary narrative (the classic examples are natural narrative introduced by the marker "That reminds me of the story about . . ."; a parallel marker that has been extensively literaturized is "Once upon a time . . ."). It is significant in this regard that Machado de Assis' interlocutors situate themselves in the street (a "natural" setting), that their narrative is triggered by the chance passing of the black-dressed mistress, and by the fact that only the "natural" interlocutors speak—that is, there is no extranatural narrative commentary by Machado de Assis as either literary author or omniscient literary narrator. Moreover, the natural narrator narrates the "singular event" not as he saw or experienced it but as it was told to him by the distraught lawyer in his desperate attempt to understand the occurrence and to know how to handle it. All of these layers are a sort of interpretational deferral of meaning of the event being related, to the extent that each can and does give the particulars but none can explain them—not the lawyer, not his confidant-turned-narrator, not the silent author. The narrator can only say, "I have invented nothing. It's the pure truth."

By contrast, the one person who *can* explain things, the woman, not only refuses to do so in the real-life world posited by the story but also fails to have any direct or indirect speaking role in the natural narrative transmitted by the literary text (her lover does, as he is paraphrased repeatedly by the narrator). From the point of verisimilitude, one can say this silence derives from the narrator's opportunity to interview the woman. In terms of the semiological strategies of the literary text, however, her lack of voice in the story, like Machado de Assis' failure to exercise the authorial prerogative he uses elsewhere in his fiction to comment on events or others' natural narratives about those events, can only be seen to reinforce the image in the story of ambiguous, enigmatic events that are in a certain sense semantic voids. One can talk about them, with extensive reference to concrete particulars, but one can never explain them in a way that will satisfy the driving need to understand complex human experience.

Other major works

NOVELS: *Madalena*, 1860; *Resurreição*, 1872; *A mão e a Luva*, 1874 (*The Hand and the Glove*, 1970); *Helena*, 1876; *Iaiá Garcia*, 1878 (*Yava Garcia*, 1976); *Memórias Póstumas de Bras Cubas*, 1881 (*Epitaph of a Small Winner*, 1951); *Quincas Borba*, 1891 (*Philosopher or Dog*, 1954); *Dom Casmurro*, 1900 (English translation, 1953); *Esaú e Jacó*, 1904 (*Esau and Jacob*, 1965); *Memorial de Aires*, 1908 (*Counselor Ayres' Memorial*, 1982).

PLAYS: *Desencantos*, 1864; *Quase Ministro*, 1864; *Tu Só, Tu, Puro Amor*, 1881; *Teatro*, 1910.

POETRY: *Crisálidas*, 1864; *Falenas*, 1870; *Americanas*, 1875; *Poesias Completas*, 1901.

NONFICTION: *Páginas Recolhidas (Contos Ensaios, Crônicas)*, 1899; *Relíquias da Casa Velha (Contos Crônicas, Comêdias)*, 1906; *Critica*, 1910; *Correspondência*, 1938.

Bibliography

Caldwell, Helen. *The Brazilian Othello of Machado de Assis.* Berkeley: University of California Press, 1960. The first book-length study in English to deal with Machado de Assis. Focuses on his masterpiece *Dom Casmurro* and shows how Machado apparently utilized a modified version of *Othello*'s plot structure. Also discusses numerous other examples of the influence William Shakespeare had on

Machado de Assis' work. Caldwell was the first critic to argue that the novel's heroine, Capitu, was not necessarily guilty of adultery, as generations of readers had assumed.

_____. *Machado de Assis: The Brazilian Master and His Novels.* Berkeley: University of California Press, 1970. A concise survey of Machado de Assis' nine novels and his various narrative techniques. Also includes good discussions of his primary themes, a useful bibliography, and some comments on his plays, poems, and short stories.

Dixon, Paul. *Retired Dreams: Dom Casmurro, Myth and Modernity.* West Lafayette, Ind.: Purdue University Press, 1989. Though he limits his critical discussion to *Dom Casmurro,* Dixon leads his reader to see Machado de Assis as cultivating a radically new style of writing, one that featured ambiguity as the most "realistic" aspect of language and that conceived of language as a system of tropes only arbitrarily connected to physical reality. Dixon also suggests that Machado de Assis was critical of his society's patriarchal codes and that, as evidenced in the relationship between the novel's two major characters (Bento and Capitu), he implies the virtues inherent in a more matriarchal approach to sociopolitical organization.

Fitz, Earl E. *Machado de Assis.* Boston: Twayne, 1989. The first English-language book to examine all aspects of Machado de Assis' literary life (his novels, short stories, poetry, theater, critical theory, translations, and nonfiction work). Also includes sections on his life, his place in Brazilian and world literature, his style, and his themes. Features an annotated bibliography and argues that Machado de Assis—largely because of his ideas about the connection between language, meaning, and reality—is best appreciated as a modernist.

Gledson, John. *The Deceptive Realism of Machado de Assis: A Dissenting Interpretation of "Dom Casmurro."* Liverpool: Francis Cairns, 1984. Focusing on what the majority of critics have judged to be Machado de Assis' greatest novel, *Dom Casmurro,* Gledson argues against interpreting the author either as a modernist or as a precursor of the "New Novel" in Latin America and in favor of regarding him as a master (if unique) realist. Sees him as a subtle and artful stylist whose work accurately reflects the prevailing social and political tensions of his time.

Nist, John. "The Short Stories of Machado de Assis." *Arizona Quarterly* 24 (Spring, 1968): 5-22. Nist hails Machado de Assis as not only a great novelist but also perhaps the outstanding prose fiction writer of either North or South America during the late nineteenth and early twentieth centuries. Surveys a number of his most celebrated stories, including "The Psychiatrist," "A Woman's Arms," and "Midnight Mass." Nist also notes the economy of means that marks the author's style, the ironic and philosophic base of his fiction, his alleged "pessimism," and the modernist ethos inherent in his ambiguous vision of human reality.

Nunes, Maria Luisa. *The Craft of an Absolute Winner: Characterization and Narratology in the Novels of Machado de Assis.* Westport, Conn.: Greenwood Press, 1983. An excellent study of Machado de Assis' novelistic techniques, his skill at characterization, and his primary themes. Offers good summaries of his novels and shows both how they compare to each other and how their author grew in sophistication and skill. Argues that the essence of Machado de Assis' genius, like that of all truly great writers, lies in his singular ability to create powerful and compelling characters.

David W. Foster
(Revised by *Earl E. Fitz*)

JAMES ALAN McPHERSON

Born: Savannah, Georgia; September 16, 1943

Principal short fiction

Hue and Cry, 1969; *Elbow Room*, 1977.

Other literary forms

With Miller Williams, James Alan McPherson has edited and contributed essays and a short story to a volume of essays, stories, poems, and pictures entitled *Railroad: Trains and Train People in American Culture* (1976). After 1969, McPherson also contributed several essays to the *Atlantic Monthly* and to *Reader's Digest.*

Achievements

Even though McPherson has not published many collections of short fiction, his adroit characterizations and his strong sense of place have attracted many readers and influenced a number of writers. His work has begun to be anthologized and has appeared in the *Atlantic Monthly*, *Playboy*, *The New York Times Magazine*, *The Harvard Advocate*, *Reader's Digest*, *The Iowa Review*, *The Massachusetts Review*, and *Ploughshares.* His association with the Writer's Workshop at the University of Iowa and his teaching of courses in fiction writing have given him a forum from which he influences beginning writers from across the United States. Though earlier critics noted similarities between McPherson and other African-American writers such as James Baldwin and Ralph Ellison, critical attention has later been placed on his unique use of language and his ability to create a mythical dimension to his stories. Because of this, his fiction has begun to be examined in a much wider context than it has previously.

Biography

James Alan McPherson earned degrees from Morris Brown College (B.A.), Harvard Law School (LL.B.), and the Iowa Writers' Workshop (M.F.A.). He has taught at the University of Iowa, the University of California, Harvard University, Morgan State University, and the University of Virginia. Besides being a contributing editor of *The Atlantic Monthly*, he has held jobs ranging from stock-clerk to newspaper reporter. *Elbow Room* won the 1978 Pulitzer Prize for fiction and was nominated for the National Book Award. The story "Gold Coast" won the prize for fiction awarded by the *Atlantic Monthly* in 1968. In the early 1980's, McPherson began teaching fiction writing in the Writers' Workshop at the University of Iowa in Iowa City.

Analysis

James Alan McPherson is one of the writers of fiction who form the second major phase of modern writing about the black experience. Indebted, like all of his generation, to the ground-breaking and theme-setting work of Richard Wright, Ellison, and Baldwin, McPherson shies away from doctrinaire argumentation about racial issues. Rather, he uses these issues to give his work a firmly American aura which includes not only a preoccupation with what it means to be a black person in modern America but also with how the individual responds to a culture which often is plagued by subtle and not-so-subtle racial discriminations. Hence, there are times when blackness becomes for McPherson a metaphor for the alienation experienced by the individual in contemporary society.

This comprehensive concern with American culture informs all of McPherson's work, including those pieces that are included in the prose and poetry collection compiled by McPherson and Miller Williams entitled *Railroad: Trains and Train People in American Culture*. A celebration, a lament, and a plea, this volume deals with the passing of the great era of passenger railcar service in the United States. To McPherson, the liberating motion integral to the railroad is important but so is the sense of place and time that builds for his characters much of their sense of self. In fact, McPherson's characters are often confined by the conventions of locale, yet McPherson is not a regional writer in the usual sense of the word; he can bring to life stories set in Tennessee, Virginia, Boston, Chicago, or London.

Because of the tension in this body of work between the individual and the community, McPherson's people often feel alienated, lonely, and unable fully to reach or to maintain contact with acquaintances, friends, families, or lovers. Yet, such isolation may lead to a character's growth to near-tragic stature. The integrity of the individual is thus asserted even while a narrator may worry over the deep inability of any person to penetrate into the heart and mind of another. Such recognitions contribute to the sympathetic portrayal even of unpromising characters. It should be noted that the reader is not given solutions in McPherson's fiction, only access to degrees of awareness of the mysteries of race, sexuality, identity, and love. Reading McPherson, a reader may be reminded of Baldwin's presentation of agonizingly complex racial and sexual problems, of Saul Bellow's portrayal of characters battling absurdity and despair, and of the struggle of characters both in Baldwin and in Bellow toward the ameliorating but no less mysterious experience of love.

McPherson's first volume of short fiction, *Hue and Cry*, is often a grim affair, containing stories of loneliness, destitution, defeat, sexual alienation, and racial tension. A prime example of this early work is "Gold Coast." The narrator of this story is an "apprentice janitor" in a hotel near Harvard Square in Boston, a hotel that has seen better days and is now populated with aging singles or couples who are almost as disengaged from the mainstream of Boston life as is the superintendent of the building, James Sullivan. Listening to Sullivan and observing the people in the apartments, the narrator, Robert, seeks to gather information for the stories and books he hopes to write. For Robert, being a janitor is in some ways a whim; in addition to gleaning experiential details from rubbish bins, he is constructing his life along romantic lines. Hence, Robert notes that almost nightly,

I drifted off to sleep lulled by sweet anticipation of that time when my potential would suddenly be realized and there would be capsule biographies of my life on dust jackets of many books, all proclaiming: ". . . He knew life on many levels. From shoeshine boy, free-lance waiter, 3rd cook, janitor, he rose to. . . ."

Naïve but witty, the narrator humors Sullivan, putting up patiently with the Irishman's redundant reminiscing and opinionated ramblings on society and politics. Sullivan, however, comes to rely on Robert's company; he turns from the horrors of life in the filthy apartment he shares with his obscene, insane wife to interminable conversations with Robert.

Robert's sympathetic tolerance of Sullivan emanates from his sense of the pathetic isolation of Sullivan from human contact and from Robert's recognition for the first time of the terrors of aging. Robert is the archetypal youth coming to awareness of old age as a time of foreshortened expectations and straitened life-styles, of possible despair and near dehumanization. The apprentice janitor can tolerate Sullivan and his new knowledge while his relationship with the rich, lovely Jean goes well, but Jean and he are soon torn apart by social forces. In fact, they play a game called "Social Forces," in which they try to determine which of them will break first under social disapproval of their interracial relationship. When the game defeats them, Robert first is comforted by and then pulls back from his friendship with the dejected Sullivan, who is especially upset over the loss of his dog.

When Robert finally leaves his briefly held janitorial position, he does so both with relief and with guilt over his abandonment of Sullivan. He knows, however, that he is "still young" and not yet doomed to the utter loneliness of the old man. McPherson suggests that the young, nevertheless, will inevitably come to such bleak isolation and that even the temporary freedom of youth is sometimes maintained at the expense of sympathy and kindness. There are dangers in being free, not the least of which are the burden of knowledge, the hardening of the self, and the aching realization of basic but often unmet human needs. This theme of loss is picked up in the volume's title story, "Hue and Cry," which includes this interchange between two characters:

"Between my eyes I see three people and they are all unhappy. Why?"
"Perhaps it is because they are alive. Perhaps it is because they once were. Perhaps it is because they have to be. I do not know."

These voices cannot make sense of the losses to which life dooms McPherson's characters, nor does Robert. He simply moves away from the hotel to enjoy, while he can, youth and his sense of potential.

The theme of old age and its defeats is further developed in McPherson's well-received "A Solo Song: For Doc," a story which displays well the author's rhythmic and precise control of narration conceived of as speech. The narrator, an aging waiter on a railroad line, tells a young listener about the good old days in the service and about their embodiment, a waiter called Doc Craft. "So do you want to know this business, youngblood?" begins the teller of the tale, and he goes on, "So you want to be a Waiter's Waiter? The Commissary gives you a book with all the rules and tells you to learn them. And you do, and think that is all there is to it." This "Waiter's Waiter" then proceeds to disillusion the "youngblood" by describing the difficult waiter's craft—the finesse, grace, care, and creativity required to make the job into an art and to make that art pay. The grace and dedication displayed by men of Doc Craft's generation is shown to be losing ground to the contemporary world of business in which men such as "Jerry Ewald, the Unexpected Inspector," lie in wait to trap heroes like Doc Craft and to remove them from the service that keeps them alive. The narrator specifies what kept Doc on the road: having power over his car and his customers, hustling tips, enjoying women without being married to them, getting drunk without having to worry about getting home. The shift from passenger to freight service on the railroad, however, begins the company's attempt to fire Doc and also initiates Doc's rise to heroic stature. Like the old-time railroad, Doc Craft is doomed; Ewald catches Doc on a technicality about iced tea service, and the waiter is fired.

Clearly, McPherson's thematic preoccupations and love of the railroad have coalesced in this story. Movement, adventure, freedom, self-expression, craftsmanship, commitment, exuberance, and endurance—these qualities mark both Doc Craft and the railroad as valuable American entities. Yet the passing of Doc carries McPherson's sense of the epic loss suffered by an America that has allowed the railroad, the metaphoric counterpart of imaginative integration of all kinds, to decay.

Even while remaining faithful to McPherson's characteristic themes, *Elbow Room*, his second volume, includes stories which reach a kind of comic perfection. One example is "Why I Like Country Music." The narrator, a Southern-born black, addresses to his Northern-born wife an explanation of his love of square dance music. His wife will not believe or accept this preference, but the narrator quietly insists on it. In one sense, this insistence and the narration that justifies it may be viewed as evidence of the eternal and invincible isolation of the human heart from sympathetic understanding even by loved ones. The forces of memory and of individual development work to isolate human beings from one another. Further, the narrator's insistence that the South Carolina traditions of his youth have given to him preferences and ideas alien to those of the New York-born tends to strengthen this theme of the coherence but separateness of the self.

Such thematic reverberations, however, do not form the main concern of this story. Rather, the narrator tells us of a comic case of childhood puppy love; he explains that he loves country music because it is permanently associated in his mind with a girl in his fourth-grade class whose name was Gweneth Larson. Born in Brooklyn and redolent of lemons, Gweneth is for the narrator an object of infatuated first love. The moments when he square danced with her in a school May Day celebration were etched in his mind as moments of surpassing joy and love. Far from exploring alienation, the story celebrates the endurance of such affection.

McPherson's comedy is never heavy-handed, always a matter of a light tone or a moment of incongruity. An example occurs when the narrator describes the calling of the Maypole teams to the playground for their performance:

> "Maypole teams _up!_" called Mr. Henry Lucas, our principal, from his platform by the swings. Beside him stood the white Superintendent of Schools (who said later of the square dance, it was reported to all the classes, "Lord, y'all square dance so _good_ it makes me plumb _ashamed_ us white folks ain't takin' better care of our art stuff").

It is notable, however, that this comedy, like this author's more somber stances, remains firmly focused on the human personality, which is for McPherson the incentive for narration and the core of his art.

Other major works

EDITED TEXT: _Railroad: Trains and Train People in American Culture_, 1976 (with Miller Williams).

Bibliography

Beavers, Herman. "'I Yam What You Is and You Is What I Yam: Rhetorical Invisibility in James Alan McPherson's 'The Story of a Dead Man.'" _Callaloo_ 9 (1986): 565-577. Beavers discusses the linguistic and rhetorical characteristics of McPherson's dialogue and how language shapes perceptions, specifically in "The Story of a Dead Man."

Laughlin, Rosemary M. "Attention, American Folklore: Doc Craft Comes Marching In." _Studies in American Fiction_ 1 (1973): 221-227. Laughlin discusses McPherson's use of myth and folklore, as well as his ability to create new kinds of folklore in the pages of his story based on his aesthetic use of language and his unique mythical style.

McPherson, James Alan. "Interview with James Alan McPherson." Interview by Bob Shacochis. _Iowa Journal of Literary Studies_ 4 (1983): 6-33. Shacochis focuses on questions relating to McPherson's vision of his literary role and on specific works in his collections. Contains also some discussion of McPherson's obligations as a "black-American" author.

Wallace, Jon. "The Politics of Style in Three Stories by James Alan McPherson." _Modern Fiction Studies_ 34 (Spring, 1988): 17-26. Wallace argues that in three stories by McPherson, "The Story of a Dead Man," "The Story of a Scar," and "Just Enough for the City," characters use language to construct for themselves a defense against human involvement and human communities which often threaten to weaken their sense of self.

_____. "The Story Behind the Story in James Alan McPherson's _Elbow Room._" _Studies in Short Fiction_ 25 (Fall, 1988): 447-452. Wallace argues that McPherson's stories are often attempts to create a new kind of mythology, or mythological space, in which to place the experiences of his characters in the larger context of American society. Because of this, Wallace argues that in Mc-

Pherson's work it is narrative form that matters much more than either the particulars of the story or the characters.

Cheryl Herr
(Revised by *Edward Huffstetler*)

NAGUIB MAHFOUZ

Born: Cairo, Egypt; December 11, 1911

Principal short fiction

Hams al-junun, 1939; *Dunya Allah*, 1963; *Bayt sayyi' al-sum'a*, 1965; *Tahta al-mizalla*, 1967; *Khammarat al-qitt al-aswad*, 1968; *God's World*, 1973; *Hubb fawqa hadabat al-haram*, 1979; *Ra'aytu fima yara al-na'im*, 1982; *Al-Tanzim al-sirri*, 1984; *Al-Fajr al-kadhib*, 1989; *The Time and the Place and Other Stories*, 1991.

Other literary forms

Despite his lifelong dedication to the short story, Naguib Mahfouz's reputation stems chiefly from the many novels he has produced over his lengthy career. He has also been an important influence in the Egyptian cinema, having written the screen texts for many films drawn from Arabic novels, including some of his own works. He is the author of several short plays, some of which have been performed on stage.

Achievements

By the late 1950's, Mahfouz had earned recognition throughout the Arab world as the most sophisticated author of the Arabic novel. While earlier Arab novelists had initiated this literary form, Mahfouz demonstrated a gift for presenting characters and situations that intimately captured the spirit of his native Egypt. His generally tragic works often center their interest on individuals in crisis and examine issues relating to class, ambition, and morality in government. They illustrate the personal faults or the incidents of fate that can bring tragedy to humankind; though didactic, they are usually nonjudgmental.

His partly autobiographical trilogy, *Bayna al-qasrayn* (1956; *Palace Walk*, 1990), *Qasr al-shawq* (1957; *Palace of Desire*, 1991), and *Al-Sukkariyah* (1957; *Sugar Street*, 1992), explores the many developments in three generations of a middle-class Cairo family; its frame spans the period from shortly before the beginning of World War I to almost the end of World War II. The influx of ideas, culture, and mores from the West is seen to bring disequilibrium to a largely Muslim Egypt that is still conservative. The work, like many of Mahfouz's novels, chronicles the dimensions of these changes upon individuals and Egyptian society at large. Mahfouz's university training in the study and communication of philosophy is evident in many works, most notably in his allegorical and highly controversial *Awlad haratina* (1967; *Children of Gebelawi*, 1981). He evinces a fascination with time, and his themes often draw on history. Contemporary political and social issues, both of the Middle East and of the world at large, are central to his writing. The recipient of many honorary doctoral degrees from foreign universities and prestigious awards from the Egyptian government, Mahfouz received in 1988 the Nobel Prize in Literature.

Biography

Though gregarious and accessible, Naguib Mahfouz has disclosed little about his personal life or background. His father was apparently a shopkeeper (or perhaps a minor civil servant), and Mahfouz was the youngest of seven children. At the time of his birth, the family resided in Gamaliya, an area named after a street traversing an ancient quarter of Cairo. It is this colorful, conservative environment that provides the locale for many of his works. In his preteens, the family moved to the wealthier and more European neighborhood of 'Abbasiya. His early education was in public schools, and he earned a B.A. in philosophy from Cairo University in 1934. He continued studies there for an M.A. in philosophy but withdrew for undisclosed reasons to take employment in the university's administration; shortly thereafter, he joined the bureaucracy, first working in the ministry of religious endowments. In 1971, he retired and became director of the government-controlled board of film censorship, while continuing to devote himself to his writing. He married in his early forties and has two daughters.

Mahfouz's writing career began even before his college graduation, with short stories and articles on philosophy published in the early 1930's by Cairo journals. He has produced several books, consisting of novels, novellas, short stories, and short plays; most of these first appeared in Cairo periodicals. Though very circumscribed in his travels abroad, Mahfouz has reading knowledge in English and French and has been disciplined and comprehensive in his readings in international literature of all periods; he refers to first having taken John Drinkwater's *The Outline of Literature* (1931) as a guide for readings in the works of authors representative of various literary schools and tendencies. He has acknowledged in interviews and suggests in his works that Marcel Proust, Albert Camus, and Jean-Paul Sartre, as well as the Russian realists and the absurdists, have been major Western influences upon his own production. Some works, such as *Rihlat Ibn Fattumah* (1983), a sociopolitical discussion in fictional form, draw their structure and diction from the Arab-Islamic cultural heritage.

Analysis

Naguib Mahfouz is said to have published his first short story in an obscure Cairo journal, *al-Siyasa*, in July, 1932. This was followed by a regular production in several Egyptian journals, both literary and popular. These early stories number approximately eighty, of which only a score have been republished, in a collection entitled *Hams al-junun*. They frequently present situations where sadness results from faults of character and immorality, or from ill fortune. The situations are often domestic, and the problems prosaic, such as marital infidelity or a family's descent into poverty through unemployment or the death of the wage earner.

These stories are generally didactic and sentimental and reflect the influence of the works of the then hugely popular Sheikh Mustafa Lutfi al-Manfaluti; this author's genius for archaic, sonorous, and rhythmic prose Mahfouz was, however, unable to match. Other early stories present flat and static character sketches of the lives and personalities of curious characters; these are reminiscent of the fiction of Mahmud Taymur, a prominent Egyptian writer who was himself a devotee of Guy de Maupassant. Often with characters and situations that are unconvincing and lack development, these works nevertheless suggest the pessimism and high seriousness that have characterized Mahfouz's literary production.

From the late 1930's, Mahfouz devoted himself to the writing of lengthier works. A translation from an introductory English text on the history of ancient Egypt seems to have inspired his three subsequent novels set in Pharaonic times of political unrest; these are interpreted by some commentators as allegorical criticism of the state of his nation's affairs during the last decades of its monarchy.

This historical fiction was followed in the late 1930's and 1940's by popular novels set in contemporary Cairo. In these works, the tragic and sentimental themes of the early short stories are expanded, and the author demonstrates his growing interest in character development. While these novels are still essentially cautionary and didactic in their messages, Mahfouz's authorial presence is now less evident. Flashes of humor, skillful dialogue, and lively dramatic action, most evident in the popular novel *Zuqaq al-Midaqq* (1947; *Midaq Alley*, 1966), become hereafter important elements in his fiction.

The short stories of this period, like the novels, still largely concern themselves with the issues and dilemmas that affect the poor, the bureaucracy, and the petit bourgeois. They emphasize the negative aspects of Egypt's class structure and demonstrate how the struggle for survival and advancement entails loss of morality and personal happiness. They suggest a general compassion for the underprivileged and a disapproval of the values of his compatriots who enjoy wealth and power.

The whimsical "Dunya Allah" ("God's World"), in the collection *Dunya Allah*, and available in various English translations, centers sympathetically on an aging man, an impoverished messenger in a department of the bureaucracy, who, having stolen the salaries of his colleagues, absconds to Alexandria with a young woman. Though his idyllic vacation ends with her rejection of him and his capture by the police, the thief has no cause for regret since he has achieved one brief period of happiness in an otherwise dismal life.

Mahfouz's writings of the 1950's and 1960's became increasingly complex in their structure and style and more political and obscure in their themes. As was the case with other Egyptian writers, such as Yusuf Idris, and Ihsan 'Abd al-Quddus, his works now contained subtle expressions of discontent at the repressive nature of the rule of the country's dictator, Gamal Abdel Nasser, who had led an army coup in 1952 that had overthrown the monarchy. While viewed as generally benevolent and reformist, the regime brooked no criticism from its citizenry, and brief jail sentences were served by many intellectuals whose loyalty became suspect. Caution and obfuscation were clearly necessary to escape notice or defy interpretation by the "defenders of the revolution." The stories are therefore metaphorical and the criticisms oblique, though some do lend themselves to easy equational interpretation.

For example, his "Sa'iq al-qitar" (in the collection *Bayt sayyi' al-sum'a*) presents passengers in a train; one man, reminiscent of a bear, standing for the Soviet Union, constantly challenges another, reminiscent of an "eagle," representing the United States, over the future of a woman who presumably stands for Egypt. The passengers realize that their train is rushing headlong into certain disaster. The train driver, locked in the engine compartment—clearly Nasser—refuses all advice to slow down, and seems crazed and suicidal. It is implied that the nation is helpless and headed for tragedy under his leadership.

Other short stories of the period reflect the malaise and confusion widely shared by Egyptian intellectuals. While they applauded the new international attention and prestige that the regime had won for Egypt as a leader of the neutralist Third World and were pleased at the downfall of the landowning aristocracy, they suffered from involvement in a debilitating war in Yemen, a stagnant economy, and restrictions on travel. They also chafed at the abolition of the country's political parties and freedoms of expression, while they disdained the Nasser worship of the powerful state-controlled media. Stories such as "Zaabalawi" (in the collection *Dunya Allah*) clearly suggest this malaise; it involves a sick man's search for a revered healer, a holy man who embodied inherited rather than imported values and procedures of contemporary "doctors." The dissatisfaction at the root of this story is viewed by some critics as similar in its message to that of Mahfouz's extremely controversial novel *Children of Gebelawi*, which chronicles the failures of both the religions and the governmental structures to satisfy people's needs for security and justice.

In the several months following the disastrous war of June, 1967, between Israel and the Arabs, Mahfouz wrote a variety of curious and disturbing short stories and five one-act plays, which were collected and published in 1969 in the volume *Tahta al-mizalla*. These works present characters and situations that show Egyptians to be living in a Kafkaesque and chaotic world where individuals live in distress and terror. The story reflects the trauma then affecting Egyptians from two sources—the fear of death from sporadic Israeli air attacks and the repressive policies being pursued by the Nasser regime.

While the internal message in these works was constrained and camouflaged with symbolism, their intent to reveal despair and to suggest criticism is clear. While not lending themselves to full equational interpretation, unlike some of his earlier stories, they contain enough "clues" to suggest the author's purpose, which at times extended beyond the prosaic criticism of the country's leadership into the metaphysical.

For example, the story "Tahta al-mizalla" ("Beneath the Shelter") could obviously be interpreted as an expression of the tragedy and absurdity of the human experience stemming from failure to replace brutality and chaos with an order based on morality and compassion. In this story, dramatic and tragic events unfold in the street before onlookers awaiting the arrival of a bus. These incidents, occurring in an atmosphere of unrelieved gloom and downpourings of rain in increasing intensity, suggest the progression of the recent history of the Middle East as seen from an Egyptian perspective. The onlookers are reluctant to accept as reality the strange and bloody events that they witness. To justify their own fear of involvement, they convince themselves that the changing scene is merely the action of a motion picture being shot. A final horrific event, however, convinces them that they are witnessing a reality too horrible to ignore; a head gushing blood—presumably during the 1967 war—rolls down the street before them. Belatedly seeking involvement, they call out to a "policeman" who has also been an uninvolved observer of the scenes. His response, however, is to question their identity and loyalty and to shoot them all dead. While the general intent of the story is evident, its specific symbols may be variously interpreted. It is not clear, for example, whether the uninvolved spectators are Egyptian or foreign, or whether the brutal and callous policeman is Nasser or an abstraction, such as time or fate.

Such stories, for all the interest they arouse in Arabic and the speed and frequency with which they have been published in translation, have received little interpretation. Clearly, commentators have realized that it would be an act of betrayal to reveal the purposes of an author who has taken such pains to present his ideas in so obscure and circumspect a manner.

The issue of commitment against injustice is clearly a major theme of Mahfouz's oeuvre, and in works prior to 1978, this theme often finds expression in relation to the Arab-Israeli conflict. In several works—for example "Finjan Shayy" (in the collection *Tahta al-mizalla*), the novel *Al-Hubb tahta al-matar* (1973), and the one-act play "Death and Resurrection" (from the collection *Tahta al-mizalla*, in English in the collection *Naguib Mahfouz One Act Plays*)—Mahfouz insists on the need to redress the wrongs done to the Palestinians and to continue the Arab struggle against Israel. These works all appeared before Egypt's 1978-1979 rapprochement with Israel, following which Mahfouz has been an outspoken advocate of peace and cooperation between Arabs and Israelis.

In his later stories, Mahfouz demonstrates a greater emphasis on certain themes that he had touched upon in earlier works, while developing others of a decidedly prosaic nature. The issues of time and growing old are central, most noticeably in the short novel *Qashtamar* (1988), in which the tone is decidedly nostalgic. The difficulties of life in an Egypt experiencing serious overpopulation and diminishing living standards is another occasional theme. Similarly, inflation, especially in real estate, is seen to present particular difficulties for the young while bringing opportunities for sudden wealth and social advancement for those with inherited property. Such stories often suggest personal reminiscence as much as they do imaginative creativity. They embody that mixture of pessimism, skepticism, pragmatism, and existentialism that is perhaps his most distinctive characteristic.

The chaotic and fast-changing nature of contemporary Egyptian society and its values and the resultant sense of disorientation and bewilderment has been the subject of several stories. In "False Dawn" (in the collection *al-Fajr al-kadhib*), the reader follows a young man's apparently logical search for an enemy only to discover that he has been suffering from paranoid schizophrenia caused by the confusion of change in modern society.

Mahfouz's works have consistently expressed his interest in the role of women in society. His fiction suggests that he has generally been supportive of women exerting their personal choice. Even women who become prostitutes are viewed with equanimity and understanding, if not admiration. In the early novels, the materialistic and narcissistic Hamida in *Midaq Alley*, the desperate orphan Nafisa in *Bidaya wa nihaya* (1949; *The Beginning and the End*, 1951), and the compassionate Nur in *Al-Liss wa-al-kilab* (1961; *The Thief and the Dogs*, 1984) are all women who are presented with compassion and understanding despite their prostitution.

Several of the short stories similarly center on strong-willed women; indeed, it could be maintained that Mahfouz, like many prominent Arab authors, has his female characters exemplify virtues lacking in his male figures. Mahfouz's advocacy of the right to choose or reject marriage clearly contradicts traditional male mainstream opinion in his society. For example, in the story "The Answer Is No" (from the collection *Al-Fajr al-kadhib*), a young girl who is seduced by a teacher refuses to marry him despite his dutiful proposal to her as soon as she reaches the legal age for marriage. Years later, when he becomes the principal in the school where she teaches and inquires after her marital status, she expresses no regret at her unmarried state. Similarly, in "Min taht ila Fawq" (also in *Al-Fajr al-kadhib*), an unmarried young woman, orphaned as a child and exploited by her family for whom she acts as an unpaid cook and housekeeper, decides to take employment as a servant in luxury Cairo apartments. Formerly sickly and depressed at home, she becomes happy and earns a fine salary. When her health, morale, and dress improve, she marries an electrician, whom she proudly introduces to her family; she has married by choice, and as an equal.

In his fiction, Naguib Mahfouz has assumed the role of chronicler and conscience of Egypt in the twentieth century. Since, however, many of his works examine issues that are common to all humanity, they are timeless and of universal interest.

Other major works

NOVELS: *Zuqaq al-Midaqq*, 1947 (*Midaq Alley*, 1966); *Bidaya wa nihaya*, 1949 (*The Beginning and the End*, 1951); *Bayna al-qasrayn*, 1956 (*Palace Walk*, 1990); *Qasr al-shawq*, 1957 (*Palace of Desire*, 1991); *Al-Sukkariyah*, 1957 (*Sugar Street*, 1992); *Al-Liss wa-al-kilab*, 1961 (*The Thief and the Dogs*, 1984); *Al-Summan wa-al-kharif*, 1962 (*Autumn Quail*, 1985); *Al-Tariq*, 1964 (*The Search*, 1987); *Al-Shahhadh*, 1965 (*The Beggar*, 1986); *Miramar*, 1967 (*Miramar*, 1978); *Awlad haratina*, 1967 (*Children of Gebelawi*, 1981); *Al-Maraya*, 1972 (*Mirrors*, 1977); *Al-Hubb tahta al-matar*, 1973; *Al-Karnak*, 1974 (*Karnak*, 1979); *Hadrat al-muhtaram*, 1975 (*Respected Sir*, 1988); *Afrah al-qubbah*, 1981 (*Wedding Song*, 1984); *Rihlat Ibn Fattumah*, 1983; *Qashtamar*, 1988.

Bibliography

Abadir, Akef, and Roger Allen. Introduction to *God's World*. Minneapolis, Minn.: Bibliotheca Islamica, 1973. This introduction by Abadir and Allen is followed by twenty translations selected from Mahfouz's short stories.

Johnson-Davies, Denys. Introduction to *The Time and the Place and Other Stories.* Garden City, N.Y.: Doubleday, 1991. Consists of twenty of Mahfouz's short stories selected and translated, following an introduction by Denys Johnson-Davies.

Kilpatrick, Hilary. *The Modern Egyptian Novel: A Study in Social Criticism.* London: Ithaca Press, 1974. This academic study examines Mahfouz's novels in the context of contemporary Egyptian fiction. Contains appropriate literary and critical evaluations, notes, and bibliographies.

Le Gassick, Trevor, ed. *Critical Perspectives on Naguib Mahfouz.* Washington, D.C.: Three Continents Press, 1991. Eleven articles by authorities on Mahfouz, following an introduction by the editor. The articles, four of which are in translation from Arabic, range widely over Mahfouz's contributions to the short story, the novel, and the Egyptian cinema. Complemented by bibliographies of materials in English.

Somekh, Sasson. *The Changing Rhythm.* Leiden, The Netherlands: E. J. Brill, 1973. A careful, comprehensive study of Mahfouz's major novels. Academically sound and with good bibliographies, it addresses the general reader as well as the student of Near Eastern literatures.

Trevor Le Gassick

BERNARD MALAMUD

Born: Brooklyn, New York; April 26, 1914
Died: New York, New York; March 18, 1986

Principal short fiction

The Magic Barrel, 1958; *Idiots First*, 1963; *Pictures of Fidelman: An Exhibition*, 1969; *Rembrandt's Hat*, 1973; *The Stories of Bernard Malamud*, 1983.

Other literary forms

Bernard Malamud devoted his writing career to fiction. In addition to his highly praised short stories, he wrote seven well-received novels: *The Natural* (1952), *The Assistant* (1957), *A New Life* (1961), *The Fixer* (1966), *The Tenants* (1971), *Dubin's Lives* (1979), and *God's Grace* (1982). He is also the author of many literary essays and reviews.

Achievements

Of the last half of the twentieth century, Malamud is one of the best American writers. In his seven novels and numerous short stories, he transcends the Jewish experience so ably chronicled by the so-called Jewish literary renaissance writers (such as Saul Bellow and Philip Roth) by using Jewish life as a metaphor for universal experience. Critic Robert Alter has proclaimed that short stories such as "The First Seven Years," "The Magic Barrel," "The Last Mohican," "Idiots First," and "Angel Levine" will be read "as long as anyone continues to care about American fiction written in the 20th century."

Both a traditionalist and an experimenter in his fiction, Malamud won rave reviews, literary plaudits, and many awards. *The Magic Barrel* brought a National Book Award in 1959. In 1967, *The Fixer* won for him a second National Book Award as well as a Pulitzer Prize. In addition, he was president of the International Association of Poets, Playwrights, Editors, Essayists, and Novelists (PEN Club) from 1979 to 1981.

Biography

Born on April 26, 1914, Bernard Malamud was the eldest of two sons of Max and Bertha Malamud. His parents, who had emigrated from Russia, ran a grocery store. Both Yiddish and English were spoken in the Malamud household, where much emphasis was placed on the cultural aspects of Judaism.

This milieu as well as his father's tales of life in czarist Russia provided much fodder for Malamud's fiction. He was also influenced by many trips to the Yiddish theater on Manhattan's Second Avenue, and by novels such as his favorite Horatio Alger stories and a multivolume *Book of Knowledge* that his father gave him when he was nine.

Throughout his boyhood in the back room of the family store, where he wrote stories, and his high school days at Erasmus Hall in Brooklyn, where he was an editor of the literary magazine, he was devoted to storytelling. In 1936, he was graduated from City College of New York. He had written a few stories in college and continued to write during a series of odd jobs. While working on an M.A. at Columbia University, he taught at Erasmus Hall Evening High School and wrote. In 1945, he married a Gentile, Ann de Chiara.

During the 1940's, Malamud's stories appeared in some noncommercial magazines. Then, in 1949, he sold the appropriately titled "The Cost of Living" to *Harper's Bazaar.* That same year, he moved with his family to Corvallis, Oregon, where he worked at Oregon State University. Finally adjusting from the urban to the rural life-style, Malamud developed a new perspective and a weekly routine that allowed him much quality time for writing: he taught three days a week and wrote four. Without a Ph.D., he was forced to teach composition, not literature, so his favorite course was a compromise—a night workshop in short-story writing for townspeople. His stories began to appear in such noted magazines as *Partisan Review, Commentary,* and *Harper's Bazaar.*

The Natural, his first novel, appeared in 1952 to mixed reviews. Some critics were put off by what they saw as an obscure symbolism, while others applauded the masterful use of fable and its art of ancient storytelling in a modern voice. In 1956, the *Partisan Review* made him a fellow in fiction and recommended him for a Rockefeller grant, which made it possible for Malamud to spend a year in Europe. In 1957, his next novel, *The Assistant,* was published, winning for him many awards and establishing him as a major Jewish American writer. The short-story collection *The Magic Barrel* came out in 1958, followed by his third novel, *A New Life.* In 1961, he moved to Bennington College, where he taught for more than twenty years. *Idiots First* was followed by *The Fixer,* which was researched by a trip to Russia.

From 1969 until his death in 1986, Malamud continued to publish both novels and short stories. His works include *Pictures of Fidelman: An Exhibition,* a collection of stories about one character; *The Tenants,* a novel; *Rembrandt's Hat,* another short-story collection; *Dubin's Lives,* a novel; *God's Grace,* a novel; and *The Stories of Bernard Malamud,* still another collection.

Analysis

All Bernard Malamud's fiction seems based on a single affirmation: despite its disappointments, horror, pain, and suffering, life is truly worth living. His work may be best understood in the context of mid-twentieth century American literature. When Malamud arrived upon the literary scene, he disagreed with the period's twin pillars of negativism and nihilism, and his work is a reaction to this prevailing trend. "The purpose of the writer," contends Malamud, "is to keep civilization from destroying itself." Therefore, his characters, no matter how bad their lot, push toward a better life, a new life. "My premise," notes the author, "is that we will not destroy each other. My premise is that we will live on. We will seek a better life. We may not become better, but at least we will seek betterment."

In this respect, for Malamud the most important element of fiction is form, a belief that appropriately reinforces his thematic beliefs. Literary form as "ultimate necessity" is the basis of literature. The writer's duty, he argues "is to create the architecture, the form." This element of structure, so prevalent in both his short and long fiction, runs counter to the practice of many of his contemporaries, who preferred the inherent formlessness of the so-called "new novel." The essence of this form, says Malamud, is "story, story, story. Writers who can't invent stories often pursue other strategies, even substituting style for narrative. I feel that story is the basic element of fiction."

This belief, however, raises the question of what for Malamud constitutes a good story. Here Malamud is likewise a traditionalist, returning to such nineteenth century influences as Fyodor Dostoevski, Leo Tolstoy, and Gustave Flaubert. Malamud's stories grow out of character. More often than not, the typical protagonist is the schlemiel (usually Jewish, though sometimes Italian). According to the author himself, "A Malamud character is someone who fears his fate, is caught up in it, yet manages to outrun it. He's the subject and object of laughter and pity." When Malamud began publishing his stories, the emphasis was often on case studies rather than elaborate personality development, a trend that irritates Malamud:

> The sell-out of personality is just tremendous. Our most important natural resource is Man. The times cry out for men of imagination and hope. Instead, our fiction is loaded with sickness, homosexuality, fragmented man, "other-directed" man. It should be filled with love and beauty and hope. We are underselling Man. And American fiction is at its weakest when we go in for journalistic case studies instead of rich personality development.

A typical Malamud story, then, is an initiation story, the classic American pattern. Malamud admits that his American literary roots lie in Stephen Crane, Ernest Hemingway, and Sherwood Anderson. The story usually begins with a youth—or an older man with arrested personality development—who has led an unfulfilled life because of undeveloped emotions, failed relationships, and/or questionable morality. This protagonist then encounters a father figure—similar to the Hemingway tutor-tyro technique—who guides him through his odyssey by prodding him to ask the right questions, teaching him the meaning of suffering and spirituality, and ultimately coaxing him to accept the responsibility for his own life.

Because Malamud is Jewish, his protagonists are, more often than not, Jewish as well. Given Malamud's background—his father was a Jewish immigrant and passed on his knowledge of the Yiddish tradition of storytelling—this is to be expected. Malamud himself admits, "I write about Jews because I know them. But more important, I write about them because Jews are absolutely the very *stuff* of drama." By itself, this assertion is misleading, for unlike his fellow members of the Jewish literary renaissance, Malamud is not preoccupied with the uniqueness of the Jewish experience. The Jew for Malamud is a metaphor for all human beings. "Jewishness is important to me," Malamud asserts, "but I don't consider myself only a Jewish writer. I have interests beyond that, and I feel I am writing for all men." Malamud's method, then, is synecdochic—by detailing the plight of his Jews, he reveals humans' common humanity.

Throughout his career Malamud alternated writing novels with short stories. Of the two forms, he confesses to "having been longer in love with short fiction." One aspect of the short story that Malamud especially enjoys is "the fast payoff. Whatever happens happens quickly." A related matter is compression. Short fiction, Malamud argues, "packs a self in a few pages predicating a lifetime. . . . In a few pages a good story portrays the complexity of a life while producing the surprise and effect of knowledge—not a bad payoff."

Ironically, this fastness and compression are part of the ultimate illusion of Malamud's art. For him the writing of a short story is a long task that demands constant revision. "I would write a book, or a short story," Malamud admits, "at least three times—once to understand it, the second time to improve the prose, and a third to compel it to say what it still must say."

"The First Seven Years," which first appeared in the *Partisan Review* in 1950 and later in *The Magic Barrel*, is a straightforward tale set in the favorite Malamudian milieu, the New York Jewish ghetto. Feld, the shoemaker, decides to play matchmaker for his nineteen-year-old daughter, Miriam, whom he desires to attend college. Feld's choice is Max, a college boy, but the shoemaker is disappointed to learn that Max is a materialist (he wants to be an accountant), and for this reason his daughter rejects the chosen suitor. Simultaneously, Sobel, Feld's assistant, quits his job, and Feld has a heart attack.

The story turns on a typical Malamud irony. What Feld has failed to realize is that he, like Max, is a materialist and that his dreams of his daughter having "a better life" are wrapped up in money, her marrying well. Malamud here also reverses the typical older-man-equals-tutor, younger-man-equals-tyro pattern. Apparently, Feld is teaching Sobel the shoemaker's trade, but in truth, Sobel is the instructor: he admits that he has worked cheaply and lived poorly for the past five years only to be around the woman whom he truly loves, Miriam. As Malamud might have punned, the assistant teaches the master the difference between soles and souls. Finally, Sobel agrees to remain an assistant for two more years before asking Miriam to marry him.

Malamud's symbolism is both simple and mythic. Feld suffers literally from a damaged heart and metaphorically from an organ that is too materialistic. The rebirth pattern is inherent in the story's time frame, which moves from February and winter toward spring. The seven-year cycle of fertility—Sobel's wait—suggests that he is in tune with larger forces in the universe. Interestingly, the story is also an early version of the tale on which Malamud would elaborate in *The Assistant.*

"The Magic Barrel" utilizes another familiar Malamud pattern, the fantasy. Here, he blends elements of the traditional fairy tale with Jewish folklore. The story in fact begins like a fairy tale, with the line "Not long ago there lived. . . ." In the story, Leo Finkle, a rabbinical student searching for a wife, is the prince; Salzman, the marriage broker with the "magic" barrel and his sudden appearances, is the supernatural agent; and Stella, Salzman's prostitute daughter, is the princess of the tale.

The plot is likewise reminiscent of a fairy tale as the prince finally meets the princess and through the intervention of the supernatural agent has a chance at a happy ending.

Malamud's fairy tale borrows elements from Jewish folklore. The characters are certainly stereotypical: the marriage broker, the schlemiel, and the poor daughter. The setting is the usual lower-class milieu. With Leo helping Salzman at the end (each man plays both tutor and tyro), the plot has the familiar reversal, and the story is based on the age-old subject of parent as matchmaker. Even the theme is familiar: love is a redemptive force earned through suffering and self-knowledge. Malamud also infuses his story with humor. Aside from the stock characters and stock situations, he utilizes puns (for example "Lily wilted"), hyperbole, and comic juxtaposition (prospective brides are described in the jargon of used-car salesmen). Finally, the story contains social criticism directed at the Jews. Leo Finkle, the would-be rabbi, has learned the Jewish law but not his own feelings. He takes refuge in his self-pity (a frequent Malamud criticism), he wants a wife not for love but for social prestige, and he uses his religion to hide from life.

"Angel Levine" is part fable, part fantasy, and an example of the typical Malamud theme, the brotherhood of all people. Manischevitz, a Malamudian Job-victim, seeks relief from his suffering and aid for his sick wife, Fanny. In the Malamudian world, help comes from human rather than divine sources; here, the aide is a Jewish Negro angel, Angel Levine. In his narrow religious pride and prejudice, Manischevitz can only wonder why God has failed to send him help in the form of a white person. The tailor's subsequent refusal of aid, an act saturated with egotistical pride, fails to lead to relief.

Eventually, Manischevitz, in pursuit of aid, roams into Harlem, where, finding Angel Levine in Bella's bar, he overhears the essential Malamudian lesson about the divine spark in all persons: "It de speerit," said the old man. "On de face of de water moved de speerit. An' dat was good. It say so in de Book. From de speerit ariz de man. . . . God put the spirit in all things."

Socially color-blind at last, Manischevitz can now believe that the same spirit dwells within every human, uniting them all. In a scene reminiscent of Felicity's vision at the end of Flaubert's "Un Cœur simple," Manischevitz is rewarded by the sight of a dark figure flying with dark wings. The final meaning of his experience he conveys to Fanny when he admits, "Believe me, there are Jews everywhere." Here, he is Malamud's rationalizer, mouthing the familiar theme of brotherhood.

"The Last Mohican" introduces the recurring Everyman character Arthur Fidelman (the stories about him were collected in *Pictures of Fidelman: An Exhibition*) and reveals Malamud's growth and artistry in enlarging the scope of his essentially Jewish materials. Although the setting is not New York City but Rome, the protagonist is familiar. Fidelman, "a self-confessed failure as a painter," is also a failure as a human being, a self-deluded egotist who knows little about his self. His teacher is the familiar aged Jew—this time called Shimon Susskind in typical Malamudian gentle irony, "a Jewish refugee from Israel."

The essential lesson is again brotherhood. As Susskind persists in asking for help on his own terms, Fidelman inquires, "Am I responsible for you, Susskind?" The elderly Jew replies, "Who else . . . you are responsible. Because you are a man. Because you are a Jew, aren't you?" Like Dante descending into the depths of Hell, Fidelman must enter the personal hell of his own ego to learn the powerful lesson. Fearing that Susskind has stolen his manuscript-laden briefcase, Fidelman discovers the refugee in the Jewish ghetto of Rome, "a pitch black freezing cave." Susskind admits to burning the Giotto manuscript inside the case because "the spirit was missing."

This "rebirth of the spirit" story reads less like a Jewish parable than do many of Malamud's stories. Malamud has verisimilarly set the tale in Rome, and he has obviously undergirded it with mythic dimensions by using *Inferno* motifs (using, for example, "Virgilio" Susskind and a street named Dante). Some critics even contend this is the best of the stories in *The Magic Barrel*. Perhaps this story is more believable than others, for rather than merely learning an abstract lesson, Fidelman actually begins to care about Susskind, even forgiving him.

"Idiots First," the title story of his second collection, reveals Malamud's willingness to experiment. The story is a strange combination of fantasy and fable. Although set at night in his familiar territory, this New York is more of a dreamscape, a nightmare, than a realistic environment. No character motivation is provided, key information is omitted, and one Jewish character, Ginzburg, matter-of-factly introduced à la the fairy godmother in "Cinderella," follows an elderly Jew named Mendel, has the ability to freeze people, and seems to represent God/death. Malamud has either invented a new dramatic form or reverted to an old, nineteenth century American mode known as the romance.

Mendel, convinced that he will die that night, desperately seeks thirty-five dollars in order to send his retarded son to Uncle Leo in California. What is not made clear is that Mendel seems to have made a pact with Ginzburg—he will go willingly to his death if he is given time to take care of his son. Mendel is helped not by the rich (a pawnbroker or the supposedly philanthropic Mr. Fishbein), but by the poor, a dying rabbi who gives him a coat, and by death (or Ginzburg) himself, who gives him extra time.

Whereas earlier Malamud stories usually had contrivances such as obvious symbols or preachy *raisonneurs*, "Idiots First" offers no such aid. On one level, the story seems almost metaphysical, a questioning of God/death for being so detached ("What will happen happens. This isn't my responsibility") and wrathful (Ginzburg sees wrath mirrored in Mendel's eyes) that He no longer understands "what it means human." In any case, this open-endedness and general ambiguity represent a new development.

"Black Is My Favorite Color," first appearing in *The Reporter* in 1963, is representative of another of Malamud's frequent concerns, the relationship among the races. Like "Angel Levine" before it and the novel *The Tenants* after it, this story explores the fragile love-hate bonds between Jews and African Americans.

Nat Lime, a white Jew who operates a liquor store in Harlem, professes to be color-blind ("there's only one human color and that's the color of blood"). Throughout his life, Lime has befriended "colored" people, but they all seem to resent his attempts. Buster Wilson, his would-be childhood buddy, Ornita Harris, the black woman to whom he proposes marriage, and Charity Sweetness, his current maid, all reject his overtures of friendship and more.

This story is difficult to understand. Both Lime's words and his actions indicate that he is free of prejudice. He operates a business in black Harlem, and he hires black workers. In return, he is rejected by the three black people he truly likes and helps; twice, he is beaten and robbed by blacks, once obviously for dating a black woman. Yet, through it all, Lime retains his good sense as well as his good humor, and he pursues his cleaning lady everywhere ("Charity Sweetness—you hear me?— come out of that goddamn toilet!"). Malamud appears to be indicating that prejudice and divisiveness reside in black people.

"The German Refugee," one of the few first-person stories in the Malamud canon, also illustrates the theme of brotherhood. The narrator, Martin Goldberg, relates his attempts to teach English to a German refugee, Oskar Gassner, who is scheduled to give a lecture in English about Walt Whitman's relationship to certain German poets.

Two distinct stories emerge: Oskar's anguish over his failure to comprehend English and the irony of Goldberg's failure to understand why. Thus, once again, each man is both tutor and tyro. While Martin teaches Oskar English, the German army begins its summer push of 1939. What the narrator fails to grasp is his pupil's deep involvement in his former country's fate and that of his non-Jewish wife, whom he left there.

To emphasize the irony, Malamud uses references to Whitman. Oskar ends up teaching his teacher the important lesson when he declares about the poet that "it wasn't the love of death they [German poets] had got from Whitman . . . but it was most of all his feeling for *Brudermensch*, his humanity." When Oskar successfully delivers his speech, the narrator feels only a sense of pride at what he taught the refugee, not the bonds of *Brudermensch* that have developed between them. When Oskar commits suicide, the narrator never sees that he is partially responsible.

"The Jewbird" is a modern, urban version of "The Raven." Just as the raven flew through the open window of Edgar Allan Poe's narrator and stayed to haunt his conscience, so Schwartz, this black jewbird, which looks "like a dissipated crow," flaps through the window of Harry Cohen's top-floor apartment and lingers to bedevil him. "Bird or devil," demands Poe's narrator: "how do I know you're a bird and not some kind of a goddamn devil," asks Cohen.

Malamud's beast fable, however, is concerned with more than nebulous guilt over a lost love. On one hand, the tale is lighthearted with a considerable amount of hyperbole, sarcasm, and comic banter; on the other, "The Jewbird" focuses on a heavier theme, prejudice. When Schwartz first enters the Cohen apartment, the bird announces that it is running from "anti-Semeets." At the conclusion of the story, young Maurie Cohen goes in search of the bird, which had been driven from the apartment by his father. Finding the damaged jewbird by the river, the boy asks his mother who so hurt Schwartz, and his mother replies, "Anti-Semeets." In other words, Harry Cohen is anti-Semitic.

Malamud's story, however, is still more than a parable of anti-Semitism. Harry Cohen is a cruel man and an inherently selfish father who has little to do with his son. When Schwartz begins to help Maurie with his reading, math, violin lessons, and even games, the narrator notes that the bird "took on full responsibility for Maurie's performance in school." Harry Cohen is so self-absorbed that he has been unable to function successfully as a parent.

Nathaniel Hawthorne once admitted that a few of his tales suffered from an inveterate love of allegory. The same diagnosis might apply to some of Malamud's stories. "Rembrandt's Hat," the title story from the collection that was published in 1973, is typical of the essentially two-person psychological dramas that Malamud does so well. Often in such stories, two people who apparently work closely together never grasp what is truly going on in each other. As a result, painful misunderstandings occur, with a major one and its subsequent suffering leading to self-knowledge as well as a greater understanding between the two. Feld and Sobel, Finkle and Salzman, Manischevitz and Levine, Goldberg and Gassner, Fidelman and Susskind—the names change, but the pattern remains.

In "Rembrandt's Hat," Rubin, a sculptor, and Arkin, an art historian, are colleagues at a New York art school, and they run into each other occasionally and utter polite, meaningless words. One day, Arkin makes a chance remark to Rubin that the latter's white headwear resembles a hat that Rembrandt wears in one of his self-portraits. From this point on, Rubin grows silent and starts shunning his colleague. Then, each wearing a different hat, the two art teachers go to great lengths to avoid each other. Ultimately, Arkin apologizes, Rubin weeps, and the two men resume their tenuous friendship.

The story turns on another prominent Malamud motif; like Henry James before him, Malamud uses art as a touchstone of character. For example, Fidelman's success as a human being is mirrored in his self-appraisal as an artist. Arkin, like some other Malamud characters, uses art to hide from life; it occurs to him that "he found it easier to judge paintings than to judge people." Rubin's self-portrait is sculpted in a single welded piece, a dwarf tree in the midst of an iron jungle. Thus, when Arkin makes the innocent comment, Rubin's inferiority complex interprets it as a comparison of the sculptor to the old master, Rembrandt, with the sculptor much less prominent. Finally, all the hats, from Arkin's white Stetson to Rubin's railroad engineer's cap, become self-Rorschach tests of the story's participants.

"Notes from a Lady at a Dinner Party," appearing in *Rembrandt's Hat*, is a typical Malamud tale about the relationship between the sexes. In the Malamudian world, men and women desperately seek out each other, reach the verge of true commitment, but find it difficult to communicate, often to commit. Thus, Sobel silently pursues Miriam for seven years without revealing his true feelings, and Fidelman in "Naked Nude" finds it necessary to forge paintings in a whorehouse.

At a dinner party, Max Adler finds himself attracted to Karla Harris, the young wife of his former professor who is more than twice her age. Adler and Harris develop an alluring intimacy by secretly passing notes back and forth. An artist mired in the traditional role of wife-mother, Karla flirts with Adler, who, though previously daring only in his architecture, kisses her. After planning a late-night rendezvous at a nearby motel, they both get cold feet, part, and return to their separate lives of quiet desperation.

Both Karla and Adler are different versions of Malamud's self-limiting human beings. For the most part, Adler can only express his desires in architecture, while Karla's inner self comes out only in the relative safety of watercolors and romantic notes. In Malamud's twentieth century America, then, would-be lovers still cling to the courtly love tradition. Art is a medium not solely to express one's feelings but a place to hide and sublimate. Love rarely blossoms. Adler is divorced. Karla is content to write enticing notes to strange men and keep getting pregnant by her aging husband. Other Malamud men never marry. Oskar Gassner and his wife live in two different countries and are separated by war. Mendel's wife has died. Feld claims his wife does not understand man-woman relationships. Fidelman ultimately becomes bisexual.

"God's Wrath" is another story about parent-child relationships. As with the sexes and the races, Malamud indicates that there is very little communication between parents and children. Glasser, a retired sexton, is a Lear-like figure with three daughters (by two wives) who have all been disappointments. His hopes for one having a better life are pinned on his youngest daughter, Luci, who quits college, leaves her job, and moves out of his apartment. After a long search, Glasser finally locates Luci, learning that she has become a prostitute. "God's Wrath" offers little explanation for the reason things are the way they are, except that God occasionally winks an eye. The story's conclusion is once again open-ended. Unable to dissuade his daughter from a life of prostitution, Glasser stations himself at her haunts and calls down God's wrath on her. Interestingly, at this point, Malamud switches from the past to the present tense, which indicates a sort of never-ending tension between parent and child, a perpetual inability to communicate, and the ultimate ignorance about how a parent affects a child. In the midst of a pessimistic, naturalistic universe, Malamud suggests that certain conflicts are eternal.

Malamud is an acclaimed twentieth century master of the short story. Often writing realistic fantasy, he is able to imbue his initiating Jews with a mythic dimension, while simultaneously depicting social and spiritual squalor in a realistic manner. His tales contain a great depth of feeling that is occasionally marred by obvious moralizing and transparent mythology. He evinces a deep concern for his fellow human beings. His major flaw has been called the narrowness of his subject matter, the plight of the lower-class Jew, but this problem is only a misunderstanding when one realizes that the Jew is a symbol for people everywhere.

Other major works

NOVELS: *The Natural*, 1952; *The Assistant*, 1957; *A New Life*, 1961; *The Fixer*, 1966; *The Tenants*, 1971; *Dubin's Lives*, 1979; *God's Grace*, 1982.

Bibliography

Field, Leslie A., and Joyce W. Field, eds. *Bernard Malamud and the Critics.* New York: New York University Press, 1970. The Fields present a collection of critical essays that are separated into sections on the Jewish tradition; myth, ritual, and folklore; varied approaches; and specific novels and stories. Although the material is somewhat dated, this book is a valuable guide for scholars trying to review early Malamud criticism. Contains a select bibliography and an index.

Malamud, Bernard. Introduction to *The Stories of Bernard Malamud.* New York: Farrar, Straus & Giroux, 1983. This untitled introduction by Malamud offers an invaluable insight into the mind and theories of the writer himself. After a short literary autobiography, Malamud details his belief in form, his assessment of creative writing classes, and the reasons he loves the short story.

_____. "Reflections of a Writer: Long Work, Short Life." *The New York Times Book Review* 93, no. 20 (March, 1988): 15-16. This essay, originally a lecture at Bennington College, offers numerous anecdotes and details about Malamud's life as a writer. He elaborates upon his influences, his various professions, his friends, and some of his theories.

Richman, Sidney. *Bernard Malamud.* Boston: Twayne, 1966. In the first book-length study of Malamud, Richman systematically appraises each of Malamud's works through *A New Life.* Richman also provides a chapter on Malamud's Jewishness, a select bibliography, and some personal correspondence with the writer. A must for students getting started on Malamud.

Hal Charles

SIR THOMAS MALORY

Born: Warwickshire(?), England; early fifteenth century
Died: London(?), England; March 14, 1471

Principal short fiction

Le Morte d'Arthur, 1485; the Winchester manuscript, 1934 (discovered by W. F. Oakeshott).

Other literary forms

Le Morte d'Arthur, published in 1485, is the only work that has been attributed to Sir Thomas Malory.

Achievements

Although a vast body of Arthurian legend, fable, and romance existed (in works such as the Latin *Historia Regum Britanniae* by Geoffrey of Monmouth, the French verse romances of Chrétien de Troyes, and the English Layamon's *Brut*) before Malory's *Le Morte d'Arthur*, Malory was the first writer to give unity and coherence to this mass of material. Popular for centuries after its publication by William Caxton in 1485, Malory's collection of Arthurian tales served as inspiration to many later writers such as Alfred, Lord Tennyson (*Idylls of the King*, 1859-1885) and T. H. White (*The Once and Future King*, 1958). In addition, Malory is credited with being the first English writer to use prose with a sensitivity and expressiveness that had hitherto been reserved to poetry.

Biography

Controversy surrounds the precise identity of the Sir Thomas Malory who wrote *Le Morte d'Arthur*. Long identified as a knight born in Newbold Revell, Warwickshire, who wrote his work in prison, and died in 1471, modern scholars have identified several other contenders. Opinion seems divided concerning whether he supported the York or the Lancastrian side in the Wars of the Roses which ravaged England in the fifteenth century.

Analysis

Although in 1570 Roger Ascham attributed the popularity of Sir Thomas Malory's work to an unhealthy interest in "open manslaughter and bold bawdry," the continuing popularity of *Le Morte d'Arthur* is itself evidence of this medieval author's remarkable grasp of narrative technique. The aesthetic principles governing Malory's art have been a matter of debate since the discovery of the Winchester manuscript in 1934. Eugène Vinaver, who edited the modern standard edition, *The Works of Sir Thomas Malory* (1947), has argued that Malory unraveled the complicated *entrelacement* of his French sources, focusing on narrative units which approach the unity readers expect in modern short stories. Since the appearance of his edition, critics have argued that whatever Malory's intentions, *Le Morte d'Arthur* is one work with a cumulative effect. This controversy seems to have subsided, with most scholars agreeing that Malory wrote eight separate tales rather than one unified narrative and that each of the tales exists within a well-defined cycle. Malory's work thus represents an important transition from the medieval romance to the modern narrative or short story.

"The Tale of King Arthur," Malory's first treatment of Arthur, describes Arthur's battles to consolidate England as one kingdom. Within this one large unit, there are a number of tales which, although linked to the overall theme of Arthur's conquests, illustrate Malory's narrative techniques. "The Tale of Balin," for example, is a self-contained story in which one learns all that is needed to know about Balin; on the other hand, Malory includes inscriptions on tombs, puzzling prophecies by Merlin, and other interpolations which allude to incidents in the stories of Galahad, Lancelot, and Tristram. These vestiges of the medieval *entrelacement* supply information which is not necessary to an understanding of Balin's adventures; their existence makes it impossible to claim "The Tale of Balin" an absolute unity of effect. Nevertheless, the presence of this unnecessary information does not make the story of Balin any less a self-contained and independent narrative unit. This story affords a particularly interesting example of Malory's characteristic style and use of techniques which were to find their greatest themes in "The Quest of the Holy Grail" and "The Death of King Arthur."

"The Tale of Balin" begins when a mysterious damsel appears at Arthur's court, wearing a sword that can only be drawn out of its sheath by a virtuous knight. All of Arthur's knights try and fail to unsheathe the sword. Balin, however, draws out the sword only to be told by the damsel that if he keeps it, he will destroy his best friend and the man whom he most loves. It is then that the Lady of the Lake appears, demanding that Arthur give her the heads of Balin and the sword-damsel. Hearing this, Balin claims that the sword-damsel caused his mother's death and cuts off her head. By this action Balin violates Arthur's safe conduct and loses his favor.

In the incidents which follow, Balin tries to regain Arthur's favor by conquering his enemies; however, in adventure after adventure Balin's success as a knight, the greatest in the world, is juxtaposed with prophecies of disaster and tragedy. He unintentionally causes the suicides of two sets of lovers and strikes a "dolorous stroke" in self-defense which lays waste three kingdoms. Finally, he meets his brother Balan, his best friend and the person he most loves. Disguised with unfamiliar shields, they fail to recognize each other and fight to the death. Just before they die, they recognize each other and ask to be buried in the same tomb.

While readers accept the supernatural prophecies as tragic foreshadowings, Balin refuses to believe them. Reluctant as he is to accept the validity of the prophetic warnings, he accepts the disasters themselves with a simple fortitude. At three different points in the narrative, he says: "I shall take the aventure that God woll ordayne me." This courageous acceptance of a tragic fate becomes a compelling secondary theme in the tale.

Of the foreshadowings, the most significant occurs just before the final episode in which Balin and his brother engage in fatal battle. Balin hears a horn blow "as it had ben the dethe of a best. . . . 'That blast,' said Balyn, 'is blowen for me, for I am the pryse, and yet am I not dede.'" After causing the death of innocent lovers and the waste of three kingdoms, Balin says with stark but effective simplicity that he is the prize or victim of the hunt, but he is not yet dead. At this point, he realizes that he is being pursued by supernatural forces.

In fact, this image of fate as the hunter and Balin as the prize or victim epitomizes the irony and pathos of Balin's fortunes. Through the use of tragic foreshadowing, Malory contrasts Balin's success as a knight, his demonstration of faith and virtue by winning the sword, with his human vulnerability to fate.

"The Quest of the Holy Grail" is linked somewhat loosely to "The Tale of Balin" by allusions to the failure of all knights, even Lancelot, to draw out Balin's sword, but it is principally concerned with parallelism between Galahad and his father Lancelot. Malory emphasizes Lancelot's supremacy over all earthly knights, but it is Galahad who serves as model for the followers of Christ and becomes the spiritual ideal.

Traditionally, the Grail is the name of the cup Jesus used at the Last Supper. Later, Joseph of Arimethea was supposed to have caught Christ's blood in it during the Crucifixion. A vision of the Grail was seen by a nun, the sister of one of the Knights of the Round Table, but only three knights achieve the quest—Galahad, Percival, and Bors. At the conclusion of the tale, a multitude of angels appear and bear Galahad's soul to heaven; a hand descends to take the Grail and the sacred spear which pierced Christ's body into heaven.

At the very outset of the quest for the Grail, Arthur laments that however worthy this quest may be, it will destroy the solidarity of the Round Table. Lancelot insists that the quest will bring great honor to the knights. It is a tribute to Malory's success as a storyteller that he does justice both to the spiritual ideal of the quest and the earthly, but splendid, fellowship of the Round Table.

Malory's "The Death of King Arthur" is both his greatest work and the one in which he demonstrates most independence from his sources. With profound psychological understanding, he dramatizes the conflict between two loyalties: the chivalric code with its emphasis upon comradeship and devotion to one's lord, epitomized in the Round Table, and the service of the knight-lover for his lady, the romantic theme of courtly chronicles. In rescuing Queen Guinevere whom he loves and serves as knight, Lancelot is forced to kill Sir Gareth, the brother of Gawain and the knight who loves Lancelot more than all other men. This incident is Malory's own invention; his sources describe only vaguely the death of Gawain's brothers.

Faced with the prospect of battle against Lancelot, Arthur realizes that this battle will indeed result in the destruction of the fellowship of the Round Table. His lament emphasizes the tragedy of the loss: "I am soryar for my good knyghtes losse than for the losse of my fayre queen; for quenys I myght have inow, but such felyship of good knyghtes shall never be togydirs in no company." Eugène Vinaver has commented:

. . . it is not through sin or weakness of heart that the end comes about, but through the devotion of the truest friend and the truest lover, though a tragic greatness which fixes forever the complex and delicate meaning of Arthur's epic.

Confronted with accusations by Agravain and Mordred, his bastard son and nephew, that Lancelot has traitorously loved the queen, Arthur is reluctant to take action. When he agrees to test Lancelot, it is with misgivings because, as he acknowledges, "sir Launcelot had done so much for hym and for the quene so many tymes." After Lancelot is discovered in the queen's chamber, Guinevere is sentenced to burning. Lancelot rescues her, and in the process of saving her from the flames, slays Gareth. The war which follows destroys everything.

Even after Lancelot returns the queen to Arthur, Lancelot is exiled and then attacked in France by Arthur and Gawain. While Arthur is gone, Mordred seizes the kingdom and Guinevere, whom he plans to marry. In the first battle with Mordred, Arthur wins, although Gawain receives his death wound and writes repentantly to Lancelot, begging him to come to Arthur's assistance. Arthur dies on the plains of Salisbury and with him pass the ideals of the Round Table.

When Lancelot returns to avenge the king and queen, he finds that Guinevere has entered a convent. As she explains to Lancelot, she has renounced the world because she feels that their love has caused the wars and the death of Arthur. Although she urges Lancelot to marry and to find his own happiness, he insists that he will become a hermit for her sake: "And therefore, lady, sithen you have taken you to perfection I must needs take me to perfection of right."

Finally, in an episode that seems to be Malory's invention, Lancelot learns of Guinevere's death in a dream and is told to bury her near Arthur. During her burial he swoons in sorrow. When he dies shortly afterward, consumed by grief for the king and queen, the bishop hermit relates a vision in which he sees angels raising Lancelot to heaven. At his burial his brother Ector delivers a eulogy which represents Malory's definitive statement on the chivalric ideal:

. . . thou were never matched of erthely knyghtes hande. . . . And thou were the truest frende to thy lovar that ever bestrade hors, and thou were the trewest lover of a synful man that ever loved woman, and thou were the kyndest man that ever strake wyth swerde. And thou were the gode-lyest persone that ever cam emonge prees of knyghtes, and thou was the mekest man and the jentyllest that ever ete in halle emonge ladyes, and thou were the sternest knyght to thy mortal foo that ever put spere in reeste.

It is because of Malory's handling of the Arthurian materials that the stories of King Arthur became part of English literary tradition. From the complexity of his French sources he produced narratives which remain vital and appealing to the modern reader. Perhaps, however, the best critical summary of Malory's achievement was offered by William Caxton, Malory's first editor and critic, who tells readers that in *Le Morte d'Arthur* they will find "many joyous and playsaunt hystoryes and noble and renomed actes of humanyte, gentylnesse, and chyvalryes."

Bibliography

Bennet, J. A. W., ed. *Essays on Malory.* Oxford, England: Clarendon Press, 1963. A collection of seven essays by such outstanding Middle English scholars as C. S. Lewis, Derek Stanley Brewer, and W. F. Oakeshott. Included is an essay on art and nature by Eugène Vinaver, one of the most prominent Malory scholars of his day, written in the form of an open letter to C. S. Lewis, which responds to many of the points made by Lewis in his own essay in this collection ("The English Prose *Morte*"). A lengthy examination of chivalry in *Le Morte d'Arthur* is also included.

Benson, Larry D. *Malory's Morte Darthur.* Cambridge, Mass.: Harvard University Press, 1976. Four aspects of Malory's work are examined in a work concerned chiefly with the context in which Malory wrote: a discussion of the relationship of the genre of *Le Morte d'Arthur* to Arthurian legend and traditional romances; the structure of Malory's work particularly as it relates to the English romance; a historical perspective on chivalric traditions and chivalry in Malory; and a detailed literary and historical interpretation of the tale of the Sancgreal, the book of Sir Lancelot and Guinevere, and the death of Arthur.

Kennedy, Beverly. *Knighthood in the Morte Darthur.* Cambridge, England: D. S. Brewer, 1985. A comprehensive, detailed examination of knighthood and chivalry and a meticulous discussion of *Le Morte d'Arthur* in this light. Kennedy considers different facets of knighthood, such as "The High Order of Knighthood," "Worshipful Knighthood," and "True Knighthood."

McCarthy, Terence. *Reading the "Morte d'Arthur."* Wolfeboro, N.H.: Boydell and Brewer, 1988. An excellent introduction to *Le Morte d'Arthur.* McCarthy outlines the structure of the work, book by book, with plenty of background and analysis, then offers more in-depth discussions of chivalric tradition, historical background, Malory's style, and his method of storytelling. He also suggests a selection of passages for closer study to give the newcomer to Malory a representative and manageable introduction to an occasionally difficult text.

Takamiya, Toshiyuki, and Derek Brewer, eds. *Aspects of Malory.* Totowa, N.J.: Rowman & Littlefield, 1981. Eleven essays on Malory. Examines topics such as sources of Malory, the structure of Malory's tales, and the Malory manuscript. Eugène Vinaver discusses Malory's prose style, and Richard R. Griffiths offers a new theory on the author's identity.

J. R. Brink
(Revised by *Catherine Swanson*)

THOMAS MANN

Born: Lübeck, Germany; June 6, 1875
Died: Zurich, Switzerland; August 12, 1955

Principal short fiction

Der Kleine Herr Friedemann, 1898; *Tristan*, 1903; *Tonio Kröger*, 1903 (novella; English translation, 1914); *Der Tod in Venedig*, 1912 (novella; *Death in Venice*, 1925); *Das Wunderkind*, 1914; *Herr und Hund*, 1919 (novella; *Bashan and I*, 1923; also known as *A Man and His Dog*, 1930); *Erzählung*, 1922; *Unordnung und frühes Leid*, 1926 (novella; *Disorder and Early Sorrow*, 1928); *Children and Fools*, 1928; *Mario und der Zauberer*, 1930 (novella; *Mario and the Magician*, 1930); *Stories of Three Decades*, 1936; *Die vertauschten Köpfe: Eine indische Legend*, 1940 (novella; *The Transposed Heads: A Legend of India*, 1941); *Ausgewahlte Erzählungen*, 1945; *Die Betrogene*, 1953 (novella; *The Black Swan*, 1954); *Death in Venice and Seven Other Stories*, 1954; *Stories of a Lifetime*, 1961.

Other literary forms

In addition to his short fiction, Thomas Mann wrote novels, essays, and some poetry. When he received the Nobel Prize in Literature in 1929, his novel *Buddenbrooks* (1901; English translation, 1924) was cited specifically, though many of his later novels have received wide acclaim. Especially widely read and written about are the novel *Der Zauberberg* (1924; *The Magic Mountain*, 1927), a philosophical exploration of post-World War I dilemmas, and the four volumes of *Joseph und seine Brüder* (1933-1943; *Joseph and His Brothers*, 1934-1944, 1948), a modern mythology based on biblical tales. Mann's essays, collected in *Adel des Geistes* (1945; *Essays of Three Decades*, 1947), cover a broad range of political and literary issues.

Achievements

During more than half a century of writing and publishing both fiction and nonfiction, the German writer Mann received at least a dozen honorary doctoral degrees from universities in Europe and the United States. Though Mann lost both his honorary doctorate from the Rheinische Friedrich Wilhelm Universität in Bonn and his German citizenship in 1936, when he was accused of "subversive attacks on, and the gravest insults to, the Reich," he was reinstated as an honorary doctorate at Bonn in 1947. Among his other honorary doctorates, two stand out in particular: one was his honorary doctorate from Harvard University, which he received together with Albert Einstein in 1935; the other was an honorary doctorate of natural sciences from the Eidgenössische Technische Hochschule of Zurich in 1955, a degree that especially pleased Mann because it was so unusual.

Mann received the Nobel Prize in Literature in 1929, and he received numerous other honors throughout his writing career, including the Herder-Prize of Czechoslovakia for exiled writers, in 1937. During his international travels, both before and during his exile, Mann received many personal honors. In 1935, he was the guest of former American president Franklin D. Roosevelt and his wife at a private dinner at the White House. From 1938 to 1941, he was a visiting professor at Princeton University, and in 1953, two years before his death, Mann saw Pope Pius XII in private audience.

Mann's fiction is diverse, sometimes reflecting conventions of the nineteenth century, as in Mann's early novel *Buddenbrooks*, sometimes exploring philosophical dilemmas, as in his novel *The Magic Mountain*, sometimes experimenting with stream-of-consciousness writing, as in the final chapter of his novel *Lotte in Weimar* (1939; *The Beloved Returns*, 1940), and sometimes rewriting mythology, as in the tetralogy *Joseph and His Brothers*, based on a biblical story, and the novella *The Transposed Heads*, adapted from a Hindu legend. Always, however, Mann infused a new irony into his fiction. He is a key figure in Western literature.

Biography

Thomas Mann was born on June 6, 1875, in Lübeck, Germany. He was the son of Johann Heinrich Mann, a minor politician and grain merchant, and Julia Mann (née da Silva-Bruhn), an accomplished musician, born and reared in Brazil. The dichotomy between the burgher and the artist, embodied in Mann's parents, is one of the themes of Mann's fiction, appearing in such works as the novella *Tonio Kröger*. One of five children, Mann was especially close to his older brother Heinrich, who traveled through Italy with him. The philosophical and political conflicts between the brothers fueled some of the debates in Mann's fiction, particularly in *The Magic Mountain*.

Though Mann worked briefly as an editor and an insurance agent, he was primarily a writer. When he was nineteen years old, the prestigious journal *Die Gesellschaft* published his first short story, "Gefallen"; after this first publication, Mann continued to write and publish until his death.

In 1905, Mann married Katya Pringsheim, whose father was a mathematics professor at the University of Munich. The Manns had six children: three girls and three boys. Their oldest son, Klaus, who was a writer, took his own life in 1949 at the age of forty-three.

In addition to the influence of Mann's family on his writing, there were two other sources of influence: the political climate of Europe and the social environment of the artist. It was the political climate of Europe that brought about Mann's exile. According to André von Gronicka's account of Mann's life, the "immediate cause of Mann's exile" from Germany was Mann's reading of the essay on Richard Wagner ("Leiden und Grösse Richard Wagner," "The Suffering and Greatness of Richard Wagner") at the University of Munich in 1933. Shortly after the reading, the Manns went to Holland, where they received a call from their children, warning them not to return. As a result, the Manns went into self-imposed exile, spending a brief time in Holland, Switzerland, and the south of France. In 1934, Mann made his first visit to the United States at the invitation of the publisher Alfred A. Knopf. In 1936, when

Mann lost his German citizenship, he and his wife became citizens of Czechoslovakia. In 1938, they returned to the United States, and in 1944, they became American citizens. Though Mann's writing has an international flavor, as is evident in the wide range of settings in his fiction, Mann was acutely aware of his German roots. Only briefly between 1933 and his death was he able to return to his homeland.

Mann's social environment as an artist was especially diverse. Because he published from the age of nineteen, in 1894, until his death, in 1955, he had lifelong friendships with such artists as Bruno Walter and Hermann Hesse, and he often visited other friends and acquaintances, such as Hugo von Hoffmannsthal, André Gide, Sigmund Freud, and Gustav Mahler.

In 1953, the Manns returned to Europe and went to Kilchberg, Switzerland, where they bought their last home. Though Mann had begun to show signs of ill health as early as 1945, his death was fairly sudden. On August 12, 1955, he suffered a sudden collapse. By eight o'clock that evening, he was dead.

Analysis

Thomas Mann's early stories are set in late nineteenth century and early twentieth century Europe, primarily in Germany and Italy. The protagonists are artists, disillusioned romantics with an ironic view of the cost of their art, which is an isolation from others. They are often burghers turned artist, often physically deformed, further isolating them from life around them and traditional courtship. To avoid the pain and disappointment of love, these protagonists retreat to art and nature, but in midlife, usually when they reach thirty years of age, they are suddenly overwhelmed by passion, usually for an unworthy and superficial beloved. Simultaneously, the disillusioned romantic usually comes face to face with his own superfluity, as does Mann's dilettante, in the story "Der Bajazzo" ("The Dilettante"), when he recognizes himself as "a perfectly useless human being." Though the sense of superfluity is quite often triggered by unrequited love, the object of the love, the beloved, is treated only superficially. Such is the case, for example, with Amra in "Luischen" ("Little Lizzy"), who obliviously orchestrates her husband's destruction and stares vacantly at him while he dies of grief over her mistreatment of him. Mann says of Amra that she is not "sensitive enough to betray herself because of a guilty conscience." The disillusionment, in fact, has little to do with the beloved. Rather, the disillusionment is a device to trigger the protagonist's introspection, his moment of awareness brought on by the experience. The moment of awareness for Amra's husband, Christian Jacoby, kills him. Other protagonists live on, lacking the will even to kill themselves, such as the narrator in Mann's story "Enttäuschung" ("Disillusionment"), who says of his disillusionment that it has left him "alone, unhappy, and a little queer."

Mann's protagonists yearn for experience, for connection with the day-to-day living of those around them, and for a synthesis between body and spirit, discipline and impulse, reason and passion, involvement and withdrawal, action and inaction. They are fascinated by grief, death, and disease. In Mann's story "Der Kleiderschrank"

("The Wardrobe"), for example, the dying man is drawn to the boardinghouse of a woman who has a "repulsive eruption, a sort of fungus growth, on her brow." Again, in Mann's story "Tobias Mindernickel," Tobias is fascinated by a child's bleeding injury and by his dog Esau's injury. He is so fascinated by Esau's injury that, after it has healed, he tries to reinjure the dog and, in the process, kills it.

Two works typical of Mann's early short fiction are "Der kleine Herr Friedemann" ("Little Herr Friedemann") and *Tonio Kröger*. In these works, Mann develops the Symbolist theme of the artist's solitude, the theme of the burgher turned artist, and the themes involved in the battles between body and mind, passion and intellect, action and inaction.

In "Little Herr Friedemann," the title story from Mann's 1898 collection of stories, Mann explores the themes of obsession with beauty and disillusionment with romanticism. Johannes Friedemann, a hunchback because he was dropped by his drunken nurse when he was an infant, seeks a life of fulfillment through art and nature. This pursuit is encouraged by his ailing mother, who, after fourteen years of a lingering illness, dies, leaving Friedemann with his three unmarried sisters. Like other protagonists in Mann's short fiction, Friedemann "cherishes" his grief over his mother's death and moves further into his solitary existence. To the extent that he thinks of his own death, he envisions it like his mother's death, a "mild twilight radiance gently declining into dark." At the age of thirty, after constructing a rigorously disciplined life, Friedemann becomes obsessed with a beautiful woman, Frau Gerda von Rinnlingen. Battling between passion and reason, between action and inaction, Friedemann finally summons his courage to go to Frau Rinnlingen and confess his love. He hopes that she will feel pity for him. She instead dismisses him with a "short, scornful laugh" as she clutches his arm and flings him sidewise to the ground. The rejection leaves Friedemann "stunned and unmanned" and shuddering. In this moment of awareness, he directs his anger against himself. He is filled with "a thirst to destroy himself, to tear himself to pieces, to blot himself utterly out." He drags himself to the river and, with a faint splash, drowns himself. The final image is a "faint sound of laughter" in the distance. Friedemann is among Mann's disillusioned romantics who do not survive their moment of awareness.

Friedemann, often considered a prototype of Gustave von Aschenbach in the novella *Death in Venice*, illuminates the struggle between passion and intellect, a leitmotif linking the various stories in the first volume together. It is the disillusioned romanticism embodied in Friedemann that moves Mann, in his second volume of stories, *Tristan*, toward what critics have called a "new artistic intellectualism."

In the novella *Tonio Kröger*, Mann again develops the burgher-artist theme, evident in the title name itself. The name "Tonio," for Mann, symbolizes the artistic heritage of Italy, and "Kröger" symbolizes the disciplined intellectualism of his German father. The protagonist, Tonio Kröger, is a sort of synthesis of the artist and intellectual. An outsider in his youth, Tonio later considers isolating himself from society, but he rejects the impulse, thus allowing himself to find a sort of consolation.

The novella begins as Tonio waits for his childhood friend Hans Hansen, so that they can go for a walk, something Hans has almost forgotten while Tonio has "looked forward to it with almost incessant joy." Though Tonio does not want to be like Hans, he loves Hans, not only because he is handsome but also because he is "in every respect his [Tonio's] own opposite and foil." Tonio is brooding, sensitive, and introspective, while Hans is lively, insensitive, and superficial.

Hans and Tonio are separated, years pass, and when Tonio is sixteen years old, his passion for Hans turns to Ingeborg Holm, who makes his heart throb with ecstasy. Tonio, like Friedemann in "Little Herr Friedemann," is aware that his beloved is "remote and estranged," but still he prefers her company to that of Magdalena Vermehren, who understands him and laughs or is serious in the right places. Tonio, realizing the implications of his unrequited love for Hans and later for Inge, speaks of being flung to and fro forever "between two crass extremes: between icy intellect and scorching sense."

In contrast to Hans and Inge is Lisabeta Ivanova, Tonio's close and candid artist-friend of approximately his own age. Though she offers Tonio consolation during his turmoil, she also calls him bourgeois, because he is drawn to the superficial Hans and Inge and because he wants to be ordinary. Lisabeta and Tonio explore in dialogue the implications of the artist's existence. Lisabeta, unlike Tonio, is reconciled to her role as an artist.

After thirteen years, Hans returns, and Tonio comes upon him with Inge; Hans and Inge, two of a type, get along well together. Nevertheless, when Tonio, Hans, Magdalena, and Inge all end up at a dance, Tonio tries to make Inge jealous by dancing with Magdalena. Like many of Mann's disillusioned romantics, Tonio hopes that his beloved will suddenly return the passion that he feels for her. Inge, however, is incapable of feeling passion for Tonio. She is, in fact, oblivious to his anguish and remains at the dance with Hans. Dejectedly, Tonio returns to his room.

The novella ends with a letter that Tonio writes to Lisabeta from his room at Aalsgard. In the letter, Tonio concludes that he can be happy with the unrequited love of his ideal beauty. He says to Lisabeta of his unrequited love that it is "good and fruitful." He relishes the "longing" in it and the "gentle envy." He concludes that, through the love, he experiences a "touch of contempt and no little innocent bliss." Unlike the unrequited love of Johannes Friedemann that leads to Friedemann's self-loathing and death, the unrequited love of Tonio Kröger somehow consoles and sustains him.

A significant change in Mann's later short fiction appears in his treatment of aging. In the earlier works, the protagonists tend to be thirty-year-old disillusioned romantics, characters drawn to youth as much as beauty. The culminating point of this fascination with youth is in the story "Das Wunderkind" ("The Infant Prodigy"), in which the protagonist is eight, looks nine, and is given out for seven. The child, dressed in white silk, has dark circles around his eyes and is already bored, isolated, and somewhat cynical. Nevertheless, the audience is spellbound by the prodigy's youth.

In Mann's later works, the protagonists develop a fear of aging. For example, Gustave von Aschenbach in the novella *Death in Venice* and Frau Rosalie von Tümmler in the novella *The Black Swan*, upon reaching their early fifties, fall passionately in love as they are dying, Aschenbach of cholera and Tümmler of cancer. As in Mann's early works, the beloved ones are young. In the later works, however, the protagonists dread their own aging, eventually creating young-old death masks for themselves, masks that, ironically, turn out to be their death masks. In addition to exploring the fear of aging, Mann begins to explore new ideas, such as the effects of evil on passive people, as in *Mario and the Magician*, and the implications of mythologies, as in *The Transposed Heads*.

Death in Venice has received high critical acclaim; it is often called Mann's finest novella and one of the finest novellas of Western literature. Mann explores several themes in the novella: the conflict between discipline and impulse, the fear of aging, the draw to beauty that destroys, the death wish, the draw to homoerotic love, and the battle between passion and reason.

Death in Venice is set in the early twentieth century in Munich, Germany, and Venice, Italy. The central character, Gustave von Aschenbach, is a well-known German author in his early fifties. At the beginning of the novella, Aschenbach, suffering from insomnia, takes a walk near his home in Munich. On the walk, he encounters a man near the burying ground. The man, who later appears in Venice, awakes in Aschenbach an irresistible longing to travel. This longing eventually puts him on board a ship bound for Venice, where he encounters a repulsive "young-old man," masquerading as a youth and trying to keep pace with them. The man, "pitiably drunk," approaches Aschenbach, and as the young-old man drools and stutters nonsense, the upper plate of his false teeth falls loose. Clearly disgusted by the young-old man, Aschenbach escapes. This encounter foreshadows Aschenbach's later battle against his own aging.

In Venice, Aschenbach becomes obsessed with the beautiful Tadzio, a Polish youth about fourteen years old. Mixed with Aschenbach's passion for Tadzio's beauty is a conscious fascination with Tadzio's mortality. For example, as Aschenbach watches Tadzio play, he realizes that it is not Tadzio he sees, "but Hyacinthus, doomed to die because two gods were rivals for his love." When Aschenbach recognizes Tadzio's ill health, he thinks that Tadzio will "most likely not live to grow old." This idea gives Aschenbach pleasure, but Aschenbach refuses to analyze his response. Later, upon the same realization, "compassion" struggles with "reckless exultation" in Aschenbach's heart. Though Aschenbach chooses not to explore this exultation, clearly one part of his joy lies in what critics have called "the seduction of the individual by disease and death" and the other part in Tadzio's avoidance of the aging that disgusts and frightens Aschenbach. Aschenbach feels exultation not because Tadzio will die but because Tadzio will not live to grow old.

As Venice becomes plague-ridden with Asiatic cholera, Aschenbach himself begins to look haggard. He is plagued by the odor of carbolic acid from the man from the burying ground, an odor that Aschenbach suspects others may not detect. He is repulsed by the pervasive stench of germicide and by the "odour of the sickened city." At this point, in his own battle against the physical effects of his declining health and his aging, Aschenbach dyes his hair black and "freshens up" his skin, making himself into a ghoulish "young-old man."

Aschenbach, nearing his end, has a terrifying dream about the "bestial degradation of his fall." In the dream, he realizes that he has lost the battle between passion and reason. Tadzio has smiled at Aschenbach and has, in that small gesture, left Aschenbach feeling "quite unmanned." Aschenbach, still made up into a young-old man, dies in Venice of the cholera. Aschenbach's death reinforces Mann's theme that in the battle between spirit and body, there are no winners. In death, Aschenbach satisfies his need to be free of the yearning that is opposed to his art, the "lure, for the unorganized, the immeasurable, the eternal—in short, for nothingness."

Finally, in *Death in Venice*, Mann explores again, as he does in "Little Herr Friedemann," the theme of the artist being drawn to "beauty that breaks the heart." Even while Aschenbach recognizes the superficiality of the physical attraction, even of his beloved, as he comes to the subtle realization that the lover is "nearer the divine than the beloved," he finds that beauty compelling. He concludes, as does Tonio Kröger, that "in almost every artist is inborn a wanton and treacherous proneness to side with the beauty that breaks the heart, to single out aristocratic pretentions and pay them homage." It is this homage to beauty that makes Aschenbach incapable of action and holds him in Venice to meet his death.

A novella in a different vein is *Mario and the Magician*, published between World War I and World War II. It is generally considered an attack on Fascism. The story begins with a German family visiting Italy and experiencing a series of minor humiliations. The family later becomes part of the audience of an evil hypnotist, Cipolla, who humiliates the members of his passive audience, one at a time, until one of them, Mario, shoots him, an act that leaves the audience liberated.

Early in the novella, Mann introduces the theme of peace. He says, "We all know how the world at once seeks peace and puts her to flight—rushing upon her in the fond idea that they two will wed, and where she is, there it can be at home." Peace, however, is treated ironically, in that the desire for peace keeps the passive audience from acting, even as they become the "humpbacked magician's victims. Mann's narrator soon begins to realize that in "yielding to another person's will—there may lie too small a space for the idea of freedom to squeeze into." In contrast to Johannes Friedemann, who is destroyed when he acts, the audience in *Mario and the Magician* is saved only through action.

Among Mann's last short fiction, first published between 1940 and 1955, are *The Transposed Heads* and *The Black Swan*. Significant in these last major works of short fiction are two characteristics of Mann's work. The first is one of adapting mythology in new contexts, as he does in the novella *The Transposed Heads*, an adaptation of a Hindu legend about seeking harmony between the inner and outer self. The second characteristic is one represented in the novella *The Black Swan*, in which Mann's earlier theme of the conflict between youth and age, life and death, occurs.

In *The Transposed Heads*, Mann creates his most abstract and mythic characters. Shridaman, a merchant and the son of a merchant, represents spirit and intellect, while Nanda, a smith and a cowherd, represents body and intuition. The girl represents beauty. Though Mann called this work "a metaphysical farce," it offers an integral vision of a new humanity. It is in this tale that Mann includes his clearest synthesis of the unity between "Shridaman" and "Nanda":

> This world is not so made that spirit is fated to love only spirit, and beauty only beauty. Indeed the very contrast between the two points out, with a clarity at once intellectual and beautiful, that the world's goal is union between spirit and beauty, a bliss no longer divided, but whole and consummate.

Following this vision, Mann returns to the farce, concluding, "This tale . . . is but an illustration of the failures and false starts attending the effort to reach the goal."

In *The Black Swan*, Mann retells the story of Gustave von Aschenbach of *Death in Venice* but with a new twist. The novella, set in Düsseldorf in the 1920's, tells the story of Frau Rosalie von Tümmler, a fifty-year-old widow, who is caught up in passion for her son Eduard's youthful tutor, Ken Keaton, an American expatriot. Once again, the lover is closer to the divine than the beloved. Ken Keaton is variously described by critics as insipid, mediocre, and commonplace, an amiable nonentity. Like Aschenbach, Rosalie, as she becomes increasingly obsessed with her beloved, dyes her hair and applies cosmetics to conceal her age. Like Aschenbach, she does active battle against physical aging.

Rosalie von Tümmler's daughter Anna, born with a clubfoot, paints abstract art and tries to purge all feeling from her work. It is she, recognizing her mother's unhealthy passion, who urges her mother to establish a more socially acceptable relationship with Keaton. Still, Rosalie ignores her daughter's advice.

In an ironic twist, Mann has Rosalie develop cancer of the womb before she can go to Keaton's room to consummate their relationship. The cause of the cancer is, again ironically, the agitation that she experiences during menopause, her passion for Keaton thus leading to her own death in a matter of weeks. A further irony is evident in that the rejuvenation that Rosalie feels in her passion for Keaton is, in fact, a symptom of her physical decay.

Unlike Aschenbach, however, Rosalie regains her dignity during the final weeks of her life. She yearns for the aristocratic black swans, a death symbol. The German title, *Die Betrogene*, means "the deceived," and Rosalie von Tümmler is indeed deceived, by both her passion and her body, which has sent her messages of a new vitality even while she was mortally ill. Still, unlike Aschenbach, whose passion remains unresolved, Rosalie dies a "gentle death, regretted by all who knew her."

Throughout Mann's lengthy writing career, from 1894 to 1955, the bulk of critical opinion of his work was consistently favorable. It has remained so after his death. Nevertheless, significant changes occur between his early and late short fiction. To some extent, Mann's protagonists do achieve, if not a synthesis of polarities, at least a complex worldview in which they find consolation. The shift in worldview is particularly evident in Mann's treatment of the conflicts between self-destruction and survival, between passion and discipline, and between action and inaction.

First, in the conflict between self-destruction and survival, Mann's early protagonists cannot survive their disillusionment. Johannes Friedemann in "Little Herr Friedemann" is filled with self-loathing and drowns himself. Christian Jacoby in "Little Lizzy" becomes suddenly aware of his wife's infidelity and dies instantly from shock and grief. With Mann's development of Tonio Kröger in *Tonio Kröger*, however, the disillusioned romantic finds a new, though not fully gratifying, illusion that can permit him to survive. Some critics have referred to this new worldview as Mann's artistic intellectualism. This artistic intellectualism is based on a sort of ironic realization that perhaps the wanting is superior to the having, an idea that acknowledges both the passion and the intellect. Mann explores another sort of synthesis of the conflict between self-destruction and survival in Frau Rosalie von Tümmler in *The Black Swan*. Though Frau Tümmler's passion triggers the cancer that kills her, she clearly comes to terms with her self-destructive passion. Her death is not a suicide but rather a "gentle" death, the sort envisioned by Johannes Friedemann before his disillusionment.

Second, in the conflict between passion and discipline, Mann's early protagonists are undone by their passion. Johannes Friedemann and Christian Jacoby illustrate Mann's early theme that in conflicts between passion and discipline, body and intellect, there are no winners. Though Tonio Kröger provides a respite from the conflict, as he learns to live with unrequited love, Mann explores this conflict in a new light with Gustave von Aschenbach in *Death in Venice*. Aschenbach does not act on his passion, except insofar as he does not leave the plague-ridden Venice, an inaction that, in fact, becomes a self-destructive action. Unlike Johannes Friedemann and Christian Jacoby, however, Aschenbach does not confess his love to his beloved; to that extent, he displays discipline. Nevertheless, the inaction caused by his passion leads as clearly to his destruction as if he had taken his own life, and though he dies with his self-loathing at what he calls his "bestial degradation," he has not destroyed his reputation as a novelist. Mann does a final exploration of the battle between passion and discipline in the character of Rosalie von Tümmler. Frau Tümmler, fully prepared to act on her passion despite her daughter's advice, collapses on her way to meet her beloved and consummate their passion. To that point, Frau Tümmler has lost her battle between passion and discipline, but through the remainder of her mortal illness, she has a second chance to retrieve her dignity, and she does so with grace.

Finally, in the conflict between action and inaction, Mann's protagonists become increasingly complex. In the early stories, characters who act, especially on their passion, destroy themselves. For example, when Johannes Friedemann in "Little Herr Friedemann" acts on his passion for Frau Rinnlingen, the action leads to his death. When Christian Jacoby in "Little Lizzy" acts on his wife's wishes and against his better judgment, he faces a moment of awareness that destroys him. Later, Mann's Tonio Kröger in *Tonio Kröger* opts for inaction with his beloved Inge. That inaction saves him. Mann's treatment of Gustave von Aschenbach in *Death in Venice* is among Mann's most complex explorations of the conflict between action and inaction. Had Aschenbach not acted on the yearning to travel, triggered by the stranger at the burying ground in Munich, he may not have been in Venice during the cholera epidemic. Aschenbach's failure to act by leaving Venice when he had the opportunity, however, results in his death of cholera. Mann introduces another new complexity into the conflict between action and inaction in Mario in *Mario and the Magician*. The audience sits by passively while the magician victimizes them, one after another. When Mario acts, killing the magician, his action liberates the audience. In Mann's final exploration of the conflict between action and inaction, Rosalie von Tümmler, in her decision to act on her passion, loses her option for further action on her passion, but in her final weeks of illness, she acts again, this time to reclaim her dignity. Her final action leads to her self-respect and to a gentle death.

Part of the resolution of conflicts in Mann's later short fiction undoubtedly comes from his use of his own experience in the creation of his protagonists. In fact, in 1936, when *Stories of Three Decades* was published, Mann, then officially in exile, referred to the collection as "an autobiography in the guise of a fable." In Mann's work during his years of exile, he moved increasingly toward exploring syntheses of the conflicts in his earlier protagonists. As a result, his later protagonists, as they expand their worldviews, begin to synthesize humanism, culture, and philosophy, and through these protagonists, one sees, always, Mann's ironic observations of the world.

Other major work

NOVELS: *Buddenbrooks: Verfall einer Familie,* 1901 (English translation, 1924); *Tristan,* 1903 (English translation, 1925); *Königliche Hoheit,* 1909 (*Royal Highness,* 1916); *Der Zauberberg,* 1924 (*The Magic Mountain,* 1927); *Joseph und seine Brüder,* 1933-1943 (*Joseph and His Brothers,* 1934-1944, 1948; includes *Die Geschichten Jaakobs,* 1933 [*Joseph and His Brothers,* 1934; also as *The Tales of Jacob,* 1934]; *Der junge Joseph,* 1934 [*The Young Joseph,* 1935]; *Joseph in Ägypten,* 1936 [*Joseph in Egypt,* 1938]; *Joseph, der Ernährer,* 1943 [*Joseph the Provider,* 1944]); *Lotte in Weimar,* 1939 (*The Beloved Returns,* 1940); *Doktor Faustus: Das Leben des deutschen Tonsetzers Adrian Leverkühn, erzählt von einem Freunde,* 1947 (*Doctor Faustus: The Life of the German Composer Adrian Leverkühn as Told by a Friend,* 1948); *Der Erwählte,* 1951 (*The Holy Sinner,* 1951); *Bekenntnisse des Hochstaplers Felix Krull: Der Memoiren erster Teil,* 1954 (*Confessions of Felix Krull, Confidence Man: The Early Years,* 1955).

PLAY: *Fiorenza,* 1906.

POETRY: "Gesang vom Kindchen," 1919.

NONFICTION: "Friedrich und die grosse Koalition," 1915 ("Fredrick and the Great Coalition," 1929); *Betrachtungen eines Unpolitischen,* 1918 (*Reflections of a Nonpolitical Man,* 1983); *Rede und Antwort,* 1922; *Bemühungen,* 1925; *Die Forderung des Tages,* 1930; *Lebensabriss,* 1930 (*A Sketch of My Life,* 1960); *Three Essays,* 1932;

Past Masters and Other Papers, 1933; *Leiden und Grösse der Meister*, 1935; *Freud, Goethe, Wagner*, 1937; *Achtung, Europa!*, 1938; *Dieser Friede*, 1938 (*This Peace*, 1938); *Vom künftigen Sieg der Demokratie*, 1938 (*The Coming of Victory of Democracy*, 1938); *Deutsche Hörer!*, 1942 (*Listen, Germany!*, 1943); *Order of the Day: Political Essays and Speeches of Two Decades*, 1942; *Adel des Geistes: Sechzehn Versuche zum Problem der Humanität*, 1945 (*Essays of Three Decades*, 1947); *Neue Studien*, 1948; *Die Entstehung des "Doktor Faustus": Roman eines Romans*, 1949 (*The Story of a Novel: The Genesis of "Doctor Faustus,"* 1961); *Altes und Neues: Kleine Prosa aus fünf Jahrzehnten*, 1953; *Versuch über Schiller*, 1955; *Nachlese: Prosa, 1951-1955*, 1956; *Last Essays*, 1958; *Briefe*, 1961-1965 (3 volumes; partial translation, *Letters of Thomas Mann, 1889-1955*, 1970); *Addresses Delivered at the Library of Congress*, 1963; *Wagner und unsere Zeit*, 1963 (*Pro and Contra Wagner*, 1985); *Reden und Aufsätze*, 1965 (2 volumes); *Essays*, 1977-1978 (3 volumes); *Tagebücher*, 1977-1986 (6 volumes; partial translation, *Diaries 1918-1939*, 1982); *Goethes Laufbahn als Schriftsteller: Zwölf Essays und Reden zu Goethe*, 1982.

MISCELLANEOUS: *Gesammelte Werke*, 1956 (12 volumes; includes critical writings in volumes 10-11); *Gesammelte Werke*, 1960-1974 (13 volumes; includes critical writings in volumes 9-11); *Werkausgabe*, 1980-1986 (20 volumes; includes 3 volumes of critical writings); *Frage und Antwort: Interviews mit Thomas Mann 1909-1955*, 1983; *Thomas Mann's "Goethe and Tolstoy": Notes and Sources*, 1984.

Bibliography

Lesér, Esther H. *Thomas Mann's Short Fiction: An Intellectual Biography*. Rutherford, N.J.: Fairleigh Dickinson University Press, 1989. Lesér states the purposes of her biography as twofold: "as a reference work in which each story may be read individually with its comprehensive study materials, and as an organic study of Thomas Mann's intellectual development." The chapters are arranged thematically, each integrating analyses of representative works.

Mann, Thomas. *The Thomas Mann Reader*. Edited by Joseph Warner Angell. New York: Alfred A. Knopf, 1950. This anthology contains selections from Mann's work, including short stories, essays, novellas, and excerpts from novels. The collection has introductions and some biographical information.

Von Gronicka, André. *Thomas Mann: Profile and Perspectives*. New York: Random House, 1970. The author, in his biographical analysis of Mann and his works, hopes "to offer some new insights to the specialists while helping the general reader to orient himself in Thomas Mann's vast and complex world." The book also includes two previously unpublished letters and a chronological list of significant events in Mann's life.

Votteler, Thomas, ed. "Thomas Mann: 1875-1955." In *Short Story Criticism, Excerpts from Criticism of the Works of Short Fiction Writers*. Vol. 5. Detroit: Gale Research, 1990. The entry begins with a brief introduction to Mann, but it is primarily a series of excerpts of the criticism of Mann's short fiction.

White, Andrew. *Thomas Mann*. London: Oliver & Boyd, 1965. White uses a thematic approach to the life and works of Mann. He concludes with a review of six decades of criticism.

Winston, Richard. *Thomas Mann: The Making of an Artist, 1875-1911.* New York: Alfred A. Knopf, 1981. Winston arranges the biographical information chronologically, but he intersperses chapters of thematic analysis and explication. The book, aimed at readers of literary biography, covers Mann's early years.

Carol Franks

KATHERINE MANSFIELD

Born: Wellington, New Zealand; October 14, 1888
Died: Fontainebleau, France; January 9, 1923

Principal short fiction

In a German Pension, 1911; *Bliss and Other Stories,* 1920; *The Garden Party and Other Stories,* 1922; *The Doves' Nest and Other Stories,* 1923; *Something Childish and Other Stories,* 1924 (also known as *The Little Girl and Other Stories,* 1924).

Other literary forms

Although Katherine Mansfield is best known as a writer of short stories, she also wrote poems and book reviews, which were collected and edited posthumously by her second husband, John Middleton Murry. She once began a novel, and several fragments of plays have survived. She left a considerable amount of personal documents; their bulk greatly exceeds that of her published work. Murry edited the *Journal of Katherine Mansfield* (1927; "Definitive Edition," 1954), *The Letters of Katherine Mansfield* (1928), *The Scrapbook of Katherine Mansfield* (1939), and *Katherine Mansfield's Letters to John Middleton Murry, 1913-1922* (1951).

Achievements

Although extravagant claims have been made for her, many critics insist that Mansfield's achievements were modest. She completed no novel, and, although she wrote about a hundred stories, her fame rests on no more than a dozen. Yet, in any age, her stories would be remarkable for their precise and evocative descriptions, their convincing dialogue, their economy and wit, and their dazzling insights into the shifting emotions of their characters.

In her own age, she was a pioneer. She and James Joyce are often credited with creating the modern short story. Though this claim may be an exaggeration, her stories did without the old-fashioned overbearing author-narrators, the elaborate settings of scenes, and the obvious explanations of motives and themes of earlier fiction. Instead, she provided images and metaphors, dialogues and monologues with little in between. Like T. S. Eliot's *The Waste Land* (1922), her stories seem to have had their nonpoetic dross deleted.

Her stories have influenced such writers as Elizabeth Bowen, Katherine Anne Porter, and Christopher Isherwood; the standard "*New Yorker* story" owes much to her. Most important, many decades after her death, her stories are read with pleasure.

Biography

Almost everything Katherine Mansfield wrote was autobiographical in some way. It helps a reader to know about Mansfield's life because she often does not identify her stories' locations. For example, readers may be puzzled by her combining English manners and exotic flora in her New Zealand stories.

The author was born Kathleen Mansfield Beauchamp in Wellington, New Zealand, on October 14, 1888. (In her lifetime, she used many names. Her family called her "Kass." She took "Katherine Mansfield" as her name in 1910.) Her father, Harold Beauchamp, was an importer who rose to become chairman of the Bank of New Zealand and to be knighted in 1923. In 1903, the Beauchamps sailed for London, where Kass was enrolled at Queen's College, an institution for young women much like a university. She remained at Queen's until 1906, reading advanced authors such as Oscar Wilde and publishing stories in the college magazine. Her parents brought her back to Wellington in 1906, where she published her first stories in a newspaper. She left New Zealand for London in 1908, never to return.

Her next decade was one of personal complexities and artistic growth. She was sexually attracted to both women and men. At Queen's College, she met Ida Baker, her friend and companion for much of her life. Back in London, she fell in love with a violinist whom she had known in New Zealand. After she learned that she was pregnant by him, she abruptly married George C. Bowden on March 2, 1909, and as abruptly left him. At her mother's insistence, she traveled to Germany, where she had a miscarriage. The Bowdens were not divorced until April, 1918.

In Germany she met the Polish translator Floryan Sobieniowski, who, in the opinion of biographer Claire Tomalin, infected her with gonorrhea. Most of her medical problems may have come from this infection: the removal of a Fallopian tube, rheumatic symptoms, pleurisy, and eventually tuberculosis. Back in London, Mansfield met the future editor and critic John Middleton Murry. Their on-again, off-again relationship endured until her death. They were married on May 3, 1918; after she died, Murry edited her stories, letters, and journals. Meanwhile, she was strongly affected when her brother was killed in France in 1915. His death and her own worsening health were probably strong influences on her stories.

During these years, she and Murry knew many famous writers and artists, particularly those who frequented Lady Ottoline Morrell's famous salon at Garsington: Lytton Strachey, Dora Carrington, David Garnett, Aldous Huxley, Dorothy Brett, J. M. Keynes, T. S. Eliot. She and Virginia Woolf had an off-and-on friendship and professional association; she seriously flirted with Bertrand Russell. The Murrys' most notable friendship was with D. H. and Frieda Lawrence; "Gudrun" in D. H. Lawrence's *Women in Love* (1920) is said to be based on Mansfield. Both Woolf and Lawrence were influenced by Mansfield; both made nasty remarks about her in her last years.

Another result of meeting Sobieniowski in Germany may have been reading the works of Anton Chekhov; her story "The Child-Who-Was-Tired" is a free adaptation—perhaps a plagiarism—of a Chekhov story. During 1910 and 1911, she published a number of bitter stories with German settings, collected in *In a German Pension*. For the next seven years, Mansfield experimented with many styles and published stories in journals such as *New Age, Rhythm,* and *Blue Review* before she discovered a mature voice. Her first great story, "Prelude," was published as a booklet in July, 1918, by Virginia and Leonard Woolf's Hogarth Press.

Her health had not been good for several years; her gonorrhea remained undiagnosed until 1918. From the time she learned that she had tuberculosis in December, 1917, she spent most of each year out of England. Accompanied by Murry or Ida Baker, she traveled to France, Switzerland, and Italy, trying to fight off her disease. In 1922, her search lead her to Georges Ivanovitch Gurdjieff's Institute of the Harmonious Development of Man near Paris, where she seems to have been moderately happy until she died.

During her last five years, she wrote most of the stories for which she is best known. They were often published in journals such as *Athenaeum*, *Arts and Letters*, *London Mercury*, and *Sphere*. Many were then collected in *Bliss and Other Stories* and *The Garden Party and Other Stories*.

Analysis

Katherine Mansfield's themes are not hard to discover. In 1918, she set herself the tasks of communicating the exhilarating delicacy and peacefulness of the world's beauty and also of crying out against "corruption." A reader will soon make his or her own list of themes: the yearnings, complexities, and misunderstandings of love; loneliness, particularly of independent women; the superficiality of much of modern life; the erosions of time and forgetfulness; the beauty and indifferent power of the natural world, especially plant life and the sea. Her exact meanings are not so easily pinned down, for her tone is complex: she mixes witty satire and shattering emotional reversals. Moreover, she uses dialogue and indirect speech extensively, and she does not often seem to speak directly in her own voice; the reader is not sure exactly who is speaking. It is vital for readers to understand that Mansfield (like Chekhov, to whom she is often compared) does not conceal a hidden "message" in her stories. If a story appears to point in many directions, not all of which are logically consistent, that is the way Mansfield feels the whole truth is most honestly communicated. This essay suggests some of the ways these stories may be read.

The action of her stories (again, like Chekhov's) does not surge powerfully forward. Often her stories are designed, by means of quick changes in time and by surprise turns, to lead the reader to unexpected moments of illumination or epiphanies. Her stories are economical, edited so that there is usually not one unnecessary or insignificant word. She can be witty if she chooses, but more often her stories provide arresting descriptions and startling metaphors, which evoke shifting states of happiness, yearning, or despair.

Mansfield's stories often evoke the complexities of the conversational give-and-take between women and men and the unexpected courses that passion can take. An early story, "In a Café," portrays a youthful "new woman" and her male acquaintance, a musician. They flirt as they discuss life, art, and the future. Before he leaves, he asks the girl for her violets, but once outside he drops them because he must keep his hands warm for performing. The young woman is totally happy until she sees the violets on the sidewalk. The reader knows that her love has been crushed, but, new woman that she is, she kicks the flowers and goes her way laughing.

"Epilogue II" (also known as "Violet") is more complex. At a pension in France, where the acidly worldly narrator is recovering from an attack of nerves, she reports a long conversation with an exasperating woman named Violet, who in turns tells of a conversation she has had with a man named Arthur. Violet says that, after a few dances, Arthur asked her if she believed in Pan and kissed her. It was her first adult kiss, and they immediately became engaged. The narrator can hardly believe what Violet tells her and is repelled by how easily the naïve Violet and Arthur have found each other. The story (a conversation within a conversation) ends with the narrator thinking that she herself might be too sophisticated. (In this story, Mansfield has imported a piece of conversation from real life. Some time before she wrote "Epilogue II," she startled a man by asking him if he believed in Pan.)

In "Psychology," Mansfield dissects the ebb and flow of attraction between two older artists, culminating in a moment of potential, a moment which, because of their agonizing self-consciousness, they miss. This story shows both minds, but readers are left with the woman and with another characteristically unexpected psychological twist. An older female acquaintance brings her flowers—violets again. This spontaneous gift revitalizes the woman, and with renewed hope she begins an intense letter to the man who has left her. Readers may guess that their next meeting will be no more satisfying than their last.

Mansfield often portrays more complex and ambiguous sexual and psychological relationships and, as usual, constructs her story to lead her reader in roundabout ways into unexpected territory. Though she often takes readers briefly into male minds, the story "Je ne parle pas français" has one of her rare male narrators. Raoul Duqette, a grubby Parisian writer, pimp, and gigolo, tells of an Englishman, Dick Harmon, and the woman nicknamed "Mouse," whom he brings to Paris. Not all critics agree on whom the story concerns. Although the reader learns much about the English couple's tortured relationship (Dick leaves Mouse because he cannot betray his mother, and Mouse knows she cannot return to England), many readers think that the story centers on the Frenchman. Incapable of deep emotion, Raoul spies on those with fuller lives than his own; he despises women, is sexually attracted to Dick, and is able to recognize only dimly the suffering that he has witnessed. At the end, he revels in Mouse's sorrow and imagines selling a girl like her to an old lecher.

The triangle in "Bliss" is different, and again, Mansfield mixes her tones. Bertha seems childishly happy in her marriage, her home, her child, and her arty friends. She gives a marvelous party in which sophisticated guests make inane, decadent conversation. Meanwhile, Bertha finds herself physically attracted to one of her guests, the cool Miss Fulton, and thinks that she detects Miss Fulton giving her a signal. Together in the garden, they contemplate a lovely, flowering pear tree, and Bertha senses that they understand each other intuitively. Again Mansfield surprises the reader. Bertha transfers her feelings for Miss Fulton to her husband; for the first time, she really desires him. When she overhears him making an assignation with

Miss Fulton, however, her life is shattered. In "Bliss," as elsewhere, Mansfield's brilliant and precise descriptions of the nonhuman world are always evocative. Although sometimes nature simply reveals an unsympathetic force, allied to human passions but beyond human control, some natural features demand to be interpreted as symbols, such as the phallic pear tree in this story. Phallic it is, but it may be feminine as well, for Bertha identifies with it. The story is read, however, and the pear tree cannot be explained simply. Neither can the reader's final reaction: Is Bertha trapped in an evil world? Is she a free adult at last?

Mansfield also explores the problems of lonely women, often by showing the reader their inmost trains of thought. In "The Lost Battle," a woman traveling alone is escorted to her room in a French hotel by an overbearing man who makes demeaning and insinuating remarks: a bed in a small room will be enough for her, he implies. She asserts herself and demands a better room, one with a table on which to write. She wins her struggle and is happy with her new room—its size, the view from its windows, and its sturdy table. When she overtips the boy who delivers her bags, however, her joy somehow leaves her. In a convincing but mysterious moment typical of Mansfield's stories, the woman's bravery collapses in self-consciousness, memory, tears, and desire.

Perhaps Mansfield's best-known version of the lonely woman is the central character of "Miss Brill." The reader follows Miss Brill's thoughts as she arrives at the public gardens. The first faint chill of fall and the noise of the band signals that a new season has begun. Miss Brill's sympathetic interest extends to the various sorts of people in the park; the reader senses an older, precise woman who yearns that happiness and gentleness will come for herself and others. Even some unpleasantries fail to shake Miss Brill's enjoyment, as she rejoices that everyone there is performing in some wonderful, happy play. Her illusions, however, are shattered by two insensitive young lovers who simply wish that the fussy old woman would move. Again the reader is taken into a lonely woman's mind as she undergoes a psychic shock.

In "The Daughters of the Late Colonel," the shock is muffled, and the reader does not enter the two sisters' minds so deeply so soon. The story at first appears to center on the familiar Mansfield theme of male domination. The sisters seem to react alike to the death of their domineering father. They are still under his spell. Mansfield shows her dry wit as their hesitant and ineffectual efforts to assert themselves with the nurse and their maid are pathetic and hilarious at the same time. Even sisters, however, may be alone. Not only have they lost their father and are without prospects of marriage, but also they differ so much in temperament that they will never understand each other—the older sister is prosaic, the younger one dreamy. It is only at the end of the story that each sister shows small signs of vitality. The prosaic sister hears a cry from within, muses on lost chances, and feels a hint of hope. When Mansfield takes readers into the thoughts of the younger sister, they discover that all along she has been living in a secret and extravagant imaginary world of repressed desire: her real life. For a moment, each sister thinks that some action could be taken, but the moment passes without communication. Their lives will never bear fruit.

Mansfield's wit is sometimes closer to the center of a story. In "Bliss," many early pages show a devastating view of the world of artists that Mansfield knew so well at Garsington and elsewhere. "Marriage à la Mode" is more purely a social satire. A nice, plodding husband, William, supports his wife Isabel's ambitions. They move from a cozy little house to the suburbs and entertain her artistic friends. Mansfield's acute ear for conversation enables her to give the reader the wonderful remarks that pass for wit among the arty set. The reader cheers when William, in a dignified letter, asks for a divorce. Isabel's friends mock the letter. Isabel herself realizes how shallow they are, but she runs to them laughing. The story has a moral, but its chief impact is satirical. This is also true of "The Young Girl." The title character is the disgustingly spoiled and overdressed teenage daughter of a selfish mother who is mainly interested in gambling at a casino. By the end of the story, the girl has revealed her youth and vulnerability, but a reader probably remembers the story's vapid world most vividly.

Mansfield's modernist method seldom gives the reader straightforward statements of her themes; the reader needs to interpret them carefully. Her most deliberately ambiguous and hotly debated story is "The Fly." A businessman ("the boss") is reminded of his beloved son's death in World War I and how he has grieved. Now, however, the boss is troubled because he can no longer feel or cry. At this point, he rescues a fly caught in his inkwell; the fly carefully cleans itself. Then the Mansfield surprise: the boss drops another gob of ink on the fly, admires its courage as it cleans itself again, but then drops more ink. The fly is dead. The boss feels wretched and bullies an employee. The story may remind some readers of William Shakespeare's "As flies to wanton boys are we to the gods;/ They kill us for their sport."

Murry said that "The Fly" represents Mansfield's revulsion from the cruelty of war; other critics discover her antipathy to her own father. Whatever its biographical source, the reader must try to decide his or her reaction to the boss. Where are the readers' sympathies? At first they are with the aged employee who jogs the boss's memory and perhaps with the boss himself. When readers hear of the son's death, they do sympathize with the father. What do they make of his torturing—yet admiring—the fly? Do readers despise him as a sadistic bully? Do they sympathize with him? Is the fly simply another victim of society's brutality, the boss's brutality? Are readers to see Mansfield as the fly, unfairly stricken with tuberculosis? Does the boss refuse to admit his own mortality until he sees himself as a victim, like the fly? At the very end, is he repressing such thoughts again? Critics are divided about this story, but what is clear is that its ambiguities raise a host of issues for consideration.

Another story that poses problems is "The Man Without a Temperament." The reader has trouble establishing where the story is taking place and who are its characters. Gradually it can be determined that the story takes place at a continental hotel and that the central characters are, not the grotesque guests like The Two Topknots, but The Man (Robert Salesby) and his invalid wife (Jinnie—Mrs. Salesby). The

Mansfield woman here is not only lonely but also sick—sick with something that resembles the author's own tuberculosis. The reader's difficulties are slightly compounded when Mansfield manipulates time; readers soon decide that the dislocations in the story are Robert's memories of happier days in England. This story's greatest problem, however, is what the reader is to think of Robert. At first glance, he seems without temperament; all his care is for his wife, her comfort, her health, and her whims. Soon, the tension that he is under becomes obvious. He is tortured by his memories. When his wife encourages him to take a walk by himself, he quickly agrees and almost forgets to return. The exquisite tact and humor that his wife loves so much rings hollow: Readers know that he suspects that she will not live much longer. Is he an icy, resentful, and disgusting hypocrite? Some readers may think so. Is he admirably patient and forbearing? Murry, who acknowledged that Robert was a portrait of himself, thought it was drawn with admiration.

Soon after her return to London, Mansfield wrote some stories based on her experiences among the common people of New Zealand. "The Woman at the Store" is a chilling and dramatic tale in which three travelers stop far from civilization at a dilapidated store run by a slatternly woman and her child. Although the travelers feel sympathy for the woman's hard life, they also laugh at the woman and child—laugh until the child's drawing makes clear that the woman has murdered her husband. The travelers leave quickly. "Ole Underwood," a character sketch based on a real Wellington character, lets readers see into the mind of a deranged ex-convict as he makes his way around town, driven by memories of his wife's infidelity. In both cases, Mansfield tries to get into the minds of lower-class people, people much different from those she usually depicts. Another story that deals sympathetically with the doomed struggles of a lower-class character is "The Life of Ma Parker."

When Mansfield returned in earnest to telling stories of the New Zealand life that she knew best, she produced her finest work. (The critic Rhoda B. Nathan thinks that the New Zealand stories, taken as a group, can be considered as a *Bildungsroman*, or story of an artist's growth.) The family drama of her childhood provided material for many of these stories. Her mother was attractive but delicate. Her father was forceful and successful. They lived in a substantial house in Wellington just on the edge of a poor district, then in a nearby village, and later at the edge of the sea in Wellington harbor. She was the third of five surviving children living among a number of aunts and cousins, an uncle and a grandmother.

Her two longest works of fiction, "Prelude" and "At the Bay," are strikingly different from conventional short stories. Both take a slight narrative line and string on it a number of short episodes and intense renderings of the inner lives of members—mainly female—of an extended family. In both, readers are set down among these people without preparation; they must work out their relations for themselves. In both, readers must take time to discover the rich vision that Mansfield is giving them.

In "Prelude," the reader enters the consciousness of several members of the family as they adjust to a new house in the country. (The Beauchamps moved from

Wellington to Karori in 1893). The reader is led from the minds of the child Kezia (the character who resembles the author as a girl), her hearty father (Stanley), her pregnant mother (Linda), and her unfulfilled aunt (Beryl). Their relations are strained, and they reveal their hopes, loves, and anxieties. Gradually, Mansfield's emphasis becomes clear. She gives most weight to Linda and Beryl, whose inner worlds invite a range of analysis. Analysis begins with the aloe tree. Mansfield had earlier prepared readers for this huge, ugly, ominous growth, which flowers only once every hundred years. Readers sense that the tree is somehow symbolic. Linda is fascinated by it. When she sees the tree by moonlight, its cruel thorns seem to embody the hate that she often feels, or do they embody the masculine force that she hates? Either way, the aloe tree brings out for the reader the secret that Linda keeps from everyone else: alongside her other emotions (dislike for her children, love and concern for her husband) is pure hatred. She wonders what Stanley would think of that. Beryl too has her secret self. The story ends with her taking an inventory of her attractive qualities and wondering if she can ever get beyond her poses, her false life, to the warm authentic life that she thinks is still within her. Mansfield's apparently haphazard plot has in fact been drawing the reader to two striking female visions.

"At the Bay" tells about the same household perhaps a year later. Some characters, such as Kezia, appear to have changed. Mansfield's methods, however, are much the same, though the sea that frames this story does not insist on its symbolic force so obviously as did the aloe tree. Stanley forges off to work. The women he leaves are happy that he is gone, especially Linda, his strangely passive wife, who still loves him but dislikes their children, including a new baby boy. The children and their cousins play games. Kezia almost faces death when she pleads with her grandmother not to leave them. Linda's weak brother does face his failure. Beryl has a new friend, a vivid witchlike woman with an attractive younger husband. Though Linda briefly finds love with Stanley, this story, like "Prelude," ends with two dissimilar kinds of unfulfilled love. Linda loves her baby only for a moment. Beryl yearns for sexual contact but is terrified and revolted when she finds the real thing. Perhaps at the end, the sea (as a possible symbol of female fecundity, time, and destruction) sympathizes with human desires, perhaps not. Mansfield's way of presenting her incidents and structuring her story creates intense sympathy for her characters, yet simultaneously lets readers see them, without obviously judging them, from a distance.

Two shorter New Zealand stories probably show Mansfield at her finest, and they show most clearly how her narrative surprises and moments of brilliant revelation of character and motive can be concentrated in a single phrase, in what might be called a domestic epiphany: a small moment of great importance not easily summarized. In "The Doll's House," Kezia and her sisters are given a vulgar plaything. The house is despised by Aunt Beryl but loved by the girls (Kezia is particularly enthralled by a tiny lamp in the diminutive dining room) and much admired by their schoolmates. The story seems to be about adult cruelty and juvenile snobbery. All along, however, there appear to be two social outcasts, Lil Kelvey and her silent little sister, Else, both daughters of a washerwoman and (perhaps) a criminal. When Kezia impulsively invites them to look at the house, Aunt Beryl orders them away. Lil says nothing, but her silent, wretched little sister had got one glimpse of the beautiful doll's house and remembers, not her humiliation, but that she saw the house's tiny lamp. A small human spirit asserts itself.

"The Garden Party" is based on what happened at a real party that the Beauchamps gave in Wellington in 1907. Part of its meaning concerns the relations between two social classes. The central character is Laura, clearly a Mansfield-like character, an adolescent Kezia. Laura is thrilled by the promise of festivity, but in the middle of the expensive preparations—canna lilies, dainty sandwiches, a small band to play under the marquee—she learns of the death of a poor man who lived close by in a wretched house. Readers see the clash of generations when Laura demands that the party be canceled, but her worldly mother says no. The party is a grand success. As usual in Mansfield, important matters slip the mind; Laura enjoys herself immensely, especially because her large new hat is widely admired. After the guests have left, her mother sends Laura with a basket of party food to the house of the dead man. Her journey at dusk is phantasmagoric. Her sympathies, forgotten at the party, return. She is shocked by the somber house of death and by the grieving wife, and overwhelmed by the stillness, even the beauty, of the corpse. Laura feels that she must say something: "Forgive my hat." What she says is certainly inadequate, but it seems to signal a moment of understanding and growth—or does it? Laura has found a moment of beauty in death. Is that evasive or profound? She accepts the sympathy of her brother at the very end. He understands—or does he?

Other major works

POETRY: *Poems*, 1923 (edited by J. M. Murry).

NONFICTION: *Novels and Novelists*, 1930 (edited by J. M. Murry).

Bibliography

Alpers, Antony. *The Life of Katherine Mansfield*. Rev. ed. New York: Viking Press, 1980. This volume is the standard biography, sensible, balanced, and detailed. Alpers draws on years of research and includes interviews with people who knew Mansfield, such as Murry and Ida Baker, and their comments on his earlier book, *Katherine Mansfield: A Biography* (1953). He offers some analyses, including passages on "At the Bay," "Prelude," and "Je ne parle pas français." Includes notes, illustrations, index, a detailed chronology, and a full bibliography.

Bateson, F. W. "The Fly." *Essays in Criticism* 12 (1962): 39-53. In these pages, two critics interpret "The Fly," giving it the kind of close reading usually reserved for lyric poetry. Other correspondents support and contest the original reading. Although they discuss the functions of characters and many details, they focus on the mind of the boss and a reader's reaction to him.

Berkman, Sylvia. *Katherine Mansfield: A Critical Study*. New Haven, Conn.: Yale University Press, 1951. This study has a chapter on how Mansfield used details of her family's life to write "The Aloe" and then to revise it as "Prelude." The final chapter usefully compares Mansfield to Anton Chekhov and James Joyce.

Hankin, C. A. *Katherine Mansfield and Her Confessional Stories.* New York: St. Martin's Press, 1983. Hankin's thesis is that Mansfield's stories are confessional, with the result that this book connects each story as precisely as possible to its sources in Mansfield's life. The detailed analyses of each of the major stories are more valuable than the thesis suggests. Hankin's readings are subtle and detailed, especially when they discuss the complexities of characters and symbols.

Mansfield, Katherine. *The Complete Stories of Katherine Mansfield,* edited by Antony Alpers. Auckland: Golden Press/Whitcombe & Tombs, 1974. Not the complete short stories but a full and comprehensive collection of almost all of them, scrupulously edited and arranged chronologically in natural and instructive groups. Alpers' notes provide basic facts about each story and much essential information about many of them. The notes also list all the stories not included in this collection, thus forming a complete catalog of Mansfield's short fiction.

Nathan, Rhoda B. *Katherine Mansfield.* New York: Continuum, 1988. A detailed and useful chapter on the New Zealand stories considered as a group. Includes comments on the "painterly" qualities of "Je ne parle pas français." The final two chapters discuss Mansfield's achievement with regard to other writers.

Tomalin, Claire. *Katherine Mansfield: A Secret Life.* New York: Alfred A. Knopf, 1987. A very readable biography, though without many critical comments, emphasizing the medical consequences of Mansfield's sexual freedom and treating the question of her plagiarizing "The Child-Who-Was-Tired." An appendix gives *The Times Literary Supplement* correspondence on this topic.

George Soule

MARIE DE FRANCE

Born: Normandy, France; c. 1150
Died: England(?); c. 1190

Principal short fiction

Lais, c. 1167 (*The Lays of Marie de France*, 1911).

Other literary forms

In addition to the *Lais*, Marie de France is also known for the *Isopet* (c. 1170; *Medieval Fables*, 1983), a translation of a Latin text by Aesop. Besides being a demonstration of Marie's poetic skill, the lively and witty *Medieval Fables* is historically important as the earliest existing collection in the vernacular of Western Europe of this material. She is also known for *Espurgatoire Seint Patriz* (c. 1190; the purgatory of St. Patrick), a translation of a Latin text attributed to a twelfth century Cisterian monk, to which she added a prologue and an epilogue.

Achievements

Although her identity remains unclear, France's first woman poet, known as Marie de France, emerges from the twelfth century as an important literary figure. As a writer of vernacular literature, she ranks, along with Chrétien de Troyes, among the best-known medieval writers of the period. Her ability as a writer has been noted by critics, who cite her mastery of irony and understatement, her creation of suspense and description, and her use of material from folktales. A product of her times, her work is a reflection of medieval attitudes and society.

Her best-known and most representative work, the *Lais*, is characterized by a view of the problems of a love that finds itself in confrontation with social conventions. In form, they are brief works in rhymed octosyllabic couplets. The *Lais* have been much imitated, and there are several others attributed to Marie beyond the twelve that scholars are reasonably sure are her work.

Biography

Only two facts are certain about Marie: her name and her provenance. She names herself in each of her works, and in the *Medieval Fables* she says that she is "de France." Although there are several Maries mentioned in this period, notably Marie de Champagne, daughter of Eleanor of Aquitaine and patroness of Chrétien de Troyes, the most appealing identification of Marie de France is with Marie, abbess of Shaftesbury, the natural daughter of Geoffrey of Anjou and half-sister of Henry II of England. The precise date of Marie's birth is unknown but a *floruit* of 1155-1215 seems reasonably firm. From the allusions in her works, she was obviously well educated (she mentions Priscian and Ovid), and she was aware of the conventions of "courtly" romance of her time, although her connections with and influence of and by her contemporaries are unclear.

Analysis

Marie is best known for the twelve *Lais* that represent her earliest work and also present her narrative art in its fullest variety. The *Medieval Fables* and the *Espurgatoire Seint Patriz* are clearly derivative (more or less faithful translations of earlier works) and allow very little opportunity for the development of character, ironic situations, or the exploitation of supernatural elements that are hallmarks of Marie's work. It has been suggested that, in the *Lais*, Marie is the creator of a narrative form. Although this is a debatable point and one that is difficult to support, it is reasonable to say that the form Marie gave to the *lai* became normative in the centuries that followed.

Marie states that she is writing down *lais* that she has heard from Breton *conteurs* or from other sources. The titles of some of her *Lais*, "Yonec," "Eliduc," or "Laüstic," for example, are of Celtic provenance, but it is impossible to determine precisely how much and in what ways Marie depended on her "Celtic sources." Even the etymology of the word *lai*—possibly the Celtic *laid*, Latin *leudas* (*laus* or *laudis*?), meaning a tale to be sung—is in dispute and can give little substance to theories of the origin of this genre. If there were Breton minstrels who composed and performed, possibly with musical accompaniment, the short adventures known as "Breton lays," there is very little evidence of connection between such performers and the courts of Norman England.

The general "Prologue" to the *Lais* provides Marie's definition of the genre and her own statement of purpose in writing the *Lais*. A *lai* is composed to commemorate an adventure, generally an affair of love, that had first become current as a *conte*, a tale (Prologue, vv. 33-42) which was then formulated in verse so that it could better be remembered. Marie desired to demonstrate her literary skills, which should not be hidden; she also saw in her writing a labor that would keep her from idleness and sorrow: "Who wishes to defend herself from wickedness should study and learn and undertake serious work."

Both the general Prologue as well as the prologue to "Guigemar," her first *Lai*, show an artist at once confident in her skill and defensively aware that her learning makes of her an anomaly in her culture, the object of jealousy and scorn. In a strongly worded passage, she compares her detractors to "evil, cowardly, felonious dogs/ who bite people treacherously," but she will not allow such opposition to stop her from writing. Isolated by her talents and quite possibly also isolated in her personal circumstances since "de France" indicates that she is not writing in her native land, it is not surprising that many of her characters find themselves in some form of alienation created either by their own natures, or their societies, or by the love relationship that is the core of their adventure. This is not to suggest that the *Lais* are autobiographical; rather, the theme of isolation or alienation is one of the most effectively expressed elements in the *Lais* of Marie.

Most notable in this regard is "Lanval." The protagonist, Lanval, a young knight of Arthur's court, finds himself neglected and unrewarded by the king he serves and envied by his fellows because of his prowess. His own pride prevents him from seeking help in his impoverished state and, near despair, he leaves the court to seek the consolations of solitude. He is approached by the handmaidens of a princess of the fairy realm. The princess welcomes him as a lover and promises to free him from want and loneliness as long as he keeps their relationship a secret. When he returns to court, he finds himself both the possessor of miraculous wealth and also the lover of the lady. He keeps his lady's identity a secret until he is taunted by Arthur's queen, whose efforts at seduction he has repulsed, claiming that the least of his lady's maidens is more beautiful than the queen. His words earn him the king's displeasure and it is only at the last moment that he is rescued from the penalties of *lèse majesté* by the arrival of his lady, who makes good his boast.

The theme of isolation is the most consistently developed element of "Lanval." Although Marie alludes specifically to the plight of one who finds himself a stranger in a foreign land, her implicit references to alienation are more effective. Lanval is wretched in his neglected state, but part of his plight is the result of his own prideful refusal to seek aid. His eminence in knightly skill—which should alleviate his difficulties—ironically worsens them since he earns only the envy of his fellows. Even in the consolations of love he finds himself shut out from the knightly community since he must keep secret his lady's existence. This same necessity for secrecy opens the way for the vicious taunts of the queen (spurned, she accuses Lanval of unnatural vice) that lead to Lanval's breaking of his oath to his lady. Marie's presentation of isolation in "Lanval" has a lyric force and intensity, yet Lanval is agent as well as victim; his own sexual pride is the cause of the betrayal that redoubles his isolation. The poignancy of his situation is balanced by the aesthetic distance that Marie provides in indicating that much of Lanval's distress can be attributed to his own nature. At the same time, she emphasizes the exclusivity of the love relationship, the effect of which is heightened by the use of the supernatural, since, in gaining the fulfillment of love, Lanval must leave behind the society that both nurtured and scorned him. Lanval's lady comes from the fairy realm, and it is to her land that Lanval is taken in the end. In this and in many others of the *Lais* of Marie, the denouement is ambiguous at best.

If Marie's lovers are isolated in and by their loves, they are also, initially, deprived of love. In "Guigemar," "Laüstic," "Yonec," "Les Deus Amanz" ("The Two Lovers"), and "Milon," the protagonists either spurn love initially ("Guigemar") or are the victims of jealous mates (as are the wives in "Guigemar," "Laüstic," "Yonec," and "Milon") or of too-possessive parents (the daughter in "The Two Lovers"). The jealous husband in "Laüstic" is Marie's most distinct portrayal of this character type. He is aware that his wife is in love with their neighbor and that, although the two never meet, they exchange gifts and glances from the windows of their towers. The wife dissembles, claiming only her joy in the song of a nightingale (*L'eostic*) as the reason for her frequent risings at night. Her husband then sets his whole entourage to trap the nightingale. He confronts his wife with the bird, and when she demands it, he kills it and flings the corpse at her so that her shift is bloodied. The lady entombs the bird in a gem-ornamented casket and sends it, as a sign that their affair must end, to her lover who treasures the casket as a relic.

In "Laüstic," Marie maintains dramatic contrast and tension between the highly idealized passion of the lovers and the debasing jealousy of the husband; between the two codes—social and amatory; and between the fragility of the affair and the violence unleashed on it and its symbol, the nightingale, by the opposing passion of jealousy. The husband has "right" on his side as Marie attests in the words she chooses to conclude her description of the lover: "He loved his neighbor's wife." Nevertheless, the husband's rage is so exaggerated and his vengeance aimed at a bird is so incongruous, that there is little to relieve his negative portrait. Marie does not wholly exonerate the lovers, especially the lady, who dooms the affair by her lack of prudence and her transparent guile. However sincere the lovers' passion might seem to be, it is no more concrete than the song of the nightingale. Even if, as some critics maintain, the lovers are only playing at love, the husband is sincere, and if the song of the bird corresponds to the love affair, the bird's corpse and, yet more graphically, the blood on the lady's garment correspond to the violence with which reality can destroy an ideal. Marie focuses the interplay of passions by means of the nightingale, a multiplex image whose song exemplifies unrestrained passion, destroyed nevertheless by the passions of which it becomes the focus.

The nightingale is one of several concrete focusing images that Marie uses in the *Lais*. Others are the lovers' knots in "Guigemar" which can only be untied when the lovers are reunited; the ring and coverlet in "Le Frêne" ("The Asa Tree"), signs of the heroine's noble birth; the sea in "Eliduc" with its complex referents of passion and isolation; and the double image of the interwoven honeysuckle (*chèvrefeuille*) and hazel in "Chèvrefeuille" ("The Honeysuckle"). In the latter tale, which recounts an episode from the legend of Tristan and Iseult, Tristan, banished from court, uses a carved hazel twig wreathed with honeysuckle to convey this message: "Fair friend, thus it is with us/not you without me, nor I without you." This image functions both within the *lai* and between the *lai* and the reader, who receives the message in the same moment as does Iseult. The elegant simplicity of the verse, which English cannot convey, reinforces the image of interdependence of the hazel and the honeysuckle.

Not all of the *lais* deal with faithfulness in love. Two, "Equitan" and "Bisclayret," are tales of disloyalty and punishment. "Equitan" is as close to a *fabliau* as one can find among Marie's *Lais*: a pleasure-loving king commits adultery with his seneschal's wife. The two conspire to murder the husband, but they are destroyed in the trap they set for him. "Bisclayret" is the tale of a werewolf who, betrayed by his wife, is forced to remain in wolf-form while his wife lives with her lover. He is befriended by his king, and when the guilty couple come to court, he avenges himself, and his wife is forced to allow him to return to his human form. In both instances, the penalties for disloyalty in love are harsh and swiftly dealt out. At the same time, vengeance is insufficient since the survivor in both cases had been truly in love. There is thus a double condemnation of disloyalty—the simple wish fulfillment of justice meted out and the more complex implicit condemnation presented in the fate of the regretful survivor.

"Eliduc," the longest of Marie's *Lais*, is one of the most problematical. Based on the folk motif of the "man with two wives," this *lai* presents a seemingly unresolvable dilemma and a barely probable solution. The happily married Eliduc, unfairly exiled, falls in love with the daughter of the king whose service he has entered. When he is allowed to return home, he is welcomed by his king and his wife Guildeluec whom he still loves; but he yearns for Guilliadun, the princess. He returns to the land of his exile, ostensibly to aid Guilliadun's father, and she elopes with him. Their ship is caught in a storm, and the sailors blame Guilliadun's presence for their ill-fortune. When she learns that Eliduc is married, she falls unconscious and all believe her to be dead. Eliduc has her placed in a hidden chapel and visits her bier daily. Guildeluec learns of the visits, comes to the chapel, and finds Guilliadun. The princess is magically revived by an herb Guildeluec discovers by chance, and Guildeluec enters a convent to allow the lovers to marry. In their later years, Eliduc and Guilliadun also enter the religious life, and all spend their last years in holiness and charity.

The denouement of "Eliduc" is purest romantic wish fulfillment, although Guildeluec's abdication is not without overtones of much grimmer possibilities. Marie never suggests that the passionate affair is tarnished by any implicit contrast with the wife's sacrifice; Eliduc's new love is taken for granted. He can be considered an analogue to those other characters in Marie's *Lais* who are deprived of love. Although he is content in marriage, the new affair is the love of free consent, the romantic passion somewhat inaccurately called "courtly love." Guilliadun is exonerated by her innocence of Eliduc's obligations and, furthermore, she is quite similar to the lover of Lanval. Her role is analogous to that of a fairy princess: she lives in a realm apart, her lover is drawn or compelled to come to her, and her power is absolute. The element of conflict between "ideal" love and social reality is also present, but here a near-miraculous decision resolves the dilemma. The denouement moves the story from the secular context entirely, since it is only in the realm of *caritas*, Christian charity, that the complex loves of the "Eliduc" can exist.

No one *lai* of Marie can be selected as supremely characteristic of her work. All show the cool, ironic detachment that tempers the allegiances and responses of the readers as they observe her characters in their respective dilemmas of love. The "Eliduc," however, may be seen as a compendium of motifs, technique, and thematic emphasis. From the all-powerful princess, the isolation and deprivation of the protagonist, the celebration of free passion tempered by the ironic observation of its consequences, to the validation of faithfulness in loving even when the *context* of that love must be transposed to a higher realm, "Eliduc" shows Marie at her best.

Perhaps the best evaluation of the *Medieval Fables* of Marie, her translation of a Latin text of Aesop, is that which, in one scholar's words, describes her work as a depiction not of "humanity" but of "feudalism." The moral application of a typically Aesopian tale, the lamb confronted by the wolf who chooses any imagined grudge as an excuse to devour his victim, is appropriate to twelfth century society.

Marie's contribution to this genre was to bestow contemporary referents on these ancient tales and render them skillfully in the octosyllabic couplets popular with the readers and the listeners of her milieu.

Marie's *Espurgatoire Seint Patriz* is also a translation, this time of a Latin text attributed to Henry of Saltrey, a twelfth century Cistercian monk. Marie followed her Latin text very closely, adding a prologue and an epilogue of her own and a very small number of lines not in the original for purposes of clarification. The work narrates the adventures of an Irish knight, Owein, who serves as interpreter for an English monk who is establishing a monastery in Ireland. He visits the entrance to Purgatory established by the second St. Patrick, is allowed to enter, witnesses the various torments inflicted on sinners, and is himself menaced by demons. Later he is shown the Terrestrial Paradise. He survives the ordeal and lives for twelve years more as a lay Brother at the monastery established by the Englishmen. Although Marie states that she is translating the story for the purpose of spiritual edification, the *Espurgatoire Seint Patriz* has attractive literary qualities as well. It is vividly descriptive of Owein's experiences, and scholars have noted its resemblance to a tale of knightly adventure. The established sequence of Marie's works (the *Lais*, the *Medieval Fables*, and *Espurgatoire Seint Patriz*) might suggest a turning-away on her part from purely secular works, but thematic and stylistic similarities, such as the journey, elements of the supernatural, the concern with moral obligations, and the verse form, show a basic consistency in her works. Although it pleased her to instruct, Marie did not allow didacticism to overshadow her impulse to produce a well-wrought narrative.

Other major works

TRANSLATIONS: *Isopet*, c. 1170 (*Medieval Fables*, 1983); *Espurgatoire Seint Patriz*, c. 1190.

Bibliography

Burgess, Glyn S. *The "Lais" of Marie de France: Text and Context*. Athens: University of Georgia Press, 1987. A detailed study of the twelve *lais* contained in manuscript Harley 978 of the British Library. The study notes thematic and textual parallels in the *lais*, with the author's hope that they will help scholars in future evaluations of the authorship of these works (given the possibility that the twelve *lais* were not all written by the same person). Burgess discusses the problem of internal chronology and focuses attention on key terms in Marie's use of language. Includes extensive notes for further study, a bibliography, and an index.

Donovan, Mortimer J. *The Breton Lay: A Guide to Varieties*. Notre Dame, Ind.: University of Notre Dame Press, 1969. A readable and well-documented general discussion of the Breton lay. Chapter 1 is devoted to Marie de France and the tradition of the Breton lay as it relates to her work.

Ferguson, Mary H. "Folklore in the *Lais* of Marie de France." *Romantic Review* 58 (1966): 3-24. A catalog of folklore motifs. This article can be a useful introduction to this aspect of the *Lais*.

Marie, de France. *Fables.* Edited and translated by Harriet Spiegel. Toronto: University of Toronto Press, 1987. Provides the text and English translation for the *Medieval Fables.* This book has an especially interesting introduction with informative notes, in which Spiegel suggests that Marie herself could have gathered and recorded these fables for the first time. Spiegel includes a discussion of Marie's role in adapting existing tales, and her comments on the meaning of "translation" in regard to the *Medieval Fables* are particularly thought-provoking.

Mickel, Emanuel J. *Marie de France.* New York: Twayne, 1974. A good, full-length study of Marie de France, her works, and the intellectual background of the twelfth century for the general reader as well as the student of medieval literature. Contains individual chapters on Marie's identity, the narrative *lai,* sources and plot summaries for the various *Lais,* an interpretation, and the structure and style of the *Lais.* Includes a chronology of the time period, useful notes and references for further study, a select bibliography (with many foreign language sources), and an index.

_____. "Marie de France's Use of Irony as a Stylistic and Narrative Device." *Studies in Philology* 71 (1974): 265-290. Mickel discusses Marie's gentle irony as an inherent element in several of the plots in the *Lais*; he also considers her use of irony as an important part of her skill as a writer. Detailed presentation of the question with examples.

_____. "A Reconsideration of the *Lais* of Marie de France." *Speculum* 46 (1971): 39-65. A careful consideration of the various *Lais* from the point of view of Marie's concept of love. Many of the same points are made in chapter 7 of Mickel's book, *Marie de France* (above).

Amelia A. Rutledge
(Revised by *Susan L. Piepke*)

PAULE MARSHALL

Born: Brooklyn, New York; April 9, 1929

Principal short fiction
Soul Clap Hands and Sing, 1961; *Reena and Other Stories*, 1983.

Other literary forms
Paule Marshall is best known for her 1959 novel *Brown Girl, Brownstones*, which tells the story of Barbadian immigrants striving to surmount poverty and racism in their new home, as seen through the eyes of the young heroine, Selina Boyce, daughter of a hardworking, ambitious mother and an easygoing, romantic father.

Ten years after her first novel, *The Chosen Place, the Timeless People* (1969) was published, followed by *Praisesong for the Widow* (1983) and *Daughters* (1991). Marshall has also written a number of essays on African-American women writers and her own experience as an artist.

Achievements
Marshall's first novel, *Brown Girl, Brownstones*, ushered in a whole new approach to the African-American female protagonist; only Gwendolyn Brooks's *Maud Martha* (1953) and the earlier *Their Eyes Were Watching God* (1937) by Zora Neale Hurston had focused on an African-American woman's search for identity within a black community and her own conscious, interior life. Marshall also has explored the experience of Americans of West Indian origin. Her writing is lyrical, capturing the grace and idiom of her protagonists. She was awarded a Guggenheim Fellowship in 1960, the Rosenthal Award from the National Institute of Arts and Letters in 1962, for *Soul Clap Hands and Sing*, a Ford Foundation grant for 1964-1965, a National Endowment for the Arts grant for 1967-1968, and the Before Columbus Foundation American Book Award in 1984 for *Praisesong for the Widow.*

Biography
Paule Marshall was born in Brooklyn in 1929, the daughter of Samuel and Ada Burke, émigrés from Barbados who arrived in the United States shortly after World War I. She thus grew up in a culture with its roots in the Caribbean, which she visited for the first time when she was nine years old, an experience that had a strong influence on her future writing. She wrote poetry as a child and listened to the talk of women, both preparing her for her career as a powerful and poetic writer. In the opening of *Reena and Other Stories*, she describes the influence of her mother, women relatives, and other female friends on her experience in an essay called "From the Poets in the Kitchen":

They taught me my first lesson in the narrative art. They trained my ear. They set a standard of excellence. This is why the best of my work must be attributed to them; it stands as testimony to the rich legacy of language and culture they so freely passed on to me in the workshop of the kitchen.

Marshall attended Brooklyn College, receiving a B.A. cum laude in 1953; she was also a member of Phi Beta Kappa. She wrote her first novel, *Brown Girl, Brownstones*, while a graduate student at Hunter College. She married Kenneth E. Marshall in 1950; they had a child, Evan, but the marriage failed and a divorce was granted in 1963. In the meantime, Marshall worked as a librarian for the New York Public Libraries and as a staff writer for *Our World* magazine in New York; she also published her first collection of short stories for Atheneum, *Soul Clap Hands and Sing*. With the help of grants from the Ford Foundation and the National Endowment for the Arts, she completed her second novel, *The Chosen Place, the Timeless People*, which, like her earlier work, was critically well received but commercially only marginally successful.

On July 30, 1970, Marshall married Nourry Menard, and that fall she took the position of lecturer on creative writing at Yale University. She has also been a lecturer on black literature at several colleges and universities, including the University of Oxford, Columbia University, Michigan State University, Lake Forest College, and Cornell University. In 1983, Marshall's third novel, *Praisesong for the Widow*, was published by Putnam; this work won the Before Columbus Foundation American Book Award in 1984. The Feminist Press published *Reena and Other Stories*, which includes the novella *Merle*, excerpted from *The Chosen Place, the Timeless People*, and the short stories "Brooklyn" and "Barbados," which originally appeared in *Soul Clap Hands and Sing*. Other stories in *Reena and Other Stories* appeared in various periodicals. This collection was reprinted in 1985 by Virago Press under the title *Merle: A Novella and Other Stories*. In 1991, Marshall published the novel *Daughters*, which was also greeted with great critical acclaim. Her influence on, and significance to, both African-American literature and feminist scholars is gradually being recognized in the academy, but only time will tell if she will ever receive the popular attention that she so richly deserves.

Analysis

Paule Marshall's work has been concerned from the beginning with a number of major themes: the experience of growing up African American in the United States, the clash of cultures between Westerners and African Americans, West Indians and inhabitants of the American mainland, and the relationships between men and women.

Marshall's first collection of shorter works is *Soul Clap Hands and Sing*, which contains four longer short stories, almost novellas. They are given the title of the setting: "Barbados," "Brooklyn," "British Guiana," and "Brazil." In each, the main character is an older man, and the stories explore how that man has failed to live his life fully, for whatever reasons. This failure is indicated by the title of the collection, which is taken from the William Butler Yeats poem "Sailing to Byzantium," which includes the lines "An aged man is but a paltry thing/ A tattered coat upon a stick, unless/ Soul clap its hands and sing." In each case, it is the failure of the man to allow his soul to "clap hands" that has led to the emptiness or aridity of his life. Thus, he is forced to realize his failure to live truly through the intervention of a woman who, in some way, exposes his inadequacies.

For example, in "Barbados," Mr. Watford, who has returned to his native island after having worked single-mindedly throughout his adult life in the United States just so he can return for this purpose, lives like a white colonizer. He has built a house, bought plantation land, and planted coconut trees, which he tends faithfully, despite years of accumulated fatigue. He has never completely finished his house, however, and he lives in total isolation, proud of the fact that he needs no one and no one needs him. It takes a young native woman, foisted on him as a servant, to reveal the paucity of his life, the emptiness of his days. He recognizes that he has not been able to bear the responsibility for the meaninglessness of his life, but when he goes to confront the young woman with the hope of some renewal, he is capable only of attacking her verbally, to which she responds, "you ain't people, Mr. Watford, you ain't people." It is this that destroys him: that he has not been able to be a part of the people who bore him, and has not found sustenance living the same way as those who oppressed him.

In "Brooklyn," an aging Jewish professor, who has been banned from teaching by the red-baiters of the McCarthy era, attempts to coerce a young black woman who is taking his class to spend some time at his summer home. She refuses but in the end returns to his class for the final and takes him up on his invitation, only to express her outrage but also the freedom that she now feels. She has also felt an outcast from her own people, while unable to trust the whites. Now she has the courage to live not as her parents have taught her but as she chooses. Professor Max Berman, on the other hand, is forced to recognize that it is his failure to believe in or stand up for anything that has resulted in his loneliness and failure. Interestingly, in the first story the female protagonist is not given a name, while in the second she is named only in dialogue as Miss Williams.

"British Guiana" explores the present of Gerald Motley, a man who is indeed a motley collection of races; he could have been taken for white, because of the British army officer who was one of his ancestors, or black, for the slave woman that officer had used, or East Indian, from some Hindu who also had a part in his creation. He has achieved a certain amount of success as the head of a radio station, but he knows that he has failed to live his life fully. Although as a young man he had shown a great ability and had rejected his middle-class background to organize a strike, he had been bought off by a job in radio, which forces him to copy the whites who have colonized his country. When he attempts to penetrate the jungle, to prove himself to himself, he is prevented by another motley person, Sybil, an African-Chinese woman with whom he is involved. He is forever conscious of his betrayal of himself and also of Sybil's part in this, which results in a life of cynicism and taking the easy way. At the end of the story, when Sybil, whom he might have married, returns to visit, his last act is to bargain with her for a protégé who despises him but deserves a chance. In the conclusion, he realizes that he is going to die a failure by his own doing.

The final story in the book, "Brazil," reminds the reader of Carson McCullers' "Ballad of the Sad Café," in that it is the story of what appears to be a strange love affair between a white woman of epic proportions and a black dwarf. In this story, the dwarf is a performer who goes by the name of O Grande Caliban and has teamed up with a blonde of Germanic appearance to perform a comic and athletic act. He, however, has decided that it is time to retire, but his mistress does not wish to do so. One of the interesting things about the story is the breaking of the traditional white reader's expectations; it is the undersized black man who is trying to end a relationship with the Aryan-looking female. He has become so famous as Caliban, however, that no one, not even his wife, knows him as he had been. He has been living a lie so long that he cannot convince people of the truth anymore, and so he ends by destroying everything.

Reena and Other Stories is a collection of previously printed works gathered together for the first time in 1983 by the Feminist Press. It begins with Marshall's autobiographical essay, "From the Poets in the Kitchen," which had originally been published in *The New York Times Book Review*'s series called "The Making of a Writer." This essay celebrates the women in Marshall's life who helped form her thought and shape her voice. The collection includes two of the stories discussed above, "Brooklyn" and "Barbados," previously published in *Soul Clap Hands and Sing*. Also included is a novella, *Merle*, which has been excerpted from her 1969 novel *The Chosen Place, the Timeless People* but was extensively reshaped and rewritten. Marshall wrote autobiographical headnotes to each story, which help to place them in the context of her experience and development as a writer.

For example, the first story in the collection, "The Valley Between," was as Marshall explained, "my very first published story, written when I could barely crawl, never mind stand up and walk as a writer." In it, the characters are white, a deliberate decision as Marshall herself was at the time married to Kenneth E. Marshall, a marriage she describes as "an early, unwise first marriage," and she wished to disguise the autobiographical elements in it. It is the story of a marriage falling apart because the wife (and mother of a small child) continues to grow, while the husband wishes her to remain the same, to be nothing more than a wife and mother. Published in August, 1954, it is a story well before its time in its depiction of the stifling expectations placed upon a woman of talent and energy.

The title story, "Reena," is unusual in that it was commissioned by *Harper's Magazine* for a special supplement on "The American Female," published in October of 1962. Intended by the editors to be an article on the African-American woman, the story instead became a thinly disguised fiction concerning the women whom Marshall knew best: "those from an urban, working-class and lower middle-class, West Indian-American background who, like [Marshall herself], had attended the free

New York City colleges during the late forties and fifties."

A first-person narrator named Paulie recounts her meeting again after twenty years with a friend from her childhood, Reena, formally named Doreen but—being a child who shapes her own life as best she can in a world that discriminates against women, African Americans, and particularly African Americans from the West Indies—had transformed herself into Reena, "with two ees!"

The meeting place is at the funeral of Aunt Vi, Reena's aunt, a woman who represents the strong, nurturing, enduring women "from the poets in the kitchen," and who will reappear in Marshall's fiction. Having been out of touch for so long, Reena and Paulie have much to discuss, and much of the story is Reena's recounting of what has been happening in her life: the struggle for meaningful work; her relationship with her family, particularly her mother; relationships with white men (usually unsuccessful) and with black men, who have to learn how to relate to and accept a strong, educated, ambitious black woman; childbearing; radical politics; and loneliness. In almost essayistic form, this story provides an intimate glimpse into the struggle, suffering, and successes of this group of African-American women.

"To Da-duh, in Memoriam" is based on a visit that Marshall made to her maternal grandmother in Barbados when she was nine. Da-duh is another of the ancestor figures who populate Marshall's fiction, like Aunt Vi in the previous story and Merle in the story of that same name; as Marshall says, "Da-duh turns up everywhere."

An example of this appears in the final selection in the collection, the novella *Merle* excerpted from *The Chosen Place, the Timeless People*. Merle is "Part saint, part revolutionary, part obeah woman," a woman who, wherever she goes, exhorts people to resist oppression, while on a personal level she is "still trying to come to terms with her life and history as a black woman, still seeking to reconcile all the conflicting elements to form a viable self."

Merle is the woman whom Paule Marshall creates in various guises, calling into being a new character for twentieth century American literature. In her compelling portrayal of women in her works, she brings to life for her readers a vision of the direction the world should be going by showing readers the people whom the world desperately needs to listen to and perhaps emulate.

Other major works

NOVELS: *Brown Girl, Brownstones*, 1959; *The Chosen Place, the Timeless People*, 1969; *Praisesong for the Widow*, 1983; *Daughters*, 1991.

Bibliography

Brown, Lloyd W. "The Rhythms of Power in Paule Marshall's Fiction." *Novel: A Forum on Fiction* 7, no. 2 (Winter, 1974): 159-167. This essay focuses on Marshall's short story "To Da-Duh, in Memoriam," tracing Marshall's concern with the problems of African-American women, tied to her commitment to feminism and racial equality. Brown argues that Marshall sees power as both a political goal of ethnic and feminist movements and a social and psychological phenomenon that affects racial and sexual roles, shapes cultural traditions, and molds the individual psyche.

Christian, Barbara. "Sculpture and Space: The Interdependency of Character and Culture in the Novels of Paule Marshall." In *Black Women Novelists: The Development of a Tradition, 1892-1976*. Westport, Conn.: Greenwood Press, 1980. A close and intelligent reading of the works through *The Chosen Place, the Timeless People*. Christian emphasizes Marshall's ability to create distinct characters who are affected by culture and society and who in turn affect these two important elements. Includes a general bibliography and an index.

Collier, Eugenia. "The Closing of the Circle: Movement from Division to Wholeness in Paule Marshall's Fiction." In *Black Women Writers, 1950-1980*, edited by Mari Evans. Garden City, N.Y.: Anchor Press/Doubleday, 1984. Collier finds in Marshall's writing a movement from the separated, segmented self to a discovery of wholeness and completion; this healing and wholeness is found within the context of the community. Contains good discussions of the short fiction. The first of two essays on Marshall in Evans' collection, which should be required reading for anyone interested in African-American women writers. Contains a bibliography of criticism on Marshall and an index.

Kapai, Leela. "Dominant Themes and Technique in Paule Marshall's Fiction." *College Language Association Journal* 16 (September, 1972): 49-59. Examines Marshall's use of folk tradition in her novels through *The Chosen Place, the Timeless People* and also in the short story "Reena." Kapai claims that Marshall puts being a human being, the universal human experience, before racial identity and states that Marshall is aware of her Western heritage, even as she writes out of her personal experience as an African American. Contains some good, close readings.

McClusky, John, Jr. "And Called Every Generation Blessed: Theme, Setting, and Ritual in the Works of Paule Marshall." In *Black Women Writers, 1950-1980*, edited by Mari Evans. Garden City, N.Y.: Anchor Press/Doubleday, 1984. This essay, the second on Marshall in Evans' book, gives an overview of Marshall's achievement, evolution, and her state and future directions in writing.

Washington, Mary Helen. Afterword to *Brown Girl, Brownstones*. New York: Feminist Press, 1981. This essay places Marshall firmly in the African-American tradition, traces the roots of the Barbadians about whom she writes, analyzes the characters of Silla and Selena Boyce in the novel, and discusses Marshall's use of the oral tradition.

Mary S. LeDonne

BOBBIE ANN MASON

Born: Mayfield, Kentucky; May 1, 1940

Principal short fiction
Shiloh and Other Stories, 1982; *Love Life*, 1989.

Other literary forms
Bobbie Ann Mason has written novels, literary criticism, and popular culture journalism. She has also been the subject of numerous interviews.

Achievements
Mason has earned a place in American literature with her short stories. She won the Ernest Hemingway Foundation Award for first fiction in 1983 for her first collection of short stories, *Shiloh and Other Stories*. That collection also earned for Mason nomination for the National Book Critics Circle Award (1982), the American Book Award (1982), and the International Association of Poets, Playwrights, Editors, Essayists, and Novelists' PEN/Faulkner Award for Fiction (1983). Mason's writing for newspapers and magazines includes work as a society columnist for the *Mayfield Messenger* in Kentucky and as a writer of fan magazines for Ideal Publishing Company in New York City. She has also written "Talk of the Town" articles for *The New Yorker*.

Mason's novels have reinforced her reputation as a fine writer. The first of her novels, *In Country* (1985), was particularly well received, and a film (also titled *In Country*) based on the book was released by Warner Bros. in the fall of 1989. Often compared with Ann Beattie, Raymond Carver, and Frederick Barthelme, Mason writes fiction that reads like life. Her characters struggle with jobs, family, and self-awareness, continually exuding a lively sense of being. Those who people her stories often transcend circumstance without losing their rootedness in place. Most often, her characters struggle to live within a relationship but are, in the final analysis, alone. In fiction that resonates with rock 'n' roll music and family conflicts, her descriptions leave a reader sometimes feeling uncomfortably aware of a truth about families: caring does not guarantee understanding or communication.

Biography
Bobbie Ann Mason was born in rural Kentucky, and her Southern background appears to have been a major force in shaping her fiction. She attended a country school through the eighth grade and then attended Mayfield High School. Her descriptions of country schools in "State Champions" certainly ring true, and apparently her novel *Spence + Lila* (1988) fictionalizes a part of her parents' experience. Another aspect of her high school life echoes in her fiction: her love of rock 'n' roll.

Mason majored in journalism at the University of Kentucky in Lexington, where she wrote for the university paper, *The Kernel*. While in college, she also wrote the summer society column for the *Mayfield Messenger*. After graduating with a B.A. degree in 1962, she spent fifteen months in New York City working for Ideal Publishing Company writing for fan magazines such as *Movie Life* and *TV Star Parade*. In addition to her degree in journalism, Mason earned an M.A. degree in literature from the State University of New York at Binghamton in 1966, as well as a Ph.D. in literature from the University of Connecticut in 1972. In her doctoral dissertation, she analyzed the garden symbolism in *Ada or Ardor: A Family Chronicle* (1969), by Vladimir Nabokov. Nabokov's artistry in presenting the details of his characters' lives apparently touched a chord in Mason. While pursuing her Ph.D., she met Roger B. Rawlings at the University of Connecticut; they were married in 1969.

From 1972 to 1979, Mason was an assistant professor of English at Mansfield State College (which later became Mansfield University) in Pennsylvania, where she taught journalism as well as other English courses. She had been writing short stories during this period and had received encouraging responses from editors who, nevertheless, rejected her stories for publication. In 1979, Mason stopped teaching to write fiction. She settled in rural Pennsylvania, sometimes giving readings and sometimes writing for *The New Yorker*. Her life, with its movement from rural to urban and back to rural living, mirrors a typical concern of her fiction: the tension between rural and urban life. Apparently her own feelings match those of many of her protagonists. In interviews, Mason has said that she considers herself an exile.

Analysis

The short stories of Bobbie Ann Mason are for the most part set in small towns in Kentucky. The stories explore the lives of lower-middle-class people from small towns or farms. Kentucky, a North/South border state, is emblematic of Mason's concerns with borders, separations, and irrevocable decisions. Mason's stories typically explore a conflict between the character's past and future, a conflict that is often exemplified in a split between rural and urban leanings and a modern as opposed to a traditional life. Most often, the point of view in Mason's short fiction is limited omniscient. She is, however, adept with first-person narration as well. Readers are most often left with a sense of her characters' need to transcend their life scripts through action, most often a quest.

"Shiloh," for example, is a story about love, loss, and history. A couple, Leroy and Norma Jean, have been married for sixteen years. They married when Norma Jean was pregnant with their son Randy, a child who died as an infant. Leroy is home recuperating from an accident he had with his truck. His leg is healing, but he is afraid to go back to driving a truck long distances. He takes on traditionally feminine activities in the story: he starts doing crafts, watches birds at the feeder, and remains the passenger in the car even after his leg has healed enough for him to drive.

The accident that forced Leroy to remain at home for months recuperating is the second crisis point in the couple's marriage. The earlier crisis had been their baby's death. After the baby died, Leroy and Norma Jean remained married but emotionally isolated from each other: "They never speak about their memories of Randy, which have almost faded, but now that Leroy is home all the time, they sometimes feel awkward around each other, and Leroy wonders if one of them should mention the child. He has the feeling that they are waking up out of a dream together." Now that Leroy is at home, he "sees things about Norma Jean that he never realized before." Leroy's staying at home so much leads to several important changes for Norma Jean: she begins to lift weights, takes a writing course, and curses in front of her mother. In response to the repeated suggestion of Norma Jean's mother, the couple drives to the Shiloh battleground for a second honeymoon trip. At Shiloh, Norma Jean tells Leroy that she wants to leave him. The history of Shiloh is significant to the story of this marriage. Shiloh, an early battle in the Civil War, proved that the Civil War would be a long and bloody one. The story concludes with Leroy merging family history with battleground history and Norma Jean literally flexing her muscles. Their civil war will be Leroy fighting for union and Norma Jean seeking her independent self.

A contemporary history lesson in the fear of polio and communists, "Detroit Skyline, 1949" narrates in first person the summer spent by a nine-year-old girl, Peggy Jo, and her mother as they visit the mother's sister and her family in Detroit. The story reveals the conflict between rural and city life through the perceptions and desires of Peggy Jo. Seeing her aunt's neighborhood for the first time, Peggy Jo immediately knows that she wants to live "in a place like this, with neighbors." When she plays with the neighbor child, however, Peggy Jo is made to feel incompetent because she does not know how to roller skate, so she instead spends her time watching television and examining articles and pictures in her aunt's scrapbook.

Peggy Jo feels isolated that summer. She observes the smoothness with which her mother and aunt converse, how natural their communication is. When she attends a birthday party for the neighbor child, Peggy Jo notes: "I did not know what to say to the children. They all knew each other, and their screams and giggles had a natural continuity, something like the way my mother talked with her sister, and like the splendid houses of the neighborhood, all set so close together." For Peggy Jo there is little "natural continuity" of speech or gesture within her aunt's household that summer. Her own comments are most often cut short, silenced, or discredited by the others. By the end of the summer, Peggy Jo realizes that her "own life [is] a curiosity, an item for a scrapbook."

Another of Mason's stories concerning rural isolation is "Offerings," in which the isolation is redemptive for Sandra, who stays in the couple's country home instead of traveling with her husband, Jerry, to Louisville, "reluctant to spend her weekends with him watching go-go dancers in smoky bars." She instead spends her time growing vegetables and tending her cats, ducks, and dogs. Her cobweb-strewn house is not her focus; the outdoors is. The offerings that Sandra makes are many: to her mother, tacit agreement to avoid discussing the separation from Jerry; to her grandmother, the fiction of Jerry's presence; and to the forces of nature around her, her tamed and dependent ducks. Sandra finds grace through the natural world, exemplified within the final image of the story: dewy spider webs that, in the morning, are trampolines enabling her to "spring from web to web, all the way up the hill to the woods." She cannot be honest with her grandmother and avoids truth in conversation with her mother, but she feels at peace and at home with her yard, the woods, and the wildlife there.

In "Residents and Transients," Mason's narrator is also married to a man who has gone away to work in Louisville. Mary, the narrator, is finding her place within a relationship as well as a location. Several images in this story reinforce the theme of stability as opposed to movement. The cats Mary cares for on the farm represent her dilemma of moving to Louisville. To Stephen, her lover, she explains that she has read about two basic types of cats, residents and transients. She cites difference of opinion by researchers over which type is truly superior: those who establish territories and stay there or those who show the greatest curiosity by going from one place to another. Mary is drawn to the stability of her parents' old farmhouse, feeling the pull of traditional value of place. The single image that most succinctly and horrifically mirrors her dilemma is a rabbit, seen in the headlights as she is driving home. The rabbit at first appears to be running in place, but she realizes that its forelegs are still moving despite the fact that its haunches have been run over. Throughout the story, Mary has been literally running in place, running from her relationship with her husband by taking a lover and running from her life with her husband by remaining in her parents' old home.

Mary's position at the end of the story is mirrored by the image of the odd-eyed cat, whose eyes shine red and green. The narrator has been waiting for some signal to move. Her husband's words do not convince; Mary thinks of them as words that are processed, computerized renderings. She needs more than words; she needs an integrated part of her world to spur her to act. Because her husband is no longer an integral part of her world, she listens and looks for other cues. Apparently, the dying rabbit has spurred her to action. The story ends with Mary "waiting for the light to change."

Within Mason's second collection of short fiction, *Love Life*, the reader sees continued the skillful treatment of people's decisions and perceptions. As in the first collection, *Shiloh and Other Stories*, there are two first-person narratives, both with young women narrators. "State Champions" is a reminiscence of twenty years past, so it offers a perspective different from that of other works. "State Champions" further explores Mason's theme of rural versus urban experience by recounting the success of the Cuba Cubs, Kentucky state champions in basketball in 1952. The twelve-year-old narrator, Peggy, had seen the team as glamorous, certainly larger than life. As an adult in upstate New York, Peggy is surprised to hear that team referred to as "just a handful of country boys who could barely afford basketball shoes." Although Peggy had shared in the excitement of the championship season, "State Champions" presents her perceptions of being different from the rest even at that time. She rebelled against authority at school by talking back to the history teacher. She surprised her friend Willowdean with the assertion that she did not want to get pregnant and get married, a normal pattern for the girls at the high school. From her adult perspective, Peggy ascribes her own struggle for words with Glenn, the boy she cared about in 1952, to her status as a "country kid":

> I couldn't say anything, for we weren't raised to say things that were heartfelt and gracious. Country kids didn't learn manners. Manners were too embarrassing. Learning not to run in the house was about the extent of what we knew about how to act. We didn't learn to congratulate people; we didn't wish people happy birthday. We didn't even address each other by name.

Ironically enough, what triggers Peggy's recollection of the state championship year is the comment by the New Yorker about the poor country boys' basketball team, certainly a comment not springing from a mannered upbringing.

In "Coyotes," Mason provides a third-person account from the perspective of a young man, Cobb, who embodies the ambivalence and sensitivity often seen in Mason's characters. He has asked Lynnette Johnson to marry him, and he continues to look for signs and indications that marriage is the right thing to do. Cobb sees a young clerk in a drugstore showing her wedding ring to a young couple. Their conversation was flat: no congratulations, no excitement. The matter-of-fact nature of the exchange haunts Cobb. He wants his marriage to be the subject of excitement, hugs, celebration. Marriage in general presents itself as a risk, leading him to look further for signs that his own marriage will work. He wonders if Lynnette will find more and more things about him that will offend her. For example, he fails to tell her about having hunted after she told him that his sweatshirt, on which is written "Paducah, the Flat Squirrel Capital of the World," is in bad taste. He is reassured by their similarities—for example, the fact that they both pronounce "coyote" with an *e* sound at the end. Lynnette's past, with a mother who had attempted suicide, is something he recognizes to be significant to them, but he nevertheless speaks confidently with Lynnette about their future. Lynnette fears that her past will somehow intrude on their future, and so, in fact, does Cobb. Their relationship is, as is typical of Mason's fiction, freighted with all those tangled possibilities.

Past and future as conflicting forces also form a theme of "Private Lies," in which the male protagonist, Mickey, reestablishes his relationship with his former wife and decides to search for the child they gave up for adoption eighteen years before. Mickey's wife, Tina, has compartmentalized their lives with a regular television schedule and planned activities for their children. Tina has forbidden him to tell their children about his daughter. Mickey, however, cannot ignore the eighteenth birthday of his daughter given up to adoption. The story concludes with Mickey and his former wife, Donna, on the beach in Florida, the state in which they gave their daughter up for adoption. Donna insists that she does not want to find their daughter and that searching is a mistake. She nevertheless accompanies him to Florida, where Mickey seeks to stop telling lies (by silence) and where Donna still seeks to avoid the search, exemplified by her refusal to look inside shells for fear of what she may find in them. Mickey seeks the daughter that will be his bridge between past and future. He seeks to make a new present for himself, a present free of Tina's control.

Much of Mason's short fiction concerns people facing the need for resolution between their pasts and their futures. Using memorable and realistic detail, Mason fleshes out the lives of her characters, who never cross the line to maudlin confession. Her stories typically lack resolution, making them uncomfortably true to life.

Other major works

NOVELS: *In Country*, 1985; *Spence + Lila*, 1988.

NONFICTION: *Nabokov's Garden: A Nature Guide to Ada*, 1974; *The Girl Sleuth: A Feminist Guide to the Bobbsey Twins, Nancy Drew, and Their Sisters*, 1975.

Bibliography

Brinkmeyer, Robert H., Jr. "Never Stop Rocking: Bobbie Ann Mason and Rock-and-Roll." *Mississippi Quarterly: The Journal of Southern Culture* 42, no. 1 (1988-1989): 5-17. Footnoted from seven other articles and interviews, this essay explores Mason's use of rock music as a significant expression of contemporary culture.

Morphew, G. O. "Downhome Feminists in *Shiloh and Other Stories*." *The Southern Literary Journal* 21, no. 2 (1989): 41-49. In a considered treatment of Mason's down-home feminists, Morphew notes that the heroines want space within relationships, not equal pay for equal work. The essay notes differences between the actions of Mason's educated and uneducated heroines.

Rothstein, Mervyn. "Homegrown Fiction: Bobbie Ann Mason Blends Springsteen and Nabokov." *The New York Times Biographical Service* 19 (May, 1988): 563-565. This essay reports Mason's love of rhythm and blues in high school and notes the semiautobiographical details of *Spence + Lila*.

Ryan, Maureen. "Stopping Places: Bobbie Ann Mason's Short Stories." In *Women Writers of the Contemporary South*, edited by Peggy W. Prenshaw. Jackson: University Press of Mississippi, 1984. An overview of Mason's themes and character portraits, this sampling provides a brief treatment of many different works.

Wilhelm, Albert E. "Private Rituals: Coping with Change in the Fiction of Bobbie Ann Mason." *Midwest Quarterly* 28, no. 2 (1987): 271-282. This article includes interview commentary from Mason as well as analysis of the rituals in several of the stories. Wilhelm examines "Shiloh" most closely of the works he treats.

Janet Taylor Palmer

W. SOMERSET MAUGHAM

Born: Paris, France; January 25, 1874
Died: Nice, France; December 16, 1965

Principal short fiction

Orientations, 1899; *The Trembling of a Leaf: Little Stories of the South Sea Islands*, 1921; *The Casuarina Tree*, 1926; *Ashenden: Or, The British Agent*, 1928; *Six Stories Written in the First Person Singular*, 1931; *Ah King*, 1933; *East and West*, 1934; *Cosmopolitans*, 1936; *The Mixture as Before*, 1940; *Creatures of Circumstance*, 1947; *Here and There: Selected Short Stories*, 1948; *The Maugham Reader*, 1950; *The Complete Short Stories of W. Somerset Maugham*, 1951; *The World Over*, 1952; *Seventeen Lost Stories*, 1969.

Other literary forms

A dedicated professional, W. Somerset Maugham earned more than three million dollars from his writing, a phenomenal amount for his day. Between 1897 and 1962, a career spanning eight decades, Maugham published twenty novels, four travel books, more than twenty stage plays, an autobiography of ideas, and innumerable essays, *belles-lettres*, and introductions, in addition to more than one hundred short stories, of which about ninety are readily accessible in different editions. Much of his work has been adapted for use by television and cinema.

Achievements

Maugham is best known for his urbanity, his wit, his controlled sense of writing, and his ability to describe not only objectively but also so realistically that he has been accused of lifting stories directly from life. Many of his stories do spring from real incidents or actual people, but the perceptions and surprise plot twists are always Maugham-inspired. In fact, Maugham is expressly known as a master of the surprise or twist ending to an inextricably woven plot in his short stories, many of which have been converted to film. His early work, under the influence of Oscar Wilde and his cult of aesthetes, shows a refined and civilized attitude toward life. Several of his novels illustrate the demanding sacrifices that art necessitates of life or that life itself can become, in turn, an art form, thereby demonstrating the "art of living" (*The Razor's Edge*, 1944).

Maugham was curiously denied many conspicuous honors (such as knighthood) usually conferred on a man of letters of his distinction, but he was awarded by the Royal Society of Literature the title of Companion of Literature, an honor given to "authors who have brought exceptional distinction to English letters." Furthermore, the occasion of his eightieth birthday was celebrated with a dinner at the Garrick Club, a distinction given to only three writers before him: Charles Dickens, William Makepeace Thackeray, and Anthony Trollope.

Biography

When William Somerset Maugham was eight, his mother died, and his father, a solicitor for the British Embassy in Paris, died two years later. Shy and speaking little English, Maugham was sent to Whitstable in Kent to live with an uncle, the Reverend Henry MacDonald Maugham, and his German-born wife, and thence almost immediately to King's School, Canterbury. These wretched and unhappy years were later detailed in Maugham's first masterpiece, the novel *Of Human Bondage* (1915). A stammer which stayed with him for life seems to have originated about this time. At seventeen, Maugham went to Heidelberg and attended lectures at the university. His first play, *Schiffbrüchig* (1902), was written during this year abroad and performed in Berlin.

Returning to London, he began the study of medicine at St. Thomas' Hospital, where the misery of the nearby Lambeth slums profoundly impressed him. He took his medical degree in 1897, the same year *Liza of Lambeth*, his first novel, was published, then abandoned medicine. By 1908, Maugham had an unprecedented four plays running simultaneously in London, and by 1911, he had become successful enough to buy a fashionable house in Mayfair.

In 1915, he married Syrie Barnardo Wellcome. Divorced in 1927, they had one daughter, Liza, who became Lady Glendevon. During World War I, Maugham served as a medical officer in France and as an agent for the British Secret Service in Switzerland and Russia, where he was to prevent, if possible, the Bolshevik Revolution. During and after the war, he traveled extensively in Hawaii, Samoa, Tahiti, China, Malaysia, Indochina, Australia, the West Indies, various Central and South American countries, and the United States. In 1928, Maugham settled on the French Riviera, buying Villa Mauresque. Maugham died in Nice, France, on December 16, 1965.

Analysis

W. Somerset Maugham first claimed fame as a playwright and novelist, but he became best known in the 1920's and 1930's the world over as an international traveler and short-story writer. Appearing in popular magazines such as *Nash's*, *Collier's*, *Hearst's International*, *The Smart Set*, and *Cosmopolitan*, his stories reached hundreds of thousands of readers who had never attended a play and had seldom read a novel. This new public demanded simple, lucid, fast-moving prose, and Maugham's realistic, well-defined narratives, often set amid the exotic flora of Oceania or Indochina, were among the most popular of the day.

The Trembling of a Leaf: Little Stories of the South Sea Islands collected six of these first "exotic stories" and assured Maugham fame as a short-story writer on equal footing with his established renown as novelist and dramatist. It was actually his second collection, coming twenty years after *Orientations*, whose title clearly bespeaks its purposes. Apparently, Maugham had found no suitable possibilities for short fiction in the meantime until, recuperating from a lung infection between World War I assignments for the British Secret Service, he took a vacation to Samoa and Hawaii:

I had always had a romantic notion of the South Seas. I had read of those magic islands in the books of Herman Melville, Pierre Loti, and Robert Louis Stevenson, but what I saw was very different from what I had read.

Although Maugham clearly differentiates life as he saw it in the South Seas from life as he had read about it in the writings of his "romantic" predecessors, his stories of British Colonials, of natives and half-castes in exotic environments, are reminiscent of these authors and also of Rudyard Kipling. Maugham's assessment of Kipling, the only British short-story writer he thought comparable to such greats as Guy de Maupassant and Anton Chekhov, neatly clarifies their similar subject, as well as their ultimate stylistic differences. Kipling, Maugham writes,

opened a new and fruitful field to writers. This is the story, the scene of which is set in some country little known to the majority of readers, and which deals with the reactions upon the white man of his sojourn in an alien land and the effect which contact with peoples of another race has upon him. Subsequent writers have treated this subject in their different ways, but . . . no one has invested it with more romantic glamour, no one has made it more exciting and no one has presented it so vividly and with such a wealth of colour.

Maugham's first South Sea stories are essentially criticisms of the "romantic glamour" of Kipling and his predecessors, especially Stevenson, his most immediate literary forefather in terms of location. Rather than repeat their illusions, Maugham tries to see the "alien land" as it really is, without poetic frills. "Red," which Maugham once chose as his best story, is a clear example of this process.

A worldly, gruff, and overweight skipper of a bedraggled seventy-ton schooner anchors off one of the Samoan Islands in order to trade with the local storekeeper. After rowing ashore to a small cove, the captain follows a tortuous path, eventually arriving at "a white man's house" where he meets Neilson. Neilson seems a typical character out of Robert Louis Stevenson, a life deserter unable either to return to his homeland or to accommodate himself completely to his present situation. Twenty-five years ago he came to the island with tuberculosis, expecting to live only a year, but the mild climate has arrested his disease. He has married a native woman called Sally and built a European bungalow on the beautiful spot where a grass hut once stood. His walls are lined with books, which makes the skipper nervous but to which Neilson constantly and condescendingly alludes. Offering him whiskey and a cigar, Neilson decides to tell the skipper the story of Red.

Red was Neilson's romantic predecessor, Sally's previous lover, an ingenuous Apollo whom Neilson likes to imagine "had no more soul than the creatures of the woods and forests who made pipes from reeds and bathed in the mountain streams when the world was young." It was Red who had lived with Sally in the native hut, "with its beehive roof and its pillars, overshadowed by a great tree with red flowers." Glamorizing the young couple and the lush habitat, Neilson imagines them living on "delicious messes from coconuts," by a sea "deep blue, wine-coloured at sundown, like the sea of Homeric Greece," where "the hurrying fish were like butterflies," and the "dawn crept in among the wooden pillars of the hut" so that the lovers woke each morning and "smiled to welcome another day."

After a year of bliss, Red was shanghaied by a British whaler while trying to trade green oranges for tobacco. Sally was crestfallen and mourned him for three years, but finally, somewhat reluctantly, she acceded to the amorous overtures of the newcomer Neilson:

> And so the little wooden house was built in which he had now lived for many years, and Sally became his wife. But after the first few weeks of rapture, during which he was satisfied with what she gave him, he had known little happiness. She had yielded to him, through weariness, but she had only yielded what she set no store on. The soul which he had dimly glimpsed escaped him. He knew that she cared nothing for him. She still loved Red. . . .

Neilson, admittedly "a sentimentalist," is imprisoned by history. His books, a source of anxiety to the skipper, are a symbol of what Maugham believes he must himself avoid: useless repetition of and bondage to his forebears. As creation, Neilson does repeat Stevenson; but as character, he shows the absolute futility of this repetition. The dead romance assumes priority from the living one, and priority is everything. For the sentimentalist Neilson, tropical paradise has become living hell and the greatest obstacle preventing his own present happiness, the fulfillment of his own history, is his creation of an insurmountable predecessor, one whose "romantic glamour" is purer and simpler than his own reality.

The final irony, that the skipper, now bloated and bleary-eyed, is in fact the magnificent Red of Neilson's imagination and that when Sally and he meet they do not even recognize each other, snaps something in Neilson. The moment he had dreaded for twenty-five years has come and gone. His illusions disintegrate like gossamer; the "father" is not insurmountable:

> He had been cheated. They had seen each other at last and had not known it. He began to laugh, mirthlessly, and his laughter grew till it became hysterical. The Gods had played him a cruel trick. And he was old now.

In "Red," Neilson's realization of failure and waste do prompt some action, possibly an escape from the cell of his past. Over dinner, he lies to Sally that his eldest brother is very ill and he must go home. "Will you be gone long?" she asks. His only answer is to shrug his shoulders.

In its natural manner, Maugham's prose in these stories never strains for effect; each could easily be retold over coffee or a drink. Like Maupassant, Maugham is a realist and a merciless ironist, but while his narrator observes and his readers chuckle, characters such as Neilson grapple in desperate roles against the onrushing determination of their lives. In the style of the best "magazine" stories, incidents in Maugham inevitably build one on top of the other, slowly constraining his protagonists until, like grillwork, they all but completely bar them from realizing their individual potential and freedom. Maugham's predilection for the surprise ending helps some find a final success, but not all; most end as we have believed they would— like the cuckolded Scotsman Lawson in "The Pool" who, after losing job, friends' respect, wife, and self, is "set on making a good job of it" and commits suicide "with a great stone tied up in his coat and bound to his feet."

Lawson, another "great coward" in the Stevenson mold, has married a beautiful half-caste and, naïvely assuming human nature the same the world over, has treated her as he would a white woman. By providing primarily in terms of his own culture's expectations, Lawson unwittingly shoulders "the white man's burden," that bequest of Kipling's, until he becomes himself a burden. Maugham implies, with great irony, that if Lawson had been less "a gentleman" and had taken the girl as a mistress, his tragedy might have been averted. As the reader must see the "alien land" for what it really is, so must they see its peoples.

"Rain," Maugham's best-known short story, develops many of these same themes. Pago-Pago is unforgettably described, but no one could confuse it with the romanticized "loveliness" of Neilson's island. When the rain is not falling in torrents, the sun is oppressive. Davidson, the missionary, and Sadie, the prostitute, act out their parts with the same furious intensity. Neither is banalized; Maugham neither approves nor condemns. Only the "mountains of Nebraska" dream foreshadows Davidson's lust. (With its overtones of sexual repression, this dream makes "Rain" a notable pioneer in Freudian fiction.) Other than that, however, Davidson's sincere religious fervor seems convincingly real, inspired though it is by his "mission," yet another example of "the white man's burden." In the ensuing struggle between spiritual and "heathen" sensuality, the ironic stroke is that the prostitute wins; up to the last few pages, the story's outcome looks otherwise. Finally, Davidson must admit that he cannot proscribe human nature, not even his own. Neither saint nor sinner, he is simply human. On a more universal level than either "The Pool" or "Red," "Rain" shows that of human nature, only its unaccountability is predictable.

Maugham's detachment and moral tolerance, as well as assuring Davidson's and Sadie's vitality as characters, benefits his handling of the tale. The restraint exercised in *not* portraying for the reader either of the two "big scenes," Sadie's rape or Davidson's suicide, gives Maugham's story "Rain" an astounding dramatic power. The "real life" genesis of "Rain" is well known, how Maugham jotted down his impressions of a few passengers aboard ship traveling with him in the winter of 1916 from Honolulu to Pago-Pago and then four years later made a story from it. Of his prototype for Sadie Thompson he wrote:

> Plump, pretty in a coarse fashion perhaps not more than twenty-seven. She wore a white dress and a large white hat, long white boots from which the calves bulged in cotton stockings.

This practice of taking characters and situations directly from life is nowhere better elaborated in Maugham than in the volume entitled *Six Stories Written in the First Person Singular.* The personal touch—clear in the book's title— leaves a strong impression of reality. Whereas "Rain" seems a small classic in its theme, conflict, effective setting, and dramatic ending, it has one difficulty: the reader is unable to sympathize clearly with any one character, and this detracts from a greater, warmer effectiveness it might have. When the narrator as detached observer is introduced as character, however, there is no such problem with sympathy. This creation, the consistent and subsequently well-known cosmopolite, the story*teller* for his stories, is one of Maugham's finest achievements.

In "Virtue" the narrator—here differentiated as "Maugham"—browses at Sotheby's auction rooms, goes to the Haymarket, and dines at Ciro's when he has a free morning; he was once a medical student and is now a novelist. In "The Round Dozen," he is a well-known author whose portrait appears in the illustrated papers. He is at Elson, a tattered seaside resort "not very far from Brighton," recovering from influenza. There, "Maugham" coincidentally observes a well-known bigamist—whose portrait at one time had also graced the pages of the press—capture his twelfth victim. In "Jane," the versatile man-of-the-world is introduced as a writer of comedies, while in "The Alien Corn" he is a promising young novelist who has grown middle-aged, written books and plays, traveled and had experiences, fallen in and out of love. Throughout *Six Stories Written in the First Person Singular*, "Maugham" is intermittently away from London, "once more in the Far East." Such frank appeals to verisimilitude (in other words, that "Maugham" is in fact Maugham) succeed extremely well.

In "The Human Element," the narrator is a popular author who likes "a story to have a beginning, a middle, and an end." He meets Carruthers, whom he does not much like, one night at the Hotel Plaza in Rome during the late summer "dead season." Carruthers is inhumanly depressed and tells Maugham why: he has found his life's love, the woman he would make his wife, Betty Weldon-Burns, living in Rhodes "in domestic familiarity" with her chauffeur.

Carruthers, also a short-story writer, has been praised by critics for "his style, his sense of beauty and his atmosphere," but when "Maugham" suggests he make use of his experience for a story, Carruthers grows angry: "It would be monstrous. Betty was everything in the world to me. I couldn't do anything so caddish." Ironically, the story ends with Carruthers' excuse that "there's no story there." That "Maugham" has in fact just made a story of it suggests that life can and does provide limitless possibilities for art if we are only ready to accept them.

Maugham specifically delineates these dual creative principles, life and art, in his introduction to the six stories in the collection. Defending the practice of drawing fictional characters from personal experience, Maugham cites Henri Beyle (Stendhal), Gustave Flaubert, and Jules Renard. "I think indeed," he writes, "that most novelists and surely the best, have worked from life." The concern of Maugham's South Sea stories, to convey what he "saw" rather than what he "had read," is continued here on a higher plane. Maugham qualifies that there must also be art:

A real person, however eminent, is for the most part too insignificant for the purposes of fiction. The complete character, the result of elaboration rather than of invention, is art, and life in the raw, as we know, is only its material.

Illustrating the unaccountability of human behavior (for how could he endeavor to account for it?), "Maugham" remains a detached observer of life. Critics have wished for more poetry, loftier flights of imagination, more sympathy for his characters, and even occasional indirection; the lack of these things constitutes the limitation of Maugham's style. Rejecting both the atmospheric Romanticism of his predecessors and the exhaustive modernism of his contemporaries, Maugham's short stories do not seek to penetrate either landscape or life. His reader, like his narrator, may experience admiration, annoyance, disgust, or pity for the characters, but he does not share or become immersed in their emotions. This point of view of a calm, ordinary man, so unusual for the twentieth century, is instructive, teaching careful and clear consideration of life's possibilities, its casualties and successes, banalities and gifts. In this way, objective understanding is increased by reading Maugham much as intersubjective facilities are by reading James Joyce, D. H. Lawrence, or the other moderns.

Other major works

NOVELS: *Liza of Lambeth*, 1897; *The Making of a Saint*, 1898; *The Hero*, 1901; *Mrs. Craddock*, 1902; *The Merry-Go-Round*, 1904; *The Bishop's Apron*, 1906; *The Magician*, 1908; *Of Human Bondage*, 1915; *The Moon and Sixpence*, 1919; *The Painted Veil*, 1925; *Cakes and Ale*, 1930; *The Narrow Corner*, 1932; *Theatre*, 1937; *Christmas Holiday*, 1939; *Up at the Villa*, 1941; *The Hour Before Dawn*, 1942; *The Razor's Edge*, 1944; *Then and Now*, 1946; *Catalina*, 1948; *Selected Novels*, 1953.

PLAYS: *A Man of Honour*, 1903; *Lady Frederick*, 1907; *The Explorer*, 1908; *Jack Straw*, 1908; *Mrs. Dot*, 1908; *The Noble Spaniard*, 1909; *Penelope*, 1909; *Smith*, 1909; *Loaves and Fishes*, 1911; *The Land of Promise*, 1913; *Landed Gentry*, 1913; *The Tenth Man*, 1913; *Caroline*, 1916 (as *The Unattainable*, 1923); *Our Betters*, 1917; *Caesar's Wife*, 1919; *Home and Beauty*, 1919 (also as *Too Many Husbands*); *The Unknown*, 1920; *The Circle*, 1921; *East of Suez*, 1922; *The Constant Wife*, 1926; *The Letter*, 1927; *The Sacred Flame*, 1928; *The Breadwinner*, 1930; *For Services Rendered*, 1932; *Sheppey*, 1933; *Collected Plays*, 1952 (3 volumes, including 18 plays).

NONFICTION: *The Land of the Blessed Virgin*, 1905 (also known as *Andalusia*, 1920); *On a Chinese Screen*, 1922; *The Gentleman in the Parlour*, 1930; *Don Fernando*, 1935; *The Summing Up*, 1938; *Books and You*, 1940; *France at War*, 1940; *Strictly Personal*, 1941; *Great Novelists and Their Novels*, 1948; *A Writer's Notebook*, 1949; *The Writer's Point of View*, 1951; *The Vagrant Mood*, 1952; *The Travel Books*, 1955; *Points of View*, 1958; *Purely for My Pleasure*, 1962; *Selected Prefaces and Introductions*, 1963.

Bibliography

Burt, Forrest D. *W. Somerset Maugham*. Boston: Twayne, 1985. This volume asserts that Maugham has long been an underestimated and neglected writer in terms of an assessment of his value and position in the literary canon and that there has been a more serious appraisal of his works since his death. Includes a chronology, a basic biography (in the early chapters), and a focus on the literary works from a critical standpoint.

Calder, Robert L. *W. Somerset Maugham and the Quest for Freedom*. London: Heine-
mann, 1972. This impressive study primarily emphasizes critical and thematic
assessment of the novels, breaking them down into categories of genre ("Novels
of Apprenticeship") or categories of thematic focus ("Artist-Hero Novels"; "Aspects of the Maugham *Persona*"). This work also exhaustively delineates several
of the important issues with which Maugham was concerned—that is, the absolute importance of money, the nature of marriage and bondage, the interest in
Indian mysticism (*The Razor's Edge*), and the nature of individual freedom. Also
provided are four informative appendices, including material on Maugham's role
in Allied espionage (1917) and a discussion of recurring images of bondage and
freedom in his works.

Cordell, Richard A. *Somerset Maugham: A Writer for All Seasons*. 2d ed. Bloomington: Indiana University Press, 1969. Cordell, who was Maugham's friend and confidant, provides an in-depth examination of the writer's life and works. Cordell
disputes the labelling of Maugham as "enigmatic" and "inscrutable," charging
instead that Maugham was just the opposite. This volume includes a substantial
section devoted to a discussion of Maugham's short stories along with chapters on
three of the "autobiographical novels," plays, other fiction, and critical reception.

Curtis, Anthony. *Somerset Maugham*. Windsor, England: Profile Books, 1982. An excellent forty-seven page pamphlet-sized volume that provides both an intensive
and lucid overview of the writer, his genres, his life, and his themes. It also clearly
distinguishes Maugham as preeminently a writer of short fiction. An insightful
and brief introduction to the author that also includes an index of his available
short stories.

Jonas, Klaus W., ed. *The Maugham Enigma*. New York: Citadel Press, 1954. An informative background collection of articles, essays, biographical notes, and book
reviews by numerous authors on Maugham. It covers the author as dramatist,
novelist, "teller of tales," and essayist and it also includes some interesting reminiscences and notes on writing from Maugham himself.

Naik, M. K. *W. Somerset Maugham*. Norman: University of Oklahoma Press, 1953.
The underlying concept of Naik's approach to a discussion of Maugham's life and
work is that it reveals a basic "conflict between the two strains of cynicism and
humanitarianism" in the author himself. Naik begins with a definition of this
conflict, discusses biographical data, and then examines the various genres of the
author in terms of his overall premise.

Kenneth Funsten
(Revised by *Sherry Morton-Mollo*)

GUY DE MAUPASSANT

Born: Château de Miromesnil, France; August 5, 1850
Died: Paris, France; July 6, 1893

Principal short fiction

La Maison Tellier, 1881 (*Madame Tellier's Establishment and Short Stories*, 1910); *Mademoiselle Fifi*, 1882 (*Mademoiselle Fifi and Other Stories*, 1922); *Clair de lune*, 1883; *Contes de la bécasse*, 1883; *Les Sœurs Rondoli*, 1884 (*The Sisters Rondoli and Other Stories*, 1923); *Miss Harriet*, 1884 (*Miss Harriet and Other Stories*, 1923); *Contes du jour et de la nuit*, 1885 (*Day and Night Stories*, 1924); *Toine*, 1885 (*Toine and Other Stories*, 1922); *Yvette*, 1885 (*Yvette and Other Stories*, 1905); *Monsieur Parent*, 1886 (*Monsieur Parent and Other Stories*, 1909); *La Petite Rogue*, 1886 (*Little Rogue and Other Stories*, 1924); *Le Horla*, 1887 (*The Horla and Other Stories*, 1903); *Le Rosier de Madame Husson*, 1888; *L'Inutile Beauté*, 1890 (*Useless Beauty and Other Stories*, 1911); *Eighty-eight Short Stories*, 1930; *Eighty-eight More Stories*, 1932; *Complete Short Stories*, 1955.

Other literary forms

Although he became famous above all for his well-crafted short stories, Guy de Maupassant also wrote poems, plays, and three successful novels: *Une Vie* (1883; *A Woman's Life*, 1888), *Bel-Ami* (1885; English translation, 1889), and *Pierre et Jean* (1888; *Pierre and Jean*, 1890). His preface to *Pierre and Jean* has attracted a considerable amount of attention over the years because it reveals the profound influence that Gustave Flaubert exerted on Maupassant's development as a writer. Maupassant was not, however, a major literary theoretician, and many critics have agreed with Henry James's perceptive comment that Maupassant as a "philosopher in his composition is perceptibly inferior to the story-teller." Maupassant also wrote several volumes of fascinating letters to such eminent writers as Flaubert, Ivan Turgenev, and Émile Zola.

Achievements

Maupassant is generally considered to be the most significant French short-story writer. Unlike other important nineteenth century French prose writers such as Honoré de Balzac and Flaubert who are better known for their novels than for their short stories, Maupassant created an extensive corpus of short stories that reveals an aesthetically pleasing combination of wit, irony, social criticism, idealism, and psychological depth. Although his short stories deal with readily identifiable situations and character types in France during the 1870's and 1880's, they explore universal themes such as the horrors of war and the fear of death, hypocrisy, the search for happiness, the exploitation of women, and contrasts between appearance and reality. His characters illustrate the extraordinary diversity in modern society, from prostitutes to adulterous husbands and wives and from peasants to aristocrats. Even during his lifetime, his short stories were appreciated both within and beyond the borders of France. He had the special ability of conveying to readers the universal elements in everyday situations. He used wit and an understated style in order to create aesthetically pleasing dialogues. His work exerted a profound influence on many major short-story writers, including Thomas Mann, Katherine Mansfield, and Luigi Pirandello.

Biography

Henri-René-Albert Guy de Maupassant was born on August 5, 1850, in the Château de Miromesnil in the French province of Normandy. He was the first child of Gustave and Laure de Maupassant. Guy de Maupassant spent his childhood and adolescence in Normandy. His parents grew to dislike each other intensely, and they eventually separated. Laure did not want Gustave to play any role in rearing either Guy or their second son, Hervé. She was an overly protective mother, and she did not allow Guy to attend school until he was thirteen years old. Until he became a student in 1863 at a Catholic seminary school, Guy's only teacher was the local parish priest. Guy became indifferent to religion, and at the age of seventeen he was expelled from the seminary school because of behavior judged to be unacceptable by his teachers. He completed his secondary studies in 1869 at a boarding school in Rouen.

In 1867, Maupassant met the celebrated novelist Flaubert, whom Laure had known for almost twenty years. Some fanciful critics have suggested that Flaubert was not only Maupassant's literary mentor but also his biological father. Although there is no evidence to support this hypothesis, Maupassant did react with extreme displeasure and perhaps with excessive sensitivity to the frequently repeated remark that Flaubert had been his father.

Maupassant began his law studies at the University of Paris in 1869, but with the outbreak of hostilities in the Franco-Prussian War in 1870, he enlisted in the French army. He served in Normandy, where he experienced firsthand the humiliation of the French defeat and the severity of the Prussian occupation. After his return to civilian life, he became a clerk in the Naval Ministry. He remained in government service until 1880, when he resigned his position in the Ministry of Public Instruction so that he could dedicate all of his efforts to writing.

Starting in 1875, Flaubert became Maupassant's literary mentor. At first, Maupassant slavishly imitated his master's style, but gradually he began to explore themes and situations such as the tragic effect of war and occupation on French society, which Flaubert had chosen not to treat. Maupassant received further intellectual stimulation by frequenting Flaubert's weekly literary salon, which was attended at various times by such eminent writers as Turgenev, Zola, Alphonse Daudet, and Edmond de Goncourt. In late 1879, Maupassant and five other French authors agreed that each would write a short story on the Prussian occupation of France for a volume to be entitled *Les Soirées de Médan* (1880; the evenings in Médan). Maupassant's contribution was "Boule de Suif." The other contributors to this volume were

Zola, Joris-Karl Huysmans, Paul Alexis, Henry Céard, and Léon Hennique. Almost all critics agreed with Flaubert's assessment that "Boule de Suif" was "a masterpiece of composition and wit." This extremely favorable reaction encouraged Maupassant to become a very prolific writer of short stories and novels. During the 1880's, he earned a good living as a writer, but gradually his health began to deteriorate as a result of syphilis, which he had contracted in the 1870's and which his doctors had failed to diagnose until it was too late for him to be cured. On January 2, 1892, Maupassant tried to kill himself. After this unsuccessful suicide attempt, he was committed to a psychiatric asylum at Passy, in Paris, France, where he died on July 6, 1893.

Analysis

Although his active literary career began in 1880 and lasted only ten years, Guy de Maupassant was nevertheless an extraordinarily productive writer whose short stories dealt with such diverse themes as war, prostitution, marital infidelity, religion, madness, cultural misunderstanding between the French and the English, and life in the French provinces, especially his native Normandy. His short stories varied greatly in length from only a few pages to more than forty pages. His short stories are extremely well organized, and there is much psychological depth in his insights into the complex motivations for his characters' behavior. His work explores the full spectrum of French society. He describes characters from various professions and social classes with sensitivity and humor. Although Maupassant was himself very pessimistic, rather chauvinistic, and also distrustful of organized religions, his characters do not simply mirror his own philosophy. He wrote about topics of interest to his French readers in the 1880's, but he also enriched his short stories with psychological and moral insights, which continue to fascinate readers born several generations after his death. Maupassant examined how ordinary Frenchmen and Frenchwomen, with whom readers can readily identify, reacted to unexpected social, historical, moral, and business situations. His short stories mirror life because in fiction as in life things never turn out exactly as one thinks they will.

Although Maupassant wrote on a wide variety of topics, the major recurring themes in his short stories are war, prostitution, and madness. Why Maupassant explored these themes instead of others is problematic. In their excellent biographies of Maupassant, Paul Ignotus and Francis Steegmuller showed that the Prussian occupation of France had been a traumatic experience for him. Even his mentor Flaubert realized that Maupassant was promiscuous, and he warned his disciple of the physical consequences of sleeping with prostitutes. By the middle of the 1880's, Maupassant began to write very frequently about characters who fear losing their minds. This would, in fact, happen to Maupassant himself, but not until late 1891. Although it is tempting to interpret Maupassant's short stories in the light of his personal experiences, such an approach is not very useful for literary criticism. Other Frenchmen of his day were scarred by the Prussian occupation of France or frequented houses of prostitution, but they did not possess his literary talents. His biography may well explain his preference for certain themes, but it does not enable readers to appreciate the true value of his short stories.

Maupassant wrote more than two hundred short stories. Even in a relatively long essay, it would be impossible to do justice to all of his major works. This article will examine four representative short stories in order to give readers a sense of Maupassant's refined artistry. These works are "La Folle" ("The Madwoman"), "Boule de Suif," "La Maison Tellier" ("Madame Tellier's Establishment"), and "Le Horla" ("The Horla").

"The Madwoman" and "Boule de Suif" both describe personal tragedies that can result from war and military occupation. These two short stories are significantly different in length. In Albert-Marie Schmidt's 1973 edition of Maupassant's short stories, "The Madwoman" is four pages long, whereas "Boule de Suif" fills forty pages. Both, however, describe women who are victimized by the arbitrary abuse of power during the Prussian occupation of France. The structure of "The Madwoman" consists of a story within a story. The narrator is an unnamed man from Normandy. He tells his listener, Mathieu d'Endolin, that hearing woodcocks reminds him of a terrible injustice that took place during the Prussian occupation of Normandy. This odd reference to woodcocks is explained only at the end of this short story. The narrator speaks of a woman who went mad from grief after her father, husband, and baby had all died within a month of one another in 1855. She went to bed, became delirious, and screamed whenever anyone tried to take her out of her bed. The narrator is a sensitive man who feels pity for this woman. He wonders if she still thinks about the dead or if her mind is now "motionless." Her isolation from the world is absolute. She knows nothing about the world outside her room. During the Prussian occupation of the town in which the narrator and this madwoman live, German soldiers were assigned to the various houses. The madwoman and her maid had to receive twelve soldiers.

For reasons that are totally incomprehensible to the narrator, the German officer in charge of the soldiers in this house convinced himself that the madwoman would not talk to him because she held Germans in contempt. He orders her to come downstairs, but the madwoman cannot understand his demand. He interprets her silence as a personal insult, and he orders his soldiers to carry the woman in her bed toward a nearby forest. For nine months, the narrator learned nothing about the fate of this woman. During the fall hunting season, he went to the forest and shot a few woodcocks. When he went to retrieve these woodcocks, he found a human skeleton on a bed. The awful truth is revealed to him. The madwoman had died from exposure to the cold, and "the wolves had devoured her." The narrator does not end this tale by denouncing the Germans but rather by praying that "our sons will never again see war" lest other innocent victims suffer similar tragedies. Readers from any country or generation can identify with the hopes of his narrator. Readers and the narrator know all too well that many innocent victims have been killed in war. "The Madwoman" is a powerful short story that expresses one's revulsion over the death of any innocent victim of war.

Although his most famous short story, "Boule de Suif," also deals with the horrors of war, "Boule de Suif" is a much more complicated tale, and it has eleven major characters. At the beginning of "Boule de Suif," Maupassant evokes the terror felt by many French citizens who came to fear the abuse of power by the occupying soldiers. This short story begins in the Norman city of Rouen. The Prussian general in Rouen grants ten inhabitants of this city special permission to travel by coach from Rouen to Dieppe. Their intention is to reach the port of Le Havre from which they can leave France for safety in England. Their motivation is clear. They hope to lead better lives in a free country.

The ten travelers are from different social classes. There are three married couples. Mr. and Mrs. Loiseau are wine merchants whose integrity has been questioned by many of their customers. Mr. and Mrs. Carré-Lamodon are well-to-do owners of cotton mills, but Maupassant describes Mr. Carré-Lamodon as a hypocritical politician. The Count and Countess of Bréville are very rich, but their noble title is of questionable value. Rumor has it that King Henry IV of France had impregnated an ancestor of the Brévilles. In order to avoid an unpleasant situation, he made the lady's husband a count and appointed him as the governor of Normandy. This placated the husband. In the coach, there are also two nuns, an inoffensive leftist named Cornudet who is more interested in drinking beer than in reforming society, and finally a prostitute named Boule de Suif. Her name, which means "ball of tallow," evokes her rotund figure. Although the three respectable couples feel superior to Boule de Suif, they do not hesitate to accept food from her once they realize that she alone had brought food for this trip.

When their coach stops in the village of Tôtes, a German officer orders the ten passengers to stay in the local inn until Boule de Suif agrees to sleep with him. As a patriotic Frenchwoman, she refuses to yield to this blackmail. The next day she goes to church and asks God to grant her the strength to remain faithful to her moral principles and to France. She assumes that the other passengers will support her, but she is wrong. The married couples and the two nuns conspire to put pressure on Boule de Suif. The elder of the two nuns is especially reprehensible because she distorts the clear meaning of several biblical passages in order to convince Boule de Suif that it would be praiseworthy of her to sleep with the Prussian officer. Boule de Suif feels abandoned by her fellow citizens and by two representatives of her church. In despair, she yields to the Prussian's ultimatum. The three married couples and the two nuns celebrate this action by drinking champagne. Their insensitivity and general boorishness are obvious to the reader, who feels much sympathy for the victim. As they are traveling from Tôtes to Dieppe, Boule de Suif begins to weep, and the others take out their newly purchased picnic baskets filled with cheese, sausage, and bread, but they do not offer to share their food with Boule de Suif, who had been so generous during the earlier trip. A silent rage builds within her, but the proud Boule de Suif says nothing. She realizes that they are unworthy of her.

Ever since its publication in 1880, "Boule de Suif" has been considered Maupassant's masterpiece. Its structure is admirable, and the parallel scenes of eating in the coach serve to reinforce in the reader's mind Boule de Suif's alienation from the other passengers. Her patriotism causes her to sacrifice herself for them, but now they want nothing to do with her. Both "Boule de Suif" and "The Madwoman" reveal Maupassant's artistry in describing the unpredictable and destructive effect of war and occupation on innocent victims.

Although the title character in "Boule de Suif" is a prostitute, the story's main theme is war and not prostitution. In Maupassant's equally celebrated short story "Madame Tellier's Establishment," the principal theme is prostitution, but Maupassant develops this theme with much sensitivity and wit. Madame Tellier runs a bordello, but she is a shrewd businesswoman who does a fine job in marketing. She hires prostitutes representing the different types of feminine beauty "so that each customer could find there the satisfaction" of his sexual fantasies. The men in her town feel very much at ease in her bordello, and she treats her prostitutes and clients as members of her extended family. One Friday evening, however, the routine is disrupted when her customers see a sign with the words "Closed Because of First Communion" at the entrance of her business. Madame Tellier has decided to close her bordello for a day so that she and her five employees can attend the first Communion of her niece, who lives in the rural community of Virville.

The train ride to Virville contains a marvelously comic scene. Seated with Madame Tellier and her five prostitutes are a traveling salesman and an elderly peasant couple, who are transporting three ducks not in cages. The husband and wife watch with disbelief as the five prostitutes take turns sitting on the salesman's lap while playing with the ducks. The salesman then takes out brightly colored garters, and he cajoles the prostitutes and even Madame Tellier into allowing him to place the garters on their legs. All of this is accompanied by much laughter. The peasants cannot believe their eyes. As they get off the train with their ducks, the wife tells her husband: "They are sluts on their way to the wicked city of Paris." She is partially correct, but their actual destination is the nearby village of Virville.

After they have breakfast on her brother's farm, Madame Tellier leads her prostitutes into the local church for the first Communion services. The parishioners have never before seen such gaudily dressed women. The worshipers find it difficult to concentrate on the Mass. The prostitute named Rosa thinks of her first Communion; she begins to cry, and her tears become contagious. First the other prostitutes, then Madame Tellier, and finally all the adults in the church begin to weep uncontrollably, and the tears do not end until the elderly priest has distributed Communion to the last child. He is so moved by their tears, which he interprets as the expression of profound religious emotion, that he decides to give a sermon. For him, this is "a sublime miracle" that has made him the "happiest priest in the diocese." He speaks of the "visible faith" and "profound piety" of the out-of-town visitors. Although this priest would most probably have expressed himself differently had he known of their profession, readers cannot question his sincerity or the reality of the religious emotions experienced by the worshipers in this small church.

After the Mass, life returns quickly to normal for the ever-practical Madame Tellier. She tells her brother that they must take the midafternoon train so that she can reopen her business within a few hours. That evening, there is a festive atmosphere in her bordello. Much champagne is drunk, and Madame Tellier is unusually generous. She charges her customers only six francs for a bottle of champagne instead of the normal rate of ten francs. This is a well-structured short story in which scenes in the bordello precede and follow the first Communion sequence. Maupassant describes characters from widely different professions and social classes in a nonjudgmental manner. The refined artistry and style of "Madame Tellier's Establishment" may explain why Thomas Mann, who was himself renowned for his short prose works, concluded that Maupassant "would be regarded for centuries as one of the greatest masters of the short story."

"The Madwoman," "Boule de Suif," and "Madame Tellier's Establishment" are all effective third-person narratives, but Maupassant also experimented with other narrative techniques. In 1886, he wrote two versions of a short story that he entitled "The Horla." Both versions describe the mental illness of a Frenchman who believes that an invisible being called "the Horla" has taken possession of his mind. In the first version, a psychiatrist named Dr. Marrande asks seven colleagues to listen to a patient who is sure that the Horla entered his locked bedroom, drank milk and water, and then took over his personality. The psychiatric patient assures his listeners that he "saw" the Horla: he looked in a mirror but did not see his own image. After the patient stops talking, Dr. Marrande makes a very strange remark for a psychiatrist: "I do not know if this man is mad or if we are both mad or if our successor has actually arrived." The first version of "The Horla" is ineffective for several reasons. First, it lacks a clear focus because both Dr. Marrande and his patient speak of their reactions to the Horla. Second, Dr. Marrande's comment that he may have gone mad does not inspire much confidence in him. Third, the very nature of this narration does not enable readers to experience the gradual development of the patient's psychiatric problems.

Maupassant wisely decided to revise this short story into a first-person narrative presented in the forms of diary entries written by the patient himself. In his first entry, dated May 8, the diarist seems to be a calm individual who mentions in passing that a Brazilian boat has just passed by his house, which overlooks the Seine. He soon develops a fever, has trouble sleeping, and writes of a recurring nightmare. He dreams that a being is on his bed and is trying to strangle him. This nightmare returns several nights in a row. For the month of June, he is on an extended vacation, and he considers himself cured. When he returns home, however, he has new nightmares. This time, a being is trying to stab him. Although he keeps his bedroom locked at night, a spirit always drinks the water and the milk left in carafes by his bed. Gradually, he comes to accept the presence of this thirsty spirit. By mid-August, however, he concludes that a spirit has taken over his mind. The spirit orders him to read a book and an article on invisible spirits from Brazil that like to drink water and milk. In a desperate effort to free himself from the Horla, he traps the Horla in his bedroom and then burns down his house. It does not occur to him to think of his servants, who are asleep in his house. They die in the fire, and the diary does not indicate what happened to the diarist. Has he been arrested for murder or has he been committed to an insane asylum? In his very last entry, the diarist assures the reader that if the Horla is still alive, he will have to commit suicide. The second version of "The Horla" is very effective because it enables the reader to experience the gradual transformation of the diarist from a sensible person into a terrified and self-destructive individual who no longer appreciates the value of human life.

Although some critics have hypothesized that the second version of "The Horla" somehow prefigures the serious psychological problems that Maupassant himself would develop five years later, this is a fanciful interpretation. Maupassant did not try to kill himself until January, 1892, and he was still perfectly lucid when he wrote "The Horla" in 1886. This first-person narrative is a powerful short story that enables readers to experience the process by which a person can develop a serious mental illness. "The Horla" had a profound effect on generations of readers. In 1938, Arnold Zweig wrote of his recollection of this short story, which he had read years earlier:

> I still remember my emotion and admiration. I do not even need to close my eyes to see the white ship passing his country-house from which the strange guest, the split ego, invaded the life of the sick person.

Maupassant is still admired for his well-structured and beautifully written short stories. He is generally considered to be the best French short-story writer, although since the early years of the twentieth century, his works have been held in much higher esteem outside France (especially in England, the United States, and Germany) than in his homeland. It is not clear why so many French critics have been less than enthusiastic in their assessment of his short stories. Perhaps the critical standing of Maupassant would be higher than it is today among French critics if he had explored a wider variety of themes. Readers should not forget that Maupassant died at the relatively young age of forty-two. His short literary career of only ten years did not give him sufficient time to develop the extraordinary breadth and diversity of a writer such as Victor Hugo, whose literary career spanned more than six decades. Despite the relatively limited number of themes that he explored in his short stories, Maupassant wrote short stories of such stylistic beauty and psychological depth that they still continue to please readers and to inspire creativity in short-story writers from many different countries.

Other major works
NOVELS: *Une Vie*, 1883 (*A Woman's Life*, 1888); *Bel-Ami*, 1885 (English translation, 1889); *Pierre et Jean*, 1888 (*Pierre and Jean*, 1890); *Forte comme la mort*, 1889 (*Strong as Death*, 1899); *Notre cœur*, 1890 (*The Human Heart*, 1890).
POETRY: *Des Vers*, 1880 (*Romance in Rhyme*, 1903).
NONFICTION: *Au Soleil*, 1884 (*In the Sunlight*, 1903); *Sur l'eau*, 1888 (*Afloat*, 1889);

La Vie errante, 1890 (*In Vagabondia,* 1903).

MISCELLANEOUS: *The Life Work of Henri René Guy de Maupassant,* 1903 (17 volumes); *The Works of Guy de Maupassant,* 1923-1929 (10 volumes); *Lettres de Guy de Maupassant à Gustave Flaubert,* 1951.

Bibliography

Artinian, Artine. *Maupassant Criticism in France, 1880-1940.* New York: Russell & Russell, 1941. Despite its title, this important book explores critical reactions to Maupassant's works both in France and outside France. Artinian also includes thoughtful comments on Maupassant by some of the most important American and European writers of the 1930's. An essential work for all critics interested in Maupassant. Contains a very thorough bibliography.

Ignotus, Paul. *The Paradox of Maupassant.* London: University of London Press, 1966. In this fascinating but subjective interpretation of Maupassant's genius, Ignotus believes that Maupassant was a paradoxical writer because he was obsessed with sex and was nevertheless a creative genius. At times, Ignotus' arguments are not terribly convincing, but this book does discuss very well Maupassant's ambivalent attitudes toward his literary mentor Gustave Flaubert.

Steegmuller, Francis. *Maupassant: A Lion in the Path.* New York: Random House, 1949. In this extremely well-documented biography of Maupassant, Steegmuller described very well both the nature of Flaubert's influence on Maupassant and the contacts of Maupassant with such major writers as Émile Zola, Ivan Turgenev, and Henry James.

Sullivan, Edward. *Maupassant the Novelist.* Princeton, N.J.: Princeton University Press, 1945. This volume is a very thoughtful analysis of Maupassant's novels. Sullivan argues persuasively that Maupassant's novels do deserve as much critical attention as his more famous short stories have received over the years. Contains a solid bibliography.

Wallace, Albert H. *Guy de Maupassant.* New York: Twayne, 1973. Wallace presents an excellent analysis of recurring themes in Maupassant's major works. He discusses with much subtlety Maupassant's representations of war and madness. This well-annotated book is an essential introduction to the thematic study of Maupassant's major works.

Edmund J. Campion

CHRISTOPH MECKEL

Born: Berlin, Germany; June 12, 1935

Principal short fiction

Im Land der Umbramauten, 1961; *Tullipan,* 1965; *Die Noticen des Feuerwerkers Christopher Magalan,* 1966; *Die Gestalt am Ende des Grundstücks,* 1975 (*The Figure on the Boundary Line,* 1983); *Licht,* 1978; *Suchbild: Über meinen Vater,* 1980 (*Image for Investigation About My Father,* 1987); *Ein roter Faden: Gesammelte Erzählungen,* 1983; *Der wahre Muftoni,* 1982; *Plunder,* 1986; *Snow Creatures and Other Stories,* 1990; *Zuend and Other Stories,* 1990.

Other literary forms

Christoph Meckel first gained renown and critical acclaim for his poetry appearing in such collections as *Nebelhörner* (1959), *Wildnisse* (1962), and *Säure* (1978); he is continually praised as one of the leading poets in contemporary German literature. Furthermore, his graphic art has appeared in more than thirty one-man exhibitions on three continents and has been published in various cycles as woodcuts, engravings, and drawings under several titles, such as *Moël* (1959), *Das Meer* (1965), and *Anabasis* (1982). He has also written several radio plays and essays.

Achievements

Meckel has been most highly regarded for his poetry, having received the prestigious Rainer Maria Rilke Prize for Poetry (1979) and the Georg Trakl Prize of the City of Salzburg (1982), as well as a dozen other prizes or subventions for his writings and honors for his graphic art. In fact, as early as the 1950's, he began creating prose fiction, as well as poetry and visual art. Meckel's early prose works drew curious interest and mixed critical acclaim, earning for Meckel the reputation of a fantast, a comic, even that of a dilettante. Individual short stories were initially placed with various periodicals or appeared in special printings with small publishing houses. The success of his more serious fiction, such as *Licht* and *Suchbild,* has caused him to be recognized as a major writer, and his works have regularly appeared with major West German publishers.

Biography

Christoph Meckel was born in Berlin on June 12, 1935, son of the German poet Eberhard Meckel. His early years were spent in the warmth of a loving and well-to-do family, but within ten years he had experienced the collapse of the Third Reich, and with it that of his stable family life. While waiting for his father's return from a French prisoner-of-war camp in North Africa, the family became refugees, frequently moving between Berlin, Erfurt, and Freiburg. Despite poverty and a contentious father, Meckel survived the tumultuous early postwar years.

Though standard biographies report that he studied painting and graphics at the art academies in Freiburg (1954-1955) and in Munich (1956), he admits in *Bericht zur Entstehung einer Weltkomödie* (1985) that he was duly unimpressed with the quality of instruction and thus taught himself the intricacies of his craft through patience and experience. With the exception of the Near East, he has traveled extensively throughout the world: besides Munich, Paris, and Rome (and his alternating residences in Berlin and southeastern France), he has lived for brief intervals in the United States, Mexico, Africa, Australia, and Southeast Asia. These travels are mirrored in the majority of his works as—in his own term—"vagabondage," the wandering from one landscape or climate to another.

Although Meckel has not written an autobiography as such, several of his works seem to be based on events or experiences from his life. *Suchbild*, for example, relates his childhood, his experiences as a youth at the end of World War II, his relationship with a distraught father, and the eventual literary successes which overshadowed the father's earlier poetry. If the biological father is here rejected, Meckel discovers a more suitable progenitor in *Nachricht für Baratynski* (1981); the forgotten nineteenth century Russian poet is resurrected through biography and fiction as literary kin to Meckel to clarify the latter's aesthetics and support him in his undertaking. (Incidentally, *Nachricht für Baratynski*, while composed of fictional elements, can best be understood as an essay, rather than as a "story" or literary prose fiction.)

Further biographical information can be gathered in the *Bericht zur Entstehung einer Weltkomödie*. Like other works by Meckel, this so-called report on the origins of a world comedy is not easily catagorized in literary terms. While it purports to be a biography of Meckel the graphic artist (and pointedly not that of Meckel the writer), it is scarcely the objective work that a "report" would insinuate, and it is woefully incomplete as a biography: names and dates are frequently omitted, and the entire narration is superficially divided into three parts, the "report," followed by "notebooks" and an "appendix." Indeed, the reader finds mention of the external events of Meckel's life, his development as a graphic artist, his methods and ultimate goal: to create a World Comedy consisting of nine hundred etchings (*Radierungen*), from the origins of the early collection *Moël* in 1959 to the completion of *Anabasis* in 1982—a period of twenty-five-years.

Still, the literary aspects, the taste of fiction, is familiar to Meckel's readers. He reproduces in words and images the themes which are evident in his visual art: the moods, weather, people and objects, personal recollections, and historical events which underlie his work. This prose piece, like *Suchbild*, can be read as flawed autobiography—though the style and narrative techniques, the evocation of subjectivity through brief anecdotes and mood pictures make a "good story." As autobiography it is disappointingly incomplete; as a report it is fragmented and too subjective. Yet as literature it is evocative, revealing, creating character, mood, and impact which engage the reader. With its irony and humor, *Bericht zur Entstehung einer Weltkomödie* is similar to another of Meckel's fictional biographies, the notes of Christopher Magalan, the fireworks maker.

Analysis

Christoph Meckel's preoccupations with both graphic art and literature have proven to be mutually beneficial. In preparation for an illustration, for example, Meckel collects moods and events in written form as the basis for his visual art. Conversely, his literature benefits from the images that he has seen or "dreamed," as he so often expresses it. To the repeated frustration of literary critics and scholars, Meckel's prose works also elude traditional literary categories. Each is frequently a composite of his complete artistic expression: a prose work may be introduced or illustrated with his own engravings and further enhanced by the inclusion of poems or songs. Especially in his longer fiction, Meckel has insistently avoided the term "novel," preferring instead the broader category of "narration," which allows him more auctorial freedom to combine poetry and graphics with his prose.

Meckel and his works are often characterized as clever, witty, and inventive. Perhaps the most concise description of Meckel's traits comes from his translator and collaborator, Christopher Middleton, who emphasizes Meckel's exuberance. This term is meant to convey not only Meckel's enthusiasm for writing but also his inventiveness and the resultant variety of characters, themes, and forms. A common misconception of Meckel's works centers on precisely this exuberance, this playful aspect of much of his prose. Here several critics have noted that this abundance of imagination often results in no more than interesting tableaux, devoid of a cohesive plot and sustained tension. Others have complained about the aspect of "play," finding no redeeming value in these fanciful creations. In Meckel's defense, this imaginative world is created spontaneously, and, when successful, encourages a similar spontaneity of thought and action on the part of the reader. The world of routine and boredom suddenly is infused with new life; much in the traditional Romantic sense, each reader can create his or her own world through imagination and active participation. It is in this vein that a reader can begin to appreciate Meckel's unique contribution to modern literature.

Meckel's short prose includes both the realistic and the tragic, as well as the fantastic and fanciful. The latter clearly are fictive; with the former, however, the temptation to consider them autobiographical is irresistible: indeed, they deal with writers or storytellers and are set in locations where Meckel himself has resided. This is the nature of his art: the stories are sensitive, seemingly based on personal experience, thus convincing—yet they must be recognized as fiction.

Meckel's first significant piece of short fiction, *Im Land der Umbramauten*, contains three short stories and twenty-one anecdotal prose pieces centering on the thoughts and deeds of Herr Ucht, a confessed magician. Ucht invents objects and scenarios, purportedly the title story of this volume. Here, in the land of the Umbramauts, the reader learns the geography, topography, characteristics, traditions, and myths—in short, everything one would wish to know in this imaginative travelogue, so reminiscent of Cornelius Tacitus' *Germania* (A.D. 98). Unusual features of this country include wandering mountains and lakes amid the generally barren landscape of a perpetual twilight, fierce winds and giant dogs which threaten the inhabitants. The pivotal chapter, placed exactly in the middle of the narration, concerns Sambai-Sambai, the wandering storyteller. His yarns captivate and entertain the Umbramauts yet also activate and engage their imaginations, much as Meckel himself attempts to do with this slim volume. Though these stories are the result of a clever and active fantasy, they are not, finally, memorable. They concern the magician's creations—wisps of fancy—not individual characters or events which might capture the reader's sympathy or interest, with which he might identify.

Still, noteworthy in this prose work are the descriptions of the artists, Ucht and Sambai-Sambai, and their function. They are storytellers, creators, magicians, who make life more interesting and thoughtful. Yet their responsibility does not end with the creation of their characters (as is repeated later in the story "Tullipan"). In short, authors must be completely aware of their characters' capabilities before they set them into the world, for otherwise they might inadvertently harm themselves or others.

Following this first major prose publication, Meckel wrote "Die Krähe" ("The Crow"), arguably the most popular and frequently anthologized of Meckel's short pieces. One fine summer day, the narrator happens upon a hunter in the forest, who is seeking to capture a tiger. Agreeing to help, the narrator soon learns that the tiger has metamorphosed himself into a bear, then into an elephant, a wolf, a black fox, and finally a man-sized crow. Eventually, the narrator meets and becomes friends with the crow; together they elude the hunter and make their way through the forests and villages. When they come to a city, however, the crow's unusual size attracts attention, and the two are chased through the streets by an unruly mob. Attempting one last transformation, the crow slowly becomes a huge black cat, blind and thus harmless. The city dwellers, overcome by suspicion and fear, stone the helpless cat to death, while the unharmed narrator quickly leaves the city, never to return. In "The Crow," Meckel's strength as a narrator is evident: characterized by simplicity of style, an innocent and magical narrative stance leads the reader into a fairy-tale world. This atmosphere of naïveté and innocence, the wondrous mood, are unexpectedly dashed by a grotesque scene of senseless murder, thus earning for the piece the designation as an anti-fairy-tale. Regardless of its literary categorization, the story's implications reflect a timeless moral, as well as a possible reference to contemporary world events.

Tullipan is literally a figment of the narrator's imagination—an invented personality through whom the author can live vicariously—who appears one day at the door. Though harmless and lovable, Tullipan is not a "mature" character; his refreshing innocence estranges him from the townspeople and the narrator. Though Tullipan is able to survive and live happily ever after in a remote castle, the townspeople and the narrator ultimately regret their loss.

Another artist-figure of note is outlined in *Die Noticen des Feuerwerkers Christopher Magalan*, a humorous encomium to the fictitious nineteenth century genius of fireworks. Magalan's brilliant career is cut short during an aerial display, when he suddenly disappears in smoke and flames; the worst is assumed, since he is never seen again. Magalan's biography, written by a certain C. E. McKell, is accompanied by original sketches and an interview with the scholar L. Kuchenfuchs. This playful sketch scarcely conceals its author, Christoph Meckel—in the guises of Christopher Magalan and C. E. McKell—while recalling the Romantic age, Meckel's true artistic and spiritual home.

A more serious investigation of life's meaning is presented in *The Figure on the Boundary Line*. Alone as the houseguest of an absent friend, the protagonist, a writer, observes a lone figure in the woods bordering his property. The writer discovers that this person, seemingly poor and hungry, is perfectly content, that he wants and needs nothing. Gradually, the writer becomes more deeply involved with this man's simple routine, spending more time each day on the border of the property, until one day he completely disappears with the unknown figure, leaving only his diary as a clue to his fate. Metaphorically speaking, both men live at the extreme, at the boundary of property and a complicated, modern life-style. It is precisely this life-style, from which the writer was originally recuperating, that the writer ultimately rejects when he joins the outsider's uncomplicated existence.

The appearance of *Licht* in 1978 marked a new departure for Meckel; this is the first serious narrative of extended length since the novel *Bockshorn* (1973). Its plot is simple: upon the discovery of a love letter from his companion Dole to an anonymous recipient, the narrator, Gil, sees his world destroyed. Both Gil and Dole, globe-trotting journalists dedicated to their careers, share their spare moments and thus create a separate world of love, hope, and trust. This world is dashed by the presence of the letter. Before Gil can accept and begin to reconstruct their relationship, he receives yet another letter, this one announcing the accidental death of Dole. Reviewers chastised Meckel for the lack of epic narration in the center of the story, while overlooking its necessity: the subjective memories of the narrator throughout the piece purposely clash with the objective reality of the love letter at the beginning and the death notice at the conclusion. Despite the negative reviews, this work established Meckel as a serious writer of prose fiction.

With his next work, *Suchbild*, Meckel enjoyed his greatest success. Perhaps his most ambitious, complex, and compelling work, this "wanted poster" is an attempt to identify his own deceased father, the poet Eberhard Meckel. Initially, the son recounts those many childhood memories which constitute his love for his father. Upon the discovery of his father's war diaries, however, Meckel realizes that the father had compromised his principles and become a conformist to Nazi ideology. The son's faith and trust are shattered, and he must find adequate means of expressing his loss. In addition to introductory quotes, his own engraving as frontispiece, the diary entries and his personal memories, Meckel expands the scope of the work by including an afterword, composed as a fairy tale; in it, the father as magician ultimately destroys the world he loves through thoughtless acts. This narration represents the high point of all those "father books" around 1980, in which children of Nazi sympathizers took their parents to task for betraying their professed ideals under pressure or from conviction.

Der wahre Muftoni provides a humorous respite for Meckel and his readers, following the two previous narratives. The dead brother of Susanne, the narrator, reappears as a diminutive figure reminiscent of Tom Thumb. As he grows to his former adult size, the two siblings become lovers and lead a scandalous life of glamour and adventure. The brother is a perfect charlatan and lovable thief, a "Muftoni." Finally, however, he begins to shrink, until he is no larger than Susanne's little finger. His final request is that he be placed in a bottle and cast out to sea—until he can return once again in adult size. While Meckel's story can be seen as a delightful parody of sensational adventure novelettes, the "immoral" freedom and spontaneity of the Muftoni inject vitality into an otherwise pedestrian tale.

As defined by Meckel, *Plunder* are those superfluous objects which inhabit one's world. Neither consumer items nor those with practical value, they are the useless, impractical mementos which one invests with value, and which in turn provide one's life with its distinctive meaning. These objects by their subjective appeal—for example, a mildewed spoon, tin soldiers long lost, a stolen bath towel from a favorite hotel—represent a healthy chaos in the ordered ennui of modern society. Interestingly, much of the book consists of anecdotes or stories that the narrator and his companion, Caroline, tell each other. Like the plunder mentioned above, these stories are unique, without utilitarian value, yet in their very telling they represent at once play, trust, mutual esteem, and affection between the man and woman. Aside from content and intent, the act of narration provides a valuable human bond between narrator and listener.

When asked why he writes, Meckel once replied that the best of all possible worlds was not good enough for him, that he wanted to create his own heaven on earth, and to communicate the fact that he was alive. This he has done, even in his less successful works. Though he has written short fiction as brief as a one-page anecdote and as long as a 120-page novelette, his most memorable works are those which engage the reader's sense of play or sympathy, his contemplation and involvement with his fictional world. Only through this shared spontaneity, this exuberance, can people actively create their own worlds and thus escape the stifling regimentation of everyday existence.

Other major works
NOVELS: *Bockshorn*, 1973; *Die Messingstadt*, 1991.
POETRY: *Tarnkappe*, 1956; *Nebelhörner*, 1959; *Wildnisse*, 1962; *Säure*, 1978; *Anabasis*, 1982; *Souterrain*, 1984; *Anzahlung auf ein Glas Wasser*, 1987; *Das Buch Shiralee*, 1989.
NONFICTION: *Nachricht für Baratynski*, 1981; *Bericht zur Entstehung einer Weltkomödie*, 1985.
MISCELLANEOUS: *Werkauswahl: Lyrik, Prosa, Hörspiel*, 1971.

Bibliography
Bedwell, Carol B. "Bread and Brilliance: Utility Versus Poetic Ecstasy in Meckel's

'Der Zünd.' " *Seminar: A Journal of Germanic Studies* 20 (November, 1984): 290-298. The author provides a close reading of an early story by Meckel and focuses on the creative process as one of its themes.

Grant, Alyth. "When Is Biography an Autobiography? Questions of Genre and Narrative Style in Christoph Meckel's *Suchbild.*" *Seminar: A Journal of Germanic Studies* 26 (September, 1990): 189-204. Grant finds that Meckel's *Suchbild* is a mixed genre work, that it not only presents his father's story but also reveals much about the author himself. An analysis of Meckel's narrative style reveals that he employs two distinct styles, one for the biographical and one for the autobiographical sections of the book.

Hanlin, Todd C. "A Biography for the 'New Sensibility': Christoph Meckel's Allegorical *Suchbild.*" *German Life and Letters* 39 (1986): 235-244. Hanlin discusses Meckel's *Suchbild* as a merging of two forms of biography, that of the artist and that of the parent, and sees the work both as an allegory for the behavior of the fathers during the Nazi period and an allusion to the potential danger in the "indifference" and "inertia" of the author's own contemporaries.

Rockwood, Heidi M. "Writing as a Magician's Game: The Strange Early World of Christoph Meckel." *Studies in Twentieth Century Literature* 8 (Spring, 1984): 197-210. Rockwood focuses on Meckel's use of the metaphor of "playing a game" in four of his short stories and concludes that the author, while recognizing its possible dangerous implications, nevertheless regards the element of play as essential for retaining one's "basic humanity."

Shapiro, David. "The Figure on the Boundary Line." *The New York Times Book Review*, November 25, 1984, 8. This review of the first book-length English translation of Meckel's work provides a good insight into a limited selection of the author's better known stories.

Todd C. Hanlin
(Revised by *Stella P. Rosenfeld*)

HERMAN MELVILLE

Born: New York, New York; August 1, 1819
Died: New York, New York; September 28, 1891

Principal short fiction

The Piazza Tales, 1856; *The Apple-Tree Table and Other Sketches*, 1922.

Other literary forms

Herman Melville's sixteen published books include novels, short stories, poetry, and sketches. He is best known for his novels, particularly *Moby Dick* (1851), *The Confidence Man* (1857), and *Billy Budd, Foretopman* (1924).

Achievements

By the middle of the twentieth century, names such as *Moby Dick* and Captain Ahab were well known in the popular culture of America. Yet, one must look to the 1920's and the revival in Melville's work (notably *Moby Dick*) to see the beginning of what came to be Melville's immense stature in American literature. His most significant works received little popular or critical acclaim in his lifetime. One reason for this may have been friction with nineteenth century American tastes. Problems also stemmed, however, from Melville's fascination with forces that seemed (to him) to lie below the placid optimism of his contemporary American culture. Readers were disturbed by the author's tendency to view outward appearances as pasteboard masks that concealed a truer, darker reality. It should come as no surprise that modern students sense an invitation to allegorize Melville's works. Many believe that Melville, himself, perceived life in a symbolic way.

Many of the short pieces that Melville wrote for various magazines represent conscious attempts, through symbol and irony, to express disturbing layers of meaning beneath a calm surface. In 1855-1856, Melville finished a novel, *The Confidence Man*, rendering a bleak view of the possibility of faith in the world as he knew it. Although Melville openly wrote verse throughout his life, the manuscript that would become his novella, *Billy Budd, Foretopman*, was packed away by his widow and not discovered until the 1920's.

Melville completed *Moby Dick* some forty years before Sigmund Freud began to penetrate the veneer of conventional surfaces in his quest for the causes of hysteria—the salient behavioral aberration of repressive nineteenth century Europe. Yet, Melville (like his contemporary Nathaniel Hawthorne) had already begun to probe beyond the level of mundane appearances in his fiction. Even though some of Melville's stories are lengthy by today's standards, the finest of them exhibit exceptional merit in the short-story genre. "Benito Cereno" and *Bartleby the Scrivener*, for example, reveal a rich complexity and density which rivals modern masterpieces of the form.

Biography

Herman Melville withdrew from school at the age of twelve after the death of his father. He worked in various jobs—in a fur and cap store (with his brother), in a bank, on a farm, and as a teacher in country schools. He made two early sea voyages, one on a merchant ship to Liverpool in 1839, and one to the South Seas aboard the whaler *Acushnet*, in 1841. After about eighteen months, Melville and a friend deserted the whaler, and Melville spent a month in the Taipi Valley on the island of Nuku Hiva. Melville escaped the island aboard an Australian whaler but was imprisoned when he and ten other crewmen refused service. Again, he escaped, spent some time on the island of Mooréa, then several months in Hawaii. Eventually, he joined the U.S. Navy and returned home in 1844.

Out of these early sea adventures came Melville's two successful early novels, *Typee: A Peep at Polynesian Life* (1846) and *Omoo: A Narrative of Adventures in the South Seas* (1847). His experiences aboard the whaling ships led to a novel that was not to be successful in his lifetime, *Moby Dick*. The failure of *Moby Dick* and *Pierre: Or, The Ambiguities* (1852) left Melville financially and morally drained, but he would continue to produce fiction for a while, including the short stories that were guardedly constructed to seem unruffling to the sensibilities of the time but carried submerged patterns and disturbing undertones.

While still in the limelight of his early success, Melville married Elizabeth Shaw, daughter of a Massachusetts chief justice. They were to have four children; three died in young adulthood and the eldest son committed suicide in his eighteenth year (1867).

Melville was continually plagued by doubt, unrest, and marital problems. His later years were spent trying to adjust to his decline in status and seeking a comfortable living. In 1856, his father-in-law subsidized Melville's travels to the Mediterranean, the Holy Land, and England, where he visited Nathaniel Hawthorne. Unable to secure a naval commission during the Civil War, Melville sold his estate in Massachusetts and settled in New York. Finally, in 1866, he became an inspector in the New York Custom House until, some twenty years later, an inheritance enabled him to retire. He died September 28, 1891, at the age of seventy-two.

Analysis

After the critical and commercial failure of *Moby Dick* and *Pierre*, Herman Melville, who was then supporting his wife and children, his mother, and his four sisters, was desperate for money. So when he received an invitation from *Putnam's Monthly Magazine* to contribute short stories at the rate of five dollars a page, he accepted. He also sold short stories to *Harper's New Monthly Magazine*. Both magazines, however, had very strict editorial policies banning any material which might conceivably offend even the most sensitive reader on moral, social, ethical, political, or religious grounds. This was a shattering limitation to Melville, whose deepest personal and artistic convictions were bound up in the defiant heroes and themes of highly unconventional metaphysical speculation of *Mardi and a Voyage Thither*,

Moby Dick, and *Pierre*. He genuinely questioned many of the ideas which, although they are freely debated today, were sacrosanct in the nineteenth century. These included the existence of a personal God outside the human spirit, the importance of material goods, the existence of absolute good and absolute evil, and the right of established civil and religious authorities to impose sanctions against those who expressed ideas that differed from the ideas of the majority. Obviously, neither *Putnam's Monthly Magazine* nor *Harper's New Monthly Magazine* would publish stories which dealt openly with opinions that would be objectionable to many of their readers. This left Melville in an apparently unresolvable dilemma: ignore his own strongest beliefs, or allow those dependent on him to live in poverty.

Melville not only found a solution; he also found one which, while not ideal from an artistic standpoint, gave him a great deal of rather diabolical satisfaction. Melville's short stories—all of which were written during this period and under these conditions—present bland and apparently harmless surfaces under which boil the same rebellion and the same questioning of established ideas that characterize his most controversial novels. Furthermore, these stories reflect, in allegorical terms, the same dilemma which produced them. Beneath apparently innocuous surface plots, Melville's short stories center on the image of an anguished human being who is cursed with the ability to see more than the world sees; faced with the hostility which results from his challenge to the established beliefs of a complacent majority, his protagonist either fights against, withdraws from, or surrenders to the world.

One of the most effective devices which allowed Melville to achieve his artistic purpose was his use of reassuringly respectable elderly gentlemen as narrators. In the very act of allowing them to tell their own stories, Melville injected a subtle but savage mockery which both expressed and concealed his own attitudes. For example, the narrator of Melville's best-known short story, *Bartleby the Scrivener* (1856), which was collected in *The Piazza Tales*, is an elderly lawyer reminiscing about an incident which had occurred some time earlier. The lawyer's own blindness to the deeper meanings of life is suggested in the first paragraph of the story, when Melville describes Bartleby as "one of those beings of whom nothing is ascertainable." As the reader discovers, it is primarily the physical, external facts of Bartleby's life which are unknown; but to the materialistic lawyer, these are everything. He sees only surface reality, never inner truth, a point which is underlined in the narrator's next sentence: "What my own astonished eyes saw of Bartleby, *that* is all I know of him. . . ."

The lawyer begins his story by describing the office on Wall Street which he occupied at the time of Bartleby's appearance. The significance of "Wall Street" becomes apparent immediately; the lawyer has surrounded himself with walls, and his windows command no other view. When the lawyer hires Bartleby as a scrivener, or copier of law documents, he assigns Bartleby a desk near a window which faces a wall only three feet away. On one side of Bartleby's desk is a ground glass door separating him from the other two copyists; and on the other side, the lawyer places a folding screen. Having imposed upon Bartleby his own claustrophobic setting, the lawyer gives him law documents to copy. For a while all goes well; Bartleby copies documents neatly and efficiently. On the third day, however, the lawyer asks Bartleby to examine his writing.

In ordering him to examine his writing, the lawyer means that Bartleby should read through the copy he has made while someone else reads aloud from the original. This is an extremely boring task, but an accepted part of every scrivener's work. Bartleby replies, "I would prefer not to." The lawyer reacts with characteristic indecision: he feels impelled to expel Bartleby from his office, but does nothing because he is unnerved by Bartleby's total lack of expression, by the absence of "anything ordinarily human about him."

Several days later, when Bartleby again refuses to examine his copy, the lawyer appeals to him in the name of two ideals which are of great importance to the lawyer himself: common usage and common sense. Bartleby is unmoved. Instead of asserting his own authority, the lawyer appeals not only to his other two scriveners but even to his office boy. All these uphold the lawyer's view. He then calls upon Bartleby in the name of "duty"; but again, Bartleby fails to respond to the verbal cue.

The lawyer's inability to cope with Bartleby is anticipated in the story by his tolerance of the Dickensian eccentricities of his other two scriveners. The older one, Turkey, works well in the morning; but after a lunch which is implied to be mostly liquid, he becomes reckless, irascible, and messy. The younger copyist, Nippers, is dyspeptic. His irritability takes place in the morning, while the afternoons find him comparatively calm. Thus, the lawyer gets only one good day's work between them. Nevertheless, he always finds some rationalization for his lack of decisiveness.

The first rationalization he applies to his indecision regarding Bartleby is the difficulty of coping effectively with passive resistance. The lawyer feels that Bartleby's unaccountable displays of perversity must be the result of some involuntary aberration, and he reflects that tolerating Bartleby "will cost me little or nothing, while I lay up in my soul what will eventually prove a sweet morsel for my conscience." Even on the comparatively rare occasions when he is sufficiently irritated to confront Bartleby with a direct order to do something which Bartleby "would prefer not to," the lawyer always retires with dire resolutions, but no action.

One Sunday morning, as the lawyer walks toward Trinity Church "to hear a celebrated preacher," he decides to stop at his office. There he finds Bartleby in his shirt sleeves, together with evidence that he has been using the office as his home. The lawyer feels at first a sense of melancholy and pity at Bartleby's loneliness; but as the full realization of Bartleby's isolation dawns on the lawyer, his feelings turn to fear and repulsion. He reflects that Bartleby never reads, never converses, but only works and stands for long periods staring out at the dead walls. Bartleby's presence in the office at night and on Sunday, when the usually bustling Wall Street is silent and uninhabited, reminds the lawyer of Bartleby's essential unlikeness to his own concept of humanity, which revolves around surface society. The lawyer rationalizes his unsympathetic response to these circumstances by reflecting that such depths of soul-sickness as Bartleby's repel the human heart because common sense rejects the idea of pity where there is no realistic hope of offering aid.

The lawyer makes an attempt, on Monday morning, to bring Bartleby inside the narrow circle of external reality which is all the lawyer is capable of comprehending. He asks Bartleby for details of his life: place of birth, family, and the like. Bartleby refuses with his usual "I prefer not." The lawyer notices that he and his other copyists have begun to use that expression, and he fears that the influence of Bartleby will spread throughout the office. Bartleby further irritates the lawyer the next day by refusing to do even the one task he had, until then, been willing to do: copying law documents. When the lawyer asks the reason, Bartleby replies, "Do you not see the reason for yourself?" The lawyer does not see; and ironically, he attributes Bartleby's refusal to copy to trouble with his eyes. When Bartleby finally makes it clear, some days later, that his refusal is final, the lawyer decides to order him to leave. Yet he feels a sense of pity for the scrivener because "he seemed alone, absolutely alone in the universe."

The lawyer gives Bartleby six days in which to get ready to leave; at the end of that time, Bartleby is still there. The lawyer gives him money, and, ordering Bartleby to be gone by the next day, leaves the office assuming that he will obey. The lawyer's self-congratulations on his masterly application of the doctrine of assumption end abruptly the next day when the lawyer discovers the scrivener still in the office. Then the lawyer rationalizes that it is his predestined fate to harbor Bartleby, and that his charity will be amply repaid in the next world. The gibes of his friends and professional associates, however, undermine his resolve, and again he orders Bartleby to depart. When he does not, the lawyer finally takes decisive action. He packs up his own belongings and moves to a new office, leaving Bartleby alone in an empty room.

The lawyer soon finds, however, that he is not yet free of Bartleby. The landlord of the lawyer's former office, unable to move Bartleby from the building even after the new tenant has expelled him from the office itself, applies to the lawyer for help. The lawyer offers Bartleby several different jobs, and even suggests that he make his home with the lawyer for a time. Bartleby, however, replies that he "would prefer not to make any change at all." The lawyer flees the building and stays incommunicado for several days. When he cautiously returns to his office, he finds that Bartleby has been removed to the Tombs, a prison in New York City. The lawyer visits the Tombs to offer comfort, but Bartleby will not speak to him. He adjures Bartleby to look at the blue sky and the green grass, but Bartleby replies, "I know where I am," and refuses to speak again. The lawyer leaves Bartleby in the prison yard, and on his way out arranges for him to be well fed but Bartleby refuses to eat. When the lawyer visits Bartleby again, several days later, he finds the scrivener curled up in a ball with his head against the prison wall, dead.

The narrator concludes the story by relating a rumor he has heard to the effect that Bartleby was once employed in a Dead Letter Office. He reflects on the melancholy nature of such work, handling letters containing messages of charity and hope which arrived too late to relieve those to whom they had been sent. "On errands of life," reflects the lawyer, "these letters speed to death." The story ends with the line, "Ah Bartleby! Ah, humanity!"

Although the lawyer seems to be an honest and humane man, he is actually guilty of what Melville considers society's most prevailing sin: self-deception. He labels his pusillanimity, prudence; his indecisiveness, tolerance; his curiosity, concern; as if by doing so he can create a reality which corresponds to his own illusions. He goes to a fashionable church not to worship the God in whom he professes to believe, but "to hear a famous preacher." When he is upset by Bartleby's presence in his office on a Sunday, he does not turn to God for help. Rather, he stays away from church because his perturbation makes him unfit for the only function of church-going that he is aware of: the social function. He constantly thinks in terms of material entities, particularly money and food. Yet the lawyer is not an evil man. By the standards of the world, he is exceptionally charitable and forbearing. He feels for Bartleby's suffering, even if he never understands it; and if the help he offers his scrivener is not what Bartleby needs, still it is all the lawyer has to give. That is Melville's point: even the best of those who think conventional thoughts, order their lives by conventional rules, and never question conventional commonplaces like "common sense" and "common usage," are incapable of understanding a man like Bartleby. Bartleby is the only character in the story who makes a point of looking at the walls, who is actually aware of the limitations with which society, represented by the lawyer, has boxed him in. Bartleby's refusal to value meaningless tasks simply because they are important to a shallow and materialistic society reflects Melville's own rage at being ordered to produce literary pabulum by a society which will not even try to understand his ideas. Bartleby is placed in the same economic dilemma which produced the story in which he appears: produce what society values, regardless of your own needs and beliefs, or die. The solitary Bartleby died; and Melville, equally oppressed by being tied down to a family of dependent women and children, wrote *Bartleby the Scrivener.*

Not all the protagonists of Melville's short stories withdraw from the world. The narrator-protagonist of "The Fiddler," for example, responds to the world's contempt for his poetry by abandoning his art and attempting to become a happy failure. The story opens as the young poet, Helmstone, storms out of doors after reading an unfavorable review of his recently published work. He meets a friend, Standard, who introduces him to Hautboy. The three attend a circus, where Helmstone rages at seeing the applause which the world has denied to his poetry being awarded to the antics of a clown. He marvels at the evident enjoyment of Hautboy, whom Helmstone identifies as a man of taste and judgment. Helmstone and Standard later visit Hautboy's home, where he entertains them by playing common tunes on a fiddle. Despite the simplicity of the tunes, Helmstone is struck by Hautboy's style; and Standard finally explains that Hautboy is actually a musical genius who has given up the fame he once had and retired to happy obscurity. The poet, resolved to imitate him, tears up his manuscripts, buys a fiddle, and goes to take lessons from Hautboy.

In "The Fiddler," Hautboy serves as a lesson in the worthlessness of fame because, having had it and rejected it, he is so outstandingly happy. This allows the poet to rationalize his own failure into a deliberate choice to turn his back on the world's opinion of his poetry. In this story, however, as in *Bartleby the Scrivener*, the narrator's conformity to the standards of the world (in this case, by ceasing to produce poetry which the world does not appreciate) is an act of self-deception. Either Helmstone's poetry is meritorious but misunderstood by a world whose applause is reserved for clowns, in which case he has betrayed his art by abandoning it, or his poetry is genuinely inferior, in which case he has renounced nothing because he has had nothing, and his attitude of choice is a sham. This, of course, reflects another aspect of the situation which produced "The Fiddler." If the kind of literature Melville would have preferred to write was in fact the truth, then in ceasing to write it he was betraying himself; if it was not the truth, he was deceiving himself.

These two examples illustrate the complexity and depth which underlie the surface smoothness of Melville's short tales. His stories are allegorical in nature, expressing his ideas as parables rather than as expositions. Melville often makes his points by means of emblematic symbols, such as the walls in *Bartleby the Scrivener* and the clown in "The Fiddler." In his short stories, as in his novels, Melville emphasizes subjectivity, relativity, and ambiguity. Different characters see the same situation from different perspectives, and there is no omniscient force within the story which can resolve the resulting conflict. Reality is not static and absolute, but shifting and relative; and ultimate truth, if it exists at all, is unattainable.

Other major works

NOVELS: *Typee: A Peep at Polynesian Life*, 1846; *Omoo: A Narrative of Adventures in the South Seas*, 1847; *Mardi and a Voyage Thither*, 1849; *Redburn: His First Voyage*, 1849; *White-Jacket: Or, The World in a Man-of-War*, 1850; *Moby Dick: Or, The Whale*, 1851; *Pierre: Or, The Ambiguities*, 1852; *Israel Potter: His Fifty Years of Exile*, 1855; *The Confidence Man: His Masquerade*, 1857; *Billy Budd, Foretopman*, 1924.

POETRY: *Battle-Pieces and Aspects of the War*, 1866; *Clarel: A Poem and Pilgrimage in the Holy Land*, 1876; *John Marr and Other Sailors*, 1888; *Timoleon*, 1891; *The Works of Herman Melville*, 1922-1924 (volumes 15 and 16).

NONFICTION: *Journal Up the Straits*, 1935; *Journal of a Visit to London and the Continent*, 1948; *The Letters of Herman Melville* (1960; Merrill R. Davis and William H. Gilman, editors).

Bibliography

Branch, Watson Gailey, ed. *Melville: The Critical Heritage*. Boston: Routledge & Kegan Paul, 1974. This volume contains reviews and essays that present an overview of critical response of Melville's work in his lifetime. Includes criticism of the novels and *The Piazza Tales*, as well as some general estimates.

Bryant, John, ed. *A Companion to Melville Studies*. New York: Greenwood Press, 1986. Articles contributed by various scholars compose this thorough volume, which includes a biography, and discussions of the short stories and other works. Some articles give insight into Melville's thought on religion and philosophy and discuss his impact on modern culture.

Dillingham, William B. *Melville's Short Fiction 1853-1856.* Athens: University of Georgia Press, 1977. Dillingham provides footnoted, readable explications of the stories, with moderate allusion to possible sources and other works.

Fisher, Marvin. *Going Under: Melville's Short Fiction and the American 1850's.* Baton Rouge: Lousiana State University Press, 1977. Explores the short fiction works with Melville's cultural milieu of the 1850's as a backdrop. Fisher discusses "The Fiddler," "The Lightning Rod Man," and *Bartleby the Scrivener,* among other short works.

Leyda, Jay. *The Melville Log: A Documentary Life of Herman Melville, 1819-1891.* New York: Harcourt, Brace, 1951. This compilation of documents (letters, diary entries, and other materials) is carefully prepared chronologically with pages headed by year. It is published in two volumes and includes biographical sketches of Melville's associates.

Newman, Lea Bertani Vozar. *A Reader's Guide to the Short Stories of Herman Melville.* Boston: G. K. Hall, 1986. Newman includes "The Encantadas." Each chapter is divided into sections: publication history, circumstances of composition, relationship to other works, profile of interpretive criticism, and bibliography.

Parker, Hershel, ed. *The Recognition of Herman Melville: Selected Criticism Since 1846.* Ann Arbor: University of Michigan Press, 1967. This volume contains selected reviews and criticism that chronicle Melville's gradual recognition as a great writer.

Joan DelFattore
(Revised by *Mary Rohrberger*)

PROSPER MÉRIMÉE

Born: Paris, France; September 27, 1803
Died: Cannes, France; September 23, 1870

Principal short fiction

Mosaïque, 1833 (*The Mosaic,* 1905); *La Double Méprise,* 1833 (*A Slight Misunderstanding,* 1905); *La Vénus d'Ille,* 1837 (*The Venus of Ille,* 1903); *Colomba,* 1840 (English translation, 1853); *Carmen,* 1845 (English translation, 1878); *Nouvelles,* 1852 (*Stories,* 1905); *Dernières nouvelles,* 1873 (*Last Stories,* 1905).

Other literary forms

While Prosper Mérimée is best remembered as an important innovator of the short-story form in France, he was, as befits a member of the French intelligentsia of the mid-nineteenth century, a contributor to all of the literary genres. He dabbled in poetry; wrote astonishing plays, romances, and a major novel; contributed as a journalist to the art and literary criticism of his time; distinguished himself as a translator of Russian literature into French; and is largely responsible for introducing Russian literature to the French reading public.

Achievements

In Mérimée, readers encounter an amazingly versatile writer, scholar, and public official. Best known for his short stories, which, as Henry James once commented, are full of "pregnant brevity" and a "magical after-resonance," Mérimée also belonged to the French Romantic generation. With the Romantics, he shared a taste for exoticism, folk culture, and local color, and he practiced unsparingly that uniquely Romantic form of irony, whereby writers distance themselves from their work, mocking themselves and their own creations. In his desire, however, to shock the bourgeoisie, indulge in complex wordplays, and mock Romantic conventions, he resembles the writers of the later Young France movement. Simultaneously, his objectivity and the concision of his narratives link him with realism. Renowned as a writer of short fiction, he has also been praised for his painstakingly researched reconstruction of the past in his historical works and his innovations in dramatic theory and practice. Named to the French Academy in 1844, Mérimée was a cosmopolitan figure in the cultural life of Europe. His work was favorably reviewed by contemporary English periodicals.

Biography

Prosper Mérimée was the son of a wealthy art professor and painter; his mother was well known for her own work in the arts as a child-portraitist. Therefore, early in his life, Mérimée was surrounded not only by the arts but also by the atmosphere in which art thrives: there were constant discussions and arguments among friends, an intermingling of art forms, and, above all, an acknowledgment of the art of living. Like his close friend Stendhal, he lived through the Romantic period in France without ever becoming too deeply involved himself, although some of his plays show discernible tendencies to cater to the public's taste of the moment. For many Romantics, art was a game, and in this sense Mérimée excelled: his first publications were elaborate put-ons. *Le Théâtre de Clara Gazul* (1825; the theater of Clara Gazul) purported to be a collection of plays by a Spanish actress and enjoyed great success in Paris. Two years later, Mérimée published *La Guzla* (an anagram of Gazul), a collection purporting to be translations into French of Balkan ballads and folk songs; his techniques were so sophisticated that Alexander Pushkin translated the collection into Russian and published it in his own country before the hoax became known. The success of these anonymous works as well as of others confirmed to Mérimée that his true artistic talent lay in the development of shorter fiction since the genre permitted him to exploit his quick wit, cleverness, and extraordinary powers of observation.

In 1829, at the age of twenty-six, Mérimée signed his real name to several short stories that took the reading public by storm: "Mateo Falcone," "Tamango," and "Le Vase étrusque." Several plays were equally successful, bringing Mérimée more and more into the public eye, where his family, friends, and connections paid off with a series of political posts. In 1833, he was appointed chief inspector of historical monuments; the position provided his aesthetic preoccupations an outlet. Thanks to his energetic dedication to his task, which required him to sacrifice his own personal artistic ambitions, Mérimée was instrumental in helping to preserve and upgrade French treasures of Roman and Gothic art.

Mérimée's life was filled with successes, including being elected a French Senator, remaining close to the emperor Napoleon III and his wife Eugénie, and being elected early (1844) to the Académie Française. Although he was able to indulge himself in every way, his upbringing in the world of art helped guide him instinctively toward ventures that were both noble and aesthetic; he was a learned critic, linguist, and historian with many diverse interests. While his detractors criticized his calm dispassion, contemporary critics, armed with Mérimée's vast correspondence, perceive that this dispassion was also a pose, concealing an artfully nurtured sensitivity.

Analysis

Typical of Prosper Mérimée's art is "Mateo Falcone," first published in 1829, and included in the volume *Mosaïque*. Set in Corsica, it is a story of rigorous family pride and personal honor. While Mateo Falcone and his wife are away caring for their flocks, their ten-year-old son Fortunato remains at home alone. A bandit, however, pursued by soldiers, arrives and gives the young boy some coins in exchange for the latter's promise to hide him. Moments later, the soldiers arrive and question Fortunato, who disavows any knowledge of the bandit. The captain, nevertheless, is a clever person; he shows the boy a lovely silver watch that will be his if he reveals the presence of the fugitive. Unable to resist, Fortunato grasps the watch and reveals the hiding place. Mateo and his wife return at this point and hear the bandit cursing the greedy child and his family. Profoundly shocked, Mateo asks his wife if Fortunato is truly his son, for if so, Fortunato is the first member of his race to have betrayed another. Consanguinity confirmed by the mother, father and son walk into the underbrush where Fortunato is ordered to pray and is shot. One of Mérimée's first published works in prose, this short story is powerful precisely because of the author's meticulous control of the material. There are no digressions, no self-serving descriptions, no gratuitous details. Mérimée's sober and rigorous discipline is in marked contrast to the exuberant mood of Honoré de Balzac, his contemporary. The tone of detachment heightens the intensity of primitive passion, giving a mythical quality to the story.

Another tale of Corsican passion is *Colomba*, which deals with the notion of vengeance that overpowers all other considerations. After Napoleon's defeat at Waterloo, Lieutenant Orso returns to his native Corsica to learn that his father has been killed. Rumors suggest that the Barricini family is responsible, although the official accounts exonerate them. Because of his European experience and culture, and because his long absence from the island may have dulled his native instincts, Orso's first response is to accept things as they are. His sister Colomba, however, has been eagerly awaiting his return to avenge her father, and she will not allow Orso's complacency. Similar to Electra in Jean-Paul Sartre's *Les Mouches* (1943; *The Flies*, 1946), Colomba drives her brother to action, and thus the cycle begins again. With all the classical intensity of such a work as Pierre Corneille's *Horace* (1640), Mérimée's story builds as the characters fall victim to a terrifying and overpowering thirst for blood.

Perhaps the best known of Mérimée's short stories is *Carmen*, the story of the love of a soldier, Don José, for Carmen, the bohemian he is supposed to escort to prison. Infatuated, he allows her to escape and then suffers the humiliation of being demoted for his ineptitude. His love for Carmen prompts him to abandon his career and seek her out, join her, and earn his livelihood as a smuggler. Since he exults in his love for her, he can accept his new life, and he savors his exclusive possession of such a fascinating woman. She, on the other hand, is a bohemian, both capricious and willful, dominated by fate and tradition. When Carmen's husband reappears unannounced, Don José kills him from jealousy since he cannot endure the sight of Carmen with another man. Later, when Carmen throws down her wedding ring in a temper, Don José kills her in a fit of jealous rage. Mérimée adopted for this story the point of view of a young archaeologist, whose scientific detachment makes these extraordinary characters more believable and the overpowering presence of fate in the story more compelling. *Carmen* had many imitators and served as the basis for Georges Bizet's opera of the same name, presented in Paris in 1875.

Finally, *The Venus of Ille* must be mentioned because it develops Mérimée's notions of the supernatural and marks an important step in the evolution of the genre toward its climax in the works of Guy de Maupassant. On the Spanish border in the foothills of the Pyrenees, a collector discovers a lovely statue of Venus, which he cherishes all the more strongly when the local townspeople express their fear of it as an omen of evil. The collector's son is a devotee of the game of *pelote*; on his wedding day he joins some friends in a game, and in order not to be encumbered by the wedding ring which he will soon be placing on his bride's hand, he places the ring on the hand of the statue, where it is forgotten. Later, at the wedding ceremony, another ring must be used. That same afternoon, he returns to the garden to attempt to recover the ring, but it will not come off the statue's finger. In panic because he feels bewitched, the son joins his bride in their room, where he hopes to be comforted and distracted. Once in bed, however, he is kissed by the statue, whose embrace kills him in full view of his bride, who then goes mad. The dispassion of the author in leading the reader from the festive atmosphere of the opening pages to the horror of the conclusion, and his subtle foreshadowing of the hand of fate are excellent examples of Mérimée's art.

Contrary to Gustave Flaubert and his preoccupation with subject matter that could be considered normal, ordinary, or plausible, Mérimée was fascinated by the *élan vital* of the Mediterranean world. Strong, colorful people from Italy, Corsica, and Spain inhabit his universe; they have violent, primitive passions and are imbued with tradition and a keenly developed sense of honor. In contrast to his contemporaries, Mérimée applied to his prose that dispassionate artistic perspective that neither praises, condemns, nor judges.

Other major works

NOVELS: *La Famille de Carčajal*, 1828; *Chronique du règne de Charles IX*, 1829 (*A Chronicle of the Times of Charles the Ninth*, 1830).

PLAYS: *Le Théâtre de Clara Gazul*, 1825; *La Jaquerie*, 1828; *L'Occasion*, 1829; *Le Carrosse du Saint-Sacrement*, 1829; *Les Deux Héritages*, 1850.

POETRY: *La Guzla*, 1827.

NONFICTION: *Histoire de don Pedre Ier, roi de Castille*, 1848 (*The History of Peter the Cruel*, 1849; 2 volumes); *Les Faux Démétrius*, 1852 (*Demetrius, the Impostor*, 1853); *Lettres à une inconnue*, 1874 (*Letters to an Unknown*, 1874); *Correspondance générale*, 1941-1964 (17 volumes).

MISCELLANEOUS: *The Writings of Prosper Mérimée*, 1905 (8 volumes).

Bibliography

Bowman, F. P. *Prosper Mérimée: Heroism, Pessimism, and Irony*. Berkeley: University of California Press, 1962. Provides an analysis of the heroes depicted in Mérimée's works, a study of his basically pessimistic ideas about life and human fate, and a discussion of the way Mérimée's concepts of hero and life express themselves in the formal aspects of his writing. The comic and the ironic, Bowman claims, mask a deep sensitivity. Instead of trivializing the role of the writer, they allow him to maintain an intense awareness of his emotions and fears and to achieve a balance between sensitivity and will. Includes a bibliographic note and extensive references throughout the text.

Dale, R. C. *The Poetics of Prosper Mérimée*. Paris: Mouton, 1966. An exploration of the creative theory that underlay Mérimée's practice. Although the focus is more on Mérimée's theory as revealed in his letters and criticism than on his fictional works, the study does offer a number of insights that can be applied to the fiction. According to Mérimée, Dale concludes, the writer's fictional works incorporate a worldview that reflects his own psyche or inner self. The study is well substantiated by references to the author's voluminous correspondence and includes a brief bibliography.

Raitt, A. W. *Prosper Mérimée*. London: Eyre and Spottiswoode, 1970. An essential study of the life, times, and works of Mérimée, for both the specialist and the general reader. Raitt combines a biography with critical chapters analyzing Mérimée's major writings. Illustrations, appendices, a comprehensive bibliography, and an index enhance this book as an invaluable source of material on the French author.

Smith, Maxwell A. *Prosper Mérimée*. New York: Twayne, 1972. A readable introductory study of the author's life and works. Especially relevant to the study of the short prose fiction are chapters 6 through 11. Biographical and critical material are supplemented by a chronology of Mérimée's life, a select bibliography, and an index.

Stowe, Richard. "Prosper Mérimée." In *European Writers*. Vol. 6 in *The Romantic Century*, edited by Jacques Barzun and George Stade. New York: Charles Scribner's Sons, 1985. This brief study combines a biographical overview with a discussion of the style and content of Mérimée's major works, including the short fiction. The select bibliography includes editions, collected works, bibliographies, translations, correspondence, and biographical critical studies.

Tilby, Michael. "Languages and Sexuality in Mérimée's *Carmen*." *Forum for Modern Language Studies* 15, no. 3 (1979): 255-263. An analysis of the fictional world of *Carmen*, focusing on its tight and natural organization.

Robert W. Artinian
(Revised by *Anna M. Wittman*)

YUKIO MISHIMA
Kimitake Hiraoka

Born: Tokyo, Japan; January 14, 1925
Died: Tokyo, Japan; November 25, 1970

Principal short fiction

Hanazakari no mori, 1944 (includes plays); *Kaibutsu*, 1950; *Tōnorikai*, 1951; *Manatsu no shi*, 1953 (*Death in Midsummer and Other Stories*, 1966); *Eirei no Koe*, 1966 (includes essays).

Other literary forms

Yukio Mishima wrote more than eighty short stories; twenty novels; more than twenty plays, several in the manner of the classical Nō dramas, as well as plays for the Kabuki theater; several essay collections; two travel books; a bit of poetry; and a handful of works that defy clear-cut classification.

Achievements

The collected works of Mishima form thirty-six volumes, more than the literary production of any other writer of his time. The Japanese writer best known outside Japan, from the viewpoint of Western critics he is the most gifted of the post-World War II writers. Mishima also combined his knowledge of classic Japanese literature and language with his wide knowledge of Western literature to produce plays for the Kabuki theater and the first truly successful modern Nō plays.

While uneven in some volumes, style is the most distinctive feature of Mishima's work. His writing is characterized by beautiful but rarely lyric passages. Figures of speech, notable in his later works, are also present in his juvenilia. He consistently used ornate language, though he could also write realistic dialogue.

A Nobel Prize hopeful at least two times, Mishima is among those Japanese writers closest to attaining the rank of master of twentieth century fiction.

Biography

Kimitake Hiraoka, who began using the pseudonym Yukio Mishima in 1941, was the son of a middle-class government official who worked in Tokyo. When Mishima was less than two months old, his paternal grandmother, Natsu, took the boy to her living quarters; his mother, Shizue, felt helpless to protest, and his father, Azusa, appeared to be totally subjected to his mother's will.

In 1931, Mishima was enrolled in the Gakushūin (the Peer's School), a school attended largely by young aristocrats. In due time, he was graduated at the head of his class and received a silver watch from the emperor personally at the Imperial palace. By this time, his literary gifts had already become evident, and his first long work, "Hanazakari no mori" ("The Forest in Full Bloom"), was published in 1941.

In 1946, Mishima entered the Tokyo Imperial University to study law. After being employed for a time at the Ministry of Finance, he resigned in 1948 to devote full time to writing. The publication of *Kamen no kokuhaku* (1949; *Confessions of a Mask*, 1958) established him as a literary figure.

The 1950's were eventful years in Mishima's life. During this decade, he produced several novels, two of them major successes. He also traveled to the United States, Brazil, and Europe, and his visit to Greece in particular was a highlight because of its classical associations. During these years, *Shiosai* (1954; *The Sound of Waves*, 1956), a best-seller, was published and film rights were sold, and *Shiroari no su* (1956; the nest of the white ants) established his reputation as a playwright. He also began a bodybuilding program (having been a spare, sickly child) and married Yoko Sugiyama in 1958.

During the first half of the 1960's, writing plays occupied Mishima's time. He trained at the Jieitai bases (Self-Defense Forces) and traveled periodically. He was a strong contender for the Nobel Prize in 1968, the year that his mentor Yasunari Kawabata won it. The short story "Yūkoku" ("Patriotism"), in which the hara-kiri (ritual suicide by disembowelment) of a young patriot is described, was published in 1961. He also acted in his first film, a gangster story.

By this time, Mishima's obsession with death was manifested both in word and in deed. He developed a plan for organizing a private army to be used somehow in his death, a step labeled foolish by his friends and ignored by others. During the final five months of his life, he completed the third and fourth books of his tetralogy *Hōjō no umi* (1969-1971; *The Sea of Fertility*, 1972-1974), and on November 25, 1970, he delivered the final volume to the magazine that was publishing it in installments. Later that day, following his plan and schedule implicitly, Mishima went to the Ichigaya Self-Defense headquarters with a group of his Shield Society (a private legion) and, following a nationalistic speech, committed ritual seppuku.

Analysis

The world will never know what course the literary career of Yukio Mishima might have taken had he not died at age forty-five. Nevertheless, he was the best known of post-World War II writers among critics and readers outside Japan, and he received a fair share of attention within his own country. Not all of his work was of equal literary merit, but a certain unevenness is almost certain for a prolific writer.

Apart from his style, usually ornate and meticulously wrought, Mishima's success stemmed in part from his effectiveness in capturing the sense of void and despair that typified many Japanese during the postwar period. Another key to his success lay in his unusual interest in Japanese cultural tradition. His abilities, unique among his peers, enabled him to write in the genre of classical Kabuki and Nō plays.

Mishima's early works represent a period that both clarified the directions in which his talents would go and developed features that would become trademarks of his later works. He came to realize that poetry was not to be his major effort. In 1941, the year he was graduated from the Peer's School, he published his first long work, "The Forest in Full Bloom" in October, at the age of sixteen. The maturity of style in this juvenile work amazed his mentors and peers. The sophisticated word choice is noteworthy, but its maturity goes much farther; it establishes the major theme of his life's work, for he was well on his way to evolving the aesthetic formula that would distinguish his work: longing leads to beauty; beauty generates ecstasy; ecstasy leads to death. Likewise, the sea, an important motif throughout his writing, is associated with death. Indeed, as Donald Keene has noted, Mishima seemed to be "intoxicated with the beauty of early death."

Preoccupation with death is obvious even in the title of the short-story collection that constitutes Mishima's major short fiction, *Death in Midsummer and Other Stories*. The title story, "Death in Midsummer," takes an epigraph from one of Charles Baudelaire's poems that translates as "Death affects us more deeply under the stately reign of summer." The psychological realism of Mishima's presentation of the family's reactions to three deaths in the family is the focus of the story. Masaru and Tomoko Ikuta have two sons, Kiyoo and Katsuo, and a daughter, Keiko. Yasue, Tomoko's sister-in-law, is baby-sitting the children while Tomoko takes an afternoon nap. Despite warnings to the children against wandering away, during a brief moment when Yasue is preoccupied with other thoughts, two of the children disappear, leaving the three-year-old Katsuo alone, crying. When Yasue realizes what has happened, she is stricken with a heart attack and dies. Informed of Yasue's accident, Tomoko "felt a sort of sweet emptiness come over her. She was not sad." (This is only one of several passages in which a dearth of feeling is expressed.) Only then does she inquire about the children; she finds Katsuo, who informs her that "Kiyoo . . . Keiko . . . all bubbles." Tomoko is afraid; she sends her husband a telegram telling him that Yasue is dead and that the two children are missing, although by now it is clear that the children have drowned.

Masaru prepares to go down to the resort where the family was vacationing. Devoid of any emotion, he feels more like a detective speculating on the circumstances of death than a distraught father. Intuitively, he senses that the children are dead, not simply missing. When he arrives at the resort, he hears that three people have died, and his thoughts turn to how to approach his wife. Funeral preparations are made. Tomoko is conscious of the incongruity of her almost insane grief alongside her businesslike attention to detail and her large appetite at such a time. She vacillates between a feeling of guilt and her knowledge that she did not cause the deaths. Dissatisfied, she believes that Yasue is lucky to be dead because she does not have to feel that she has been "demoted and condemned" by relatives. Mishima here intrudes to comment that although Tomoko does not know it, it is her "poverty of human emotions" that is most troubling her.

On the surface, life returns to normal, but Tomoko associates almost everything with the tragic accident, while Masaru takes refuge in his work. Tomoko questions the fact that "she was living, the others were dead. That was the great evil. How cruel it was to have to be alive." Autumn comes and goes; and life becomes more peaceful, but Tomoko comes to feel as if she is waiting for something. To try to assuage her empty feelings, Tomoko seeks outside activities. She asks herself why she had not "tried this mechanical cutting off of the emotions earlier." Winter comes. Tomoko, who is to have another child, admits for the first time that the pain of the lost children was gone, but she cultivates forgetfulness in order not to have to deal with her feelings further. After two years, one summer day, Tomoko asks Masaru to return with her to the beach. Grudgingly, he consents. Tomoko is silent and spends much of her time gazing at the sea, as if she were waiting for something. Masaru wants to ask but then realizes that "he thought he knew without asking."

As with much Japanese literature, the cycle of the seasons is prominent. Deaths come in midsummer, when things should be flourishing and in full bloom. When winter comes, the final ritual of burying the ashes of the dead is completed. Tomoko becomes pregnant, and Momoko is born the following summer. Again, it is summer when she returns to the beach. The cryptic ending is typical of some, not all, of Mishima's work. One may speculate that the return to the beach in the summer is a sign of acceptance or an effort by Tomoko to come to terms with her own identity. Possibly, her waiting represents some sense of communication with the spirits of the dead or even indicates a longing for her own death. A less gloomy interpretation of the return to the beach, however, may recall Baudelaire's line suggesting that death in summer is out of place; death is for the winter, when nature too is desolate.

More often anthologized, the story "Shigadera Shōnin no Koi" ("The Priest of Shiga Temple and His Love") manifests Mishima's familiarity with classical Japanese literature. At the same time, the central theme of the story is one that is common in the West but relatively rare in Japanese literature: the inner conflict between worldly love and religious faith. A brief account in a fourteenth century war chronicle of an elderly priest falling in love with the imperial concubine provides the subject matter of the story.

It is the motivation of the concubine and the priest—rather than the events—that is the focus of the story. The priest is an exemplar of virtue; he is old and doddering, physically a "bag of bones"; it is unlikely that he would become infatuated with a beautiful young woman. When the concubine comes to the area to view the springtime foliage, the priest "unwittingly" glances in her direction, not expecting to be overwhelmed by her beauty. He is, however, and he realizes that "what he had imagined to be completely safe had collapsed in ruins." Never had he broken his vow of chastity, but he realizes that this new love has taken hold of him. The concubine, having forgotten their meeting, is reminded of it when she hears a rumor that an old priest has behaved as if he were crazed after having seen her. She, too, is without blemish in that, while she performed her duties to the emperor, she has never given her love to any suitor.

The priest is now tormented by the implications of this love in relation to his attaining enlightenment. He longs to see the lady once more, confident in his delusion that this will provide escape from his present feelings. He goes to her garden, but when the concubine sees him, she orders that his presence be ignored; she is frightened when he continues to stand outside all night. The lady tells herself that this is a one-sided affair, that he can do nothing to her to threaten her security in the

Pure Land. Finally, she admits him, and her white hand emerges from beneath the dividing blind that separates them, as custom decrees. She waits, but the priest says nothing. Finally, he releases her hand and departs. Rumor has it that a few days later, the priest "achieved his final liberation" and the concubine begins copying rolls of religious sutras. Thus, the love story between these two who both are faithful to the tenets of *Jōdo* Buddhism focuses on the point at which the ideal world structure that each one envisioned was in this incident "balanced between collapse and survival." If nothing more, the story reflects the aesthetic formed early in Mishima's life, which holds that beauty causes ecstasy which, in turn, causes death.

The story "Yūkoku" ("Patriotism") which was made into a film, is the first of several that focus on ideals of young military officers of the 1930's. To understand this work, it is important to grasp the meaning of the translation of the word "patriotism." The word *yūkoku* means grieving over a country rather than loving a country (*aikoku*), which is a positive emotion. Thus, it is autobiographical in that it expresses Mishima's own grief over the country that he perceived to be in disorder. "Patriotism," according to Mishima's own evaluation, contains "both the best and the worst features" of his writing. The story concerns a young lieutenant, Shinji Takeyama, who commits seppuku because he feels that he cannot do what he has been ordered to do: lead an attack on the young rebels in the Ni Ni Roku Incident, an unsuccessful coup d'état that occurred on February 26, 1936, in Tokyo. Although Mishima was only eleven years old at the time of the incident, its influence on him provided the germ for two other works, a play *Tōka no Kiku* (1961; tenth-day chrysanthemums) and *Eirei no Koe* (voices of the heroic dead). These works confirm Mishima's growing dedication to imperialism. The story contains what is possibly the most detailed account of the samurai rite of seppuku in all Japanese literature.

Almost everything spoken or written by Mishima fits into a personal cosmology that evolved and was refined throughout his life; the living out of this system led to his death: beauty leads to ecstasy, ecstasy to death. Literature was central to Mishima's cosmos and was virtually inseparable from it. To understand one is to comprehend the other. Mishima was obsessed with death, and to create beauty in his works, in his system, led inevitably to his death.

Other major works

NOVELS: *Kamen no kokuhaku*, 1949 (*Confessions of a Mask*, 1958); *Ai no kawaki*, 1950 (*Thirst for Love*, 1969); *Kinjiki*, 1951, and *Higyō*, 1953 (combined as *Forbidden Colors*, 1968); *Shiosai*, 1954 (*The Sound of Waves*, 1956); *Kinkakuji*, 1956 (*The Temple of the Golden Pavilion*, 1959); *Kyōko no ie*, 1959; *Utage no ato*, 1960 (*After the Banquet*, 1963); *Gogo no eikō*, 1963 (*The Sailor Who Fell from Grace with the Sea*, 1965); *Hōjō no umi*, 1969-1971 (*The Sea of Fertility: A Cycle of Four Novels*, 1972-1974; includes *Haru no yuki*, 1969 [*Spring Snow*, 1972], *Homba*, 1969 [*Runaway Horses*, 1973], *Akatsuki no tera*, 1970 [*The Temple of Dawn*, 1973], and *Tennin gosui*, 1971 [*The Decay of the Angel*, 1974].

PLAYS: *Kantan*, 1950 (English translation, 1957); *Yoro no himawari*, 1953 (*Twilight*

Sunflower, 1958); *Dōjōji,* 1953 (English translation, 1966); *Aya no tsuzumu,* 1955 (*The Damask Drum,* 1957); *Aoi no ue,* 1956 (*The Lady Aoi,* 1957); *Hanjo,* 1956 (English translation, 1957); *Shiroari no su,* 1956; *Sotoba Komachi,* 1956 (English translation, 1957); *Kindai nōgakushū,* 1956 (includes *Kantan, The Damask Drum, The Lady Aoi, Hanjo,* and *Sotoba Komachi; Five Modern Nō Plays,* 1957); *Tōka no kiku,* 1961; *Sado kōshaku fujin,* 1965 (*Madame de Sade,* 1967); *Suzakuke no metsubō,* 1967; *Wagatomo Hittorā,* 1968 (*My Friend Hitler,* 1977); *Chinsetsu yumiharizuki,* 1969.

NONFICTION: *Hagakure nyūmon,* 1967 (*The Way of the Samurai,* 1977); *Taiyō to tetsu,* 1968 (*Sun and Steel,* 1970).

Bibliography

Keene, Donald. *Fiction.* Vol. 1 in *Dawn to the West: Japanese Literature of the Modern Era.* New York: Holt, Rinehart and Winston, 1984. Keene's section on Mishima contains both biographical data and critical evaluations of a large number of Mishima's works. He quotes important passages from various works and from conversations that he had with Mishima. Includes notes, a bibliography, and a detailed index.

_____. *Landscapes and Portraits: Appreciation of Japanese Culture.* Tokyo: Kodansha International, 1971. The section on Mishima and his work comments on various of his works but especially on *Confessions of a Mask,* because, atypically, this novel is autobiographical, providing insight into his thinking and his relation to his own work. As in most works, Mishima's preoccupation with death is explored. Includes a short reading list but no index.

Miyoshi, Masao. *Accomplices of Silence: The Modern Japanese Novel.* Berkeley: University of California Press, 1974. Chapter 6 in part 2, "Mute's Rage," provides studies of two of Mishima's major novels, *Confessions of a Mask* and *The Temple of the Golden Pavilion,* as well as comments on works that Miyoshi considers to be important. Includes notes and an index.

Nathan, John. *Mishima: A Biography.* Boston: Little, Brown, 1974. In this very readable biography, Nathan's personal acquaintance with Mishima as one of the writer's several translators is evident. The chapters are organized according to chronological periods in Mishima's life. In addition to a chronological listing of the major plays and novels, this volume contains a helpful index.

Scott-Stokes, Henry. *The Life and Death of Yukio Mishima.* New York: Farrar, Straus & Giroux, 1974. Following a personal impression of Mishima, Scott-Stokes presents a five-part account of Mishima's life, beginning with the last day of his life. The author then returns to Mishima's early life and the making of the young man as a writer. Part 4, "The Four Rivers," identifies the rivers of writing, theater, body, and action, discussing in each subsection relevant events and works. Part 5 is a "Post-mortem." Supplemented by a glossary, a chronology, a bibliography, and an index.

Ueda, Makoto. *Modern Japanese Writers and the Nature of Literature.* Stanford,

Calif.: Stanford University Press, 1976. Mishima is one of eight Japanese writers treated in this volume. While Ueda discusses certain novels in some detail, for the most part his discussion centers on philosophical and stylistic matters and suggests that Mishima's pessimism derived more from his appraisal of the state of human civilization than from his views on the nature of literature. Includes a brief bibliography and an index.

Victoria Price